METHODS OF RHETORICAL CRITICISM

METHODS OF
RHETORICAL CRITICISM

A TWENTIETH-CENTURY PERSPECTIVE

Third edition, revised
Edited by
Bernard L. Brock, *Wayne State University,*
Robert L. Scott, *University of Minnesota,* and
James W. Chesebro, *Queens College and the Speech Communication Association*

Wayne State University Press, Detroit, 1989

Library of Congress Cataloging-in-Publication Data

Methods of rhetorical criticism : a twentieth-century
    perspective. — 3rd ed., rev. / edited by Bernard L. Brock,
    Robert L. Scott, James W. Chesebro.
        p.   cm.
    Includes bibliographies and index.
    ISBN 0–8143–2300–6
    1. Oratory.   2. Criticism—20th century.   I. Brock,
Bernard L.   II. Scott, Robert Lee, 1928—   .
III. Chesebro,   James W.
PN4061.S37   1990
801'.955—dc20   89–35152
                                                 CIP

About the cover photos
Left to right:
    first row—Richard M. Nixon
    second row—Abraham Lincoln
    third row—Ronald Reagan

Cover art and design by Mary Primeau.

CONTENTS

PREFACE TO THE THIRD EDITION

In the preface to the first edition we observed that "the criticism of rhetorical discourse is steadily assuming a more vital role in American life" and that "our very environment is taking on a rather distinctly rhetorical character." Almost twenty years later not only are these observations still true, but with the increase in electronic technology people as symbol users have become further separated from their natural condition. Today, the public's primary source of rhetorical criticism continues to be popular journalism. We are also pleased to note that critics in such academic departments as English, political science, sociology, journalism, history, and communication, instead of moving further apart in their approaches to criticism, are coming closer together.

Even though the organization for the book has changed drastically from the first edition, the original impetus for the book continues unchanged.

The increased use and diversity of criticism has resulted in such a proliferation of terms and methods that the field of rhetorical criticism appears chaotic to the novice. One is apt to be driven either to oversimplify critical form so as to include all methods or to make criticism so individual as virtually to exclude any method. We would hope that this book responds to the current confusion in criticism by hitting between these two extremes. No one should believe that his favorite nomenclature or method for dealing with those phenomena is apt to be universally adopted. We certainly have no such illusion that ours will be so adopted—not even in that fraction of consciousness of humanity and its ways that we know as academic departments of speech-communication. We do believe, however, that there has been a rather strong and useful tradition of rhetorical criticism in such departments. Moreover, we believe that that tradition has been affected by some important evolutionary forces.

In order to describe those forces and to make possible a way of looking at them that may prove useful for many interested in rhetorical criticism, we have undertaken to assemble this book. A key assumption is that Thomas S. Kuhn is right in arguing that modes of thought dominate the structures scientists find in the reality they describe and manipulate. He calls these modes "paradigms." We believe that Kuhn's concept is useful in considering the regularities in what rhetorical criticism has been in departments like ours and, more importantly, in understanding the situation that critics are in regarding their tradition and present inclinations. We have argued that rhetorical criticism has taken certain shapes in the past and that the present indicates certain potentials for the future. Those arguments will have to stand as readers use and scrutinize this book. We hope that even if many are inclined to reject the way we have typified the reality presented to us by critical activity, these readers will find their rejections meaningful acts in reformulating the reality.

It is gratifying to us that this book has proved useful enough to warrant a third edition. Coping with the diversity of rhetorical criticism is a task that will confuse the experienced, as well as the inexperienced, critic. We have no illusion that we have done so perfectly. At best we have provided a set of concepts with which other critics, old and young, may find at least momentarily helpful (as the metaphor *perspective* suggests) but that must be transformed concretely as they grapple with discourse, that is, with the tough verbal fibers with which men and women make and remake their communities.

In the first edition we declared that a "tradition" dominant in rhetorical criticism for about forty years had fragmented and that criticism was "preparadigmatic." Although we found criticism even more diverse when we constructed the second edition of this book, we clung to the notion that rhetorical critics were still in a preparadigmatic state.

We seemed to assume—looking back, we might now say *unwisely* assume— that the state of criticism was fundamentally unsatisfactory because it lacked a desirable feature, that is a practical agreement that if not universal, was at least regular enough to permit a clear, general description of ends and means.

We are more inclined now to see diversity as a sign of strength rather than weakness and to predict that although differences will at times seem to be less marked and important and at times more, diversity will continue to mark rhetorical criticism as *criticism*, that is, as practice continually being turned to fresh ends and adapting means. We shall continue to be fascinated by theorizing about the practice of rhetorical criticism, that is, by attempts to find fruitful regularities to guide critical efforts; but we do not expect to utter just the right phrase to end such attempts, nor do we expect anyone else to do so.

In this edition, as in the first two, we continue to generalize sets of concepts—labeling each a *perspective*. Within each perspective we find subsets. These we illustrate by selecting essays of two sorts: essays arguing for the efficacy of ways of working (call these theory) and essays that criticize some part of the rhetoric that constantly flows around us (call these practice).

To save pages, we have not added a bibliography at the end of the book, as we did in the first two editions. We intend that the footnotes will serve students who want to inquire further into the stuff that underlies our attempts, finding, we hope, that our conceptualizing is justified to some degree. At any rate, it is to the vigor of the many persons noted and many others mentioned but no less important that we must credit the usefulness of this book.

Where we were once a pair we now are three. As our labels go, neither Brock nor Scott has converted the other. The first remains "dramatistic" and the second "experiential," whereas Chesebro declares himself a dramatist with postmodern tendencies.

1

AN INTRODUCTION TO RHETORICAL CRITICISM

"Greenhouse Effect Threatens American Agriculture," "Budget for AIDS Doubles," and "Divorce Rate Drops 20%" are titles that leap out at us as we leaf through newspapers or magazines. In response we may feel a mixture of curiosity, disdain, or any number of emotions. But if we focus even momentarily on what is written, we are apt to respond in *some* way.

Not all of our responses are critical. Nor are all of the articles we glance at critical. Every day our experiences make us aware of circumstances that seem to cry out for explanations. What we feel moving within us at these moments of special questioning may be called "the critical impulse." But what is this impulse? It is difficult to pinpoint. Perhaps it is a queasy feeling or the urge to run or to strike out. Often it manifests itself by verbalizing agreement or disagreement. At other times the critical impulse is formed into a guarded intellectual statement.

The Province of Criticism

All living organisms respond to their environment, assess life-threatening and life-sustaining forces, and react accordingly. In this sense, the critical impulse is universal. Although what we call the critical impulse is a vague feeling that cannot be defined with precision, the human being sets some boundaries for him- or herself as critic. How does one "size up" a situation in a critical sense?

Initially, the critical impulse manifests itself as a quest for more information and understanding. The more we know about some human enterprise and the more salient it is to our interests, the more likely we are to feel the critical impulse.[1] In fact, consciously or unconsciously we potentially take a significant step toward the role of critic when we actively seek additional knowledge about our world. Yet this observation raises the question, "Can't one just know about something without criticizing it?" Our position is that (1) knowing about something and (2) recognizing that the object of interest has in some respect become entwined with human purposes in the creation of a human product will lead to criticism. However, such a conception of knowledge requires that types of knowing be recognized.

The impulse to know things in and of themselves is more appropriately referred to as the scientific impulse. We may make several observations about the scientific impulse with a fair degree of confidence. First, the impulse predates what nearly everyone today calls "science." Ways of knowing things in and of themselves and the knowledge that scientific procedures presuppose were both so rudimentary and sketchy until the last few centuries that science in a contemporary sense was scarcely possible. Another way of saying all of this is that science itself has a history and preconditions. A second assertion we can make is that

[1]See, e.g., Lawrence W. Rosenfield, "The Experience of Criticism," *Quarterly Journal of Speech* 60, 4 (December 1974): 489–96.

designating something as a science, or even as an object of scientific scrutiny, entails an arbitrary narrowing of focus. Thomas H. Huxley recognized this problem when he was explaining the Darwinian theory of natural selection in accounting for the evolution of species. The idea of "nature" (another way of saying, "things in and of themselves") must be restricted to those parts of the phenomenal world in which the human being does not play "the part of immediate cause."[2]

While both the critical and scientific impulse share a common quest to know, the critic and scientist differ in terms of their central object of attention. Of the phenomena that surround them, human beings do not undertake to criticize those that might be called natural. The vibrations of the air may be considered to be an aspect of the physics of sound. The phenomena of pitch and overtone may be taken to be constituents of harmony and counterpoint. But it is to musical composition and performance that the critic turns. If a human being were to say, "I am a critic of the rocks and hills, of bees and flowers," the statement would strike us as whimsy. Rather, it is to the creations of human beings themselves that we turn when moved by the critical impulse.

Within the realm of human constructions, the critic's domain is likely to span topics from both the "fine arts" and the "practical arts." Of the "fine arts," one can quite readily compose a list of some that are relevant to criticism: theatre and literature, sculpture and music, cinema and dance. These we tend to call "art." And although we are not so likely to list them initially, we commonly find references to the art of war (or, less often, the art of peace), to the art of government, or even to the art of marriage. These human relationships in which we find ourselves involved, although unique as particular occurrences, partake of traditions, of institutions, of plans; they are, in short, human constructions.

The distinction we tend to make between "fine art" and "practical art" is beguiling. Notice that although we may criticize the practice of the art of government or the performance of a musical composition, in the former case we are less likely to think of ourselves as critics or our product as criticism. Our feeling is that—like natural phenomena, which are not subject to criticism—the practical arts are instruments to aid the human being's living, whereas the fine arts express the human being's humanity. Right here, however, the line between the fine and the practical begins to fade. Our mass media systems, for example, seem to dissolve the distinction. There are ways in which a television program can be viewed as an artistic experience, yet it can simultaneously and readily serve pragmatic ends. The human life is defined by both the fine and practical arts. Certainly, the line between the fine and practical arts becomes even more obscure if a critic seeks to answer the question, "What is the good life?"

Clearly, we cannot settle such questions here, but we may point out that the critical impulse has again manifested itself in our responses and, we trust, in our readers'. Human beings do not simply live in an environment; they create instruments and institutions for living, which they use, discard, and recreate. They see and assess what they do. In fact, human beings seem scarcely able to keep themselves from responding critically to the products of the human imagination.

While the desire to understand what human beings have created is an essential feature of the critical impulse, we are only likely to identify a response as

[2]Thomas H. Huxley, "The Struggle for Existence in Human Society," *Evolution and Ethics* (New York: Appleton-Century-Crofts, 1899), 202.

critical if it entails the use of other more particular "ways of talking." To merely express an interest in what human beings have created is unlikely to qualify as a critical assessment.

A critic is also likely to view a human act as a product of human specific drives, desires, and motivations. Knowing *why* people have acted as they have makes a difference in how we assess actions. The objectives or ends sought alter how a critic judges a human enterprise. A television program is evaluated from one perspective if it is designed to be comedy and quite another way if it seeks to reflect the tragic.

Of course, critics have no direct access to the inner motivations of others. The creator or author of any human product may likewise be unaware of, or unable to articulate, the reasons for a given action. In some cases, the stated motives given for an action may strike us, for any number of reasons, as misleading. Literary critics use the term *intentional fallacy* to capture the host of issues that can emerge whenever one claims to identify and understand all that motivates others. While never completely avoided, the perils of the intentional fallacy are countered, in part, when the intentions of others are based not only on what others say but are on a comprehensive assessment of explicit behaviors, the means employed, the circumstances under which an act is initiated, and the social outcomes produced. Yet even the use of such a comprehensive list of variables is likely to leave a critic with the feeling that at best, only a *persona* of a human being has been captured at a given moment in time.[3] Second-guessing motives is always a risky business. A thoughtful critic is constantly aware of the inherent limitations involved whenever a psychological profile is created to account for the actions of others.

Nonetheless, critics frequently find it impossible to avoid such concerns. Why people act always seems to make a difference in how we judge what occurs. And a central element of the critical impulse is directed toward understanding human motivations and intentions.

Beyond its concern for intentions, the critical impulse involves evaluation.[4] As we noted at the outset of this chapter, every organism must assess its circumstances and determine which forces act in its favor and against its survival. In this sense, the evaluative component embedded in the critical impulse is a survival technique, and perhaps an inherent dimension of all human beings. Kenneth Burke has stated the case in this fashion: "We must name the friendly and unfriendly functions and relationships in such a way that we are able to do something about them." "In naming them," Burke reasoned, "we form our characters, since the names embody attitudes; and implicit in the attitudes there are the cues of behavior."[5]

Yet judgments about the products of others have social consequences. Evaluations of others can often be awkward, upsetting, and difficult for both the critic and those being judged. The popularity of "nonjudgmental" schools of psychology, the emergence of the human sensitivity movement, and attention devoted to

---

[3]See, e.g., Edwin Black, "The Second *Persona*," *Quarterly Journal of Speech* 56, 2 (April 1970): 109–19.

[4]See, e.g., Philip Wander and Steven Jenkins, "Rhetoric, Society, and the Critical Response," *Quarterly Journal of Speech* 58, 4 (December 1972): 441–50.

[5]*Attitudes toward History*, rev. ed. (Boston, MA: Beacon Press, 1959), 4 (originally published 1937).

interpersonal communication all underscore the social issues involved whenever one person judges another.[6] We find such concerns completely legitimate. In a humane society, the critical impulse should not destroy another person's sense of self-worth or ability to select an exciting and productive range of individual choices. Nonetheless, judgments remain an essential component of human existence. When we interact with others, they can influence and shape the directions of our lives, often in beneficial ways but sometimes with less than desirable outcomes. Moreover, we can simply disagree with the attitudes and proposed actions others outline for our society. Accordingly, when the discussion turns to topics such as politics, religion, questions of aesthetics, social programs, and economics, we encounter issues, issues requiring that we form and articulate judgments if we are to remain in control of our own destinies. Try as we may, the evaluative component appears to remain an enduring feature of any critical impulse.

The evaluative dimension of the critical impulse is dramatically tempered when we recognize that a critical judgment is also a reason-giving activity. Reactions to any human activity can certainly include a bold statement such as, "I hate it!" Such an expression is clearly a statement of taste and preference. It is only critical in the sense that it reveals an inclination, establishes differences, and prepares for confrontation. If the full history of criticism is appreciated, statements of taste and preference do not qualify as criticism.[7] Statements that solely assess the worth of a human endeavor without also providing reasons and evidence for such judgments are many things, but not criticism. We hold criticism to be an art of evaluating with knowledge and propriety. Criticism is a reason-giving activity; it not only posits a judgment, the judgment is explained, reasons are given for the judgment, and known information is marshaled to support the reasons for the judgment.[8]

Finally, the critical impulse is directed towards some social objective or end. If you will, criticism is action-oriented; it seeks to change the human condition. For the arts and entertainment critic, criticism is designed to encourage or discourage an action, namely the attendance of, participation in, or viewing of, a play, television show, or concert. For the political critic, criticism functions to affect voting behavior. More broadly stated, as Scott has previously argued, "One of the strongest claims we can make for rhetorical criticism generally is its merit in clarifying values in specific pieces of discourse and relating these to societal tendencies."[9] Accordingly, criticism is an inherently ethical activity, for future actions can be affected by the work of the critic.

Rather than define "criticism," we have discussed the vague notion of a critical impulse, arguing that such an impulse manifests itself naturally as a human being becomes knowledgeable about any human activity and sees that this activity is salient to her or his purposes as a fully functioning human being. We would argue that a human being cannot completely repress the critical impulse,

[6]See, e.g., Ronald B. Adler and Neil Towne, *Looking Out/Looking In: Interpersonal Communication* (New York: Holt, Rinehart & Winston, 1987), 248.

[7]See, e.g., Joseph Priestly, *A Course of Lectures on Oratory and Criticism,* ed. Vincent M. Bevilacqua (Carbondale, IL: Southern Illinois University Press, 1965), esp. 73–78.

[8]See, e.g., Wayne Brockriede, "Rhetorical Criticism as Argument," *Quarterly Journal of Speech* 60, 2 (April 1974), 165–74.

[9]Robert L. Scott, "Focusing Rhetorical Criticism," *Communication Education* 33, 2 (April 1984): 89–96, esp. 93.

because it is a part of learning how to act toward something or someone. Knowing about something necessarily includes knowing how to behave toward it. Knowing how to behave toward something does involve a series of evaluations, but such evaluations are themselves instructive when the critical impulse is also viewed as a reason-giving activity directed toward a socially beneficial objective.

Rhetoric as an Object of Criticism

Rhetoric may be defined as the human effort to induce cooperation through the use of symbols. Most definitions tend to give rise to troublesome questions of inclusion and exclusion; this definition is no exception.

First, the limits of rhetoric are imprecise. The simple request, "Please pass the salt," is an example of the use of symbols to induce cooperation. On the other hand, such requests, if repeatedly ignored, may be reinforced with angry shouts and kicks. Although normally we would exclude simple, conventional requests and physical coercion from the concept of rhetoric, no one can draw the boundaries easily. If the notion of voluntary cooperation, that is, that which involves choice on the part of those responding to symbolic inducements, is necessary to define rhetoric, then certainly the everyday conventions that groups respond to are germane; moreover, threats of coercion are much more common than coercion itself and often succeed. The question, "Has one *really* cooperated if one accedes to conventional requests, social conditioning, or to threats?" calls attention to the difficulty of making distinctions and also to the need for criticism.[10]

Second, an ambiguity of this sort appears in the question, "Does rhetoric refer to the process of inducing cooperation or to the product of that process?" The obvious answer is that it refers to both, but the answer does not reduce the ambiguity. Historically and currently, the word has been and is used in both senses.

Traditionally, one thinks of criticism in terms of the products of human creation. One is used to thinking of criticism in regard to paintings, novels, and speeches. Indeed, at one time, *rhetorical criticism* and *speech criticism* were synonymous. When the living voice was the only practical public means to induce cooperation, speeches nearly exhausted the possibilities of rhetoric. The printing press ended that circumstance. Although the marvels of electronic media have again brought the living voice and visage back to prominence, the forms of presentation stagger the capacity of speeches to contain them. The emergence of a global information network and computerized communication systems have also redirected our attention back to the word itself as a dynamic mode for inducing cooperation. Without the preciseness some might desire, we conclude that rhetoric encompasses all of these means for inducing cooperation.

The products of rhetoric, then, are multitudinous. Part of the task of rhetorical criticism is to find a focus, to pick products that will be fruitful to criticize.

But the very idea of product—though traditional for the critic—may be detrimental to the deepest fulfillment of the critical impulse if it is taken as a limit. This conclusion is especially apparent if one follows carefully the implications of the existence of any product—say, an ordinary public speech. Where does the

---

[10]See, e.g., James R. Andrews, "The Rhetoric of Coercion and Persuasion: The Reform Bill of 1832," *Quarterly Journal of Speech* 56, 2 (April 1970): 187–95.

speech start? Where does it end? Does it start in the mind of the speaker as he or she interacts with a given social and physical environment? Immediately we are likely to see relationships between a speaker's thought—its formation and expression—and similar thoughts, formations, and expressions. We are apt to become aware that the context in which the speech occurs is a rhetorical context. The critic may find her- or himself less interested in commenting on specific speeches as speeches than in typifying the verbal and nonverbal forms that permeate many speeches and seem to constitute some discernible social conventions.[11] Our effort here is not to typify a particular kind of criticism but rather to point out that one's focus may easily shift from a distinct product toward the process that apparently brings the product into being.

The rhetorical critic may be concerned with such traditional objects as speeches and editorials;[12] or she or he may be interested in scrutinizing less tra ditional objects, such as novels and plays,[13] from a rhetorical point of view. The rhetorical critic may sense that some event or campaign or movement formed of congeries of rhetorical products will yield to his or her efforts.[14] For others, our channels of communication may be viewed as significant determinants of the meanings of our symbols and of how these symbols induce cooperation.[15] Or, a nonverbal activity, such as the sexual act, may be cast as a source of rich and diverse sets of discourses.[16] Whatever the rhetorical critic's endeavor, however, it is aroused by her or his sense of the importance of the human being's effort to induce cooperation through the use of symbols. Since the critic will wish to bring across his or her own point of view regarding symbolic inducements, the critic's communication will probably display a deeply rhetorical characteristic. To say that critical comment on rhetoric will likely be rhetorical itself, however, leads to the question, "What are the dimensions of rhetorical criticism?"

Dimensions of Rhetorical Criticism

Any number of schemes can be used to characterize rhetorical criticism as a form of discourse. Rhetorical criticism can be viewed as a series of components, with each component influencing the final product we call rhetorical criticism. Yet when the critic works well, the nature of rhetorical criticism as a unique whole emerges, with all subordinate parts yielding to an overall organic unity.

---

[11]See, e.g., Franklyn Haiman, "The Rhetoric of the Streets: Some Legal and Ethical Considerations," *Quarterly Journal of Speech* 53, 2 (April 1967): 99–114; Robert L. Scott and Donald K. Smith, "The Rhetoric of Confrontation," *Quarterly Journal of Speech* 55, 1 (February 1969): 1–8; and Parke G. Burgess, "The Rhetoric of Black Power: A Moral Demand?" *Quarterly Journal of Speech* 55, 2 (April 1969): 122–33.

[12]See, e.g., Meredith W. Berg and David M. Berg, "The Rhetoric of War Preparation: The New York Press in 1898," *Journalism Quarterly* 45, 4 (Winter 1968): 653–60.

[13]See, e.g., Ray Lynn Anderson, "The Rhetoric of Science Fiction," Ph.D. diss. (University of Minnesota, Minneapolis, 1968).

[14]See, e.g., Leland Griffin, "The Anti-Masonic Persuasion," Ph.D. diss. (Cornell University, 1950).

[15]See, e.g., W. Lance Haynes, "Of That Which We Cannot Write: Some Notes on the Phenomenology of Media," *Quarterly Journal of Speech* 74, 1 (February 1988): 71–101; and Walter J. Ong, *Orality and Literacy: The Technologizing of the Word* (New York: Methuen, 1982).

[16]See, e.g., Michel Foucault, *The History of Sexuality,* volume 1, *An Introduction* (New York: Vintage Books/Random House, 1980) (originally published in 1978).

The critic's attention is drawn to a certain phenomenon. Yet the critic's perception is not universally shared. In part, the function of the rhetorical critic is to indicate, to point out, to draw the attention of others to, a particular case or type of symbolic inducement. Since the critic is not working with something that is solely physical, she or he must reveal whatever is the critic's object of attention. In this respect, a dimension of rhetorical criticism is descriptive.

With more or less awareness of the implications of her or his activity, the critic endows with meaning the symbolic inducement to which the critic attends. We say that the critic endows it because the meaning shaped in his or her descriptions is one among several possibilities. In the very act of choosing from among the welter of the critic's experiences what aspects are to be set forth as constituting a symbolic inducement—the impact of a single speech, the career of a speaker, the outlines of a campaign, the sort of argument that typifies a repeated experience in like circumstances, and so on—the critic begins to shape the meaning of the symbolic inducement for anyone who attends to her or his critique. When the selective nature of criticism is recognized, the interpretative dimension of rhetorical criticism emerges.

Finally, criticism contains a judgmental dimension. In some way or another, implicitly or explicitly, the critic says that the rhetoric, product or process, is well done or ill. Accordingly, a dimension of criticism is evaluation. On what basis does the critic judge? We shall turn to that question shortly.

The primary dimensions of rhetorical criticism are description, interpretation, and evaluation. Certain statements within rhetorical criticism may appear explicitly descriptive, others predominantly interpretative, and some solely evaluative. These dimensions tend to merge into one another. Each shapes the next and reflects back on the other.

Purposes of Rhetorical Criticism

Rhetorical criticism may serve any number of objectives or ends. The background of the critic, the object of criticism, circumstances, the techniques used by the critic, and the action proposed by the critic all shape and determine what rhetorical criticism is designed to do and actually does. Yet some of the purposes and ends served by rhetorical criticism appear more universal than others.

The process of calling attention to a phenomenon, interpreting it, and judging it, will inevitably result in a product that is designed, more or less consciously, to be persuasive. The critic says implicitly, "See as I see, know as I know, value as I value." If we are correct in our interpretation of the critical act, then when that act is directed towards rhetorical objects, which are themselves potentially persuasive, the critic enters into the arena of argument inhabited by the object being criticized.

Just as the critic may choose to deemphasize the evaluative function of criticism, he or she may wish to minimize the persuasive potential of her or his criticism. Nevertheless, the critic should be prepared to recognize the possible social consequences; for if rhetoric seeks to induce cooperation of others, the seeking and the cooperation achieved will have social consequences.

In addition to a persuasive purpose, clearly, in the critical impulse there lies the motivation to learn about things. The pedagogical function of rhetorical criticism stretches back to antiquity. Choosing model speeches for the students to imitate was an early critical act. The question was, "What speeches are worth saving and studying?" In addition to the basic evaluation necessary, interpretation was needed, that is, the student had to understand the speech in his or her own way, if imitation of it was not simply to be slavish. [17]

Closely allied to the pedagogical function is the theoretical. Criticism may serve theoretical motivations and ends in two ways: first, it may give rise to insights that can then be phrased as principles for further use or hypotheses for further testing. Second, criticism may serve as a test. If conventional principles are sound, they should be confirmed in the practice of good communicators. [18]

In addition to learning about rhetoric, one may undertake the study of rhetorical criticism to learn about other matters, such as those skilled in other forms of symbolic action. One's motivation may be historical, biographical, or cultural. Indeed, rhetorical materials are artifacts and, therefore, are the evidence for reconstructing the lives and ways of the people who produced the materials. The rich diversity of purposes that can guide rhetorical criticism are amply illustrated in the balance of this volume. We ultimately consider five basic approaches to rhetorical criticism, and each is governed by a different set of purposes and ends. For some, rhetorical criticism is undertaken to manage societal interactions more effectively, for others rhetorical criticism promotes individual understandings, while some undertake critical analyses of rhetoric to reveal the dynamic processes of society itself. Another group hopes that rhetorical analyses will reveal the influence of society itself as a socializing agency, while others quite clearly believe that rhetorical criticism can create new political alignments within our social systems. We undertake a detailed consideration of each of these more specific purposes of rhetorical criticism in the chapters that follow.

Criteria for Rhetorical Evaluation

If evaluation continually manifests itself in criticism, the question, "On what grounds shall I evaluate?" is inevitable. The question is difficult to deal with.

The difficulty first arises out of the multiplicity of purposes that criticism can serve. If, at its best, a piece of criticism subordinates the ordinary purposes to a unique whole, the criteria appropriate to the critical act may be unique. But if we leave the matter at this point, we have simply refused to answer an honest question: "Is there no standard common to all acts of rhetorical criticism?"

The most common standard asserted is that of effect. Since rhetorical acts are normally viewed as instrumental—as indeed the phrase "inducing cooperation" may be taken—is not success in using the instrument the final measure? If, for example, the purpose of a presidential campaign is to elect the candidate, the candidate who gets elected has mounted a good campaign.

As tempting as this pragmatic evaluation may be, the critic who invokes it so simply is likely to find her- or himself in some embarrassing positions. May not the success in a campaign, for example, be attributed more to the ineptness of

---

[17]For an excellent discussion of the classical notion of *imitatio*, see Donald Leman Clark, *Rhetoric in Greco-Roman Education* (New York: Columbia University Press, 1957), chap. 6.

[18]For a more extended treatment of the issues involved, see Karlyn Kohrs Campbell, "Criticism: Ephemeral and Enduring," *Communication Education 23*, 1 (January 1974): 9–14.

the opposition than to the adequacy of the winner? Are not some of the most successful persuaders, on the face of what they say, disreputable, and some of the best unsuccessful? Would the criterion of effect lead us to conclude that Adolph Hitler was one of the finest speakers of history, and Demosthenes among the poorest? Was Martin Luther King, Jr. successful?

The answers to these questions are not simple, but two conclusions are indicated. First, we tend to shift our perspective. For example, we can say that Hitler was good in one respect and bad in another or that Martin Luther King, Jr. was overwhelmingly successful, given the circumstances within which his rhetoric worked. Second, in spite of the difficulties that the criterion of effect entails, it is impossible to do without this criterion altogether. Although the question, "Is one success as good as another?" indicates the ultimate shortcomings of that criterion, the very question assumes some weight when applied to the notion of effect.

We have scarcely discussed all of the difficulties. Some of these arise from traditional uncertainties, such as linking causes with effects in any circumstances. Again, the difficulties are compounded by the necessity to focus on a few causes and effects among many, since it is an impossible task to be aware of all the possible causes and effects of any complex, human action. The shifting of perspective mentioned in the last paragraph may be one of turning from immediate effects to long-run effects.

Motivated in part by the difficulties of assessing effect and in part by their concept of rhetoric, some critics examine the process of persuasion and then appeal to artistic criteria to evaluate. Such an appeal may be thought of as the doctrine of effectiveness in contrast to the doctrine of effect. Authority for this doctrine is drawn from Aristotle, who defines rhetoric as "the faculty of observing in any given case the available means of persuasion." Focusing on the means, not the ends, the point of rhetoric is "not simply to succeed in persuading, but rather to discover the means of coming as near such success as circumstances of each particular case allow."[19]

Appealing to artistic criteria assumes that there are well-recognized principles that can be embodied concretely in particular works. Today many critics might question such an assumption. Indeed, it is because of such an inclination to question the notion that there are clearly recognized, artistic principles to which the critic may appeal that we have undertaken this book.

If a critic is to appeal to the doctrine of effectiveness, what will be the source of his or her critical criteria? The very assumption of principles to be appealed to as criteria suggests that authority or tradition will be their source. But why should a critic follow a particular tradition or authority? Two reasons are given as possible explanations, although they are not always clearly distinct from one another. The first is that the authority or tradition seems consistent with practice, which may be a way of appealing obliquely to the doctrine of effect. The second is that the authority or tradition seems internally consistent and the principles are coherent with one another and with the sense of good practice with which the critic and the critic's immediate culture feel comfortable.

In considering traditional criteria, whatever the theoretical vocabulary may be, one senses the potential interactions of product and process in the doctrines of effect and effectiveness. We do not mean to suggest the comfortable compromise

[19]Aristotle, *Rhetoric* (trans. W. Rhys Roberts), 1355b26, 1355b10.

of a platitudinous "At best all work together," which is obviously true but not helpful. What we see is a circularity, in which the appeal to good practice helps to establish principle and the appeal to principle helps to determine good practice. Often the observation of circularity is offered as a refutation of the efficacy of whatever exhibits that characteristic. We do not offer our observation in a refutative sense, however. We believe that such circularity is inevitably a part of building a tradition. If a critic rejects a tradition, she or he will probably do so either because it fails to do what it promises or because the critic appeals to standards that are outside the tradition.

Often rhetorical critics appeal to standards that are outside rhetoric. The tendency to make ethical judgments about the goodness of rhetoric is often such an appeal; perhaps it is inevitably such an appeal. In any case, critics often do submit rhetoric to ethical or moral judgments.

The doctrine of effect leads to the judgment of rhetoric as good pragmatically; that is, whatever the given ends, the rhetorical means seem causally important in reaching them. The doctrine of effectiveness leads to the judgment of rhetoric as a qualified good; that is, given a sense of good means, the rhetoric in question is an embodiment of such means. To make a moral judgment of rhetoric may be to extend the doctrine of effect—to argue that some ultimate goals are or are not enhanced by the rhetoric in question. On the other hand, such a judgment may be focused on means, on the assumption that some means are per se valuable whereas others are destructive to human value.

Recently some critics have argued that although most ethical evaluations of rhetoric have indeed been an appeal beyond the rhetorical itself to nonrhetorical standards, the critic may find an intrinsically rhetorical ethic. We cannot argue the questions raised by such a potentiality here; but the notion, as it is now being worked out, is one of the most exciting problems in contemporary rhetorical theory.[20]

The Pattern of This Book

Our organizing principle for examining the structure and evolution of rhetorical criticism was articulated by Thomas S. Kuhn in his landmark book, *The Structure of Scientific Revolution*.[21] Invoking terminologies frequently employed to describe cultural change, Kuhn has maintained that change within a community of scientists is ultimately revolutionary. He has rejected the well-established notion that scientific knowledge grows by a gradual accumulation of knowledge; in such a process errors are sifted out and replaced by fresh hypotheses, which are verified and developed into an orderly, unified pattern. If the unified pattern does not exist, this view contends, the hypothesis is assumed to be the goal of a progression proceeding from the ingrained ignorance and misinformation of prescientific culture to the full explanation of nature in and of itself.

Kuhn has argued that science grows by fits and starts—that fundamental to change, which may not be progress at all, is the construction of a fresh

[20]For an excellent idea of the potentialities envisioned, see Parke G. Burgess, "The Rhetoric of Moral Conflict," *Quarterly Journal of Speech* 56, 2 (April 1970): 120–30; and Karlyn Kohrs Campbell, "The Rhetoric of Woman's Liberation: An Oxymoron," *Quarterly Journal of Speech* 59, 1 (February 1973): 74–86.

[21]Chicago, IL: University of Chicago Press, 1962.

"paradigm." By paradigm he means an imaginative picture of what reality is like. Rather than being noncultural, scientists form a community, or community of interests. When a number are convinced of the efficacy of a particular paradigm, usually resulting from the insight of an unusually creative thinker, the work of "ordinary science" begins. Ordinary science is the clarifying and testing of innumerable hypotheses implied by the paradigm. As this work progresses, the inadequacies, the lacunas, and the contradictions of the paradigm become more apparent and more bothersome. At first these are simply ignored— for they can be ignored until scientists have worked out other problems from among the myriad hypotheses that can be stated in the various branches of science. Finally, however, the old paradigm breaks down from the weight of its inadequacies, which are really the dissatisfactions (one might almost say "the lack of faith") of scientists in it. Other paradigms compete for the loyalties of scientific workers—for "working to the pattern of a paradigm" is an excellent definition of such loyalty.

Whether or not the sort of rhetorical criticism that grew up in speech and communication departments of colleges and universities in the United States during the past sixty years would qualify as *paradigmatic* is probably arguable. But a strong tradition, the roots of which are best revealed by Herbert Wicheln's 1925 essay, "The Literary Criticism of Oratory,"[22] did grow. The inadequacies of the tradition were undoubtedly always apparent, but they began to impress themselves on more and more rhetorical critics in the 1960s.[23] Searching for alternative frames of reference, critics have turned in a number of directions. By gathering together both theoretical essays about criticism and examples of criticism, we shall try to indicate some of the most promising of these directions, letting critics who take them speak for themselves.

We believe that the efforts we shall try to describe are preparadigmatic. Whether or not any of the critical probings now apparent will build into a fresh paradigm is not clear. Therefore, our dividing the book into five general sections—traditional, experiential, dramaturgical, sociological, and postmodern perspectives—should not be taken as an attempt to fix the outlines along which criticism must proceed.

Within the traditional perspective we have identified two approaches: the neo-Aristotelian and the historical. The former applies Aristotelian concepts to the characteristics of the *role* of a source of communication to explain the nature and effects of a communicative act. The historical approach seeks to establish a relationship between public communication and historical events by focusing on a communicator who is cast as a dominant individual or leader capable of interpreting and expressing the circumstances and struggle of people during a given era. Accordingly, people who speak out in a time of crisis are particularly likely to arouse the interest of the traditional critic.

We have observed four general tendencies among rhetorical critics that deemphasize the traditional approach in favor of alternative conceptions of rhetorical criticism: first, a shift in rhetorical criticism from a speaker- to critic-centered mode of analysis; second, a movement away from a managerial to a

---

[22]In A. M. Drummond, ed., *Rhetoric and Public Speaking in Honor of James A. Winas* (New York: Century, 1925), 5–42.

[23]See, e.g., Edwin Black, *Rhetorical Criticism: A Study in Method* (New York: Macmillan, 1965).

symbolic interactionist theory of rhetoric as the starting point and core of rhetorical criticism; third, an effort to place and explain rhetoric within a societal framework; and fourth, a shift in the conception of rhetorical criticism from an artistic and scientific model to a persuasion-oriented and ideological ideal in which rhetorical criticism is directed toward explicit political ends.

Criticism that features and emphasizes the orientation of the critic as a unifying and defining feature of rhetorical criticism we have called the "experiential" perspective. The experiences of critics—the rhetorical standards that they have established throughout years of extensive reading and varied contacts—are drawn on creatively as starting points for their rhetorical criticisms. Experiential criticism is probably more diverse than any other perspective, but two approaches that stand out within this perspective we identify as "eclectic" and "epistemic."

Criticism that has shifted from a neo-Aristotelian to symbolic interactionist theories of rhetoric we have called the "dramaturgical" perspective.[24] Criticism functioning from a dramaturgical perspective holds symbol using to be the core from which a critic describes, interprets, and evaluates all elements and patterns of human communication. While the specific approaches employed here could theoretically vary tremendously, three approaches have decisively occupied the attention of rhetorical critics, which we have called the "dramatistic," "fantasy theme," and "narrative" approaches.

Criticism that attempts to place, define, and assess rhetoric within a societal context we have identified as the "sociological" perspective. Criticism operating within a sociological perspective views human communication as a generating force and one reflective of society and accordingly assesses human communication in terms of societal structures, traditions, norms, and conventions. Four approaches have gained particular attention among rhetorical critics, which we have identified as the "sociolinguistic," "generic," "social movements," and "feminist" approaches.

Criticism that conceives of the critical endeavor as profoundly persuasive and ideological and directed toward a realignment of political relationships we have called the "postmodern" perspective. While mutually interdependent from a theoretical viewpoint, two approaches have dominated the postmodern perspective, which we have identified as the "constructionist" and "deconstructionist" approaches.

In each section of this anthology we shall endeavor, first, to explain the critical perspective; second, to represent it with theoretical essays; and third, to illustrate it with criticism embodying the relevant theory.

We believe that agreement was complete enough and practice consistent enough to justify our referring to the traditional perspective of rhetorical criticism as a paradigm. But in organizing the breaks from tradition into four categories, we do not mean to imply that these are clearly unified countertraditions.

---

[24]For a concise summary of the principles that equate symbolic interactionism and the dramaturgical, see Erving Goffman, *The Presentation of Self in Everyday Life* (Garden City, NY: Doubleday Anchor, 1959), esp. xi–xii, 1–16, 238–55. Goffman's comparative methodological analysis is particularly relevant here (pp. 240–41). Also see Barry R. Schlenker, *Impression Management: The Self-Concept, Social Identity, and Interpersonal Relationships* (Monterey, CA: Brooks/Cole, 1980), esp. 33–43; and Alfred R. Lindesmith and Anselm L. Strauss, *Social Psychology, rev. ed., (New York: Holt, Rinehart & Winston, 1956), esp. 56–61.*

We do think that the nature of these tendencies, the assumptions underlying them, and their theoretical implications are well enough formed to warrant the categories and subcategories we shall make. But we also believe that the circumstance of criticism is quite fluid and that the tendencies involved may form themselves in ways we can scarcely predict.

The critic, of course, must form his or her own discourse. As Edwin Black has tellingly argued, the critic's own style will be essential in forming a critique.[25] The rhetorical critic should gather reference books dealing with such details of writing as style and usage. While we are particularly interested in the new explorations individual critics may forge, this is not intended to be a handbook on the mechanics of writing critical essays. Our final chapter, ''Decisions in Rhetorical Criticism,'' should not be taken in that vein. We hope this text goes behind the mechanics of writing criticism to the theory and method involved. We have sought to identify perspectives and approaches that are likely to be of value to the rhetorical critic. We hope to raise some important questions about junctures at which the critic must make decisions that will shape specific pieces of criticism. We believe that the essays included within this volume are apt to remain important to the substance of rhetorical criticism into the foreseeable future. At the same time, we have included essays that should stand as illustrations not only of each method but of critical writing.

[25]This argument seems to us one of the main thrusts of Black's foreword to the 1978 edition of *Rhetorical Criticism: A Study in Method.* (See esp. p. xiv.)

2

THE TRADITIONAL
PERSPECTIVE

We have discussed a "critical impulse," suggesting that it inheres in the process of making some phenomenon a part of human experience; in fact, the critical impulse is central to the human experience. The impulse can be studied because people continually conventionalize and institutionalize it to serve their needs.

In the academic work of speech communication departments, the "critical impulse" was formalized into a traditional perspective for rhetorical criticism during the first half of the twentieth century. Herbert Wichelns laid the cornerstone with his essay, "The Literary Criticism of Oratory."[1] The basic outlines Wichelns laid down were given the fullest detail by Lester Thonssen and A. Craig Baird in *Speech Criticism*.[2] Essays representative of criticism of this tradition are in the three-volume series, *A History and Criticism of American Public Address*, sponsored by the Speech Association of America.[3]

The traditional perspective solidified into a paradigm during the ferment of departmentalization of higher education in the United States. In the late nineteenth and early twentieth centuries, some of the traditional, broad disciplines began to splinter; and fields such as psychology, sociology, and political science established unique identities. Speech communication, or what some people called oratory and drama, was part of this process. In 1898 Brander Matthews wrote that "an oration or a drama, shall be judged not as literature only, but also in accordance with the principles of its own art."[4] Matthews accepted a link between speech and literature and attempted to establish unique characteristics for oratory and drama. The drive for differentiation was intensified as the discipline of speech communication became increasingly separate from English departments. The separation was symbolized by the formation of the National Association of Academic Teachers of Public Address in 1915 (renamed the Speech Association of America in 1946 and the Speech Communication Association in 1970).

In his formative essay, after reviewing available critical work, Herbert Wichelns opens his essay by stating "we have not much serious criticism of oratory."[5] He also identifies the central concern of both literary and rhetorical criticism. He states, "All the literary critics unite in the attempt to interpret the permanent value that they find in the work under consideration."[6] Wichelns then describes the focus of rhetorical criticism, "It is not concerned with permanence,

---

[1]"The Literary Criticism of Oratory," in *Rhetoric and Public Speaking in Honor of James A. Winans*, ed. A. M. Drummond (New York: Century, 1925).

[2]*Speech Criticism* (New York: Ronald, 1948; 2d ed., New York: Waldo Braden, 1970).

[3]W. Norwood Brigance, ed., *A History and Criticism of American Public Address*, vols. 1 and 2 (New York: McGraw-Hill, 1943); Marie Hochmuth Nichols, ed., *A History and Criticism of American Public Address*, vol. 3 (London: Longmans, Green, 1955).

[4]"The Relation of Drama to Literature," *Forum*, January 1898, 630–40; also in *Essays on Rhetorical Criticism*, ed. Thomas R. Nilsen (New York: Random House, 1968), 4.

[5]Wichelns, 182.

[6]Wichelns, 208.

nor yet with beauty. It is concerned with effect. It regards a speech as a communication to a specific audience, and holds its business to be the analysis and
appreciation of the orator's method of imparting his ideas to his hearers."[7]

He sought to establish a framework for such criticism. For two reasons we
believe that it is fair to cite Wichelns's essay as the beginning of the paradigm
that later dominated. First, he sets forth a difference between literature and rhetoric that is still generally accepted—rhetoric is concerned with effect and literature with permanence. Second, his fundamental outline for criticism was
accepted by most rhetorical critics for at least thirty years.[8]

In *Speech Criticism*, the first book in the field devoted solely to the theory
and methods of criticizing speeches, Lester Thonssen and A. Craig Baird extended the traditional perspective as defined by Wichelns. Although the authors
surveyed much of the history of rhetoric and drew examples from twentieth-
century criticism, essentially they took the Aristotelian rhetorical theory and historical method suggested by Wichelns and developed them into a more complex
series of patterns. For example, they present a framework for the analysis of
"rhetorical art and practice" that well reflected and in turn helped form the
rhetorical criticism that clearly remained dominant for over twenty years: "Systematically considered, these studies have usually evaluated orators with reference to one or more, or a combination of all, the following concepts: (1) the
nature of oratory; (2) the constituents of the speaking situation; (3) the offices or
duties of the orator; (4) the types of oratory; (5) the traditional parts of the art of
rhetoric; (6) the effect of the oratory."[9] Then they enlarge on these concepts in a
detailed outline.[10]

Finally, in 1955 Marie Hochmuth Nichols published the third volume of *History and Criticism of American Public Address*, supplementing William Norwood Brigance's two volumes released in 1943. These works include the critical
efforts of forty scholars in the field of speech communication and demonstrates
the application of the basic patterns to traditional criticism. However, the application was uneven and at times deviated significantly from the ideal. Wichelns—
and later Thonssen and Baird—stressed making judgments about the effects of
rhetoric; but many of these critical essays tended to stress description, stopping
shy of explicit evaluation. The thrust of traditional criticism apparently brought
many critics to look on their art as that of identifying conventional rhetorical
strategies and presenting an account of the speaker and the times.

Within the traditional perspective, two approaches to criticism stand out: the
neo-Aristotelian and the historical. Some critics weave the two approaches into a
unified work, but often they stand quite separately. The roots of these approaches can be found in Wichelns's discussion of three types of criticism. The
first is "predominantly personal or biographical" and "goes behind the work to
the man" (historical). The second "attempts to hold the scales even between the
biographical and the literary (rhetorical) interest. . . . The third is occupied with
the work and tends to ignore the man" (neo-Aristotelian).[11]

[7]Wichelns, 209.
[8]Herbert A. Wichelns, "The Literary Criticism of Oratory," in *The Rhetorical Idiom*,
ed. Donald C. Bryant (New York: Russell & Russell, 1966), 5.
[9]Thonssen and Baird, 290.
[10]Thonssen and Baird, 292–93.
[11]Wichelns, 183.

The Neo-Aristotelian Approach

The nomenclature common to traditional criticism is derived from Aristotle's *Rhetoric*. To stress that the pattern is *derived* from, but not synonymous with, the ancient source, Edwin Black labels it "neo-Aristotelian."[12]

In his 1925 essay, Herbert Wichelns listed the necessary elements for neo-Aristotelian criticism: "The speaker's personality as a conditioning factor, . . . the public character of the man, . . . a description of the speaker's audience, . . . the leading ideas with which he plied his hearers—his topics, the motives to which he appealed, the nature of the proofs he offered, . . . the surviving texts to what was actually uttered, . . . the speaker's mode of arrangement and his mode of expression, . . . his habit of preparation and his manner of delivery, . . . diction and sentence movement, . . . the effect of the discourse on its immediate hearers."[13] The Aristotelian concepts of "ethos," "pathos," and "logos" and the classical canon of "invention," "arrangement," "style," and "delivery" stand out as both the categories and standards for criticism. This impressive list of topics became the rhetorical ideal for the neo-Aristotelian critic, who, after 1948, drew from the heavily detailed Aristotelianism of Thonssen and Baird's *Speech Criticism*.[14]

The ideal prescribed by Wichelns was quite ambitious because its method essentially required the critic to describe and analyze in depth all aspects of the historical and rhetorical elements that surround a rhetorical act. In practice few critics were able to achieve the ideal, even though the neo-Aristotelian approach dominated the literature of rhetorical criticism for thirty years. In studying the three volumes of *History and Criticism of American Public Address*, Black concluded that fifteen of the fifty essays employ this pattern and that the neo-Aristotelian influence significantly affected many of the remaining twenty-five essays.[15]

The Historical Approach

Wichelns's three types of criticism describe a continuum of emphasis, one end of which is "predominantly personal or biographical." We label this emphasis "historical." The neo-Aristotelian approach tends to shortcut the demanding traditional criticism by focusing on the work from an Aristotelian point of view; the historical approach tends to reduce the complete traditional pattern by concentrating on the *historical* elements of the person and the times. The historical approach assumes a causal relation between events in history and public address. Viewing public address as both formed by, and formative of, the events of history, the historical critic analyzes the interrelationship of rhetoric and its times as essential to his or her study. Wichelns explains the historical approach by describing a criticism of Edmund Burke:

[12]*Rhetorical Criticism: A Study in Method* (New York: Macmillan, 1965 repr. Madison: University of Wisconsin Press, 1978; esp. p. 31.

[13]Wichelns, 212–13.

[14]Walter Fisher ("Methods in Rhetorical Criticism," *Southern Speech Communication Journal* 35, 2 [Winter 1969]: 101–9 reads Wichelns in much the same way we do.

[15]Edwin Black, *Rhetorical Criticism: A Study in Method* (New York: Macmillan, 1965), 28.

We may begin with that type of critic whose interest is in personality, who seeks the man behind the work. . . . The second part of Birrell's essay on Burke will serve for the mental character sketch (the first half of the essay is biographical); . . . these [aspects] emphasize the concrete nature of Burke's thought, the realism of his imagination, his peculiar combination of breadth of vision with intensity; they pass to the guiding principles of his thought: his hatred of abstraction, his love of order and of settled ways. But they do not occupy themselves with Burke as a speaker, nor even with him as a writer; their first and their last concern is with the man rather than with his works, and their method is to fuse into a single impression whatever of knowledge or opinion they may have of the orator's life and works. These critics, in dealing with the public speaker, think of him as something other than a speaker. Since this type of writing makes but an indirect contribution to our judgment of the orator, there is no need of a more extended account of the method, except as we find it combined with a discussion of the orator's works.[16]

A variation on the traditional historical approach was introduced by Ernest Wrage who believed that public address in the United States should be approached as a study in the history of ideas. From his perspective the critical act is viewed as "tracing out an American intellectual pattern." Earlier editions of this book included his essay "Public Address: A Study in Social and Intellectual History"[17] as representative of the theory of the historical approach and his essay "The Little World of Barry Goldwater" as an application of that approach.[18] These essays still merit careful study. Wrage contrasted neo-Aristotelian criticism with his approach: "One seeks to explain factors which contributed to personal persuasion; the other yields knowledge of more general interest in terms of man's cultural strivings and heritage," Wrage then united the rhetorical perspective and the historical approach: "To adopt the rhetorical perspective is actually to approximate more closely a genuinely historical point of view when analyzing and interpreting speeches as documents of ideas in social history."[19]

Characteristics of the Traditional Perspective

In spite of their different emphases, the neo-Aristotelian and the historical approaches share a common heritage, perspective, and several assumptions. Their common heritage starts with the dictates of the classical rhetoricians, especially Aristotle's famous definition of rhetoric as "the faculty of observing in any given case the available means of persuasion."[20] In its subsequent development, rhetorical criticism served as an illustration and refinement of what has become known as the "classical canon." The point of departure for traditional criticism is indicated by Wichelns: "One must conceive of the public man as influencing the men of his own times by the power of his discourse."[21] It is in this light that the neo-Aristotelian critic studies the progress of any identifiable influence that originates with the speaker, while the historical critic studies the ideas presented

[16]Wichelns, 183–4.
[17]*Quarterly Journal of Speech* 33, 4 (December 1947): 451–57.
[18]*Western Speech* 27, 4 (Fall 1983): 207–15.
[19]Wrage, "Public Address," 454–55.
[20]1355[b]26. Aristotle's *Rhetoric* is readily available in several editions. We are citing the translation by W. Rhys Roberts, which may be found in an inexpensive Modern Library edition by Random House.
[21]Wichelns, 213.

by the speaker as an integral part of their times. We refer to the traditional perspective with its focus on the speaker as the center of interest as a *speaker orientation*. The traditional critic is likely to see the historical approach as posing such questions as, "What strategies or rhetorical principles or ideas does the speaker employ in making messages?" "How did the speaker adapt to the audience?" "How did the times, background, and training influence the speaker?" "How did the speaker take advantage of the historical setting and occasion?" It is not simply that the traditional perspective examines interaction among the speaker, message, occasion, setting, and audience but that the interaction is consistently viewed through the speaker's eyes. Aristotle's principles are cast as choices that a speaker must make. If the question, "Is the rhetoric good for society?" evolves, the critic is likely to put it aside as not relevant since the approach itself "gives the speakers their purposes." Thus, the traditional perspective tends to be amoral, attempting to raise and answer technical problems.

The traditional critic is apt to scrutinize historical rather than contemporary public address because the former lends itself to greater objectivity and the details of the events are better documented.[22]

If critics strive for objectivity and believe that rhetorical principles reflect a relatively stable reality, it follows that an accurate reconstruction of history is their goal.

The orientation, assumptions, and consensus describing the traditional perspective are summarized in the following outline:

1. *Orientation*. The critic concentrates on the speaker (or the apparent source of discourse). Her or his purpose is to consider the speaker's response to the rhetorical problems that the speaking situation poses.
2. *Assumptions*
    a. Society is stable: people, circumstances, and rhetorical principles are fundamentally the same throughout history.
    b. Rhetoricians have discovered the essential principles of public discourse.
    c. Rhetorical concepts are reasonably discrete and can be studied apart from one another in the process of analyzing rhetorical discourse.
    d. A reasonably close word-thought-thing relationship exists. Rhetorical concepts accurately reflect and describe an assumed reality.
3. *Consensus*. Rhetoricians generally agree that Aristotle identified the fundamental rhetorical process.

All dividing and labeling of human activity is arbitrary to some degree, but we believe the traditional perspective is evident in much twentieth-century rhetorical criticism. This perspective was dominant and unchallenged for nearly twenty-five years; so well established was it that we have chosen to call it "paradigmatic" in that its norms circumscribed acceptable critical activity. The subordinate approaches, which we call the neo-Aristotelian and the historical,

---

[22]As one well-known traditional critic warned—though one may suspect with at least a touch of humorous hyperbole—any speaker studied should "be safely dead and buried, the principal reason being the prime necessity of critical perspective" (Loren Reid, "The Perils of Rhetorical Criticism," *Quarterly Journal of Speech* 30, 4 [December 1944]: 419).

are often separated but sometimes merged as critics approach the ideal set by Wichelns.

Students interested in additional examples of traditional criticism should study applications in the three volumes of *A History and Criticism of American Public Address* as the most convenient source. Almost any essay consciously published as rhetorical criticism from 1925 until 1960 will probably illustrate the paradigm.

Revival of the Traditional Perspective

One should not conclude that the elements that made the traditional perspective vigorous are by any means moribund, either in theory or in practice. A brilliant application of neo-Aristotelian principles and a discussion of the relevancy of these principles may be studied in a pair of essays by G. P. Mohrmann and Michael Leff.[23] Few would deny that their reading of Abraham Lincoln's "Cooper Union Address" quickens interest and insight into this highly significant speech. The theoretical discussion in their analysis of the text reinvigorates the tradition and relates it to the growing interest in what is being called "generic criticism," a term we discuss and illustrate later in this book.

Nor are Mohrmann and Leff the only persons drawing imaginatively from neo-Aristotelianism. In 1972 Forbes Hill applied those principles in criticizing a speech by Richard Nixon with an aim, in part, of providing a sharp contrast with the reading made by several other critics.[24] The existence of these varied critiques and the ensuing exchange between Forbes Hill and Karlyn Kohrs Campbell over the contrasting readings and the efficacy of the methods offer a stimulating case study for students of rhetorical criticism.[25]

Finally, students should not miss Barnet Baskerville's argument for the significance and the integrity of a historical reading of rhetorical materials.[26] Our analysis leads us to present this historical impulse as one of two approaches within a more complete tradition. We recognize that this position can be taken as a negative judgment even though we intend to describe what critics actually do.[27] Baskerville argues that historical essays are fully as useful as rhetorical essays

---

[23]"Lincoln at Cooper Union: A Rationale for Neo-classical Criticism," *Quarterly Journal of Speech* 10, 4 (December 1974): 459–67; and "Lincoln at Cooper Union: A Rhetorical Analysis of the Text," *Quarterly Journal of Speech* 60, 3 (October 1974): 346–58. (Notice that Mohrmann and Leff use "neo-classical" rather than "neo-Aristotelian." They seem to make this move to distinguish their analysis from that of Edwin Black, who used the latter term. One or both of these parties might well object to our having collapsed their efforts into a unit.)

[24]"Conventional Wisdom—Traditional Form: The President's Message of November 3, 1969," *Quarterly Journal of Speech*, 58, 4 (December 1972): 373–86.

[25]Campbell and Hill, "Conventional Wisdom—Traditional Form: A Rejoinder," *Quarterly Journal of Speech*, 58, 4 (December 1972): 415–60. Campbell's critique of the speech appears in her book, *Critiques of Contemporary Rhetoric* (Belmont, CA: Wadsworth, 1972), 39–49. See the footnotes of essays cited here for other readings to fill in a fascinating picture of differing ways of working.

[26]"Must We All Be 'Rhetorical Critics'?" *Quarterly Journal of Speech* 63, 2 (April 1977): 107–16.

[27]See Bernard L. Brock, "Brock on Baskerville," *Quarterly Journal of Speech*, (The Forum), 69, 1 (February 1978): 97–98, with a reply by Baskerville, 99–100.

on any subject and that they are therefore not offshoots of anything[28] but things capable of standing alone.

The revival of the traditional perspective also includes a renewal of interest in public address. Two volumes edited by Bernard K. Duffy and Halford R. Ryan, *American Orators before 1900* and *American Orators of the Twentieth Century,* provide strong evidence of this renewal.[29] Duffy and Ryan argue that speeches "are fascinating windows to the past" and that they are fragments of "unvarnished truth that would otherwise remain hidden beneath the veneer of popular history." They go on to indicate that "the history and culture of the United States have been shaped by orators."[30]

Further evidence of the traditional renewal is Stephen E. Lucas's article, "The Renaissance of American Public Address: Text and Context in Rhetorical Criticism." After acknowledging the "assault on neo-Aristotelianism," Lucas proceeds to argue, "studies in public address can focus on historical or contemporary rhetorical phenomena, can range from mere chronicle to the most audacious interpretation and assessment, can—indeed, should—adopt whatever critical posture works best to explicate the object of inquiry."[31] We should point out that the renewal Lucas points toward builds on more than the traditional perspective as it was initially practiced and as we have described it. This renewal has extended to the point that in 1983 traditional scholars initiated the journal *Rhetorica: A Journal of the History of Rhetoric* that focuses on academic articles written primarily from their perspective. However, this traditional renewal may combine a traditional interest with experiential, dramaturgical, and sociological perspectives that we will soon discuss.

Applications of the Traditional Perspective

In the first two editions of this book we stressed the separation of the two traditional approaches by presenting two essays for each approach. We chose Herbert Wichelns's "The Literary Criticism of Oratory" and Marie Hochmuth Nichols's "Lincoln's First Inaugural" to illustrate neo-Aristotelian criticism. We have already commented on the significance of Wichelns's work, and we encourage readers to study the complete essay.

In this edition Marie Hochmuth Nichols's essay will represent the neo-Aristotelian approach because she represents the neo-Aristotelian tradition at its best. She does an excellent job of discussing all of the elements initially set forth by Wichelns, weaving history and rhetorical analysis together quite effectively. In the process the essay typifies the common neo-Aristotelian bent, stressing description and interpretation rather than evaluation.

We have already indicated that in previous editions a pair of essays by Ernest Wrage represented the historical approach. These essays, which play an important role in the history of public address, should be studied; but in this edition

---

[28] The problem of presenting compatible yet contrasting views of "history" and "criticism" has stimulated a number of writers. We believe that an especially worthy effort is Bruce E. Gronbeck, "Rhetorical History and Rhetorical Criticism: A Distinction," *Speech Teacher* 24, 4 (November 1975), 309–20.

[29] New York: Greenwood, 1987.

[30] Duffy and Ryan, xv–xvi.

[31] *Quarterly Journal of Speech* 74, 2 (May 1988): 243.

they have been replaced by two articles that illustrate the revival of traditional criticism and public address. The historical rhetorical approach is represented by Halford R. Ryan's essay "Harry S Truman." In his review of *American Orators of the Twentieth Century,* Stephen Lucas identified Ryan's essay as one of the outstanding articles in the volume. Ryan's analysis of Truman's rhetorical presidency makes this period come alive for those who do not remember this colorful president.

The final essay will illustrate how in the revival of traditional criticism the historical method unites with other approaches. In "The Historiographical Dilemma in Myrdal's American Creed: Rhetoric's Role in Rescuing a Historical Moment," E. Culpepper Clark and Raymie E. McKerrow combine historical and ideological criticism in examining Gunnar Myrdal's argument that the American Creed and democratic liberalism would bring about improvement in race relations in the United States.

The traditional perspective represents a special formalizing of the critical impulse, which came to be questioned as other forms of the impulse took shape. To study the breaks from tradition, however, we believe that the dominant mode must be understood and appreciated. We present the following selections illustrating the traditional perspective as a means of gaining that understanding and appreciation, and as useful in themselves as well.

THE NEO-ARISTOTELIAN APPROACH

LINCOLN'S FIRST INAUGURAL

Marie Hochmuth Nichols

Part I

"Spring comes gently to Washington always," observed the poet-historian, Carl Sandburg. "In early March the green of the grass brightens, the magnolia softens. Elms and chestnuts burgeon. Redbud and lilac carry on preparations soon to bloom. The lovemaking and birthing in many sunny corners go on no matter what or who the blue-prints and personages behind the discreet bureau and departmental walls."[1] Spring of 1861 was little different from other springs in physical aspect. March 4th dawned as other March 4th's, no doubt, wavering between clearness and cloudiness. At daylight clouds hung dark and heavy in the sky. Early in the morning a few drops of rain fell, but scarcely enough to lay the dust. A northwest wind swept down the cross streets to Pennsylvania Avenue. The weather was cool and bracing, and on the whole, "favorable to the ceremonies of the day."[2] The sun had come out.

But if, on the whole, spring had come "gently" as usual, there was little else that bespoke the same rhythm. Out of the deep of winter had come the somewhat bewildered voice of President Buchanan asking, "Why is it . . . that discontent now so extensively prevails, and the union of the States, which is the source of all these blessings is threatened with destruction?"[3] Spiritually and morally, the city, indeed the nation, were out of tune, cacophonous, discordant.

Would there be a harmonizing voice today from the gaunt "orator of the West," about to take the helm of the nation? "Behind the cloud the sun is shining still," Abraham Lincoln had said three weeks before, as his train meandered across the Illinois prairies taking him on an "errand of national importance,

From *American Speeches* by Wayland Maxfield Parrish and Marie Hochmuth Nichols (New York: 1954) Copyright 1954 by Longmans, Green and Co., Inc. Reprinted by permission of David McKay Co., a Division of Random House, Inc.

Dr. Nichols was professor of speech at the University of Illinois.

[1]Carl Sandburg, *Abraham Lincoln: The War Years* (Harcourt, Brace and Co., 1939), I, 120.

[2]*New York Times*, March 5, 1861, p. 1, col. 1.

[3]James Buchanan, "Fourth Annual Message, December 3, 1860," *The Works of James Buchanan*, collected and edited by John Bassett Moore (Philadelphia: J. B. Lippincott Co., 1910), XI, 7.

attended . . . with considerable difficulties."[4] Trouble had not come suddenly to the nation, of course. Only a year previously the country had been "eminently prosperous in all its material interests."[5] Harvests had been abundant, and plenty smiled throughout the land. But for forty years there had been an undercurrent of restlessness. As early as 1820, an occasional voice had urged the necessity for secession. Again in 1850, with somewhat greater vehemence, voices were raised as the distribution of newly acquired Mexican territory took place. Then came the repeal of the Missouri Compromise in 1854, the civil war in Kansas and the Sumner-Brooks combat in the Senate in 1856, the Dred Scott decision in 1857, and John Brown's spectacular raid at Harper's Ferry in 1859, all giving rise to disorder, unrest, and threats of secession as abolition sentiment mounted. Finally, came the election of 1860, and the North appeared to have "capped the mighty pyramid of unfraternal enormities by electing Abraham Lincoln to the Chief Magistracy, on a platform and by a system which indicates nothing but the subjugation of the South and the complete ruin of her social, political and industrial institutions."[6] It was not merely that Lincoln had been elected president, but the "majorities" by which he was elected were "more significant and suggestive than anything else—more so than the election itself— for they unmistakably indicate the hatred to the South which animates and controls the masses of the numerically strongest section of the Confederacy."[7] Senator Clingman of North Carolina found the election a "great, remarkable and dangerous fact that has filled my section with alarm and dread for the future," since Lincoln was elected *"because he was known to be a dangerous man,"* avowing the principle of the "irrepressible conflict."[8] Richmond observers commented that a party "founded on the single sentiment, the exclusive feeling of hatred of African slavery," was "now the controlling power in this Confederacy," and noted that the question "What is to be done . . . presses on every man."[9] In Charleston, South Carolina, the news of Lincoln's election was met with great rejoicing and "long continued cheering for a Southern Confederacy."[10]

Scarcely more than a month had passed when South Carolina led off in the secession movement. Her two senators resigned their seats in the United States Senate on November 10, 1860, and on December 20 an Ordinance of Secession was adopted,[11] bringing in its wake secessionist demonstrations throughout the South.[12] By the first of February of the new year, Mississippi, Florida, Alabama,

---

[4]Speech at Tolono, Illinois, February 11, 1861, as reported in *New York Daily Tribune,* February 12, 1861, p. 5, col. 3.

[5]Buchanan, *loc. cit.*

[6]*New Orleans Daily Crescent,* November 13, 1860, as quoted in *Southern Editorials on Secession,* edited by Dwight Lowell Dumond (New York and London: The Century Co., 1931), p. 237.

[7]*New Orleans Daily Crescent,* November 12, 1860, as quoted in *Southern Editorials on Secession,* p. 228.

[8]Speech of Senator Thomas L. Clingman of North Carolina in the Senate, December 3, 1860, *The Congressional Globe,* Second Session, 36th Congress, Vol. 30, p. 3.

[9]*Richmond Semi-Weekly Examiner,* November 9, 1860, as quoted in *Southern Editorials on Secession,* p. 223.

[10]*The Daily Herald,* Wilmington, N.C., November 9, 1860, as quoted in *Southern Editorials on Secession,* p. 226.

[11]Daniel Wait Howe, *Political History of Secession* (New York: G. P. Putnam's Sons, 1914), p. 449.

[12]J. G. Randall, *Lincoln the President* (New York: Dodd, Mead and Co., 1945), I, 215.

Louisiana, Texas, and Georgia had "repealed, rescinded, and abrogated" their membership in the Union by adopting secession ordinances, standing "prepared to resist by force any attempt to maintain the supremacy of the Constitution of the United States."[13] The other slaveholding states held a position of "quasi neutrality," declaring that their adhesion to the Union could be secured only by affording guarantees against wrongs of which they complained, and dangers which they apprehended.[14] Already by the end of 1860, secessionists at Charleston were in possession of the post office, the federal courts, the customhouses, and forts Castle Pinckney and Moultrie.[15]

It was not without clamor and fanfare that senators took their leave from familiar places. When, on December 31, Senator Judah Benjamin of Louisiana reported that he would make a parting secession speech, "every corner was crowded"[16] in the Senate galleries. His closing declaration that "you can never subjugate us; you never can convert the free sons of the soil into vassals . . . never, never can degrade them to the level of an inferior and servile race. Never! Never!"[17] was greeted by the galleries with "disgraceful applause, screams and uproar."[18] As the galleries were cleared because of misbehavior, people murmured in departing, "Now we will have war," "D—n the Abolitionists," "Abe Lincoln will never come here."[19] Critics observing the national scene remarked, "The President . . . enters upon one of the most momentous and difficult duties ever devolved upon any man, in this country or any other. No one of his predecessors was ever called upon to confront dangers half as great, or to render a public service half as difficult, as those which will challenge his attention at the very outset of his Administration."[20]

January of 1861 came without hope, and with little possibility of the cessation of unrest. Occasionally the newspapers scoffed at the recommendation of the *Richmond Inquirer* that an armed force proceeding from Virginia or Maryland should invade the District of Columbia and prevent the peaceful inauguration of Abraham Lincoln, dismissing it as the "exaggeration of political rhetoric."[21] The capital of the nation was beset by rumor, clamor, occasional attempts at compromise, and general misbehavior. "I passed a part of last week in Washington," observed a Baltimore reporter, "and never, since the days of Jerico [sic], has there been such a blowing of rams' horns as may now be heard in that distracted city. If sound and clamor could overthrow the Constitution, one might well expect to see it go down before the windy suspirations of forced breath that shock and vibrate on all sides." Almost everywhere he met "intemperate and alarming disciples of discord and confusion." "War, secession, and disunion are on every lip; and no hope of compromise or adjustment is held out by any one. The prevailing sentiment in Washington is with the South."[22]

[13]*New York Times*, February 11, 1861, p. 4, col. 2.
[14]Ibid.
[15]Randall, loc. cit.
[16]*New York Times*, January 1,, 1861, p. 1, col. 1.
[17]*Congressional Globe*, Second Session, 36th Congress, Vol. 30, p. 217.
[18]*New York Times*, January 1, 1861, p. 1, col. 1.
[19]Ibid.
[20]*New York Times*, February 11, 1861, p. 4, col. 2.
[21]*The National Intelligencer* (Washington), January 3, 1861, p. 3, col. 2.
[22]*New York Times*, January 15, 1861, p. 1, col. 5.

As secession went on apace in the South, Wendell Phillips declared in Boston's Music Hall that he hoped that all the slave states would leave the Union.[23] Horace Greeley, impatient after forty years of Southern threat, disclaimed a "union of force,—a union held together by bayonets," and would interpose "no obstacle to their peaceful withdrawal."[24] Meanwhile, however, a few held out for compromise. On December 18, Senator Crittenden of Kentucky introduced a series of compromises in the Senate,[25] but action seemed unlikely. And when, on January 7, Senator Toombs of Georgia made a "noisy and ranting secession speech, and at the close was greeted with a storm of hisses and applause, which was continued some time," Crittenden's "appeal to save the country," presented in "good taste," created "little or no additional favor for his compromise measure."[26] While Crittenden appealed in the Senate, a peace conference met in Washington at the invitation of Virginia, with its announced purpose "to afford to the people of the slaveholding States adequate guarantees for the security of their rights."[27] Although delegates assembled and conducted business, ultimately submitting to the Senate a series of resolutions, it appeared from the beginning that "no substantial results would be gained."[28] It was clear that the sympathies of the border states which had not yet seceded "were with those which had already done so."[29] Ultimately, the propositions were rejected by the Senate, just as were the Crittenden resolutions, in the closing days of the Congress. In all, it appeared to be an era of "much talk and small performance," a dreary season of debate, with "clouds of dusty and sheety showers of rhetoric," a nation trying to live by "prattle alone," a "miserably betalked nation."[30]

When Lincoln left Springfield, February 11, to wend his way toward Washington, another President, Jefferson Davis, elected on February 9 to head the newly organized Southern Confederacy, was traveling from Mississippi to the Montgomery Convention of slaveholding states to help complete the act of secession, his trip being "one continuous ovation."[31] "The time for compromise is past," observed Davis, as he paused at the depot at Montgomery to address the crowd, "and we are now determined to maintain our position, and make all who oppose us smell Southern powder, feel Southern steel."[32] Clearly, people could agree that Lincoln was to inherit "a thorny wilderness of perplexities."[33] Would he "coerce" the seceded states and ask for the restoration of federal properties in possession of the secessionists? Would he respond to pressure "from all sides" and from a "fraction of his own party" to consent to "extension" of slavery, particularly below the line 36° 30'? Would he listen to "compromise" Republicans in Congress and only "*seem*" to compromise, "so as not to appear

[23]*New York Times*, January 21, 1861, p. 1, col. 4; see also, complete text of speech in ibid., p. 8, cols. 5, 6, and p. 5, cols. 1, 2.

[24]Horace Greeley, *Recollections of a Busy Life* (New York: J. B. Ford and Co., 1868), p. 398.

[25]*Congressional Globe*, Second Session, 36th Congress, Part I, Vol. 30, pp. 112–14.

[26]*New York Times*, January 8, 1861, p. 1, col. 1; see also, *Congressional Globe*, Second Session, 36th Congress, Part I, Vol. 30, pp. 264–71.

[27]Howe, op. cit., p. 465.

[28]Ibid., p. 467.

[29]Ibid., p. 467.

[30]*New York Daily Tribune*, March 13, 1861, p. 4, col. 4.

[31]*New York Daily Tribune*, February 18, 1861, p. 5, col. 6.

[32]Ibid., p. 5, col. 6.

[33]Ibid., March 4, 1861, p. 4, col. 2.

obstinate or insensible to the complaints of the Slaveholders''?[34] Would he stand by the Chicago Republican platform, severe in its strictures on the incumbent Democratic administration's acceptance of the principle that the personal relation between master and slave involved ''an unqualified property in persons''?[35] Would he stand by the part of the platform which pledged ''the maintenance inviolate of the rights of the States, and especially the right of each State to order and control its own domestic institutions according to its own judgment exclusively''?[36] Was the belief that he had so often uttered representative of the true Lincoln: ''A house divided against itself cannot stand''?[37]

On March 4 as the newspapers gave advance notice of what was to transpire during the day, there was a note of fear and uncertainty in regard to the safety of the President-elect, along with the general eagerness about the outlines of Lincoln's course of action to be announced in the inaugural. ''The great event to which so many have been looking forward with anxiety—which has excited the hopes and fears of the country to an extent unparalleled in its comparatively brief history—will take place to-day,'' observed the *New York Times*. ''The occasion has drawn to the Federal Capital a greater crowd, probably, than has ever been assembled there on any similar occasion. . . . Whether the ceremonies will be marred by any untoward event is, of course, a matter of conjecture, though grave fears are expressed on the subject.''[38] While visitors to Washington were seeking to get a glimpse of the tumultuous Senate in all-night session, General Scott and his advisers were together planning to take the ''greatest precaution'' for preventing ''any attack upon the procession or demonstration against Mr. Lincoln's person.''[39] Rumors of the presence of a ''large gang of 'Plug Uglies' who are here from Baltimore,''[40] circulated freely. Whether they were in Washington to make an attack on the person of the President or to ''create a disturbance, and plunder private persons''[41] was a matter for general speculation. Whatever the purpose, General Scott and his advisers had decided to leave nothing undone to secure the safety of the President-elect. Riflemen in squads were to be placed in hiding on the roofs commanding buildings along Pennsylvania Avenue. Orders were given to fire in the event of a threat to the presidential carriages. There were cavalry regulars to guard the side-street crossings, moving from one to another as the procession passed. From the windows of the Capitol wings riflemen were to watch the inauguration platform. General Scott would oversee the ceremonies from the top of a slope commanding the north entrance to the Capitol, ready to take personal charge of a battery of flying artillery stationed

---

[34]*New York Daily Tribune*, February 18, 1861, p. 6, col. 1.

[35]M. Halstead, *A History of the National Political Conventions of the Current Presidential Campaign* (Columbus, Ohio: Follett, Foster and Co., 1860); p. 138.

[36]Ibid.

[37]''A House Divided: Speech Delivered at Springfield, Illinois, at the Close of the Republican State Convention, June 16, 1858,'' in *Abraham Lincoln: His Speeches and Writings*, edited with critical and analytical notes by Roy P. Basler (Cleveland, Ohio: The World Publishing Co., 1946), p. 372.

[38]*New York Times*, March 4, 1861, p. 4, col. 1.

[39]*New York Times*, March 4, 1861, p. 1, col. 2.

[40]Ibid.

[41]Ibid.

there. District militia in three ranks were to surround the platform to keep back the crowd. Armed detectives in citizen's clothing were to be scattered through the great audience.[42]

The occasion must have seemed strange to the man who had been accustomed to being carried on the shoulders of admirers on speaking occasions in his years as a stump orator in the West, and to being the idol of many a torchlight procession during the combats with the "Little Giant" in the tumultuous debates of 1858. Even the Capitol grounds where the crowds had begun to assemble had a strangely unfamiliar look in contrast to its fixity during his years as congressman in 1847 and 1848. "The old dome familiar to Congressman Lincoln in 1848 had been knocked loose and hauled down," noted Sandburg. "The iron-wrought material on the Capitol grounds, the hammers, jacks, screws, scaffolds, derricks, ladders, props, ropes, told that they were rebuilding, extending, embellishing the structure on March 4, 1861." "On the slope of lawn fronting the Capitol building stood a bronze statue of Liberty shaped as a massive, fertile woman holding a sword in one hand for power and a wreath of flowers in the other hand for glory. Not yet raised to her pedestal, she looked out of place. She was to be lifted and set on top of the Capitol dome, overlooking the Potomac Valley, when the dome itself should be prepared for her."[43] The carpenters had set up a temporary platform fronting the Senate wing for the occasion, with a small wooden canopy covering the speaker's table.[44] "The crowd swarmed about all the approaches leading to the capitol grounds," observed a witness, "while the spacious level extending from the east front of the capitol was one vast black sea of heads."[45] There were between 25,000 and 50,000 people there, waiting with expectancy.[46] "Every window in the north front of the Capitol was filled with ladies. Every tree top bore its burden of eager eyes. Every fence and staging, and pile of building material, for the Capitol extension was made a 'coyn of vantage' for its full complement of spectators."[47] It was noticeable that "scarce a Southern face is to be seen"[48] in the crowd, "judging from the lack of long-haired men."[49] While the crowd waited for the administration of the oath of the Vice-President, which took place in the Senate chambers, it was entertained with martial music, and "by the antics of a lunatic, who had climbed a tall tree in front of the capitol and made a long political speech, claiming to be the rightful President of the United States." Policemen were detached to bring him down, but he merely climbed higher and "stood rocking in the wind, and made another

[42]Ibid.; see also, Sandburg, *The War Years*, I, 120–21; Randall, *Lincoln the President*, I, 293, 294; William F. Baringer, *A House Dividing* (Springfield, Ill.: Abraham Lincoln Association, 1945), pp. 331–34; *The Diary of a Public Man*, Prefatory notes by F. Lauriston Bullard, Foreword by Carl Sandburg (Chicago: Privately printed for Abraham Lincoln Book Shop, 1945), pp. 73, 74; Clark E. Carr, *Stephen A. Douglas, His Life and Public Services, Speeches and Patriotism* (Chicago: A. C. McClurg and Co., 1909), p. 123.

[43]Sandburg, *The War Years*, I, 120.

[44]Baringer, op. cit., p. 333.

[45]Correspondence of the *Cincinnati Commercial*, as quoted in *The Chicago Daily Tribune*, March 8, 1861, p. 2, col. 4.

[46]*New York Daily Tribune*, March 5, 1861, p. 5, col. 4.

[47]*Chicago Daily Tribune*, March 9, 1861, p. 3, col. 2.

[48]*New York Times*, March 4, 1861, p. 1, col. 2.

[49]*Chicago Daily Tribune*, March 5, 1861, p. 1, col. 2.

speech."[50] The ceremonies over indoors, the major figures of the occasion were seen emerging, Abraham Lincoln with James Buchanan by his side.

As Lincoln and Buchanan took places on the right side of the speaker's stand, Chief Justice Taney, who soon would administer the oath of office, took a seat upon the left. Many in the audience were seeing Lincoln for the first time. "Honest Abe Lincoln," the folks back home called him, or just "Old Abe" was the affectionate cry at the Chicago "Wigwam" as thousands cheered and shook the rafters "like the rush of a great wind, in the van of a storm,"[51] when he was nominated. Walt Whitman thought "four sorts of genius, four mighty and primal hands, will be needed to the complete limning of this man's future portrait—the eyes and brains and finger-touch of Plutarch and Eschylus and Michel Angelo, assisted by Rabelais."[52] "If any personal description of me is thought desirable," Lincoln had written two years before, "it may be said I am, in height, six feet four inches, nearly; lean in flesh, weighing on an average one hundred and eighty pounds; dark complexion, with coarse black hair and gray eyes. No other marks or brands recollected."[53] He was "not a pretty man," his law partner, Herndon, thought, "nor was he an ugly one: he was a homely man, careless of his looks, plain looking and plain acting." But he had that "inner quality which distinguishes one person from another."[54] "I never saw a more thoughtful face," observed David Locke, "I never saw a more dignified face, I never saw so sad a face."[55] Emerson had found in him the "grandeur and strength of absolute simplicity," when, on occasion, he had heard him speak, seen his small gray eyes kindle, heard his voice ring, and observed his face shine and seem "to light up a whole assembly."[56] "Abraham Lincoln: one of nature's noblemen," he was sometimes toasted.[57]

"It was unfortunate," says the noted Lincoln scholar, J. G. Randall, "that Lincoln was not better known, North and South, in March of 1861. Had people more fully understood his pondering on government, reverence for law, peaceful intent and complete lack of sectional bitterness, much tragedy might have been avoided."[58] "Gentle, and merciful and just!"[59] William Cullen Bryant was eventually to write. But now, in 1861, there was something unknown about Lincoln to many. It is true that after the Lincoln-Douglas debates he had gained recognition beyond the limits of his state. The Chicago *Democrat* called attention to the

[50]Correspondence of the *Cincinnati Commercial*, as quoted in *The Chicago Daily Tribune*, March 8, 1861, p. 2, col. 4.

[51]Halstead, op. cit., pp. 149–51.

[52]*The Complete Writings of Walt Whitman* (New York: G. P. Putnam's Sons, 1902), II, 244.

[53]Lincoln to J. W. Fell, Springfield, Illinois, December 20, 1859. *Complete Works of Abraham Lincoln*, edited by John G. Nicolay and John Hay (New York: The Tandy-Thomas Co., 1905), V, 288, 289.

[54]Herndon MS fragment, quoted in Randall, op. cit., p. 28.

[55]*Remembrances of Abraham Lincoln by Distinguished Men of His Time*, collected and edited by Allen Thorndike Rice (8th ed.; New York: Published by the North American Review, 1889), p. 442.

[56]John Wesley Hill, Abraham Lincoln, *Man of God* (4th ed.: New York: G. P. Putnam's Sons, 1930), p. 306.

[57]Carl Sandburg, *Abraham Lincoln, The Prairie Years* (New York: Harcourt, Brace and Co., 1926), 1, 199, 200.

[58]*New York Times Magazine*, February 6, 1949, p. 11.

[59]"Abraham Lincoln," in *The Poetical Works of William Cullen Bryant*, edited by Parke Godwin (New York: D. Appleton and Co., 1883), II, 151.

fact that "Mr. Lincoln's name has been used by newspapers and public meetings outside the State in connection with the Presidency and Vice Presidency, so that it is not only in his own State that Honest Old Abe is respected." "Even his opponents profess to love the man, though they hate his principles," it observed.[60] Again the *Illinois State Journal* took pride in reporting his growing fame. In "other states," it said, he had been found "not only . . . an unrivalled orator, strong in debate, keen in his logic and wit, with admirable powers of statement, and a fertility of resources which are equal to every occasion; but his truthfulness, his candor, his honesty of purpose, his magnanimity . . . have stamped him as a statesman whom the Republicans throughout the Union may be proud of."[61] In 1860, in New York, the "announcement that Hon. Abraham Lincoln, of Illinois, would deliver an address in Cooper Institute . . . drew thither a large and enthusiastic assemblage," and William Cullen Bryant thought that he had only "to pronounce the name of Abraham Lincoln" who had previously been known "only by fame" in order to secure the "profoundest attention."[62] Lincoln had faced thousands of people along the way to Washington, at Indianapolis, Cleveland, Philadelphia, Albany, Harrisburg, and elsewhere, being greeted enthusiastically. Still, "in general," observed Randall, "it cannot be said that he had a 'good press' at the threshold of office. Showmanship failed to make capital of his rugged origin, and there faced the country a strange man from Illinois who was dubbed a 'Simple Susan,' a 'baboon,' or a 'gorilla.' "[63] "Our Presidential Merryman," *Harper's Weekly* had labeled him,[64] later carrying a caricature recounting the fabricated story of his incognito entry into Washington. "He wore a Scotch plaid Cap and a very long Military Cloak, so that he was entirely unrecognizable," the caption read.[65] Men like Stanton thought of him as a "low, cunning clown."[66] And the Associated Press reporter, Henry Villard, remembered his "fondness for low talk," and could not have persuaded himself "that the man might possibly possess true greatness of mind and nobility of heart," admitting to a feeling of "disgust and humiliation that such a person should have been called upon to direct the destinies of a great nation."[67]

In the South, there had been little willingness to know the Lincoln they "should have known," the Lincoln who "intended to be fair to the Southern people, and, as he had said at the Cooper Union in February of 1860, 'do nothing through passion and ill-temper,' 'calmly consider their demands, and yield to them' where possible."[68] The South had made up its mind that whatever the North did to ingratiate Lincoln with them was done in deceit. "Since the election of Lincoln most of the leading Northern Abolition papers have essayed the herculean task of reconciling the Southern People to his Presidential rule," observed the *New Orleans Daily Crescent*. "Having succeeded to their heart's content in electing him—having vilified and maligned the South through a long

---

[60]Quoted in *Daily Illinois State Journal*, November 15, 1858, p. 1, col. 1.

[61]Ibid., November 12, 1858, p. 2, col. 1.

[62]*New York Times*, February 28, 1860, p. 1, col. 1.

[63]Randall, op. cit., I, 292.

[64]Vol. V (March 2, 1861), p. 144.

[65]Ibid. (March 9, 1861), p. 160.

[66]*The Diary of a Public Man*, pp. 48, 49.

[67]*Memoirs of Henry Villard* (Boston: Houghton, Mifflin Co., 1904), I, 144.

[68]J. G. Randall, "Lincoln's Greatest Declaration of Faith," *New York Times Magazine*, February 6, 1949, p. 11.

canvass, without measure or excuse—they now tell us that Mr. Lincoln is a very good man, a very amiable man; that he is not at all violent in his prejudices or partialities; that, on the contrary, he is a moderate, kindly-tempered, conservative man, and if we will only submit to his administration for a time, we will ascertain that he will make one of the best Presidents the South or the country ever had! 'Will you walk into my parlor said the spider to the fly.' " "Mr. Lincoln may be all that these Abolition journals say he is. But, we do not believe a word they say," the *Crescent* continued. "We are clearly convinced that they are telling falsehoods to deceive the people of the South, in order to carry out their own selfish and unpatriotic purposes the more easily. They know that, although Lincoln is elected to the Presidency, he is not yet President of the United States, and they are shrewd enough to know that grave doubts exist whether he ever will be. The chances are that he will not, unless the South is quieted. . . . "[69]

The South found it easier to view Lincoln as a stereotype, a "radical Abolitionist," an "Illinois ape," a "traitor to his country." Then, too, the escape through Baltimore by night could "not fail to excite a most mischievous feeling of contempt for the personal character of Mr. Lincoln throughout the country, especially at the South."[70]

Thus appeared Lincoln, who "without mock modesty" had described himself en route to Washington as "the humblest of all individuals that have ever been elevated to the presidency."[71]

Senator Baker of Oregon advanced to the platform and announced, "Fellow-Citizens: I introduce to you Abraham Lincoln, the President-elect of the United States of America."[72]

Mr. Lincoln had the crowd "matched"[73] in sartorial perfection. He was wearing a new tall hat, new black suit of clothes and black boots, expansive white shirt bosom. He carried an ebony cane with a gold head the size of a hen's egg. He arose, "walked deliberately and composedly to the table, and bent low in honor of the repeated and enthusiastic cheering of the countless host before him. Having put on his spectacles, he arranged his manuscript on the small table, keeping the paper thereon by the aid of his cane."[74] In a clear voice he began:[75]

> Fellow-citizens of the United States:
> In compliance with a custom as old as the government itself, I appear before you to address you briefly, and to take, in your presence, the oath prescribed by the Constitution of the United States, to be taken by the President "before he enters on the execution of his office."
> I do not consider it necessary at present for me to discuss those matters of administration about which there is no special anxiety or excitement.
> Apprehension seems to exist among the people of the Southern States, that by the accession of a Republican Administration, their property, and their peace, and

[69]*Southern Editorials on Secession,* p. 229.

[70]*The Diary of a Public Man,* p. 46.

[71]"Address to the Legislature of New York, at Albany, February 18, 1861," in *Complete Works of Abraham Lincoln,* VI, 140.

[72]*New York Times,* March 5, 1861, p. 1, col. 3.

[73]Sandburg, *The War Years,* I, 122.

[74]*New York Times,* March 5, 1861, p. 1, col. 3.

[75]The text of the inaugural being used is that contained in *Abraham Lincoln: His Speeches and Writings,* edited by Roy P. Basler, pp. 579–90.

personal security, are to be endangered. There has never been any reasonable cause for such apprehension. Indeed, the most ample evidence to the contrary has all the while existed, and been open to their inspection. It is found in nearly all the published speeches of him who now addresses you. I do but quote from one of those speeches when I declare that "I have no purpose, directly or indirectly, to interfere with the institution of slavery in the States where it exists. I believe I have no lawful right to do so, and I have no inclination to do so." Those who nominated and elected me did so with full knowledge that I had made this, and many similar declarations, and had never recanted them. And more than this, they placed in the platform, for my acceptance, and as a law to themselves, and to me, the clear and emphatic resolution which I now read:

"*Resolved,* That the maintenance inviolate of the rights of the States, and especially the right of each State to order and control its own domestic institutions according to its own judgment exclusively, is essential to that balance of power on which the perfection and endurance of our political fabric depend; and we denounce the lawless invasion by armed force of the soil of any State or Territory, no matter under what pretext, as among the gravest of crimes."

I now reiterate these sentiments: and in doing so, I only press upon the public attention, the most conclusive evidence of which the case is susceptible, that the property, peace and security of no section are to be in any wise endangered by the now incoming Administration. I add too, that all the protection which, consistently with the Constitution and the laws, can be given, will be cheerfully given to all the States when lawfully demanded, for whatever cause—as cheerfully to one section as to another.

There is much controversy about the delivering up of fugitives from service or labor. The clause I now read is as plainly written in the Constitution as any other of its provisions:

"No person held to service or labor in one State, under the laws thereof, escaping into another, shall, in consequence of any law or regulation therein, be discharged from such service or labor, but shall be delivered up on claim of the party to whom such service or labor may be due."

It is scarcely questioned that this provision was intended by those who made it, for the reclaiming of what we call fugitive slaves; and the intention of the law-giver is the law. All members of Congress swear their support to the whole Constitution—to this provision as much as to any other. To the proposition, then, that slaves whose cases come within the terms of this clause, "shall be delivered up," their oaths are unanimous. Now, if they would make the effort in good temper, could they not, with nearly equal unanimity, frame and pass a law, by means of which to keep good that unanimous oath?

There is some difference of opinion whether this clause should be enforced by national or by state authority; but surely that difference is not a very material one. If the slave is to be surrendered, it can be of but little consequence to him, or to others, by which authority it is done. And should any one, in any case, be content that his oath shall go unkept, on a merely unsubstantial controversy as to *how* it shall be kept?

Again, in any law upon this subject, ought not all the safeguards of liberty known in civilized and humane jurisprudence to be introduced, so that a free man be not, in any case, surrendered as a slave? And might it not be well, at the same time to provide by law for the enforcements of that clause in the Constitution which guarantees that "the citizens of each State shall be entitled to all privileges and immunities of citizens in the several States"?

I take the official oath to-day, with no mental reservations, and with no purpose to construe the Constitution or laws, by any hypercritical rules. And while I do not choose now to specify particular acts of Congress as proper to be enforced, I do suggest that it will be much safer for all, both in official and private stations, to conform to, and abide by, all those acts which stand unrepealed, than to violate any of them, trusting to find impunity in having them held to be unconstitutional.

It is seventy-two years since the first inauguration of a President under our national Constitution. During that period fifteen different and greatly distinguished citizens, have, in succession, administered the executive branch of the government. They have conducted it through many perils; and, generally, with great success. Yet, with all this scope for [of] precedent, I now enter upon the same task for the brief constitutional term of four years, under great and peculiar difficulty. A disruption of the Federal Union, heretofore only menaced, is now formidably attempted.

I hold, that in contemplation of universal law, and of the Constitution, the Union of these States is perpetual. Perpetuity is implied, if not expressed, in the fundamental law of all national governments. It is safe to assert that no government proper, ever had a provision in its organic law for its own termination. Continue to execute all the express provisions of our national Constitution, and the Union will endure forever—it being impossible to destroy it, except by some action not provided for in the instrument itself.

Again, if the United States be not a government proper, but an association of States in the nature of contract merely, can it, as a contract, be peaceably unmade, by less than all the parties who made it? One party to a contract may violate it—break it, so to speak; but does it not require all to lawfully rescind it?

Descending from these general principles, we find the proposition that, in legal contemplation, the Union is perpetual, confirmed by the history of the Union itself. The Union is much older than the Constitution. It was formed in fact, by the Articles of Association in 1774. It was matured and continued by the Declaration of Independence in 1776. It was further matured and the faith of all the then thirteen States expressly plighted and engaged that it should be perpetual, by the Articles of Confederation in 1778. And finally, in 1787, one of the declared objects for ordaining and establishing the Constitution, was "to form a more perfect Union."

But if [the] destruction of the Union, by one, or by a part only, of the States, be lawfully possible, the Union is *less* perfect than before the Constitution, having lost the vital element of perpetuity.

It follows from these views that no State, upon its own mere motion, can lawfully get out of the Union,—that resolves and ordinances to that effect are legally void, and that acts of violence, within any State or States, against the authority of the United States, are insurrectionary or revolutionary, according to the circumstances.

I therefore consider that in view of the Constitution and the laws, the Union is unbroken; and to the extent of my ability I shall take care, as the Constitution itself expressly enjoins upon me, that the laws of the Union be faithfully executed in all the States. Doing this I deem to be only a simple duty on my part; and I shall perform it, so far as practicable, unless my rightful masters, the American people, shall withhold the requisite means, or, in some authoritative manner, direct the contrary. I trust this will not be regarded as a menace, but only as the declared purpose of the Union that it will constitutionally defend and maintain itself.

In doing this there needs to be no bloodshed or violence; and there shall be none, unless it be forced upon the national authority. The power confided to me will be used to hold, occupy, and possess the property and places belonging to the government, and to collect the duties and imposts; but beyond what may be necessary for these objects, there will be no invasion—no using of force against or among the people anywhere. Where hostility to the United States, in any interior locality, shall be so great and so universal, as to prevent competent resident citizens from holding the Federal offices, there will be no attempt to force obnoxious strangers among the people for that object. While the strict legal right may exist in the government to enforce the exercise of these offices, the attempt to do so would be so irritating, and so nearly impracticable with all, that I deem it better to forego, for the time, the uses of such offices.

The mails, unless repelled, will continue to be furnished in all parts of the Union. So far as possible, the people everywhere shall have that sense of perfect security which is most favorable to calm thought and reflection. The course here indicated will be followed, unless current events and experience shall show a modification or change to be proper; and in every case and exigency my best discretion will be exercised according to circumstances actually existing, and with a view and a hope of a peaceful solution of the national troubles, and the restoration of fraternal sympathies and affections.

That there are persons in one section or another who seek to destroy the Union at all events, and are glad of any pretext to do it, I will neither affirm nor deny; but if there be such, I need address no word to them. To those, however, who really love the Union, may I not speak?

Before entering upon so grave a matter as the destruction of our national fabric, with all its benefits, its memories and its hopes, would it not be wise to ascertain precisely why we do it? Will you hazard so desperate a step, while there is any possibility that any portion of the ills you fly from have no real existence? Will you, while the certain ills you fly to, are greater than all the real ones you fly from? Will you risk the commission of so fearful a mistake?

All profess to be content in the Union, if all constitutional rights can be maintained. Is it true, then, that any right, plainly written in the Constitution, has been denied? I think not. Happily the human mind is so constituted, that no party can reach to the audacity of doing this. Think, if you can, of a single instance in which a plainly written provision of the Constitution has ever been denied. If, by the mere force of numbers, a majority should deprive a minority of any clearly written constitutional right, it might, in a moral point of view, justify revolution—certainly would, if such a right were a vital one. But such is not our case. All the vital rights of minorities, and of individuals, are so plainly assured to them, by affirmations and negations, guarantees and prohibitions, in the Constitution, that controversies never arise concerning them. But no organic law can ever be framed with a provision specifically applicable to every question which may occur in practical administration. No foresight can anticipate, nor any document of reasonable length contain express provisions for, all possible questions. Shall fugitives from labor be surrendered by national or by State authority? The Constitution does not expressly say. May Congress prohibit slavery in the territories? The Constitution does not expressly say. Must Congress protect slavery in the territories? The Constitution does not expressly say.

From questions of this class spring all our constitutional controversies, and we divide upon them into majorities and minorities. If the minority will not acquiesce, the majority must, or the government must cease. There is no other alternative; for continuing the government, is acquiescence on one side or the other. If a minority, in such case, will secede rather than acquiesce, they make a precedent which, in turn, will divide and ruin them; for a minority of their own will secede from them whenever a majority refuses to be controlled by such minority. For instance, why may not any portion of a new confederacy, a year or two hence, arbitrarily secede again, precisely as portions of the present Union now claim to secede from it? All who cherish disunion sentiments, are now being educated to the exact temper of doing this.

Is there such perfect identity of interests among the States to compose a new Union, as to produce harmony only, and prevent renewed secession?

Plainly, the central idea of secession, is the essence of anarchy. A majority, held in restraint by constitutional checks and limitations, and always changing easily with deliberate changes of popular opinions and sentiments is the only true sovereign of a free people. Whoever rejects it, does, of necessity, fly to anarchy or to despotism. Unanimity is impossible; the rule of a minority, as a permanent arrangement, is wholly inadmissible; so that, rejecting the majority principle, anarchy or despotism in some form is all that is left.

I do not forget the position assumed by some, that constitutional questions are to be decided by the Supreme Court; nor do I deny that such decisions must be binding in any case, upon the parties to a suit, as to the object of that suit, while they are also entitled to very high respect and consideration in all parallel cases by all other departments of the government. And while it is obviously possible that such decision may be erroneous in any given case, still the evil effect following it, being limited to that particular case, with the chance that it may be overruled, and never become a precedent for other cases, can better be borne than could the evils of a different practice. At the same time, the candid citizen must confess that if the policy of the government upon vital questions, affecting the whole people, is to be irrevocably fixed by decisions of the Supreme Court, the instant they are made, in ordinary litigation between parties, in personal actions, the people will have ceased to be their own rulers, having to that extent practically resigned their government into the hands of that eminent tribunal. Nor is there in this view any assault upon the court or the judges. It is a duty from which they may not shrink, to decide cases properly brought before them; and it is no fault of theirs if others seek to turn their decisions to political purposes.

One section of our country believes slavery is *right,* and ought to be extended, while the other believes it is *wrong,* and ought not to be extended. This is the only substantial dispute. The fugitive slave clause of the Constitution, and the law for the suppression of the foreign slave trade, are each as well enforced, perhaps, as any law can ever be in a community where the moral sense of the people imperfectly supports the law itself. The great body of the people abide by the dry legal obligation in both cases, and a few break over in each. This, I think, cannot be perfectly cured; and it would be worse in both cases after the separation of the sections, than before. The foreign slave trade, now imperfectly suppressed, would be ultimately revived without restriction, in one section; while fugitive slaves, now only partially surrendered, would not be surrendered at all, by the other.

Physically speaking, we cannot separate. We cannot remove our respective sections from each other, nor build an impassable wall between them. A husband and wife may be divorced, and go out of the presence, and beyond the reach of each other; but the different parts of our country cannot do this. They cannot but remain face to face; and intercourse, either amicable or hostile, must continue between them. Is it possible, then, to make that intercourse more advantageous or more satisfactory, after separation than *before?* Can aliens make treaties easier than friends can make laws? Can treaties be more faithfully enforced between aliens than laws can among friends? Suppose you go to war, you cannot fight always; and when, after much loss on both sides, and no gain on either, you cease fighting, the identical old questions, as to terms of intercourse, are again upon you.

This country, with its institutions, belongs to the people who inhabit it. Whenever they shall grow weary of the existing government, they can exercise their *constitutional* right of amending it, or their *revolutionary* right to dismember or overthrow it. I cannot be ignorant of the fact that many worthy and patriotic citizens are desirous of having the national Constitution amended. While I make no recommendation of amendments, I fully recognize the rightful authority of the people over the whole subject to be exercised in either of the modes prescribed in the instrument itself; and I should under existing circumstances favor rather than oppose a fair opportunity being afforded the people to act upon it.

I will venture to add that to me the Convention mode seems preferable, in that it allows amendments to originate with the people themselves, instead of only permitting them to take or reject propositions, originated by others, not especially chosen for the purpose, and which might not be precisely such as they would wish to either accept or refuse. I understand a proposed amendment to the Constitution, which amendment, however, I have not seen, has passed Congress, to the effect that the federal government shall never interfere with the domestic institutions of the States, including that of persons held to service. To avoid misconstruction of what I have said, I depart from my purpose not to speak of particular amendments, so far as to say that holding such a provision to now be implied constitutional law, I have no objection to its being made express and irrevocable.

The Chief Magistrate derives all his authority from the people, and they have conferred none upon him to fix terms for the separation of the States. The people themselves can do this also if they choose; but the executive, as such, has nothing to do with it. His duty is to administer the present government, as it came to his hands, and to transmit it, unimpaired by him, to his successor.

Why should there not be a patient confidence in the ultimate justice of the people? Is there any better or equal hope, in the world? In our present differences, is either party without faith of being in the right? If the Almighty Ruler of nations, with his eternal truth and justice, be on your side of the North or on yours of the South, that truth, and that justice, will surely prevail, by the judgment of this great tribunal, the American people.

By the frame of the government under which we live, this same people have wisely given their public servants but little power for mischief; and have, with equal wisdom, provided for the return of that little to their own hands at very short intervals.

While the people retain their virtue and vigilance, no administration, by any extreme of wickedness or folly, can very seriously injure the government in the short space of four years.

My countrymen, one and all, think calmly and *well*, upon this whole subject. Nothing valuable can be lost by taking time. If there be an object to *hurry* any of you, in hot haste, to a step which you would never take *deliberately*, that object will be frustrated by taking time; but no good object can be frustrated by it. Such of you as are now dissatisfied, still have the old Constitution unimpaired, and, on the sensitive point, the laws of your own framing under it; while the new administration will have no immediate power, if it would, to change either. If it were admitted that you who are dissatisfied, hold the right side in the dispute, there still is no single good reason for precipitate action. Intelligence, patriotism, Christianity, and a firm reliance on Him, who has never yet forsaken this favored land, are still competent to adjust, in the best way, all our present difficulty.

In *your* hands, my dissatisfied fellow countrymen, and not in *mine,* is the momentous issue of civil war. The government will not assail *you.* You can have no conflict, without being yourselves the aggressors. *You* have no oath registered in Heaven to destroy the government, while *I* shall have the most solemn one to "preserve, protect and defend" it.

I am loth to close. We are not enemies, but friends. We must not be enemies. Though passion may have strained, it must not break our bonds of affection. The mystic chords of memory, stretching from every battle-field, and patriot grave, to every living heart and hearthstone, all over this broad land, will yet swell the chorus of the Union, when again touched, as surely they will be, by the better angels of our nature.

With "more of Euclid than of Demosthenes"[76] in him, his delivery was not that of the spellbinder, agitator, or demagogue. His voice was a tenor that "carried song-tunes poorly but had clear and appealing modulations."[77] Habitually a

[76]Randall, op. cit., I, 49.
[77]Sandburg, *The Prairie Years,* I, 305.

little "scared"[78] when he spoke, he was "pale and very nervous"[79] on this occasion, but his "cheerfulness was marked."[80] "Compelled by nature, to speak slowly,"[81] his manner was "deliberate and impressive"[82] and his voice "remarkably clear and penetrating."[83] There was little evidence in his voice of the fear that might have come as the result of knowing that there were "heavy bets" about his safety.[84] Some of the spectators noted a "loud, and distinct voice, quite intelligible by at least ten thousand persons below him";[85] others found it a "clear, ringing voice, that was easily heard by those on the outer limits of the crowd";[86] still others noted his "firm tones of voice," his "great deliberation and precision of emphasis."[87] Sandburg might have remarked that it gave out "echoes and values."[88]

As Lincoln read on, the audience listened respectfully, with "intense interest, amid a stillness almost oppressive."[89] In the crowd behind the speaker sat Horace Greeley, momentarily expecting the crack of rifle fire.[90] At one point he thought it had come. The speaker stopped. But it was only a spectator crashing down through a tree.[91] Otherwise, the crowd in the grounds "behaved very well."[92] Buchanan sat listening, and "looking as straight as he could at the toe of his right boot."[93] Douglas, close by on Lincoln's right, listened "attentively," showing that he was "apparently satisfied" as he "exclaimed, *sotto voce*, 'Good,' 'That's so,' 'No coercion,' and 'Good again.' "[94] Chief Justice Taney "did not remove his eyes from Mr. Lincoln during the entire delivery."[95] Mr. Cameron stood with his back to the President, on the opposite side to Mr. Douglas, "peering off into the crowd."[96] Senator Seward and the other Cabinet officers-elect "kept themselves in the background."[97] Senator Wigfall of Texas, with folded arms "leaned conspicuously in a Capitol doorway," listening to the Inaugural, plainly wearing "contempt, defiance, derision, on his face, his pantomimic posture saying what he had said in the Senate, that the old Union was a corpse and the question was how to embalm it and conduct the funeral

---

[78][W. H. Herndon and J. W. Weik], *Herndon's Life of Lincoln*, with an introduction and notes by Paul M. Angle (Cleveland: The World Publishing Co., 1949), p. 220.

[79]*The Diary of a Public Man*, p. 74.

[80]Correspondence of the *Cincinnati Commercial*, as quoted in *Chicago Daily Tribune*, March 8, 1861, p. 2, col. 4.

[81]Herndon and Weik, op. cit., p. 273.

[82]*New York Tribune*, March 5, 1861, p. 5, col. 4.

[83]Ibid.

[84]*New York Times*, March 4, 1861, p. 1, col. 2.

[85]*National Intelligencer*, March 5, 1861, p. 3, col. 3.

[86]*New York Times*, March 5, 1861; p. 1, col. 3.

[87]Correspondence of the *Cincinnati Commercial*, quoted in *Chicago Daily Tribune*, March 8, 1861, p. 2, col. 4.

[88]Sandburg, *The Prairie Years* I, 306.

[89]Frederick W. Seward, *Seward at Washington, as Senator and Secretary of State* (New York: Derby and Miller, 1891), I, 516.

[90]Greeley, op. cit., p. 404.

[91]*Diary of a Public Man*, p. 74.

[92]Ibid.

[93]*New York Times*, March 5, 1861, p. 1, col. 3.

[94]Ibid.

[95]Ibid.

[96]Correspondence of the *Cincinnati Commercial*, as quoted in *Chicago Daily Tribune*, March 8, 1861, p. 2, col. 4.

[97]Ibid.

decently."[98] Thurlow Weed moved away from the crowd, reporting to General Scott at the top of the slope "The Inaugural is a success," as the old general exclaimed, "God be praised! God in his goodness be praised."[99] To a newspaper reporter surveying the scene, there was a "propriety and becoming interest which pervaded the vast assembly" and "impressed every spectator who had the opportunity of overlooking it."[100] The crowd "applauded repeatedly" and "at times, rapturously,"[101] particularly at points where he "announced his inflexible purpose to execute the laws and discharge his whole constitutional duty."[102] When Lincoln declared, "I hold that in the contemplation of international law, and of the Constitution, the Union of these States is perpetual," the "cheers were hearty and prolonged."[103] When he said, "I shall take care that the laws of the Union be faithfully executed in all the States," he was met with a "tremendous shout of approval."[104] But the "greatest impression of all was produced by the final appeal,"[105] noted one of the reporters. "With great solemnity of emphasis, using his gestures to add significance to his words," Lincoln remarked "You have no oath registered in Heaven to destroy this Government, while I shall have the most solemn one to preserve, protect and defend it," and the crowd responded with "round after round of cheering."[106] Finally, after Lincoln had addressed his "words of affection" to the audience, ending his address, "men waved their hats, and broke forth in the heartiest manifestations of delight. The extraordinary clearness [sic], straightforwardness and lofty spirit of patriotism which pervaded the whole address, impressed every listener, while the evident earnestness, sincerity and manliness of Mr. Lincoln extorted the praise even of his enemies."[107] "The effect of the Inaugural on the country at large remains to be awaited and to be gathered from many sources," observed a reporter, "but it is conceded on all hands that its effect, already noticeable on the vast gathering here, upon the city, and the tone of feeling here is eminently happy, and the source of great gratulation on every side."[108]

Chief Justice Taney stepped forward, shrunken, old, his hands trembling with emotion, and held out an open Bible. Lincoln laid his left hand upon it, raised his right hand, and repeated with a "firm but modest voice"[109] the oath: "I do solemnly swear that I will faithfully execute the office of President of the United States, and will, to the best of my ability, preserve, protect, and defend the Constitution of the United States." Lincoln was now President. Below, the crowd "tossed their hats, wiped their eyes, cheered at the tops of their voices,

[98]Sandburg, *The War Years,* 1, 123.
[99]Seward, op. cit., pp. 516, 517.
[100]*New York Daily Tribune,* March 5, 1861, p. 5, col. 4.
[101]*Chicago Daily Tribune,* March 8, 1861, p. 2, col. 4, quoted from *Cincinnati Commercial.*
[102]*New York Daily Tribune,* March 5, 1861, p. 5, col. 4.
[103]*Chicago Daily Tribune,* March 8, 1861, p. 2, col. 4, quoted from *Cincinnati Commercial.*
[104]*Chicago Daily Tribune,* March 8, 1861, p. 2, col. 4, quoted from *Cincinnati Commercial.*
[105]Ibid.
[106]Ibid.
[107]*Chicago Daily Tribune,* March 8, 1861, p. 2, col. 4, quoted from *Cincinnati Commercial.*
[108]*Chicago Daily Tribune,* March 9, 1861, p. 3, col. 2.
[109]*New York Times,* March 5, 1861, p. 1, col. 3.

hurrahed themselves hoarse," and "had the crowd not been so very dense, they would have demonstrated in more lively ways, their joy, satisfaction and delight."[110] Over on the slope the artillery boomed a salute to the sixteenth President of the United States.[111] The crowd ebbed away, and Lincoln rode down Pennsylvania Avenue with Buchanan, bidding him good-bye at the Presidential mansion.[112]

The address had taken thirty-five minutes in delivery, and now it was all over, at least until the nation in general turned in its response. Lincoln had spent six weeks in preparing it—six weeks and many years of lonely thought, along with his active experience on the circuit and the stump. Like the "House Divided Speech" and the "Cooper Union Address" it was deliberately and cautiously prepared, undergoing revision up to the moment of delivery. "Late in January," he told his law partner, Herndon, that he was "ready to begin"[113] the preparation of the Inaugural. In a room over a store, across the street from the State House, cut off from all intrusion and outside communication, he began the preparation. He had told Herndon what works he wanted to consult and asked to be furnished "Henry Clay's great speech delivered in 1850; Andrew Jackson's proclamation against Nullification; and a copy of the Constitution." He "afterwards" called for a copy of Webster's reply to Hayne, a speech which he regarded as "the grandest specimen of American oratory."[114] "With these few 'volumes,' and no further sources of reference,"[115] he began his work on the address.

On February 2, 1861, he wrote a friend, George D. Prentice,[116] editor of the *Louisville Journal*, "I have the document blocked out; but in the now rapidly shifting scenes I shall have to hold it subject to revision up to the time of delivery."[117] He had an original draft printed by one of the proprietors of the *Illinois State Journal* to whom he entrusted the manuscript.[118] "No one else seems to have been taken into the confidence of Mr. Lincoln as to its contents until after he started for Washington on February 11."[119] Upon reaching Indianapolis, he presented a copy to O. H. Browning who had accompanied him from Springfield. According to Browning, "before parting with Mr. Lincoln at Indianapolis, Tuesday, he gave me a copy of his inaugural address, and requested me to read it, and give him my opinion, which I did. I thought it able, well considered, and appropriate, and so informed him. It is, in my judgment, a very admirable document. He permitted me to retain a copy, under promise not to show it except to Mrs. Browning."[120]

---

[110]Ibid.
[111]Sandburg, *The War Years*, I, 122.
[112]Baringer, op. cit., p. 334.
[113]Herndon and Weik, op. cit., p. 386.
[114]Ibid.
[115]Ibid.
[116]*Lincoln Lore*, No. 308 (March 4, 1935).
[117]Louis A. Warren, "Original Draft of the First Inaugural," *Lincoln Lore*, No. 358 (February 17, 1936).
[118]Ibid.
[119]Ibid.
[120]*The Diary of Orville Hickman Browning*, edited with an introduction and notes by Theodore Calvin Pease and James G. Randall (Springfield, Ill.: Illinois State Historical Library, 1925), I, 1850–1864, 455, 456.

Upon arriving in Washington, Lincoln submitted a copy to Secretary Seward with the same invitation to criticize it.[121] According to Louis A. Warren, "As far as we know these two men are the only ones who made any suggestions about certain revisions in the original copy,"[122] even though a few others may have seen it.[123]

Reporters showed an avid interest in the preparation of the Inaugural, sometimes reporting inaccurately on the various stages of its preparation. Recording the activities of the President on Saturday night, March 2, one reporter erroneously observed: "Mr. Lincoln sent for Senator Seward, and at 11½ o'clock that gentleman reached the hotel. Mr. Lincoln read to him the Inaugural for the first time, and then asked his advice. Senator Seward took it up section after section and concurred heartily in a great part of it. He suggested a few modifications, an occasional emendation and a few additional paragraphs, all of which were adopted by Mr. Lincoln, and the Inaugural was declared complete and perfect by Senator Seward, who then retired."[124] On Sunday, the reporter remarked, "Mr. Lincoln stated this evening that the Inaugural could not be printed, as some points might require modifying or extending, according to the action of the Senate to-night. His son is now writing copies of what is finished, one of which will be given to the Associated Press when he commences reading it."[125] On the same day there were "reports of efforts in high quarters to induce the president to tone down his inaugural, but it is not affirmed that they were successful."[126]

A final report on the preparation of the Inaugural records the activities on the morning of March 4th: "Mr. Lincoln rose at 5 o'clock. After an early breakfast, the Inaugural was read aloud to him by his son Robert, and the completing touches were added, including the beautiful and impassioned closing paragraph."[127]

As J. G. Randall has observed, "if one would justly appraise Lincoln's first presidential state paper, this inaugural of 1861 deserves to be read as delivered and to be set over against the alternative statements that Lincoln avoided or struck out in revision. Statements pledging maintenance of Federal authority were toned down and shorn of truculence, while promises of conciliation were emotionally underlined."[128] Mr. Browning advised "but one change," supposed by some authorities to be "the most important one in the entire document."[129] "Mr. Seward made thirty-three suggestions for improving the document and nineteen of them were adopted, eight were used after Mr. Lincoln had modified them, and six were discarded *in toto*."[130] Finally, Lincoln, "without suggestion from any one made sixteen changes in the original draft."[131]

---

[121]Seward, op. cit., p. 512.

[122]*Lincoln Lore*, No. 358.

[123]John G. Nicolay and John Hay, *Abraham Lincoln, A History* (New York: The Century Co., 1914), III, 319. Nicolay and Hay observe that "Judge David Davis read it while in Springfield," and "Francis P. Blair, Sr., read it in Washington, and highly commended it, suggesting no changes."

[124]*New York Times*, March 4, 1861, p. 1, col. 1.

[125]*New York Times*, March 4, 1861, p. 1, col. 2.

[126]*New York Daily Tribune*, March 4, 1861, p. 5, col. 1.

[127]*New York Times*, March 5, 1861, p. 1, col. 1.

[128]Randall, op. cit., I, 309.

[129]Warren, loc. cit.

[130]Ibid.

[131]Ibid.

And so, however much the country might criticize as it scanned the Inaugural, Lincoln could respond, as he did to the Douglas taunt in 1858, that the "House Divided Speech" had been "evidently well prepared and carefully written."[132] "I admit that it was. I am not master of language; I have not a fine education; . . . I know what I meant, and I will not leave this crowd in doubt. . . ."[133]

Lincoln did not have to wait long for a response from the country at large. As he delivered the address, little audiences unseen by the speaker dotted the land, clustering around newspaper offices and waiting for telegraphic reports of what was in the Inaugural. Between Washington and New York, the American Telegraph Company had placed at the disposal of the Associated Press three wires for the communication of the address.[134] Similar arrangements had been made with other key cities. The delivery of the Inaugural commenced at 1:30 P.M., Washington time, and the "telegraphers promptly to the minute" began its transmission. "The first words of the Message were received by the agents of the Press at 1:45, and the last about 3:30," observed the *New York Times*.[135] "Such rapidity in telegraphic communication has never before been reached in this country."[136] By four o'clock, "the entire document was furnished to the different newspapers,"[137] and special editions of the press were in the hands of readers within an hour. "People of all parties in this city, as elsewhere, were on tip-toe all day to know what was going on at Washington, and especially to hear what President Lincoln would say in his Inaugural," observed the *New York Times*.[138] "At length it was announced that the procession had reached the Capitol, and then, while the President was delivering his speech and the reporters were transmitting it by telegraph, there was a long period of unalloyed expectancy. Meantime, men given to talking, in the many crowds, discussed all sorts of topics, connected with the questions of the day, before little groups of gaping listeners. There was many a prophet among them, not without honor, before the Message was received, who knew exactly what it was going to contain, and foretold with marvelous preciseness the points which Mr. Lincoln would dwell on.

"It was nearly 5 o'clock when the eloquence of these worthies was suddenly quenched as by a wet blanket, and the wet sheets of the latest edition, with the President's Inaugural in black and white, leaped forth from the presses into the hands of all who could get copies. Then there was wild scrambling around the counters in publication offices, a laying down of pennies and a rape of newspapers, and the crowds began to disperse, each man hastening to some place remote from public haunt, where he might peruse the document in peace. The newsboys rushed through the city crying with stentorian lungs 'The President's

---

[132]Speech of Senator Douglas, delivered in Chicago, July 9, 1858, in *The Political Debates between Abraham Lincoln and Stephen A. Douglas*, with an introduction by George Haven Putnam (New York: G. P. Putnam's Sons, 1913), p. 24.

[133]Speech in reply to Douglas at Chicago, Illinois, July 10, 1858, in *Abraham Lincoln, His Speeches and Writings*, edited by Roy P. Basler, p. 392.

[134]*New York Times*, March 5, 1861, p. 8, col. 5.

[135]Ibid.

[136]Ibid.

[137]Ibid.

[138]*New York Times*, March 5, 1861, p. 8, cols. 4, 5.

Message!' 'Lincoln's Speech!' 'Ex-tray Times!' 'Get Lincoln's Inau-gu-ra-a-a-il!' And an hour later everybody had read the Message and everybody was talking about it."[139]

Out in Mattoon, Illinois, a similar scene was being enacted. A roving reporter, heading south from Chicago to observe the reactions of the crowds, made a "tour of the town" and stopped at hotel lobbies, where the speech, fresh from the press, was being "read and re-read, silently and aloud, to groups of ardent listeners . . . As the reading in a crowd progresses, when the reader comes to the place where Mr. Lincoln 'puts his foot down,' down goes likewise every foot in the circle."[140]

The home folks whom Lincoln had bade an affectionate farewell three weeks before were among the most anxious of the unseen audiences. Whereas they spoke only for themselves at the time of the tearful departure, they were now ready to speak for the nation. "The Inaugural Address of our noble Chief Magistrate has electrified the whole country," they said. "It has satisfied people of all parties who love the Union and desire its preservation. In this city it gives almost universal satisfaction."[141] In Quincy, the scene of one of the debates of 1858, the address was received with "much enthusiasm," and the Republican Gun Squad fired thirty-four guns;[142] in Peoria, "so great was the anxiety felt to see what Mr. Lincoln said, that people came forty miles to get copies of the message,"[143] reading it with "much enthusiasm."[144]

But occasionally there was a dissenting voice back home, particularly in the Democratic press, as there was generally throughout the North. While the *Chicago Daily Tribune* was "quite sure that no document can be found among American state papers embodying sounder wisdom and higher patriotism,— breathing kindlier feelings to all sections of the country,"[145] the Chicago *Times* denounced the Inaugural as "a loose, disjointed, rambling affair," concluding that the Union was now "lost beyond hope."[146] While the *New York Times* observed that "conservative people are in raptures over the Inaugural," and that "Its conciliatory tone, and frank, outspoken declaration of loyalty to the whole country, captured the hearts of many heretofore opposed to Mr. Lincoln,"[147] the New York *Herald* found that "the inaugural is not a crude performance—it abounds in traits of craft and cunning. It bears marks of indecision, and yet of strong coercion proclivities . . . It is neither candid nor statesmanlike; nor does it possess any essential dignity or patriotism. It would have caused a Washington to mourn, and would have inspired a Jefferson, Madison, or Jackson with contempt."[148] There were those in Maine who found it a "poor, weak, trashy affair, a standing disgrace to the country, and a fit commentary on the fanaticism

---

[139]Ibid.
[140]*Chicago Daily Tribune*, March 8, 1861, p. 2, col. 3.
[141]*Illinois State Journal*, March 6, 1861, p. 2.
[142]*Chicago Daily Tribune*, March 6, 1861, p. 1, col. 3.
[143]Ibid.
[144]Ibid.
[145]*Chicago Daily Tribune*, March 5, 1861, p. 1, col. 1.
[146]Quoted in Randall, op. cit., p. 306.
[147]*New York Times*, March 5, 1861, p. 1, col. 4.
[148]Quoted in the *New York Daily Tribune*, March 7, 1861, p. 6, col. 6.

and unreasonableness which made him President."[149] Some in Pennsylvania found it "one of the most awkwardly constructed official documents we have ever inspected," and "pitiably apologetical for the uprising of the Republican party, and his own election to the Presidency, by it."[150] And there were those in Ohio "who never expected to see a Black Republican peaceably inaugurated in this White Republican country . . . but now the Rubicon is passed," and the Inaugural, "like its distinguished author," is "flat-footed. It is more *magazinish* in *sound* than in *style*, smelling strongly of gunpowder, and is '*coercion*' all over, as the South understands that word."[151]

"It is an interesting study" said a Douglas journal, the Peoria *Daily Democratic Union*, on March 7th, "to look over the various journals that have come to our table since the delivery of President Lincoln's Inaugural Address, and notice the different manner in which they speak of it." "All of these criticisms of the Address cannot be correct, for they clash materially; and that fact demonstrates very plainly that some of them were either the offspring of prejudice, or were written by men incapable of judging of the merits of this first state paper of President Lincoln."[152]

Whereas there was difference of opinion in the North, much of it stopped short of vehement denunciation. However, the South saw little hope from Lincoln, and expressed itself accordingly. "Mr. Lincoln's Inaugural Address is before our readers," observed the *Richmond Enquirer*, "couched in the cool, unimpassioned, deliberate language of the fanatic, with the purpose of pursuing the promptings of fanaticism even to the dismemberment of the Government with the horrors of civil war . . . Civil war must now come. Sectional war, declared by Mr. Lincoln, awaits only the signal gun from the insulted Southern Confederacy, to light its horrid fires all along the borders of Virginia."[153] The *Richmond Dispatch* was equally strong: "The Inaugural Address of Abraham Lincoln inaugurates civil war, as we have predicted it would from the beginning . . . The sword is drawn and the scabbard thrown away . . . ere long Virginia may be engaged in a life and death struggle. . . . "[154] The *Baltimore Sun* observed, "The Inaugural, as a whole, breathes the spirit of mischief," and found "no Union spirit in the address."[155] "We presume nobody is astonished to hear that Secessionists regard the Inaugural as a 'declaration of war,' " noted one observer. "Before the Inaugural has been read in a single Southern State, it is denounced, through the telegraph, from every Southern point, as a declaration of war."[156] "I have heard but one construction of Mr. Lincoln's declaration of his intention to 'hold, occupy, and possess the property and places belonging to the Government, and to collect the duties and imposts,' " observed a special

[149]*The Bangor Union*, as quoted in *New York Daily Tribune*, March 8, 1861, p. 6, col. 5.

[150]*The Philadelphia Evening Journal*, as quoted in *New York Daily Tribune*, March 7, 1861, p. 7, col. 3.

[151]*Cleveland Plain Dealer*, as quoted in *Chicago Daily Tribune*, March 9, 1861, p. 1, col. 3.

[152]Quoted in *Northern Editorials on Secession*, edited by Howard Cecil Perkins (New York: D. Appleton-Century Co., 1942), II, 643.

[153]Quoted in *New York Daily Tribune*, March 7, 1861, p. 7, col. 2. See also, *Southern Editorials on Secession*, pp. 474, 475.

[154]*Southern Editorials on Secession*, p. 475.

[155]Quoted in *New York Daily Tribune*, March 7, 1861, p. 7, col. 1.

[156]*New York Times*, March 7, 1861, p. 4, col. 2.

correspondent in Richmond. The Inaugural "is received with much disfavor," and "is regarded, if not as a declaration of war, as at least the expression of a determination to coerce the seceding States into compliance with the demands of the Federal Government."[157] Reporting from Charleston, South Carolina, another correspondent observed, "The part which, of course, attracted most attention and was read and re-read with deep interest, was that wherein Mr. Lincoln declares that to the best of his ability, he will take care, according to his oath and the Constitution, that 'the laws of the Union are faithfully executed in all the States,' and that he will use the power confided to him to 'hold, occupy and possess the property and places belonging to the Government, and to collect the duties and imposts.' " The verdict was, according to this correspondent, "that rebellion would not be treated tenderly by Mr. Lincoln, and that he was quite another sort of man from James Buchanan."[158]

At least a minority of the people of the South responded less vehemently. Occasionally a roving reporter, mingling among the crowds in Southern cities, reported less fury. From Montgomery came word that Alexander Stevens had found the Inaugural "the most *adroit* State paper ever published on the Continent," and "a great moral impression has been produced"[159] in both Charleston and Montgomery. In Savannah, Georgia, "Not a word have we yet heard uttered against its tone," observed a reporter, predicting "a powerful and sweeping effect at the South."[160] Now and then a reporter noticed "a pretty general disappointment that the document contained so little 'blood and thunder.' "[161] "That the document should be calm and dignified in tone and style, logical in its conclusions, and plain and kind in its treatment of the great topic of the day, was annoying to the Rebels, who hoped to find in the address a provocation for extreme action."[162]

While the country at large read the speech and responded both favorably and unfavorably, Senator Clingman of North Carolina and Stephen A. Douglas engaged in debate over its meaning in the United States Senate. "If I understand it aright, all that is direct in it, I mean, at least, that purpose which seems to stand out clearly and directly, is one which I think must lead to war—war against the confederate or seceding State"[163] remarked Clingman. Douglas, on the other hand, who had "read it carefully" could not "assent to the construction" of the senator from North Carolina, believing he could "demonstrate that there is no foundation for the apprehension which has been spread throughout the country, that this message is equivalent to a declaration of war."[164]

Just as the country searched the Inaugural for the sentiments it contained, it also examined and appraised the language and style in which it was couched. The Toronto *Leader* could not admire the "tawdry and corrupt schoolboy style," even as it gave "credit" for its "good sense."[165] An Albany, New York, observer found it "useless to criticize the style of the President's Inaugural when

[157]*New York Daily Tribune*, March 9, 1861, p. 6, col. 2.
[158]*New York Daily Tribune*, March 9, 1861, p. 6, col. 1.
[159]*New York Daily Tribune*, March 12, 1861, p. 6, col. 1.
[160]*New York Daily Tribune*, March 11, 1861, p. 6, col. 2.
[161]*New York Daily Tribune*, March 9, 1861, p. 6, col. 1.
[162]Ibid.
[163]*Congressional Globe*, Second Session, 36th Congress, Vol. 30, Part II, p. 1436.
[164]Ibid.
[165]Quoted in *New York Daily Tribune*, March 7, 1861, p. 7, col. 3.

the policy it declares is fraught with consequences so momentous." Nevertheless, he paused to describe it as a "rambling, discursive, questioning, loose-jointed stump speech." It consisted of "feeble rhetorical stuff."[166] While papers unfriendly to Lincoln were finding it "inferior in point of elegance, perspicuity, vigor, talent, and all the graces of composition to any other paper of a like character which has ever emanated from a President of the Republic,"[167] papers that were friendly found the contrary to be the case. "It is clear as a mountain brook," commented a Detroit reporter. "The depth and flow of it are apparent at a glance."[168] In Boston, the *Transcript* reporter commented at length. "The style of the Address is as characteristic as its temper. 'Right words in their right places'; this is the requirement of good rhetoric. Right words at the right times, should be the test by which we try the speech of statesmen; and this test Mr. Lincoln's address will bear. It has not one flaming expression in the whole course of its firm and explicit statements. The language is level to the popular mind,—the plain homespun language of a man accustomed to talk with 'the folks' and 'the neighbors,' the language of a man of vital common sense, whose words exactly fit his facts and thoughts."[169] Occasionally, the concluding paragraph was singled out for praise. In Indianapolis, the reporter of the *Daily Journal* remarked: "The closing sentence, the only attempt at rhetorical display in the whole address, is singularly and almost poetically beautiful."[170]

Part II

Given the circumstances that brought forth the Inaugural Address, and removed in time from the passions which agitated the country, what may one say of Lincoln's address on March 4, 1861? The historian has often examined it for its effects, and has concluded that "Though not fully appreciated then, this was one of the great American inaugurals."[171] And the literary critic has sometimes observed its final passage, finding in it poetic beauty and enduring worth. Unlike the historian, we are not concerned merely with the Inaugural as a force in the shaping of American culture; nor are we concerned with its enduring worth as literature. The Inaugural was a speech, "meant to be heard and intended to exert an influence of some kind on those who heard it,"[172] or those who read it. We must, therefore, be concerned with evaluating the Inaugural as a speech, a medium distinct from other media, and with methods peculiarly its own. We must be concerned with discovering in this particular case "the available means of persuasion" and with evaluating their worth.

Let us view the Inaugural as a communication, with a purpose, and a content presumably designed to aid in the accomplishment of that purpose, further

[166]*Albany Atlas and Argus,* as quoted in *Northern Editorials on Secession,* II, 628.

[167]*Jersey City American Standard,* as quoted in *Northern Editorials on Secession,* II, 625.

[168]*Detroit Daily Tribune,* as quoted in *Northern Editorials on Secession,* II, 623.

[169]Quoted in *New York Daily Tribune,* March 7, 1861, p. 7, col. 1.

[170]Quoted in *Northern Editorials on Secession,* II, 619.

[171]J. G. Randall, "Lincoln's Great Declarations of Faith," *New York Times Magazine,* February 6, 1949, p. 23.

[172]Wayland M. Parrish and Marie Hochmuth Nichols, *American Speeches,* (New York, David McKay, 1954), p. 3.

supported by skillful composition in words, and ultimately unified by the character and manner of the person who presented it.

We must not casually assume that Lincoln's purpose is easily discernible in the occasion itself. It is true, of course, that this was an inaugural ceremony, with a ritual fairly well established by fifteen predecessors, "Yet, with all this scope for [of] precedent," Lincoln was keenly aware that he entered upon the same task "under great and peculiar difficulty. A disruption of the Federal Union, heretofore only menaced, is now formidably attempted." If we are to discern the purpose that Lincoln had when he addressed the American people on March 4, 1861, we must recall the experiences of the nation between his election as President and the day of his inauguration. During that time, he had been made keenly aware of Southern resentment to a "sectional" President. The rapid movement of the Secessionists followed closely on the announcement of his election, and of the ascendancy of the Republican party to a position of power. The South viewed the Republican platform as an instrument for its "subjugation" and the "complete ruin of her social, political and industrial institutions."[173] By its acts of secession, and its establishment of a provisional government of its own, the lower South raised the very practical question: What is the authority of the federal government in regard to maintaining itself and in regard to reclaiming those federal properties possessed by retiring members?

Lincoln had also been made keenly aware of the doubts and skepticism that prevailed regarding his ability to lead his party and the nation. "I cannot but know what you all know," he had observed on his way to Washington, "that without a name, perhaps without a reason why I should have a name, there has fallen upon me a task such as did not rest even upon the Father of this Country . . . "[174] In addition, he was keenly aware of both Northern and Southern distrust of his moral character and integrity. Even to members of his party, he was a "funny man," given to stories in bad taste, and an Illinois wag. And to the South, he was at best thought to be as radical as the most rabid of the left-wing Republicans, hence a "dangerous man."[175] That he was aware of the prevailing sentiments regarding him as a man is reflected in his casual remark en route to Washington when, for a moment, his address was misplaced. In a worried search, he described the Inaugural as "my certificate of moral character, written by myself."[176]

Although from the time of his election he was urged to state his views on the passing events, Lincoln had remained silent. That his silence was not due to a lack of anxiety is easily apparent. "Allusion has been made," he noted on his way to Washington, "to the interest felt in relation to the policy of the new administration. In this I have received from some a degree of credit for having kept silence, and from others some deprecation. I still think that I was right . . .

"In the varying and repeatedly shifting scenes of the present, and without a precedent which could enable me to judge by the past, it has seemed fitting that

[173]*New Orleans Daily Crescent,* November 13, 1860, as quoted in *Southern Editorials on Secession,* p. 237.

[174]"Address to the Legislature of Ohio at Columbus, February 13, 1861," *Complete Works,* VI, 121.

[175]Speech of Senator Clingman of North Carolina in the Senate, December 3, 1860, *The Congressional Globe,* Second Session, 36th Congress, Vol. 30, p. 3.

[176]Ward Hill Lamon, *Recollections of Abraham Lincoln, 1847–1865,* edited by Dorothy Lamon Teillard (Washington, D.C.: Published by the editor, 1911), p. 36.

before speaking upon the difficulties of the country I should have gained a view of the whole field, being at liberty to modify and change the course of policy as future events may make a change necessary.

"I have not maintained silence from any want of real anxiety."[177]

What, then, was Lincoln's purpose? Clearly, he intended to take the occasion of the inauguration to declare the position of the Republican party in regard to the South, to announce his considered judgment in regard to the practical questions raised by the movement of secession, and, in all, to give what assurance he could of his personal integrity.

In evaluating the inaugural, we must keep in mind its purpose, for the purpose of the speech controlled Lincoln's selection of materials, his arrangement, his style, and his manner.

Let us turn to the speech itself in order to note the materials and methods he employed to sustain his purpose. Considering the general predisposition of the South to view the incoming administration with suspicion, and considering the fact that Lincoln had not spoken for his own party since his nomination, he found it necessary to take a moment to "press upon the public attention the most conclusive evidence of which the case is susceptible," the idea of the integrity of the Republican party and his own integrity as its helmsman. Wise judgment could scarcely have dictated otherwise, for the lower South had gone out of the Union partly on the grounds that it expected no fair consideration from the newly born party, and the border states were contemplating similar measures. Lincoln attempted to conciliate his audience by assuring the country that "the property, peace and security of no section are to be in any wise endangered by the now incoming Administration." In order to do this he called attention to the fact that he was taking a solemn oath in "your presence"; he committed himself again to previously spoken words[178] that have "all the while existed, and been open to their inspection"; to the Republican platform pertaining to the "maintenance inviolate of the rights of the States, and especially the right of each State to order and control its own domestic institutions according to its own judgment exclusively";[179] and to the clause "plainly written in the Constitution," pertaining to delivering up "on claim of the party to whom such service or labor may be due"[180] the escaping fugitive. He concluded his opening remarks with a reiteration of the avowal that he took the "official oath to-day, with no mental reservations, and with no purpose to construe the Constitution or laws, by any hypercritical rules." This was neither the material nor the method of a "deceitful" or "dangerous" man. By it, Lincoln was attempting to touch off those favorable responses that accrue to the appearance of honesty, straightforwardness, and obedience to the Constitution. One must remember that Lincoln's pledge of faith could not have given satisfaction to the Abolitionist group within his own party with whom he was constantly identified by the South; it did, however, serve to differentiate him from the radical element and hence to reassure the states yet within the Union. From the standpoint of persuasiveness

[177]"Address to the Legislature of Ohio at Columbus, February 13, 1861," *Complete Works*, VI, 121, 122.

[178]"Mr. Lincoln's Reply," First Joint Debate, at Ottawa, August 21, 1858, *The Political Debates between Abraham Lincoln and Stephen A. Douglas*, p. 209.

[179]Halstead, op. cit., p. 138.

[180]Article IV, Sec. 2.

Lincoln was undoubtedly wise in taking the advice of Seward to omit the two paragraphs immediately following his opening statement in the original draft of the Inaugural:

> The more modern custom of electing a Chief Magistrate upon a previously declared platform of principles, supersedes, in a great measure, the necessity of restating those principles in an address of this sort. Upon the plainest grounds of good faith, one so elected is not at liberty to shift his position. It is necessarily implied, if not expressed, that, in his judgment, the platform which he thus accepts, binds him to nothing either unconstitutional or inexpedient.
>
> Having been so elected upon the Chicago Platform, and while I would repeat nothing in it, of aspersion or epithet or question of motive against any man or party, I hold myself bound by duty, as well as impelled by inclination to follow, within the executive sphere, the principles therein declared. By no other course could I meet the reasonable expectations of the country.[181]

To have used the paragraphs would undoubtedly have incited anew the suspicion that he was merely a "sectional" President and an "abolitionist" or "party man."

Having spent time in an attempt to gain a fair hearing for the rest of his address, Lincoln next took up the question for which the whole country awaited an answer, namely, What is the duty and the policy of the Republican administration in regard to Secession? Without delay, he laid down the proposition, "I hold, that in contemplation of universal law, and of the Constitution, the Union of these States is perpetual. Perpetuity is implied, if not expressed, in the fundamental law of all national governments"; hence "no State, upon its own mere motion, can lawfully get out of the Union,—that *resolves* and *ordinances* to that effect are legally void, and that acts of violence, within any State or States, against the authority of the United States, are insurrectionary or revolutionary, according to circumstances." Furthermore, "if the United States be not a government proper, but an association of States in the nature of contract merely, can it, as a contract, be peaceably unmade, by less than all the parties who made it?"

To the North, the mere assertion of the principle of perpetuity would have been sufficient; no further proof would have been necessary. But to the lower South, already out of the Union, and to the border states and upper South contemplating similar action, clearly assertion was not sufficient. Therefore, Lincoln found his proposition "confirmed by the history of the Union itself." The Union, he pointed out, was "much older than the Constitution"; it was "formed in fact, by the Articles of Association in 1774"; it was "matured and continued by the Declaration of Independence in 1776"; it was "further matured and the faith of all the then thirteen States expressly plighted and engaged that it should be perpetual, by the Articles of Confederation in 1778"; finally "in 1787, one of

---

[181]For changes in the Inaugural, see MS of early printed version with secretarial reproductions of the changes, and accompanying letter of John Hay to Charles Eliot Norton, dated March 25, 1899, explaining the nature of the revisions, in Widener Library of Harvard University. See also, John G. Nicolay and John Hay, *Abraham Lincoln*, III, 327–344; Louis A. Warren, "Original Draft of the First Inaugural," *Lincoln Lore*, No. 358 (February 17, 1936) and No. 359 (February 24, 1936). See, *The Robert Todd Lincoln Collection of the Papers of Abraham Lincoln*, Library of Congress. Microfilm in University of Illinois Library. This collection contains the most important source for the various working sheets of the Inaugural.

the declared objects for ordaining and establishing the Constitution, was '*to form a more perfect Union.*' " Although Lincoln's support of his proposition was factual, the facts themselves carried with them the respect and loyalty that had always attached to the founding fathers who were held in esteem for their vision and their wisdom.

Having stated the principle that guided him, Lincoln continued logically with its application, holding that "to the extent of my ability I shall take care, as the Constitution itself expressly enjoins upon me, that the laws of the Union be faithfully executed in all the States." In discussing the policy of the government in enforcing the laws of the Union, Lincoln does not speak as the master or the mere advocate handing down a bloodless decision, but as a servant performing a "simple duty," the "American people" being "my rightful masters." As a skilled persuader, he was undoubtedly aware that lines of argument will often meet with varied responses according to whether they are put forward by those toward whom one feels sympathetic or antagonistic.[182] Nowhere in the Inaugural does Lincoln seek more earnestly to be conciliating and mild. He was aware that legalism alone would not sustain his purpose. He could have used the bold and confident assertion that appeared in the original draft of the Inaugural:

> All the power at my disposal will be used to reclaim the public property and places which have fallen; to hold, occupy and possess these, and all other property and places belonging to the government and to collect the duties and imposts; but beyond what may be necessary for these objects, there will be no invasion of any State.

Even in the original draft, Lincoln had avoided the use of the names of specific forts to which he had reference. Pickens and Sumter were in a precarious position and were peculiarly explosive topics of discussion. However, Lincoln yielded even further in tempering his remarks, accepting the suggestion of O. H. Browning, and finally choosing only to say:

> The power confided to me will be used to hold, occupy, and possess the property and places belonging to the Government, and to collect the duties and imposts; but, beyond what may be necessary for these objects, there will be no invasion, no using of force against or among the people anywhere.

Furthermore, "Where hostility to the United States, in any interior locality, shall be so great and so universal, as to prevent competent resident citizens from holding the Federal offices," he would make "no attempt to force obnoxious strangers among the people for that object," even though the "strict legal right may exist." And, the mails "unless repelled" would continue to be furnished. In doing this, "there needs to be no bloodshed or violence," he assured the country, and promised that "there shall be none, unless it be forced upon the national authority." Nowhere did Lincoln assert a power or a practice that he believed impossible of enforcement, or that he believed could be interpreted as "coercion" in its baldest and most belligerent form.

Having announced his specific policy, Lincoln turned to those "who really love the Union," neither affirming nor denying that there were those "who seek to destroy the Union at all events," being "glad of any pretext to do it." In his original draft, he had intended pointedly to observe, "Before entering upon so grave a matter as the destruction of our national Union, would it not be wise to

---

[182]Robert K. Merton, *Mass Persuasion* (New York: Harper and Brothers, 1946), p. 109.

ascertain precisely why we do it?'' In his final draft, however, he blotted out the word "Union" and substituted for it the unifying and figurative word "fabric," further inserting the words "with all its benefits, its memories and its hopes," thereby seeking to heighten feeling by suggesting appropriate attitudes.

Having passed the climax of his remarks, Lincoln moved, in the last half of the Inaugural, to a reasoned discussion of related topics. He denied that any right plainly written in the Constitution had been violated, observing that majorities and minorities arise as a result of that class of questions for which no specific constitutional answer has been provided. The alternative to accepting the "majority principle" was always either "anarchy or depotism." Not even the Supreme Court could serve as the final arbiter on questions "affecting the whole people," for unless it limited its activity to making decisions on specific "cases properly brought before them," the "people will have ceased to be their own rulers." He argued the impracticability of secession, contrasting it with the simple act of divorce between husband and wife who may remain "beyond the reach of each other," and concluded that "Physically speaking, we cannot separate." Not even war was a satisfactory solution to difficulties, for "you cannot fight always," and after much "loss on both sides, and no gain on either," the "identical old questions" are again to be settled. "This country, with its institutions, belongs to the people who inhabit it," he insisted, urging that when the whole people "shall grow weary of the existing government, they can exercise their *constitutional* right of amending it, or their *revolutionary* right to dismember or overthrow it."

Lincoln's appeal throughout was to the "patient confidence in the ultimate justice of the people." "Is there any better or equal hope, in the world?" he asked, even as he noted the human tendency of parties in dispute to insist with equal confidence on being in the "right." Rising to the position of impartial leader, he sought faith in a higher law, and in a disinterested Ruler: "If the Almighty Ruler of nations, with his eternal truth and justice, be on your side of the North or on yours of the South, that truth, and that justice, will surely prevail, by the judgment of this great tribunal, the American people."

Lincoln ended his address with both a challenge and a declaration of faith. "In *your* hands, my dissatisfied fellow countrymen, and not in *mine,* is the momentous issue of civil war. The government will not assail *you.*" He was just about to take an oath, and to him an oath was a solemn pledge, not only in word, but in truth. It was an avowal of morality, binding him not only to duty to the people but to God, "the Almighty Ruler of nations." "*You* have no oath registered in Heaven to destroy the government," he pleaded in an attempt to secure the cooperation of all those who could help him in fulfilling the pledge he was to take, "while *I* shall have the most solemn one to 'preserve, protect and defend' it." His final appeal was to feeling rather than to reason. He undoubtedly realized that when men cannot achieve common ground through reason, they may achieve it through the medium of feeling. "I am loth to close," he observed. "We are not enemies, but friends. We must not be enemies. Though passion may have strained, it must not break our bonds of affection." No longer the advocate, or even the President performing official duties, Lincoln, taking the advice of Seward, became the affectionate father, the benevolent and hopeful counselor, trusting not only in reason, but calling on "memory," the "patriot grave," the "heart and hearth-stone," "the better angels of our nature" to "swell the chorus of the Union."

Whereas the disgruntled may have "found too much argumentative discussion of the question at issue, as was to have been expected from a man whose whole career has been that of an advocate,"[183] obviously others could not have failed to notice that Lincoln sought valiantly to employ all the "available means of persuasion." He had sought to reach his audience not only through reason, but through feeling and through the force of his own ethical ideals.

Any fair-minded critic, removed from the passions of the times, must find himself much more in agreement with those observers of the day who believed the Inaugural met the "requirements of good rhetoric" by having "right words in their right places" and "right words at the right times,"[184] than with those who labeled it "feeble rhetorical stuff," and found it "inferior in point of elegance, perspicuity, vigor, talent, and all the graces of composition to any other paper of a like character from a President of the Republic."[185] One who studies the revisions in phrase and word in the various drafts of the Inaugural must become aware that Lincoln was concerned not only with using the right argument, but with using words cautiously, and purposefully, to obtain a desired effect from his listeners and from his potential readers. To the rhetorician, style is not an aspect of language which can be viewed in isolation or judged merely by the well-attuned ear. Nor is it sufficient to apply such rubrics as clarity, vividness, elegance as absolute values, or as an adequate description of style. Words are an "available means of persuasion," and the only legitimate question is: Did Lincoln use words effectively to achieve his specific purpose?

Although Lincoln may have lamented that he did not have a "fine education" or that he was not a "master of language,"[186] he had a keen sensitiveness for language. He "studied to see the subject matter clearly," said an early teacher, "and to express it truly and strongly. I have known him to study for hours the best way of three to express an idea."[187] And when his partner, Herndon, attempted the grandiose in expression, Lincoln sometimes remarked, "Billy, don't shoot too high—aim lower and the common people will understand you. They are the ones you want to reach—at least they are the ones you ought to reach. The educated and refined people will understand you any way. If you aim too high your ideas will go over the heads of the masses, and only hit those who need no hitting."[188] Lincoln had become adept at stump speaking, and knew how to use language to make himself clear and to make a point. That he knew the power of language to fire passions and to cloud understanding is amply demonstrated in his remarks at Indianapolis when he was en route to Washington. "Solomon says there is 'a time to keep silence,' " he observed, "and when men wrangle by the month with no certainty that they mean the same thing, while using the same word, it perhaps were as well if they would keep silence. The words 'coercion' and 'invasion' are much used in these days, and often with some temper and hot blood. Let us make sure, if we can, that we do not misunderstand the meaning of those who use them. Let us get exact definitions of

---

[183]*The Diary of a Public Man*, p. 75.
[184]*The Boston Transcript*, as quoted in *New York Daily Tribune*, March 7, 1861, p. 7, col. 1.
[185]*Jersey City Standard*, as quoted in *Northern Editorials on Secession*, II, 625.
[186]Speech in reply to Douglas at Chicago, Illinois, July 10, 1858, in *Abraham Lincoln: His Speeches and Writings*, edited by Roy P. Basler, p. 393.
[187]Herndon and Weik, op. cit., p. 99.
[188]Ibid., p. 262.

these words, not from dictionaries, but from the men themselves, who certainly deprecate the things they would represent by the use of words."[189] Lincoln was keenly aware that words themselves were often grounds for argument, systems of attitudes suggesting courses of action.[190] Then, too, Lincoln knew that his "friends feared" and "those who were not his friends hoped, that, forgetting the dignity of his position, and the occasion, he would descend to the practices of the story-teller, and fail to rise to the level of a statesman."[191]

The desire for clearness, the desire to subdue passion, the desire to manifest the integrity and dignity befitting a statesman in a responsible position—these are the factors that influenced Lincoln in his composition of the Inaugural, and to appraise his style without constant awareness of them is likely to lead the critic far afield. Let us consider Lincoln's style, then, as a system of symbols designed to evoke certain images favorable to the accomplishment of his purpose and, in so far as he could, to prevent certain other images from arising.

One of the most marked characteristics of Lincoln's style is its directness. By it he attempts to achieve the appearance of candor and honesty, traits that were eminently significant to the success of the Inaugural, considering the doubts and suspicions that were prevalent regarding his integrity. From the opening sentence to the conclusion one notes the unmistakable honesty and straightforwardness that reside in direct address. "I appear before you," he remarks, "to address you briefly, and to take, in your presence, the oath prescribed by the Constitution of the United Sates . . . " Again he observes, "I have no purpose, directly or indirectly, to interfere with the institution of slavery in the States where it exists"; "I now reiterate these sentiments"; "I take the official oath to-day, with no mental reservations";"*You* have no oath registered in Heaven to destroy the government, while *I* shall have the most solemn one to 'preserve, protect and defend' it." Direct and forthright throughout, he could scarcely have used words to better advantage in emphasizing his honesty and integrity.

What doubts there were pertaining to inadequacies traceable to his humble origins and his lack of formal education must in some wise have been dispelled by his clearness, his accuracy, and his freedom from the awkward expression or the simple idiom of the Western stump speaker. Lincoln had felt his inadequacies when he addressed an Eastern audience of educated men at Cooper Union and was uncomfortable. In his Inaugural, prepared for an audience representative of the whole country, he had been cautious and careful to use language that was sustained in its dignity. Seward, sometimes known for his polished expression, had given him some aid in the choice of the proper word. Lincoln accepted advice in such word changes as "acquiesce" instead of "submit," "constituted" instead of "constructed," "void" instead of "nothing," "repelled" instead of "refused," and he also accepted such a change of phrase as "imperfectly supports the law itself" for " is against the law itself." Although the changes are minor, they reflect Lincoln's desire for correctness and conciseness. On his own better judgment, he deleted the one extended metaphor that appeared in the

---

[189]"Address to the Legislature of Indiana at Indianapolis, February 12, 1861." *Complete Works,* VI, 112, 113.

[190]Kenneth Burke,"Two Functions of Speech," *The Language of Wisdom and Folly,* edited and with an introduction by Irving J. Lee (New York: Harper and Brothers, 1949), p. 40.

[191]L. E. Chittenden, *Recollections of President Lincoln and His Administration* (New York: Harper and Brothers, 1904), p. 88.

original draft. "I am, rather for the old ship, and the chart of the old pilots," he had originally written, with some of the tang and flavor of his speech in addressing popular Western audiences. "If, however, the people desire a new, or an altered vessel, the matter is exclusively their own, and they can move in the premises, as well without as with an executive recommendation." The figure was not equal in elevation to the rest of his remarks. His final draft read simply, "I cannot be ignorant of the fact that many worthy and patriotic citizens are desirous of having the national Constitution amended. While I make no recommendation of amendments, I fully recognize the rightful authority of the people over the whole subject . . . " Such phrasing, simple in its dignity, undoubtedly was more appropriate and suited to his needs.

That Lincoln sought to control the behavior of his audience and the reader through the appropriately affective word is apparent throughout his address. There are times when even the level of specificity and concreteness, usually thought to be virtues of style, is altered in favor of the more general word or allusion. For instance, Lincoln had originally intended to say, "why may not South Carolina, a year or two hence, arbitrarily, secede from a new Southern Confederacy . . . ?" Finally, however, he avoided being specific, altering his remarks to read "why may not any portion of a new confederacy, a year or two hence, arbitrarily secede again . . . ?" Again, the ridicule in his assertion, "The Union is less perfect than before, which contradicts the Constitution, and therefore is absurd," is eliminated and reason is substituted: "The Union is *less perfect* than before the Constitution, having lost the vital element of its perpetuity." Lincoln sometimes chose the longer statement in preference to the sharp, pointed word or phrase, if by a longer expression he could avoid truculence or the pointing of an accusing finger. Such a phrase as "be on your side of the North or on yours of the South," aided considerably in creating an image of impartiality, and was to be preferred for the shorter, but divisive phrase, "be on our side or yours." The changes that Lincoln made in the direction of fullness rather than compression were designed to aid in clearness, exactness, and completeness, for the country expected him to express himself fully on the disturbing problems of the time.

The close of Lincoln's address, often cited for its poetic beauty, reflects not only his aesthetic sense, but perhaps more importantly, his power of using words to evoke images conducive to controlling response. As is very well known, Lincoln was not merely trying to be eloquent when he closed the address. He achieved eloquence and cadenced beauty through his direct attempt to be "affectionate," Seward having reminded him that perhaps feeling should supplement reason, and having suggested a possible conclusion:

> I close. We are not we must not be aliens or enemies but ~~countrym~~ fellow countrymen and brethren. Although passion has strained our bonds of affection too hardly they must not ~~be broken they will not~~ I am sure they will not, be broken. The mystic chords of memory which proceeding from ~~every ba~~ so many battle fields and ~~patriot~~ so many patriot graves ~~bi~~ pass through all the hearts and hearths ~~all the hearths~~ in this broad continent of ours will yet ~~harme~~ again harmonize in their ancient music when ~~touched as they surely~~ breathed upon ~~again~~ by the ~~better angel~~ guardian angel of the nation.[192]

---

[192]Facsimile of the original suggestion of Seward as reprinted in *Abraham Lincoln: His Speeches and Writings,* edited by Roy P. Basler, pp. 589, 590.

An image of great-heartedness, great humility, and great faith resulted when Lincoln rephrased Seward's suggestion in his own style. It was his final declaration of faith and had in it the emotional intensity that often accompanies the hoped-for but unknown. It was his final plea for a course of action befitting "friends."

Let us conclude our remarks on Lincoln's style by emphasizing that it reflected the same purposefulness that was characteristic of the arguments contained in the address. Through directness, clearness, dignity, and appropriately affective words, he sought to aid himself in achieving his ends.

One further means of persuasion may be noted, namely, that of his manner in oral presentation. Lincoln's delivery, of course, was significant chiefly to those who composed his immediate audience, and not to any great extent to the much larger audience throughout the country, except in so far as eyewitnesses and newspaper reports conveyed impressions pertaining to the character and personality of the speaker. It is undoubtedly true that Lincoln's manner contributed heavily to his effectiveness on this particular occasion. It may even be true that, had the whole country been immediately present, it would have found further grounds for trust. Ethical stature often shows itself not only in the selection of argument or the composition of words, but in those "echoes and values" that emanate from physical presence alone. "If I were to make the shortest list of the qualifications of the orator," Emerson once remarked, "I should begin with *manliness;* and perhaps it means here presence of mind." [193] It must be remembered that when Lincoln advanced to the platform to deliver his Inaugural, he did so in face of threats on his life. That he manifested little fear is apparent from practically all of the newspaper accounts of the day. The most usual observation indicated that "the great heart and kindly nature of the man were apparent in his opening sentence, in the tone of his voice, the expression of his face, in his whole manner and bearing." [194] In the judgment of many, he "gained the confidence of his hearers and secured their respect and affection." [195] Lincoln appears to have had a sense of communication, a complete awareness of what he was saying when he was saying it. His thought emerged clearly and appeared to be in no way obstructed by affectation or peculiarities of manner. With dignity and firmness coupled with mildness and humility he sought to enforce his plea by those powers that reside in personality. That they have stimulus value one can scarcely question.

Thirty-nine days after Lincoln delivered his Inaugural Address, Fort Sumter was fired upon. Civil war had begun. Lincoln had sought to save the Union by carefully reasoned argument, by regard for the feelings and rights of all the people, and by a solemn avowal of justice and integrity. That the inaugural alone could not prevent the war is surely insufficient ground to condemn it for ineptness. "In speechmaking, as in life, not failure, but low aim, is crime." [196] There were many divisive forces, and these had gained great momentum by the time Lincoln addressed the American people. The South accepted the burden of his challenge, "In *your* hands, my dissatisfied fellow countrymen, and not in *mine,* is the momentous issue of civil war."

---

[193] "Eloquence," *The Complete Works of Ralph Waldo Emerson* (New York: Sully and Kleinteich, 1875), VIII, 123.

[194] Chittenden, loc. cit.

[195] Ibid., p. 90.

[196] Parrish and Nichols, op. cit., p. 12.

THE HISTORICAL APPROACH

HARRY S TRUMAN (1884–1972), THIRTY-THIRD PRESIDENT OF THE UNITED STATES

Halford R. Ryan

Harry S Truman had the distinct rhetorical disadvantage of following one of the greatest presidential persuaders in U.S. history, Franklin D. Roosevelt. Although Truman was not as eloquent as his predecessor and would always thereby suffer in comparison, he was nevertheless an effective speaker as president of the United States.

Truman was not unacquainted with oratorical skills upon ascendancy to the Oval Office. He began his speaking career by addressing Masonic lodges in Missouri. He ran for judge of the Jackson County Court as a Democrat in 1922, and he appealed effectively to the veteran voters from World War I. But many of his close friends and political pals agreed that he was not a particularly effective orator. He lost the judgeship race in 1924 due to a national Republican sweep into power from the presidency, with Calvin Coolidge, right down to Jackson County, Missouri. Truman, however, was elected Jackson County presiding judge in 1926, and he was never thereafter defeated in a political race. Voter loyalty to the Democratic party and to its candidates probably accounted more for Truman's elections than did his oratory. Although his speeches were not stirring or stylistic, they were characterized by a straightforward style that stressed the facts and the issues at hand. This rhetorical habit of plain speaking served him well in the presidency.

Just being a Democrat in the 1934 Senate race helped Truman win his seat. Truman ran against the Republican conservative incumbent and for Franklin D. Roosevelt and his popular New Deal. During the depression, the choice was abundantly clear to the voters. Truman was not a noted orator in the Senate, nor were his speeches widely printed or closely read; however, he was a conscientious worker on senatorial committee business.

The campaign for his Senate seat in 1940 was arduous, often bitter, and close. He emerged from the primary by a narrow margin of 8,000 votes and beat the

From *American Orators of the Twentieth Century: Critical Studies and Sources,* edited by Bernard K. Duffy and Halford R. Ryan (Westport, CT: Greenwood Press, 1987), 397–404. Copyright © 1987 by Bernard K. Duffy and Halford R. Ryan. Reprinted with permission.

Dr. Ryan is a professor of speech communication at Washington and Lee University.

Republican candidate by some 44,000 ballots. Truman had to campaign extensively, and, again, he was somewhat helped by being a New Deal Democrat. His political prominence on the national level increased under his leadership of the Truman committee, which investigated what could be called today the seamy side of the military-industrial complex of World War II. Indeed Truman was chosen as FDR's running mate in 1944 not so much for his oratorical abilities as for his loyalty to FDR and to the New Deal and for his popular and praiseworthy work on the Truman committee. Truman campaigned as the vice-presidential candidate, but Roosevelt won the votes. And then, on April 12, 1945, Harry S Truman became president of the United States.

Truman as a Rhetorical President

President Truman relied on persuasive presidential oratory to articulate his key administrative policies and to seek support for them. In this category of significant policy speeches were the Truman Doctrine, the Korean war, and the firing of General MacArthur. In addition to these addresses, the miracle of 1948 merits special mention: his convention acceptance speech, his whistle-stop campaign, and his Inaugural Address. His valedictory speech appropriately summarizes his seven-year tenure in the White House.

One of President Truman's most important addresses was his so-called Truman Doctrine speech to a joint session of Congress on March 12, 1947. This speech was Truman's economic, political, and rhetorical response to mounting communist infiltration and subversion in Greece and Turkey, and it also was the impetus for his containment policy and cold war rhetoric. He organized his speech around four main ideas: (1) Greece needed economic and political aid in order to survive as a democracy, (2) so did Turkey, (3) the United States was the only power capable of meeting that need, and (4) Congress needed to approve the specific funds. Truman used a number of logical appeals in the form of factual examples to underline the urgent situation, and he employed numerous emotional appeals—centering around pity and indignation for the embattled Greeks and Turks and focusing on fear, righteousness, and anger against the communists—to bolster his argument. As an example of the cold war rhetoric, Truman polarized his language: the United States was portrayed as good and the communists as bad. This hard-line speech was generally well received by the American people and even by some newspapers that did not normally support Truman, and a bipartisan Congress passed the enabling legislation. The cold war containment policy, which was enunciated in the Truman Doctrine speech, was one of Truman's major legislative accomplishments.

President Truman delivered several important addresses on the Korean war, which was uppermost in his and America's thoughts for most of his last two years in office. North Korean forces invaded South Korea in July 1950, and Truman delivered his first rhetorical response on July 19, 1950. In his usual manner, he went directly to the facts of communist "aggression," "contempt," and "challenge." He gave a short history of how the crisis arose, which was narrated in the cold war polarity between good (the United Nations and the United States) versus the bad (the Soviet Union). He bolstered his justification for sending U.S. troops to Korea by citing letters from Generals Collins and MacArthur. In the latter part of the speech, he dealt with the economic and military measures he sent to the Congress for enactment, and he tried to still domestic fears about shortages of food and rationing of materials. He indicated in his speech that the war aim was "to put down lawless aggression" and "to stop the fighting in Korea." The rationale for these responses to the Korean intervention was based on the lessons one learned from the 1930s: "Appeasement leads only to further aggression and ultimately to war." The same general themes were stressed in his speech at the War Memorial Opera House in San Francisco on October 17, 1950, where he made his famous statement, "The only victory we seek is the victory of peace."

Suddenly, however, the military situation changed dramatically when the Chinese communists entered the fray to help the North Koreans who were losing the war. Truman took to the airwaves on December 15, 1950, to announce a national emergency. He again stressed the themes of nonappeasement and no more Munichs, and he clearly identified the Soviet Union as the real culprit. The rest of the speech dealt with domestic issues on how Americans should respond to the Korean setback in their new emergency situation.

In these speeches, President Truman gave good reasons for U.S. involvement in the Korean war. However, his main problem was that he used the term *victory* in a nebulous sense. A close reading of his speeches suggests a realistic victory goal as the *status quo ante bellum*. But many Americans probably did not listen or read that closely, and so they inferred that Truman meant an all-out military victory in its traditional sense rather than a holding action. As the Korean war wore on without significant battlefield progress, Truman became the target of political attacks from the Republicans, who had their eyes on the 1952 presidential election, and from General Douglas MacArthur. The general became combative under his constitutional constraints; he made unauthorized statements about the conduct of the war—unwise and improper as he saw it—and he finally wrote a letter, which was insubordinate to Truman, to Congressman Joseph Martin, who read it on the floor of the House. Truman's rhetorical problem was that he never adequately prepared Americans for a new kind of war in which there was no traditional victory, and his political enemies capitalized on that rhetorical mistake. In the atomic age, Truman wanted to avoid another world war, and perhaps it was too much to ask of the man that he should persuade others to believe that the United States probably could not win another world war, assuming it could even be won, at a price the United States would be willing to pay.

Fortunately for the country and for its principle of civilian control over the military, Truman occupied the Oval Office when it was necessary to remind America's would-be Caesar, General MacArthur, that he was a general only. In his constitutional role as commander-in-chief, Truman fired MacArthur for actions of insubordination, but as chief executive, he wanted to explain his presidential action to the country. For his radio speech on April 11, 1951, Truman chose between two sets of speech drafts. One came from the State Department, and it stressed Secretary of State Dean Acheson's belief that the now-unpopular Korean war was being waged to avoid a world war III. The other draft was produced by Truman's own speech team of David Bell and Charles Murphy, who stressed MacArthur's insubordination to the president as the reason why he was fired. From a rhetorical perspective, it was unfortunate that Truman used Acheson's State Department draft, which mentioned only obliquely in a few sentences toward the end of the speech why MacArthur was fired. The strategy was not overly successful with the radio audience. Americans expected to hear why Truman fired MacArthur, a popular World War II hero; instead they heard why soldiers should remain fighting an unpopular war. Support for the president's speech was weak as gauged by the caustic White House reaction mail: "Your speeches stink and you stink," "Your lousy speech over the radio trying to clear yourself of the blundering mistakes you made at the expense of General MacArthur are as stupid and dumb as your daughter's sand paper singing voice." Truman also continued to cast his language in cold war rhetoric with phrases such as "Communist doubletalk" and "Commie language." Although the president had every right to sack MacArthur, this speech was one in which Truman did not successfully communicate the real basis for his legitimate action but chose instead to try to defend the Korean war. That rhetorical strategy was unwise because he did not meet audience expectations.

The conditions under which President Truman delivered his 1948 convention acceptance address, which some critics believe was his most stirring speech, would not ordinarily be conducive to such an oratorical achievement. The weather in Philadelphia was hot and humid; the Dixiecrats had walked out, and the "doves of peace"—pigeons, actually, that were released into the hall—caused a commotion in the convention, and some even dove for Speaker Sam Rayburn's bald head. Finally, at 2:00 A.M. on July 15, Truman began to address the exhausted delegates. He delivered his speech from a bare-bones outline of twenty-one pages, which allowed him to extemporize in vivid interpolations and emotional ab-libs. Truman was not a good manuscript speaker, but off-the-cuff Truman soon had the weary delegates on their feet and applauding his remarks. He told the delegates that he and vice-presidential nominee Senator Alban Barkley would "win this election and make the Republicans like it—don't you forget that!" because "they are wrong and we are right." He reminded the working man and the farmer that they should vote Democratic, or else they would be "the most ungrateful people in the world!" Then Truman ticked off the legislation he had requested, unsuccessfully, from the Republican Eightieth Congress—price controls, housing, minimum wage—and he reminded the delegates what he got, "Nothing. Absolutely nothing." He then ripped into the Republican platform, which promised the legislation its Congress had refused him, and he asserted: "I wonder if they can fool the people of the United States with such poppycock as that!" The president administered his rhetorical coup de grâce to the Republicans when he pledged to call the Eightieth Congress back into session in order to pass the Republican platform. That was the high point of his rousing speech, and the convention audience greeted his adroit political move with thunderous approval. In his conclusion, he aptly stated the theme of his speech, and indeed the theme of the coming campaign, in his parting sentence: "The country can't afford another Republican Congress."

The speech statistics for the 1948 campaign suggest the role his oratory played in persuading the people: 26 addresses in major cities and approximately 250 whistlestop talks. These talks, from the rear platform of a railroad observation car, were actually quite refined in their rhetorical technique. Truman would speak for about five minutes or so on local interests and issues, then introduce Mrs. Truman as "the Boss," and then finally his daughter Margaret. This folksy touch drew the crowds and pleased the people. But the substance of his rhetoric persuaded the voters. Truman ran against the "Do-Nothing Eightieth Congress," and this gave the voters a scapegoat on which to vent their frustrations rather than on him. He made specific appeals on economic issues that touched the voters' lives, such as at Worcester, Massachusetts, on October 27: "The Republicans believe in what they call the 'trickle down' theory. They want the big, rich, and wealthy, the privileged special interest groups to get the lion's share of the income and let the scraps fall down for the rest of us.'' He never failed to call for specific action, such as to an audience in New York City on October 28: ''Now I want to say this to you, that if you believe in government of, by, and for the people, if you believe in your own self-interest, the best thing for you to do on November 2d is to go to the polls early and vote the straight Democratic ticket, and then the country will be safe for another 4 years.'' In truth Truman outhustled his complacent opponent, Governor Thomas Dewey.

On January 20, 1949, President Truman delivered his Inaugural Address. He and his speech writers turned their attention from the domestic issues of the past campaign to foreign affairs, for which the speech would serve as a state paper. In typical Truman style, the address was arranged around several points—this time four. The importance of these four points is that to some degree they still guide U.S. foreign policy. First, Truman pledged support for the United Nations and its peacekeeping function. The Korean war was a logical extension of that commitment. Second, he promised support for world economic recovery and continued help for war-ravaged Europe. Third, he pledged U.S. efforts to strengthen freedom-loving countries against aggression with the NATO security plan. Last, he offered American science and industry to help the underdeveloped nations. The speech contained his usual cold war rhetoric, but it was toned down for the occasion. Truman merely juxtaposed democratic values with their communistic counterparts in order to tell his audiences, domestic and foreign, that only the United States and its allies stood for peace against communist aggression.

Truman's Valedictory Address, delivered to the nation on January 15, 1953, was a personal and sometimes poignant statement of his major trials and triumphs in the Oval Office. The speech is particularly useful in revealing the motivations of the president's major policies in his own language. Two main issues concerned him. The first was the beginning of the containment policy, begun in Greece and Turkey in 1947, and expanded to the Marshall Plan, the Berlin airlift, and NATO. The second issue was his nemesis: Korea. Truman repeated in this speech the same kind of rhetorical reasoning he had used in his other major speeches on Korea. He decided, on the basis of his knowledge of European political leaders' unwise appeasement policies in the era of the 1930s for Hitler, Mussolini, and the Japanese, that that kind of appeasement should not be repeated in areas threatened by communist aggression and takeover, especially in the case of Korea. However, Truman's claim that the UN forces had successfully met and repelled the aggression there sounded hollow to some Americans who were accustomed to traditional military victories. From Truman's viewpoint, however, the assertion was warranted because his goal of limited war, as earlier delineated, was a useful political and military response to the realities of the time, but many people failed to perceive it that way. Nor was Truman particularly successful in persuading them to that viewpoint. There was also a certain soberness in the later part of the speech in which he tried to reassure the country that the cold war would cease when the communist world collapsed. The speech reveals that Truman had come to terms with that unsolvable cold war problem but that American people, then as now, had difficulty in adjusting to that uncomfortable reality.

Truman was famous for public profanity. He wrote to a Methodist minister who complained about the chief executive's language but decided not to mail the letter; that emphatic language was a prerogative the president would never forgo.

Truman in private was Truman in public. Some critics objected to such honesty in speech, but something must be said for his lack of duplicity. In hindsight, Americans now know that he was little better or worse than his predecessors or his successors in using profane language; they just hid it from view. That seems to be Truman's major mistake: he was not a hypocrite.

The effectiveness of President Truman's delivery seemed to depend on whether he spoke from a prepared text or extemporaneously—he called it off the cuff. By most accounts, Truman was not an effective manuscript speaker. What happens to most other manuscript speakers happened to him: his rate was too fast, his phrasing was poor, his pitch tended to be unvarying, he often slurred and mispronounced words, and his voice was faintly nasal. In short, he did not have FDR's wonderfully modulated radio voice. Although his speech staff tried repeatedly to coax him to change his delivery habits, Truman apparently had little motivation or willingness to do so. On the other hand, he was effective as an extemporaneous campaign speaker or any other time he spoke without relying on a written text. In this area, he was probably FDR's superior. Freed from the obligation of saying words on paper, HST was able to be his greatest asset, himself, because he could communicate energetically, enthusiastically, and effectively with his live audiences. Freed from the constraints of a written manuscript style, Truman communicated in a direct conversational style. He maintained the dignity of his position, yet he was able—through a folksy style, coupled with direct eye contact and vigorous gestures—to appeal to the issues on the listeners' minds. This common man, with his common language, made the voters believe their best interests were served by the man communicating with them. President Truman's delivery in the 1948 whistlestop campaign was one of the vital elements in its and his success. The direct and vigorous style of delivery—but not finely polished or presented—that Truman had learned and practiced on the Missouri stump in his early political career served him well in campaigning, often from the rear platform of an open-air railroad observation car. Voters saw and heard a feisty, scrappy, and unpretentious president who talked with them in a straightforward and down-to-earth fashion and who earnestly and sincerely delivered his political remarks. They liked what they saw and heard.

Truman's rhetorical style was plain. He believed he should communicate in clear, unadorned, and ordinary language, and he instructed his speech writers to compose his major addresses accordingly. Consequently his rhetoric is practically devoid of the "purple patches of prose" one might associate with FDR or JFK. No memorable Truman lines come to mind. Truman was also fond of the debater-like first, second, and third method of signposting his major points, and his speeches read more like lawyers' briefs than eloquent orations.

Truman was not an ideal presidential orator. Yet he was a major political orator, if not an eloquent one, who persuaded Americans to accept or tolerate ideas that have had a lasting legacy in postwar American political thought and action.

Information Sources

Research Collections and Collected Speeches   The Harry S Truman Library, Independence, Missouri, is a rich repository of rhetorical artifacts for the speech scholar. Truman's home, burial site, and museum are also located there. The materials in the library are typical of the holdings of the other presidential libraries.

There are copies of the speech drafts up to Truman's reading copy, and many of these contain his emendations; one can utilize the sound recordings and motion picture films to criticize his delivery; there is a photographic file; and the White House kept the invaluable public reaction mail to the president's major speeches and addresses. The library also holds the usual secondary materials: oral histories, diaries of Truman's contemporaries, theses and dissertations, and other germane research guides and aids. The Harry S Truman Library Institute makes available a number of grants-in-aid for scholarly investigation of Truman and his presidency.

*American Rhetoric from Roosevelt to Reagan: A Collection of Speeches   ARRR
and Critical Essays.* Edited by Halford Ross Ryan. Prospect Heights, Ill.:
Waveland Press, 1983.
The Public Papers of the Presidents: Harry S Truman. 8 vols. Washing-   PPP
ton, D.C.: Government Printing Office, 1964.

Selected Critical Studies   Brembeck, Cole S. "Harry Truman at the Whistlestops."
Quarterly Journal of Speech 38 (1952): 42–50.
Brockreide, Wayne, and Scott, Robert L. *Moments in the Rhetoric of the Cold War.* New
York: Random House, 1970.
Hensley, Carl Wayne. "Harry S. Truman: Fundamental Americanism in Foreign Policy
Speechmaking, 1945–46." *Southern Speech Communication Journal* 40 (1974): 180–
90.
McKerrow, Ray. "Truman and Korea: Rhetoric in the Pursuit of Victory." *Central States
Speech Journal* 28 (1977): 1–12.
Ryan, Halford Ross. "Harry S Truman: A Misdirected Defense for MacArthur's Dis-
missal." *Presidential Studies Quarterly* 11 (1981): 157–66.
Underhill, William R. "Harry S Truman: Spokesman for Containment." *Quarterly Journal
of Speech* 47 (1961): 268–74.
White, Eugene E., and Henderlider, Clair R. "What Harry S. Truman Told Us about His
Speaking." *Quarterly Journal of Speech* 40 (1954): 37–42.

Selected Biographies   Donovan, Robert J. *Tumultuous Years: The Presidency of Harry S.
Truman,* 1949–1953. New York: Norton, 1982.
McCoy, Donald R. *The Presidency of Harry S. Truman.* Lawrence: University Press of
Kansas, 1984.
Miller, Merle. *Plain Speaking: An Oral Biography of Harry S. Truman.* New York: Put-
nam, 1974.
Truman, Harry S. *Memoirs.* 2 vols. Garden City, N.Y.: Doubleday, 1955–56.
Underhill, Robert. *The Truman Persuasions.* Ames: Iowa State University Press, 1981.

Chronology of Major Speeches

See "Research Collections and Collected Speeches" for source codes.

"Truman Doctrine," Washington, D.C., March 12, 1947; *ARRR,* pp. 80–85;
PPP, pp. 176–80.

Inaugural Address, Washington, D.C., January 20, 1949; *PPP,* pp. 112–19.

Special message to Congress on Korea, Washington, D.C., July 19, 1950;
PPP, pp. 527–36.

Address at the War Memorial Opera House, San Francisco, October 17, 1950;
PPP, pp. 673–79.

"Far Eastern Policy," Washington, D.C., April 11, 1951; *ARRR,* pp. 86–91;
PPP, pp. 223–27.

Valedictory, Washington, D.C., January 15, 1953; *PPP,* pp. 1197–1202.

THE HISTORIOGRAPHICAL DILEMMA IN MYRDAL'S AMERICAN CREED: RHETORIC'S ROLE IN RESCUING A HISTORICAL MOMENT

E. Culpepper Clark and Raymie E. McKerrow

The past is hidden . . . beyond the reach of intellect, in some material object (in the sensation which that material object will give us) of which we have no inkling.

Marcel Proust

Three Foreigners stand out for their incisive interpretations of American character: Alexis de Tocqueville, Lord James Bryce, and Gunnar Myrdal. All three had enormous impact on the way Americans have thought of themselves. So influential was their work that the 1946 "Harvard Report" on higher education in American society argued that core education include an examination of democracy in America, its values and institutions, from the detached perspectives of these observant foreigners.[1] Of the three, however, none had greater political and social impact than Myrdal. Working under a lavish grant from the Carnegie Corporation, the young Swedish economist assembled a team of scholars in the late 1930s to produce a massive study of race relations in America. What was originally envisioned as a two-year project wound up taking nine years from inception to completion. Titled *An American Dilemma*, the study first appeared in 1944, but was obscured by world war. A decade later, Myrdal's study was cited in the famous footnote 11 to *Brown vs. Board of Education* and immediately won the admiration of liberal America and the opprobrium of most white southerners.

Myrdal's work not only affected American constitutional history but also had profound implications for the way the chief narrators of American thought—historians and journalists—came to think about race relations. The effect was nowhere more evident than among young southerners who reached intellectual

From *Quarterly Journal of Speech* 73 (August 1987): 303–16. Used by permission of the authors and the Speech Communication Association.

E. Culpepper Clark is professor of speech communication at the University of Alabama; Raymie E. McKerrow is professor of speech communication and associate dean of arts and sciences at the University of Maine.

[1] Harvard Committee on the Objectives of a General Education in a Free Society, *General Education in a Free Society* (Cambridge: 1946), 219, cited in David W. Southern, *Gunnar Myrdal and Black-White Relations: The Use and Abuse of an American Dilemma, 1944–1969* (Baton Rouge: Louisiana State University Press, 1987), 197. The original idea for this essay began with a paper prepared for the SCA Regional Research Seminar, "Ideology and Public Argument," Birmingham, Alabama, May 19–21, 1983.

maturity in the late thirties and early forties. Older southern liberals, like Virginius Dabne, Mark Ethridge, and William Terry Couch, would have difficulty embracing the progressive vision of race relations constructed by Myrdal. Newer liberals, like C. Vann Woodward, Ralph McGill, and Harry Ashmore, would embrace change. Couch, who as editor of the University of North Carolina Press courageously broke new intellectual ground in the 1930s and who later became a bitter critic of Myrdal, spoke the dissonance of the older generation when he observed, "modern modes of thinking—modes characteristic of current sociological and anthropological thinking—have penetrated the South as well as other places. Many of us would agree with Myrdal, and as he says, this leaves us divided in our minds and, so far, we have been unable to overcome this division and see our way clearly to a place where we can stand."[2]

Following Myrdal's lead, one group of historians in particular came to think of the southerner not as some regional aberration but more fundamentally as American. With Myrdal, they saw enlightenment principles of equality, what the Swede styled the American Creed, operating as a counterforce to existing racial practice in the South. The resulting dilemma produced a creative tension that ineluctably drew southern whites toward racial accommodation. The path may have been fraught with danger and the progress painfully slow, but the direction was nonetheless forward.[3] Myrdal's notion that the southern dilemma had progressive implications for race relations dominated social thinking for twenty years, in large measure because it argued for gentle social engineering and eschewed revolutionary change and in part because the massive book, more than a thousand pages of text and half again that many in appendixes and footnotes, seemed to ground the American Creed in the new empiricism of the social sciences. The book also benefited from the democratic passions stirred by the very war that had obscured its birth. An exhaustive study by David Southern shows how Myrdal's view became a compelling metaphor for public discourse and how it sustained and justified the preeminent position of a liberal elite in shaping the terms of the South's great mass movement for human equality.

With the radicalization of the Civil Rights Movement after 1965, especially with the intensification of racial conflict, historians and social scientists discredited the Myrdalian emphasis on ideological consensus and guilt-actuated gradualism. Despite their myriad voices and incessant squabbling over definitions of racism and its implications (and because of it), these scholars produced no

---

[2]Quoted in Daniel Singal, *The War Within: From Victorian to Modernist Thought in the South, 1919–1945* (Chapel Hill: University of North Carolina Press, 1982), 301. Singal's study contains an excellent analysis of the move to modernist and liberal thought in the South. Among the architects of that movement were U. B. Phillips, Broadus Mitchell, Ellen Glasgow, Howard Odum, Couch, Rupert Vance, a number of the Nashville Agrarians, Faulkner, Guy Johnson, Arthur Raper, and Robert Penn Warren. Most of these did not make the transition from segregationist to integrationist thought on race relations. Couch represented the group's splenetic view of Myrdal when he conceded the Swede's impact on thought but demurred as to its originality and said that it was exceptional "only in that it was published under highly favorable and most reputable auspices, and is more comprehensive, more thorough, and more readable than the mass of material sharing its attitude." In Rayford Whittingham Logan, ed., *What the Negro Wants* (Chapel Hill: University of North Carolina Press, 1944), xv.

[3]The best single collection of this thought is in Charles G. Sellers, Jr., ed., *The Southerner as American* (Chapel Hill: University of North Carolina Press, 1960). The single most influential essay expressing the Myrdalian idea is C. Vann Woodward, "Equality: America's Deferred Commitment," *American Scholar* 27 (1958): 459–72.

alternative vision to rival the earlier dominance of Myrdal's value-centered theory of social change.[4] These critics of Myrdal are not to be faulted. Much of their work is at once more sophisticated and more cautious than the bold, value-laden sociology of Myrdal. The real difference between Myrdal and his critics is the public difference. His was an optimistic sociology, a rhetorical vision capable of operating synergistically with the democratic passions unleashed by war against Germany, Italy, and Japan. So powerful was his grand idea that now it is viewed nostalgically, almost wistfully, as a time of innocent hope forever lost, a time when doing good and changing laws was charged with higher moral purpose. The view of Myrdal's critics, on the other hand, is pessimistic, rooted in dashed hopes, neosegregation, and a general perception of social disintegration.

While critics seem to speak with all the confusion of Babel, they are agreed on one point—the Myrdalian perspective, for all its power to reveal the agonies of a white liberal elite, is limiting. Its emphasis on consensus helped obscure from journalistic interpretation the dramatic tensions occurring among the masses (Kluxers, Citizens Councillors, and blacks of a variety of persuasions) while at the same time holding out promise of conservative change for a small group of liberals and their monied allies. The damage it did to the writing of history was equally significant and forms the subject of this essay. Operating from the coercion of first premises (all men are created equal), the Myrdalian perspective carries with it all the liabilities of deterministically constrained history. Under its terms, victory for the Whig-Liberal ideology is a necessary outcome, not a problematic to be reenacted by each generation with the power to win or lose on its own terms. To be sure, a deterministic perspective on history is not identified with any particular ideology. Whether Marxist or Whig-Liberal or Freudian, the perspective assumes that the historical context in which the ideology operates precludes options for influence by active agents. The Myrdalian approach, however, is a textbook case of the constraints imposed by the Whig-Liberal ideology on the ability to see history whole. As one sociologist put it, Myrdal's was only a slightly "softer" determinism than the earlier sociological views of William Graham Sumner or Robert E. Park.[5]

The antidote to deterministic coercion in the writing of history is the adoption of an alternate stance, one which acknowledges the presence of discontinuity in the flow of history.[6] Michel Foucault urges that every discourse should be received in its original upsurge, in its own complexity. Where "genesis," "continuity," and "totalization," are "the great themes of the history of ideas," Foucault's approach highlights the "analysis of contradictions, comparative descriptions, and the mapping of transformations" that constitute lived

[4]The works attacking Myrdal's thesis are too numerous to cite. For an excellent discussion of the subject see Southern, *Gunnar Myrdal*, 261–92.

[5]See Stanford M. Lyman, *The Black American in Sociological Thought: A Failure of Perspective* (New York: Putnam, 1972), 99–120, 176–82. Cited in Southern, 304.

[6]Michel Foucault, trans. A. M. Sheridan Smith, *The Archaeology of Knowledge* (New York: Harper and Row, 1972). For an analysis of the relationship between rhetoric and history, see Ray E. McKerrow, "Rhetoric as History: An Archaeological Perspective," unpublished paper presented at the University of Alabama at Birmingham, February 21, 1981. Also see Dominick LaCapra, *History and Criticism* (Ithaca: Cornell University Press, 1985), especially Chapter 1, "Rhetoric and History," 15–44; Hayden White, *Theories of History*, William Andrews Clark Memorial Library Seminar Papers (Los Angeles: University of California, 1978), Michael C. McGee, "The Fall of Wellington: A Case Study of the Relationship between Theory, Practice and Rhetoric in History," *Quarterly Journal of Speech* 63 (1977): 28–42.

experience.[7] In this context, historians should simply describe contradictions rather than trying to dissipate them through a preconceived terministic screen.[8]

Foucault's approach is at best an ideal, and has been superceded in his own writings by a more generalized "genealogical" approach.[9] As Larry Shiner observes, the archaeological approach "becomes not merely a critique of the conventional history of ideas and a clever suggestion for its replacement by a diagnostics of discursive practices, but above all a *parody* of the search for method."[10] Nevertheless, the spirit that animates Foucault's critique, and the message that history can be seen in terms of discursive practices, should not be lost sight of as historians rush to make the past more usable by making it more continuous. It is the paradox of doing history. What draws us to it is similarity; what makes it history is difference.

In this essay we describe how an influential group of historians, writing for the most part in the 1950s, used Myrdal's determinism to explain why and how the South lost its second encounter with Reconstruction. We isolate this particular interpretation not only because it is an archetypal case of ideological determinism but also because the historians who used it (many of whom would later change their minds as to its utility) have been among the most persuasive of the twentieth century; for example, C. Vann Woodward, George Brown Tindall, Oscar Handlin, and Carl Degler. In fact, so persuasive was their appropriation of the idea that many undergraduate classes are still dominated by its vision. We then suggest an alternative approach to historical documents that counteracts the instinctive yet ahistorical urge to discover similarities even out of obvious conflict and contradiction. In the concluding portion, we use what is best termed a *rhetorical stance*, owing to its concentration on discursive practices, to examine a speech urging defiance of the Supreme Court's 1954 ruling. The analysis reveals the importance of eschewing a dogmatic, constrained view of history in the interpretation of events.

The Deterministic Perspective

In the early days of World War II, John Temple Graves, editor of the Birmingham *Age-Herald*, surveyed the South's leading thinkers to find out why the

---

[7]Foucault, 138. For further readings on Foucault, see Dominick LaCapra and Steven L. Kaplan, eds., *Modern European Intellectual History* (Ithaca: Cornell University Press, 1982); Alan Megill, *Prophets of Extremity* (Berkeley: University of California Press, 1985); R. Anchor, "Realism and Ideology: The Question of Power," *History and Theory* 22 (1983): 107–19; M. Clark, *Michel Foucault: An Annotated Bibliography* (New York: Garland, 1982); L. Grossberg, "The Ideology of Communication: Post-Structuralism and the Limits of Communication," *Man and World* 15 (1982): 83–101; C. Lemert, *Michel Foucault: Social Theory as Transgression* (New York: Columbia University Press, 1982); K. Racevskis, *Michel Foucault and the Subversion of Intellect* (Ithaca Cornell University Press, 1983); C. Scott, "History and Truth," *Man and World* 15 (1982): 55–66; M. Shapiro, *Language and Political Understanding: The Politics of Discursive Practices* (New Haven Yale University Press, 1981); and L. Shiner, "Reading Foucault: Anti-Method and the Genealogy of Power-Knowledge," *History and Theory* 21 (1982): 382–98.

[8]Kenneth Burke, *Language as Symbolic Action* (Berkeley: University of California Press, 1966), 44–62.

[9]For a review of Foucault's genealogical approach see Shiner, 386–392; Megill, 232–237.

[10]Shiner, 385–386; Megill, 228.

region seemed so belligerent. Indeed, an Alabama congressman had quipped, "They had to start selective service to keep our Southern boys from filling up the army." Lister Hill, one of Roosevelt's principal champions in the Senate, thought southerners would go to war for anything "that pertains to their rights and their country . . . not merely because they are a people quick to action once their emotions are aroused but because they are willing to make great sacrifice in this struggle for democracy just as their forebears risked their lives." Oliver Cromwell Carmichael, then Chancellor of Vanderbilt University and later president of the University of Alabama during the Autherine Lucy episode, pontificated that "the greater belligerence of the South towards this war is due to its greater abhorrence of dictatorship and greater love of liberty and freedom."[11]

These testimonies to the South's prejudice for freedom and liberty notwithstanding, Graves got a more pointed answer from Howard Odum, the man who at Chapel Hill had done so much to make regionalism a respected subject for scholarly inquiry. Odum explained, "Southerners give the appearance of wanting to believe in something and when believing in it, to fight for it . . . Much of our belligerency is against those who do not believe as we do. It is defense." Odum believed the South to have been "invaded so often since the Civil War by thousands of reformers and accusers that it is automatically prepared to defend itself,"[12] Graves titled his book *The Fighting South,* and as a characterization of the South's conduct in World War II and its commitment to massive resistance in the following decade, the title seemed appropriate. But the defensiveness in the bellicosity left historians to wonder whether the South was up to its old habit of "losing battles"; whether in the chest-thrusting boast of more Medals of Honor or in the defiant cries of never! Never! NEVER! one could sense a deeper fear.

Historians who followed the Myrdalian thesis viewed this apparent urgency to protect the collective regional self as an expression of futility and ultimately of resignation. They believed that the South never had a chance of maintaining its segregated institutions; that massive resistance had all the accompaniments of revolution but it was alas a wheel without a hub, an act of sound and fury. These deterministically inclined historians embraced democratic-liberalism as a continuous thread in American history—any effort to resist the influence of this ideology was seen as little more than a fraudulent parody of the central theme. Even the southern strike for independence in 1860 was seen as just another ripple on a surging tide of American liberalism. Speaking for this historiographical tradition, Louis Hartz wrote, "The political thought of the Civil War symbolizes not the weakness of the American liberal idea but its strength, its vitality, and its utter dominion over the American mind. The strange agonies the Southerners endured trying to break out of the grip of Locke and the way the nation greeted their effort, stand as permanent testimony to the power of that idea."[13]

A clear application of a "continuity" theme in writing about the Second Reconstruction is found in George Tindall's essay "The Central Theme Revisited,"

---

[11]John Temple Graves, *The Fighting South* (New York: G. P. Putman's Sons, 1984), 5 and 9–10.

[12]Graves, 16–17.

[13]Louis Hartz, *The Liberal Tradition in America: An Interpretation of American Political Thought since the Revolution* (New York: Harcourt, Brace, 1955), 177.

an idea he worked out in the early fifties and continues to support.[14] In this essay Tindall took on one of the more prevalent arguments raised by self-styled southern moderates. Their argument claimed that if the North continued to agitate the issue of civil rights in the South, southern moderates would be driven to the wall and hardcore *segs* (segregationists) would prevail. While "granting some force to this argument," Tindall nonetheless insisted "that criticism has other effects in a libertarian society, especially when the criticized share many of the assumptions on which the criticism is based." Having conceded this premise, the South was destined to remain on the defensive, standing in front of, only to step aside from, one schoolhouse door after another. As Tindall saw it, "criticism of southern racial practice has repeatedly generated temporary intransigence, but in the long run and more significantly it has also compelled self-justification and a slow but steady adjustment by white southerners in the direction of the American faith in equality of opportunity and rights."[15]

Tindall's expression typified the growing tendency to view the southerner as American—as a person inevitably, inexorably influenced by the American Creed. Of course, the move toward this view had been triggered by Myrdal's *American Dilemma*. Taking the optimistic view, Myrdal believed southerners had taken a permanent subscription to what he called the American Creed or that "great national suggestion"—a creed born of enlightenment equalitarian views. Myrdal even went so far as to call it a "state religion." Having bought the premise of equality, and perforce the political ideology it entailed, the southerner, Myrdal believed, was to be incapable of thinking "constructively along segregation lines" or of conceptually understanding "how a segregation system could be rationally organized. For this would imply an open break with the principles of equality and liberty."[16]

The deterministic perspective is a seductive one. The ideology symbolized by the "American Creed" operates as one of those covering laws that help explain why certain public advocates win and others lose—it provides a decision theory. One can chart its effects as southern governors retreated into the premise of equality even as they cried segregation now and forever. Adherence to the creed accounts for the South's inability to generate a political theory grounded in assumptions of racial inferiority. As Eric Vogelin observed, "racial symbolism has comparatively little chance in a society which has gone through an 18th century revolution, because the collective element in racialism is hardly compatible with the belief in the value of the sovereign person and the indestructible soul, and its rights and liberties."[17] The price of adherence, or so Myrdal argued, was the inability to think "constructively" along lines other than those compatible with the tenets of equality.

Not that the South was without advocates of racism as political doggerel, but because these racists found it difficult to deny the American Creed explicitly, they had to find ways of disparaging blacks that did not turn on the Creed itself. Thus, the more important debate, the actual speaking of the public mind, centered on euphemisms for, or assumed consequences of, visceral notions of racial

---

[14]George B. Tindall, "The Central Theme Revisited," in *The Ethnic Southerners* (Baton Rouge: LSU Press, 1976), 59–87.

[15]Tindall, 74–75.

[16]Gunnar Myrdal, *An American Dilemma: The Negro Problem and Modern Democracy* (New York: Harper and Row, 1962), 800.

[17]Quoted in Tindall, "The Central Theme," 74.

inferiority. During Reconstruction and after, advocates of white supremacy had to argue such points as Negro corruption, ignorance, and incompetence, reflecting as they did questions of taste and manners, or more basically questions of class as opposed to race. Despite the later career of Jim Crow and the pervasive racism which underlay it, the debate was forced to issues more suggestive of remediation than grounds for permanent racial enslavement. If blacks were ignorant, educate them. If blacks were corrupt, reform them. If blacks were incompetent, train them. And while racism might retard efforts at remediation, nowhere in the reconstructed South did a regime develop, acceptable to the nation as a whole, that was grounded in an articulated theory of racial supremacy. Acceptance of the American Creed made the articulation of such a theory both logically and practically impossible.

The deterministic perspective explains why the South *failed* to develop an articulable political ideology. More important, the deterministic view also explains why the South *could not* develop an "exportable ideology"[18]—a set of beliefs grounded in an assumption of racial inferiority that, transcending southern borders, would supplant the prevailing ideological force of the American Creed. It was in this same deterministic spirit of historiographical and intellectual consensus that Stanley Elkins argued the American Constitution to have become a "shining moral abstraction" with an attendant "withering away of the state." America was an idea, not an institutional arrangement.[19] As "idea," the American Creed functioned as a *given,* a taken-for-granted, an unarticulated assumption governing actions. This quality of "givenness" was both the genius of American politics and its weakness; that is, the inability to successfully export one's own ideological premises.

While the "givenness" of the American Creed functioned at a national level to preclude the emergence of a new, exclusively provincial, ideology in the South, the same quality of givenness, when applied to racial thought, had a profound influence on the white southerner's capacity for argument. Racism also functioned as an absolute given, as an instinctive, visceral attitude that was beyond debate. Those who accept a racist attitude believe it to be in the nature of things. In the experience of one of the authors, growing up in South Georgia meant that the local barber would make occasional racial jokes and slurs, but as years of experience have informed the author, it would never have occurred to the barber that beneath that head of hair was a mind in need of persuading, that he would have to explain the *common understanding.* After all, the boy, later the author, was white. Such taken-for-granteds create a kind of passivity in the face of outside agitation. Interviews with former and present members of the Citizens Councils (commonly called White Citizens Councils) find few of them believing their cause to be lost.[20] Despite the continued advance of civil rights, they still await that revulsion of feeling which will return the South, if not the nation, to

[18]Daniel J. Boorstin, *The Genius of American Politics* (Chicago: University of Chicago Press, 1953), 8–35. Boorstin was attempting to explain why Americans were disadvantaged in the ideological struggle of the Cold War. In so doing, he hit upon the notion that because the American Creed was a "given," there was no ideological blueprint available to export.

[19]Stanley M. Elkins, Intro. by Nathan Glazer, *Slavery, A Problem in American Institutional and Intellectual Life* (New York: Grosset and Dunlap, 1963), 144.

[20]Interviews conducted by students at the University of Alabama under the direction of the first author and funded by an NEH Educational Programs Grant, 1978–79.

its original course. They need not argue, as their vision of racial relations is in the nature of things.

But citizen councillors were only the latest in a long line of southerners who failed to develop an alternative or exportable ideology. The givenness of race had a profound effect on the father of American equalitarianism himself. As the historian Winthrop Jordan explained:

> Jefferson's derogation of the Negro revealed the latent possibilities inherent in an accumulated popular tradition of Negro inferiority: it constituted, for all its qualifications, the most intense, extensive, and extreme formulation of anti-Negro 'thought' offered by any American in the thirty years after the Revolution. Yet Thomas Jefferson left to Americans something else which may in the long run have been of greater importance—his prejudice for freedom and his larger equalitarian faith. It was this faith which must have caused him to fall gradually more silent on a subject which many of his fellow intellectuals were taking up with interest. For Jefferson more than for any of his known contemporaries, the subject was not an easy or a happy one.[21]

Thus, the given, or that "accumulated popular tradition of Negro inferiority," combined with Jefferson's notions of equality to paralyze the mind of the South, thereby making it incapable of developing an exportable ideology.

If the historians we have cited are to be believed, an army of southern advocates encountered an idea whose time arrived in the eighteenth century, and as in Hugo's dictum, the army was overmatched by the idea. While outside critics concentrated their attack on the institutional arrangement of Jim Crow, the South flailed away at an idea they shared in common with the enemy or were reduced to the lamest form of counterstroke—the argument *tu quoque,* that the North was just as guilty. From the deterministic perspective there was an inevitability to the demise of massive resistance and the system it defended. As we have seen, some southern intellectuals prophesied as much in the forties and fifties, while Ralph McGill, a belated convert to the Myrdal view, could write in the early sixties: "The walls are broken—not down. But each day there is a further crumbling of them. Segregation is a Humpty-Dumpty. It will not be put back together again. It lies there in the ruins. Guerilla fighting will go on in some areas for an unpredictable time. Extreme racial attitudes will not be easily diffused. But, curiously, it is they that are becoming segregated in today's society." Comparing the massive resisters to an earlier generation of southerners, McGill concluded, the older generation "did not, or would not, understand that the conscience of the world had condemned slavery. So it is with segregation. Civilization and morality are bored with it."[22] On this analysis, the South would not rise again, at least not in any way resembling its former self.

Still the question must be asked, was everything as certain as the deterministic perspective would have it? Was the South engaged in some tragicomedy where the audience knows what the characters are powerless to know? More recent studies of massive resistance have tended to discount the inexorable force of an idea such as the "American Creed." The most exhaustive treatment to date

---

[21]Winthrop D. Jordan, *White over Black: American Attitudes toward the Negro* 1550–1812 (Chapel Hill: University of North Caroline Press, 1968), 481.

[22]Ralph McGill, *The South and the Southerner* (Boston: Little, Brown, and Co., 1963), 237.

even doubts the failure of massive resistance, arguing instead that it served to stabilize southern institutions in the face of growing national criticism. "Even the eventual abandonment of massive resistance," concluded Numan Bartley, "rested upon pocketbook ethics and conservative inclinations. The white South was yet to face the 'American dilemma' or to demonstrate confidence in the principles of liberal democracy."[23] Yet the answer to the question of historical causation more likely lies somewhere between pocketbook ethics and the coercion of an idea.

Historians in general have not been unmindful of the difficulty in relating historical determinism to material conditions. Gordon Wood, on confronting the problems raised by such an interpretation of the American Revolution, demonstrated an appreciation for rhetoric's reality by suggesting a symbiotic relationship between ideas and the socio-economic milieu in which they operate.[24] Wood believed ideas in the Anglo-American community to be constant, with the important variable between mother country and colonies being the social stability of the mother country as contrasted with the colonies. Thus, ideas which had become habitual and conventional in England could spark a revolution in a region more unsettled and socially unstable. But even here one does not break the deterministic hold of ideas; there remains an inevitability to the Whig worldview that excludes competing views; ideological consensus and economic conflict have the relationship of smoke to fire, the one inseparable from the other.

The determinism that influences the historical practices of those who follow the Myrdalian thesis and others, especially historians writing in the "consensus" tradition,[25] draws attention to what Dominick LaCapra refers to as "documentary history."[26] In a penetrating critique of the limits of documentary practices, LaCapra notes that "in the recent past, much attention has been paid to mechanisms of diffusion and the documentation of how texts and other artifacts are circulated and used in society, but little notice has been granted to the precise process whereby complex texts undergo transformation into specific use and exchange values—a process whose investigation would confront the historian with problems not reducible to a truncated documentary framework."[27] Doing history by focusing sole attention on governmental artifacts, diaries, and other archival documents gives the appearance of an objective, comprehensive appraisal, but it does not account for how discursive texts may have influenced events. As LaCapra observes, "the difficulty is that a restricted documentary or objectivist model takes what is in certain respects a necessary condition or a crucial dimension of historiography and converts it into a virtually exhaustive definition. It also diverts attention from the way 'documents' are themselves texts that 'process' or rework 'reality' and require a critical reading."[28]

[23]Numan V. Bartley, *The Rise of Massive Resistance: Race and Politics in the South during the 1950s* (Baton Rouge: LSU Press, 1969), 345.

[24]Gordon Wood, "Rhetoric and Reality in the American Revolution," *William and Mary Quarterly*, 3rd Ser., 23 (1966): 3–32.

[25]The "consensus" tradition refers to historians writing in the post-World War II era who sought to restore the notion that an intellectual consensus dominated and motivated American political history. They believed American history to be the product of intellectual agreement or shared values more than economic struggle or class conflict.

[26]La Capra, *History and Criticism*, 18.

[27]La Capra, *History and Criticism*, 18–19.

[28]La Capra, *History and Criticism*, 19.

Discontinuity—A Rhetorical Perspective

To break the tyranny of ideas in history, especially as practiced by those following Myrdal's thesis, and the narrowness of the documentary methods that support the tyranny, requires that the historian adopt a perspective which acknowledges the force of discontinuities. At the same time, it requires a perspective that acknowledges the potential force documents may have in changing perceptions of the reality in which they participate. Insofar as discourse is seen as relevant historical evidence of an era's beliefs and actions, the perspective is a rhetorical one. In their emphasis on the history of ideas, and in keeping with their documentary approach to outlining that history, many historians tend to read too much into documents—the documents being the record of a discourse. Rather than taking the discourse at its face value, energy is spent seeking to determine what is behind the document, what it really means. Unfortunately, the only way to make that determination is to cast oneself into a future transformation that the past qua past could not have known, to find some future and therefore continuous connection that the past could not have assumed. Intent on discovering "what really happened," these historians miss the interaction between the documentary analysis and the "rhetorical" impact that the document may have had on the development of future events.[29]

To preserve the continuous flow of ideas, these historians are constrained to search for similarities rather than differences. In a trenchant critique of this approach, Foucault argues that "for the history of ideas, the appearance of difference indicates an error, or a trap; instead of examining it, the clever historian must try to reduce it: to find beneath it a smaller difference, and beneath that an even smaller one, and so on until he reaches the ideal limit, the non-difference of perfect continuity."[30] Consonant with the search for similarities, historians must devalue those differences which separated massive resisters from advocates of civil rights, they must show why a given outcome obtained in the absence of revolutionary change and the creation of new institutions. They are driven by the future perfect, oblivious to the rhetorical transformations emerging from out of the past. To prove their outcomes, they must assume a greater intellectual consensus capable of resolving lesser differences—a consensus always greater than may exist in fact. This, in essence, is the driving principle behind the Myrdalian perspective on southern race relations. As LaCapra has suggested, the documentary mode that supports consensus historiography is a necessary but by no means exclusive approach to doing history.

The alternative, suggested in Foucault's "archaeology," a parody of method in its own right, is to recognize the existence of discontinuities, of occurrences or documents that do not fit the "grand plan." It is not necessary to follow Foucault's delineation of an archaeological method (in fact, he abandoned the method once it was written) to appreciate the message explicit in his approach: "Archaeology does not seek to rediscover the continuous, insensible transition that relates discourses, on a gentle slope, to what precedes them, or follows them. It does not await the moment when, on the basis of what they are not yet, they became what they are; nor the moment when, the solidity of their figure

---

[29]La Capra, *History and Criticism,* 21, 35–44; Murray Edelman, *Political Languages* (New York: Academic Press, 1977), 11.

[30]Foucault, 171.

crumbling away, they will gradually lose their identity."[31] Although the allusion may oversimplify the actual practice of consensus or determinist historians, there is a semblance of truth in Foucault's suggestion that such historians have succumbed willingly, almost enthusiastically, to knowing who won. They seem to be locked in "a Sisyphean struggle with the rock of the post hoc fallacy," and as in the myth, the mean's becomes the end.[32]

But the question must be asked, is Foucault so stern in his rebuke of the history of ideas as to leave us barren of examples as to how the historian should proceed? It is one thing to adopt a rhetorical perspective; quite another to do it. Here let us depart from Foucault to state our belief that some historians have managed the task of reading discourse in its exteriority and have produced excellent intellectual history as a result. Some years ago Herbert Butterfield warned historians of the dangers inherent in forcing a Whig consensus on history. In so doing he urged historians to treat the historical record as a clash of wills out of which emerges something that probably no man ever willed, to, as it were, move into the dialectic of the discourse minus a knowledge of its resolution.[33]

Some have accomplished Butterfield's suggestion. Bernard Bailyn's *Ideological Origins of the American Revolution* achieved results that should have pleased Butterfield or Foucault.[34] Submersing himself in the discourse of the pamphlets, he was able to detect the sham and the spurious from the genuine in terms of historical antecedents. He learned that classical allusions were window-dressing, not antecedent arguments; he learned that familiarity with enlightenment ideas did not necessitate a future-anterior connection; that if connections were to be made, it was with the less "trendy" group of opposition writers. And while Bailyn may have erred, in strict accordance with Foucault's schema, by searching for antecedents and by talking about the contagion of liberty as future project, his approach escapes censure because the point of departure was the discourse. More important, the analysis of the discourse was not governed by an antecedent-future connection.

Still, what most troubled Foucault in his archaeological period, as it should all students of public address, rhetoric, and history, is the compelling urge to search out continuities, especially when working willy nilly in a deterministic mode. Foucault's goal, though difficult, is not unattainable. He did not seek "to restore what has been thought . . . in its very identity" nor to achieve "a reading that would bring back, in all its purity, the distant, precarious, almost effaced light of the origin."[35] Rather, the goal is to recognize that there are discontinuities, that the manner in which the discourse of a given time appropriates ideas follows no necessary or continuous pattern. The manner in which Jefferson appropriated Enlightenment notions of the free man is, as Edmund Morgan so vividly

[31]Shiner, 385–86; Megill, 228; Foucault, 139; The search for similarity is not, in itself, the focus of the problem, as a rhetorical perspective can be applied to similarities as well as differences. The problem, in this instance, is that historians lock onto similarities to the exclusion of dissimilarities.

[32]E. Culpepper Clark, "Argument and Historical Analysis," in J. Robert Cox and Charles A. Willard, *Advances in Argumentation Theory and Research* (Carbondale: Southern Illinois University Press, 1982), 302.

[33]Herbert Butterfield, *The Whig Interpretation of History* (New York: W. W. Norton, 1965).

[34]Bernard Bailyn, *Ideological Origins of the American Revolution* (Cambridge: Harvard University Press, 1967).

[35]Foucault, 1939–40.

demonstrates, not the manner in which the Second Reconstruction appropriated those ideas.[36] Even conceding a larger American Creed at work, it did not necessitate the failure either of massive resistance or of racial politics. Indeed, if we move back into the discourse of the 1950s, we might discover the true angst of the period, an uncertainty as to which values might prevail. Just as the geist of the German people cannot be said to have necessitated Hitler and National Socialism any more than Gustav Stresseman and the Weimar Republic, neither should an American Creed be said to have ordained the South of Martin Luther King over that of George Wallace. Each generation has the ability to appropriate for good or ill the language it inherits through its discourse. There are no necessary outcomes. The power of the American Creed notwithstanding, its rhetorical force should not be "oversold" as an explanation of the South's failure to create a viable rhetoric of segregation.

A Case in Point

The uncertainty of the outcome of racial strife in the 1950s is a matter in constant need of reassertion. Too few of our students remember it, and having achieved something of a constitutional victory, too many of us are self-congratulatory. The right people won. But massive resisters were not *then* on the verge of losing. They had won at Tuscaloosa in 1956, and although Little Rock proved unsettling, resisters had passed a spate of legislation to stop the perceived insanity of racial mingling. The discourse of the 1950s is replete with a tone of hope that the "givenness" of the southern "tradition" would hold.

Speeches of defiance echoed throughout the South. A year before his death in 1960, Hugh Morrow, Sr., a wealthy Birmingham industrialist, addressed the Alabama legislature. Morrow had been President of the Sloss-Sheffield Steel and Iron Company and a former member of the legislature himself. He was truly one of Birmingham's "big mules." The opening portions of his speech begged the indulgence due an old man's reminiscence and rambled through the slights and slurs of his generation's racial humor. The point of his speech, however, was to lecture the august assembly on the need for resisting the Supreme Court's sociological and psychological usurpation of the law. "Well, who is this Myrdal?" he queried. "I'll tell you. He is a product of one of those South-hating, tax exempt, multi-million dollar, leftist, 'intellectual disease carrier' foundations." Contrasting unfavorably the character and thinking of the federal judiciary with that of an indigenous black like Booker T. Washington, Morrow went on to quote Senator James O. Eastland, who lamented the "'tragic commentary on the intelligence and judgment of members of the Supreme Court that they would override the Constitution on the opinions of such psychological authority.'"[37]

Following these and other attempts to assassinate the character of those who were considered architects of the 1954 court ruling, Morrow appealed to that greatest teacher of all—history. Observing the subtleties of language, the old man noted that the Court "did not hand down a 'desegregation' decision; it handed down an 'integration' decision." He then quoted "some talented writer"

[36]Edmund S. Morgan, "Slavery and Freedom: The American Paradox," *Journal of American History* 59 (June 1972): 5–29.

[37]"Address of Honorable Hugh Morrow," Alabama Legislature, Montgomery, Alabama, October 6, 1959, Regular Session, Legislative Document #5, 13 and 16.

to the effect that " 'one may search the history of all nations, peoples, governments and minority populations and there will be found examples of genocide, extinction, enslavement, torture and exile, but there will not be found one single instance whose government has forced one race against its will to integrate with another.' "[38] Though a bleak view of history, one would be hardpressed to doubt its accuracy. From the vantage of the fifties, one would be equally encouraged to think the extension of civil rights to blacks was far from inevitable.

Shouting the defiant words of Mark Ethridge, a journalist Myrdal himself had termed liberal, Morrow proclaimed, " 'There is no power in the world—not even the mechanical armies of the earth—which could now force the Southern white people to abandonment of the principle of social segregation.' "[39] And yet, no sooner did these words stir the assembly to visions of heroic resistance than Morrow conceded, wittingly or unwittingly, that it was to be the sacrificial heroism of Thermopylae. Describing the Spartan youth who complained to his mother that his sword was too short, Morrow drew a thrill of admiration from the mother's reply: " 'My son,' she said, 'don't let that bother you . . . just take another step forward.' " Whereupon Morrow urged the legislators not to be "unduly disturbed or deterred by the dark sociological cloud forming overhead; let it speak what it may (bayonet or prison), just take another step forward."[40]

Morrow's language gives us pause in accepting the inevitability of Myrdal's thesis. Morrow's discourse is not the rhetoric of resignation that Myrdal and the historians foretell. Rather, this is typical fare for a people being urged to sacrifice *in extremis*, to take that next step that would insure the continuation of the struggle. Clearly, the rhetoric comprises a mixed, if not confused appeal. Morrow's own conclusion best captures this paradoxical spirit: "The South forever tragic, forever triumphant, forever doomed, and yet forever on the march, finds herself today, with her back to the wall, facing the dire necessity of making a last stand in defense of the true way of life."[41]

There may be an additional error if one were to label Morrow's rhetoric as paradoxical or even enigmatic. It is so only if we view winning to be the opposite of losing and we are forced to this conclusion only if we seek to go behind Morrow's words to find some continuity with what transpired in the years following the speech. With the civil rights legislation of 1964 and 1965 and the 1970 court orders on desegregation, it was clear that Morrow's world was gone. Whether the relative position of the black person had improved is still open to debate, but the world of segregation was at an end. In retrospect, therefore, Morrow had lost, but only in retrospect. The Spartan fantasy, which was not infrequently employed by an older patrician order in the South, was defiant, even vigorous, and looked to a future restoration of southern sanity.[42] If one looks at Morrow's words, as would Foucault, in their exteriority, then one can only assume that value and meaning for Morrow were to be found in the act of defending and resisting, not in the outcome of winning or losing. Winning or losing, while important, was essentially irrelevant. It was a Spartan case of returning with one's shield or on it. Looked at in this manner, there is vitality in the act of

[38]"Address," 16.

[39]"Address," 16–17.

[40]"Address," 18.

[41]"Address," 18.

[42]Fred Hobson, *Tell about the South: The Southern Rage to Explain* (Baton Rouge: Louisiana State University Press, 1983), 131.

Morrow's speaking. Depending on one's point of view, the old man's words may have been a menace or a promised good; whatever, they cannot be ignored as the idle talk of a pre-destined loser; they were, as John Temple Graves would have styled it, "fighting words."

Conclusion

Students of rhetoric have long recognized the tension that emerges from the desire to find similarities between past and present experience, which after all is history's attraction, and the dissimilarities that in fact constitute history.[43] We have argued that the acknowledegment of discontinuity liberates the text from the reductionist urge to similarity and restores the primacy of the text as a unique product in time. We have traced the work of historians who, influenced by Gunnar Myrdal, saw the demise of massive resistance as inevitable because the resisters spoke against the continuous and seemingly irresistible force of an American Creed. The view of these historians has been influential, even among rhetorical scholars, because it shows the power of a major premise in public argument and demonstrates how the seizure of common ground reduces opposition to ideological paralysis. But what ideology robs from history with its emphasis on similarity, the rhetorical perspective returns; namely, the vitality of struggle and the uncertainty of the future. The perspective is not a "method." It is a "stance" that treats the document as if it were a multi-faceted prism; not to be found as it lies in the present, hiding the facets of its underside, but to be picked up and turned so as to refract the light of the past in wholly unexpected ways.

By examining the speech of Hugh Morrow, a leading proponent of resistance, we have sought to demonstrate the possibilities inherent in such an approach. It is not new, of course. Good historians, after years of archival work, either by design or willy nilly, have discovered in the discourse of a given period those facts and concepts and narratives that reveal the ironical twists and turns of our past. But good historians equally have fallen victim, often unawares and sometimes by choice, to the determinism that proceeds from the coercive influence a dominant ideology has over textual readings. Our purpose is fulfilled if we have made explicit the approach that is implicit in the best historical works. By willfully encountering a discourse in its own terms, as opposed to the terms of its present manifestation or past inheritance, the historian enters a dimension of language that is individuated and time specific. The act is historical/hermeneutical, not critical. In sum, the historian is doing history. The end aimed at by adopting a rhetorical perspective is at once no more possible, and perhaps as possible, as the process whereby scientists attempt to recreate origins in a laboratory— whether possible or not, the process itself yields fleeting glimpses into the nature of being.

---

[43]For an analysis of historiographical issues as they relate to rhetorical theory, see Eric W. Skopec, "Systems Theory as a Historiographic Perspective," *The Pennsylvania Speech Communication Annual* 38 (1982): 9–13.

3

THE EXPERIENTIAL
PERSPECTIVE

In the introductory essay to this book, we cited Thomas Kuhn's notions of paradigm and the breakdown of faith in paradigms as accounting for the historical pattern of science. We have adapted these notions to twentieth-century rhetorical criticism and have described and illustrated a traditional perspective. Now we shall try to account for what appears to be a breakdown of faith in the paradigm.

In the 1940s and 1950s a few voices were raised decrying the traditional approach to rhetoric and communication. The General Semanticists were the most vocal early group of protesters.[1] However, not until the 1960s could one say that a serious break from traditional rhetoric and criticism had developed. Edwin Black's *Rhetorical Criticism: A Study in Method* (1965) stands out as the book that announced the end of the neo-Aristotelian hegemony.[2]

Interesting evidence of the shift can be derived from studying Barnet Baskerville's bibliographical essay "Selected Writings on the Criticism of Public Address." To the essay, first published in 1957, Baskerville added an "Addendum, 1967."[3] A comparison of the two essays is informative.

In 1957 Baskerville testified to "an abundance of critical literature on speaking" without "a corresponding interest in discussing the act of criticism itself." Throughout the essay he clearly implied that the traditional neo-Aristotelian and historical modes dominated criticism. But a decade later he wrote, "It is probably not inaccurate to observe that we have more distinguished essays *on* criticism than essays *in* criticism" (emphasis Baskerville's).[4] The shift in emphasis was not brought about by a decrease in the number of essays in criticism but by an outpouring of articles on the shortcomings of existing work and recommendations for new directions. This shift from the application of an accepted theory to speculation about acceptable theory is consistent with Kuhn's description of a breakdown of faith in a paradigm.

Reasons for a loss of faith are always complex, but perhaps we can identify a few of the interrelated causes of the break from a well-established tradition.

First, providing a comprehensive rhetorical criticism as initially outlined by Wichelns and made more elaborate by Thonssen and Baird is a challenge that few critics have met successfully. In practice, critics developed many shortcuts—providing only a historical analysis, focusing on a few Aristotelian topics, or being descriptive only—which reduced the adequacy of the method. Many critics who have decried traditional criticism have objected actually to its incomplete application.

---

[1]See, for example, Irving Lee, "Four Ways of Looking at a Speech," *Quarterly Journal of Speech* 28, 2 (April 1942): 148–55.

[2]*Rhetorical Criticism: A Study in Method* (New York: Macmillan, 1965; repr. with a new foreword, Madison: University of Wisconsin Press, 1978).

[3]Baskerville's essay first appeared in *Western Speech* (Spring 1957) and is reprinted together with "Addendum, 1967" in *Essays on Rhetorical Criticism*, ed. Thomas R. Nilsen (New York: Random House, 1968).

[4]Ibid., 174 and 184.

A second, more profound reason for the breakdown lies in a growing agreement that speakers (or writers or publicists) are as much a result of cultural forces as they are active participants in explaining rhetorical processes and effects. The critic, then, becomes interested in the sociocultural process itself, looking at discourse as something that permeates various sources yet is larger and more pervasive than any one or all of them. Thus, the traditional speaker orientation proves inadequate as the critic's interest in the speaker recedes and the socio-politico-economic environment as a source of rhetorical potency increases.

Third, critics recognize that any particular meaning derived from a message is not inherent or universal. The intentions of a source alone cannot explain the diverse ways people respond to a message. Rather, meaning is understood as a response to the message and its concomitants. Moreover, critics become aware of themselves as interpreters of events in which they are interested. They are aware of the multitude of focuses possible and the selective nature of their own perspective. Any picture they present will be but one of several possibilities. Such a line of reasoning does not imply that any one interpretation is just as good as another; that question is not central to this tendency. Therefore critics must ask themselves what unique insights they can give into the phenomena that attracts their concern. The result of their work must justify itself. In short, to borrow a phrase from psycho-historian Robert Jay Lifton, critics become aware of "an ever expanding use of the self as one's research instrument."[5]

The fourth reason is simply an amalgam of the second and third: a larger, more complex and representative unit of analysis is sought. The complex interaction of speaker, audience, context, and society over a period of time is what interests many critics today. Thus, an extended political campaign or social movement may become a focus for their studies. Initially, critics attempted to adapt the traditional method to their expanded interest, but many soon began to look elsewhere for a more appropriate theory and a new perspective.

The break with faith in the traditional paradigm has been neither smooth nor complete. For several decades the field of rhetorical theory and criticism seemed chaotic, with many specifying alternatives to the traditional approaches while paying little attention to the general flow of other proposals.[6] However, today we believe that a number of tendencies that we will call *perspectives* have emerged.

Initially (i.e., in the first two editions of this book), we saw the break with traditional criticism going in two directions—"experiential" and "New Rhetorics." The experiential perspective will be described in this chapter; the "New Rhetorics," which have experienced recent modifications, are treated in the "dramaturgical" perspective and will be the subject of chapter 4. In the last ten years two additional perspectives have emerged—"sociological" and "postmodern"—and they will be presented in chapters 5 and 6.

Before proceeding with the perspectives we would like to present two cautions. First, our perspectives represent one way of organizing rhetorical criticism. We realize that other ways of explaining the field are possible, but we believe that

[5]*History and Human Survival* (New York: Random House, 1970), 5.

[6] This shift away from traditional criticism is reflected in the third volume of *A History and Criticism of American Public Address,* which was published twelve years after volumes 1 and 2. Black's analysis of neo-Aristotelian criticism in *Rhetorical Criticism,* 27–35, suggests in footnotes 27–31 that volumes 1 and 2 are more narrowly traditional than volume 3. Further, Black uses Martin Maloney's criticism of Clarence Darrow from volume 3 as an example of a definite departure from the traditional perspective.

the literature over the past forty years supports this analysis. Any tensions or dialogue generated by such groupings may create a further evolution of critical thought and practice.

A second caution: we do not intend our ordering to suggest any priority of value among the perspectives. The experiential perspective will be discussed first, based on the observation that in the 1960s more critical essays followed this perspective, whereas it was not until the 1970s and 1980s that the dramaturgical perspective was developed fully and was employed with greater frequency. The sociological perspective evolved throughout the 1960s and 1970s and reached a high point in the 1980s. The postmodern perspective was discovered by rhetorical critics in the early 1980s and is just now gaining strength within this field. It is important to note that all five critical perspectives currently flourish in journals publishing rhetorical criticism.

The Experiential Perspective

In describing the breakdown of the traditional perspective, we suggested that many critics reacted against the constraints of traditional criticism—its rules, its objectivity, its speaker orientation, and its tie to historical documents. Many critics wanted to select their own focus of attention, reason more creatively, and make a greater variety of judgments. So a practice in rhetorical criticism developed that had more of a critic orientation than a speaker orientation. It was more experiential in nature.

A fundamental urge that seems to mark what we are calling the *experiential perspective* is the exploration of symbol using as personally experienced. Two strains or approaches dominate this perspective. One is eclectic, in which the critic sorts out and communicates what are perceived as the diverse forces involved in a given rhetorical act. A second strain focuses on how an experiential perspective generates knowledge; that is, this perspective stems from the now-familiar phrase "Rhetoric is epistemic." As we label the two approaches, we are aware that they are really only different in emphasis—they are not distinctly separate categories. Eclectic criticism is not prescriptive since it draws on theories, vocabulary, and knowledge in a variety of disciplines: epistemic criticism is quite eclectic as it treats rhetoric as the basis for knowledge. Yet we find it useful to discuss two central tendencies in experiential criticism.

Earlier we indicated that most critics developed shortcuts in the comprehensive traditional method outlined by Wichelns and adapted by Thonssen and Baird and that the complex, process nature of the rhetorical situation made critics realize that they could not achieve the objectivity assumed in traditional criticism. Some critics began to argue that they were starting with their perceptions of a rhetorical situation and were selecting from their rhetorical training and experience the analytic tools and standards appropriate for assessing any given rhetorical act. Black suggests this attitude toward criticism in the conclusion to *Rhetorical Criticism* when he says that rhetorical criticism is "the process by which, through the medium of language, a private attitude becomes a public faith." And when he closes the book, he states, "We simply do not know enough yet about rhetorical discourse to place our faith in systems [paradigms], and it is only through imaginative criticism that we are likely to learn more."[7]

[7]Black, 177.

One could accept Black's position and argue that "experiential" criticism is simply a "stop-gap" position until we learn more about the rhetorical process. Then we will be able to act differently. If that is a good gloss on the book published in 1965, Black himself seems to retreat from that reasoning in the foreword to the 1978 reprinting. In fact, from that forward one might glean a superb expression of the attitude that seems to us to drive the approach we are attempting to describe. Black says from his retrospective view, "Behind the composition of *Rhetorical Criticism: A Study of Method* was an idea that was too dimly understood by its author to possess the book as firmly as it would if the book were to be written now. That idea is that critical method is too personally expressive to be systematized."[8]

A number of critics have taken positions similar to the one Black later saw as his own. One of the first was Mark Klyn, who wrote in his essay "Toward a Pluralistic Rhetorical Criticism" that "rhetorical criticism . . . only means 'intelligent writing about works of rhetoric'—or about works which are not 'rhetoric' in any formal sense but which can be illuminatingly treated from such a standpoint—in whatever way the critic can manage it. It does not imply a prescriptive mode of writing, any categorical structure of judgment, or even any judgmental necessity."[9]

It would be far from the spirit of either Klyn or Black to present them as saying, in effect, that one need only to toss out all methods in order to see truth face to face. It seems possible that a critic could become objective by giving his or her allegiance to a method and thus become a neutral manipulator of instruments (an ideal that is fast being taken as a myth in what we often call "the exact sciences"). This stance must be guarded against.

The result will not be subjectivism but intersubjectivism or agreement among observers regarding a matter of truth. Black cautions, "To say that criticism is a personal instrument is not to say that it is a private one. Critics do address a public, and they thereby incur public responsibilities."[10] A similar insight seems to us to motivate Wayne Brockriede in his often-cited article, "Rhetorical Criticism as Argument." He writes, "A person can function as critic either by passing judgment on the [concrete rhetorical] experience or by analyzing it for the sake of a better understanding of that experience or some more general concept of theory about such experience."[11] In any case, Brockriede holds—and we agree—that the critic should present an argument. The meaning of an argument, as Brockriede has made clear several times, is always open; the critic as arguer is an important concept if the experiential perspective is not to veer toward whim.

The triad of critical procedures we posited in our opening essay—description, interpretation, and evaluation—influence the arguments made by any rhetorical critic, but the experiential critic will tend to assimilate descriptive and evaluative tendencies to the interpretive.[12] Another way to put the point is this: what the

---

[8]"Author's Foreword," x.

[9]Nilsen, 147.

[10]"Author's Foreword," xii.

[11]"Rhetorical Criticism as Argument," *Quarterly Journal of Speech* 60, 2 (April 1974): 165.

[12]A pair of essays that will reward careful study are David L. Swanson's "A Reflective View of the Epistemology of Critical Inquiry," *Communication Monographs* 44, 3 (August 1977): 207–19; and "The Requirement of Critical Justification," *Communication Monographs* 44 (November 1977): 306–20. Swanson carefully labels his work "meta-critical"

world is, is always problematic and open to a variety of interpretations. Thus critics examining rhetorical discourse can only—in this view—describe and evaluate that discourse from their individual interpretative perspectives. A reflexiveness dominates the critical act: criticism can and should only seek momentary interpretative closure in such a way as to remain open to further interpretation.

The point of view expressed in the last paragraph is essential to the experiential perspective. Interpretation is the key word and attitude that accompanies experiential criticism and is probably essential to contemporary theorizing about rhetoric and to all the critical points of view we discuss. Interpretation, of course, is an act, and the significance of the term is appropriately highlighted in Malcolm Sillar's essay "Rhetoric as Act," in which he elevates "rhetoric to the status of an act."[13] The separation of "facts" from "mere rhetoric" has plagued rhetorical thinking throughout the history of Western culture. Taking the distinction at face value would seem to imply that the best criticism would be a sort of peeling away of the latter to reveal the former. Sillar's argument, widely accepted today among rhetorical theorists and critics, is that everything the human can experience as meaningful is permeated with human participation, that is, what "means" does not stand apart from us but is embodied by us. To use the key word— acting in the world creates meaning.

Given this point of view, the experientialist stresses that the rhetorical critic is fundamentally a participant. The critic, then, must argue. Insofar as critical arguments constitute judgment (and, as we said, experientialists may subordinate that element of their critical statements), that judgment cannot be taken as objective measuring, but rather as an invitation to experience rhetorical phenomena as the critic has.

We suggest that experiential criticism may be seen as primarily eclectic. Within the flow of eclecticism, some critics utilize rhetoric as the starting point for understanding knowledge, and we label this tendency the epistemic approach. But given the nature of this perspective, dividing the whole must be even more precarious than most acts of categorizing. If for no other reason than momentary convenience and the conventions of bookmaking, some sort of division seems necessary.

The Eclectic Approach

The tendency to pick and choose from the parts of the culture that appeal to one is as ancient in Western thought as its records. Rudyard Kipling put the matter amusingly in these lines:

When 'Omer smote 'is bloomin' lyre
He's 'eard men sing by land an' sea;
An' what he thought 'e might require
'E went an' took—the same as me!

---

rather than "critical," signaling that he is discussing the basis on which theorizing about criticism might proceed rather than setting forth critical theory. But in the first of these essays, he suggests that what we call "experiential criticism" bears a dim likeness to the outline that he tries to bring forward in bolder relief (p. 213). Throughout the second essay, it is clear that Swanson prefers criticism that interprets; but it is also clear that he believes that the act of interpretation as a critical act needs considerable explication in order to sort out the implications of various stances one may take toward it.

[13]"Rhetoric as Act," *Quarterly Journal of Speech* 50, 3 (October 1964): 277–84.

Less graciously, many see the eclectic urge as akin to a lack of good sense rather than pilfering. The mind that is committed to the unity of thought as the highest mark of goodness is apt to object that one cannot dismember a system or a method, which, if worthwhile, is an organic whole, without obviating the very feature that makes it viable.

The conscientious eclectic is apt to be more interested in the immediacy of experience than the abstract integrity of a system or method. Such a person will argue that methods are but more-or-less-complete sets of tools with instructions by which to build scaffoldings and framework. They will argue that when what is made is made, the tools are laid aside, the scaffolding torn down, and the framework absorbed. When the eclectic critic does use a method, it is an "open-ended" one that does not force or prescribe a specific and provides the critic with a great deal of creative decision making. The eclectic approach stresses the critic's ability to assemble and absorb ways of working, subordinating these to the task at hand. The attitude of eclectic experientialism is well indicated by movie critic Pauline Kael: "I believe we respond most and best to work in any art form [and to other experience as well] if we are pluralistic, flexible, relative in our judgments, if we are eclectic. But this does not mean a scrambling and confusion of systems. Eclecticism is the selection of the best standards and principles from various systems of ideas. It requires more orderliness to be a pluralist than to apply a single theory. . . . Criticism is exciting because you must use everything you are and everything you know that is relevant."[14] The ideal eclecticism may seldom be attained, but then ideals generally are striven for, rather than reached.

We have chosen two essays to illustrate eclecticism generally, both by Lawrence W. Rosenfield. In his theoretical essay "The Anatomy of Critical Discourse," Rosenfield responds to the "ferment in rhetorical criticism" by challenging "critics to formulate more carefully their goals and methods." In his attempt at such a formulation, he creates a sort of matrix that may function as an open system for the critic as "expert-spectator" who can choose from numerous methodological alternatives. The guides he offers are of the sort that quicken the possibility of the scrupulous pluralism that Pauline Kael lauds.

In "A Case Study in Speech Criticism: The Nixon-Truman Analog," Rosenfield demonstrates one way in which the eclectic critic may work to maximize insights that hold promise of transferring from the case at hand to other cases. Although it seems to us that experiential criticism is not generally inclined toward "building theory," Rosenfield's work demonstrates that the possibility is not closed.

The Epistemic Approach

Within the experiential perspective a second tendency has evolved that we label *epistemic*. After describing in the first edition of this book the breakdown of the traditional paradigm, we observed a tendency for critics to communicate an insight into a given rhetorical act through the use of a nonrhetorical concept or theory, so we called this approach "sociocultural-psychological." At that point critics used Freudian psychology or Hegelian dialectic as a basis for the

[14]*I Lost It at the Movies* (Boston: Little, Brown, 1964), 309.

organization and analysis of their criticism. Critics developed an extended analogy, which they found heuristic in a given case. The two essays we included to illustrate the theory and application of sociocultural-psychological criticism were Kenneth Burke's "Mind, Body, and the Unconscious"[15] and "The Rhetoric of Hitler's 'Battle.' "[16] We felt they were excellent examples of Freudian theory and its application to rhetorical criticism.

This critical tendency, in the second edition, took the form of explaining some rhetorical act in terms of its economic, social, or psychological context. This concern for context, which we identified in the breakdown of the traditional perspective, became the starting point for what we labeled as the "social reality" approach to criticism. Scholars probed the economic, social, and psychological conditions to reveal symbolic systems through which people interact to create these conditions. The two essays that illustrated the "social reality" approach were "The Rhetoric of 'Rocky': A Social Value Model of Criticism" and "The Rhetoric of 'Rocky': Part Two" by Janice Hocker Rushing and Thomas S. Frentz.[17] These essays presented and applied a five-phase social value model of rhetorical criticism designed to be a heuristic vehicle for analyzing the reciprocal relationship between societal values and film. We still believe that the four essays from the two earlier editions reward close study as part of an evolution of rhetorical criticism.

These earlier critical tendencies have now manifested themselves in the epistemic approach. This approach was first defined by Robert L. Scott in his article, "On Viewing Rhetoric as Epistemic," where he concluded, "Man must consider truth not as something fixed and final but as something to be created moment by moment in the circumstances in which he finds himself and with which he must cope. . . . In human affairs, then, rhetoric . . . is a way of knowing: it is epistemic."[18]

We have already indicated that the experiential critic sees reality as intersubjective rather than objective. Other scholars joined Scott in articulating that reality is intersubjective. For example, Arthur Hastings identified metaphor as central to one's view of reality: "We can say that every culture's view of reality is a metaphorical view which is structured into various frameworks of perception, values, beliefs, feelings, and behaviors—all connected to language patterns."[19] Hastings goes on to argue that "a culture itself is a broad metaphor, and within a culture, subcultures have their own metaphors for relating to aspects of experience."[20]

Ten years later, in revisiting his earlier essay, Scott states, "the claim of knowing rhetorically is that of creating actuality."[21] The actuality created is an

[15]*Language as Symbolic Action* (Berkeley: University of California Press, 1966).

[16]*The Philosophy of Literary Form* (Baton Rouge: Louisiana State University Press, 1941).

[17]"The Rhetoric of 'Rocky': A Social Value Model of Criticism" and "The Rhetoric of 'Rocky': Part Two," *Western Journal of Speech Communication* 42, 2 (Spring 1978): 63–72 and 42 3 (Fall 1978): 209–21.

[18]"On Viewing Rhetoric as Epistemic," *Central States Speech Journal* 18, 1 (February 1967): 9–17.

[19]"Metaphor in Rhetoric," *Western Speech* 34, 3 (Summer 1970): 187.

[20]Ibid., 194.

[21]"On Viewing Rhetoric as Epistemic: Ten Years Later," *Central States Speech Journal* 27, 4 (Winter 1976): 258–66.

individual's perspective, and essays such as David Berg's "Rhetoric, Reality, and Mass Media" not only show the importance of perspective but also suggest the role of the mass media in creating an individual's reality. As Berg writes, "The briefest reflection ought to verify sufficiently that, for most of us, the great issues of the day—Vietnam, Arab-Israeli confrontations, the national economy—are known only indirectly and usually via the mass media."[22] Berg concludes that "rhetorical criticism, consequently, if it is to remain a viable instrument for social analysis, must take cognizance of the media's influence on human communication behavior."[23]

Scott's two essays on "rhetoric as epistemic" initiated a dialogue on nature of "truth" and "reality" that has a significant impact on rhetoric and criticism. Scott and Brummett[24] defend one of the polar positions and argue that truth is relative because it is humanly generated through rhetoric. Cherwitz and Croasmun, advancing the opposing position, argue that rhetoric is tied to an objective reality and must be judged by external standards for truth. Later Cherwitz with James Hikins offers "perspectivism"—"that reality is independent of human attitudes, beliefs, and values"—as a compromise,[25] and Celeste Condit Railsback attempts to bridge the opposing positions with a "bounded network theory of language" in which "truth is simply a description which adequately portrays a given event, situation, or substance, given a language structure and the structure of the purposes of the agents doing the describing."[26] It is important to note that even with the compromise positions, truth is related to a perspective that is developed through rhetoric, which is really the essence of Scott's initial position. This "perspectivism" is also the key to epistemic rhetorical criticism.

The significance of this dialogue is recognized by Michael Leff, after reviewing the articles on rhetorical theory for 1976 and 1977, when he states, "There appears to be an emerging consensus in support of Scott's view that rhetoric is epistemic" and "An epistemic view of rhetoric signifies a major break in the modern rhetorical tradition."[27] Further, Alan Brinton summaries the dialogue well and raises issues that all parties should consider.[28]

The epistemic critic seeks to understand and possibly evaluate how a rhetor strategically uses language to develop a perspective or worldview. Three essays have been selected to illustrate the epistemic approach. Scott's "On Viewing Rhetoric as Epistemic: Ten Years Later" will set forth the theoretical position and raise and attempts to answer three questions: Is there one way of knowing or many? What sort of knowing does rhetoric seek to achieve? and Is rhetorical relativism vicious? Robert L. Scott's and James F. Klumpp's "A Dear Searcher into Comparisons: The Rhetoric of Ellen Goodman" and James W. Chesebro's

[22]"Rhetoric, Reality, and Mass Media," *Quarterly Journal of Speech* 58, 3 (October 1972): 255–56.

[23]Ibid., 263.

[24]"Some Implications of 'Process' or 'Intersubjectivity': Postmodern Rhetoric," *Philosophy and Rhetoric* 9 (1976): 21–51.

[25]"Rhetorical Perspectivism," *Quarterly Journal of Speech* 69, 3 (August 1983): 249–66.

[26]"Beyond Rhetorical Relativism: A Structural-Material Model of Truth and Objective Reality," *Quarterly Journal of Speech* 69, 4 (November 1983): 351–63.

[27]"In Search of Ariadne's Thread: A Review of the Recent Literature on Rhetorical Theory," *Central States Speech Journal* 29, 2 (Summer 1978): 73–91.

[28]"On Viewing Knowledge as Rhetorical," *Central States Speech Journal*, 26, 4 (Winter 1985): 270–81.

"Computer Science as a Rhetoric" illustrate two ways to apply the epistemic approach. Scott and Klumpp demonstrate how Ellen Goodman's newspaper columns "dynamically build meaning" and in the Burkeian sense provide "equipment for living" for ordinary people. Chesebro argues that computers are rhetorical and epistemic rather than scientific and ontological as he demonstrates that at all levels computers are pragmatic human constructs for communication. Chesebro illustrates a common trait of experiential critics in choosing for his subject and data material that is not usually considered rhetorical in nature.

Characteristics of the Experiential Perspective

Rejecting, consciously or unconsciously, traditional rhetorical criticism, many critics have taken themselves and their own perceptions as a starting place. The critic takes the interactions of the sociopolitical-economic environment and the rhetorical forces as infinite and believes that the mind and experience must be drawn on creatively to form coherent views of the phenomena of discourse. Experientialism, of course, entails assumptions different from those of traditional criticism.

First, from this perspective society is viewed as being in a continual state of process or change. Thus, any statement critics make to describe, interpret, or evaluate discourse must be quite tentative, since discourse is a part of the ever-shifting reality. Interested in relationships, experiential critics focus on things that by definition are relative to point of view; the nature of social reality and a scrupulous appreciation of their own way of working tends to bring experientialists to assimilate descriptive and evaluative gestures to larger patterns of interpretation. To the traditional rhetorical critic, to judge justly was the preferred end of critical action (even though description was quite often the way station achieved). To the experiential critic, to interpret openly in such a way as to encourage further individual interpretations seems preferable.

The tentativeness of experientialists goes well beyond normal scholarly reserve: they hold no theory as absolute and believe that all rules can be disregarded if the circumstances warrant. Experiential critics do not see process simply as cycle, which would imply that the discarded principles can be reclaimed. Instead they are likely to see each day and its experiences as unique, requiring critical insight to understand the skein of passing phenomena and, especially, to act wisely in the face of changing circumstances.

Second, experiential critics, in contrast to traditional critics, tend to believe that an infinite number of concepts, strategies, and postures are available for the study of the rhetorical act; and they believe that a close interaction between the critic and the act itself is necessary for the selection of the correct concepts, strategies, and postures in given instances. As the world is a state of process that must be lived to be real, so is rhetorical theory. Thus, fresh concepts and strategies, as well as different combinations of the old, must evolve if the critic is to work well.

A third assumption characteristic of the experiential critic follows from understanding both rhetoric and criticism as being interpretations of phenomena. This means that any critical vocabulary—in fact, any system of symbolizing—is arbitrarily established and does not reflect merely an external reality. Experiential critics are as likely as any others to be concerned about maintaining a close word-thought-thing relationship, because only through language can they communicate their interpretations. However, they are especially sensitive to the impact that the arbitrary process of selecting a symbol can have on the perceptive process. The word-thought-thing relationship is reciprocal. Not only does the referent influence the selecting of the word, but the word influences the understanding of what is referred to. Thus, the experiential critic is likely to stress the arbitrary nature of all interpretations of phenomena.

Clearly, the experiential stance obligates critics to be eclectic in their methods. That stance, however eclectic, does function within the compass of an orientation and a set of assumptions. That compass is a rough consensus. So let us restate the experiential perspective in the three-part manner we have chosen.

1. *Orientation.* No single element or rhetorical principle can be assumed as the starting point for criticism. Thus, the critic, depending on his or her sensitivity and knowledge, must make the fundamental choice of emphasis.

2. *Assumptions*
    a. Society is in a continual state of process.
    b. An infinite combination of concepts, strategies, and postures are available for the study of public discourse.
    c. Any system of categorizing is arbitrary and does not accurately reflect an assumed external reality for extended periods of time.

3. *Consensus.* No special pattern exists for the study of public discourse. Therefore, discourse must continually be studied afresh.

We have argued that what we call experiential criticism represents a break from the traditional paradigm, and we believe the following essays will help clarify the nature and potentialities of the experiential perspective. In chapters 4, 5, and 6 we explain and illustrate with further essays other directions established after the break of faith in the traditional paradigm.

THE ECLECTIC APPROACH

THE ANATOMY OF CRITICAL DISCOURSE

Lawrence W. Rosenfield

The recent ferment in rhetorical criticism generated by Professor Black's provocative *Rhetorical Criticism: A Study in Method* challenges critics to formulate more carefully their goals and methods. The attempt to raise critical procedures from an *ad hoc* status to something more systematic is not new,[1] but at least among rhetorical critics, it seems today to hold a place of special interest.

The discussion of some of the logical features of criticism contained in this essay responds to the call for a more formal understanding of the critical act. It is an effort to abstract the implicit assumptions of those whom we would clearly want to call critics, to consider the ways in which it would make sense for an ordinary but responsible user of the English language to talk about the behavior of critics and about their products (criticism).

It is the contention of this essay that criticism is most sensibly conceived of as a special form of reason-giving discourse. The nature of reason-giving in criticism becomes intelligible if we treat four particular questions concerning criticism: (1) What do we commonly mean when we call someone a "critic"? (2) What features of criticism distinguish it from other intellectual endeavors? (3) What kinds of questions does criticism seek to answer? (4) By what modalities (formulae) are reasons produced in criticism? Answers to these four questions, and hence support for the central assertion, constitute the bulk of this study.[2] Let us begin by raising the first question and asking of whom we are talking when we speak of "the critic."

Whenever the word "critic" comes up in conversation, a variety of images is liable to come to mind. Some think of the book reviewer or the drama critic for a newspaper. Others, who equate "critic" with "carper," are reminded of a

From *Speech Monographs*, XXV, 1 (March 1968), 50–69. Used by permission of the author and the Speech Communication Association
Dr. Rosenfield is professor of speech at Queens College, New York.

[1]Cf. L. H. Levy, *Psychological Interpretation* (New York, 1963), p. 30; R. McKeon, "The Philosophic Bases of Art and Criticism," *Critics and Criticism, Ancient and Modern*, ed. R. S. Crane (Chicago, 1952), pp. 147–175; L. Thonssen and A. C. Baird, *Speech Criticism* (New York, 1948).

[2]The reader should beware of confusing the remarks made in this essay about the nature of criticism with handbook directions on how to *do* criticism or with empirical descriptions of how criticism is *done*. The aim here is simply to offer a topology which suggests the characteristic formal relationships normally encountered by critics.

sour, negative individual who cannot be pleased. Still others (particularly if they are conversant with too many Master's theses in public address) may imagine that "the speech critic" is a kind of reporter of public address in history.[3] Clearly, common usage has made the term so vague as to be practically meaningless. Is it possible to restrict the meaning of "critic" by adopting semantic boundaries which enable us to distinguish the legitimate critics from those for whom the label represents simply encomium (or invective)? To do so we would need to ascertain what actions we may ordinarily expect of one who is fulfilling the office of critic. If we investigate what I have chosen to call the "critical posture," or the stance habitually assumed by one who is fulfilling the logical requirements of critic, we can reach some consensus as to the behavior of the critic; we will then be in a better position to understand "criticism" itself. In order to clarify what is meant here, it may be helpful to draw a rough comparison between events discussed by critics and those events we commonly call "athletic." We shall discover that in the main the critical posture resembles the "spectator" half of an agent-spectator dichotomy.[4]

First of all, it is easy enough to understand that some sporting events are not only played but are observed as well—by individuals we call "spectators." And it is common that these spectators, if they are genuine fans, do more than simply purchase a ticket of admission so that they may sit in proximity to the athletic activity. They will also devote a certain time and effort to contemplating and discussing the events they observe. That is to say, the role of the spectator often entails reflection and communication about the athletic events. For instance, the baseball fan may attend winter Hot Stove meetings where particular plays will be recalled and mulled over; likewise, the Monday Morning Quarterbacks derive a certain satisfaction from assembling to debunk the maneuvers executed in recent football games.

This same quality of spectatorship seems to be common among those whom we might call fans of aesthetic events, whether their particular "sport" be painting or public communication.[5] One characteristic of the rhetorical critic, then, is his interest in observing and discussing instances of rhetorical discourse, be they speeches, essays, or advertisements, from the vantage of the spectator.

Another characteristic which critics share with at least some sports fans is that both show an appreciation for the execution of the event or object.[6] The

[3]Cf. E. G. Bormann, *Theory and Research in the Communicative Arts* (New York, 1965), pp. 227–238, for a discussion of the confusion which often arises between the role of historian and that of critic.

[4]Cf. N. Smart, "Sense and Reference in Aesthetics," British Journal of Aesthetics, III (October, 1963), 363–366; L. W. Beck, "Agent, Actor, Spectator and Critic," *The Monist,* XLIX (April 1965), 167–182; D. Van de Vate, Jr., "Disagreement as a Dramatic Event," *The Monist,* XLIX (April 1965), 248–261.

[5]Nothing esoteric is meant by "aesthetic." I intend only to convey the notion that the logical conditions mentioned here apply to the full range of interests open to the critic: dramatic productions, musical performances, traditional "fine art," as well as to orations and political dialogues. "Aesthetics" is derived from the Greek *aisthetikos* (of sense perception), and I use the term to suggest that the phenomena which provoke discussion by spectators are of the order which manifest themselves to the perceptions.

[6]The notion of execution should not be confused with the idea of intent. The football pass may have been an accident and still have been well executed. "Skill in execution" is not synonymous with "doing what the creator intended." Cf. M. Eshleman, "Aesthetic Experience, The Aesthetic Object and Criticism," *The Monist,* L. (April 1966), 281–291.

involvement of some fans is limited to being loyal followers of a favorite team; they are mainly concerned to share in the exaltation of the home team's victories. For such "part-time" fans, the outcome of a contest is of paramount interest. True enthusiasts, however, seldom gather merely to report the results of games; they do not confine their comments to the immediate, utilitarian aspects of athletic events. Such fans derive satisfaction from watching a film replay of a game whose final score they already know, a satisfaction we may label as appreciation. This appreciation, whether in the fan or the critic, is not inherently related to enthusiasm or suspense over outcome.

A third similarity between the posture of the critic and that of the athletic fan is that heightened appreciation (and hence increased satisfaction or pleasure) accompanies increased knowledge of the events or objects observed. The football fan who knows more than the formal rules of the game (e.g., understands the tactics of blocking assignments and the relative merits of the T-formation and the single wing) derives a satisfaction from second-guessing the coach which the less informed "rooter for the home team" misses. In other words, consciousness of artistic principles contributes to appreciation.

A final commonality follows from the notion of heightened appreciation. Some spectators, because of especially fine training or acute sensitivity, attain the status of "experts." In the athletic sphere such persons are often hired to act as sportscasters and sports-writers, and in the aesthetic realm they may be called upon to act as "critics" in giving reviews of books, plays, and the like. However, their titles do not derive from the fact that they are appointed or paid to perform these tasks. Rather, it is because of their competence that they are asked to assume the critic's office. An expert can be an amateur and still be a fine sports analyst or critic. What matters is exceptional understanding. Accordingly, "critical posture" refers to *the capacity a person has to act as an expert commentator,* and the critic, if he is nothing else, must be one who is capable of fulfilling this role.

Simple *capacity* to render commentary is not yet criticism. The expert-spectator who relishes the events he observes but does not relate his appreciation to others is not a critic, for "criticism" normally refers to the critic's verbal commentary on the event. Criticism is therefore the special variety of discourse which results when a person who has adopted a critical posture makes assertions, i.e., statements by an expert about "the way things are."[7] How then may we distinguish critical discourse from the general range of assertive discourse?

One procedure would be to examine several instances of discourse which we would definitely wish to call criticism and seek to discover its typical features. I refer the reader to two short essays dealing with a speech delivered by General Douglas MacArthur to a joint session of Congress (and through direct broadcast, to the nation) on April 19, 1951. The first essay is by journalist Richard Rovere,

---

[7]This places literary and rhetorical critics in the peculiar position of producing verbal objects as comment on other verbal objects (e.g., novels, plays, speeches, etc.), so that both types of critic are in fact engaged in producing discourse about discourse. Cf. A. Hillbruner, "Criticism as Persuasion," *The Southern Speech Journal,* XXXVIII (Summer 1963), 260–267; E. Black, "Moral Values and Rhetorical Criticism," lecture delivered at University of Wisconsin, July 12, 1965; Thonssen and Baird, pp. 13–14.

the second by Herbert Wichelns, a professor of speech.[8] Let them represent clear cases of discourse we would ordinarily consider rhetorical criticism. What characteristics make them intuitively admissible as criticism?

Richard H. Rovere

As a literary critic and political observer, I view the speech solely from the literary and political points of view. I am not qualified to criticize oratory or elocution.

As a piece of composition, the speech seemed to me a good deal but not a great deal better than the general run of public prose in the United States today. MacArthur has eloquence of a kind, but it strikes me as a rather coarse eloquence. He never shades his meanings, never introduces a note of humor, never gives the feeling that he is one man, only one, addressing himself to other men. His language is never flat and bloodless; neither is it flabby and loose-jointed, as so much writing of this sort is. But to me there is rather a fetid air about it. It does not leave me with the impression that a cool and candid mind has been at work on difficult matters of universal concern. Instead, it leaves me with the impression that a closed and in a sense a rather frantic mind has been at work to the end of making an appeal to history—not neglecting to use any of the rulebook hints on how to do it. I think not of history but of second-rate historian as I read the speech.

Form and content are, if not inseparable, very closely related. Politically, MacArthur's speech seemed extremely weak to me. This is not, I think, because I am opposed to his politics; I believe he could have made out a much stronger case for himself. But he never came to grips with the issues. For example, he wanted to have it that he was being persecuted for "entertaining" his particular views. This, of course, is rubbish. He got into trouble not for the political and military views he entertained (no doubt he was right in saying they were entertained by many of his colleagues) but for seeking to usurp the diplomatic function. He never sought to answer the objections to his position that rest on political and economic facts recognized by both sides; that if we followed him, we would be abandoned by several allies; that if Russia invaded Europe, which he has admitted might be an early consequence of his policy, the industrial balance would favor the Communist world; that, like it or not, American power does have its limitations. MacArthur's policy may be sounder than Truman's. But the contention cannot be sustained without facing these stubborn facts about the world today. MacArthur, in his speech, never faced them.

Herbert A. Wichelns

Demosthenes had the problem too; how much to spell out, how formal and explicit to make his proposals. At times Demosthenes judged it best not to "make a motion" but merely to offer comment and advice at large. MacArthur made a similar choice. In the main he chose not to debate, in the sense of formulating proposals

---

[8]Both essays are drawn from F. W. Haberman, "General MacArthur's Speech: A Symposium of Critical Comment," *Quarterly Journal of Speech*, XXXVII (October 1951), 321–331. They are reprinted in C. C. Arnold, D. Ehninger, and J. C. Gerber, *The Speaker's Resource Book* (Chicago, 1961), pp. 283–286. Cf. also P. Wylie, "Medievalism and the MacArthurian Legend," ibid., XXXVII (December 1951), 473–478; P. R. Beall, "Viper-Crusher Turns Dragon-Slayer," ibid., XXXVIII (February 1952), 51–56; K. R. Wallace, "On the Criticism of the MacArthur Speech," ibid., XXXIX (February 1953), 69–74; M. H. Nichols, *Rhetoric and Criticism* (Baton Rouge, La., 1963), pp. 68–69.

and defending them in full. Instead he indicated the heads for debate, leaving no doubt as to the direction of his policy. Definite proposals were few, and sharply limited to Formosa and Korea. Supporting reasons were very sparingly given, and sometimes confined to bare assertions (as on the extent of China's present military commitment and Russia's probable course). But the call for a harder and more aggressive policy is plain from the beginning ("no greater expression of defeatism"). The chief support for that policy is neither logical argument nor emotional appeal, but the self-portrait of the speaker as conveyed by the speech.

It is an arresting portrait. Certain colors are of course mandatory. The speaker respects Congress and the power of this nation for good in the world. He is free from partisanship or personal rancor. He sympathizes with the South Koreans and with his embattled troops. He prefers victory to appeasement. He seeks only his country's good. He hates war, has long hated it. If these strokes are conventional, they take little time, except for the last, on which the speaker feels he must defend himself.

More subtle characterizing strokes are found in the "brief insight into the surrounding area" which forms a good half of the speech. Here the General swiftly surveys the nature of the revolution in Asia, the island-frontier concept and Formosa's place in the island-chain, the imperialistic character of the Chinese communities, the regeneration of Japan under his auspices, the outlook for the Philippines, and the present government of Formosa. All this before reaching Korea. Most of these passages have no argumentative force. But all together they set up for us the image of a leader of global vision, comprehending in his gaze nations, races, continents. The tone is firmest on Japan ("I know of no nation more serene, orderly and industrious"), least sure on the Philippines, but always positive.

Rarely indeed have the American people heard a speech so strong in the tone of personal authority. "While I was not consulted . . . that decision . . . proved a sound one." "Their last words to me"—it is the Korean people with whom the General has been talking. "My soldiers." The conduct of "your fighting sons" receives a sentence. A paragraph follows on the General's labors and anxieties on their behalf. The pace at which the thought moves, too, is proconsular; this is no fireside chat. Illustration and amplification are sparingly used; the consciously simple vocabulary of the home-grown politician is rejected. The housewife who "understood every word" was mistaken; she missed on *epicenter* and *recrudescence* and some others. But having by the fanfare been jarred into full attention, she understood quite well both the main proposition of the speech—a harder policy—and the main support offered—the picture of a masterful man of unique experience and global outlook, wearing authority as to the manner born.

One feature these comments display, which is often noted as an essential of critical discourse, is that both contain verdicts (sometimes called judgments or evaluations). Not all assertive discourse contains appraisal as criticism does. Scientific reports, for instance, display an exploratory impulse rather than an evaluative one.[9] Nor is this to say that critical essays must reach a settled and final verdict, for clearly Wichelns is at pains to avoid assessing MacArthur's speech as good or bad. But criticism does eventuate in, or at least has as an ultimate objective, assessment. Professor Black has put it most succinctly:

> At the culmination of the critical process is the evaluation of the discourse or of its author; a comprehensive judgment which, in the best of criticism, is the fruit of patient exegesis. . . . Even the purely technical objective of understanding how a

[9]Bormann, pp. 227–229; E. Black, *Rhetorical Criticism: A Study in Method* (New York, 1965), p. 4.

discourse works carries the assumption that it does work, and that assumption is an assessment. Similarly, to understand why a thing has failed is at least to suspect that it *has* failed, and that suspicion is an assessment. There is, then, no criticism without appraisal; there is no "neutral" criticism. One critic's judgment may be absolute and dogmatic, another's tentative and barely committal, but however faint the judicial element in criticism may become, it abides.[10]

If Black is correct, we ought seldom to find a critic engaging in description of a rhetorical event for its own sake; and if we do, we ought perhaps proceed most cautiously in determining whether to label the product "criticism."[11]

Clearly our two samples of criticism meet the criterion of making assessments. Rovere is explicit:

> . . . the speech seemed . . . a good deal but not a great deal better than the general run of public prose . . . There is a rather fetid air about it. . . , Politically [the] speech seemed extremely weak.

Wichelns' appraisal is more complex. Avoiding any "good-bad" evaluation, he invites us to accept his verdict on how the speech was executed (i.e., what made it work as it did). In Wichelns' judgment the speech called for a harder policy and this call was supported by the speaker's self-portrait. Both Rovere and Wichelns present us with settled, though not necessarily final or definitive, assertions as to the character and/or worth of the speech; their critical comments betray momentary terminations (benchmarks) in their thought processes, terminations which are expressed in the form of verdicts.

Once we grant that the assertive discourse of criticism strives for appraisal, we should concurrently examine the "reasons" offered to justify the verdicts. The bulk of both critical essays consists of reasons justifying the judgments. Notice, for example, Wichelns' assertion that MacArthur's main form of proof was his own self-portrait. It is supported by three contentions: that it was an arresting portrait, employing both "mandatory colors" and "subtle . . . strokes"; that the speech otherwise is lacking in argument and abounding in assertion; and that the speech was couched in the language of personal authority. From these Wichelns is enabled to conclude that the speech offered "the picture of a masterful man of unique and global outlook" as support for MacArthur's claims.

Dealing as we are with evaluative discourse, it is only natural to speculate further about the relationship linking verdicts and reasons. Imagine for instance the following situation: a friend says, "I read the novel *Tom Jones* last week." You treat this statement as a factual report. But were your friend to co-append, "It struck me as a rather shallow book," there is an immediate change in conditions. You may then decide to treat the combined statements as criticism, with the second sentence serving as an appraisal and the first now transformed from a

[10]Black, "Moral Values. . . . " Cf. Hillbruner, pp. 264–266; P. W. Taylor, *Normative Discourse* (Englewood Cliffs, N.J., 1961), p. 52; W. Righter, *Logic and Criticism* (New York, 1963), pp. vii–3; Bormann, p. 229; J. Holloway, "Symposium: Distinctive Features of Arguments Used in Criticism of the Arts," *Proceedings of the Aristotelian Society* (supplement), XXIII (1949), 173.

[11]A. Isenberg, "Critical Communication," *Philosophical Review*, LVIII (April 1949) 331. See also the following articles in *The Monist*, L (April 1966): M. Scriven, "The Objectivity of Aesthetic Evaluation," 159–187; H. Osborne, "Reasons and Description in Criticism," 204–212; H. Morris-Jones, "The Logic of Criticism," 213–221; P. Wilson, "The Need to Justify," 267–280.

report into part of the justification for the judgment. Furthermore, it would be extremely odd if your friend were to utter the second statement and at the same time deny having ever read the novel, having had any contact with anyone who had read it, or having had access to any critical comments about it. Obviously, we expect a critical verdict to be in some way conditional upon the reasons offered in its support. We are not yet in a position to see why reasons are expected or to determine how they function as support, but that they do so function to make criticism a reason-giving activity is evident.[12]

A valuable first step in grasping the logical structure underlying this conditional relation of reasons-and-verdict is to realize that criticism is an exercise in forensic reasoning. The critic's commentary is analogous to that of the trial lawyer who bases claims as to the proper verdict in a case on his interpretation of the facts in the light of some legal code. What tactics are open to the legal advocate? He may in some circumstances accept a set of legal standards (canons or laws) and apply them rigorously to the facts in the case. He may on the other hand feel that the laws as they are commonly interpreted hurt his case. In that event he could propose a new interpretation of the laws which does more justice to the position he is defending; or if his mind functions after the fashion of an Erskine, he could seek to "make law" by questioning the established norms and attempting either to amend them or to substitute a code of his own choosing as the standard of evaluation. Again, some circumstances may be such that the counsel will accept a verdict contrary to his position but then go on to try to mitigate the thrust of the verdict by showing how special factors in the case deserve attention. Or perhaps there is a conflict in the legal code such as a contradiction between two laws. In the case of such an overlap, the advocate may argue for the priority of one law over another. In each of these instances the essential forensic tactic is to measure facts or observations against a code or canon.

A similar juxtapositioning of observations and normative standards constitutes the essence of critical activity:

> The code may be the law of the land, the theory of probabilities, the standards of historical research, *the canons of artistic excellence* [my italics], or their own standards for distinguishing truth from error. Whoever judges in these ways, then, needs two distinct kinds of knowledge: (1) knowledge about the facts or events he is to judge and (2) knowledge about the standards against which he is to measure the facts or events.[13]

We may thus expect that reasons offered in critical discourse will lay claim to being the product of a "measurement" (comparison of data observed and norm). This does not mean that the verdict need follow inevitably from the comparison, only that it will claim such a juxtapositioning as a warrant for its own worth.

---

[12]Let us momentarily disregard a related problem, whether one's verdicts must follow inevitably from one's reasons, as in a valid syllogism, or whether there is some looser connection between the evaluations and the justificatory reasons, perhaps a relation of appropriateness instead of one of correctness. What matters here is that both components are inseparable parts of the critic's assertions, no matter what their bearing on each other. Cf. Righter, pp. 74–84; M. Weitz, "Reasons in Criticism," *Journal of Aesthetics and Art Criticism,* XX (Summer 1962), 427–437; B. C. Heyl, "The Critic's Reasons," ibid., XVI (Winter 1957), 169–179.

[13]J. F. Wilson and C. C. Arnold, *Public Speaking as a Liberal Art* (Boston, 1964), p. 97. Cf. Weitz; Isenberg, pp. 330–335; Taylor, pp. 9–14.

If the notion of forensic reasoning as the foundation of critical strategy is plausible, we have further grounds for rejecting some evaluations which are offered as specimens of criticism. Though tradition recognizes as "movie reviews" the placement of stars next to film titles in newspapers (four stars equivalent to "excellent," one star meaning "terrible"), we need not accept such markings as criticism (or if we do, as more than decapitated criticism). Again, what should one make of an argument which runs, "I feel that MacArthur's speech was unsatisfactory because the General once insulted me"? Such a remark is ordinarily disturbing. In part this is because the comment does not fulfill forensic requirements: the reason offered, although it explains why the commentator holds the position he does, is not admissible as a justification for the verdict. In this case the norm (such as it is) violates the critical posture, and there is in addition a failure to juxtapose the norm to facts about the speech.

Observe how Wichelns illustrates the forensic pattern. He opens his essay by distinguishing between speeches which offer advice and those which join a debate. He thereby establishes the norm. He then spends the remainder of his first paragraph drawing attention to those facts about the speech which place it in the category of speeches of advice. In his next paragraph Wichelns formulates the principle that some remarks are mandatory on this kind of occasion—and then observes the extent to which MacArthur met those demands. In his third paragraph the critic implies that some rhetorical tactics reveal a proconsular image and then presents facts which enable him to ascribe such an image to MacArthur. The forensic pattern is evident throughout Wichelns' essay.

But the notion of forensic reasoning highlights one curious feature of criticism: although both norms and observations are logically essential, they need not be expressed separately. This aspect of criticism is illustrated in the dialogue concerning *Tom Jones*. When your friend justifies his evaluation of the novel with "I read the novel last week," where is the standard of judgment? Clearly, if it exists at all it is only implicit. One might suspect that your friend really meant, "I read the novel, and it did not measure up to my taste in novels," but that would only be speculation. Or take Rovere as a case in point. True, he announces at the outset that his standards will be "literary" and "political" ones. But then he goes on to call MacArthur's eloquence "coarse" and to say that MacArthur's language is neither "flat and bloodless" nor "flabby and loosejointed." Are these observations or verdicts? And what are Rovere's standards for eloquence? Apparently, Rovere demands that the reader accept the existence and the excellence of the norms on faith. The norms do not appear in the criticism, though they are presupposed by Rovere's comments.

This fusion of otherwise distinct components is not an accident of composition. When Rovere condemns MacArthur's prose for its unshaded meanings, its lack of humor, its fetid language, is he hypothesizing that "the occurrence of these three elements results in coarse eloquence" after the fashion of the experimental scientists? Or is he calling to attention these particular observable features which, in these particular rhetorical circumstances, lend an air of coarseness to this particular speech? Rovere is obviously affirming his possession of standards of eloquence; but the application of the standards to a particular aesthetic event is, as we shall discover when we treat the modalities of analysis, far more complex than the measurement of the length of a metal pipe. In aesthetic judgments the standards often defy expression as general propositions for any but the most gross (and hence, trivial) features. And the standards applied are bound to the particulars of the single event because the events are too diverse and complicated to be comprehended by universal precepts. Such is the case of Rovere seeking to illuminate the coarseness of MacArthur's prose. He would be unable to provide general rubrics for what makes prose coarse because too many factors enter in; but he is able to account for the "coarse eloquence" in this case, and he does so.[14]

To answer what features of criticism distinguish it from other types of reason-giving discourse, we have so far maintained that the term "criticism" is most sensibly reserved for that assertive discourse produced by expert-spectators whose judgments as to the execution of (in this case) rhetorical phenomena are supported by forensic arguments. We may now consider the two remaining questions posed at the beginning of this essay. Let us for present purposes exclude from attention questions concerning the goals of rhetorical criticism or the origin and validity of rhetorical canons, interesting as these questions may be. In this essay we shall take for granted that the rhetorical critic possesses certain *a priori* objectives; he engages in the critical act for the sake of some preestablished end(s) which need not be specified here. We shall also presume that if called upon to do so, the critic could vindicate by means extrinsic to the realm of criticism (e.g., by metaphysical justification of some sort) his adoption of what-ever rhetorical concepts he employs in his criticism.[15] Our interest is not in why he acts and believes as he does, but in how he exploits the critical opportunities available to him.

We are consequently obliged to examine the array of methodological options open to the rhetorical critic. At least two method-related questions invariably confront the critic in the exercise of his office: 1) what shall be the major focus of his critical analysis (what data will he find primarily relevant)? 2) what sorts of measurements or readings shall he take on the rhetorical transactions under investigation (in what fashion shall he transpose and describe the data he chooses to fix upon)? How he elects to answer these questions will in part in-fluence both the nature and function of the critical reasons produced. Let us first address ourselves to the alternative foci open to the critic of "public address."

If we schematize an instance of public communication encountered by the critic, we intuitively recognize four gross variables: the sources(s) or creator(s) of the message, the message itself, the context or environment in which the mes-sage is received (including both the receivers and the social "landscape" which spawns the message), and the critic himself (who, especially in the study of public address of the past, is in a sense a unique receiver). For the sake of con-venience, let us label the variables "S" (source), "M" (message), "E" (envi-ronment), and "C" (critic). Obviously, in a total interpretation of the communicative act all four variables are relevant. But equally obvious from past critical practice, such all-encompassing analysis will be rare if not impossible for the single critic. Perhaps the two most thoroughly examined messages in the English language are Shakespeare's *Hamlet* and Lincoln's *Gettysburg Address;* the very fact that criticism of these two is not yet exhausted attests to the

---

[14]Righter, p. 22.

[15]Cf. Taylor, pp. 128–138; McKeon, pp. 489–490; K. Burke, *A Grammar of Motives* (New York, 1945), p. 472; E. Olson, "The Poetic Method in Aristotle: Its Powers and Limitations," *Aristotle's Poetics and English Literature*, ed. E. Olson (Chicago, 1965), pp. 187–191.

impracticality of completely enveloping one verbal act with another. We are therefore forced to recognize that critics will have to concentrate on some permutation of the four variables as a means of making their critical tasks manageable.

For the rhetorical critic the one indispensable factor is M, the message. Exclusive concern for S, the source, is the biographer's business; study of E, the environment, is the historian's; studies relating speakers to audience apart from the substance of the message (as in explorations of the role of status or leadership in public affairs) are performed mainly by sociologists. The rhetorical critic sees the entire communicative transaction as somehow "suspended" from the language of the message under examination. For the rhetorical critic the verbal utterance constitutes a kind of linguistic architecture which supports and gives form to the total rhetorical act. In this belief the critic differs from the historian and sociologist, who may choose to treat the verbal factors as mere artifacts of the event. The rhetorical critic not only fastens his observation to M; he does so in the conviction that the message is fundamental to an appreciation of the entire event.[16]

The critic therefore occupies himself with some combination of variables which focus on the message: S-M, M-E, M-C, S-M-E, S-M-C, or M-E-C. These are combinations which constitute genuine critical options. It is not the critic's task to inspect these variables in isolation; neither is it sufficient for him to report that they all converged in a particular instance of public discourse.

Consider first the nature of the M-C focus, which represents an unashamedly introspectionist stance. This focus seeks to gauge the critic's personal response to the aesthetic object.[17] The critic who directs his attention to the M-C relationship will conceive of himself as a kind of sensitive instrument, and his analysis will be comprised primarily of reports of his own reactions to the work apart from any impact the work may have had on any particular "public." In this vein, Anatole France remarked that the good critic

> . . . is he who relates the adventures of his soul among masterpieces. . . . The truth is that one never gets out of oneself.[18]

Rovere's commentary suggests that he adopted a focus such as the one described by France.

The M-C orientation grounds its validation on the premise that communication is essentially a unique event, a private transaction between message and receiver which can never be known to a third party. The critic is simply one more receiver of the message, albeit more sensitive than the typical, untrained

[16]Cf. T. Clevenger, Jr., "Research Opportunities in Speech," *Introduction to the Field of Speech*, ed. R. F. Reid (Chicago, 1965), pp. 222–224.

[17]Cf. Heyl, p. 170; R. Wellek and A. Warren, *The Theory of Literature* (New York, 1949); W. Embler, "The Language of Criticism," *Etc.*, XXII (September 1965), 261–277. This cryptic account is obviously not the entire story. The critic is not privileged simply to report his pleasure and/or pain on confronting the discourse. He is in some manner obligated to explain how and why the work *justifies* his particular response. It is also important to note that contemporary literary critics who claim to focus entirely on the work itself are in fact often employing the M-C paradigm; their failure to recognize the implications of their critical orientation results occasionally in rather odd exigeses.

[18]Anatole France, "The Literary Life," *The Book of Modern Criticism*, trans. and ed. L. Lewisohn (New York, 1919), pp. 1–3. Cf. I. A. Richards, *Principles of Literary Criticism* (New York, 1925), pp. 5–24.

receiver. If one accepts the notion that critical interpretation is so uniquely personal, it then follows that no interpretation can expect to be more than a justification of the critic's own state of mind as he responds to the aesthetic object.

And if communication is inherently a private matter, then one's faith in the critic's explication and overall taste constitutes at least as important a means of support for the verdicts offered as do the critic's stated reasons for his evaluation. Hence, in the case of Rovere, we need to trust his sensitivity as much as we need to be persuaded by his analysis of the prose. It is even possible to imagine that the primary function served by reasons submitted by an observer with the M-C focus is to demonstrate to a reader the observer's competence as a critic, to "exhibit his credentials," to make authoritative judgments.[19] Such a conception of M-C analysis may account for the propensity of prominent critics to set forth lists of their favorite books, or of the best plays or speeches of all time. Having achieved eminence, they need no longer justify their selections, but are able to telescope or even abort their arguments in favor of short explications of why a particular book, play, or novel pleased them personally.

The next three foci are related to each other in their denial of an introspectionist critical stance and their advocacy of greater detachment. The S-M focus concentrates on understanding discourse as an expression of its creator. Most often the critic attempts to trace out the creative process by which the speaker externalized and structured the feelings, thoughts, and experiences contained within himself. The relation of source to message has prompted two general schools of criticism. One (which actually concentrates on the S →M relationship) seeks to account for the rhetor's behavior as a function of the factors which influenced him: his education, the books he read, the persons who inspired him, and the like.[20] The other variation of the S-M focus, S←M, is best typified by neo-Freudian critics who treat the aesthetic event as symptomatic of the artist's personal life and psychodynamics. The critic, in other words, acts as a kind of lay psychoanalyst, using the message as a key to understanding and evaluating the creator of the message.[21]

The M-E focus also incorporates two divergent streams of critical practice. In the one instance (M←E), "environment" is interpreted broadly (as by historians and literary critics) to encompass the age and the civilization in which the message originated. The historian of ideas attempts to set the historical background in which particular works or clusters of works were produced, showing how the messages are themselves a reflection of their era. This emphasis finds its rationale in the assumption that to the extent that an aesthetic event can be considered

[19]Embler, p. 265; M. Beardsley, *Aesthetics: Problems in the Philosophy of Criticism* (New York, 1958), pp. 129–134.

[20]Cf. M. H. Abrams, *The Mirror and the Lamp: Romantic Tradition* (New York, 1953), pp. 21–25; J. Thorp, "The Aesthetics of Textual Criticism," *PMLA*, LXXX (December 1965), 465–482; L. D. Reid, "Gladstone's Training as a Speaker," *The Quarterly Journal of Speech*, XL (December 1954), 373–380; L. Crocker, "The Rhetorical Training of Henry Ward Beecher," *The Quarterly Journal of Speech*, XIX (February 1933), 18–24.

[21]Cf. H. D. Duncan, *Communication and Social Order* (New York, 1962), pp. 3–16; M. Maloney, "Clarence Darrow," in *A History and Criticism of American Public Address*, ed. M. K. Hochmuth, III (New York, 1955), 262–312; H. M. Ruitenbeek (ed.), *Psychoanalysis and Literature* (New York, 1964); N. Kiell (ed.) *Psychological Studies of Famous Americans* (New York, 1964); W. S. Scott, *Five Approaches of Literary Criticism* (New York, 1962), pp. 69–73; R. L. Buxhman, "On the Uses of Psychology: Conflict and Conciliation in Benjamin Franklin," *History and Theory*, V (#3, 1966), 225–240.

typical of its age, it will provide valuable insight into the intellectual and social trends of that age.[22] Another direction which critics with an M-E focus have chosen to follow, one which has gained its widest acceptance among critics with a bent toward social science, interprets "environment" in a more prescribed sense, referring to the specific audience which the message had. These critics consider the "functional" relationship which existed between the discourse and its receivers. They seek to determine how the receivers used the messages presented to them as stimuli. The assumption underlying the functional (M→E) approach to the M-E relationship is that, whatever the speaker's intention, the auditor attends to a speech in a manner which fulfills his own personal needs. An old man may attend a July 4th celebration, not prepared to be persuaded or inspired to increased patriotism, but simply because the ceremonial oratory reminds him of the speeches he heard on similar occasions in his youth. Similarly, the daily newspaper may function for some readers as a means by which they maintain an intimate contact with their favorite celebrities. For such readers, news of a Hollywood scandal is as welcome as a letter from home. In cases such as these, the M-E critic might concern himself with determining expectations of the audience as well as the extent to which those expectations were fulfilled by the discourse.[23]

Although it is possible for a rhetorical critic to employ any of the three foci so far mentioned, the bulk of traditional speech criticisms has not explored dyadic relationships but the triadic formulations of S-M-E. Essentially, this "pragmatic" orientation treats the message as an effort at persuasion and ventures to assess the artistic skill of the speaker in achieving his persuasive goals with his audience.[24] The extensive use of the S-M-E framework can be justified if we accept the notion that public address is, literally, discourse addressed to a public by a speaker who is carrying on public business by his act of communication. Because the critic takes for granted the Janus-like quality of public address, revealing simultaneously the communicator and the social environment to which he seeks to adapt himself, the S-M-E critic emphasizes in his study the mediating nature of the message in moving (or failing to move) the audience toward the speaker's vision of how the demands of occasion ought to be met and resolved.[25]

The three foci—S-M, M-E and S-M-E—comprise a set because they share one quality which distinguishes them from the introspectionist reports of the M-C

---

[22]For example, V. L. Parrington, *Main Currents of American Thought* (New York, 1927) 3 vols.; R. T. Oliver, *History of Public Address in America* (Boston, 1965); M. Meyers, *The Jacksonian Persuasion* (New York, 1960); A. O. Lovejoy, *The Great Chain of Being* (Cambridge, Mass., 1936); D. M. Chalmers, *The Social and Political Ideas of the Muckrakers* (New York, 1964); G. Orwell, "Boys' Weeklies," in *A Collection of Essays* by George Orwell (Garden City, N.Y., 1954), pp. 284–313; Scott, pp. 123–126.

[23]Cf. Heyl, p. 169; D. Katz, "The Functional Approach to the Study of Attitudes," *Public Opinion Quarterly*, XXIV (Summer 1960), 163–204; J. K. Galbraith, *Economics and the Art of Controversy* (New York, 1955), pp. 3–31; L. W. Lichty, "The Real McCoys and It's [sic] Audience: A Functional Analysis," *Journal of Broadcasting*, IX (Spring 1965), 157–165; B. DeMott, "The Anatomy of Playboy," *Commentary*, XXIV (August 1962), 111–119.

[24]Abrams, pp. 16–21; W. N. Brigance, "What is a Successful Speech?" *The Quarterly Journal of Speech Education*, XI (April, 1925), 272–277; Black, *Rhetorical Criticism*, pp. 36–58; Thonssen and Baird, pp. 448–461.

[25]D. C. Bryant, "Rhetoric: Its Scope and Function," *Quarterly Journal of Speech*, XXXIX (December 1953), 401–424.

focus. This shared quality is a stress on objective, verifiable, critical statements. By placing the spectator outside the critical equation, each method attempts to make of criticism a dispassionate report of what actually "is," a judicious, unbiased account of properties which inhere in the communicative event itself. In so doing they imply that the critic should strive to produce an analysis of the essential nature of the phenomenon apart from any idiosyncrasies in his personal responses.[26]

None of the three "impersonal" approaches so far mentioned can serve the ends of the introspectionist, and hence, none of the three finds encourages critical reasons employed mainly to establish the critic's own credentials as a sensitive observer. Instead, the critic who strives for a dispassionate and reliable report of the rhetorical act will find that the reasons he gives in support of his verdicts function primarily to call to the attention of others those characteristics of the original communication which merit their further contemplation. The method is similar to that of the football announcer who uses an instant replay camera. A team scores a touchdown, and seconds later the television commentator says, "As we play back the scoring play, notice the excellent footwork of the man with the ball." The listener-viewer is thus primed to observe for himself a feature of the event which the expert-commentator feels merits attention. The same ostensive function applies to the selection of reasons by the impersonal, rhetorical critic; his reasons do not report, nor do they simply support a conclusion—they call on the reader to observe for himself.

The last two foci available to the critic, S-M-C and M-E-C, reject the cleavage between introspection and impersonal functions of critical discourse. Justification for these two foci stems from the recognition of contemporary science that the very act of observation alters the event observed and so distorts the information one is able to obtain about the event. The distortions can never be overcome by more precise observations or measurements, but can only be acknowledged by specifying a degree of uncertainty and looseness in one's formulations.

As applied to the critical act, such a position holds that criticism is inevitably the product of the critic's encounter with the rhetorical event, that the locus of criticism is neither critic nor ontic event but the critic's intrusion upon the event. Such an intrusion may not directly influence the agents involved in the communication; we may wish to admit, for instance, that as he prepared his first inaugural address Thomas Jefferson probably did not significantly alter his behavior in conscious anticipation of twentieth-century rhetorical critics. But neither should we misconstrue the dilemma faced by the critic who would do more than resurrect the data of the past. His problem is less one of succumbing to personal bias than it is of taking and formulating precise measurements on the event under investigation.[27] Our final two foci suit the critic who has reconciled himself to the inevitable impossibility of making meticulously accurate statements about the

[26]B. Harrison, "Some Uses of 'Good' in Criticism," *Mind,* LXIX (April 1960), 206; A. H. Hanney, "Symposium: Distinctive Features of Arguments Used in Criticism of the Arts," p. 169.

[27]A. G. Van Melsen, *The Philosophy of Nature* (New York, 1953), p. 226; L. Brillouin, *Science and Information Theory* (New York, 1962), p. 232; F. C. Frick, "Some Perceptual Problems from the Point of View of Information Theory," *Psychology: A Study of a Science,* II (New York, 1959), 77; J. Rothstein, "Information and Organization as the Language of the Operational Viewpoint," *Philosophy of Science,* XXIX (October 1962), 406–411; J. Ruesch, "The Observer and the Observed: Human Communication Theory," *Toward a Unified Theory of Human Behavior,* ed. R. R. Grinker (New York, 1956), pp.

events he observes, who wishes instead the maximum fidelity possible within the limits imposed on him by the nature of perception and critical language. His framework for observation indexes neither the event *in vacuo* nor his own response to the event, but the relation which joins him to the rhetorical act.

The critic who adopts the S-M-C focus assumes that a speech will no more exist "out there" in some ontic world than a symphony resides "in" a musical score or a drama "in" a manuscript.[28] Instead, he believes that we can discern an artistic intention in a work of art; and the aesthetic experience, be it to speech or symphony, is the experiencing and articulation of that artistic intention. Artistic intention is understood as the peculiar way in which the elements of the message cohere in the movement of confrontation with the observer-critic.

There are objective clues in the messages as to the meaning which will be actualized by the interaction of observer and thing observed. It becomes the critic's task to investigate that cooperation of elements and ratios in the message which gives rise to the artistic meaning-as-experienced. In other words, speaker, speech, and observer momentarily coalesce as the elements of the rhetorical event unite to move toward some terminal condition. The critic's objective is to explicate that condition and the communication factors which contribute to or retard the transaction. The critic seeks to determine the nature of the demands made by the rhetorical event upon the beholder of the event. He is of course obligated to be alert to his own predilections as an instrument of observation, but his attention is focused outward upon artistic intention rather than inward as with introspection.[29]

The source enters into this equation because it is posited that the artist's intention(s) in creating the message may provide a key to understanding the artistic intention embodied in the message. The critic assumes that the speaker, by virtue of his close connection with the message, is something of an authority on the event; that is, the speaker often possesses special knowledge about the speech which adds depth to the critic's own interpretation. Hence, a comparison of artist's intentions with artistic intentions may prove a valuable aid in centering interest on the decisive qualities of the work of art.

Consider, for example, John Kennedy's television address to the nation on the Cuban missile crisis in 1962: we might regard the policy enunciated on that occasion as rhetorically inappropriate. However, if we knew that Kennedy was privy to secret information indicating that the Russians would withdraw their missiles if we took a strong line, this knowledge would help clarify the forceful posture Kennedy chose to adopt and possibly alter our critical assessment of the artistic intention evidenced in the discourse. We might now see the message as primarily a warning to Russia rather than as a report to the nation.

Notice that the S-M-C focus does not obligate the critic to accept the artist's personal conception of his creation; the purpose of uncovering Kennedy's

---

36–54; M. Bunge, *Casuality: The Place of the Casual Principles in Modern Science* (New York, 1963), pp. 348–349; P. Frank, *Philosophy of Science* (Englewood Cliffs, N.J., 1957), pp. 207–231; A. Moles, *Information Theory and Esthetic Perception* (London, 1958).

[28]Cf. A. G. Pleydell-Pearce, "On the Limits and Use of 'Aesthetic Criteria,'" *Philosophical Quarterly*, IX (January 1959), 29–30.

[29]Cf. E. Berne, *Transactional Analysis in Psychotherapy* (New York, 1961); Ch. Perelman and L. Olbrechts-Tyteca, "Act and Person in Argument," *Philosophy, Rhetoric and Argumentation*, ed. M. Natanson and H. W. Johnstone, Jr. (University Park, Pa., 1965), pp. 102–125.

purpose in speaking is not to whitewash Kennedy but to understand the parameters within which his verbal behavior operated. We might still find that Kennedy chose an inappropriate rhetorical strategy. Or we might conclude that Kennedy was himself not fully aware of the real significance of the discourse he produced. Our search does not necessarily tell us anything about the ultimate character of the message, for the artist's intentions are ancillary to our primary concern, which is artistic intention.[30] We seek to discover the speaker's point of view; the symptoms of artistic and intellectual choice thereby revealed may lend depth to our apprehension of the design of the message.

Like its S-M-C counterpart, M-E-C rests on a conception of the critical act as an encounter. And it also recognizes the importance of artistic intention, of the demands made by the work upon the recipient of the message. The primary distinction between the two frameworks is the emphasis that the M-E-C focus places on the rhetorical event as an act, a performance which is only fully consummated in that instant when message is apprehended by receiver. Just as a play is not theatre until it is being performed for an audience, so the rhetorical artifact (such as a speech manuscript) becomes discourse only when it is experienced in a public "arena" or forum.[31] The rhetorical critic therefore necessarily fastens his attention not on the moment of creation but upon the moment of reception, realizing all the while that by his intrusion he is mutilating the confrontation of message and audience.

One consequence of this shift in emphasis is that the M-E-C critic is less concerned with the speaker's influence on the message than is the S-M-C critic. As the French symbolist Paul Valéry has contended:

> There is no true meaning to a text—no author's authority. Whatever he may have wanted to say, he has written what he has written. Once published, a text is like an apparatus that anyone may use as he will and according to his ability: it is not certain that the one who constructed it can use it better than another.[32]

Although there are important differences between symbolist literary criticism and the traits of M-E-C rhetorical analysis, they are in this respect similar.

Whereas the S-M-C focus concentrates on the aesthetic demands of the event upon *an* auditor (the potential interpretation which any sensitive recipient might make), M-E-C considers the aesthetic demands made by the event upon *the* auditors (the likely meaning of the message for a given public). To illustrate, the S-M-C critic would seek to assess the enduring worth of medieval morality plays, taking account of their original cast as inculcators of religious faith; the M-E-C critic, on the other hand, would distinguish between the meaning of a

---

[30]Cf. R. Kuhns, "Criticism and the Problem of Intention," *Journal of Philosophy*, LVII (January 7, 1960), 5–23; S. Gendin, "The Artist's Intentions," *Journal of Aesthetics and Art Criticism*, XXIII (Winter 1964), 193–196; E. Roma III, "The Scope of the Intentional Fallacy," *The Monist*, L (April 1966), 250–266.

[31]M. O. Sillars, "Rhetoric as Act," *The Quarterly Journal of Speech*, L (October 1964), 277–284; H. Arendt, *Between Past and Future* (Cleveland, 1963), pp. 143–172; S. K. Langer, *Problems of Art* (New York, 1957), pp. 1–58; S. C. Petter, *The Work of Art* (Bloomington, Indiana, 1955); M. Natanson, "The Claims of Immediacy," in *Philosophy, Rhetoric and Argumentation*, ed. M. Natanson and H. W. Johnstone, Jr. (University Park, Pa., 1965), pp. 10–19; W. Sacksteder, "Elements of the Dramatic Model," *Diogenes*, LII (Winter 1965), 26–54; P. K. Tompkins, "Rhetorical Criticism: Wrong Medium?" *Central States Speech Journal*, XIII (Winter 1962), 90–95.

[32]Paul Valéry, *The Art of Poetry* (New York, 1958), p. 152.

morality play for its original audience and its meaning (perhaps totally different) for a typical contemporary auditor. Constrained thus by context, the M-E-C critical focus is more particularized, with the critic acting as a kind of surrogate for the audience he projects into the communicative event.[33]

Nor is the M-E-C frame simply a variation of the more objective message-environment focus. M-E analysis offers a predominantly historical interpretation of "how it was" when the public confronted the speech. The M-E critic seeks to understand the nature of the transaction as it in fact originally occurred. He may even go so far as to evaluate the speech using the rhetorical norms of the period and society in which the speech was delivered. He has a tendency to work back from the context to the message as he engages in assessment.

In contrast, an historistic interpretation might be more appropriate to an M-E-C focus. The M-E-C critic would try to go beyond understanding the message *as* the original participants understood it and attempt also to understand it *better than* they did.[34] He would seek to determine "how it would have to be" if one were to derive the fullest significance implicit in the rhetorical event. It is likely that an observer with an M-E-C orientation would follow a course of action in which he first analyzed the message, then projected from his analysis a description of the public for whom the message would be most appealing, and finally compared the bulk of the actual audience with his composite ideal auditor.

It is suggestive for us to bear in mind that both frames originate in the physicist's efforts to accommodate his formulations to the inherent uncertainty of the cosmos. We might therefore expect S-M-C and M-E-C critics to be somewhat more heedful of the limitations of their investigations and less inclined to construct a brief for a particular interpretation. They might be somewhat more prone to employ their reasons as part of a calculation of the validity of particular rhetorical concepts. Their primary objective would then be to modify rhetorical theory to accommodate their clinical observations rather than to establish their own credibility or assist readers to derive increased satisfaction from the rhetorical event under discussion. We would expect critics with this cast to be more tentative in their reason-giving, since their comments would operate less in an advocative capacity and more as a special kind of scientific discourse. Such a critic might very well take the view that if his reasons are sound those to whom he reports will *probably* attach greater value to his judgments. He would therefore seek to determine the strength of his reasons.[35]

Let us conclude consideration of alternative critical foci by reminding ourselves that the focus adopted by the critic determines what kind of questions he

---

[33]The problem of a possible shift in meaning for morality plays is raised in F. J. Coleman, "A Phenomenology of Aesthetic Reasoning," *Journal of Aesthetics and Art Criticism*, XXV (Winter 1966), 197–203.

[34] The distinction has been alluded to by R. L. Scott in his review of E. Black's *Rhetorical Criticism* (*The Quarterly Journal of Speech*, LI [October 1965], p. 336). Scott suggests that one may go to extremes in appealing to the immediate audience as a decisive measure of rhetorical merit, that in such instances the critic may be more concerned with direct measures of audience response such as shift-of-opinion ballots than with the speech itself. An extremist M-E critic might indeed tend to fit such a description, but an M-E-C critic would be unlikely to find himself in such a posture.

[35]E. H. Hutten, "Uncertainty and Information," *Scientia*, IC (#9–10, 1964), 199–206; J. J. Kupperman, "Reasons in Support of Evaluations of Works of Art," *The Monist*, L (April 1966), 222–236; J. Rothstein, *Communication, Organization, and Science* (Indian Hills, Colo., 1958). The problem we face at this point in the discussion is that no clear instances of this critical stance are available as of this date.

will find most interesting. Insofar as the critic chooses to relate the rhetorical event to its creator he will ask: How did the message come to be? Is it symptomatic of the speaker? What are the capacities of the rhetor as an artist? How does the man shape the message? The critic who regards the message as the initial stimulus in his formula will ask himself a complementary set of questions: How does the message reflect its context? What evidence is there that the message as created was appropriate to the climate in which it was employed? How did the message serve to influence its environment? How and why does my experience with this message differ from the likely experiences of other recipients? These are all legitimate questions for a critic to ask; but his decision as to which shall occupy his attention will be at least partially influenced by the focus he has chosen to adopt.

Although many more problems pertaining to the logic of rhetorical criticism remain, this essay will treat only one more topic, the procedures available to the critic for relating norm and observation. This topic is essential since reasoning-giving has been shown to be the fundamental aspect of the logic of critical discourse.

We can imagine judgments which do not entail even the possibility of supporting reasons, but we ordinarily treat such evaluations as capricious remarks when uttered by critics. The manner in which a critic relates fact and criterion is of some moment if we hope to understand the character of his reason-giving. For our purposes, the term "modality" will refer to any characteristic manner (or formula) for joining observations and norms so as to produce justificatory reasons in criticism. The term's meaning is thus roughly comparable to the sense of "function" as used in calculus.[36] To explain this special use of "modality" it is necessary to begin with a clarification of the term "juxtapose."

Earlier in this essay the critic was compared to the lawyer pleading a case. It was then suggested that a critic's primary task is to formulate justificatory bases for his verdicts by "juxtaposing" descriptions and norms. The term "juxtapose" is purposely vague, and it must be understood in light of John Dewey's observation that criticism

> . . . is judgment engaged in discriminating among values. It is taking thought as to what is better and worse in any field at any time, with some consciousness of *why* the better is better and *why* the worse is worse.[37]

Now determination of better-and-worse may take several forms. One might "grade" a speech according to various criteria or rank it with respect to other speeches and along designated scales, or he might simply classify it by type as part of a general act of recognizing features (when one labels a speech "epideictic," what he in fact does is provide a shorthand notation of several qualities we expect to find in epideictic oratory).[38]

Whatever the informative pattern evident in criticism, we expect that two related features of the critical act will remain constant. The critic will first have alternative speeches in mind as he approaches the object of study. Better-and-worse

---

[36]Cf. R. P. Agnew, *Analytical Geometry and Calculus with Vectors* (New York, 1962), pp. 111–117.

[37]Cited in M. K. Hochmuth (ed.), *History and Criticism of American Public Address,* III (New York, 1955), 4.

[38]Hanney, p. 170; Righter, pp. 64–69; Kupperman, pp. 229–233; Levy, p. 11.

implies better-or-worse-than something else. To say that Adlai Stevenson was a great speaker suggests that the critic can discriminate between the speeches of Stevenson and those of some not-so-great speakers. To find fault with Lyndon Johnson's style suggests that the critic has in mind alternative stylistic tactics which Johnson might employ to improve his style.

The second implication to be drawn from Dewey's comment is that the alternative(s) the critic has in mind will take the form of particular speeches or aspects of speeches. To illustrate suppose we feel that "good" speeches generally require transitions between main points. Should we find a speech lacking transitions is it perforce a "bad" speech? Obviously not. Some speeches do not need transitions. Hence, the rubric "good speeches have transitions" is merely a guiding principle which serves to canalize critical observations; it is a reminder to consider the possibilities of an alternative speech containing transitions. To judge a discourse deficient in its use of transitions we need to have in mind how the addition of transitions might improve the speech; we must have an alternative image of a speech which is better, in particular ways, than the one we are observing. The "juxtaposition" called for in criticism is not straightforward application of rules to events in the manner by which we measure the length of an object against a yardstick. There is instead an oblique, two-step process by which the critic either generates or selects an appropriate alternative discourse and then compares that specific alternative to the discourse under analysis. The two modalities we shall consider represent general procedures for so joining observations and rhetorical norms.

A model modality is employed when the critic starts by generating some sort of paradigm which he will use as a basis of comparison. Laymen commonly speak of models in reference to airplanes, toy houses, or sets of blueprints. They tend to associate the term with miniatures, objects and/or plans drawn to scale.[39] However, the more appropriate sense of "model" in criticism is one which roughly corresponds to "prototype" or to "exemplar of a kind." Drawing on his rhetorical theory, the critic generates a model representing his conception of what would have constituted the ideal speech for the situation. He then compares his archetype with the speech which was actually delivered in order to determine the degree and the nature of the disparity between paradigm and actual speech. The comparison precipitates a kind of diagnosis; if the model conforms to the critic's rhetorical theory (as we must assume it does if it is to be regarded as a paradigm), then disparity between the norm-discourse and the actual one should provide some insight into both the aesthetic excellence and the rhetorical weaknesses evident in the discourse being inspected.

This notion of the norm as a model presupposes that the critic can himself create a prototype which is neither a stock image ("the speech for all occasions") nor yet a capricious whim. His model must be one which in its essentials conforms to his rhetorical theory. As we noted earlier, no rhetorical theory is so detailed that it can account for every aspect of every speech except in general outline. The well-wrought model requires a sensitive creator who can use his theory as a point of departure in developing in his imagination the model uniquely suited to assess a particular message. The search for an explanation for the extent and character of deviation from the paradigm model will then constitute the invention of critical reasons.

[39]M. Black, *Models and Metaphors* (Ithaca, N.Y., 1962), pp. 219–224.

Both Rovere and Wichelns illustrate the model modality of reason-giving. Rovere contrasts MacArthur's speech by means of a treatment of issues demanded by the controversy; on that basis he decides MacArthur's effort is inappropriate to the occasion. Wichelns, too, seems to reason from an implicit prototype insofar as he comments on attributes present and lacking, mandatory and optional in MacArthur's prose. If Wichelns is unwilling to discuss the appropriateness of MacArthur's tone of authority (and his silence on this score is revealing), he is at least willing to address himself to MacArthur's skill in executing the tactic; and such comments, responsibly made, entail a theoretical conception of how public image is conveyed in a speech.

The essential feature of the second tactic of comparison, the analog modality, is that the norm employed is some actual discourse and not a theoretically derived prototype. Imagine the behavior of a critic who wished to characterize the rhetoric of Fidel Castro on those occasions when Castro justifies his failure to hold popular elections. The critic might use his rhetorical theory to generate a model of what would be appropriate for Castro to say; he might, on the other hand, be reminded of the rhetoric of another revolutionary in similar circumstances, say Cromwell dissolving Parliament. In the latter case, the critic might choose to juxtapose Castro's discourse to Cromwell's. His norm would no longer be paradigmatic, for he would have no *a priori* grounds for judging either Castro or Cromwell the more worthy rhetorician.

In lieu of such assessments, the critic would use Cromwell's speeches for topological purposes, much as he would a road map. Cromwell's discourse would serve to focus and guide the critic in his interpretation of Castro. Critical judgments would thus assume the form of statements of more-and-less or better-and-worse respecting particular qualities evident in the discourses. Perhaps Cromwell is more likely to engage in personal invective while Castro is more discursive in justifying his policies.

An illustration of the analog modality is found in Professor Laura Crowell's criticism of the speaking of John Pym, the English Parliamentarian. Crowell is contending that a distinctive feature of Pym's address is his interpretation of new events within the context of already-accepted materials and attitudes:

> To people whose world was changing from medievalism to modernism under their feet, the words of a man who consistently saw events in larger context and who had details ready at hand on Biblical, philosophical, legal, financial, and parliamentary matters were extremely comforting. A cocksure age is ready for persuasion to new proposals, easily abandoning the present, not fearing the leap. But a skeptical age, such as Pym's, asks a persuasion that keeps its hold upon the present even while raising questions; it needs to feel the security of the past even while rising to meet new problems.[40]

The contrast between the debate of Pym's time and contemporary debate over, say, social welfare enables the critic in this case to highlight a quality in Pym's discourse which might not be readily evident were one to attempt to conceive the ideal rhetorical strategy for Pym solely on the basis of a rhetorical theory.

The analog relation of two particulars without direct recourse to a set of precepts entails a special role for rhetorical theory in the interpretive act. In the

[40]L. Crowell, "The Speaking of John Pym, English Parliamentarian," *SM,* XXXIII (June 1966), 100.

model modality the critic's norm is generated and constrained by theoretical precepts. In the analog situation rhetorical theory constitutes a shorthand account of those rhetorical categories which are typically helpful to the act of comparison. In the latter instance the critic is less concerned with creating a prototype than he is with "characterizing" an actual discourse.[41]

The analogical modality opens realms of critical analysis which have been for the most part neglected by rhetorical critics. Let us imagine that a critic, having assessed Castro in the light of the rhetorically similar Cromwell, decides to compare him with some apparently unrelated speaker, such as William Faulkner accepting the Nobel Prize for literature. There is no logical reason why such a comparison would be fruitless, yet it is clear that such a juxtaposing would yield results quite different from the comparison of Castro and Cromwell. Theoretically, the possibilities of analysis are infinite. Why not compare messages across cultures (say inaugural addresses of Presidents and coronation speeches of Kings), or across genres (John Adams the speaker and John Adams the writer of diaries)? Why not juxtapose various rhetorical forms, such as Ingersoll's witty ripostes at the Lotus Club and the cryptic visions of a religious mystic? Or why not contrast totally different rhetorical objects (Burke to the electors of Bristol and Martin Luther King to a college audience)?

The model modality finds its optimal use in confirming or qualifying rhetorical theory, where the analog modality, because of its factorial character, provides a point of departure which enables the critic to derive new categories and precepts from his investigation. The model-based critic is asking whether the rhetorician met certain criteria which were established by a given rhetorical system; the analog critic compares and contrasts, searching out theoretical explanations to accommodate his discoveries. In both instances theory assists the critic in his task and is in turn refined by the act of criticism. But it is clear that slatternly reliance on rhetorical canons to perform critical tasks is futile in either modality. Even where the canons suggest no obvious fault in a particular discourse, it is always possible that the astute critic could imagine a better speech or pamphlet, it is always possible that a felicitous comparison might expose qualities beyond the scope of the rhetorical theory at hand.[42]

Conclusion

This essay began by asserting that criticism is distinguished as a form of discourse by its peculiar reason-giving qualities. The ensuing discussion of this assertion holds two implications for speech scholars. The first is the suggestion, implicit in our analysis of the terms "critic" and "criticism," that rhetorical criticism does not operate *in vacuo*. Speech criticism can be best understood within the broader context afforded by a general conception of criticism's logical

---

[41]Levy, pp. 65–66.

[42]In at least one instance the model-analog distinction breaks down and the modalities seem to fuse. That is where the critic relies on a touchstone as a standard of comparison. The touchstone, or "classic of its kind," at once represents an ideal and is at the same time an actual discourse which could conceivably be replaced in its role of prototype by some other discourses yet to be discovered. That the touchstone fulfills this dual role may explain its attraction for many critics as well as the rarity of its appearance as an effective critical tool. Cf. Wilson, pp. 272–276.

features. It has been argued that among the formal aspects which unite speech criticism with other varieties of critical discourse is the expert-spectator posture assumed by all critics. Another feature common to all criticism and setting it apart from the bulk of public discourse is its reliance upon forensic reasons-in-support-of-verdicts as its primary method for advancing contentions.

The second implication derives from our consideration of critical foci and modalities: it is possible to discern a finite set of relatively clear-cut methodological options open to the critic. There is, in other words, a system of alternatives inherent in critical endeavor; criticism is not the "blooming, buzzing confusion" it may at times seem. Thus, for example, conceiving of the critical act as encompassing the four gross components of the communicative event enables us to specify in at least loose terms the kind of questions to which a given critic has addressed himself. Indeed, the recognition that various critics will give primary emphasis to particular combinations of S, M, E and C helps us to understand (although not necessarily to resolve) controversies which pit critics of one focus against those of another. We are at least aware that the issue in the debate is often not so much the validity of the critics' arguments or the acuity of their observations as it is the importance each school attaches to particular relationships among the four communicative variables.

We have also considered the two fundamental modalities open to the critic as he relates his artistic criteria to the rhetorical event. We have seen that the common conception of the critic as one directly applying his canons in the manner of a measure applied to an object is overly simplified. The relation of criteria to object is oblique, entailing the critic's own conception of what the rhetorical work might had been. And this need for a one-to-one comparison again reminds us that the critic's selection from among the methodological options available will influence the character of his discourse.

Criticism, in sum, reveals itself to be a peculiarly open-ended, frustrating, but no incomprehensible endeavor. If the general condition of the critical act is diversity of substantive and methodological options, there are still reasonable limits to the range of those options. In the final analysis it is perhaps this vast complexity of opportunity that makes understanding the formal facets of critical method tenuous and difficult, yet at the same time renders understanding virtually indispensable to the student of criticism.

A CASE STUDY IN SPEECH CRITICISM: THE NIXON-TRUMAN ANALOG

Lawrence W. Rosenfield

One of the most controversial public addresses of modern American history is also one on which rhetorical scholars have remained strangely mute. I refer to the radio-television broadcast by the then vice presidential candidate Richard Nixon on September 23, 1952, the famous "Checkers" speech in which Nixon explained to the American public his use of a special campaign fund.[1] There also exists a remarkably similar address, a broadcast by ex-President Harry S Truman on November 16, 1953 in which Truman answered charges that while president he had allowed a Communist agent, Harry Dexter White, to hold high governmental office. The generic resemblance of the two speeches (both may be classified as mass-media apologia) invites what may be called analog criticism—comparing the speeches in such ways that each address serves as a reference standard for the other. The objective of such a method of comparison and contrast is two-fold: to specify the fundamental anatomical features which relate the two speeches (engage in a *factorial* analysis of the category of apologetic discourse exemplified by the messages) and to assess the relative artistic merit of each speech, compared to the other.[2]

Comparison of these particular speeches is fruitful on several counts. First, an element of objectivity (especially important when discussing contemporary partisans like Nixon and Truman) is introduced when the speeches are played off against each other in the critic's analysis. Second, the identification of similar qualities in the two messages suggests to the critic certain constants operating in an otherwise undefined form—use of instantaneous electronic media to answer accusations. In these two instances we have cases of relatively early efforts by public officials to cope with the rhetorical problems raised by the demands of apologiae nationally broadcast. Where we discover similarities in the messages, we have grounds for attributing those qualities to the situation or the genre rather than to the individual speaker. And should we at some future date find modified tactics in apologetic speeches, we would be in a position to determine whether an evolution occurred in the form itself. Finally, because the surface conditions of these two speeches are so similar, the critic will be alert to the distinctive qualities of each. And having recognized those differences, he will be justified in evaluating the configuration of unique features in each speech as evidence of the individual speaker's artistry in responding to the exigencies of the situation.

The remainder of this paper is divided into five sections. A brief sketch of the incidents surrounding the two speeches is followed by discussion of similarities in the rhetorical contexts which gave rise to the speeches, by specification of the

From *Speech Monographs*, XXXV, 4 (November 1968), 435–450. Used by permission of the author and the Speech Communication Association

Dr. Rosenfield is professor of speech at Queens College, New York.

[1]The only formal scholarly reference to it is Professor Baskerville's sketch of the "Nixon affair" in F. W. Haberman (ed.), "The Election of 1952: A Symposium," *Quarterly Journal of Speech*, XXXVIII (December 1952), 406–408.

[2]For further discussion of the analog method as a tool for speech criticism see Rosenfield "The Logic of the Critical Act" in D. Burke (ed.), *Rhetoric, Philosophy, and Literature: An Exploration* (West Lafayette, IN, 1978).

common elements in the two addresses, by consideration of their divergent features, and by discussion of the critical and theoretical implications of the entire rhetorical analysis.

The Nixon fund affair occurred during the 1952 Eisenhower-Stevenson presidential race. On Thursday, September 18, the *New York Post* featured a story headlined "Secret Nixon Fund." It opened as follows:

> The existence of a "millionaire's club" devoted exclusively to the financial comfort of Senator Nixon, GOP Vice Presidential candidate, was revealed today.[3]

Democratic National Chairman Mitchell, in a "great show of indignation over corruption," promptly demanded that all details of the fund, including contributors and expenditures, be made public, and he called on candidate Eisenhower to remove Nixon from the Republican ticket. The next morning the battle was joined when Nixon responded to the charges in a whistle-stop speech in Marysville, California, characterizing them as a smear by Communists and crooks.[4]

This puerile exchange might have been muffled in the campaign cacophony had not the Republicans been touchy on matters ethical. They had pinned their election hopes on a "crusade to clean up the corruption mess in Washington." Hence, they felt themselves being hoisted on their own petard as the charges against Nixon spread and as several prominent newspapers began to give editorial support to the proposal that Nixon be dropped from the ticket. Should they retain Nixon, the "crusade" might take on the shabby appearance of a huckstering attempt to horn in on the proceeds of corruption. But dropping him would imply a plea of "no contest" on the corruption charge and would open them to scorn for having nominated a crook. In either event they would forfeit the corruption issue. The Republicans chose to skirt these painful alternatives and to throw the question of Nixon's future open to a national plebiscite—they purchased a half hour of national broadcast time and instructed Nixon to clear himself of the charges with the electorate.[5]

Thus it was that on September 23, a bare five days after the charges were leveled, Richard Nixon addressed in his own defense the largest television audience to that time, sixty million people. The speech had three sections: a denial of unethical conduct in maintaining a campaign fund, a revelation of Nixon's personal financial history, and a partisan counterattack on the ethical qualifications of the Democrats' nominees. The response to the speech was immediate and fantastic: the public was virtually unanimous in its support of Nixon. Within hours the Republican panic had turned to glee; the "crusade" issue was more vital than ever, and Democrat Stevenson was straining to account for his own personal campaign fund. With a single speech Richard Nixon had won a decisive initiative for his party.[6]

Ex-President Harry S Truman's ordeal smacked somewhat less of Armageddon and more of a joust; and the outcome was for several reasons less distinct than in Nixon's case. On November 6, 1953, Republican Attorney General Brownell charged in a Chicago speech (some claimed it was a smokescreen to

---

[3]Richard M. Nixon, *Six Crises* (Garden City, 1962), pp. 80–81.
[4]Nixon, pp. 83–84; *New York Times*, September 20, 1952, p. 9.
[5]Nixon, pp. 95–112.
[6]Nixon, p. 118; A. Hillbruner, *Critical Dimensions; The Art of Public Address Criticism* (New York, 1966), p. 60

draw attention away from recent Republican congressional election losses) that one Harry Dexter White, an alleged Communist spy now dead, had been promoted to a sensitive position with the International Monetary Fund during the Truman administration despite knowledge of his spying activities by "those who appointed him."[7] Truman at first denied ever having seen such reports on White. In the verbal sparring of the next few days both parties hedged. As bits of evidence came to public attention, Truman acknowledged that an unfavorable report had been received concerning White but claimed that at the proper time he had "fired" White. Later Truman shifted again to claim that he had "forced White's resignation." For his part, Brownell watered his accusation to one of "laxity" by the Truman administration in meeting Communist infiltration.

The immediate stimulus for Truman's national broadcast was a subpoena served on November 10 by Representative H. H. Velde (Illinois Republican) directing Truman to testify before the House Un-American Activities Committee regarding the White controversy.[8] Truman rejected the subpoena as his "duty under the Constitution" and chose instead to make his broadcast to fifty million people on Monday, November 16.

Like Nixon, Truman divided his remarks into three parts. He explained his refusal to testify before the H.U.A.C., justified his handling of Harry Dexter White's promotion, and attacked Brownell for having raised the issue. There were no immediate political stakes in the Brownell-Truman clash, so reaction to the speech was undramatic. In the ensuing week F.B.I. Director J. Edgar Hoover's testimony before the Senate Internal Security Committee cast some doubt on the interpretations Truman had offered in his speech. But, by November 18, Eisenhower signaled an end to the confrontation when he expressed hope that the whole issue concerning Communist internal subversion would be history by 1954. Within a week public interest had waned as congressional investigators turned from the White case to other allegations of espionage. Editorials tended to scold both Brownell and Truman for intemperate statements; then most newspapers dropped the matter. In retrospect Truman's can be considered a qualified victory. Though not as conclusive in its effects as Nixon's, his speech served to clear him of the main accusations and ended public interest in the circumstances of White's advancement.

These sketches of the two controversies provide sufficient background to enable the reader to consider the rhetorical context from which the two speeches grew.

A prime resemblance between the two speaking situations can be found in the expectations of the two national broadcast audiences. The period 1952–1953 was not marked by any striking shifts in American public opinion on major political issues,[9] and virtually the same individuals comprised the bulk of the two audiences.

---

[7]*New York Times,* November 7, 1953, p. 1.

[8]Velde apparently acted in a fit of enthusiasm without consulting Republican congressional leaders. In any event the main effect of the subpoena, besides giving Truman an excuse to mount a national forum, was to embarrass the Eisenhower administration. During his November 11 press conference, President Eisenhower noted in typical fashion that he "personally wouldn't have issued a summons" to an ex-President. Cf. *New York Times,* November 12, p. 14

[9]Cf. N.O.R.C. public opinion surveys 312, 315, 329, 334, 339, 348 for the period 1951–1953 (The Roper Public Opinion Research Center, Williamstown, Mass.); A. O. Hero, Jr., "The American Public and the United Nations, 1954–1966," *The Journal of Conflict Resolution,* X (December 1966), 436–475.

The reputations of the two speakers were also such that the public would probably expect much the same rhetorical posture of each. With careers punctuated by flamboyant partisan utterance, there was little hint in the political biographies of Nixon and Truman that either was disposed to seek bipartisan consensus of the sort made popular by Dwight Eisenhower or Lyndon Johnson. Each stood in the public mind as a partisan "slugger," a staunch, uncompromising combatant for his party. As often as not it had been Truman's and Nixon's public remarks that had caused each to perform in the limelight of controversy. Richard Nixon was blessed with a kind of notoriety for pugnacious campaign tactics and for his role in the Alger Hiss investigations. "Irascible" is perhaps the most apt description of Harry Truman's prior public address. It was not without reason that the rallying cry of his 1948 presidential campaign had been, "Give 'em Hell, Harry!" And a public which remembered Mr. Truman's threat to punch the nose of a music critic who had panned daughter Margaret's singing would presumably expect the ex-President to deliver some pungent remarks in an address of self-defense.

Subjected to a personal attack centering on charges of past misconduct in public office, each speaker was placed in a Demosthenic posture; he must go before the citizenry to clear himself of accusations leveled by political assailants. The appropriate argumentative strategy was clearly forensic. The listeners could expect arguments of accusation and defense relating primarily to the interpretation of past facts. To this extent one may say each speaker was propelled by the logic of his situation toward the same, overall rhetorical strategy.

Though it was common practice in ancient Greece for the accused to speak directly to his judges, the use of electronic media for such a purpose was unorthodox in mid-century America. By their decisions to by-pass the customary medium of contemporary public dialog, the press, and to go instead directly to the people, Nixon and Truman tell us something about the intense character of their situations. Their choice may have been in part simply a symptom of things to come; we appear to rely more and more on the air waves for our contact with current affairs. But one cannot escape the feeling that in these two instances the central figures found the struggle so intense (if not climactic) that they felt it necessary to avoid the inevitable distortion of messages which results from the intervention of the newsprint channel.[10] At any rate, they chose to risk the outcome of their battles on single national broadcasts.

In retrospect a fourth similarity of context becomes apparent: both conflicts were short, sharp, and quickly resolved. The Nixon debate lasted from September 18 to September 24, the day Eisenhower announced that Nixon was vindicated. The Harry Dexter White affair merited headlines from November 7 to November 19.[11]

Finally, the broadcasts were in each case watersheds in the controversies. Nixon's speech caused the collapse of sniping at his campaign funds; Truman's speech was the last public mention of the possibility that a congressional committee might subpoena an ex-President. In view of their importance in each conflict, it is especially remarkable how brief the speeches were. Truman spoke for

---

[10]C. E. Swanson, J. Jenkins, and R. L. Jones, "President Truman Speaks: A Study of Ideas vs. Media," *Journalism Quarterly,* XXVII (Summer 1950), 251–262. J. Ericson, "The Reporting by the Prestige Press of Selected Speeches of Senator Goldwater in the 1964 Presidential Campaign," unpubl. diss. (University of Wisconsin, 1966).

[11]Although reverberations were felt afterward in connection with other congressional investigations, it is fair to say that Truman's role in it was a scant two weeks.

twenty-three minutes and Nixon's speech ran just under a half hour. One is reminded by contrast of the protracted, even leisurely paced, nineteenth-century oratorical struggles. These modern clashes seem abrupt in any such comparison.

We cannot with assurance attribute the differences between contemporary and former controversies either to qualities inherent in current issues or to the development of electronic media. The cost of air time limits the length of speeches, but it does not prevent continuance of debate by other means. But we can say that the contextual factors here mentioned—a forensic issue, use of broadcast facilities to carry a case directly to the public, relatively limited exposure time, and the sharp, decisive quality of the encounter—seem not coincidentally present in the two cases we are examining. If we as yet have no basis for determining which of the factors were antecedent and which were consequent, which were essential and which accidental, we can at least hypothesize that other contemporary apologiae are likely to display the same combination of attributes. The two speeches under investigation asked national audiences of roughly the same backgrounds to decide the guilt or innocence of two colorful political spokesmen. In choosing to risk defense on a single short speech transmitted directly to the public, the two speakers revealed something of the urgency they must have attached to their acts. What then, may we expect when men of such stripe find it necessary to speak as advocates in their own behalves under circumstances such as these? For a tentative answer we may turn to the messages actually presented by Nixon and Truman.

Both speeches adhered to classic forensic strategies, and both displayed martial overtones. In his denial of the charges, Nixon resorted to arguments of motive and fact (*quale sit* and *an sit*). At the outset he asserted that the appropriate standard for judging his acceptance of campaign contributions must be purity of motive:

> I say that it was morally wrong—if any of that $18,000 went to Senator Nixon, for my personal use. I say that it was morally wrong if it was secretly given and secretly handled.[12]

Having demonstrated that these moral precepts were not violated in his use of the funds, Nixon proceeded to a factual iteration of personal financial affairs. These considerations ranged from his need to work in the family grocery store as a boy through the current unpaid balance on his home mortgage. The point of the narrative was clear: there was no evidence of campaign funds diverted to personal use. Nixon denied the accusation with facts.

For Harry Truman, argument by fact was not an option. The public already had reason to believe that at the time he was promoted Harry Dexter White was at least suspected by authorities of subversive activities. Truman employed forensic arguments of motive and value (*quale sit* and *quid sit*) in his defense. He contended that White's promotion was engineered so as to minimize the security risk while at the same time keeping secret an ongoing F.B.I. investigation of

---

[12]This and all following quotes from the Nixon speech are from an official speech transcript prepared by four National Broadcasting Company stenographers and printed in the *New York Times* of September 24, 1952, p. 22. The *Times* text was verified by comparison with a text appearing in *Vital Speeches of the Day*, XIX (October 15, 1952), 11–15. A variant text can be found in *U.S. News and World Report*, XXXIII (October 3, 1952), 66–70. For a discussion of the problem of textual authenticity see E. G. Bormann, *Theory and Research in the Communicative Arts* (New York, 1965), pp. 173–191.

subversion. Hence, the motives for Truman's past acts were honorable. He justified his refusal to appear before Representative Velde's committee by appealing to a higher value—such an appearance would represent a threat to the constitutional separation of the three branches of government because it would subject past executive decisions to Congressional review. Implicit in Truman's argument was the premise that constitutional prerogatives take precedence over investigations of national security breaches.

Forensic strategy normally entails accusation as well as defense. Whether from habit or because they perceived that their situations demanded such tactics, both Nixon and Truman chose invective as their mode of attack. It seems more than coincidental that their speeches abound in *ad hominum* innuendoes concerning the moral qualities of their accusers, that in each case roughly the last third of the speech is almost entirely devoted to this kind of forensic offensive.

According to Truman, the Eisenhower administration was guilty of "shameful demagoguery"; Mr. Brownell degraded his office by engaging in political trickery and skullduggery, by lying to the American people, by smearing a defenseless and patriotic American (Chief Justice Fred Vinson, now dead), and by displaying "mealy-mouthed" cowardice. Truman also drew a red herring across the issue when he slipped in a reference to Senator Joseph McCarthy:

> It is now evident that the present administration has fully embraced, for political advantage, McCarthyism. I'm not referring to the senator from Wisconsin—he's only important in that his name has taken on a dictionary meaning in the world. And that meaning is the corruption of truth, the abandonment of our historical devotion to fair play. It is the abandonment of the "due process" of law. It is the use of the big lie and the unfounded accusation against any citizen in the name of Americanism and security. It is the rise to power of the demagogue.[13]

The excerpt intrigues. Was Truman accusing the administration of merely aping McCarthy, or was he suggesting that McCarthy exerted a substantial influence in the government? His meaning was conveniently vague. What stands out in Truman's attack is that it is unanswerable, for it substitutes name-calling for an assessment of motive. Brownell, for instance, could only reply to the charge of being mealy-mouthed by hurling a more insulting label at Truman; it was here, as always, futile to treat such an accusation as a "charge" in the traditional, legal sense.

Although not as explicit, Richard Nixon proved more adept than Truman in his use of innuendo. The ex-President pinned the label "liar" on Brownell outright;

[13]The Truman text is from the transcript in the November 17, 1953 *New York Times*, p. 26. Variant texts can be found in *U.S. News and World Report*, XXXV (November 27, 1953), 104–106 and the *Kansas City Times*, November 17, 1953, pp. 1–2. The *New York Times* version gives internal evidence of being the most accurate account of what Truman actually said except for its omission of the bracketed words in the following sentence (spoken in reference to the late Chief Justice Vinson): "But I deeply resent these cowardly in[sinuations against one who is] dead." Philip C. Brooks, Director of the Harry S. Truman Library of Independence, Missouri, agrees that the selected text is the most accurate one available (there being no reading copy of the text): but in a personal letter he refers to the *New York Times* version as a "press release text," thus casting doubt on its accuracy. Since no tape recording seems to exist, close stylistic analysis which would demand the exact words uttered by Truman on the occasion has not been attempted. See J. Thorp, "The Aesthetics of Textual Criticism," *PLMA*, LXXX (December 1965), 465–482; R. W. Smith, "The 'Second' Inaugural Address of Lyndon Baines Johnson: A Definitive Text," *SM*, XXXIV (March 1967), 102–108.

candidate Nixon was content with a telling sideswipe at his opposition. Twice, as if in tossing it off in passing, Nixon reminded the public that his Democratic counterpart, vice-presidential candidate Sparkman, had his wife on the Senate payroll. Nixon in both instances hastened (almost too quickly, one might feel)[14] to add, "I don't condemn him for that," "that's his business." The critic detects the swish of a matador's cape here. Nixon's nobility ("I'm for fair play") is deftly juxtaposed to the crass conduct of Sparkman. Nixon doesn't plunge the sword—he is content to draw blood. Standing aside, as it were, Nixon left the audience to judge who was in fact honorable in the use of Senate funds, but by means of the sharp contrast the auditor was offered only one option.

This distinctive habit of juxtaposing black and white distinguished Nixon's acrid invective from Truman's forthright smears. Consider the following passages:

> . . . I love my country. And I think my country is in danger. And I think that the only man that can save America at this time is the man that's running for President on my ticket, Dwight Eisenhower. You say, why do I think it's in danger? And I say, look at the record. Seven years of the Truman-Acheson Administration and what's happened? Six hundred million people lost to the Communists, and a war in Korea in which we have lost 117,000 American casualties.

> You wouldn't trust a man who made the mess to clean it up. That's Truman. And . . . you can't trust the man who was picked by the man who made the mess to clean it up, and that's Stevenson.
> And so I say, Eisenhower, who owes nothing to Truman, nothing to the big-city bosses—he is the man that can clean up the mess in Washington.
> I'm going to campaign up and down America until we drive the crooks and the Communists and those that defend them out of Washington, and remember, folks, Eisenhower is a great man. Believe me, he's a great man, and a vote for Eisenhower is a vote for what's good for America.

What is striking is Nixon's habit of joining off-handed insults of the opposition with knight-in-shining-armor depictions of him and his. By this uneasy combination of dropped lines and stereotypes a Nixon insult was made at once more provocative—and more suspect—than the ingenuous efforts of Mr. Truman. For listeners there was the satisfaction of discerning the *act* of attack often tinged, one may believe, with distaste at being told so bluntly and sweepingly that untarnished good imbued Republicans and unrelieved corruption permeated the Democratic Party.

In addition to common forensic strategies and *ad hominum* ploys, a third general similarity characterized the two speeches: the manner in which documentation was employed to support arguments. Had this been an oratorical contest between Nixon and Truman, one might be tempted to ask which speaker displayed the better looking set of facts. Nixon's speech is of course best remembered for the section which began:

> And I'd like to tell you this evening that just about an hour ago we received an independent audit of this entire fund . . . and I have that audit here in my hand.

---

[14]Nixon documents his deliberate intent in his book. See *Six Crises*, p. 118.

The section ended with the famous anecdote which caused the speech to receive the popular title "the Checkers Speech": the story of how Nixon had accepted only one personal gift while in public office—the cocker spaniel, Checkers.[15] The section occupied the entire middle third of the address and contained all of the documentation used in the speech.

Is it only coincidental that all of Harry Truman's documentation, such as it was, was also located in the middle third of his speech? Truman did not have any records in his hands. Instead he announced his presentation of inartistic data in this way:

> I have had my files examined and have consulted with some of my colleagues who worked with me on this matter during my term of office.

Truman then "reported" his findings as a narration interwoven with interpretation; his evidence tended to uphold the assertion that his decisions were the most expedient under the circumstances. He ended his narration with the death of White in 1948, after White's appearance before H.U.A.C.

Why both speakers should lump all documentation in the middle of their speeches, and why both should assign the same relative space to presentation of evidence I am not sure. The simple enumeration of quasi-documentary data found in both cases might be taken as proof of the contention that ours is an age which puts its faith in facts rather than reason, and that contemporary rhetorical strategies often reflect that trust.[16] It is in any case somewhat beside the point for the critic to test by the traditional logical criteria the soundness of conclusions drawn from such selective, factual data as Nixon and Truman presented.

It seems clear that in one sense it was less important that the materials these speakers presented should provide absolute corroboration of their assertions than that the core of each case should contain a disclosure of new data. These data constituted artifacts; their presence lent an air of scientific proof (note the actuarial tone of Nixon's revelations) which could serve an important rhetorical end in and of itself. Professor Baskerville has argued that Senator Joseph McCarthy relied on an illusion of scientific proof to gain belief.[17] I suggest that if we leave aside matters of inferential soundness we can detect both Nixon and Truman benefiting from public acceptance of confirmation-by-a-heap of-new-information.[18] And this interpretation gains plausibility when one recalls that the "charges" being answered alleged the *existence* of a fund and the motive of an act.

One final resemblance between the two apologiae is related to the use of documentation. Aside from the "good looking" new data presented, there were,

---

[15]Nixon admits that he planted this anecdote as another barb at the Democrats. The inspiration for the ploy was F. D. R.'s "Fala" speech during the 1944 presidential campaign. Six *Crises*, p. 103.

[16]Cf. W. S. Howell, "The Declaration of Independence and Eighteenth-Century Logic," *William and Mary Quarterly*, XVIII (October 1961), 463–484; R. Weaver, *The Ethics of Rhetoric* (Chicago 1953); Dwight Macdonald, "A Critique of the Warren Report," *Esquire*, LXIII (March 1965), 59ff.

[17]B. Baskerville, "The Illusion of Proof," *Western Speech*, XXV (Fall 1961), 236–242.

[18]This "faith in the fact" hearkens back in the American rhetorical tradition at least as early as the age of Muchraker journalism, Cr. D. M. Chalmers, *The Social and Political Ideas of the Muckrakers* (New York, 1964); G. Ashenbrenner, "The Rhetoric of the Muchrakers," unpubl. thesis (University of Wisconsin, 1967).

strictly speaking, no new arguments in either speech. All the key ideas, and even the insults, can be found scattered in public statements made by the two speakers in the weeks prior to their television addresses. As early as September 19, for example, Nixon was claiming that the charges against him were a "smear by Communists and crooks" intended to make him relent in his campaign. On that same day Nixon also made references to Mrs. Sparkman's drawing a Senate salary.[19]

The finding that major speeches grew out of series of minor speeches, that the act of rhetorical invention was in fact an act of *selection* from previously used ideas is not unusual in rhetorical criticism. Studies of the major speeches of Grady, Bryan, Martin Luther King, and many others reveal the same thing: the oratorical masterpiece delivered at a crucial juncture in history reveals the orator not so much rising to heights of inspiration as choosing judiciously from a repertory of past ideas an appropriate mix of materials.[20] If our small sample is at all typical, the speech in the moment of crisis is most likely to represent a climax, a summing up, of those rhetorical thrusts which seem to have been most effective with the public on previous dry runs.[21]

In the speeches under examination here, two possible implications seem to follow from the similar inventive processes. One is that under conditions of contemporary American public address little fresh adaptation of *content* is to be expected in a climactic message. Whether Nixon or Truman spoke to a whistle-stop crowd in Idaho, a group of reporters, or a national audience, the substance of the speaker's remarks remained the same. In either case adaptation was from the outset constantly directed to the American public as a whole rather than to the immediate audience.

The central place scholars have accorded speakers' adaptation of arguments to *specific* audiences may be somewhat less justified in explaining the characteristics of television apologiae than we might at first think. Indeed, the only original element in either of the speeches examined here was the inclusion of new facts. Disclosure of new information may be more significant as a rhetorical phenomenon in discourse prepared for a mass audience than are specific tactics of adaptation to the immediate audience.

To the extent that this implication holds, it suggests another. What distinguished Nixon's television apologia from Nixon's remarks to the press during the week prior to his speech was not the substance but the form. The *manner* in which Nixon chose to array for a national audience the ploys he had by trial and error found successful on more limited platforms cannot alone account for the potentialities of his broadcast address. The elements of rhetorical artistry unique

[19]*New York Times*, September 20, 1952, p. 9

[20]Cf. Baskerville, *Q.J.S.*, p. 407; T. D. Harrison, "The 'New South' Revisited," paper presented at "debut" session of S.A.A. National Convention, December 1965; D. H. Smith, "Martin Luther King, Jr., Rhetorician of Revolt," unpubl. diss. (University of Wisconsin, 1964); R. T. Oliver, *History of Public Speaking in America* (Boston, 1965), pp. 484–485.

[21]The critic may if he chooses, examine the process whereby Nixon and Truman "discovered" the materials they eventually used—but only if he reckons with the clusters of earlier minor statements made by both men. In limiting the scope of the critical study to the television addresses themselves, the rhetorical critic must perforce adjust his notion of invention to one which emphasizes the means each speaker employed in selecting materials already available rather than broadening the concept of invention to include research procedures the speaker may originally have used.

to apologiae will be better seen if we turn from consideration of overall strategies to individual differences Nixon and Truman manifested in their tactics of array and emphasis.

Close reading confirms that there were indeed fundamental differences in the fabrics of the two speeches. Three formal qualities become prominent when one undertakes to depict the artistic genius of each discourse: the inferential patterns, the foci of attack, and the relative emphases on public or personal affairs. These three elements seem to set Nixon apart from Truman as an apologist.

The first impression one draws on comparing the two speeches is that where Truman's message displays a kind of dynamic, structural progression, Nixon's is hortatory and reminds one of the stone blocks cemented into an edifice. The instrument of Truman's kinetic coloration seems to be his tendency to fuse acceptable (from the point of view of the audience) universal principles and conditional propositions into short, direct, enthymematic inferences. In the following passage the first two sentences form the theoretical ground from which Truman, in the third sentence, drew the consequence. Let us assume that most auditors accepted the principle of maintaining the independence of the executive branch of government. By articulating that principle, Truman prepared them to accept the truth of his fourth and fifth sentences which extended the principle to cover his behavior as chief executive.

> The separation and balance of powers between the three independent branches of government is fundamental in our constitutional form of government. A congressional committee may not compel the attendance of a President of the United States, while he is in office, to inquire into matters pertaining to the performance of his official duties. If the constitutional principle were otherwise, the office of the President would not be independent. It is just as important to the independence of the executive that the actions of the President should not be subjected to questioning by the Congress after he has completed his term of office as that they should not be questioned while he is serving as President. In either case, the office of President would be dominated by Congress, and the Presidency might become a mere appendage of Congress.

There is a logical gap between premise and conclusion, but if we accept the notion of enthymematic inference it is not difficult to imagine that an auditor who fully granted the explicit major premise would be prepared to fill in for himself the implicit minor premise. Truman's "if" statement thus serves in this instance to intensify adherence to the basic principle and to prepare hearers to make the necessary logical leap.

A like inferential movement occurred in a section where Truman justified his disposal of the White case.

> But following receipt of the F.B.I. report and the consultations with members of my cabinet, it was decided that he would be limited to membership on the board of directors of the International Monetary Fund. With his duties thus restricted, he would be subject to the supervision of the Secretary of the Treasury, and his position would be less important and much less sensitive—if it were sensitive at all—than the position then held by him as Assistant Secretary of the Treasury.
>
> Tonight I want the American people to understand that the course we took protected the public interest and security and at the same time permitted the intensive F.B.I. investigation then in progress to go forward. No other course could have served both of these purposes.

Truman asked the audience to look to the consequences of his alternatives; he asked them to grant the worth of his dual objectives, and he devoted his verbal effort to convincing them (by mention of the F.B.I. report and cabinet consultations and by showing how the Secretary of the Treasury could better control White's activities) that the chosen policy was the most expedient.

It is no insult to Nixon to observe that his disposition suggests that of a catechism: he puts the question he wants the audience to consider and then he speaks to the question as if reading from a trial brief.

> But then, some of you will say, and rightly, "Well, what did you use the fund for, Senator? Why did you have to have it?"
> Let me tell you in just a word how a Senate office operates. . . .

> But then the question arises, you say, "Well, how do you pay for these and how can you do it legally?"
> And there are several ways that it can be done, incidentally, and it is done legally in the United States Senate and the Congress. The first way is to be a rich man. I don't happen to be a rich man, so I couldn't use that.
> And now I'm going to suggest some courses of conduct.
> First of all, you have read in the papers about other funds, now. Mr. Stevenson apparently had a couple.

These excerpts not only represent juncture points in Nixon's speech—they are also frames which shape the arguments. Given such overpowering lead-ins there is little room for an auditor's imagination to function. His mind remains riveted as the argument unfolds. Viewed as a performance-in-time, the inferences are pre-determined by the transitions, and the discourse stubbornly resists efforts by an auditor to participate independently in the communicative act. There are undoubted merits in such structure; but the organization does not permit enthymematic reasoning as did Truman's. It was perhaps this catechetical feature of Nixon's recital which lent that "harsh and boney" quality of pre-packaged argument, not fully digested by the speaker, which some respondents discerned in his address.

Opponents were for both men objects of scorn, but Nixon and Truman differed in the breadth with which they defined the enemy camp. For Truman the "enemy" was a single man—Herbert Brownell. At times, as in the opening words of the speech, he depicted Brownell as a tool of the administration, but for the most part his invective sought out Brownell alone.

> There can't be any doubt that Mr. Brownell was talking about me. Now let me talk about Mr. Brownell and this phone charge he has made.
> His charge is false, and Mr. Brownell must have known it was false at the very time he was making it.
> Mr. Brownell has made a great show of detail. . . . As Mr. Brownell should have learned by this time. . . .

> There is one aspect of this affair that should be clear to everyone. That is the obvious political motivations of this attack on me.
> In the launching of this attack on me, the Republican attorney general worked hand in glove with the Republican National Committee. The manner and the timing of what has been done made it perfectly clear that the powers of the attorney general have been prostituted for hopes of political gain.

In all cases Truman's tactic was to *accuse* Brownell, thus using consistently an overall forensic strategy. The cumulative impact of Truman's strategy would leave one who took the ex-President's words at face value with the feeling that the confrontation was between Truman and Brownell alone. Both the partial and the neutral auditor were given grounds for believing that Brownell unjustly maligned Mr. Truman. The entire force of Truman's argument was thus channeled to turn the attack back upon his accuser.

The clear focus of Truman's invective can be seen from these figures: of 15 accusatory references in the speech, 7 concern Brownell's personal behavior (he lied, fooled the public, is the source of malicious charges); 3 accuse Brownell of cheapening his office; 4 charge that the administration used Brownell as its tool in this affair; 1 places Brownell in conspiracy with the Republican National Committee. Again, where Truman stated the charges against him, he invariably coupled those statements with counter-charges that Brownell lied in his accusation. Had he not been so consciously mounting an offensive against Brownell, Truman might have contented himself at those points with a simple denial of the charges, but roughly 45 percent of the Truman speech concentrated on the "sordid" role of Brownell. This is gross evidence of the sharp focus of Truman's invective.

The characteristics of Truman's attack are the more noteworthy because of the comparative diffusiveness of Nixon's invective. Where Truman carefully leveled his sights on a particular object of scorn, Nixon must appear to all but his most devoted listeners to be lashing out at a penumbral host of specters. Consider the swath cut by the following excerpts.

> My fellow Americans: I come before you tonight as a candidate . . . and as a man whose honesty and integrity has been questioned.

By whom? Nixon never makes clear who is accusing him.

> I am sure that you have read the charge, and you've heard it.

Again there is no recognition of a particular source for the charge.

> And the record will show that [he had not exerted influence on behalf of fund contributors], the records which are in the hands of the Administration.

Is the source of the charges somehow in league with the Administration?

> . . . and let me say that I recognize that some will continue to smear, regardless of what the truth may be.

Here again, the sources of attack are everywhere; perhaps reasonably, Nixon seemed to see himself in a state of seige. Yet, however justified such a belief may have been, its expression could not contribute to a well-focused counter-attack.

> One other thing I probably should tell you, because if I don't they'll probably be saying this about me too . . . [Nixon here employs the "Checkers" gambit.] And you know, the kids love the dog, and I just want to say this, right now, that regardless of what they say about it, we're going to keep it.

> . . . I remember, in the dark days of the Hiss case, some of the same columnists, some of the same radio commentators who are attacking me now and misrepresenting my position, were violently opposing me at the time I was after Alger Hiss.

Is the squabble between Nixon and the press? Or is it the case that the unnamed columnists are joining forces with other sinister agents to destroy Nixon? No listener could tell *from the discourse,* for the last excerpt is as close as Nixon came to identifying his attackers.

Failure to name accusers would not be significant (it probably has certain redeeming features) were it not that a concomitant limitation must thereby be placed upon the impact of an apologia. Nixon could not thus control the vector of his counterattack as precisely as Truman. Hence the tone of Nixon's reply tended toward the petulant, as though the man were lashing out at unknown conspirators seeking to victimize him. A rough classification of approximately 20 attack-statements in Nixon's speech shows that one-third were references to unspecified opponents, another third were scattered digs at Mr. Sparkman, the State Department, Mr. Stevenson, etc., and the final third were epideictic magnifications of corruption in the Truman administration. There was, in short, no concerted effort on Nixon's part either to isolate the source of the accusations or to provide the audience an explanation for such attacks.

It may be objected that Nixon's two-fold goal of clearing himself and scoring election points would force him to employ this particular pattern in invective. But the pattern, it turns out, is a Nixon pattern, not one peculiar to the situation. As befits a campaigner, Nixon showed greater concern with the faults of his political opposition in 1952 than with the source and nature of accusations against him. But the consequences of this unfocused invective appear to have stretched beyond the political contest of 1952. Some years later Nixon was to refer to this apologia as the event which made possible his election as vice president and at the same time denied him the presidency in 1960.[22] It may be that the reputation for immaturity which attached itself to Nixon had its origins in the undisciplined, unfocused attacks found in this speech.

A third notable difference also distinguishes the two speeches. The tone of the public man doing public business pervades the Truman address, whereas Nixon offers a revelation of the personal morality of a private man. This difference in tone grew in part out of the exigencies of each speaker's self-defense; however, both men spoke as public officials, so the contrast may also be taken as in some degree an index to the habitual rhetorical postures of the men.

As Harry Truman dealt with it, Brownell's accusation concerned the conduct of a public official in the execution of his office; the official happened to be named Truman.

> When I became President, I took an oath to preserve, protect and defend the Constitution of the United States. I am still bound by that oath and will be as long as I live. While I was in office, I lived up to that oath. . . . Now that I have laid down the heavy burdens of that office, I do not propose to take any step which would violate that oath or which would in any way lead to encroachments on the independence of that great office.

Was Truman using the office to shield himself from public scrutiny? Let us grant that he was not, that he was sincere in perceiving the demand that he testify as a genuine threat to the independence of chief executives. Corroboration for this interpretation is provided by Truman's other references to himself. Virtually all of the new data he provided, for example, were designed to show the calculated

[22]Nixon, *Six Crises,* pp. 125–129.

wisdom of the policy he eventually chose to follow. His mentions of himself served chiefly to enliven and personalize the image of an official struggling to arrive at a rational course of action. In the two instances where he mentioned himself as a person, it was to diminish his personal significance and to place the issue in the larger perspective of public affairs.

> First, I would like to tell you, the people of America, why I declined to appear before that committee. On the surface, it might seem to be an easy thing to do, and smart politics, for Harry Truman, now a private citizen of Independence, Missouri, to use the committee as a forum to answer the scurrilous charges which have been made against me. Many people urged me to do that. It was an attractive suggestion and appealed to me.
>
> But if I had done it, I would have been a party with the committee to an action which would have undermined the constitutional position of the office of President of the United States.
>
> If this were a matter which merely involved the name and reputation of Harry S Truman, private citizen of Independence, Missouri, I would not be as concerned as I am. I can take care of myself. I believe that the American people know me well enough from my service as captain of Battery D in World War I to my service as President of the United States to know that I have always acted with the best interests of my country at heart.
>
> But Mr. Brownell knows that, in this matter, when the final decision was mine, I relied on my principle advisers. . . .
>
> There is one aspect of this affair that should be clear to everyone. That is the obvious political motivations of this attack on me.

Clearly, Truman preferred the *persona* of the office, and he allowed it to slip for only the briefest, most stereotyped glimpses of the real man behind the mask.

Almost the reverse was the case with Richard Nixon. Let us grant to him, too, the sincerity of his utterance. It still remains that his self-references all highlight the human creature, Dick Nixon, not the United States Senator, a public figure seeking election to another office:

> It was not a secret fund. As a matter of fact, when I was on "Meet the Press"— some of you may have seen it, last Sunday—Peter Edson came up to me, after the program, and he said, "Dick, what about this fund we hear about?" And I said. . . .

Nixon *could* have generalized his argument to a discussion of the dilemma faced by the public official who must avoid temptations to corruption even as he seeks campaign contributions. He began on this course when he briefly considered the difficulty of running a Senator's office on the meager funds allotted by Congress.[23] But in the main he chose to present an autobiographical recitation of The Life and Hard Times of Young Dick Nixon.

The baring of one's finances (Nixon called it baring his soul) is not lightly undertaken in our commercial society; it surely requires some self-sacrifice. Its spectacular quality leads one to wonder whether it was rhetorically essential to Nixon's apologia or whether it offers a special kind of reading on the speaker. A

---

[23]Professor Baskerville argues in the *Q.J.S.* symposium that Nixon ought to have taken this tack. I would not go so far, but would simply point out the ultimate rhetorical consequences of the path Nixon chose to follow.

few, but only a few, public figures publicly report the full details of their finances. My own inclination is to believe that the prominence of creature-Nixon
in this discourse served dual ends. It would seem unlikely, for instance, that a
struggling young couple renting an eighty-dollar-a-month apartment in Fairfax,
Virginia could be benefiting from graft. The material presented is persuasive,
even for the doubter; and it is touching. But at the same time the information
offered is not entirely relevant, for it fails to address itself to the issue: "Was
there a misuse of campaign funds?" Nixon had already treated that issue in his
denial of dishonesty, in his description of the needs of a modern Senate office,
and in his report of the audit. The impression remains that Nixon was more
ready to display his personal self than is common among civic men.

This same impression is further confirmed when we notice that the homey
tone pervaded Nixon's speech as thoroughly as the public tone colored Truman's
address. In both cases there was, for example, the matter of justification for
conduct. Nixon explained that he could have put his wife on his Senate payroll,
as Sparkman had done:

> . . , but I have never done that for this reason: I have found that there are so
> many deserving stenographers and secretaries in Washington that need the work
> that I just didn't feel it was right to put my wife on the payroll.

Or consider Nixon's explanation of why he intended to continue to fight the
smears:

> Because, you see, I love my country. And I think my country is in danger.

Nixon, it appears, persistently, as though habitually, accounted for his public
behavior by reference to his personal sentiments. It seems reasonable to suggest
that Harry Truman would probably have sought other, equally effective justifica-
tions and proofs had he been in Nixon's place. At any rate, his apologia was far
less creature-centered than Nixon's.

It may be that this distinction between the image of a public figure and that of
the private man accounts for the observer's subjective impression that Harry Truman's message all adds up to a public warning while Richard Nixon's message
amounts to an extended claim: "They're out to get me." And this difference in
the core of the messages may provide an additional clue as to why the "Checkers" speech, so effective with the immediate audience, could another day function as a barrier to Nixon's presidential ambitions.

The Nixon plea sacrificed the mystique of the public man. It displayed him as
a living, breathing citizen—perhaps too suggestive of Dagwood Bumstead. News
commentator Eric Sevaried may have expressed the long-range public judgment
aptly when he tried to explain the defeat of homey though honest and capable
candidates for office:

> We say in a democracy that we like the ordinary man. But we don't like him that
> much.[24]

When Nixon spoke to 60,000,000 people of his desire to help one deserving
steno rather than hire his wife, even his loyal followers must have wondered

[24]Eric Sevaried, Columbia Broadcasting System election returns program, November 8,
1966.

whether he expected to be believed totally and literally. With whatever sincerity, Nixon ensnared himself by his rhetorical choices: he portrayed himself as at least a touch too simple for a complex age and too insensitive to the demands of a national, public occasion. It seems even fair to say that not every listener's smirk was one of superiority, but some were smirks of embarrassment. Nixon's response to attack, though emotionally appealing, was not fully appropriate to the public man, at least in this century.

Let us now extrapolate from the foregoing analysis those characteristics which appear to shed light on the two speeches under investigation. Conceivably, these features may represent parameters which will define other apologiae presented via the mass media.

There are four similarities in the two discourses which I take, at this time, to represent constants in the apologetic equation. Recognizing that these similarities may be accidental, may reflect some underlying kinship of the two speakers, or may be genuine symptoms of the demands of the apologetic form, we may tentatively hypothesize that the broadcast apologia is likely to be a part of a short, intense, decisive clash of views. We may further predict that a speaker who chooses to argue in his own defense over the airwaves is unlikely to limit himself to defensive remarks. In all probability he will take the opportunity to engage in some form of invective. We may perhaps be more than ordinarily aware of the invective in these two addresses because of the speakers' reputations; therefore, future criticism ought to study the extent to which invective is a staple of the genre. A heaping of data without careful attention to their artistic use may or may not be unique to modern apologetics, but the lumping of facts in the middle third of both speeches seems more than coincidental. It may be that either the circumstances surrounding broadcasting or the forensic demands of apologiae exert particular influences in these connections. Finally, the apologists' tendency to reassemble previously used arguments for presentation from the national rostrum (as evidenced in the fact that these two speeches are simple composites of earlier remarks) may hold implications both for our conception of rhetorical invention and for the critic's selection of facets for interpretation.

Whether or not the similarities we have just reviewed represent constants in the apologetic equation, we may regard as variables the dimensions of individual difference which were observed. Here emerged three ways by which speakers may put their personal imprints on messages: the manner in which the inferential pattern controls the form of the address, the degree in which the speaker channels his attack and thereby directs his listeners' aggression, and the ratio of public-personal explanations which becomes prominent in messages employing otherwise intimate electronic media.[25] There may of course be other factors influencing the character of modern broadcast apologiae, and we cannot discount the probability that as men gain experience in the use of electronic media the forms and styles of apologiae will change. Be that as it may, the elements of form and style amplified here deserve further study in apologiae and other genres of rhetorical discourse.

Finally, we are in a position to draw some conclusions concerning specific qualities of the two speeches here analyzed. First, it seems patently unfair to

[25]Cf. J. M. Ripley, "Television and Recreational Patterns." *Television Quarterly*, II (Spring 1963), 31–36. M. McLuhan, *Understanding Media: The Extensions of Man* (New York, 1965), pp. 297–337.

hold either Mr. Nixon or Mr. Truman in contempt, as many have, because either "injected personalities" into his remarks. Even granting the mercurial nature of the two speakers, there is a possibility that resort to invective is virtually inevitable given the unique configuration of forces operating upon the apologist. Secondly, if we wish to judge the logical validity or weight of evidence in either speech, we shall need to distinguish formal standards (which are often drawn from the courtroom) from the relativistic norms inherent in apologetics or in the age. To accuse Mr. Nixon of inadequate support for his contentions is to overlook the impact of his evidence on his audience. If accusations are to be mounted in this connection they are better directed to a society which contents itself with piles of evidence in place of rigorous argument.[26]

Lastly, while recognizing the unfairness of many journalistic criticisms of Richard Nixon, it does seem reasonable to contend that the most curious shortcoming of his "Checkers" speech, when compared with Truman's address, was its endurance in the public mind, its capacity to outlast the demands of the occasion. Whereas Harry Truman's discourse was totally relevant to specific rhetorical objectives, Nixon in a single stroke demolished both the opposition's case and injured his own standing as a public man. "Checkers" resulted in immediate victory for the campaigner; yet its traces admittedly continue to plague the political figure.[27]

[26]On this matter of loose standards of assessment in a given society see Aristotle, *Rhetoric*, 1354a 15–24.

[27]Cf. E. Black, *Rhetorical Criticism* (New York, 1965), pp. 162–164.

THE EPISTEMIC APPROACH

ON VIEWING RHETORIC AS EPISTEMIC: TEN YEARS LATER

Robert L. Scott

It is my belief that the humanists themselves have betrayed the humanities. Through a mistaken loyalty to a cramped and academic sense of order, the humanists have turned their backs on men and expelled the native turbulence and greatness from their studies. Thus the humanities have been distorted, and their crucial, enabling principle—the principle of personal influence and personal example—has been neglected and betrayed in a long servile imitation of the sciences.

William Arrowsmith[1]

In the ten years that have passed since my essay "On Viewing Rhetoric as Epistemic" was published in *CSSJ*.[2] I have noticed a warming interest among rhetoricians in clarifying a fresh role for rhetoric. Such interchanges as I am thinking of do not always take "epistemic" as a key term, but sooner or later such questions must be faced, as Douglas Ehninger correctly discerned in the "colloquy" between us in the *Quarterly Journal of Speech* a year ago.[3] Gary Cronkhite suggests "psychoepistemology" (how people come to believe what they believe) as the larger framework within which communication must find its role and argues that rhetoric is fundamentally a critical study.[4] I read Roderick Hart and Don Burks' concept of "rhetorical sensitivity" as saying that a certain style of interacting with others, the rhetorical, is demanded not only *because* one understands the demands of the human circumstances but also *in order to* understand humanely.[5] Barry Brummett's examination of the dialectical tensions of

From *Central States Speech Journal* 27 (Winter 1976): 258–66. Used by permission of the author and the Speech Communication Association.
Robert L. Scott is professor of speech communication at the University of Minnesota.

[1]"The Shame of the Graduate Schools," *Harpers Magazine,* 232 (Mar. 1966), 51–52.
[2]*Central States Speech Journal,* 18 (Feb. 1967), 9–16.
[3]"A Synoptic View of Systems of Western Rhetoric," *Quarterly Journal of Speech,* 61 (Dec. 1975), 439–453.
[4]"Rhetoric, Communication, and Psycho-epistemology," in *Rhetoric: A Tradition in Transition,* ed. Walter R. Fisher (East Lansing, Michigan: Michigan State Univ. Press, 1974), pp. 261–278.
[5]Roderick P. Hart and Don M. Burks, "Rhetorical Sensitivity and Social Interaction," *Speech Monographs,* 39 (June 1972), 75–91.

intersubjectivity and process, leading to what I take to be a synthesis of the concepts, gives a formative role to rhetoric that is not simply the instrumental role of persuading an audience (all though it does not preclude that traditional role).[6] Finally, Wayne Booth's book, *Modern Dogma and the Rhetoric of Assent*, correctly both recognizes the source of belief, which, when taken as dogma, precludes any role for rhetoric, except the manipulative use by the superior, and argues for the creative role of assent.[7] For rhetoric to be a rhetoric of assent, it must be viewed as epistemic.

My effort is neither to give an exhaustive list of sources nor to annotate the few I've mentioned, but rather to illustrate what I take to be an important growing concern. In a recent dissertation, Walter Carleton has examined in detail what he takes to be a "school" of rhetoricians and philosophers who may be identified by their similarities in attempting to develop an epistemic function for rhetoric, he concentrates chiefly on the work of Richard McKeon.[8]

My 1967 essay was probing rather than definitive; neither is this effort definitive. I shall simply try to clarify three questions: Is there one way of knowing or many? What sort of knowing does rhetoric strive to achieve? Is rhetorical relativism vicious?

An early reader of this essay was puzzled: Just why these three questions? His query is a fair one; the answer must be autobiographical. The questions are those that have been raised constantly by students and colleagues in discussing my 1967 essay. The questions, and the contexts of the discussions, led me to think that I needed to deal with a logical dimension of the way in which rhetoric might be epistemic. The third question, especially, pointed to that conclusion. Critics recognized the point-of-view I expressed as thoroughly relativistic and had learned to distrust relativism as the opening wedge for self-interest, wishfulness, and even sheer chaos.

To my surprise the essay I sketched turned out to re-affirm the basically ethical thrust of the earlier article. My experience leads me to assert at this point that it is fundamentally an ethical dimension of one's thoughts and actions that rhetoric reveals. This essay seems to me to be an example of its own thesis: I set out with a clear idea, but in the course of working through that idea and of communication with others about it I became aware of what I now consider an error. My reformulation caused me to gain fresh insight into the three guiding values worked out in the earlier essay and, I hope, to re-establish them here via routes quite different than those I followed in 1967.

Often the freshness that typifies what knowing is for an individual helps that person at least for a moment possess as a living concept what might otherwise pass for a cliché. The ethical knowledge that rhetoric strives toward achieving is that of commitment. Few words are as overworked as that one. And few concepts so vitally need freshening. A social context makes commitment relevant, and, to keep it from being simply blind self-interest, wishfulness, or chaotic, rhetoric must focus on assent. Dissent, of course, may be the result. Revaluing *commitment* is the fundamental burden of the second section of this essay.

---

[6]"Some Implications of 'Process' or 'Intersubjectivity': Postmodern Rhetoric," *Philosophy and Rhetoric*, 9 (Win. 1971), 21–51.

[7]South Bend, Indiana: Notre Dame Univ. Press, 1974.

[8]"On Rhetoric as a 'Way of Knowing': An Inquiry into Epistemological Dimensions of a New Rhetoric," Diss. Pennsylvania State Univ. 1975.

To assent or dissent truly one must know intersubjectively. But intersubjectivity, a topic taken up again below, has two rather opposite expressions: in science the agreement of independent observers helps establish a conclusion just because the observers do not communicate; to communicate and to agree or disagree is to know differently. Rhetoric aims at knowledge that is social and ethical; it has the potential of creating commitment. Is it, however, the sole means of such knowing? And that is the first question posed for this paper.

Is There One Way of Knowing or Many?

Many. Thus it is important to seek to understand rhetoric as *a* way of knowing, not *the* way. This answer is ambiguous. Are the asserted "many ways" simply a multiplicity? Or are they somehow coordinated? And if coordinated, is there a hierarchical relationship, perhaps such that "the many" are subordinate to, and even aspects of, a single way?

I would say that there is a plurality rather than a multiplicity. To what degree the various ways may be coordinated is a question I cannot answer. I suspect that any person richly aware of and seeking to work out the ramifications of an epistemology will seek to relate his or her scheme to other schemes and tend to appropriate into the favored scheme ever increasing expanses of borderline territory. Jean Piaget believes that "each discipline sooner or later has to work out its own epistemology."[9] Whether or not the "dream," which does not seem to Piaget unattainable, that is, "'transdisciplinarity,' which would not only cover interactions or reciprocities between specialized research projects, but would place these relationships within a total system without any firm boundaries between disciplines,"[10] is indeed attainable, it seems to me better to concentrate on various ways of knowing without committing oneself in advance to some archetechtonic idea.

Of course traditionally, the notion of "knowing" that is not also bound to a final unity is defective. That position might be readily admitted except that it has tended to stop thought along any line other than that that makes some immediate claim to rectify the defect. The result is what Piaget, and many others, call "reductionism"; just such a tendency is now widely held as unsatisfactory.

Pluralism, on the other hand, can be taken as just another name for relativism, and once one has the latter label, it is the slightest step to insert the modifier "mere" or even "vicious" before it. The ground on which we may deal with dismissing or condemning a rhetorical relativism will be the concern of the third section of this essay.   •

In concluding this section, there is another ambiguity to consider: if the epistemic potential of rhetoric is one among a plurality of ways of knowing, is it a constituent of some acts of knowing or of all acts of knowing? Answering that rhetoric may be a constituent of any act of knowing is perhaps a more guarded claim than to say "all"; that answer is consistent with the notion of plurality since it does not preclude other constituents nor demand some proper scheme in which it must find its subordinate, articulated place. The claim is one to potentiality rather than actuality. That is to say, that a rhetorical perspective will

[9] "The Epistemology of Interdisciplinary Relationships," in *Interdisciplinarity: Problems of Teaching and Research in Universities*, ed. Léo Apostel, et al., Paris: Office of Economic Co-Operation and Development Publications, 1972, p. 129.
    [10] Ibid., p. 138.

give one a purchase not otherwise available on what may be known, but it is not demanded to say that one "knows" at all. Rather, the attitude suggested by Hart and Burks, "rhetorical sensitivity," may be usefully extended to say that if persons take seriously the possibilities that may be opened by rhetorical interchange and their commitments to the reality of social life, then developing the sensitivity necessary to seek rhetoric as a way of knowing is to enable one to take more fully the responsibilities generated by living with others.

As Grace de Laguna writes, "There is a sense in which the human being is born into a world constituted as human through the activities of his forbears, and sustained by the interrelated activities of his fellow-beings. But it is not *his* unless he makes it his, and it is only by enlarging his own being, to internalize the structure of this world within himself, that it becomes his world."[11] Discovering and validating are reciprocal processes. Rhetoric is one way that ordinary human beings may quicken these. In seeing rhetoric from this angle as a way of knowing, among other ways, one's vision will be much too limited by taking a speaker-oriented rhetoric only. An active auditor who seeks speakers is as real as speakers who seek audiences; if there is a new, social rhetoric, it must be rooted firmly in an enlarged notion of rhetorical roles.[12]

What Sort of Knowing Does Rhetoric Seek To Achieve?

If the recourse to a plurality of epistemologies in claiming an epistemic role for rhetoric is to potentiality, the claim of knowing rhetorically is that of creating actuality. Seeing in a situation possibilities that are possibilities for us and deciding to act upon some of these possibilities but not others must be an important constituent of what we mean by human knowledge. The plural pronoun in the foregoing sentence is vital. As social beings, our possibilities and choices must often, perhaps almost always, be joint.

Two qualifications are important to the claim made for rhetoric, and both should be apparent from what I've argued already, but perhaps need to be made explicit: creating situations as decisive and deciding among alternatives are not the concern of rhetoric exclusively; seeing possibilities and making decisions are not sequential steps in the sense of first all of the one and then all of the other but rather repeated phases that may be constantly enriched in rhetorical interchange. It is precisely in understanding how human action is *decisive* that rhetoric makes its contribution to knowing.

The position taken here, obviously, is one that is becoming increasingly common: reality is socially constructed.[13] But if one takes that position certain concomitants must be faced. Our freedom to decide questions, and indeed, what we

[11]*On Existence and the Human World* (New Haven, Conn.: Yale Univ. Press, 1966), pp. 104–105.

[12]I have tried to make this point several times, See my "On *Not* Defining 'Rhetoric,'" *Philosophy and Rhetoric*, 6 (Spr. 1973), 90, and the "colloquy" between Ehninger and myself (n. 3, above). This trust is clearly discernible in Cronkhite's essay (n. 4, above) and, although not always explicitly, in the other work I referred to at the outset of this essay.

[13]Perhaps the best known book that develops the idea in detail is Peter L. Berger and Thomas Luckmann, *The Social Construction of Reality* (Garden City, New York: Doubleday and Co., 1966). See also Ernest G. Bormann, "Fantasy and Rhetorical Vision: The

take to be problems presenting questions to us for decision, are to some degree fixed by historical forces that predate any of the lives of the actual persons that may be involved at decisive moments. The fact of having culture with its traditions does not seem problematic at all; what may be problematic is the very notion of freedom to decide questions. Yet we notice that traditions do not simply exist, they are lived. A culture may precede and persist after any finite number of persons living in that culture at a particular time, but that culture must be lived to be a culture.

In short, we can come to grips with our tradition; it is from one angle simply there, transparent because it is pervasive. But the living of cultural demands makes them opaque to some degree so that they reflect, so to speak, what they are and what we are. What is reflected will inevitably contain disparate features, and those features are what we can treat as problems-to-be-solved and take ourselves as decisive. Therein lies our freedom, which, although scarcely absolute, is nonetheless experienced and attested to in social change.

The opacity of living is what bids forth rhetoric. A remark in passing by Hans-Georg Gadamer seems to me to be an important insight: the "concept of clarity belongs to the tradition of rhetoric."[14] But few terms are more relative than that one, nor call forth more strongly a human element. Nothing is clear in and of itself but in some context for some persons.

Rhetoric may be clarifying in these senses: understanding that one's traditions are one's own, that is, are co-substantial with one's own being and that these traditions are formative in one's own living; understanding that these traditions are malleable and that one with one's fellows may act decisively in ways that continue, extend, or truncate the values inherent in one's culture; and understanding that in acting decisively one participates in fixing forces that will continue after the purposes for which they have been immediately instrumental and will, to some extent, bind others who will inherit the modified traditions. Such understanding is genuinely knowing and is knowing that becomes filled out in some particulars by participating rhetorically.

If one sees rhetoric as a way of embracing a tradition such that one is able to accept or reject some of its demands and simultaneously to recognize that these decisions bind oneself to others as well as to the past in seeking change, then the reasons why rhetoric is only potentially a way of knowing may also be seen. The possibility of failure is constant. Failure may result simply from ineptness or from the force of circumstances that defeat the best of intentions and efforts. But failure may also arise from ethical shortcomings. The task of the rhetorical theorist is to specify the values that will make an ethical rhetoric and continually to try to rescue these from the realm of easy cliché. The indirect method of each of these three sections is an effort to meet that task. The values will be labeled explicitly in the conclusion.

Thus far I have used the terms "knowing" and "understanding" as if they were interchangeable. Although I may have been correct in respect to ordinary

---

Rhetorical Criticism of Social Reality," *Quarterly Journal of Speech*, 58 (Dec. 1972), 396–407, for one rhetorician's development of a schema that is postulated directly on what is becoming more and more strongly a cornerstone of contemporary thought.

[14]*Truth and Method*, 2nd Ed., 1965, ed. Garrett Barden and John Cumming (New York: The Seabury Press, 1975).

usage in doing so, still the words do carry somewhat different weights, or can be made to deviate somewhat from one another, and the nuances that seem to me to cling to "understanding" make me prefer it to ascribe to rhetoric as epistemic. By "knowing" we may stress a sense of from-the-outside-in, taking knowledge as an external anchor point that may bring one into a consistent relationship with the world that is more than oneself. By "understanding" we may stress the sense of from-the-inside-out, taking understanding as a human and personal capacity to embrace what is outside the self, creating rather than finding meaning in the world.

The problem is the ancient one of the objective and the subjective. Today it is nearly commonplace to assert that those terms are after all dialectical terms; neither makes sense without the other. An object is an object only to a subject; and a subject can be subject only if it is able to contrast itself with, to differentiate itself from, objects. No one need doubt the power of "being objective" since that attitude has been a driving force behind modern science and technology. But it is an attitude that places subjects in certain relationships for certain reasons, in short, the subjective remains and is often today recognized in the intersubjective. Intersubjectivity in science is continually appealed to in such devices as "agreement among observers," "replication of experiments," and "professional standards of judgment." Again the dialectic is suggested in the opposite expressions of intersubjectivity, as the matter was put in the introduction of this essay.

It will not do, however, to press the opposites in the dialectical tension rather than the integration possible in individual actions. Those actions, indeed even of scientists, create traditions and communities. In the common intersubjective devices of science we see at least dimly the epistemic role of rhetoric, for all of these depend on communities of experience and commitment that do not exist automatically "in nature," so to speak, but are formed as all communities are formed, by the interactions of people. Although many aspects of the interactions that make scientific communities, e.g., the "invisible colleges" that some historians and sociologists of science are finding so significant these days,[15] are not rhetorical, other aspects are.

Stephen Toulmin has remarked sharply on the strange dupleness that inflicts our perceptions of what we call knowledge on the one hand and our sense of self as "knower" on the other. "In principle," he writes, "a proper grasp of our epistemic situation should reinforce confidence in the best-founded of our beliefs; in practice, it often leaves us in a bewildered and universal skepticism."[16] The way out of this impasse, Toulmin suggests, is "to bring to light . . . [an] *epistemic self-portrait:* the particular picture of human beings as active intelligences which governs . . . [a] stance toward the objects of human understanding."[17] My claim is that any "epistemic self-portrait" that approaches completeness must include rhetoric.

---

[15]See for example the "Postscript—1969" to Thomas Kuhn, *The Structure of Scientific Revolutions*, 2nd Ed. (Chicago: Univ. of Chicago Press, 1969), pp. 176–177.

[16]*Human Understanding: The Collective Use and Evolution of Concepts* (Princeton, New Jersey: Princeton Univ. Press, 1972), p. 2.

[17]Ibid., p. 3.

What sort of knowledge does rhetoric seek to achieve? The understanding of what it means to be persuaded and to persuade.[18] Such an understanding is both general and specific: general, in that one's own grasp of oneself as a social being with others in society is essential to being human, and specific in that one must continually face concrete situations in which one will act to affirm some commitments. None of these statements is meant to deny that one will continually behave scarcely aware of the patterns that behavior takes let alone with highly conscious grasp of the reasons for those patterns. But the fact that much, probably most, of our behavior is well fixed through complex reinforcements does not mean that we cannot become focally aware of these patterns and their consequences. When we do become so aware, then we can act critically, and usually rhetorically, to reaffirm or modify them, in short, to become more fully committed.

In an analysis much like the one here, Thomas Farrell pictures the Cartesian bequeathed attitude of detachment as descriptive of modern science. Farrell would move beyond that attitude in assessing the rhetorical dimension of social knowledge as taking a community of belief as necessary.[19] The requisite attitude to balance *detachment* in knowing would be *attachment* in understanding.

Although modern science is founded on the firm belief that experience must be instructive, Hans-Georg Gadamer argues that the typical attitudes of science leave "experience" incompletely understood; he undertakes to rectify the situation. Among his remarks, this one is particularly useful: "Experience teaches us to recognize reality. What is properly gained from all experience, then, is to know what is. But 'what is', here, is not this or that thing, but 'what cannot be done away with'. . . . "[20] What cannot be done away within a community is commitment to the norms of that community. Commitment and rhetoric stand in a reciprocal relationship: commitment generates rhetoric, and rhetoric generates commitment.

Is Rhetorical Relativism Vicious?

No. One may, of course, eat gluttonously or quote Shakespeare filled with vain pride in the sound of one's own voice. Likewise one may argue with wanton disregard for the fabric of social commitments or, perhaps, in blithe ignorance of the possibilities of either reaffirmation or reform. But the gratuitous abuse of rhetoric seems of less concern to thoughtful people than the sheer relativism of the point of view that takes rhetoric as epistemic. For these people, relativism seems to make abuse not simply an occasional occurrence but likely. At least such objections are typical of the discussions I have often had with colleagues and students since my effort in 1967.

The difficulty rests in the belief that relativism obviates the very idea of knowledge. From this point of view knowledge must be *a priori*, that is, we must know in some general or universal sense, before we can know at all in any

---

[18]Henry W. Johnstone, Jr., has written that "man is a persuading and persuaded animal, and . . . whenever he steps outside the forum in which rhetoric loses sway, he is in danger of losing his human dignity." "The Relevance of Rhetoric to Philosophy and of Philosophy to Rhetoric." *Quarterly Journal of Speech,* 52 (Feb. 1966). 45.

[19]"Knowledge, Consensus, and Rhetorical Theory," *Quarterly Journal of Speech,* 62 (Feb. 1976), see esp., 6–7, although the entire essay is highly pertinent to grasping the idea of rhetoric-as-epistemic.

[20]*Truth and Method,* p. 320.

specific sort of way. This point of view seems to be entitled in the traditional way of putting the question, What is knowing? The question itself suggests that the best answer, perhaps the only answer, is defining knowing as a state-of-being and, in clarifying the answer, indicating the conditions for that state. However, such moves involve us in an infinite regress unless we take some conditions as clear and necessary, that is, as axiomatic.

An axiomatic point of view can be taken as either substantial or methodological. It is in the latter form that an axiomatic epistemology has had its greatest modern impact, that is, in the ideal of "scientific method." What has been the predominant interpretation of such a method, however, is sharply under attack today.[21]

Taking prior axioms, in either a substantial or a methodological sense, precludes rhetoric's claim to being epistemic. And the implications of a rhetoric based on some prior, enabling sense of Truth are ones that persons in our field have often accepted uncritically; this point I argued in 1967.

Fundamentally, the objection to relativism is that no standards for judgment are possible and therefore sheer chaos is loosed among humankind since reduced to opinion alone, no opinion can claim legitimately any priority over any other opinion.

At least two counter-arguments may be posed against the abstract and deductive fear of relativism; both arguments appeal to common experience and both seem to me potent.

Although no one needs to doubt the severe shock of what is often called "senseless crime," the greater portion of evil in the history of humankind stems from what its perpetrators take to be quite good sense. The justification of injury to others, especially when that injury is wide scale, finding expression in social and economic dominance or violence, is ordinarily rooted in the certainty of some commanding Truth taken as axiomatic. The fact that one group, especially at some later point in time, is inclined to give unpleasant names to the ideas of order that have driven others—for example, blaming the horror of religious wars on mistaken dogmas—does not lessen the potency of certainty as enabling extreme actions. If one may repair to standards of judgment that are fixed outside the individual conscience or even the interests of an immediate community, then one does not bear the burden of responsibility in making decisions. It is that relief from individual or communal responsibility that is the chief attraction of what is sometimes called, I believe mistakenly, "objective reality."

Although clearly I cannot detail an account-book for human history and must leave my appeal to the reader's own sense of history, even in the abstract it seems to me that contingency is much less to be feared in creating chaos, wantonly or whimsically, than the spirit of axiomatic detachment.

A second line of argument to relieve the stigma of relativism runs precisely contrary to the supposed self-evident assumption on which the stigmatizing rests. Relativism, supposedly, means a standard-less society, or at least a maze of differing standards, and thus a cacophony of disparate, and likely selfish, interests.

---

[21]The literature that might be cited here is vast. The books cited above by Kuhn and Toulmin are relevant. In speech-communication one may find the concern well argued and documented by Daniel J. O'Keefe, "Logical Empiricism and the Study of Human Communication," *Speech Monographs*, 42 (Aug. 1975), 169–175. Another aspect of the current reassessment may be seen in the essay-review by Gerald R. Miller, "The Person as Actor—Cognitive Psychology on the Attack," *Quarterly Journal of Speech*, 62 (Feb. 1976), 82–87.

Rather than a standard-less society, which is the same as saying no society at all, relativism indicates circumstances in which standards have to be established co-operatively and renewed repeatedly. Since agreement seems to be at least as common in the everyday world as disagreement and, further, necessary to the working out of individual interests even in the most simple of societies, relativism would be likely to quicken a sense of commitment to creating agreement.

To accept relativism does not mean starting continually from scratch but rather recognizing one's traditions as such, recognizing that traditions need to be lived to be traditions, and, further, teaching one that one's traditions are only traditions.

Ironically enough, one interpretation of relativism, rather than casting individuals adrift in a standard-less world, fixes them in a strict determinism. This sort of relativism, often called "historicism," emphasizes the immediacy of one's own history and that of one's particular culture. We are what we are because of what our forebears have been; we act as we must given the expectancies our particular lives have endowed us with and in accordance with the limits of our societal norms. Other persons and other societies differ from us because of their cultural determinants. No culture can claim any rational priority and any contest of interests must be settled by whatever tests of sheer strength that may be brought to bear in the circumstances.

One need not deny historical determinism. One only needs to deny, and I have tried consistently to do so, the rigidity of such determinations. Shifts in cultural consciousness, both revolutionary and evolutionary, seem consistently present in human experience. Furthermore, what we call "a culture" or "a society" is marked only more-or-less distinctly; or, to put the matter a little differently, there are membranes that bound the circumferences of such bodies, but these membranes are permeable.

My suggesting that there are two dimensions of relativism—that among societies and that within a society—probably has not relieved the tension felt by those who use the word as a pejorative or who fear being so labeled. And there is a third dimension.

Even those who take the position that there must be some unified hierarchy of stable standards in order to achieve decent individual and social lives will agree that such standards must be applied in specific sets of circumstances. Few will deny that in practice, at least, applications are seldom, if ever, possible in such a way that the standards are engaged without discomfort. Some degree of discomfort seems inevitable in the very necessity of having to make a judgment. The existence of some set of circumstances in the guise of a case to be settled seems to suggest rather strongly the human participation of relating standards to particular, concrete events. Of course one might say wishfully that if we possessed knowledge of the proper sort then no such cases would arise for the judgment of some parts of society by other parts. The dialogue in Plato's *Gorgias* is actuated to a major degree around the proposition attributed to Socrates that the wrong-doer should prefer punishment to escaping punishment. I call that argument wishful since it may be interpreted as relieving members of a society of the burden of making judgments of others. That burden is particularly heavy if one is convinced of the contingency of any judgment.

None of the foregoing is intended to deprecate self-criticism. Rather I hold that a community to sustain itself, both through reaffirmation and reform, must be formed of members who will take the responsibility of examining critically the binding forces, the norms, of the community and of recognizing that the traditions accepted and extended entail living consistently with the social demands. The task is not lightened by recognizing that social demands can be repressive. On the other hand, as important as self-criticism may be, we should also recognize that a community may impose its demands quite invidiously by insisting on self-criticism as an instrument of social conformity.

Rhetorical relativism is not an easy process promising dependable outcomes. It may be just as well that the very label tends to make us fearful, for that emotion may be an indication of reluctance to impose solutions rather than to create and share them jointly. The attitude suggested is that appropriate to taking the responsibility of persuading others and, concomitantly, being open to persuasion.

Conclusion

In 1967 I argued that understanding rhetoric-as-epistemic entailed three values: tolerance, will, and responsibility. In answering the three questions that I posed at the outset of this essay, I have tried to argue in such a way as to reaffirm these values in turn as the logical outcomes of the analysis in each of the three sections above. These values should have meanings for individuals, but they have meaning only in a reality that is social. If Gadamer is correct in saying that "the experience of meaning which takes place in understanding always includes application,"[22] then rhetoric as a means of understanding social reality and as a means of acting effectively within a community is assured. Put differently: rhetoric may be the art of persuasion, that is, it may be seen from one angle as a practical capacity to find means to ends on specific occasions; but rhetoric must also be seen more broadly as a human potentiality to understand the human condition.

It is the broader scope of rhetoric that has interested rhetoricians intensely in the last decade. Recently Donald P. Verene has written that "the philosophy of science and the sciences has become a definite field of philosophical inquiry; a counterpart to this, a philosophy of the humanities, has not developed."[23] Verene would see such a philosophy developed, and it is in this relation that viewing rhetoric as epistemic becomes a vital concern.

[22]*Truth and Method*, p. 345.
[23]"Vico's Philosophy of Humanistic Imagination: Its Significance for Theory of Knowledge," *Social Research*, (Fall, 1976).

A DEAR SEARCHER INTO COMPARISONS: THE RHETORIC OF ELLEN GOODMAN

Robert L. Scott and James F. Klumpp

Then reach me my breeches off the chair, said my father to Susannah—There is not a moment's time to dress you, Sir, cried Susannah—the child is as black in the face as my—as your what? said my father, for like all orators, he was a dear searcher into comparisons.

—Laurence Sterne, *Tristram Shandy*[1]

Although not all pose such dramatic dilemma as the guilt of nakedness confronting the imminence of death, moments of moral choice are common to our lives. When value confronts value and values confront facts, when the issue is response, responsibility, and action, we feel the rhetorical impulse. We declare our opinions, we give or seek advise. Because such moments are rhetorical, they bind the private moment of choice with the nearly incessant stream of social communication. Sterne has Tristram Shandy see such a moment in retrospect, and in recreating that moment he can do so with a smile. His moment is not neutral, not a shapeless recounting of time passing and passed, but a human story—something with temper, tone, and thrust, an energy that carries the story forward through its events and into others' lives. That is the rhetorical impulse par excellence.

In understanding the relation of private choice to public communication, the title of one of Richard Weaver's essays—"Language Is Sermonic"—comes quickly to mind.[2] Weaver writes that the locus of rhetorical action rests in the ways we bring our particular time and space situations into the context of the flow of cultural meaning. Perhaps the title overstresses one of the preacher's rhetorical tasks, but we find much in the analogy to illuminate the object of our study—syndicated columnist Ellen Goodman.

Goodman intrigues us for several reasons. Her focus is overtly the point where public meets private. "I think it's . . . important for all of us to be able to make links between our personal lives and public issues," she wrote in the introduction to her first published collection of columns. "The most vital concerns can't be divided into internal and external affairs."[3] Her sense for the ways in which the private and public are bound together seems to us to be the sophisticated understanding of an accomplished rhetor.

If Goodman illuminates the rhetorical moment we seek to understand, she is no less an excellent example of the process that we see as central to our contem-

From *Quarterly Journal of Speech* 70 (February 1984): 69–79. Used by permission of the authors and the Speech Communication Association.

Mr. Scott is a professor of speech communication, University of Minnesota, and Mr. Klumpp is an associate professor of speech communication, University of Maryland.

[1]Bk. 4, chap. 14. The idiom "black in the face" is now archaic. Our contemporary idiom for the condition is "blue in the face."

[2]Reprinted in *Language Is Sermonic: Richard M. Weaver on the Nature of Rhetoric*, eds. Richard L. Johannesen, Rennard Strickland, and Ralph T. Eubanks (Baton Rouge: Louisiana State Univ. Press, 1970), pp. 201–25. Similar ideas are expressed in Weaver's essay "The Cultural Role of Rhetoric," reprinted in the same volume (pp. 161–84).

[3]*Close to Home* (New York: Simon and Schuster, 1979), pp. 15–16.

porary understanding of rhetoric. Sterne's choice of preposition to describe the reverend in his rhetorical moment may seem a bit strange, but precisely right in describing Goodman's mastery of comparison—not a searcher *after,* nor *for,* but *into* comparisons.

Finally, although we are not certain she would embrace our comparisons, we believe that her writing attains a character that we see in many columnists and would call "religio-political symbolizing." We believe that people often treat their favorite columnists in this mode. We feel safe in asserting, for example, that those who read the columns on the op-ed pages of our newspapers read selectively: cheering for their favorites and scoffing at—if reading at all—the others. In short, people go to columnists much as they go to church—some regularly, some occasionally, and most to have well-established opinions celebrated. Columnists also act a good deal like preachers. There was a day when political, social, and economic essayists got yards of columns rather than a few inches; but then there was a day when preachers had their congregations for a few hours rather than a few minutes. The moral of the story, in the two familiar senses of the word "moral," has to come quickly to the point in the pulpit or on the op-ed page. Of course, not all columnists are as patent in the religio-political mode as Richard Cohen in his recent confession as a loathesome feeder-at-the-public-trough, bidding others to come forward by displaying himself as a weak vessel, but columnists in general work by identifying some strongly valued principle and exhorting fidelity to it.[4] Lapses, hopeful signs, exemplars, sanctified writ, and a strong sense of caring are as familiar to the work of columnists as to that of ministers, rabbis, and priests.

The scene within which columnists write, that is, the symbolic working through of social, political, and/or economic motives, is familiar enough as a secular equivalent of religious experience. Our ways of viewing the world must have palpable value for us; values must be reaffirmed and the momentary business of living must be seen in their lights. The religious vein in American thinking has been broad and deep—from Puritan motives well set before voyaging from England, to the sanctifying of the Revolution, through the bitterness of the Civil War, and to the affirming and reaffirming of Manifest Destiny. In the twentieth century we find the mixing of the sacred and secular on at least two levels: the deep, assumptive structure of our motivations and the clear, direct, surface appeal to religious values.[5]

The constant reworking of the various strands of ongoing rhetoric that form the fabric of our public lives is so common that we scarcely think of columnists as Jeremiahs, as we shouldn't. Despite the American penchant for sanctifying the terms clustering with "individual," it is the shared celebration of experience

---

[4]"Tax Deductions: One Man's Confession," *Minneapolis Tribune,* 3 March 1981, p. 3.

[5]The working out of religious motives in American political and social life has been studied with an interesting fervor lately. Sacvan Bercovitch examines the Puritan strain and the particular form it takes in his *The American Jeremiad* (Madison: Univ. of Wisconsin Press, 1978). The general tendency to see our political problems and solutions in sacred terms is well pictured in Robert Bellah, *The Broken Covenant, American Civil Religion in Time of Trial* (New York: Seabury Press, 1975). A particular manifestation of this religio-political linkage is in Ernest G. Bormann's "Fetching Good out of Evil: A Rhetorical Use of Calamity," *Quarterly Journal of Speech,* 63 (1977), 130–39. That the forces which energize action from the motives runs both ways is well shown by Roderick P. Hart in his *The Political Pulpit* (West Lafayette, Ind.: Purdue University Press, 1977).

that creates our reality.[6] The columnist's role is in the chorus that cements our symbols into shared patterns through constant reinforcement of the social knowledge of our everyday experience. Both their writing and our reading of it are a celebration of rhetorical form that provides a sense of identity with groups and causes more potent than we. These forces mingle and create culture.

Thus we seek to understand the strategies by which Ellen Goodman brings her view of the world to our attention. We believe that in finding those strategies we will learn much about the rhetoric of our columnists, religio-political symbolizing, and the role of rhetoric in the ongoing decisions of life.

Comparison in Ellen Goodman's Columns

A variety of descriptive phrases might be applied in trying to understand how Ellen Goodman's columns work, but we are satisfied that none strikes nearer the heart of her method than "a dear searcher into comparisons." When Goodman observes something, perhaps something quite simple—a roadside sign, a scene in a movie, or even her own frustration at being stranded at home in a blizzard—it does not remain a simple event for long. Consider the latter case. Cut off by the blizzard from the familiar working environment of her office, she senses a principle—we are all prisoners of our routines—and the probe to define its form begins: "She was not, of course, the only one strung out on a clothesline of routines."[7] Even when the principle can be stated as a proposition, as in the sentence that headlined this column ("Routines Can Be a Self-Imposed Prison"), the comparison is important. The homely metaphor of the clothesline is given a dramatic and strongly valued nuance in the term that suggests chemical dependency—strung out.

The richness of Goodman's comparisons is in the constant turning, as with puzzle pieces, to perceive a more profound pattern in the oddities of shape. As she yields to the snow, she struggles with the realization that "she can't imagine writing at home.":

[6]Our allusion here is to the process which considers human action to be grounded in "reality" as rhetorically construed knowledge. This view features the importance of rhetoric's function as a ritualistic celebration (the term here encompasses celebrations of derogation as well as praise) of interpretations and the importance of understandings thus established in human action.

Contemporary rhetorical theory has approached this function from several directions. One major thrust has been the work in the epistemic function of rhetoric. Robert L. Scott's "On Rhetoric as Epistemic," *Central States Speech Journal*, 18 (1967), 9–17, provided the initial impetus for the contemporary development of this strain. The relevant literature is too diverse to cite economically, but is well summarized in Michael C. Leff, "In Search of Ariadne's Thread: A Review of the Recent Literature on Rhetorical Theory," *Central States Speech Journal*, 29 (1978), 73–91.

A second closely related strain develops the idea of a social knowledge created in, and brought to bear with, the rhetorical encountering of experience. This work owes much to Peter L. Berger and Thomas Luckmann's *The Social Construction of Reality: A Treatise in the Sociology of Knowledge* (Garden City, N.Y.: Doubleday, 1966). A particular rhetorical formulation is in Thomas B. Farrell's "Knowledge, Consensus, and Rhetorical Theory" *Quarterly Journal of Speech*, 62 (1976), 1–14 and "Social Knowledge II" *Quarterly Journal of Speech*, 64 (1978), 329–34.

[7]"Routines Can be a Self-imposed Prison," *Minneapolis Tribune*, 10 February 1978, p. 7A.

Theoretically, she only needed a loaf of paper, a jug of ink and an idea [allusion]. But actually she needed a sense of order and place [contrast]—all of which was separated from her by square miles of snow. She couldn't ponder Big Questions at home any more than she could eat snails with a serving fork [analogy]. She didn't have the right utensils to get the ideas out of the shells.[8]

In this case, Goodman constructs the mosaic puzzle after turning the parts to find the interlocking edges, a process that invites readers to find themselves in the parts of the emerging picture.

At other times, the puzzle comes apart. Goodman finds something, again sensing a principle that is intermeshed, and invites our understanding in the process we thought of in simpler, sexist days as the delight of small boys. She comments after having enjoyed the movie, "Don't misunderstand me. I thought '9 to 5' was wonderfully funny." But she remembers the boss's speech and the metaphor that drove that speech struck with her. As is often the case, she was restless until she had it in pieces. "Alas, he then says, it's too bad women didn't have a chance to play football. Without that training, somehow they never quite understand what 'teamwork' is all about." The regular reader of Goodman's columns knows that he or she will very quickly be told what teamwork is all about. It is all about a contrast in values: human and corporate, at least insofar as the values of corporate life are represented by the "sports model." Goodman worries humorously but genuinely about the exploitation of women: "As for this veteran, whenever I hear the pep talk about teamwork, I wonder just for whom the team is working. In the movie, when our Mr. Hart extolls the virtues of teamwork . . . , the women in the office can't even get off the bench." But she also wonders "why so many men sign up. It's possible that they've been brainwashed by high-school coaches, old war movies or the promise of the big-bucks trophy.[9] In any case, a metaphor yields to Goodman's skilled unpacking. If the game is symbolic, Goodman is quite willing to show us how to make a fresh game of it.

Comparison, of course, brings out dissimilarities as well as similarities. Probably no one can exercise a strong habit of comparing without inevitably coming to a number of sharp contrasts. Ellen Goodman is no exception. In "TV Turns Families into Audiences," Goodman analyzes a familiar problem—the extent and effects of the family's time with television—but finds a feeling of potential potency:

I grant you that there are a lot of things that touch on our families that are totally out of our individual control. We can't regulate foreign affairs. We can't set the price for oil. We have about as great a chance of controlling inflation as we do of capping Mount St. Helens.

But a television set has a dial and a plug. And we have hands. It is absurd to let our feelings of impotence in the world start creeping into our private lives.[10]

Now that is the stuff that sermons are made of. That is a preacher's way of bringing a message home, pointing it directly to the responsibilities of believers.

In Goodman's work, comparison serves both the quick thrust that may bring a smile and make an arresting opening ("Well, folks, it's time to round up the

[8]"Routines."

[9]"Pep Talk Isn't for Women," *Minneapolis Tribune*, 28 December 1980, p. 8A.

[10]*Minneapolis Tribune*, 8 July 1980, p. 6A.

usual suspects'''[11]), and the long thoughtful gaze ("It is possible that this man, too, is an island by default—another member of our Outward Bound who has become, in defense, a fearful caretaker of his only acre, grooming and landscaping. And isolated''[12]).

One can say that a comparison ordinarily sets the key for a Goodman column. Here we have in mind the musical sense of *key:* something that sets a reference point and suffuses the whole with a quality. Although Goodman is usually responsive to her social environment for a focus, and often finds the verbal cues she needs in some bit of discourse, the moral of her sermon emerges from exploring the key metaphor.

Comparison as a Form of Argument

When we say that the comparison suffuses the *whole* with a *quality,* we stress the sense in which a subtle force in a column fuses seemingly disparate elements into a unified interpretation. We believe that the fusion makes the message compelling—that the force of what is commonly thought of as "reality" is a product of the reader's encounter with an interpretation performed in the key of the comparison. Goodman, for example, often uses comparison to join the familiar with the abstract, an experience compels attention to a principle. She recalls the most common of experiences—the birth of a friend's baby: "The arrival of Julia was personal, almost selfish pleasure, the kind that comes when another small person joins the cast of characters. . . . But there was more than that." In the joy of this moment familiar to readers she "felt again some pleasure toward—rather than simple fear and horror of—the irrational side of human nature."[13]

Comparisons also guide interpretation by borrowing an image from one sort of experience to set the form of another. "I know a man who has spent this year getting himself in shape," she reports. "He has taken up self-improvement the way other people take up jogging. . . . In an era when every man is an island, this one is striving to be Bermuda."[14] A reader of Goodman knows that an exploration of "island-ness" in all its facets is forthcoming.

Finally, the tone of a piece often is urged in a metaphor, usually evolving as the image is shaped and reshaped throughout. Tone must not be thought of as something superficial; it instructs us in the proper attitude of response. "T.G.I.O.," she says of the 1980 election, "Thank God It's Over."[15]

Often her metaphors make their point by joining familiarity, intricacy, and a sharply bitter tone. We are warned to look carefully, and touch even more carefully, for more than barbs may be beneath the contrasting surfaces in the "story of Mary Cunningham and William Agee." She writes, "The Cunningham-Agee story is an updated version of the favorite male fantasy about women who sleep their way to the top. It is absolutely ripe with hostility toward uppity women, especially young uppity women." Here the Agees and Cunninghams acquire significance from the shape of a common experience and the tone of response is set

---

[11]"The ERA on Trial Again in Illinois," *Minneapolis Tribune*, 13 May 1980, p. 8A.
[12]"Islands in a Society of Impermanence," *Minneapolis Tribune*, 12 May 1978, p. 6A.
[13]"Is 'Planned Parenthood' Rational?" *Minneapolis Tribune*, 1 December 1978, p. 4A.
[14]"Islands in a Society of Impermanence.
[15]"We Were an Audience, Not Electorate," *Minneapolis Tribune*, 7 November 1980, p. 10A.

in the male-female comparison. A series of examples of the sort of social situations that men can exploit with impunity invites us to compare expectations of men with those of women. Goodman writes, "Women do not have a set of separate-but-equal unfair advantages. It is plain old hostility that assumes that a woman can only get to the top on her back instead of her merit." And, as if to say "if you want a dirty story I'll show you the real dirt," Goodman continues: "I'm not naive. The workplace is not a convent; people meet and fall in love over stranger things than blueprints. But nobody calls the reporters in when yet another boss sleeps with his secretary. If you look at the sexual harrassment statistics, it's women at the bottom who are considered fair game." A moral judgment is made, another comparison introduced, and injustice far more significant than the familiar case is carefully displayed and denounced:

> There's an old proverb: Whether the rock hits the pitcher or the pitcher hits the rock, it's going to be bad for the pitcher.
> Well, no matter what happens, or why, in this sort of collision, it's the less powerful person who gets shattered. In corporate America, Mary Cunningham was just another pitcher.[16]

Her audience knows the proverb, of course, before encountering Goodman's reference, but columnist and audience now see it in a particular light and thus come to know the Agees and Cunninghams in a new light. A rhetorical experience is shared, an interpretation formed, a belief reinforced, and a faith renewed.

We are convinced that many find Goodman convincing. Such a statement is interesting because, as we noted, most often the columnist's audience already believes. The strangeness one may sense in the remark springs from a concept of rhetoric as linguistic expression of idea subject to verification of the truth of its contents. From the time of George Campbell to the present, textbooks in rhetoric and logic have tended to view argument using forms of analogy as weak. After all, as Campbell observed in 1776, experience is direct but analogy is based on some remote similitude.[17]

Goodman's use of comparisons scarcely seems to fit Campbell's formula that analogy "is more successful in silencing objections than evincing truth, and on this account may more properly be styled the defensive arms of the orator than the offensive." What her practice does do is to show that argument at its best engages a listener or reader, making the person an active thinker, a partner in creating a reality that can be experienced. Campbell's fundamental error, an error common still, is in misunderstanding experience as a private act. When experience attains significance, i.e. meaning emerges in an interpretive process that joins history, culture and context to data, experience becomes in a significant sense social.

The columns of Ellen Goodman gives us an example of an interpretive rhetoric for which comparison is foundational. The various modes of comparison serve

---

[16]"Fantasies about Promoted Women," *Minneapolis Tribune*, 17 October, 1980, p. 10A.

[17]*Philosophy of Rhetoric*, Bk. I, Chap. v, Pt. 2. Currently, a strong interest in metaphor is rapidly changing our perceptions of its nature—basically from that of adding color *to* thought to foundational *for* thought. See, e.g., George Lakoff and Mark Johnson, *Metaphors We Live By* (Chicago: Univ. of Chicago Press, 1980) and Mark Johnson, ed., *Philosophical Perspectives on Metaphor* (Minneapolis: Univ. of Minnesota Press, 1981). We do not claim to be breaking ground, but rather to be adding to the campaign. We do believe that the attitude Campbell represents has yet to be abandoned.

(1) as instructions, that is, attitudes, by which those sharing in the rhetoric interpret the data of their experiences, and (2) as revelations of tensions among experiences, that is, principles, that must be brought to bear in interpreting the communicative force of utterances. The claim being made here is one that has become quite familiar in the last few years: rhetorical itself is epistemic.

Such a perspective implies a focus on the audience as rhetors—that the audience jointly creates meaning in the rhetorical act, rather than sequentially receiving rhetoric and then responding to it. We often make meaning as individuals; when we make meaning jointly we are communicating; when we make meaning jointly in public circumstances so as to enhance cooperation, our communication is rhetorical. The participation of an audience is not a heretofore unknown element in rhetoric, but we believe that it has been framed in an epistemology basically inhospitable to its full import.[18]

We start our understanding of argument in a different place—that rhetoric is an essential part of experiencing. Goodman's is not a propositional rhetoric persuading to material truth, but a moral rhetoric seeking followers. Facing the exigencies of life, Goodman's readers seek her insight and she ministers to them. At issue in the rhetorical conflict within which she serves is not a store of propositional truths stable until altered by effective persuasion, but a series of moral principles which her audience employs to respond to their exigencies. A moment with Ellen Goodman is a rehearsal for the encountering of experience.

We think of our clergy as both preachers—those who proclaim—and ministers—those who attend and serve. The characterization is equally true of our secular clergy. Goodman rhetorically encounters her experience to help us encounter our own. She is convincing to the extent that we do follow. We think that comparison is an essential part of her success. Perhaps this is so because the decisions of life are at heart comparisons. No two life decisions are identical, so we compare situations to develop an orientation to them. In science we can apply covering law to understand, but in life we must compare, not apply. We may compare experience with proverbs, with mores, or with other experiences, but we will always find our answers in comparisons.

The differences between application and comparison are instructive. We mean first of all that situations are unique in their space and time moment. Thus, our mores and our previous experiences only prepare us to negotiate, not to impose, an orientation to our new situations. Such a distinction implies not only a comparison of mores with situation, but also a comparison of one set of mores with another to determine which better guides us. It is this triangulation—one way with another in terms of experience—that leads both to action and to a more

---

[18]The concept of an audience active in interpreting as an essential part of rhetoric is also not novel. The Committee on Rhetorical Invention of the National Developmental Conference on Rhetoric provided a statement of the implications of the concept over a decade ago (*The Prospect of Rhetoric*, eds. Lloyd F. Bitzer and Edwin Black [Englewood Cliffs: Prentice-Hall, 1971], pp. 228–36). They note that with their conception of invention "the distinction between speaker and audience loses its sacredness. . . . Even in conventional speaker-audience situations, the 'acceptance' by the audience of a proposition must often depend on the audience's reinventing the communication for itself." The epistemological requirements of such a conception of rhetoric are explored by Barry Brummett, "Some Implications of 'Process' or 'Intersubjectivity': Postmodern Rhetoric," *Philosophy and Rhetoric*, 9 (1976), 21–51. Brummett explains that "sense data by themselves are not experience. Experience is sensation plus *meaning*."

generalized sense of morality. Obviously, the next step in such an explanation is a sense of the contingent, of probability.

We have now returned to a concept that is familiar in our traditional understanding of rhetoric. It is important, however, to realize that we have reached the concept by a different route—not as an imperfect but inevitable relative of certainty but as an outgrowth of the rhetorical encounter with the novel but similar. Ellen Goodman convinces by comparison. If we examine the substance of what we call her "argument," we find the substance of her audience's encounters—experiences demanding response, proverbs, mores of her society, metaphors of understanding.

Comparison as Equipment for Living

We have described a technique of comparison that we believe characterizes Ellen Goodman's syndicated columns and have suggested that in the context of an epistemic rhetoric, in which audience/rhetors use rhetoric in their ongoing life situations, the search into comparisons gives rhetoric a form that lives beyond the reading of the column. We sense more, however, in a Goodman column.

In reading Goodman we begin to feel (to borrow Bruce Gronbeck's term and, we hope, his temper) just a little Burkeish.[19] We have found in teaching the rhetorical theory of Kenneth Burke one of his most haunting concepts to be the question: What does the poem do for the poet?[20] The contemporary rhetoric we have adopted shifts the purpose of working rhetoric from propositional persuasion to what Burke calls symbolic action. We would thus paraphrase Burke: What does the rhetoric do for the rhetors? In searching Goodman's strategies to answer this question, we learn more about what can be characterized as epideictic—providing the converted with the interpretive instruments for their rhetorical situations.

One of the dimensions of comparison in a Goodman column is the grafting of situations from different places and times. The typical Goodman column joins two rhetorical moments. There is the moment when "everyman" encounters the life situation.

> The man is keeping his options open. He has been doing it for some time now and it is, I suppose, what he does best. Through the decade I have known him, he has let good women and great chances slip through his hands like water. But he has held onto his options like a lifeline. . . . He once described life to me as a kind of one-plate buffet table. If you fill up your plate at the beginning, you won't have any more room at the end of the table. What, he asked earnestly, if the shrimp cocktail is in the last dish?[21]

We get a glimpse of values, to be sure, but we get more. We study the ways in which rhetoric and the values we share in rhetorical moments shapes our modes of living. Our allegiance to these metaphors of experience intensifies their lives as our shapers.

---

[19]"John Morley and the Irish Question: Chart-Prayer-Dream," *Speech Monographs*, 40 (1973), 287.

[20]*Philosophy of Literary Form: Studies in Symbolic Action* (1941: rpt. New York: Vintage Books, 1957), p. 62.

[21]"How Far to Keep One's Options Open?" *Minneapolis Tribune*, 2 November 1979, p. 10A.

There is an earlier rhetorical moment, however, the moment when we learn or are persuaded to take these metaphors with their attendant values as our own. Often these moments are times of self-persuasion, as when the son stood at the funeral of his father, dead at fifty-four from a heart attack, and rued the father's time on the treadmill:

> "Locked in," the son had told me at this father's funeral. "He spent his whole life locked in." His father's plate was overloaded, and he had fallen under the weight. So, the son mixed guilt with terror. He built his father's life story into his own life plan. Where his father was locked in, he would be open. Where his father had burdens, he would have space.[22]

These are, if you will, the *first* moments of the motive celebrated, where our experiences, or more likely other people's experiences, become a lesson for us.

At other times, this earlier rhetorical moment is placed in Goodman's socio-politico-economic world, inhabited by those who have more traditionally been seen as rhetors—those persuaders who convince us to buy their product, whether this product is a candidate, an idea, a value, or an economic good. It may be the government, but more likely corporate America—the shopping center security net, or the "only a [single family] house is a home" bunch. Goodman, like any good preacher (and we might add any good rhetorical critic), seeks to innoculate us against those who would out-maneuver us with their slick rhetorical tricks.

Messages from the pulpit deal with the forces that shape the on-going moments of our lives. They convince us to give those forces their proper name, to see them in a certain way. Furthermore, they seek to give us a sense of power over those forces. If we act properly—consistent with the values we share with the minister—we will find greater peace. There is in the sermonic message a dialectic of battle and peace that carries into the ongoing moments of life's decisions.

In Ellen Goodman's columns the two moments perform the sermonic pattern. Burke's title *Rhetoric of Motives* describes—in spirit if not the letter of intent—Ellen Goodman's rhetoric. Goodman's strategy we would call a rhetoric of de-bunking. Her sermons prepare us to alter our ongoing rhetorical encounters with life, to alter our motives, by her search *into* comparisons. She helps us to see the metaphors with which we perform these life rhetorics. Her glimpses of the earlier moments are to rob them of their power over us—to help us see the sinister in these motives that push us on our way and so to point the avenue for changing these values in our own lives.

In this way a conflict is joined, and conflicts—internal and social—are at the heart of our lessons. Another dimension of the search into comparisons, the image of good, evil, and action—of values—is at work here. To illustrate, we consider at length a single column: "They Pushed Credit; Now They Lecture."[23]

Analogies in this column are important. But our experience in using the column with college classes indicates clearly that the reader's first critical impulse is toward the conflict specifically implied in the third-person plural pronoun of the title which is used throughout. Take the first paragraph as illustrative: "They've dubbed it the Great Credit Crunch as though it were a new breakfast

---

[22]"How Far?"
[23]"They Pushed Credit, Now They Lecture," *Minneapolis Tribune*, 18 April 1980, p. 8A.

cereal. Like polished admen, they even insist that it will be good for our health, though a bit hard to digest." A question begs to be answered: Who are *they?* Although scarcely beyond quibble, the answer is not difficult: commercial money-lending institutions. Even more important and much more patent is that the structure of the column pits the "us" of the first three paragraphs (that becomes "we" transmuted to "your" in the fourth) against "them." Goodman uses deftly the familiar suggestion—not explicit, to be sure, but we think unmistakable—of "whoever is not with us is against us."

The analogy of the first paragraph is the key to her strategy in this column. "The Great Credit Crunch" suggests a breakfast cereal to Goodman and she presses the analogy to get at the essence of what has happened to credit:

> Well, I suppose the comparison isn't a bad one. After all, the same cereal companies that got our kids hooked on some sugar-coated floating bits of empty calories now market high fiber health cereals. The same people who got us used to the squishy white bread you could roll into a one inch ball are now guilt-tripping us back to bran.
>
> So, too, the people who gave us the credit munchies are now bringing us the Crunchies.
>
> A decade ago the banks started sending out credit cards we never asked for and extending credit lines that we never applied for. Stores stopped asking for money, except monthly. And money people started hard-selling credit.

Two other elements essential to the persuasion of the column appear in her working out of the analogy: the motif of drug addiction that runs throughout the column (the "got our kids hooked" of paragraph two becomes explicitly "credit junkies" in paragraph eleven) and guilt (by paragraph sixteen, she writes, "The friendly folk at the First and the Second and the Chase and the rest make us feel guilty for doing what they wanted").

The motif of addiction postures the distribution of responsibility: "they" exploit "us." Their street goods may seem inconsistent—going from "squishy white bread" to "back to bran" or from easy, cheap credit to tough, expensive credit, but beneath it all "they" consistently take advantage of "us." At the same time, we are asked to also chide ourselves—"of course, nobody tortured us until we bought on time." The socio-economic conflict has now become internal and the subject is guilt. What should the guilt lead to?

Preachers know about guilt; Goodman certainly does. And good preachers know that guilt is a powerful force; like powerful forces generally, it is open to exploiting. Goodman objects to the exploitation of guilt by the powerful manipulators. Her fundamental message comes down to this: Do not let yourself be their scapegoat. Goodman skewers the justification behind the effort to make "us" feel guilty. The "polished admen" switched us one way, and now they are switching us another:

> Now, the people who made a profit pushing the addiction are protecting their margins by marketing the cure. We are learning the true meaning of the American motto: Fly Now, Pay Later.
>
> Credit cards are being repossessed, credit lines are being redrawn and applications are being denied. Just when the demand for credit is highest, the supply is lowest.
>
> This is no surprise. When money-lending is profitable, they giveth; when it is not, they taketh away. That's money biz. But what is remarkable is the ease with which the same people who once extended credit are now extending lectures.

We are being told, with a slightly paternalistic nod, that we never should have overindulged. We are being sermonized on the evils of becoming borrowers by our former lenders, as well as leaders.

They are making use of our guilt. Goodman does not suggest that we are innocent, although she can be taken as sympathetic—less sinning than sinned against is an old phrase that would capture her attitude. She does suggest that we should not be *their* scapegoats.

To expiate the guilt arising from sin, we need someone to intercede to help us develop the assessment of guilt, the values to shape our actions, and the works to perform them. Traditionally, of course, the preacher plays such a role and the sermon traditionally clarifies our transgression to foster decent acts of expiation. "You can kick the habit," we tell the junkie, "but first you have to stand before us and declare that you want to." Asking forgiveness for one's sins carries with it acknowledgement of the devil and his ways. And a good preacher prepares us to encounter the devil in the world around us and to stand up to his/her attempts to control us. We leave with the sense of recognition of evil that assures us we do control our lives.

Our casting Goodman into the role of a preacher and the column on credit into a sermon invites a dramatistic perspective. We doubt that we used "all that is there to use," but we think that all that we have used is there.[24] It is there because the elements of our culture suffuse Goodman, just as they suffuse Burke and the rest of us. Goodman has tried to clarify and to exhort. We are culture-bound creatures, but our abilities to comprehend and to communicate make it possible for us to grow in a changing culture.

Conclusion

We have tried to show how the rhetorical comparisons in Ellen Goodman's works dynamically build meaning, or, to put the matter another way, how her rhetoric is epistemic. What we have tried to point out is not so much a new rhetoric as a fresh attitude toward rhetoric. In that fresh attitude, *meaning* is not taken as a thing, that is, something done and completed, but rather as something potential and therefore emergent, invoking an active role for an auditor. We believe that Burke's insight, reflected in his phrase "equipment for living," is just about right.

Our fascination with Ellen Goodman's artistry was our starting point and our final focus. Each time Ellen Goodman writes a column, she gives us a slice of life. The protagonists of her piece are normally everyperson facing one of the decisions of life. Sometimes it's Goodman herself, sometimes it's an anonymous friend, and sometimes it's the famous or near-famous who stand surrogate. These are not political decisions and only vaguely institutional. Instead Goodman's flock face very human decisions—Shall I commit myself to others? Am I responsible for my health? How shall I face death?

The world of Ellen Goodman's people is also essentially rhetorical. Their situation presents them with decisions which they make while seeking the advice of society around them. The conflict that shapes the decisions within is reflected in the conflict of rhetoric which surrounds them. Goodman enters the conflict in an

---

[24]Burke, p. 21.

advisory role, pointing toward her way of seeing our human problems. Her advice is seldom couched as directions let alone commands. Her column on credit comes down to saying, "Don't be had!" But she ends it in these words:

> It turns out that credit cards were the Frankenberries of our financial world, and now we are breaking our teeth on the crunch. We are left paying for the dental work while the sugar dealer huffs that we should have known better.
>
> The whole atmosphere reminds me suspiciously of my favorite line from my niece's school play last week: "We live by the Golden Rule. The one who has the gold makes the rule."[25]

Between the two paths that Kenneth Burke teaches us that we take in dealing with guilt—self-mortification and scapegoating—she is clearly the adversary of the second.

She plays her role in such a way as to add to the rich mosaic of proverbs, cultural mores, and the advice of others like her. She ministers to us to help us find our way through the perplexity of life. She warns us of the misdirection of much that we see and hear and advises us to look are our exigencies from a different perspective, a perspective that is regularly captured in some comparison. She talks about our situations not only to help us decide what to do in a given case, but also to warn us against the ways of her adversaries and to make us feel better about ourselves. Her sermonic rhetoric is guidance to us as we confront the moral decisions that define the ongoing experiences of our lives.

[25]"They Pushed Credit."

COMPUTER SCIENCE AS A RHETORIC

James W. Chesebro

The scientist has occupied a preeminent position within the world culture for almost four centuries. The concepts and data of the scientist have long been presented and perceived as the end product of a logical, precise, objective, and rigorously tested set of procedures. In contrast, the conceptions guiding other disciplines have been more readily viewed as governed by social objectives, if not particular biases and self-fulfilling intentions. Indeed, many of these "nonscientific" disciplines have formally defined their philosophical orientation as epistemic and they have held their task to be the exploration of the ways in which human beings cognitively conceive the reality they encounter. The scientist, on the other hand, has been cast as exploring and describing "what is." The traditional philosophical emphasis of science has thus been the investigation of the ontological in which the nature of physical phenomena are held to determine all concepts and data derived. The role and intentions of the scientist and the methods used by scientists are designed and perceived to secure this traditional ontological end.

Yet, the foundations of all sciences, from the physical to the social scientific, have been the subject of renewed critical examinations. The ontology-epistemology distinction (Krippendorff, 1984) has functioned as one of the central bases for this challenge. Essentially, the ontological foundation of science has been denied. Science is no longer universally believed to deal with the nature of reality and with what exists independently of its observation. Increasingly, science has been cast as but one of several epistemic systems. In this view, science—its procedures, data, and conclusions—are all ultimately cast as a human construction which function as only one of the ways in which human beings understand themselves. In this view, the knowledge generated by science is not a direct reflection of some "external reality," but rather the knowledge produced by science is intimately determined by the particular motives of the knower and the means by which the knowledge is acquired.

Particularly, all of the essential ontological features traditionally assigned to science have been challenged. The challenges have included both caustic and careful reconsiderations of the ideal and actual objectives of science (Goodall & Phillips, 1981), the role and perceptions of the scientists as impartial observer (Campbell, 1975), the concept of theory-free observation (O'Keefe, 1975), the meaningfulness of the scientific method as a hypothetico-deductive and operational system (Simons, 1978), the verification and falsification systems employed in science (Kelso, 1980), the nature of scientific discourse itself (Wander, 1976), the technologies of science (Miller, 1978), and the data derived from scientific experimentation (Phillips, 1976, 1981).

For many of these critics, the epistemic nature of science has led to the conclusion that science itself can be readily cast as a rhetoric—a powerful set of humanly created concepts and symbols which constitute a way of "talking" to others—which has gained respect and power because of its persuasive use of language, its strategies and tactics, and its appeals to human values. Arguing that

From *Information and Behavior*, vol. 1, edited by Brent D. Ruben (New Brunswick, N.J.: Transaction, Inc., 1985), 74–91. (Copyright © 1985 by Transaction Publishers.) Reprinted by permission of Transaction Publishers.

"science" is "strikingly rhetorical in nature," Campbell (1975, p. 391) has confidently noted that "The argument that scientific discourse is rhetorical in nature is easy enough to make, for the materials for that argument have been provided by rhetoricians, philosophers, scientists, and literary critics." Adopting a similar tone, Kelso (1980, p. 17) has concluded that "the paradigms of science are not undistorted reflections of reality, but humanly invented representations of reality which have been embellished rhetorically to the point where, at least for the moment, they appear to be canonical." Phillips (1981, p. 363) has likewise argued that the "acceptance of scientific findings is a matter of social consent. [Scientific] proofs are not made because of the discovery of information. They are based on a process of making information appear reasonable to others."

This skeptical view of science is by no means new. Some 2,500 years ago, the Sophists posited that the only "truth" which existed was created by human beings (Jebb, 1893; Kennedy, 1963). In more contemporary writings, the skeptical view of science may be traced to a host of conceptions. Positing a prehistorical origin—if not an implicit genetic one—Russell (1945, p. 34) has argued that "most sciences, at their inception, have been connected with some form of false belief, which gave them a fictitious value. Astronomy was connected with astrology, chemistry with alchemy." These originating "false beliefs" may have established expectations which no science could realize. Moreover, as logical positivism lost favor as a scientific philosophy (Suppe, 1974), it has become less clear that scientific enterprises can ever generate data by theory-free observation (O'Keefe, 1975). Indeed, Kuhn (1962) has suggested that scientific conceptions of reality are grounded in imaginary conceptions within the mind of the observer, and therefore are subject to revolutionary change as popular conceptions change. In this vein, Burke (1965, pp. 220–224) has argued that there is a "mystic" ingredient in all of "the modern sciences of statistics." More recent critics have asked if "scientists" might not ultimately be "rhetors in disguise" (Simons, 1980), while others have blatantly charged that scientists employ an "immoral rhetoric" (Weigert, 1970) while operating under a cloak or "rhetoric of academic respectability" (Czubaroff, 1973).

Status of Computer Science

This "rhetoric of science debate" provides a context for this examination of computer science. The self-identifying association with science in the label "computer science" is perhaps the most vivid indication that computer specialists have cast themselves as scientists. This self-imposed self-definition certainly seems to suggest that computer specialists operate under a rather publically self-proclaimed link with science. McCorduck (1979, p. 28), for example, casts computer science as a "science," in which specialists are "studying their phenomena in the same way that physicists study matter." Similarly, Berleur (1978, p. 269) argues that, "Computer science is an offshoot of mathematics and is developing in direct relation to the latter. The role of mathematics in the development of computer science is comparable to that of physics with respect to energetics."

However, even these advocates of computer science as a science admit that yet another interpretation of computer science may be possible. Berleur, for example, explores the possibility that computer science is devoid of content and ultimately functions only as the study of information processing techniques. As he puts it, "In defining the content of computer science, one should not make the mistake of including everything which has to do with information. Computer science encompasses solely those problems that are related to automatic processing of information, more particularly by means of computer" (p. 270). In this context, McCorduck (1979) notes that, "there's still a controversy over whether computer science is a justifiable term" (p. 28).

The issue controlling this analysis can initially be framed in either of two ways. To what degree is computer science solely a science? or, second, To what degree is computer science a solely human created social agreement or contract emerging from, and designed to satisfy and respond to, human needs and motives? As developed here, the more substantive question focuses upon the essential nature of computer science as a discipline. The thesis developed here is that computer science is the study and application of the construction of language systems which create and sustain mutually functional interactions for human beings and computers. In this context, computer science is conceived as the study of information processing, not the study of any particular information content. Its objective, procedures, and outcomes are best understood as a form of information formatting, not unlike the specialized concerns of many in other media industries. In practice, the primary objective of computer science is to generate languages, languages which function as the means by which human ideals and various physical systems are unified.

Ultimately, computer science is more of a rhetoric than a science. In the context of the "rhetoric of science" debate, four dimensions are embedded in this conception of computer science. First, its end is decidedly determined by human needs. Computer science is designed to create interactional constructions which satisfy human needs, human motivations, and human objectives. Computer science generates the parameters required to facilitate social-mechanical or human-computer interactions. Second, as a theoretical discipline, computer science coordinates meaning systems between signal (computer) and symbolic (human) information systems. Third, in terms of its methods, computer science is pragmatic. Computer science is an instrumental study intended to facilitate and to satisfy human objectives and needs. Fourth, as a process, computer science creates and facilitates interactions between computers and human beings.

In dealing with this issue, a three-fold analysis is developed here. First, the physical basis of computer science is identified, with particular attention given to the point at which humanly created and socially shared conceptions begin to redefine the object of study of computer science. Second, the procedural basis of computer science is cast as specifically devoted to the creative, social, and humanly motivated conventions which govern the ways in which mathematics are employed. Third, the languages of computer specialists are examined on two levels. On the first and most obvious of these two levels—in its use of public and social explanatory and pedagogical rhetoric—representative metaphors of the rhetoric of computer science are identified. These metaphors create the image of computer science as a discrete and technologically powerful science. On the second and less obvious level, the languages created by computer science itself are examined. These creative and generative languages constitute a collective medium which defines the essential epistemic base of computer science as a logical-mathematical method of knowing. As this analysis unfolds, it should become clear that this three-fold analysis is employed not to debunk computer science for its failure to adhere to ideal scientific standards, but rather to identify and to reveal the sources of misunderstandings in computer-human communication in order to improve this relationship.

Several scientific bases for computer science can be identified. Phenomenally, its base is the activity and control of the electron. Procedurally, it is a discipline concerned with clear rules of procedure and inference, modeled, as Berleur notes, after mathematics. The final outcome of the phenomenal and procedural foundations of computer science is discourse, discourse designed to justify the discipline of computer science, but also the creation of new discourses which facilitate computer-human interactions. The substantive base, formal procedures, and outcomes of computer science are appropriately explored as defining features of computer science. The phenomenal basis of computer science is our first concern.

The Phenomenal Basis of Computer Science

A computer manipulates and stores electrons on a silicon chip. The presence or absence of an electron at any particular location on a chip is the technological foundation for the contemporary computer. These patterns of electrons and the control of these patterns are a central scientific foundation of computer science (Angell, Terry & Barth, 1983).

Yet, the interpretive function of the human being enters at this juncture, shifting computer science from a scientific to a social experience. People use certain analogies which give the presence or absence of electrons meaning as a communication system. For example, a light switch analogy has been employed. The presence or absence of an electron has thus been equated to the "on/off" actions possible when "communicating" with a computer. Similarly, the human vocal response of either "yes" or "no" has also been used as an analogy. In this view, the existence of an electron at a particular location on a computer chip signifies a "yes" while its absence signifies a "no."

Yet, all of these "descriptions" of the electron are not intrinsic to, or part of, the electron itself; the foundation for the analogies is not a physical or constitutive feature. These "descriptions" are figurative, not literal, analogies (Deken, 1982, pp. 45–59). Phenomenally, if an electron is present, its charge is there—it cannot be turned "on" or "off"; an absent electron is simply nonexistent—it is not "off." Likewise, an electron's presence in no way simulates the variety of ways the "yes" and "no" statements are employed by people. In order for electrons to possess such communicative messages, human beings impose these analogies upon the electrons. The imposition is arbitrary and conventional. In other words, the presence or absence of a pattern of electrons has social meaning only because human beings agree that these meanings exist in terms of an electron and that these meanings will have certain social or human interpretations and not others. The basic unit of computer communication is thus a human creation, not a communicative need or purpose found "naturally" within the machine itself.

The Procedural Basis of Computer Science

Computer science has also been perceived as a science by the virtue of its consistent use of clear rules of procedure and inference. In this sense, the use of

the scientific method has been employed as an essential definitional foundation
for the discipline of computer science. Specifically, as Berleur (1978, p. 269)
has argued, the methods of mathematics have been cast as the governing procedural principles controlling computer science.

As a self-proclaimed application of mathematics, the procedures of computer
science are subject to, and appropriately understood as governed by, the theoretical foundations of mathematics. Accordingly, insofar as computer science is
viewed as a form of mathematical information processing, its theoretical base is
directly tied to developments in mathematics.

Since the late nineteenth century, the theoretical base of mathematics has been
under constant re-examination. As mathematician Michael Guillen (1983) reports, by "the late 1800s," the role of the mathematicians-as-scientists began to
lose credibility:

> Hitherto, mathematicians had believed in the limitless and infallible capacity of
> mathematics to define the truth logically. The shortcomings discovered have ulti-
> mately served to evidence the humanness of mathematics by revealing not only its
> fallibilities but also the persistence and optimism with which modern mathemati-
> cians are struggling to overcome the limitations. (p. 3)

An even more critical view of mathematics was provided in Russell's (1919)
Introduction to Mathematical Philosophy. Indeed, by the early 1930s, Sir Arthur
Eddington's relativistic conception of mathematics began to gain prominence. In
The Nature of the Physical World (1928), Eddington had argued that physics
provided only one symbolic representation of the world and nothing more. Correspondingly, argued Eddington, mathematics could not readily justify itself as a
science which examined absolutes. In these views, measurement no longer functioned as the central objective of mathematics, nor could the symbols of mathematics be viewed as signs which were somehow directly reflective of physical
entities. Eddington had suggested that the theoretical base of mathematics was
relativistic. Indeed, the new quantum physics, which assumed that certain phenomena were absolutely undetermined, supported such a conception.

Pure or abstract mathematics was ultimately to gain independent recognition
and power in 1932 when the positron was discovered based upon the predictions
of Dirac's abstract mathematical theory. Similarly, the development and usefulness of negative, imaginary, and irrational numbers underscored the potential
power of abstract mathematics. Yet, the assumptions of abstract mathematics
were shocking, for the underlying principles of abstract mathematics essentially
held that not every mathematical statement could be proved or disproved (completeness), or would always yield the same results if valid procedures of proof
were followed (consistency), and that methods did not always exist to determine
the truth of all mathematical problems (decidability). In essence, these assumptions suggested that a finite set of procedures could not exhaust mathematics if
mathematics was perceived as a infinite set of symbols. As Hodges (1983, pp.
80–81) has so aptly noted, the "developments in many branches of mathematics
towards an *abstract* point of view" meant that "mathematical symbols became
less and less obligated to correspond directly with physical entities," and that
algebra could be "liberated" from the "traditional sphere of counting and measurement." In Hodges' view, "The effect of abstraction had been to generalize,
to unify, and to draw new analogies. It had been a creative and constructive
movement, for by changing the rules of these abstract systems, new kinds of
algebra with unforeseen applications had been invented."

The development of abstract mathematics directly affected computer science as we know it today. Indeed, as Hodges (1983, pp. 79–110) argues, abstract mathematics directly influenced and functioned as the foundation for Alan Turing's (1937) conception and design of computable numbers which made it possible to conceive of a single calculating machine performing the equivalent of human mental activity. Thus, rather than emerging from a closed, consistent, and absolute system of knowing, the contemporary computer is a product of an undeniably relativistic knowledge-based system.

While clearly useful in a host of ways, the mathematical foundations of computer science do not reside solely in complete, consistent, and decidable rules of procedure. Rather, the function of mathematics is to create relationships among the abstract and the physical or the ideal and the real (Hodges, 1983, p. 86). The mathematical system which gave rise to computer science was thus a predominantly human, creative, and constructive symbol system which sought to provide unity between an ever-changing physical reality and an ever-changing set of abstractions designed to satisfy decidedly social ends. The mathematician-as-scientist has accordingly given way to the image of the mathematician-as-artist. Guillen (1983) notes:

> Unlike scientists, who observe nature with all five senses, mathematicians observe nature with the sense of imagination almost exclusively. That is, mathematicians are as specialized, and therefore as well practiced, with this sixth sense [of imagination] as musicians are with sounds, gourmets are with tastes and smells, and photographers and filmmakers are with sights. This comparison also suggests that mathematicians are artists of the imagination just as surely as musicians, gourmets, photographers, and filmmakers are of their respective sensory domains. Through their unique creations, mathematicians inform us about reality without the intent, or ability, to actually prove that something does or does not exist. (p. 5)

In a similar fashion, Jones (1982) now casts the descriptions of physics as a "metaphor" of reality. In this sense, the original sciences which gave rise to the scientific procedures of computer science have for some time recognized a creative human motive or symbolic and rhetorical feature in the conceptions and procedures of science.

On balance, then, one must admit that a scientific feature permeates the discourse of computer scientists. At the same time, the core of computer scientific procedure is not predominantly substantive or phenomenal. Computer science is the study of information processing, not the study of any particular information content. Moreover, the procedural foundation of computer science—mathematics—functions as an extension of human creativity. In this sense, computer science is more of a rhetoric than it is a science. Accordingly, it is appropriate to identify the various ways in which computer scientists have conceived of computer systems. The process, in my view, reflects nothing less than an attempt to create complete language systems, language systems by which human beings might interact with machines in a host of diverse and fascinating ways.

The Discourses of Computer Science

The discourse of computer science operates on two levels. On one level, its discourse is public, explanatory, and pedagogical. This is the rhetoric which adjusts computer science as a discipline to the rest of society and society to the objectives of computer specialists. On a second level, the discourse of computer science is creative and generative. Computer science has created and produced a host of computer languages which determine not only how humans and computers will interact, but which specifically reveal the essential knowledge base of computer science. The public language of computer science will be our first concern.

The Explanatory Language of Computer Science   The observations of several computer reviewers and critics provide an initial indication of some of the factors currently controlling the interactions between humans and computers. These rather pointed reactions have ranged from the belief that computer specialists intentionally employ conspiratorial language to outright nonsense. Friedrich (1983, p. 39) argues, for example, "they [computer scientists] like even more to give new things names that are as mystifying to an outsider as the secret password of an esoteric cult." More explicitly, Crawford (1983, p. 153) believes that, "much of the jargon of programming and computers exists only to intimidate and exclude nontechnical people." *New York Times* computer critic, Erik Sandberg-Diment, has concluded that the discourse of computer specialists constitutes nothing less than "computerese" (1982, p. C6) and "technobabble" (1983, p. C4). He specifically observes that the computer industry is one in which "describing the use of an on-off switch may take six pages or six words, either version rarely making sense to anyone but an engineer, who understands it all by osmosis" (1983, p. C4).

Moreover, acronyms dominate the language of computer science. An acronym is a word formed from the initial letter or letters of an entire series of words. While intended to be mnemonic, the number of such acronyms so permeates the discourse of computer scientists that the original meaning of the acronyms has frequently been lost: computer dictionaries now exist to provide translations of these diverse acronyms (Consumer Guide, 1983; Meadows, Gordon & Singleton, 1983). However, even the selection of a computer manual can be a complicated issue. In a recent issue of *Popular Computing,* for example, Weal (1983) provides nine standards which should be employed when selecting such a manual. In addition, many of the computer science terms now employed as substitutes for more common everyday concepts seem to produce more confusion than clarity. There seems to be, for example, no reason why the word *documentation* (which, for most people, carries a sense of verifying) must be used as a substitute for the more commonly understood word *instructions.* Certainly such language usage is problematic for someone new to computers.

As such critical reviews suggest, a good deal of the current confusion about computers stems from the language employed by computer scientists and computer specialists. At the same time, a detailed and comprehensive survey and analysis of all of the stylistic choices, language usages, and rhetorical features of computer science is simply too ambitious a task for us to undertake here. Nonetheless, it is appropriate to identify at least a few of the features of the rhetoric of computer science which generate a fear of computers as well as prevent people from understanding both the purposes and functions of computers. While we recognize that we can only illustrate or provide some major examples of these tendencies toward miscommunication here, we hope that these illustrations will forewarn users, thereby preparing them to understand the rhetoric they are very likely to encounter. These examples may also offer computer scientists and computer specialists guidelines for reassessing their own rhetorical choices.

While computer science terminology is a very rich and detailed language system, at least three major metaphors are used repeatedly in the language of computer scientists in their textbooks, articles, scholarly papers, and in the manuals which accompany computers. Each of these three "controlling" or archetypal metaphors deserves special attention.

First, computer scientists employ a *print metaphor* to talk about computers. In a sense, computer scientists have borrowed from the technical vocabulary of other disciplines to explain a new technology. We can sympathize with such an effort: often it is possible to explain a new experience by drawing parallels to experiences already understood. In the case of computer science, electronic computers are talked about as if they were books or part of the publishing industry. Thus, for example, terminologies such as "file," "print," "print file," "save file," "edit," "recover edit," and "read" are the most frequently used commands for instructing a computer, while other terms such as "file processing" and "word processing" suggest that paper manipulations are occurring. For those outside of computer science, this print metaphor confuses, for none of the physical features of print or paper manipulation are actually used when dealing with computers.

Second, computer scientists employ a *scientific metaphor* to talk about computers. The manuals which accompany new computer components use a jargon of mathematics, electronics, and generally specialized languages when offering instructions on the use of new equipment. Consider, for example, this instruction found in one of the most popular manuals:

Connect the end of the second external drive's cable into the adapter board of the first external drive's cable although all but the last disk drive (if you are using more than one drive) should have their termination packs removed, although the drive farthest from the controller should be the one that is not modified. *Note:* It may be necessary to rotate the adapter board in order to insert it. It goes in easily if you have it positioned correctly. (Texas Instruments, 1982, p. 7)

Such instructions do not reflect the fact that the personal computer must become part of the everyday environment of the computer owner and should therefore be described in terms which reflect the place of the computer in this personal, everyday reality. Accordingly, this scientific metaphor does not clarify; it creates confusion.

Third, computer scientists employ a *passivity metaphor.* In using such a metaphor, the computer operator is implicitly told that she or he must conform to the requirements of the computer. While the ideal computer is "user friendly," the term "user" itself creates the image of someone who functions in a less than creative role. *Webster's* (1981, p. 1279), for example, defines a user as "one who consumes, expends, or takes." When combined with the fact that people new to the world of computers are "computer illiterate," a negative self-image can easily emerge for a new operator of a personal computer. Quite unconsciously, the "user" might easily experience the following kind of mental speech:

I use a computer—I don't create it, design it, or change it. I'm not the computer creator. I'm not the computer designer. I'm not the computer innovator. Of all of these active roles, I am only the recipient of the final product—I am only the user.

For those new to the world of computers, computer scientists do seem to exist in an enclave, in a world apart from others. If not a "member of this club," the closest affiliated membership that can be achieved is that of "user." Indeed, Friedrich (1983) reports that computer "hackers" refer to "anyone who simply employs a computer for some practical purpose and then shuts it off . . . derisively . . . as a 'user'" In fact, Crawford (1983, p. 153) has argued that "much of the jargon of programming and computers exists only to intimidate and exclude nontechnical people." Only within the last few years have a few people had the courage to suggest that the products of computer science create flagrantly powerful social issues potentially affecting the lifestyles of all citizens (Evans, 1979).

These irregular computer language choices are mere symptoms of a much more profound set of issues which stem from the inherent nature of any effort to develop a language equally useable by both humans and computers. While humans and computers do share common characteristics from an informational perspective, human beings and computers are structurally discrete entities. The attempt to create a link between the two classes of entities must necessarily be incomplete. The type of language structure necessary for a machine to process information differs in kind from the symbolizing processing which characterizes human communication. Accordingly, the language built into a computer must necessarily be a compromise between two different kinds of processing systems.

The Language of Computer Science as Epistemic   Computer specialists have created literally hundreds of languages designed to facilitate the human use of computer systems. Cole (1983, p. 82) reports that some "200 or more distinct computer languages" now exist. Each of these languages are designed to deal with specific kinds of information issues. Several examples illustrate the diverse uses of these languages. Combining mathematical and English conventions developed in 1956, FORTRAN (FORmula TRANslator) was initially developed for solving problems in mathematics, engineering, and science. It has more recently made its way into business, education, graphic generation industries, database management, and word-processing. Designed to satisfy other needs, specifically in business and commercial applications, COBOL (COmmon Business-Oriented Language) was developed in 1960 to provide easily learned natural words and phrases for extensive input and output report generation. Also developed in 1960, LISP (LISt Processor) is a list-processing language particularly well-suited for the manipulation of non-numeric data by artificial intelligence specialists. In contrast, BASIC (Beginner's All-Purpose Symbolic Instruction Code) was designed for nontechnical uses of computers; it is easily learned, provides immediate terminal screen responses to user input, and is inexpensive to implement and use. It functioned for several years as the dominant language built into home computers. Yet, these diverse languages only illustrate but a few of the languages developed by computer specialists. A more complete survey of computer languages might include a discussion of ALGOL, PL/I, APL, Pascal, Smalltalk, PILOT, C, FORTH, and so forth.

While diverse in number and function, computer languages share certain structural or formatting characteristics which ultimately provide a basis for describing the kind of knowledge system which these languages generate. Virtually all computer languages can be placed along five continua which reveal the essential features of computer languages as a genre. While initially described in the terminologies of the computer specialist (to reveal the essential nature of computer languages) these five continua deserve our attention.

Every computer language can be described in terms of five dimensions. First, computer languages exist along one continuum from low to high abstraction. Low level abstract computer languages allow an extensively trained programmer to manipulate the morphological, phonological, syntactical, and semantic rules of the language system. High level abstract computer languages are particularly "user friendly," making few demands upon the user's programming skills, and functioning as more prescriptive and directive systems which deal with specific problems.

Second, computer languages exist along a continuum from the highly specific to a more general system. Highly specific computer language systems are intentionally narrow and inflexible in terms of the range of computation functions which can be carried out, but this specialization also allows the language to function more powerfully (with greater speed and efficiency) within its specified area. In contrast, general computer languages are extraordinarily flexible and, ultimately, their uses far exceed the concrete plans of their designers.

Third, computer languages exist along a continuum from the highly procedural to a more problem-solving orientation. Intended to function independently of any particular user, high procedural computer languages require that specific sets of operations be used in a particular sequence to achieve certain ends. In contrast, the open-ended and heuristic approach of the problem-oriented computer language specifies what is to be accomplished without specifying the steps taken to solve the problem.

Fourth, computer languages may exist along a continuum from the ephemeral to the enduring. Ephemeral computer language systems provide immediate responses and social utility, introduce few abstractions or intermediate processing stages, and are likely to be readily understood by a general public with little or no prior exposure to computers. Enduring computer language systems provide extensive reformatting of inputted data, may manipulate data according to a host of abstract processing standards, and are ultimately designed for highly detailed and complex issues where the final outcome may be unknown to the computer user.

Fifth, computer languages may exist along a continuum from the highly structured to the unstructured. Highly structured computer languages provide explicit lines of argument and procedure, influences which are directly testable at each stage in the analysis, and in which progress can only be made if all premises leading to a conclusion can be substantiated. In contrast, unstructured computer languages may often conceal their points of origin from the user, frequently allow a user to merge diverse conclusions from logically unrelated stages in a program, and suppress the explicitness of the logical structure of the program.

These five defining dimensions of computer languages highlight the logical and mathematical nature of all computer languages. The dimensions characterizing computer languages deal with order and sequencing, reordering, quantity, scope, procedures, the explicitness of ordering and procedures, and the legitimacy of inference decisions. Each computer language requires varying degrees of skill to manipulate the language rules of the system, possesses a predetermined and clearly specified field of potential action or area of application, is capable of varying degrees of problem-solution applications, engages in varying degrees of data transformations, and provides the user with varying degrees of explicitness regarding its procedural steps. In Howard Gardner's framework, such skills characterize one type of intelligence, "logical-mathematical intelligence" (Gardner, 1983, pp. 136–44). For Gardner, the mathematician symbolizes this form of intelligence, and it seems more than appropriate to note that Gardner views computer specialist John von Neumann as one of "the greatest mathematicians of the previous generation" (p. 142). Yet, Gardner holds that logical-mathematical intelligence is but one of seven kinds of intelligence. It is ultimately only one way of knowing or one epistemic system. In contrast to the other forms of intelligence—linguistic, musical, spatial, bodily-kinesthetic, intrapersonal, and interpersonal—logical-mathematical intelligence highlights are explicit methods of problem solving as a standard for understanding or knowing Gardner characterizes this skill in this fashion:

> From students of mathematical problem solving, like George Polya, Herbert Simon, and Allen Newell, one picks up pointers. Mathematicians are advised to generalize—to proceed from the given set of objectives in a problem to a larger set which contains the given one. Conversely, mathematicians are also advised to specialize, to pass from a given set of objects to a smaller set, itself contained in the given one; to ferret out analogies, thereby finding a problem or a situation that bears instructive similarities (and differences) from the one under consideration.
>
> Other procedures are frequently mentioned. Faced with a problem too complex or unwieldly to save, the mathematician is counseled to find a simpler problem within the larger one, to seek a solution to the simpler component, and then to build upon that solution. The student is also advised to propose a possible solution and to work backward to the problem; or to describe the characteristics that a solution should have and then, in turn, try to attain each of them. Another popular method is indirect proof: one assumes the opposite of what one is trying to prove and ascertains the consequences of that assumption. More specific heuristics exist—and are drawn upon—within particular areas of mathematics. Clearly, since the most interesting problems are difficult to solve, the mathematician who can draw upon these heuristics appropriately and shrewdly is at a decided advantage. Perhaps the ability to learn and to deploy such heuristics—to supplement purely logical considerations with a sense of what might work—helps define the "zone of proximal development" in the aspiring mathematician. (p. 144)

I have thus used the computer languages created by computer specialists as the most powerful and direct indication of the epistemic framework of the discipline of computer science. These computer languages are first and foremost logical and mathematical constructions. While important in their own right, they are also highly selective constructions. As such, they reflect a highly specialized and highly incomplete kind of knowledge generated by computer science. These computer languages deflect attention from equally important knowledge systems such as spatial (the ability to detect relationships within an environment), musical (the ability to perceive pitch and rhythmic patterns), bodily-kinesthetic (such as the fine motor skills as one might see in a surgeon or a dancer), interpersonal (understanding how others feel, what motivates them, and how they interact with others), and intrapersonal (the development of a sense of identity) intelligences. In this sense, because it is profoundly logical and mathematical, computer science constitutes an incomplete way of knowing. It can tell us only about one epistemic feature which human beings employ to enact the reality in which they live. Computer scientists have celebrated in one feature of human intelligence; it is less clear that this commitment to logic and mathematics has any corresponding dimension in reality. The ontological stance of computer science remains unclear, and may indeed be an illusion of computer specialists. To emphasize the ontological status of computer science is a rhetorical act, an extension and use of the symbols of computer science to convince others of its own universality, power, and significance. At the same time, insofar as this mode of understanding is treated as a decisive or controlling framework, a rhetorical juncture is reached, for an incomplete view of reality is being cast, treated, and persuasively argued for as a central, decisive, controlling, or complete conception of what is known.

Our specializations reveal our special and unique skills, but these same specializations reveal our limits. Nonetheless, we must act upon a complex and diverse world with the specialized skills that we do possess. Such actions necessarily constitute an act of faith, in which we persuade ourselves and others that we can effectively deal with the totality of reality, even when we possess but limited and restricted skills for acting effectively. In the last analysis, our decision to specialize constitutes a profound commitment to the universal effectiveness of a limited set of symbols in a world which requires far more than one set of symbols and skills. We compensate for these limitations by imaginatively and metaphorically employing our symbols in fields of action where these symbols were never intended to function. In essence, then, we all function—computer specialists included—as rhetoricians, believing in the creative, universal, and corrective use of the symbols we are best able to master.

Conclusion

One of the tremendous breakthroughs of the twentieth century has been the creation of a mode of communication which links—albeit in a complex and partial fashion—human beings and machines. Ultimately, the contribution of computer science resides not in the creation of calculating machines, but in the creation of a signal system which human beings can employ to regulate a machine for useful ends. Computer scientists function not only as scientists and technicians, but predominantly as language creators, designing and promoting a mode of communication. Accordingly, both the potentialities and the limitations of this language or rhetorical system must be recognized. This system must be continually assessed and continually adapted to the human user, a condition which applies to all language and rhetorical systems. Ideally, a truly "user friendly" computer language would eliminate the user's need to adapt in any way to the signal system of the computer. While such extreme "friendliness" is an unattainable standard, nonetheless, if the critics are to be given at least minimum credibility, computer scientists and computer specialists have a long way to go in the direction of achieving more nearly "user friendly" computer-human systems.

References

Angell, J. B., Terry, S. C., & Barth, P. W. (1983, April). Silicon micromechanical devices. *Scientific American, 248.* pp. 48–55.

Berleur, J. (1978). Computer science, computers and education. *Impact of Science on Society, 28.* 269–74.

Burke, K. (1965). *Permanence and change: An anatomy of purpose.* Indianapolis, IN: Bobbs-Merrill. Original work published 1935.

Campbell, P. N. (1975). The *personae* of scientific discourse. *Quarterly Journal of Speech*, *61*. 391–405.

Cole, B. (1983, September). The family tree of computer languages. *Popular Computing*, *2*. pp. 82–88.

Consumer Guide. (1983). *Illustrated computer dictionary*. New York: Exeter Books.

Crawford, C. (1983, September). A great way to sharpen your thinking: Why you should learn to program. *Popular Computing*, *2*. pp. 153–56.

Czubaroff, J. (1973). Intellectual respectability: A rhetorical problem. *Quarterly Journal of Speech*, *59*. 155–64.

Deken, J. (1982). *The electronic cottage: Everyday living with your personal computer in the 1980s*. New York: William Morrow.

Eddington, A. (1928). *The nature of the physical world* (1933 ed.). New York: The Macmillan Company.

Evans, C. (1979). *The micro millennium*. New York: Viking.

Friedrich, O. (1983, January 3). Glork! a glossary for gweeps. *Time*, *121*. p. 39.

Gardner, H. (1983). *Frames of mind: The theory of multiple intelligences*. New York: Basic Books. Also, see The seven frames of mind. (1984, June). *Psychology Today*, *18*. pp. 21–24, 26.

Goodall, H. L. & Phillips, G. M. (1981). Assumption of the burden: Science or criticism. *Communication Quarterly*, *294*. 283–96.

Grossberg, L. & O'Keefe, D. J. (1975). Presuppositions, conceptual foundations, and communication theory: On Hawes' approach to communication. *Quarterly Journal of Speech*, *61*. 195–208.

Guillen, M. (1983). *Brides to infinity: The human side of mathematics*. Los Angeles, CA/ Boston, MA: J.P. Tarcher/Houghton Mifflin.

Hodges, A. (1982). *Alan Turing: The enigma*. New York: Simon and Schuster. Jebb, R. (1893). *The attic orators*. London: Macmillan.

Jones, R. S. (1982). *Physics as metaphor*. New York: New American Library.

Kelso, J. A. (1980). Science and the rhetoric of reality. *Central States Speech Journal*, *31*. 17–29.

Kennedy, G. (1963). *The art of persuasion in Greece*. Princeton, NJ: Princeton University Press.

Kripendorff, K. (1984). An epistemological foundation for communication. *Journal of Communication*, *343*. 21–36.

Kuhn, T. S. (1962). *The structure of scientific revolutions*. Chicago, IL: University of Chicago Press.

McCorduck, P. (1979). *Machines who think: A personal inquiry into the history and prospects of artificial intelligence*. San Francisco, CA: W. H. Freeman.

Meadows, A. J., Gordon, M. & Singleton, A. (1983). *The Random House dictionary of new information technology*. New York: Vintage.

Miller, C. R. (1978). Technology as a form of consciousness: A study of contemporary ethos. *Central States Speech Journal*, *29*. 228–36.

O'Keefe, D. J. (1975). Logical empiricism and the study of human communication. *Speech Monographs*, *42*. 169–83.

Phillips, G. M. (1976). Rhetoric and its alternatives as bases for examination of intimate communication. *Communication Quarterly*, *24*. 11–23.

Phillips, G. M. (1981). Science and the study of human communication: An inquiry from the other side of the two cultures. *Human Communication Research*, *7*. 361–70.

Russell, B. (1919). *Introduction to mathematical philosophy*. New York: Macmillan.

Russell, B. (1945). *A history of Western philosophy* (1964 ed.). New York: Simon and Schuster.

Sandberg-Diment, E. (1982, November 16). Primers—in old-fashioned print. *New York Times*, p. C6.

Sandberg-Diment, E. (1983, July 5). Software on a disk acts as a guide to the I.B.M. *New York Times*, p. C4.

Sandberg-Diment, E. (1983, September 13). Hacking the English language to bits and bytes. *New York Times*. p. C4.

Simons, H. W. (1978). The rhetoric of science and the science of rhetoric. *Western Journal of Speech Communication*, *42*. 37–43.

Simons, H. W. (1980). Are scientists rhetors in disguise? An analysis of discursive processes in scientific communities. In E. E. White (Ed.), *Rhetoric in transition: Studies in the nature and uses of rhetoric* (pp. 115–30). University Park, PA: The Pennsylvania State University Press.

Suppe, F. (1974). The search for philosophic understanding of scientific theories. In F. Suppe (Ed.), *The structure of scientific theories* (pp. 119–62). Urbana, IL: University of Illinois Press.

Texas Instruments Incorporated. (1982). *Disk memory drive.* Lubbock, TX: Texas Instruments Incorporated.

Turing, A. M. (1937). On computable numbers, with an application to Entscheidungsproblem. *Procedures of the London Mathematical Society, 42.* 230–65. Also, see Turing A. M. (1937). Correction. *Proceedings of the London Mathematical Society, 43.* 544–46.

Wander, P. C. (1976). The rhetoric of science. *Western Journal of Speech Communication, 40.* 226–31.

Weal, E. (1983). Does the manual measure up? *Popular Computing, 2* (9), pp. 168–69.

Webster's new collegiate dictionary. (1981). Springfield, MA: G. & C. Merriam Company.

Weigert, A. (1970). The immoral rhetoric of scientific sociology. *American Sociologist, 5* 111–19

4

THE DRAMATURGICAL PERSPECTIVE

In the late 1950s and into the 1960s the academic fields of speech communication and English, and even sociology, political science, and history were astir with talk of a "New Rhetoric." L. H. Mouat, responding to the "confusion and disagreement among rhetorical critics" and attempting to reduce such confusion for future critics, called for "a *single* set of principles" to evaluate the new rhetoric (emphasis in original).[1] Then in writing about the increasing tempo of activity, Martin Steinmann, Jr., remarked, "I say 'new rhetorics' rather than a 'a new rhetoric' because modern concepts of rhetoric are so diverse that a family of new disciplines rather than a single one seems to be evolving."[2] In the first two editions of this book, we joined Steinmann and others in stressing the plural and used the term "new rhetorics" to label a second direction in the breakdown of faith from the tradition perspective, different from the experiential perspective.

Both the experiential and New Rhetorics perspectives shared a rejection of the speaker orientation of the traditional perspective, but the "New Rhetorics" perspective also rejected the experiential focus on the critic. The "new" rhetoricians, like the traditional, followed Mouat's call for "a single set of principles" and looked toward a unified theory to shape their criticism, but their faith tended to be in a non-Aristotelian system. Some of these critics seemed to harbor the hope that their particular embryonic theory would grow to be a new paradigm for criticism, but at this point there is little evidence to suggest that any single theory will equal the acceptance or uniformity of Aristotelianism in traditional rhetorical criticism.

As we have indicated, prior to the rather clear breakdown of the neo-Aristotelian paradigm in the 1960s, some advocates not only registered their dissatisfaction with traditional theory and criticism but attempted to establish new systems that would be more compatible with contemporary views of the people and reality. Alfred Korzybski, author of *Science and Sanity*, provided one source of impetus.[3] A few critics drew from Korzybski for their critical method; they were also influenced by his disciples in the general semantics movement—such persons as Irving Lee, Wendell Johnson, S. I. Hayakawa, Anatole Rapoport, and Stuart Chase. The General Semanticists shared the belief that traditional rhetoric was prescientific and elementistic and, as a result, was the source of many problems, including mental ones.

Another writer who rejected the traditional perspective prior to the 1960s was Kenneth Burke. Initially labelled "dramatism," Burke's rhetorical philosophy evolved from literary into social criticism, with markedly sociopsychological overtones. His treatment of Aristotelian rhetoric differed from the General Semanticists', for he essentially extended the range of the Aristotelian philosophy

[1]"An Approach to Rhetorical Criticism," in *The Rhetorical Idiom*, ed, Donald C. Bryant (New York: Russell & Russell, 1966), 165.

[2]*New Rhetorics* (New York: Scribner's, 1967), iii.

[3]*Science and Sanity* (Lakewood, CT: Institute of General Semantics, 1933).

and reconceived the purpose of rhetorical criticism. Burke's rhetoric was introduced into the field of speech communication by Marie Hochmuth Nicholas in a 1952 *Quarterly Journal of Speech* essay.[4] Her essay was soon followed in the same journal by articles by Burke himself entitled "A Dramatistic View of the Origins of Language" (in three parts) and "Postscripts on the Negative."[5] With these examples before them, critics in the field of speech communication began to use a Burkeian vocabulary. Unfortunately, critics often used it mechanically, content with affixing the labels as broad descriptors, ignoring, for example, the interaction of Burkeian "ratios" or the subtle incisiveness of his well-known criticism of *Mein Kampf*, "The Rhetoric of Hitler's Battle."

Virginia Holland and Dennis Day analyzed Burke's dramatism as an extension of, rather than a departure from, traditional rhetorical theory.[6] Day even concluded, "Burke's theory of rhetoric in terms of identification is not a 'new' rhetoric."[7] To us, this effort to interpret Burke's theory simply as a fresh view of the Aristotelian tradition was a strategic effort to repair and maintain the traditional paradigm. Kuhn has pointed out that whenever a paradigm is in danger of being rejected, its proponents adapt the theory of their opponents in an effort to save the tradition. If we are correct in our judgment, the situation was ironic, for much of Burke's writing in the later 1930s and 1940s was motivated by what he considered to be the mechanical and inadequate explanations of human behavior that were then current in the writings of social sciences.

Another sign of the break from traditional rhetoric was the publication in 1959 of Daniel Fogarty's *Roots for a New Rhetoric*.[8] He believed that an amalgam of three theories—those of I. A. Richards, Kenneth Burke, and the General Semanticists—provided the basis for a unified system. Fogarty was hopeful that this new rhetoric would be paradigmatic. Even though rhetorical critics have drawn heavily on these theories, the decades of the 1960s, 1970s, and 1980s have scarcely fulfilled his hope.

Today the term *new rhetorics* has fallen into disuse. The language and drama-oriented approaches discussed in prior editions of this volume have become more complex and have actually separated into two distinct perspectives. The "new rhetorics" have been replaced by the "dramaturgical" and "sociological" perspectives. Language-oriented criticism is considered in the next part as a "sociolinguistics" approach to rhetorical criticism and as a segment of the sociological perspective. Our current object of attention is criticism based on a dramatic metaphor, which has flourished in the recent years. We have adopted

---

[4]"Kenneth Burke and the 'New Rhetoric,'" *Quarterly Journal of Speech* 38, 2 (April 1952): 133–44.

[5]"A Dramatistic View of the Origins of Language," pts.1–3, *Quarterly Journal of Speech* 38, 3 (October 1952): 251–64; 38, 4 (December 1952): 446–60; and 39, 1 (February 1953): 79–92; idem, "Postscripts on the Negative," *Quarterly Journal of Speech* 39, 2 (April 1953): 209–16.

[6]Holland, "Rhetorical Criticism: A Burkeian Method," *Quarterly Journal of Speech 39, 4 (December 1953): 444–50;* idem *"Kenneth Burke's Dramatistic Approach in Speech Criticism," Quarterly Journal of Speech* 41, 4 (December 1955): 352–58; and Day, "Persuasion and the Concepts of Identification," *Quarterly Journal of Speech* 46, 3 (October 1960): 270–73.

[7]Day, 273.

[8]*Roots for a New Rhetoric* (New York: Columbia University Teachers College Press, 1959).

the umbrella term *dramaturgical*, popularized by Bruce Gronbeck[9] as the perspective for presenting three related critical approaches—"dramatistic," "fantasy theme," and "narrative."

The Dramatistic Approach

We have chosen Kenneth Burke's key term, *dramatistic*, for one of the approaches within the dramaturgical perspective because it continues as an important method in rhetorical criticism. In rejecting the traditional speaker orientation, Burke shifted the focus of rhetoric from persuasion (the result of all the components in the rhetorical act). He highlighted the psychological constituent of rhetoric by concentrating on the analysis of motive. Among Burke's many books those that pertain most directly to rhetoric are *A Grammar of Motives*, *A Rhetoric of Motives*, *The Rhetoric of Religion*, and *Language as Symbolic Action*..[10] Yet Burke was successful in weaving all his concepts into a pattern and creating a feeling of gestalt—a feeling that one cannot fully understand his dramatistic approach without familiarity with all his works—works that span over seventy years of prolific writing.

Because of the enormous effort necessary to grasp his entire system, Burke has gained a number of interpreters and translators. An early attempt at describing Burke's rhetoric and evaluating his influence was made by Stanley E. Hyman in his essay, "Kenneth Burke and the Criticism of Symbolic Action."[11] This essay was followed by Marie Hochmuth Nichols's essay, mentioned before, and by such books as George Knox's *Critical Moments: Kenneth Burke's Categories and Critiques* and L. Virginia Holland's *Counterpoint: Kenneth Burke and Aristotle's Theories of Rhetoric*. But probably the most understandable and useful interpretation was supplied by William Rueckert in his book, *Kenneth Burke and the Drama of Human Relations*. Rueckert also edited *Critical Responses to Kenneth Burke*, a book that demonstrated Burke's tremendous influence in fields such as sociology, communication, theater, education, and literary criticism.[12]

Burke's dramatistic approach has been widely accepted as a critical method; speech communication journals reflect Burkeian concepts in a numerous ways. His theories of identification, substance, form, transcendence, representative anecdote, and pentad have been explained and interpreted.[13] Burke's ideas have

---

[9]"Dramaturgical Theory and Criticism: The State of the Art (or Science)," *Western Journal of Speech Communication* 44, 4 (Fall 1980): 315–30.

[10]*A Grammar of Motives* of 1945 and *A Rhetoric of Motives* of 1950 (er. Berkeley: University of California Press, 1969); *A Rhetoric of Religion* (Boston Beacon Press, 1961); and *Language as Symbolic Action: Essays on Life, Literature, and Method* (Berkeley: University of California Press, 1966).

[11]*The Armed Vision: A Study in the Method of Modern Literary Criticism* (New York: Knopf, 1948), 347–94.

[12]Knox, *Critical Moments: Kenneth Burke's Categories and Critques* (Seattle: University of Washington Press, 1957); Holland, *Counterpoint: Kenneth Burke and Aristotle's Theories of Rhetoric* (New York: Philosphical Library, 1959); Rueckert, *Kenneth Burke and the Drama of Human Relations* (Minneapolis: University of Minnesota Press, 1963); and Rueckert, ed., *Critical Responses to Kenneth Burke* (Minneapolis: University of Minnesota Press, 1969).

[13]Day, 270–73; Roy Ambrester, "Identification Within: Kenneth Burke's View of the Unconscious," *Philosophy and Rhetoric* 7, 4 (Fall 1974): 205–16; Ronald H. Carpenter, "A Stylistic Basis of Burkeian Identification," *Today's Speech* 20, 1 (Winter 1972): 19–

been applied in a number of specialties within speech communication. John W. Kirk explained and illustrated how Burkeian dramatism could be utilized in theatre; Don Geiger did the same for oral interpretation; William Benoit and Charles W. Kneupper for argumentation; George Cheney and Phillip K. Tompkins for organization communication; Dan Nimmo, James Combs, Lance W. Bennett, and Murray Edelman for political communication; Barbara F. Sharf for leadership in small group communication; and Donald K. Enholm, John Condon, Marcus L. Ambrester, and Glynis Holm Strause for interpersonal communication.[14] Further, critics have relied on Burkeian concepts for a variety of creative analyses. S. John Macksoud studied George Bernard Shaw's play *Saint Joan* from a Burkeian rhetorical perspective. Jeanne Y. Fisher applied Burke's dramatism to a multiple murder and suicide. Then, in what could also be called a generic criticism, Robert L. Ivie constructed a method for Burke's dramatism and applied it to selected presidential war messages. Carol Berthold followed Burke's method of agon and cluster analysis in criticizing speeches of President John F. Kennedy. Leland Griffin constructed a Burkeian dramatistic theory of social movements and applied it to the New Left. Janet Brown, Cynthia Huyink, and Julie Yingling drew on Burke's dramatism in their analysis of feminist rhetoric. James Chesebro conducted an eleven-year dramatistic analysis of

24; Weldon B. Durham, "Kenneth Burke's Concept of Substance," *Quarterly Journal of Speech* 66, 4 (December 1980): 351–64; Richard M. Coe, *Form and Substance: An Advanced Rhetoric* (New York: John Wiley, 1981); Robert L. Heath, "Kenneth Burke on Form," *Quarterly Journal of Speech* 65, 4 (December 1979): 132–43; Richard B. Gregg, "Kenneth Burke's Prolegomena to the Study of the Rhetoric of Form," *Communication Quarterly* 26, 4 (Fall 1978): 3–13; Jane Blankenship and Barbara Sweeney, "The Energy of Form," *Central States Speech Journal* 31, 4 (fall 1980): 172–83; Barry Brummett, "Burkean Scapegoating, Mortification, and Transcendance in Presidential Campaign Rhetoric," *Central States Speech Journal* 32, 1 (Winter 1981): 254–64 and "Burke's Representative Anecdote as a Method in Media Criticism," *Critical Studies in Mass Communication* 1, 2 (June 1984): 161–76; William J. Hamlin and Harold J. Nichols, "The Interest Value of Rhetorical Strategies Derived from Kenneth Burke's Pentad," *Western Speech* 32, 2 (Spring 1973): 97–102; Charles W. Kneupper, "Burkean Invention: Two Contrasting Views: Dramatistic Invention: The Pentad as a Heuristic Procedure," *Rhetoric Society Quarterly* 9, 3 (Summer 1979): 130–36.
   14"Kenneth Burke's Dramatistic Criticism Applied to the Theatre," *Southern Speech Communication Journal* 33, 3 (Spring 1968): 161–77; "A 'Dramatic' Approach to Interpretative Analysis," *Quarterly Journal of Speech* 38, 2 (April 1952): 189–94; "Systems of Explanation: Aristotle and Burke on 'Cause,'" *Rhetoric Society Quarterly* 13, 1 (Winter 1983): 41–58; "Dramatism and Argument," in *Dimensions of Argument: Proceedings of the Second Summer Conference on Argument*, ed. Ziegelmueller and Rhodes (Annandale, VA: Speech Communication Association, 1981), 894–904; "The Rhetoric of Identification and the Study of Organizational Communication," *Quarterly Journal of Speech* 69, 2 (May 1983): 143–58; "Kenneth Burke and the Inherent Characteristics of Formal Organizations: A Field Study," *Speech Monographs* 42, 2 (June 1975): 135–42; *Mediated Political Realities* (New York: Longman, 1983); "Political Scenarios and the Nature of Politics," *Philosophy and Rhetoric* 8, 1 (Winter 1975): 23–42; *The Symbolic Uses of Politics* (Urbana: University of Illinois Press, 1964); "A Rhetorical Analysis of Leadership Emergence in Small Groups," *Communication Monographs* 25, 2 (June 1978): 156–72; "Rhetoric as an Instrument for Understanding and Improving Human Relations," *Southern Speech Communication Journal* 41, 2 (Spring 1976): 223–36; *Interpersonal Communication* (New York: Macmillan, 1977); *A Rhetoric of Interpersonal Communication* (Prospect Heights, IL: Waveland, 1984).

prime time television series.[15] These articles, and others, certainly demonstrate that Burke's dramatism can be applied to rhetorical acts in a variety of fashions.

However, it is important to note that the dramatistic approach is not limited to the work of Kenneth Burke, though most scholars of dramatism acknowledge him as a philosophical and inspirational source. A good example is the book *Drama in Life: The Uses of Communication in Society*, edited by James E. Combs and Michael W. Mansfield. This book brings together in one volume such scholars as Hugh Duncan, Peter Berger, and Erving Goffman from sociology; Eric Berne and Ernest Becker from psychology; Walter Lippmann from journalism; Daniel Boorstin from history, Joseph Gusfield, Dan Nimmo, Murray Edelman, and Orrin Klapp from political science, and movie critic Pauline Kael.[16] The editors indicate in the preface, "Many contemporary social scientists have abandoned physical metaphors as inadequate, and find that the dramaturgical perspective developed by Burke has a depth and explanatory power denied to other paradigms."[17]

To illustrate dramatistic theory, we have included an essay written specifically for this book by Bernard L. Brock, "Rhetorical Criticism: A Burkeian Approach Revisited." It has been updated for this edition to reflect a shift in Kenneth Burke's dramatism to include both epistemological and ontological orientations. Brock has found Burke's concepts especially useful in the rhetorical criticism of contemporary political communication, as demonstrated in his essay, "Political Speaking: A Burkeian Approach."[18]

In previous editions of this volume, David Ling's article, "A Pentadic Analysis of Senator Edward Kennedy's Address to the People of Massachusetts,"[19] was utilized to illustrate the application of dramatistic criticism. We still recommend an examination of this essay because, in addition to utilizing Burke's pentad effectively, Ling revealed how a critic can discover and communicate an insight that would likely remain hidden except for the application of the dramatistic method. In this edition David S. Birdsell's article, "Ronald Reagan on Lebanon and Grenada: Flexibility and Interpretation in the Application of Kenneth Burke's Pentad" has been selected to illustrate how Burke's system can be applied. This criticism demonstrates a creative use of the pentad, as it unites two

---

[15]"Voices in Opposition: A Burkeian Rhetoric of Saint Joan," *Quarterly Journal of Speech* 57, 2 (April 1971): 140–46; "A Burkeian Analysis of the Rhetorical Dimensions of Multiple Murder and Suicide," *Quarterly Journal of Speech* 60 2 (April 1974): 175–89; "Presidential Motives for War," *Quarterly Journal of Speech* 60 3 (October 1974): 337–45; and "Kenneth Burke's Cluster-Agon Method: Its Development and Application," *Central States Speech Journal* 27, 4 (Winter 1976): 302–9; "A Dramatistic Theory of the Rhetoric of Movements," in *Critical Responses to Kenneth Burke: 1924–66*, ed. William H. Rueckert (Minneapolis: University of Minnesota Press, 1969), 456–78; "Kenneth Burke and *The Mod Donna*: The Dramatistic Method Applied to Feminist Criticism," *Central States Speech Journal* 29, 3 (Summer 1978): 138–46; "A Dramtistic Analysis of *Sexual Politics* by Kate Millet," *Women's Studies in Communication* 3, 3 (Summer 1979): 1–6; "Women's Advocacy: Pragmatic Feminism in the YWCA," *Women's Studies in Communication* 6, 2 (Spring 1983): 1–11; "Communication, Values, and Popular Television Series—An Eleven Year Assessment," in *Inter/Media: Interpersonal Communication in a Media World*, 3d ed., ed. Gary Gumpert and Robert Cathcart (New York: Oxford University Press, 1986), 477–512.

[16]*Drama in Life: The Uses of Communication in Society* (New York, Hastings, 1976).

[17]Ibid., xix.

[18]Rueckert, *Critical Responses*, 444–55.

[19]*Central States Speech Journal* 21, 2 (Summer 1970): 81–86.

separate events into a single drama. This article also communicates a message that might remain hidden without the application of the Burkeian method.

The Fantasy Theme Approach

The second dramaturgical approach is fantasy theme analysis. In the 1970s Ernest Bormann at the University of Minnesota, working with a number of graduate students, developed another critical method based on a dramatic metaphor that he called a fantasy theme analysis. He initially described this approach in his article "Fantasy and Rhetorical Vision: The Rhetorical Criticism of Social Reality." Bormann indicates the inspiration for the method came from Robert Bales's work in small groups when he discovered "the dynamic process of group fantasizing."[20] Bormann observes that a similar process operates in speaker-audience fantasizing and that composite dramas are formed that "catch up large groups of people in a symbolic reality" called a "rhetorical vision."[21] Bormann next argues that "individuals in rhetorical transactions create subjective worlds of common expectations and meaning" and that the rhetorical vision serves as a "coping function for those who participate in the drama."[22]

Bormann, then, rather than present a model for fantasy theme analysis raises a number of questions critics might investigate: Do the same people keep cropping up as villains? Are the same stories repeated? Where is the sacred and profane ground? What are the typical scenarios? These are just a few of the dramatic questions Bormann suggests are appropriate for a fantasy theme analysis. After raising these questions Bormann illustrates the fantasy theme approach with a brief analysis of Puritan preaching.

Immediately after its introduction, speech communication journals were flooded with fantasy theme articles, especially by persons who had been involved in its development at Minnesota. Hensley, with Bormann, applied it to religious speaking.[23] Rarick, Cragan, Shields, and Porter made political applications and employed quantitative as well as rhetorical techniques.[24]

Chesebro and Koester used fantasy analysis in movement studies.[25] John F. Cragan and Donald C. Shields solidified fantasy theme analysis when they wrote

[20]"Fantasy and Rhetorical Vision: The Rhetorical Criticism of Social Reality," *Quarterly Journal of Speech* 58, 4 (December 1972): 396–407.

[21]Ibid., 398.

[22]Ibid., 400.

[23]"Rhetorical Vision and the Persuasion of a Historical Movement: The Disciples of Christ in Nineteenth Century American Culture," *Quarterly Journal of Speech* 61, 3 (October 1975): 250–64; Bormann, "Fetching Good out of Evil: A Rhetorical Use of Calamity," *Quarterly Journal of Speech* 63, 2 (April 1977): 130–39.

[24]"The Carter Persona: An Empirical Analysis of the Rhetorical Visions of Campaign '76," *Quarterly Journal of Speech* 63, 3 (October 1977): 258–73; "Foreign Policy Communication Dramas: How Mediated Rhetoric Played in Peoria in Campaign '76," *Quarterly Journal of Speech* 63, 3 (October 1977): 274–89; "The White House Transcripts: Group Fantasy Events Concerning the Mass Media," *Central States Speech Journal* 27, 4 (Winter 1976): 272–79.

[25]"Paradoxical Views of 'Homosexuality' in the Rhetoric of Social Movements," *Quarterly Journal of Speech* 66, 2 (April 1980): 127–39; "The Machiavellian Princess: Rhetorical Dramas for Women Managers," *Communication Quarterly* 30, 3 (Summer 1982): 165–72.

and edited the book *Applied Communication Research: A Dramatistic Approach* that not only placed much of the fantasy theme research in one cover but also advanced fantasy theme theory.[26]

The method had received a great deal of attention, so it wasn't long before it spread outside the "Minnesota circle." Schrag examined TV; Kroll considered the women's movement; Doyle and Hubbard studied romance novels.[27] By the 1980s fantasy theme analysis had become an accepted approach for rhetorical study.

Seldom does a method gain a following without also becoming the target for attack. For fantasy theme analysis G. P. Mohrmann became the primary antagonist. In "An Essay on Fantasy Theme Criticism," Mohrmann attacked the theoretical roots in Bales and Freud and accused proponents of fantasy theme analysis of arguing in circles.[28] This attack was soon followed by a dialogue between Mohrmann and Bormann in which Bormann denied Mohrmann's theoretical arguments initially by saying fantasy theory was still evolving and then by defending the method on the basis of its practical results through research.[29] Of course, the issue was not resolved, but fantasy theme analysis continues to flourish.

We have selected two articles to illustrate the theory and application of the fantasy theme approach. Bormann's article "Fantasy and Rhetorical Vision: The Rhetorical Criticism of Social Reality" already discussed indicates how to conduct fantasy theme analysis. To illustrate versatility in applying fantasy theme analysis, we have selected Rita C. Hubbard's "Relationships Styles in Popular Romance Novels." This study traces the male/female relationship styles through fantasy themes over more than a thirty-year period. The study also demonstrates how rhetorical and quantitative methods can be used effectively in concert.

The Narrative Approach

The final dramaturgical approach is narrative. A forerunner of this approach can be found in J. T. Marshman's "The Use of Narrative in Speaking."[30] This article, building on the field's oral tradition, sets forth narrative as a desirable form for public speaking. However, narrative as an approach to rhetorical criticism was not discussed in the professional journals until the late 1970s and early 1980s. Then a series of articles pulled narrative out of the conventional context of literature and took a more rhetorical approach—"Storytelling and Self-confrontation: Parables as Communication Strategies," "Beyond the Narrational

[26]*Applied Communication Research: A Dramatistic Approach* (Prospect Hts., Il: Waveland, 1981).

[27]Schrag, Hudson, and Bernabo, "Television's News Humane Collectivity," *Western Journal of Speech Communication* 44, 1 (Winter 1981): 1–12; Becky Swanson Kroll, "From Small Group to Public View: Mainstreaming the Women's Movement," *Communication Quarterly* 31, (Spring 1983): 139–47; Vanderford Doyle, "The Rhetoric of Romance: A Fantasy Theme Analysis of Barbara Cartland Novels," *Southern Speech Communication Journal* 51, 1 (Fall 1985): 24–48; Hubbard, "Relationships Styles in Popular Romance Novels, 1950 to 1983," *Communication Quarterly* 33, 2 (Sprint 1985): 113–25.

[28]*Quarterly Journal of Speech* 68, 2 (may 1982): 109–32.

[29]"Coloquy—I. Fantasy and Rhetorical Vision: Ten Years Later" and "Fantasy Theme Criticism: A Peroration," *Quarterly Journal of Speech* 68, 3 (August 1982): 306–13.

[30]J. T. Marshman, *Southern Speech Bulletin* 4, 1 (September 1938): 1–6.

Frame: Interpretation and Metafiction," and "Rhetorical Fiction and the Presidency."[31] This interest in narrative continued when the *Quarterly Journal of Speech* book review section featured the article "Narrative Theory and Communication Research" based on material generally considered outside rhetorical criticism.[32] Finally, Walter R. Fisher in a series of articles—"Toward a Logic of Good Reasons," "Narrative as a Human Communication Paradigm: The Case of Public Moral Argument," and "The Narrative Paradigm: An Elaboration—and a book, *Human Communication as Narration: Toward a Philosophy of Reason, Value, and Action*, established narrative as a definite critical method.[33]

Fisher starts with the assumption that *"humans as rhetorical beings are as much valuing as reasoning animals"* and that central to this process is the giving of *"good reasons," "those elements that provide warrants for accepting or adhering to advice fostered by any form of communication that can be considered rhetorical"*[34] Fisher then defines "narration" as "symbolic actions—words and/or deeds—that have sequence and meaning for those who live, create, or interpret them." He goes on to argue that "the narrative paradigm can be considered a dialectical synthesis of two traditional strands that recur in the history of rhetoric: the argumentative, persuasive theme and the literary, aesthetic theme."[35] Fisher, further, sees narrative as competing for acceptance with the reigning "rational world paradigm" as the basis for reasoning together.[36] After relating narrative to dramatism, fantasy theme analysis, and language action, Fisher sets forth the presuppositions of the narrative paradigm:

> (1) Humans are essentially storytellers. (2) The paradigmatic mode of human decision-making and communication is "good reasons" which vary in form among situations, genres, and media of communication. (3) The production and practice of good reasons are ruled by matters of history, biography, culture, and character along with the kinds of forces identified in the Frentz and Farrell language action paradigm. (4) Rationality is determined by the nature of persons as narrative beings—their inherent awareness of *narrative probability*, what constitutes a coherent story, add their constant habit of testing *narrative fidelity*, whether or not the stories they experience ring true with the stories they know to be true in their lives. (Narrative probability and narrative fidelity are analogous to the concepts of dramatic probability and verisimilitude . . .) (5) The world as we know it is a set of stories that must be chosen among in order for us to live life in a process of continual re-creation.[37]

---

[31]W. Lance Bennett, "Storytelling in Criminal Trials: A Model of Social Judgement," *Quarterly Journal of Speech* 64, 1 (February 1978): 1–22; William G. Kirkwood, "Storytelling and Self-Confrontation: Parables as Communication Strategies," *Quarterly Journal of Speech* 69, 1 (February 1983), 58–74; James A. Pearse, *Quarterly Journal of Speech* 66, 1 (February 1980): 73–84; Walter R. Fisher, *Quarterly Journal of Speech* 66, 2 (April 1980): 119–26.

[32]Robert L. Scott, "Narrative Theory and Communication Research," *Quarterly Journal of Speech* 70, 2 (May 1984): 197–221.

[33]*The Quarterly Journal of Speech* 64, 4 (December 1978): 376–843; *Communication Monographs* 61, 1 (March 1984): 1–22 and 52, 4 (December 1985): *Human Communication as Narration*: 347–67; (Columbia, SC: University of South Carolina Press, 1987).

[34]*Human Communication as Narrative*, 57.

[35]Ibid., 58.

[36]Ibid., 62.

[37]Ibid., 64–65.

Shortly after the introduction of narrative as a critical method the *Journal of Communication* presents a symposium entitled *Homo Narrans*: Story-Telling in Mass Culture and Everday Life.[38] Fisher's article "The Narrative Paradigm: In the Beginning" opens the symposium and traces the separation of mythos and logos, imagination and thought, through the rhetoric of pre-Socratics, Plato, Aristotle, and Bacon. Logos that originally meant story became scientific or technical discourse, while mythos was downgraded to fictional myth. Fisher then argues that the narrative paradigm reunites and unifies these two strains.[39]

The second symposium article, "Re-constructing Narrative Theory: A Functional Perspective" by John Louis Lucaites and Celeste Michele Condit, reconstructs a theory of narrative by focusing on the interaction of form and function. Initially they identify the poetic, dialectic, and rhetorical functions of narrative. Poetic discourse expresses beauty; dialectic discourse discovers and presents "empirically 'verifiable' phenomena"; rhetorical discourse persuades by serving as an interpretive lens for the audience. They then ground narrative in Quintilian's discussion of *narratio* and the formal characteristics of consistency and brevity, and they discuss unity of direction and purpose as appropriate contexts for all rhetorical discourse. Lucaites and Condit conclude with cautions in the use of narrative: (1) narrative forms and functions should interact; (2) "similarities and difference of narratives should be identified across the full range of discourse genres"; (3) "social and political consequences of particular narrative forms" should be discovered. This reconstruction serves as an excellent supplement to Fisher's approach.[40]

The other participants generally reject Fisher's view that narrative is a paradigm in the Kuhnian sense, but together these articles build a strong argument for the usefulness of the narrative approach. Thomas B. Farrell focuses on the dimension of time in conversational and rhetorical narrative. Bormann examines the importance of fantasies in the psychodynamics of the narrative process. Michael Calvin McGee and John S. Nelson oppose the separation of traditional rationality and narration. W. Lance Bennett and Murray Edelman argue that new stories as narratives disguise ideological solutions as social truth.[41]

After Walter Fisher gave form to the narrative approach, very quickly others adopted it. In oral interpretation, Mary Strine and Michael Pacanowsky wrote "How to Read Interpretive Accounts of Organizational Life: Narrative Bases of Textual Authority"; and Jacqueline Taylor did "Documenting Performance Knowledge: Two Narrative Techniques in Grace Paley's Fiction."[42] In media studies, Bruce Gronbeck and Caren Deming take a narrative approach to television.[43] In political communication, Ronald Carpenter, Dennis Mumby,

[38]*Journal of Communication* 35, 4 (Autumn 1985): 73–171.
[39]Ibid., 76–87.
[40]Ibid., 90–108.
[41]Ibid., 109–71.
[42]*Southern Speech Communication Journal* 50, 3 (Spring 1985): 283–97 and 53, 1 (Fall 1987): 65–79.
[43]Caren J. Deming, "*Hill Street Blues* as Narrative," *Critical Studies in Mass Communication* 2, 1 (March 1985): 1–22; Bruce E. Gronbeck, "Narrative, Enactment, and Television Programming," *Southern Speech Communication Journal* 48, 2 (Spring 1983): 229–43.

William Lewis, and Larry David Smith applied the narrative approach to individual's, organizations', and conventions' rhetoric.[44]

As Fisher's work on the narrative paradigm gained prominence, Barbara Wanrick attacked it as taking "equivocal or contradictory positions on issues the determine how narrative rationality is to be used to assess texts" and because "the narrative rationality concept in his paradigm itself lacks narrative probability or coherence." She concluded that "narrative rationality is really a *system* of critical criteria that may be variously brought into play depending on the nature of the text to be assessed."[45] Robert C. Rowland—in "Narrative: Mode of Discourse or Paradigm?"—commended "the great value of the work of Fisher" even though he rejected narrative as a paradigm. In Rowland's view, narrative as a paradigm cannot be separated from the "rational world paradigm" because it casts the role of the expert in the public sphere as a storyteller.[46] The narrative approach may be controversial and still be in the process of being defined, but there is no question that Fisher, more than anyone else in the field, has established a line of inquiry and criticism that will remain a lively alternative for rhetorical critics.

We have chosen two articles to represent the theory and application of narrative criticism. Walter R. Fisher's "The Narrative Paradigm: An Elaboration" extends his initial theoretical statement by relating narrative to "major social scientific and humanistic theories" and applying it to the conversation between Socrates and Callicles in Plato's *Georgias*. Also, James S. Ettema and Theodore L. Glasser's "Narrative Form and Moral Force: The Realization of Innocence and Guilt through Investigative Journalism" examines prize-winning journalistic exposés for their use of narrative strategies.

Characteristics of the Dramaturgical

A single "New Rhetoric" paradigm did not merge from the break from tradition, but under the dramaturgical perspective a group of approaches do share a rough consensus and several assumptions that distinguish them from the traditional and experiential perspectives.

First, like the experiential, the dramaturgical perspective holds that society continually undergoes change. Critics working from this perspective accordingly stress interaction and change in their critical essays. However, unlike the experiential, the dramaturgical perspective assumes that stable relationships or periods of dynamic equilibrium can be discovered within the complex interactions of human beings and their social and physical context. From these stable relationships, they believe, it should be possible to construct a unified rhetoric theory.

[44]Ronald H. Carpenter, "Admiral Mahan, 'Narrative Fidelity,' and the Japanese Attack on Pearl Harbor," *Quarterly Journal of Speech* 72, 3 (August 1986): 290–305; Dennis K. Mumby, "The Political Function of Narrative in Organizations," *Communication Monographs* 54, 2 (June 1987): 113–27; William F. Lewis, "Telling America's Story: Narrative Form and the Reagan Presidency," *Quarterly Journal of Speech* 73, 3 (August 1987): 280–302; Larry David Smith "Narrative Styles in Network Coverage of the 1984 Nominating Conventions," *Western Journal of Speech Communication* 52, 1 (Winter 1988): 63–74.

[45]Barbara Warnick, "The Narrative Paradigm: Another Story," *Quarterly Journal of Speech* 73, 2 (May 1987): 172–82.

[46]Robert C. Rowland, "Narrative: Made of Discourse or Paradigm?" *Communication Monographs* 54, 3 (September 1987): 264–75.

Second, the belief in stable relationships is an assumption dramaturgical critics share with those of the traditional perspective. At the moment, a number of competing systems—or at least moves toward competing systems—mark dramaturgical criticism. If the assumption concerning the degree of social stability is correct, continued work ought to lead toward a critical consensus on a method or set of methods flexible enough to enable the critic to analyze rhetorical patterns typical of the social process.

A third assumption of the dramaturgical perspective flows from the word-thought-thing relationship. Again, this perspective and the experiential critics share a common assumption. The word-thought-thing relationship is viewed as reciprocal, that is, not only does the nature of the object (of relationship) affect the selection of words, but the use of a symbol system affects a person's perception of reality. However, the dramaturgical critic extends this assumption further than the experientialist, for the former stresses the dominance of the word in the presumed interactions of language and reality as a focal point for criticism.

Dramaturgical critics also look to a unified rhetorical theory to inform their criticism as they apply their theory in a flexible manner. Again, even though a single theory has not emerged, the foundation for such a consensus can be found in the shared orientation and set of assumptions espoused by dramaturgical critics.

So we would summarize the dramaturgical as we have the two previous perspectives.

1. *Orientation*. The critic must find stable relationships in understanding the interaction of people and their social environment.
2. *Assumptions*
    a.   Society is in process, but fairly stable relationships govern human interactions.
    b.   A flexible framework may be constructed for the systematic study of public discourses.
    c.   A specific symbol influences human beings' perception of reality.
3. *Consensus*. A unified rhetorical framework is necessary for the productive study of rhetoric and criticism.

As one considers the works that demonstrate a concern with the dramaturgical, one is inevitably struck by the rich variety of theorizing and the comparatively recent concern for critical application. Again, we must say that this situation is consistent with Thomas Kuhn's contention that the normal business of science—and we would extend the generalization to criticism—is to apply theory to as many different circumstances as possible once a paradigm is agreed on—or even if a paradigm is not agreed on. In looking at the experiential and the dramaturgical perspectives, we would conclude that both are preparadigmatic. Perhaps they are nonparadigmatic, that is, no paradigm is likely to dominate rhetorical criticism in the conceivable future.

THE DRAMATISTIC APPROACH

RHETORICAL CRITICISM: A BURKEIAN APPROACH REVISITED

Bernard L. Brock

Rhetorical criticism requires that a people make descriptive, interpretative judgments regarding the effectiveness of rhetoric. In this process critics not only need a language to describe people as they respond to their world but also a theoretical framework for understanding mankind's basic rhetorical tendencies. Kenneth Burke's dramatistic approach to rhetoric provides critics with such a language and theoretical structure; thus many critics have turned to Burke for a rhetorical theory to guide them in making critical judgments.

Burke's rhetorical philosophy evolves from the view that language is a strategic response to a situation.[1] This view underlies all his major works: *Counter-Statement* (1931) *Permanence and Change* (1935) *Attitudes toward History* (1936) *The Philosophy of Literary Form* (1941) *A Grammar of Motives* (1945) *A Rhetoric of Motives* (1950) *Rhetoric of Religion* (1961) and *Language as Symbolic Action* (1966). His prolific writing is both eclectic and complex and so has been difficult reduce to a unified rhetorical system. This task has been made even more challenging because since 1968 the focus of Burke's concern has shifted from epistemology to ontology.[2]

Structuring Burke's rhetorical theories into a system for criticism necessitates (1) identifying his philosophy of rhetoric, (2) framing a structure that reflects his philosophy, (3) showing how the dramatistic approach unites substance and rhetorical devices, and (4) describing Burke's developing ontology, Only then can one suggest specifically how the rhetorical critic might use Burke's dramatistic approach.

---

[1] Kenneth Burke, *The Philosophy of Literary Form*, (New York: Random House, 1957), 3.

[2] Discussions of Kenneth Burke's shift in rhetorical theory from epistemology to ontology may be found in Bernard L. Brock, Kenneth Burke, Parke Burgess, and Herbert Simon, "Dramatism as Ontology or Epistemology: A Symposium," *Communication Quarterly* 32 (Winter 1985): 17–33; Kenneth Burke, "Dramatism and Logology"; and Bernard Brock, "Epistemology and Ontology in Kenneth Burke's Dramatism," *Communication Quarterly* 33 (Spring 1985): 89–104; James W. Chesebro, "Epistemology and Ontology as Dialectical Modes in the Writings of Kenneth Burke," *Communication Quarterly* 36 (Summer 1988): 175–91.

Burke's Philosophy of Rhetoric

The foundation of Burke's rhetorical philosophy can be found in *Attitudes toward History*. He indicates that people assess the "human situation" and shape appropriate attitudes by constructing their conceptions of the world around them. In the process they perceive "certain functions or relationships as either friendly or unfriendly" and then, weighing their own potential against probable opposition, select their strategies for coping with the "human situation."[3] These strategies or stylized answers are symbols that reflect attitudes.[4]

By starting with people as they react symbolically to their environment, Burke arrives at the function of rhetoric—the use of words by human agents to form attitudes or to induce actions in other human agents."[5] Rhetoric originates not from "any past condition of human society" but from "an essential function of language itself." The act of using language to induce cooperation among people automatically focuses one's attention on the language or the symbols employed.[6]

Burke's focus on language is then carried over into the characteristics he attributes to human beings:

Man is
the symbol-using (symbol-making, symbol-misusing) animal
inventor of the negative (or moralized by the negative)
separated from his natural condition by instruments of his own making
goaded by the spirit of hierarchy (or moved by the sense of order)
and rotten with perfection.[7]

Burke clearly demonstrates his view that verbal symbols are meaningful acts from which motives can be derived when he discusses the relationship between symbols and action. He points out that in acting wisely "we must name the friendly or unfriendly functions and relationships in such a way that we are able to do something about them."[8] The words that one assigns to these functions and relationships not only reveal the process of sorting out the world but also communicate an attitude that is a cue for the behavior of others. Burke clearly indicates that the act of selecting one symbol over another locks the speaker's attitude into the language. For this reason verbal symbols are meaningful acts from which human motives can be derived. These motives constitute the foundation or the substance of a rhetorical act, and through the ability to identify them by the cues in verbal symbols, Burke constructs a philosophy of rhetoric.

In considering the nature of society as fundamental to Burke's philosophy of rhetoric, one can turn to *Permanence and Change*. Burke explains that "action and end" as opposed to "motion and position" and "dramatistic terms" rather than "theories of knowledge" are appropriate in discussing human conduct.[9] The human tendency toward action makes a dramatistic vocabulary appropriate to the study of people. Burke describes human society as a dramatistic process,

---

[3]Kenneth Burke, *Attitudes toward History* (Boston: Beacon Press, 1961), 3 and 4.

[4]Burke, *The Philosophy of Literary Form*, 3.

[5]Kenneth Burke, *A Rhetoric of Motives* (New York: Prentice-Hall, 1950), 41.

[6]Ibid., 43.

[7]Kenneth Burke, *Language as Symbolic Action* (Berkeley: University of California Press, 1966), 16. Kenneth Burke wrote at a time when *man* was used as a generic term for all human beings. This usage will be reflected in a number of quotation's from his work.

[8]Burke, *Attitudes toward History*, 4.

[9]Kenneth Burke, *Permanence and Change* (Los Altos, CA: Hermes, 1954), 276.

that includes the elements of hierarchy; acceptance and rejection; and guilt, purification, and redemption.

Hierarchy generates the structure of our dramatistic society. In society the social, economic, and political powers are unevenly divided. Power endows individuals with authority. Authority, in turn, establishes definite relationships among people, reflecting how much power they possess. These relationships can be viewed as a ladder of authority or the hierarchy of society.[10] As people accept their positions and work within a hierarchical structure, the structure is "bureaucratized," or given a definite organization. With the bureaucratization of the hierarchy comes order in society. This process makes hierarchy the structural principle of a dramatistic society.[11]

Another element of the dramatistic society is the concept of acceptance and rejection. Burke's philosophy of rhetoric is based upon the human's propensity to accept or reject their situation and their attempts to symbolize these reactions. The concept of acceptance follows from a positive reaction to the human situation and rejection from a negative reaction: "The essential distinction between the verbal and nonverbal is in the fact that language adds the peculiar possibility of the Negative."[12] In nature everything is positive: what exists, simply exists. The negative, or nonexistence, results from language or the separation of a symbol from what it represents. Burke further points out that historically, since there is no negative in nature, the negative in language has probably developed through the negative command, "Do not do that."[13] Language enables people to accept or reject their hierarchical positions or even the hierarchy itself. Acceptance results in satisfaction and order, whereas rejection results in alienation and disorder.

To complete the dramatistic process, the concepts of guilt, purification, and redemption must be understood. These related terms represent the effects of acceptance and rejection of the hierarchy. Whenever people reject the traditional hierarchy, they "fall" and thereby acquire a feeling of guilt. Burke feels that guilt is inherent in society because people cannot accept all the impositions of their traditional Hierarchy. Conditions change, resulting in the rejection of some of the traditional modes. Also, each social institution—family, school, church, clubs, and other "bureaucracies"—has its own hierarchy; and when two of these hierarchies are in conflict one will inevitably be rejected.[14] Since people cannot satisfy all the requirements of their traditional hierarchies, they are saddled with eternal guilt.[15]

The nature of hierarchy itself is another source of eternal guilt. Hierarchy, representing differences in authority between superiors and inferiors in society, always creates mystery. Moreover, inferiors always want to move up within the hierarchy or to change its nature. The sense of mystery that one class holds for another class and the upward tendencies of the lower classes create a guilt that is inherent in the hierarchy itself.[16]

[10]Ibid., 276.
[11]Ibid., 282 and 283.
[12]Kenneth Burke, "A Dramatistic View of the Origins of Language: Part One," *Quarterly Journal of Speech* 38, (October, 1952): 252.
[13]Ibid., 253.
[14]Burke, *Permanence and Change*, 283.
[15]Ibid., 284.
[16]Ibid., p. 287.

Burke compares the eternal secular guilt with original sin. However, neither secular guilt nor original sin result from people's "personal transgression(s), but by reason of a tribal or dynastic inheritance."[17] In spite of this fact, guilt still sets off a psychological reaction in people. Guilt reduces social cohesion and gives people the feeling of being less than whole, so that they strive to have this guilt canceled or to receive redemption. The act of purification may be either mortification or victimage. Mortification is an act of self-sacrifice that relieves guilt, whereas victimage is the purging of guilt through a scapegoat that symbolizes society's guilt. To be effective, the process of purification and redemption must be balanced: the act of purification must be equivalent to the degree of guilt if one is to receive redemption. Psychological guilt, purification, and redemption result from the rejection of hierarchy, or pollution.

Burke believes that the dramatistic nature of society may explained by considering the interrelationships among the concepts of (1) hierarchy; (2) acceptance and rejection; and (3) guilt, purification, and redemption. These relationships are also described by Burke in his poem "Cycles of Terms Implicit in the Idea of 'Order' ":

Here are the steps
In the Iron Law of History
That welds Order and Sacrifice

Order leads to Guilt
(for who can keep commandments!)
Guilt needs Redemption
(for who would not be cleaned!)
Redemption needs Redeemer
(which is to say, a Victim!).

Order
Through Guilt
To Victimage
(hence: Cult of the Kill).[18]

Another way to describe these relationships or Burke's terms for order is to say that the dramatistic process goes through the stages of order, pollution, guilt, purification, and redemption. This process, together with the belief that verbal symbols are meaningful acts in response to situations from which motives can be derived, is the philosophic foundation of Burke's system of rhetoric.

Structure in Burke's Rhetoric

Burke's dramatistic approach to rhetoric supplies a language that describes people as they respond to their world, but to be useful to critics, this language must be transformed into a more definite structure. Two concepts are basic to such a structure: identification and the pentad. These concepts can be used as

---

[17]Ibid.

[18]Kenneth Burke, *The Rhetoric of Religion* (Boston: Beacon Press, 1961), 4–5. The chapter "The First Three Chapters of Genesis" (pp. 172–272) develops these concepts in greater detail, a complex chart illustrating these relationships can be found on p. 184.

rhetorical tools to discover the attitudes expressed within a rhetorical act and to describe its dramatistic process. Identification is the major tool used to discover the attitudes and the dramatistic process; the pentad provides a structural model for their description.

In Burke's philosophy of rhetoric, verbal symbols convey the attitude of the speaker. Burke states that the basic function of rhetoric is "the use of words by human agents to form attitudes or to induce actions in other human agents."[19] In connection with this function Burke introduces *identification* which he describes in *A Rhetoric of Motives*: "A is not identical with his colleague, B. But insofar as their interests are joined, A is *identified* with B. Or he man *identify himself* with B even when their interest are not joined, if he assumes that they are, or is persuaded to believe so."[20]

Burke sees identification as an "acting together" that grows out of the ambiguities of substance. People feel social division and unity simultaneously, division because each person remains unique and unity or "consubstantiality" to the extent that the actors share a locus of motives.[21] The speakers, whose attitudes are reflected in their language, will accept some ideas, people, and institutions, and reject others; their audiences will to some extent both agree and disagree with them. To the extent that audiences accept and reject the same ideas, people, and institutions, that the speakers do, identification occurs. Speakers' language will reveal the substance out of which they expect to identify with their listeners. Consciously or unconsciously, their words will reveal their attitudes or stylized answers to the obvious divisions. The concept of identification can be used by critics to structure their insights into speakers' senses of unity by grouping strategies into "clusters." Then these "clusters" reveal the symbolic hierarchy and process of pollution, guilt, purification, and redemption that are locked into the rhetoric. Identification, the tool applied directly to verbal symbols, is the critic's key to the speaker's attitudes and the dramatistic process.

Burke labels one of his procedures as "statistical." He advises gathering lists of recurrent terms until the critic begins to sense which are essential—which terms cluster and where. Beginnings and endings, he argues, are particularly likely to reveal key terms. Critics may verify the hypotheses they construct by making a reasoned case for the consistencies of the parts and the whole, that is, for how the terms fit the apparent situation. In this work there is no substitute for intelligence and efforts, both made sensitive by wide experience. But Burke does suggest one more aid to finding and proving rhetorical structure.

Burke's well-known pentad is this aid. He used the device as a model to describe the dramatistic nature of society. In *A Grammar of Motives* Burke attempts to answer the question, "What is involved when we say what people are doing and why they are doing it?" As an explanation he introduces and defines the pentad: "We shall use five terms as generating principle of our investigation. They are: Act, Scene, Agent, Agency, and Purpose. In a rounded statement about motives, you must have some word that names the act (names what took place, in thought or deed), and another that names the scene (the background of the act, the situation in which it occurred); also, you must indicate what person

---

[19]Burke, *A Rhetoric of Motives*, 41.
[20]Ibid., 20. Emphasis Burke's.
[21]Ibid., 21.

or kind of person (agent) performed the act, what means or instruments he used (agency), and the purpose."[22]

People will disagree about the nature of these terms or what they represent, but they necessarily must provide some answer to the five questions: "what was done (act), when or where it was done (scene), who did it (agent), how he did it (agency), and why (purpose)." Thus, these terms are the key to human motives, because statements assigning motives "arise out of them and terminate in them."[23]

Burke argues that people will feature one of these terms when they express their thoughts. A person's vocabulary reveals the set that dominates thinking and speaking. Some people, for example, will ask *what* and then *who*, others *who* and then *what*. These thoughts are then reflected in symbolic relationships. In Burke's language an "act-agent" ratio properly labels the first sequence of questions, and an "agent-act" the second. Given his starting place (and starting places tend to be ending places), we can trace a constellation of ratios in a coherent, well-formed piece of rhetorical discourse. Domination by agent may reveal agent-act concern, then agent-purpose, then agent-scene. Given a person's dominant set or term, a critic may trace the complete pentad in a discourse; but probably a few ratios—and especially one term—will typify that discourse.

The pentad, together with a knowledge of identification and the innately dramatistic nature of human society, provides the critic with a vocabulary and way of proceeding. To understand the process, however, the critic must understand each term of the pentad with its corresponding philosophy and terminology.

Following from the belief that society is dramatistic in nature, the *act* for Burke is the central term in the pentad. The act answers the question, What is done? Burke explains that when the act is *featured* in discourse, the philosophy that dominates within the speech is realism.[24] In defining realism Burke cites Aristotle: "Things are more or less real according as they are more or less *energeia* (actu, from which our 'actuality' is derived)."[25] he act or realism is not just existence, it is 'taking form'." The realist grammar begins with a tribal concept and treats the individual as a participant in substance. The terminology associated with the act would suggest an emphasis upon verbs.[26]

The term *scene* corresponds with a philosophy of materialism. Burke cites Baldwin's *Dictionary of Philosophy and Psychology* to define materialism: "that metaphysical theory which regards all the facts of the universe as sufficiently explained by the assumption of body and matter, conceived as extended, impenetrable, eternally existent, and susceptible of movement or change of relative position."[27] Darwin's *The Origin of the Species* illustrates some of the terminology that accompanies the domination of the scene: *accidental variation, conditions of existence, adjustment, natural selection,* and *survival of the fittest.*[28]

The scene, which is the background or setting for the drama, is generally revealed in secular or material terms. Since it is the background, the emphasis

---

[22]Kenneth Burke, *A Grammar of Motives*, (Englewood Cliffs, NJ: Prentice-Hall, 1945), x. Italics Burke's.
[23]Ibid.
[24]Ibid., 128.
[25]Ibid., 227.
[26]Ibid., 228.
[27]Ibid., 131.
[28]Ibid., 153.

can easily shift from the scene to the act, agent, agency, or purpose. But these shifts, which will be slight if the rhetoric is consistent, will continue to reveal the determinism of the material situation characteristic with the domination of a mind by the scene.

The philosophy corresponding to *agent* is idealism. Burke again turns to Baldwin's dictionary in defining idealism: "in metaphysics, any theory which maintains the universe to be throughout the work of reason and mind."[29] Burke points to terms such as *ego, self, superego, mind, spirit,* and *oversoul* as a sign of a stress on agent. He also suggests that treating ideas—church, race, nation, historical periods, cultural movements—as "personalities" usually indicates idealism. Furthermore, the dominance of agent grows out of the spiritualization of the family. Whenever important human economic relations have become idealized or spiritualized, the agent is featured.

We have considered three terms from the pentad—*act, scene,* and *agent.* For convenience of explanation, we may draw together *agency* and *purpose* in a means-end relationship. Burke points out that "means are considered in terms of ends." But as "you play down the concept of final cause (as modern science does), . . . there is a reversal of causal ancestry—and whereas means were treated in terms of ends, ends become treated in terms of means."[30] To illustrate this shift between means and ends Burke shows that money, which is the means (agency) of obtaining goods and services, simultaneously can be the end (purpose) of work.[31]

In featuring the means, or agency, the pragmatic philosophy is dominant. Pragmatism is defined by Kant as "the means necessary to the attainment of happiness."[32] John Dewey refers to his pragmatist doctrine as instrumentalism. In modern science, method or agency dominates all other terms of the human drama. Along with modern science and pragmatism, the technologically oriented line of action has appeared and is identified with terms such as *Useful, practical,* and *serviceable.*[33] William James not only asserts that pragmatism is "a method only," but he goes on to indicate that *consequence, function, what it is good for,* and *the difference it will make to you and me* are pragmatic evaluations. However, pure pragmatism goes beyond James to transcend purpose, as in the applied sciences, when the method is built into the instrument itself. At this point agency becomes the focus of the entire means-ends relationship.

The process may be reversed, featuring *purpose* rather than agency. The philosophy corresponding to purpose is mysticism. The Baldwin dictionary describes the philosophy of mysticism: "those forms of speculative and religious thought which profess to attain an immediate apprehension of the divine essence or the ultimate ground of existence. . . . Penetrated by the thought of the ultimate of all experience, and impatient of even a seeming separation from the creative source of things, mysticism succumbs to a species of meta-physical fascination."[34]

Mysticism is readily equated to purpose when it contains such references as *the divine essence* and *the creative source.* In a mystic worldview, the element of

[29]Ibid., 171.
[30]Ibid., 276.
[31]Ibid., 108 and 276.
[32]Ibid., 275.
[33]C. Wright Mills, *Power, Politics, and People,* (New York: Ballantine, 1963), 441.
[34]Burke, *A Grammar of Motives,* 287.

unity can be emphasized to the point that individuality disappears. Identification often becomes so strong as to indicate the "unity of the individual with some cosmic or universal purpose"[35] The universal purpose becomes a compulsive force against which everything else is judged.

Aristotle and Plato reflect elements of mysticism. Aristotle's mystic absolutism can be seen in his purpose for society—happiness. Plato's mysticism goes well beyond that of Aristotle and completely equates "good" and "purpose." His concept of reality is drawn from his ideas of the "good," and the rest of the world is arranged in accordance with this ideal.[36]

In any complete discussion of human motivation, all five terms of the pentad are necessary. To the extent that these terms are represented as separate elements, there is division; however, to the extent that one term is featured and the other terms seem to grow out of this term, there is unity. As a model, the pentad can express both possibilities, unity and division.

To illustrate the operation of the pentad Burke compares it to the human hand. He likens the five terms to the fingers, which are distinct from each other and possess their own individuality; yet, at the same, time, they merge into a unity at the palm of the hand. With this simultaneous division and unity (identification) one can leap from one term to another or one can move slowly from one to another through the palm.[37] The analogy illustrates both aspects of the operation of the pentad—flexibility of movement, and unity and division. The analogy also brings out another aspect of Burke's rhetorical philosophy and structure (which will be discussed later), whereby the palm represents the unity of the terms, or substance of the speech, that is discovered by determining which of the terms is featured in the discourse.

At this point identification and the pentad merge as tools in Burke's rhetorical structure. The speaker may use the strategy of featuring the agent and then, in proving a point, proceed to an agent-scene or agent-act ratio. Then she or he may move to purpose and finally to agency. Each step represents an act that symbolizes an attitude, and the total series represents the dramatistic process in action as the speaker sees it. Using identification one can discover each step that reflects the speaker's stylized answers to the situation or strategies, and with the pentad as a model the steps can be plotted so as to describe the dramatistic process operating in the speech.

Unity of Substance and Rhetorical Devices

The structural tools of identification and the pentad bring about a unity of strategies or rhetorical devices and substance. This unity aids the critic in understanding and explaining human rhetorical tendencies.

Substance, according to Burke, is the philosophical foundation of the message in a rhetorical act. In the analogy with the hand, substance represents the palm—the place where all other elements are unified. To define *substance* Burke starts with Webster's dictionary: "the most important element in any existence; the

[35]Ibid., 288.
[36]Ibid., 292–94.
[37]Ibid., xxiv.

characteristic and essential import, purpose."[38] He concludes that substance is literally, what its name imports that which stands beneath something. The principle of substance is important in Burke's rhetorical criticism because all discourse must establish a substance that is the context for the communication or the key to the speaker's attitudes. Burke defines four types of substance: familial, directional, geometric, and dialectic. Each type of substance is established when a given term from the pentad is featured to the point that it dominates the discourse.

Geometric substance places an object in its setting as "existing both in itself and as part of its background."[39] This featuring leads to a materialistic notion of determinism, which is most consistent with the term *scene* from the pentad.

When agent is featured, a familial substance evolves. "It stresses common ancestry in the strictly biological sense, as literal descent from material or paternal sources."[40] However, the concept of family is often spiritualized so as to include social and national groups and beliefs.

Directional substance is also biologically derived; however, it comes "from a sense of free motion."[41] The feeling of movement provides a sense of motivation from within. All generalizations such as *the reasonable man* or *the economic man* fall in this category. Also, "terminologies that situate the driving force of human action in human passion"[42] and treat emotion as motive are classified as directional substance. Finally, "doctrines that reduce mental states to materialistic terms treat motion as motive," and encourage "sociological speculation in terms of 'tendencies' or 'trends.'"[43] The term *agency* follows from this context.

The last type of substance, dialectic, reflects "the ambiguities of substance, since symbolic communication is not a merely external instrument, but also intrinsic to men as agents. The motivational properties of dialectic substance characterize both 'human situation' and what men are 'in themselves.'" The ambiguity of external and internal motivation creates dialectic substance: "The most thoroughgoing dialectic opposition, however, centers in that key pair: Being and Not-Being."[44] For example, Burke shows how dialectic substance can transcend to the "ultimate abstract Oneness": "The human person, for instance, may be derived from God as a 'super-person.' Or human purpose may be derived from an All-Purpose, or Inner Purpose, etc."[45] The term central to dialectic substance is *purpose*.

Substance as the context of the discourse is the source of the subject matter for the rhetorical act, of the motives and attitudes of the speaker, and of the strategies or rhetoric devices used by the speaker. The structural tools—identification and pentad—are useful in determining and describing both the substance of the speech and the speaker's rhetorical strategies. The critic is able to uncover the substance of the speech and the rhetorical strategies used by the speaker for three reasons: (1) because verbal symbols are meaningful acts that are strategies reflecting the speaker's attitudes; (2) because these attitudes represent the speaker's acceptance and rejection of the present hierarchy of society; and (3) because

[38]Ibid., 21.
[39]Ibid., 29.
[40]Ibid.
[41]Ibid., 31.
[42]Ibid., 32.
[43]Ibid.
[44]Ibid., 34.
[45]Ibid., 35.

acceptance and rejection results in the eternal process of pollution, guilt, purification, and redemption for society. The total interrelationship of terms and processes represents Burke's dramatistic approach to rhetoric.

In addition to the dramatistic structure of his rhetorical system, Burke discusses various special rhetorical elements. The two most significant ones for rhetorical criticism are the forms of style and the levels of symbolic action. These special devices aid in describing the dramatistic process but are subordinate to the process. In *Counter-Statement* Burke indicates that form "is an arousing and fulfillment of desires."[46] Form provides sequence—one portion of the speech prepares the audience for another part. The kinds of form that Burke discusses are syllogistic and qualitative progression, repetitive form, conventional form, and minor or incidental form.[47] Because speakers will structure their speeches differently, various kinds of form aid the critic in establishing patterns for the development of the dramatistic process. Syllogistic progression is a step-by-step method of representing an argument: "To go from A to E through stages B, C, and D is to obtain such form."[48] Qualitative progression is more subtle in its development. The speaker's ideas progress through the construction of a mood or a quality rather than in a step-by step manner. Repetitive form is the process of restating a principle in a slightly different manner. The speaker may vary the details of the support with each restatement, but the principle is consistent. Conventional form is the persuasive appeal resulting from "form as form." A syllogism or analogy has appeal simply as form, independent of the argument constructed. Any work also has minor or incidental forms "such as metaphor, paradox, disclosure, reversal, contraction, expansion, bathos, apostrophe, series, chiasmus—which can be discussed as formal events in themselves."[49]

After describing the types of form, Burke indicates that there is both interrelation and conflict of forms. "Progressive, repetitive, and conventional and minor forms necessarily overlap."[50] However, the important thing is not that they overlap but that their use should be identified. The critic should discover the circumstances under which various forms are used. Not only do formal principles intermingle, they also conflict. Burke suggests that a writer may create a character who, according to the plot or the logic of fiction, "should be destroyed." But if this character is completely accepted by the audience, it may desire "the character's salvation": "Here would be a conflict between syllogistic and repetitive forms."[51] Burke also indicates that syllogistic and repetitive, as well as repetitive and conventional forms, may conflict. The form that the dramatistic process takes is another tool available to the rhetorical critic.

In describing the dramatistic process, the levels of symbolic action can also be of value to the critic. The speakers strategically select verbal symbols that represent their attitudes and which they feel will be effective in inducing "identification" with their audiences. One method of describing these symbols is to categorize them according to their level of symbolic action or level of abstraction. In *Philosophy of Literary Form* Burke considers three levels of symbolic

---

[46]Kenneth Burke, *Counter-Statement*, (Chicago: University of Chicago Press, 1957), 124.
[47]Ibid., 124–26.
[48]Ibid., 124.
[49]Ibid., 127.
[50]Ibid., 128.
[51]Ibid., 129.

action: the bodily or biological level, the personal or familistic level, and the abstract level.[52] In *Rhetoric of Religion* he discusses "four realms to which words may refer. . . . First, there are words for the natural. . . . Second, there are words for the socio-political realm. . . . Third, there are words about words,"[53] and fourth, there are "words for the 'supernatural.'"[54] Again, these levels of symbolic action and realms for words will overlap in discourse, but the critic should identify their occurrence along with the circumstances in which they occur.

Burke's special devices of form, levels of symbolic action, and realms to which words may refer represent tools for rhetorical criticism that can be used in conjunction with his dramatistic structure of rhetoric. These techniques, taken together, constitute a definite system in which the substance of the discourse and the rhetorical tools used by the speaker interlock.

Burke's Shift to Ontology

Burke's writing prior to 1968 stressed epistemology, developing and applying his rhetorical system for criticism. Then, in his article "Dramatism" in *The International Encyclopedia of the Social Science* Burke emphasized "a philosophy of language" and "a general conception of man and of human relations,"[55] increasing his concern for ontology over epistemology.

Burke clearly announced this shift in orientation in a symposium and an article in *Communication Quarterly* in 1985. He emphasized two positions: (1) that dramatism was literal, not metaphorical, and (2) that he now defines humans as "bodies that learn language."[56] Burke's development of these positions reveals three major differences in his own rhetoric as his emphasis moved from epistemology to ontology. First, the "act" becomes central to human motivation when previously any one of the five terms from the pentad could be featured.[57] Second, as language is viewed as literal, Burke's own language becomes more descriptive and less figurative in his transcendence downward from his earlier stress on, and exploitation of, the *ambiguity* of language. Burke's illustration of literal dramatism reflects this downward transcendence: "For example, if there is a shipwreck, everyone on the boat is motivated by the shipwreck (a scene-act motivation). But, every person on the boat will act differently. If there are twenty people on the boat, there will be twenty very different kinds of agent-act relationships. One person may "look out for number one." Another will try to help people. Another will pray. And, so it goes. There is an unlimited number of ways of responding to that situation. Yet, each response is a very literal response to the situation."[58] Third, in replacing his more complex and poetic definition of

[52]Burke, *The Philosophy of Literary Form*, 31–33.

[53]Kenneth Burke, *The Rhetoric of Religion* (Boston: Beacon Press, 1961), 14.

[54]Ibid., 15.

[55]Kenneth Burke, "Dramatism," in *The International Encyclopedia of the Social Sciences*, ed, D. L. Sills (New York: Macmillan/Free Press, 1968), 445–52.

[56]Bernard L. Brock, Kenneth Burke, Parke G. Burgess, and Herbert W. Simons, "Dramatism as Ontology or Epistemology: A Symposium, *Communication Quarterly* 33 (Winter 1985): 23,31.

[57]Burke, "Dramatism as Ontology or Epistemology," 24.

[58]Burke, "Dramatism as Ontology or Epistemology," 24.

human beings with "bodies that learn language," Burke moves away from the centrality of metaphor and paradox to his rhetorical system and is more concerned with "reality."[59]

Because most of Burke's writing has been devoted to his epistemic system, his ontology views are less clear. However, James W. Chesebro describes five principles that underly Burke's ontological rhetoric: "First, there is a world of external phenomena, and it is distinct from the realm of human symbol-using. . . . Second, the world of external phenomena and the realm of symbol-using are unbridgeable. . . . Third, human beings are uniquely symbol-using animals. . . . Fourth, symbols are actions which create potentialities. . . . Fifth, chaos—not the regulating of nature—is the ultimate foundation of symbol-using."[60]

The significance of Burke's shift in emphasis from an epistemological to an ontological rhetoric and the implications for the rhetorical critics are yet to be determined, but this shift now raises the question of whether or not a tension between epistemology and ontology runs throughout all of Burke's writing. Answering this question and sorting out these tendencies is a challenge for scholars in the Kenneth Burke Society.

Suggestions for the Rhetorical Critic

In executing rhetorical criticism, the critic not only describes human rhetorical efforts but also makes interpretative judgments based on rhetorical norms or principles. Burke's dramatism gives the critic a method of analysis capable of establishing, at least tentatively, rhetorical norms through repeated application. Only through such application, sufficiently wide and varied to give a thorough test to the principles that arise, can critics be certain that they have a firm basis for judgment. But the long-range task necessitates consistent use of a critical vocabulary. The point of this essay has been to outline such a vocabulary and to suggest how the terms that compose it work together and aid the critic in making rhetorical judgments. The following are some specific ways that a critic can use Burke's dramatistic rhetoric in establishing norms or principles for judgment:

1.   Each of the Burkeian rhetorical concepts can be used to discover stylistic characteristics of a given rhetorical act or speaker.
2.   The critic can observe the conditions under which various strategies are employed, thereby inductively constructing a theory about their use.
3.   Critics can identify correlations in the use of various strategies to learn more about human rhetorical tendencies and patterns. The relationship between substance and other strategies could be especially interesting.
4.   The critic should study stages in the dramatistic process—pollution, guilt, purification, and redemption—and determine how each stage is developed and stressed.

[59]Bernard L. Brock, "Epistemology and Ontology in Kenneth Burke's Dramatism," *Communication Quarterly* 33, (Spring 1985): 100–103.
[60]James W. Chesebro, "Epistemology and Ontology as Dialectical Modes in the Writings of Kenneth Burke," *Communication Quarterly* 36, (Summer 1988): 182–85.

5. Critics should also discover the circumstances in which incompatible strategies are used—for example, when two terms from the pentad receive equal stress so that no discernible substance evolves.

Kenneth Burke's dramatistic approach to rhetoric provides critics with a language and theoretical structure that allows them to describe humans as they respond to their world and to understand basic rhetorical tendencies. With such a system the critic is able to make descriptive, interpretative judgments regarding the effectiveness of rhetoric.

RONALD REAGAN ON LEBANON AND GRENADA: FLEXIBILITY AND INTERPRETATION IN THE APPLICATION OF KENNETH BURKE'S PENTAD

David S. Birdsell

On October 23, 1983, a suicide bomber set off a truck full of explosives in the American Marine compound in Beirut, Lebanon. The resulting blast killed more than two hundred Marines. The soldiers were part of a multinational peacekeeping force that included French, British, and Italian troops in addition to the Americans. Most troops were asleep when the bomb went off. There had been no active fighting immediately preceding the attack; the bomb came as a complete surprise. Aside from the tragedy of the lives lost, the attack was deeply embarrassing to the unprepared U.S. troops and the Reagan administration.[1]

Only hours later, American troops invaded and ultimately captured the Caribbean island of Grenada. The campaign was short and successful. Meaningful resistance was eliminated quickly, and American casualties were light. By ordering the invasion when it did, the administration claimed to have prevented the island's imminent takeover by Cuban infiltrators.[2] In sharp contrast to the debacle in Lebanon, the news from Grenada seemed to affirm the power and ability of the American military and the vision of the Reagan administration.

In a nationally televised foreign policy address on October 27, Ronald Reagan made his first major statement on both of these issues.[3] He claimed that, "The events in Lebanon and Grenada, though oceans apart, are closely related," supporting that contention with repeated references to the United States' national interest and the presence of hostile forces in both areas. However, an analysis of

From *Quarterly Journal of Speech* 73 (August 1987): 267–79. Used by permission of the author and the Speech Communication Association.

David S. Birdsell is assistant professor of speech at Baruch College. A version of this paper was presented at the Burke Conference, Temple University, March 6–8, 1984. The author would like to thank Kathleen Jamieson and Charles Kauffman for their helpful comments on earlier drafts of this essay.

[1]For news accounts of the attack on the Marine barracks in Lebanon, see *The Washington Post* and *The New York Times*, 24–30 October 1983. On the administration's embarrassment over the security lapse, see "President Defends Policy in Lebanon, Backs Gen. Kelley," *The Washington Post*, 21 December 1983, sec. A, p. 1.

[2]For news accounts of the Grenadan invasion, see *The Washington Post* and *The New York Times*, 27 October–1 November 1983. For the administration's claims for success, see the transcript of the Reagan speech in *The Washington Post* 28 October 1983, sec. A, p. 14. Quotations from the speech will not be individually noted. All quotations have been taken from this version of the speech.

[3]The speech was a major address that is generally thought to have been a great success for Reagan and his policies. See "Speech Seen Buttressing Support," *The Washington Post*, 28 October 1983, sec. A, p. 1. Polling results support this analysis. See "Bombing, Invasion in Eerie Focus," *The Washington Post*, 24 October 1984, sec. A., p. 10: "A Washington Post-ABC poll taken the day before his speech showed that 41 percent of the respondents approved of his [Reagan's] handling of the Lebanon situation and 53 percent disapproved. In another poll, taken the day after the speech, the figures were reversed—52 percent approved of his policy and 42 percent disapproved, even though the respondents thought, by more than 2 to 1, the Beirut bombing could have been prevented."

the speech using the terms of Kenneth Burke's dramatistic pentad reveals major differences in Reagan's framing of the two events, differences that are reconciled in the context of his elliptical remarks on foreign policy at the end of the speech.[4] Though not explicitly offered as an explanation for the margin between success in Grenada and failure in Lebanon, Reagan's characterization of qualitatively different kinds of American involvement serves to flesh out an understanding of his goals and his definition of the national interest. This in turn calls into question the administration's commitment to the ideals of multinationalism and the role of America in global politics.

The Burkean pentad helps to isolate persuasive resources in the speech. The multiple scenes, acts, agents, agencies, and purposes contained in the address provide special opportunities and challenges for a pentadic critique. The speech is divided neatly into a section on Lebanon, a section on Grenada, and a summary section. The pentadic chart that emerges is complex and "layered," featuring a different pentadic "root" for each portion of the speech. The section on Lebanon is best characterized as an examination of "scene." The section on Grenada relies principally upon a discussion of "agent." In the summary, "act" coordinates and redefines the earlier sections. Though the parts of the pentad as developed in the speech are discrete, they function as a whole, augmenting and balancing one another.

If the pentad serves to illuminate Reagan's speech, the speech serves to highlight three aspects of the critical application of the pentad. First, the terms of the pentad are inherently ambiguous; that ambiguity must be incorporated into the act of criticism to reap the full benefit of a pentadic analysis. Second, the "root" term in a given text may well shift at different stages in the text. If the Reagan speech is any indication, one term will probably come to ground the others, but this need not always be the case. Finally, the test for the most useful pentadic

---

[4]Bernard L. Brock, "Rhetorical Criticism: A Burkeian Approach," in *Methods of Rhetorical Criticism: A Twentieth Century Perspective*, ed. Robert L. Scott and Bernard L. Brock (New York: Harper and Row, 1972); see particularly 319 for mention of the pentad's notoriety. See also Bernard Brock, "Political Speaking: A Burkeian Approach," in *Critical Responses to Kenneth Burke*, ed. William H. Rueckert (Minneapolis: University of Minnesota Press, 1969), 444–55. Brock has updated his position on the pentad, "Epistemology and Ontology in Kenneth Burke's Dramatism," *Communication Quarterly* 33 (1985): 94–104. Kenneth Burke's own work on the pentad may be found in, "The Study of Symbolic Action," *The Chimera* 1 (1942): 7–16; "The Tactics of Motivation," *The Chimera* 2 (1943): 37–53; *A Grammar of Motives* (1945; reprint, Berkeley: University of California Press, 1969). Though the material in the *Chimera* articles was worked into the *Grammar*, I cite it separately since the phrasing sometimes differs somewhat from the *Grammar*. Burke has extended the notion of the pentad into a "hexad," *Dramatism and Development* (Barre: Clark University Press with Barre Publishers, 1972). This paper does not deal with the suggested sixth term, "attitude," but a hexad would be susceptible to the same analysis. See Roy S. Skodnick, "Counter-Gridlock: An Interview With Kenneth Burke," *All Area* 2 (1983): 4–35, particularly 18. Numerous critics have used or commented on the pentad. See Jane Blankenship, Edward Murphy, and Marie Rosenwasser, "Pivotal Terms in the Early Works of Kenneth Burke," *Philosophy and Rhetoric* 7 (1974): 1–24; Barry Brummett, "A Pentadic Analysis of Ideologies in Two Gay Rights Controversies," *Central States Speech Journal* 30 (1973): 250–61; William J. Hamlin and Harold H. Nichols, "The Interest Value of Rhetorical Strategies Derived from Kenneth Burke's Pentad," *Western Speech* 37 (1973): 97–102; Robert L. Ivie, "Presidential Motives for War," *Quarterly Journal of Speech* 60 (1974): 337–45. Additional references will be cited below.

explanation will often rest upon criteria external to the pentadic vocabulary. This "second judgment" reveals any pentadic analysis as a point in the critical process, not as the end of the process itself. I first present a pentadic analysis of Reagan's speech and then examine its implications for administration foreign policy and for the practice of pentadic criticism.

Criticism: The October 27th Address

Lebanon: The Dominance of Scene   Reagan's treatment of the events leading to the deaths of "more than two hundred" Marines in Beirut is rooted, as I have said, in scene. While American troops and their enemies are assigned clear positions to locate them in their physical environment, neither group's specific activities, routine procedures, or personal traits are as important as the simple fact of their bodily presence in the scene. The situation itself exerts principal control over the people encompassed within it.

This is especially plain in the earliest passages in the speech. After a brief introductory paragraph in which Reagan reminds us of the deaths on KAL flight 007, he begins to reconstruct the events leading up to the bombing.[5] At the outset, his treatment is both spatial and chronological.

> Our Marines are assigned to the south of the city of Beirut near the only airport operating in Lebanon. Just a mile or so to the north is the Italian contingent and, not far from them, the French and a company of British soldiers. This past Sunday, at twenty two minutes after six Beirut time. . . .

Much of the description centers on things: the troop encampment, the trucks on the highway, and the road itself. The driver of the truck bomb is the only agent who enters the scene, and even his action is distanced from the realm of the humanly explicable because it is "suicidal" or "insane."[6] "Marine defenders" are portrayed as incapable of dealing with the scene, or even of recognizing its dangers. There was no way our Marines could know "that there was a bomb in the truck passing on the road. There was nothing in its appearance to suggest it was any different than the cars or trucks that were normally seen on and around the airport." American efforts to materially alter the scene by erecting physical barriers are said to be similarly ineffective. The collapse of the "chain link fence and barbed wire entanglements," the only cited evidence of American effect upon the landscape, is perfectly consistent with the overall malignity of the scene.

After the eighth paragraph, the narrative shifts from the bombing itself to a discussion of the political situation in Lebanon. This long section (fully half the speech) seeks to establish the reasons for an American presence in Lebanon and, concomitantly, to justify the deaths of the Marines. The reasons for U.S.

---

[5]KAL Flight 007 was the Korean Air Lines passenger jet shot down in Soviet airspace shortly before the bombing in Lebanon.

[6]The insanity is scenic because it is entirely unpredictable in human terms and perfectly consistent with the overall situation. To feature the killing as the product of the driver as a discrete agent would be to represent scene in the action of the individual, which once again returns the critic to the explication of scene. I am simply eliminating the interim step.

involvement are put no fewer than five times.[7] American presence is carefully linked with the interests of the West, with peace, with Israel, with the military security of a portion of Beirut, and with the personal well-being of a Lebanese child.

At one level, these goals figure as a purposive rationale for American involvement, a set of programs pursued in order to alter scenic circumstances to bring them more closely into line with American policy expectations. This explanation would feature the frustration of American purposes by the malign scene. By extension, the agent phenomenalized in policy (agency) undertaken for a reason (purpose) is shown to be unequal to circumstances (scene). This interpretation is consistent with the scenic orientation outlined at the beginning of this section.

A different interpretation, also consistent with that outline, is that the nature of American involvement in the area constitutes an element of the malign scene, which would mean that the way in which the nation is involved ultimately may be hostile to American interests. The phrasing of the rationale for the Marines' presence provides a clue.

> So, why are we there? Well, the answer is straightforward: to help bring peace to Lebanon and stability to the Middle East. . . . The physical presence of the Marines lends support to both the Lebanese government and its army. It allows the hard work of diplomacy to go forward. . . . As to that narrower question: What exactly is the operational mission of the Marines? The answer is, to secure a piece of Beirut, to keep order in their sector and to prevent the area from becoming a battlefield.

Even the daily operations are argued in purposive, essential terms, rather than in procedural terms. The stated goal—stability in the Middle East—is wildly out of proportion to the stated means, an impression magnified by Reagan's own impressive list of the ways in which American efforts have been blocked. Procedures that would cause a change in scene and an explanation of the link between actions taken and goals sought are not provided. The only evidence offered for the success of U.S. policy is a little girl's return to school and, strangely enough, the bombing itself. In Reagan's words: "The multinational force was attacked precisely because it was doing the job it was sent to do in Beirut—it is accomplishing its mission."

The death of the Marines is hardly a satisfying response to the challenge of the scene in Lebanon. More disquieting is the assumption that Americans do "the job they are sent to do" primarily by dying. To explain the deaths as they are recast by Reagan, we must conclude one of three things: that the Marines are incompetent, that their efforts are hopeless, or that the nature of their presence has been radically miscalculated.[8]

Reagan repeatedly rejected the first two positions. The third option is the most satisfying, and coincides with the second explanation for the role of purpose

[7]The questions are specifically: Column 1, paragraph 10, "Why should our young men be dying in Lebanon?" Column 2, paragraph 2, "So, why are we there?" Column 2, paragraph 9, "What exactly is the operational mission of the Marines?" Column 2, paragraph 17, "[Are we] serving any purpose in being there?" Column 4, paragraph 6, "Why are we there?"

[8]Reagan has many times insisted upon the need for U.S. presence in Lebanon. See "President Defends Policy in Lebanon," The Washington Post, 21 December 1983, sec. A, p. 1.

described above. The death of the Marines is a tacit indictment of multination-alism. The "American" troops did not die because they were doing their job, the "multinational" troops did (though of course the vast majority of these were American). In the Reagan speech, the multinational context for American presence is itself described as an element of scene, little or no different from the roads surrounding the airport in Beirut. Reagan clearly subordinates the Marines to the multinational role. He lists the nations party to the original agreement and situates American troops in the midst of the process those nations initiated. "The physical presence of the Marines . . . allows the hard work of diplomacy to go forward." The Marines may work for the U.S., but they do so indirectly. American troops are working for the region rather than for America, and their effectiveness as Americans is thus scenically limited. This becomes clearer still in the next two sections where America is rehabilitated as agent and unhampered act is revealed as the source of American competence.

The multinational force just as easily could be described as an element of scene. My decision to cast the force as fundamentally scenic rests upon the way in which the multinational force is treated and with the arrangement of the rest of the speech as well. The force is described only with respect to its member-ship: there is no elaborate description of its functions or of the ways in which expressly mutinational procedures have endangered American lives. The multina-tional ethic, like the random terror in and around the airport, is simply there, and is essentially hostile to the United States. The scenic explanation (and here I would include as well the first, purposive explanation of the rationale for inter-vention from above) is more satisfying also because it comes closer to explaining the arrangement not only of one portion of the speech, but of the whole speech. American integrity is protected carefully from the ignominy of a one-on-one de-feat. Reagan could have cast the trouble in Lebanon as the activity of a malign agent/agency rather than a malign scene; however, the alternate formula would hold different implications for the argument. Should America actually be de-feated by another agent, the defeat would constitute tacit admission of inferiority to that agent, an admission inimical to the ultimate theme of American pre-eminence in Reagan's speech. The scenic emphasis avoids this problem. The scenic emphasis also links all of the hostile agents without requiring any specific arguments for treating them as a single (albeit diffuse) group. An explanation emphasizing agent would require the construction of a malign agency coordinat-ing the problems for America, a task Reagan is apparently unwilling to under-take at this point in the speech. A scenic explanation is best because it implicates all relevant agents and reveals America's difficulties as primarily positional with respect to physical and verbal commitments.[9] When liberated from these posi-tional constraints, America becomes much more effective. This is the theme ev-idenced by Reagan's explanation of the Grenadan incursion.

Grenada: The Agent Ascendant   Scene is less oppressive in Reagan's Grenada than it is in his Lebanon. The strategic importance of the area, arduously de-tailed for the Middle East, is unargued for Grenada. The importance of the

[9]Burke, *A Grammar of Motives*, 26; "The Study of Symbolic Action," 12. Burke's dis-cussion of feudalism and capitalism as "scenes" is instructive. There he treats context-of-operation as an element of scene rather than an element of agency.

island arises not from its substance, but from its associations. The Cuban presence, invited by "Maurice Bishop, a protege of Fidel Castro," provides the challenge to the United States. The differences between the malign agent of Grenada and the malign scene of Lebanon are apparent before any discussion of U.S. involvement in either situation. In Lebanon, the principal feature of the situation is random danger and unreason. In Grenada, the principal feature of the situation is the calculated mischief of the communists.

As the cause differs, so does the response. While maintaining the trappings of multinationalism established in the Beirut case, America is allowed much more freedom of movement, much more unilateral responsibility for dealing with the trouble in Grenada. Though the invasion was supposedly prompted by a local call for help, the request by the Organization of East Caribbean States remains in the background. This is very different from the description of multilateralism in Lebanon, where international commitments themselves pose a complicating and constraining element of scene. In Grenada, even though the multinational request serves as one rationale for intervention, a more important rationale is the identity of the agents. In the most succinct expression of the *post hoc* rationale for the invasion in the speech, Grenada becomes the target of invasion not because of what it has or has not done, but because of what it is:

> Grenada, we were told, was a friendly island paradise for tourism. But it wasn't. It was a Soviet-Cuban colony being readied as a major military bastion to export terror and undermine democracy. We got there just in time.

As Grenada is condemned for its chosen association with communists, so it is redeemed by the imposed American action. In other words, the agent successfully coopts the scene.

Important imbalances in the dramatic alignments arise in this portion of the speech, but they are not the same as the imbalances in the section on Beirut. Here, the American agent is perhaps over-equal to the scene/agent opposed to it. Grenada is a tiny island, and the United States a superpower. While the scene in Beirut is daunting and untamable, at least by the multinationally constrained American agent, the American agent in Grenada marshalls resources far greater than whatever might be necessary to master this less intimidating scene. The imbalances are complementary. The scene in Lebanon is balanced by the more competent agent in Grenada, just as the comparatively quiet scene of Grenada is balanced by the law-abiding agent in Beirut. The display of American force in Grenada, a dramatic over-reaction to the comparatively small provocation there, makes sense when the provocation in Lebanon is added to the balance. American force *overall* matches the enemies' provocation *overall*. The excess in Beirut matches the deficit in Grenada, and vice versa. Considering the two situations together balances the dramatic ratios. All that is missing is an encompassing term to permit direct encompassment of the two events.

The importance of having the two evaluated in tandem cannot be overstated. Troop deployment, a questionable policy on the evidence of Beirut, must be shown effective under at least some circumstances. The success in Grenada supports administration policy in the Middle East, just as the dangers of Lebanon justify American action in the Caribbean. In other words, the experience in Grenada rehabilitates the agent made suspect in Lebanon; the scene is proven malleable by proxy.

As yet, this balance is implicit. There is no organizing principle to coordinate the situations in Lebanon and Grenada. The third section of the speech reveals "act" as the coordinating principle for U.S. action.

Act as Coordinating Term   By arguing that the events in Lebanon and Grenada are closely related, Reagan creates rhetorical space for a transcendent principle that links the two situations. In the third section of the speech, the malignity of scene is plainly attributed to the Soviet Union, as was the perfidy of the agent in Grenada. The Soviet Union has a unique capacity to poison the environment quite apart from any specific actions in which it might engage. The argument for linking the two military adventures makes this clear:

> Not only has Moscow assisted and encouraged the violence in both countries, but it provides direct support through a network of surrogates and terrorists. It is no coincidence that when the thugs tried to wrest control over Grenada, there were thirty Soviet advisors and hundreds of Cuban military and paramilitary forces on the island.

Though the Cubans later fought American troops, it is plain that the fighting itself is not at issue. The simple physical presence of the communists creates an agency for Soviet domination. The contaminating elements of the Soviet presence are distinct, however, from any simplistic notion of the threat of force. While the presence of hostile troops indeed implies some potential for danger, Reagan does not focus on the likely active consequences of the foreign presence; he links his condemnation to the simple fact of the Soviets and Cubans being where they were found.

The distinction is important and more complex than the simple equation of one nation with the "good" and the other with the "bad." By basing the Soviet Union in agent/agency and the United States in act, Reagan establishes a formal difference between the two nations. The "being" of the Soviet Union and the "doing" of the United States are fundamentally incompatible. The Soviet Union contaminates with its presence. The United States redeems by its actions. Inasmuch as America embodies freedom, act is the central feature of the national character. Paraphrasing Sam Rayburn, Reagan says that freedom is "like an insurance policy—its premiums must be kept up to date. In order to keep it, we have to keep working for it and sacrificing for it just as long as we live." Under this definition of national purpose, Americans must act not only to be free, but to be truly American.

That the thrust of this theme is definition *per se* is made plain two paragraphs after the Rayburn paraphrase, when national identity is forwarded as the rationale for supporting administration policies. "We are all Americans before we are anything else, and, when our country is threatened, we stand shoulder to shoulder in support of our armed forces." Not only is America, and American character, redefined in this passage, but the military comes securely to embody act as it could not comfortably in the first portion of the speech. The Marines' frustrated act, recast as sacrifice, serves as warrant for future action. By constructing a global context for anti-Americanism, evident in scene and rooted in a malign agent/agency, the speech provides the broadest possible set of terms against which to consider American action. Situation by situation, such action may appear unbalanced; taken as a whole, however, U.S. action is appropriate and necessary. Without it, there would be no America at all.

Implications

All of the terms of the pentad are "present, in some form, in any complete statement about motives," but this does not mean that the terms are obvious, or that their relationships to one another are discoverable by formulaic rules.[10] On the contrary, the terms "can readily be made obscure"; they overlap, and "may convert into one another."[11] Since the terms are convertible, critics are well served by experimenting with various treatments of the terms within the text under study in an effort to determine which formulation will provide the fullest explanation for the relationships between those terms in that text. Such an effort will usually require the critic to marshall an understanding of the terms under a single term of the pentad, or to deal with pairs of terms (or the ratios between them) as the controlling concepts within the dramatic alignment. Identification of these controlling concepts then allows for a more extensive analysis of the implications of a text.

After exploring the ambiguity of terms in the pentad I will argue that specific symbolic acts tend to reflect a root term.[12] I also will argue that a root term is most informative when its grammatical implications are treated consistently throughout a text. Finally, I will return to Reagan's speech on Lebanon and Grenada in order to see how the pentadic alignments in the speech shed light on his framing of foreign policy agenda.

"Act, agent, agency, scene and purpose" may seem to constitute a knowable, comprehensive chart of meaning within a situation or a text, but as a practical matter, the assignment of a term to one or another component of a text depends largely upon a critic's sensibilities. The terms of the pentad are necessarily ambiguous, and are, as Burke notes, "like the five fingers. Each is distinct, yet all merge in the hand."[13] Bernard Brock's references to this analogy emphasize the principle of movement from finger to finger (whether leaping from digit to digit or moving through the palm) and the critical utility of charting the travel. Another aspect of the analogy deserves equal emphasis: In any given text the terms might be located close to the fingertips, but just as easily might be at some intermediate, liminal point between finger and palm. Determining the precise point at which a distinct motive principle emerges is a judgment not always susceptible to the same application. In other words, deciding where the purview of one term ends and another begins is a critical question that cannot be answered from within the pentad itself, but must be determined by an exterior sensibility balancing the ratios between the terms.[14]

---

[10]Burke, "The Study of Symbolic Action," 13.

[11]Burke, "The Study of Symbolic Action," 13–14.

[12]The notion of a root term is well established in previous studies. Burke organizes much of the *Grammar* by root term, 127–317. Bernard Brock has explained the utility of a root term in his discussions of the pentad. See "Rhetorical Criticism: A Burkeian Approach," 319–23. A root term may be understood as offering one kind of entitlement.

[13]Burke, "The Study of Symbolic Action," 13–14.

[14]Burke discusses the need to use various techniques to interpret the pentad in "Fact, Inference, and Proof in the Analysis of Literary Symbolism," in *Terms for Order*, ed. Stanley Edgar Hyman (Bloomington: Indiana University Press, 1964), 145–172. See also Charles Conrad, "Phases, Pentads, and Dramatistic Critical Process," *Central States Speech Journal* 35 (1984): 94–104; Robert L. King, "Transforming Scandal into Tragedy: A Rhetoric of Political Apology," *The Quarterly Journal of Speech* 71 (1985): 289–301.

This ambiguity allows for the collection of what in other contexts we might interpret as agent or agency under the heading of scene in the speech on Lebanon and Grenada. This flexible perspective on scene works to collect and explain the malign forces operating against American interests in Beirut. That the truck bomber, or the Syrian troops, in other contexts can function as pure agent, or that the anti-Israeli fighters function as agency, is undisputed. In this speech, however, they function dramatistically as elements of scene. Reagan's policy is consistent dramatistically only under a scenic interpretation of these persons and organizations.

Others have called attention to the scenic assignment of individuals.[15] For example, Jane Blankenship and her co-authors make a persuasive case that Ronald Reagan's performance in the 1980 Republican primary debates established himself as the "scene" in which the other candidates were forced to compete. My point is not that such a move is possible; non-obvious uses of pentadic terminology are well established. The implication for the practice of pentadic criticism is that a critic must consciously choose among the charts available, and pursue the implications of that chart in mapping the motives in a text. No one chart is intrinsically more "objective" than another; each is valuable in the context of a given critic's needs. Neither Blankenship's description of Ronald Reagan as the scene for the 1980 Republican primary debates nor my own assignment of the hostile forces in Lebanon to a scenic role does away with the more common understandings of "scene" and "agent."[16]

The value of focusing on a single term is not limited to instances in which scene is controlling. In his discussion of the philosophic schools, Burke makes a clear case for the broad utility of identifying a "featured" term. After identifying each term of the pentad with a different school, he argues that the worldview or essence of the school can be summed up in the term selected.[17] "Texts" can be substituted for "philosophies"—we can choose to treat a text as the accessible example of a philosophy—and the same principle can be applied to any condensation of the pentad. This condensation can be viewed as a reductive tactic (whether conscious or not) designed to obscure the various resources of persuasion and meaning, or it can be viewed as a key to the ordering of a given rhetorical system.

When searching for a featured term, care must be taken to preserve the inherent ambiguity of the terms. Burke points out that the terms can be derived from one another, "and by reason of the overlap among the terms, can reduce some of them to others."[18] This problem in finding a root term is magnified when dealing with individual texts rather than the bodies of work that Burke analyzed in "The

[15]Jane Blankenship, Marlene G. Fine, and Leslie K. Davis, "The 1980 Republican Primary Debates: The Transformation of Actor to Scene," *Quarterly Journal of Speech* 69 (1983): 25–36.

[16]Blankenship, Fine, and Davis, 25. Had Blankenship been interested exclusively in camera placement, she might well have decided to deal with Reagan as an agent and focus entirely upon the physical elements of scene. On the other hand, the broader purposes of analyzing the dynamics of persuasion in the primary campaign are better served by treating Reagan as scene and evaluating response to his candidacy as a series of responses to scene. Likewise, if I were to attempt an explanation of the different kinds of hostile forces within the malign scene in Lebanon, I would need to recast the agents and agencies as such.

[17]For the most complete statement of the various perspectives, see Burke, *A Grammar of Motives*, 127–317.

[18]Burke, "The Study of Symbolic Action," 14.

Philosophic Schools." Individual texts will be less likely to exhibit the pure characteristics of the root term.[19] I am not suggesting that pentadic analysis is uniquely appropriate to academic texts, or that unselfconscious philosophies will fail to produce a root term. I only emphasize Burke's suggestions that root terms are likely to be considerably less well-defined in specific texts. This means both that the process of pentadic analysis is harder in such cases and that the case for considering multiple "roots" is even stronger. The combination of experimentation and ambiguity allows a critic to find the most felicitous interpretation of the pentad to illuminate a given text.

Failure to consider actively and adjust to the variety of possibilities within a text can produce problems between the pentad as a device and a text as an expression of motive. Whatever term the critic decides to use will influence the nature of the criticism as surely as the pentadic alignment characterizes the subject under study. To produce conclusions that are unique to a rooted pentadic perspective, a pentadic analysis must conform to its own logic. Since in large part that logic is evolved by the critic, this requires that the critic arrive at the most complete and consistent explanation for a text, and then lay the logic out for inspection. Only in this way can the root term lend coherence to the pentadic explanation.

As I indicated earlier, the selection of a different pentadic root would change my analysis of the Reagan speech. Selecting agent or agency as the focus of my critique in an effort to discover how Reagan treats particular actors or organizations operating within the scene of the Middle East would require rethinking all of the terministic relationships in the speech. Failure to do so would be, in effect, taking elements of the speech out of "pentadic context."

In his analysis of Edward Kennedy's Chappaquiddick speech, David Ling presents a pair of pentads to explain the persuasive power of the speech.[20] Ling says that Kennedy portrayed himself as "a victim of a scene over which he had no control" in the first half of the speech, and used that tale of victimization to excuse himself from the wrath of Massachusetts voters in the second.[21] While I tend to agree with Ling's central argument on Kennedy's posture as the hapless victim of a malign scene, the arrangement of scene and agent poses problems for the argument that Kennedy favors a "philosophy" in which scene dominates. The first pentadic set (in which scene masters agent/Kennedy) is in keeping with the scenic theme, but the second set (in which agent/the voters of Massachusetts determine scene/current reaction to events, and in fact, the disposition of now curiously forgotten agent/Kennedy's public life) contradicts the thesis of a dominant scene. The contradiction can be resolved by reassigning the voters of Massachusetts to a scenic role and allowing Kennedy to continue as agent, revealing scene once again as the creative, dominant force in the drama, but Ling does not make that argument. This reinterpretation would eliminate the notion of a "second pentadic set," in favor of assigning additional characteristics to scene in the second portion of the speech.

Alternatively, we could posit a more expansive, metaphysical scene, where "It has been written a man does what he must in spite of personal consequence, in

---

[19]Burke hints at this problem himself. See "Fact, Inference, and Proof in the Analysis of Literary Symbolism," 145–52.

[20]David Ling, "A Pentadic Analysis of Senator Edward Kennedy's Address to the People of Massachusetts, July 25, 1969," in Scott and Brock, 327–35. Robert L. King comments on Ling's approach in his own analysis of the Kennedy speech, 289, 296–99.

[21]Ling, 332–33.

spite of obstacles and dangers and pressures, and that is the basis of all human morality."[22] Here the voters of Massachusetts are themselves subjected to scene. Kennedy's direct invocation of the sources of human morality makes any choice the voters might make irrelevant, tangential to the moral dilemma that is ultimately his own.

> Whatever may be the sacrifice he faces, if he follows his conscience—the loss of his friends, his fortune, his contentment, even the esteem of his fellow man—each man must decide for himself the course he will follow.[23]

In this interpretation, the people, despite the explicit invitations to participate in Kennedy's decision, would be denied more than an advisory role in the matter. All human agents would be equally subject to the mercy of the moral scene.[24]

Both re-explanations preserve the organizing power of scene that Ling posits in the first portion of his analysis. Additionally, both allow for the explanatory power of a consistent root term. This in fact provides another avenue into the analysis of Kennedy's speech as specious apology, a case made by Robert L. King in his own discussion of the Chappaquiddick address.[25] By in effect making all citizens of Massachusetts as "guilty" as he, Kennedy dodges apology in favor of extending the principle of transgression. Use of a consistent root term reveals this strong theme in the text of the speech.

Once established, a root term can help explain the interrelationships among various sets of motives. Relationships between particular terms of the pentad will not always be the same, but some relationships will occur more frequently than others. For instance, Reagan's speech derives some of its power from the simultaneous incompatibility of scene and act and compatibility of scene and agent. As notes earlier, the animosity between the Soviet Union and the United States is defined not only by associating the Soviet Union with the bad and the United States with the good, but also by their different generating principles. The "being" of the Soviet Union and the "doing" of the United States are fundamentally incompatible.

The point may be broadened to suggest that in general, that which is actively grounded will be incompatible with that which is scenically grounded. Act inaugurates change, which inevitably takes place in scene. Even changes specifically directed toward agents, agencies, and purposes can become scenic when the circumference of the encompassing situation (or of the critic's evaluation) is adjusted accordingly. Unless scene "conspires" in the change, the act will redefine the scene in a "hostile" fashion; if act is "successful" the scene will be deprived of some element specific to it. This relationship is one of probability rather than strict necessity. Act and scene are more likely to appear as dialectical opponents given the "actus" of the one and "status" of the other. If they are to be reconciled, they will be reconciled under a third term of the pentad.

---

[22]Transcript of the speech by Edward Kennedy, *The New York Times*, 26 July 1969, sec. 1, p. 10.

[23]Kennedy, 10.

[24]Kennedy explicitly invites the help of the citizenry in the speech. "And so I ask you tonight, people of Massachusetts, to think this through with me. In facing this decision, I seek your advice and opinion. In making it, I seek your prayers. For this is a decision that I will finally have to make on my own." Note that Kennedy avoids committing himself in any way to the results of the citizen participation he seeks.

[25]King, 296–99.

For much the same reason that act and scene tend to be polar terms, scene and agent are compatible terms. Scene is essentially static, and as essence, agent also describes a static set of qualities. Agent is defined in part by relation to scene; a change in either affects the definition of both. To be a featured term, agent must have some characteristics that inhere within it lest it be redefined in terms of act. For example, stories about a person's life, from childhood through old age, chronicle different stages of development. The description of the person at any one point is a description of a static collection of traits and values in a set scene. When the emphasis is upon the movement from one stage to another, the focus turns to purpose or agency, or perhaps scene: forces operating upon the agent to make it not-the-agent, to make it different. This distinction enables the critic to distinguish between that which is more precisely based upon agent and that which describes act and purpose in terms of agent. It points to another opportunity for transformation based upon shifts in pentadic root. If an agent is set against scene, then the agent attempts to achieve a goal—revealing an ultimately purposive grounding, or pursuing a character grounded in act. In neither case will agent be the featured term, but rather a vehicle for act or purpose. This tendency manifests itself in Reagan's speech by the very narrow, and arguably non-existent, distinction between the treatment of the Soviet Union as an agent on the one hand, and an element of scene on the other.[26]

These examples illustrate kinds of explanations available given the clustering of persuasive devices under a single term of the pentad. For Reagan, act serves as the benchmark of the national interest, the means to preserve freedom, and the clearest definition of national identity. Act marshalls the functions of the other pentadic terms. The other four are present, but they are coordinated by act according to the grammatical requirements of that term. Act is a synecdochic key to the substance of Reagan's speech.

The grammatical integrity of the pentadic chart allows the critic to assess at least some of the implications of the root perspective. Such an endeavor is intellectually satisfying in any case, but vital in the area of rhetorically based policy criticism. In the speech on Lebanon and Grenada, the apparently irreconcilable differences between the actively based United States and the agent/agency based Soviet Union raise a number of questions for both rhetoric and policy. First, the active definition will feature intervention as the policy alternative most likely to achieve acceptable change. If America is only as free as it acts, then passive responses will rarely be in the national interest. To argue against this perspective would require a redefinition of the state or a reversal of the dissatisfaction with scene.

Second, multinationalism will be inherently suspect because it creates agency from act, thus limiting the range of act. The role of international force in intervening between decision and act is a constraint not just upon American interests, but upon the very nature of the state under Reagan's definition. The

---

[26]Agent and agency need not be distinguished here because they perform much the same role in the speech. It might be best to think of Reagan's view of the Soviet Union as that of an agency representing and encompassing an agent. Together, they constitute a kind of purpose. Brock notes the melding of agency and purpose in the applied sciences, "Political Speaking: A Burkeian Approach, " 446. Reagan here goes one step further, folding agent back into the mixture with agency and purpose. This is the kind of persuasive reduction mentioned in note 15. Treating the Soviet Union as impersonal agency makes the task of condemnation much easier.

multinational organization's restriction on American flexibility might be perceived in its milder manifestations as a partial derogation of liberty, and in its more thorough manifestations as inimical to the nation's survival. This structural indictment of multinationalism calls into question the American commitment to any international effort that could not guarantee the U.S. unfettered pursuit of its policy goals. Such guarantees are plainly incompatible with most, if not all, international agreements. If my analysis is correct, there is reason to doubt the Reagan administration's commitment to the very principle of multinational agreement.[27]

Finally, the creation of an essential difference between the United States and the Soviet Union will tend to obscure any incremental efforts to narrow the gap dividing the two nations. Reagan begins positioning the Soviet Union as an enemy state in the first paragraph of the speech by recounting the massacre of the passengers aboard KAL Flight 007, an observation that seems almost random until the speech's later revelation of pervasive Soviet chicanery.[28] Gradually, the speech establishes Soviet involvement as the proximate source of evil in all pertinent cases. The evil is never analyzed explicitly, it is assumed. The notion of the enemy takes on a formal dimension. Its presence *must* be malign if the persuasive power of "the enemy" is to be maintained. Any rapprochement would mean that the quality of the agent's involvement would have to be reassessed in every situation, which in turn would sacrifice the synecdochic condemnation available in the mere naming of the enemy. Thus the rhetorical requirements make careful evaluation or even acceptance of an enemy's conciliatory posturing, real or duplicitous, unlikely.

Summary

The notion of a single term or ratio can provide a basis for a consistent interpretation of pentadic ambiguity within a single text and establish a grammar that the critic can use to guide the analysis of that text. A great deal of the pentad's explanatory power rests upon the assumption that the terms in fact are ambiguous, that there is no consistent rule for applying the terms across situations, and that there is not necessarily a single, "correct" rule for applying the terms in any particular situation. This perspective on the pentad stands in sharp distinction to perspectives that would seek greater specificity in the terms,[29] and also celebrates the critic's active contribution to meaning.[30] The pentad itself does not reveal substance so much as it provides a schema for directing the critic's

---

[27]Consider for example the Reagan administration's dissatisfaction with UNESCO's "unproductive" multilateralism. See William F. Buckley, *The Washington Post,* 7 January 1984, sec. A, p. 15.

[28]For more on the construction of an enemy, see Murray Edelman, *Politics as Symbolic Action: Mass Arousal and Quiescence* (Chicago: Markham Publishing Company, 1971); David J. Finlay, Ole R. Holsti, and Richard R. Fagen, *Enemies in Politics* (Chicago: Rand McNally and Company, 1967).

[29]Hamlin and Nichols, for example, demand more precision from the terms. See "The Interest Value of Rhetorical Strategies Derived from Kenneth Burke's Pentad," 98.

[30] The sentiment underlying this explicit rehabilitation of the critic is well expressed by Walter Fisher: "Criticism, as understood here, is not the arbitrary imposition of a formula complete with static equations to judge a work of art. . . . Creativity is destroyed when criticism is viewed as a scientific process." See "Method and Rhetorical Criticism," *Southern Speech Communication Journal* 35 (1969): 101–09, especially 105.

attention to the points of transformation in the narrative. The critic then is responsible for the fresh interpretation of the text.

Different pentadic formulations may be possible within a single text, each contributing to the ultimate interpretation of the text in a different but equally valuable way. This means that the critic who would make fullest use of the pentad must experiment with the ratios between the terms in order to find the most consistent or the most illuminating explanation for a given text or event. Usually, this process will isolate one term, or one ratio, as the synecdochic key to persuasion in the whole of the item under study. Merely identifying the term does not complete an act of criticism, but knowing what the term is will help the critic to make consistent conclusions, perhaps based upon other factors.

THE FANTASY THEME APPROACH

FANTASY AND RHETORICAL VISION: THE RHETORICAL CRITICISM OF SOCIAL REALITY

Ernest G. Bormann

Recent research in small group communication reveals a process that can interrelate important features of communication and rhetorical theory. Just as some psychologists and sociologists have studied the small group in order to discover features of larger social structures, so can investigations of small group communication provide insight into the nature of public address and mass communication.

For several years the small group communication seminar at Minnesota has studied the decision-making process in group discussion.[1] The seminar began with two major lines of inquiry: content analysis of group meetings and extended case studies of individual groups. Careful case studies over periods of several months provided an understanding of group process and communication which was often more complete and useful than much of the quantitative data generated by using various category systems. To develop a method for process analysis which captured the richness of case studies while allowing generalization, the seminar studied the transcripts of the small group meetings as a rhetorical critic might analyze the text of a public speech.

Most of the attempts to make a rhetorical criticism of small group communication proved relatively barren until Robert Bales published *Personality and Interpersonal Behavior* in 1970.[2] What Bales and his associates had been discovering while working with natural groups in the classroom was very like what we had been working on at Minnesota. But Bales provided the key part to the puzzle when he discovered *the dynamic process of group fantasizing.* Group fantasizing correlates with individual fantasizing and extrapolates to speaker-audience fantasizing and to the dream merchants of the mass media. Rhetorical critics have long known that rhetoric and poetic have much in common yet, still,

From *Quarterly Journal of Speech* 58 (December 1972): 396–407. Used by permission of author and the Speech Communication Association.

Ernest G. Bormann is professor of speech-communication at the University of Minnesota.

[1]For a description of the Minnesota Studies and a report of the major conclusions of the research see Ernest G. Bormann, *Discussion and Group Methods: Theory and Practice* (New York: Harper and Row, 1969).

[2]New York: Holt, Rinehart.

are different. Many have viewed persuasive discourse in dramatistic terms. Now Bales provides the critic with an account of how dramatizing communication creates social reality for groups of people and with a way to examine messages for insights into the group's culture, motivation, emotional style, and cohesion.

Bales and his associates originally developed twelve content analysis categories for the study of small groups.[3] One original category, "shows tension release," was later changed to "dramatizes." Continued work with the category of "dramatizes" led to the discovery of "group fantasy events." Some, but not all, of the communication coded as "dramatizes" would chain out through the group. The tempo of the conversation would pick up. People would grow excited, interrupt one another, blush, laugh, forget their self-consciousness. The tone of the meeting, often quiet and tense immediately prior to the dramatizing, would become lively, animated, and boisterous, the chaining process, involving both verbal and nonverbal communication, indicating participation in the drama.

What is the manifest content of a group fantasy chain? What do the group members say? The content consists of characters, real or fictitious, playing out a dramatic situation in a setting removed in time and space from the here-and-now transactions of the group. (The "here-and-now," a concept borrowed from sensitivity and encounter group practice, refers to what is immediately happening in the group. Thus a recollection of something that happened to the group in the *past* or a dream of what the group might do in the *future* could be considered a fantasy theme.)

How can a fantasy chain by interpreted? Often the drama is a mirror of the group's here-and-now situation and its relationship to the external environment. The drama played out somewhere else or in some other time often symbolizes a role collision or ambiguity, a leadership conflict, or a problem related to the task-dimension of the group. Just as an individual's repressed problems might surface in dream fantasies so those of a group might surface in a fantasy chain and a critic might interpret the manifest content with an eye to discovering the group's hidden agenda.

But the chaining can also be an expression in a given social field of the individual psychodynamics of the participants. A dramatic theme might relate to the repressed psychological problems of some or all of the members and thus pull them into participation.[4]

Bales' most important discovery for the integration of communication and rhetorical theory, however, was the process by which a zero-history group used fantasy chains to develop a common culture. The group tended to ignore comments coded as "dramatizes" which did not relate either to the group's here-and-now problems or to the individual psychodynamics of the participants. Those that did get the members of the group to empathize, to improvise on the same theme, or to respond emotionally not only reflected the members' common preoccupations but served to make those commonalities public.

When group members respond emotionally to the dramatic situation they publicly proclaim some commitment to an attitude. Indeed, improvising in a

---

[3]The original categories and the method of independent coders making a content analysis are presented in Robert F. Bales, *Interaction Process Analysis: A Method for the Study of Small Groups* (Cambridge, Mass.: Addison-Wesley, 1950). Changing the category from "show of tension release" to "dramatizes" did not change the essential procedure of coding items.

[4]Bales, *Personality and Interpersonal Behavior,* pp. 136–155.

spontaneous group dramatization is a powerful force for attitude change. Dramas also imply motives and by chaining into the fantasy the members gain motivations. Since some of the characters in the fantasies are good people doing laudable things the group collectively identifies in symbolic terms proper codes of conduct and the characteristics which make people credible message sources. A comparison with more direct here-and-now methods for establishing group norms clarifies the nature of fantasy chains. For instance, one way to discover a common ground in a zero-history group with a job to do is to confront the question directly. A member may say, "I think we all want to do a good job and we should all go to the library and do a lot of research. I know that I'm willing to do that." If the others enthusiastically respond with comments like, "Yes, that is a good idea." "Good, let's go to work," the problem is dealt with directly. The fantasy chain discovers the same common ground symbolically:

> "Last semester my roommate took this course and he never worked so hard in his life."
> "Really?"
> "Yeah, it was really great though. He took field trips to hospital labs and everything."
> "Yeah, I know this girl who took the course and she said the same thing. She said you wouldn't believe how hard they worked. But she said she really got something out of it."

Values and attitudes of many kinds are tested and legitimatized as common to the group by the process of fantasy chains. Religious and political dramas are tested. For example, if someone dramatizes a situation in which a leading political figure is a laughingstock and it falls flat, that particular political attitude and value has been exhibited and not legitimatized. However, should the group chain out on that drama improvising on other laughable situations in which the politician has participated, the group will have created a common character which they can allude to in subsequent meetings and elicit a smiling or laughing emotional response. (They have created an inside joke but they have also created an attitude towards a given political position.) As Bales describes it:

> The culture of the interacting group stimulates in each of its members a feeling that he has entered a new realm of reality—a world of heroes, villains, saints, and enemies—a drama, a work of art. The culture of a group is a fantasy established from the past, which is acted upon in the present. In such moments, which occur not only in groups, but also in individual responses to works of art, one is "transported" to a world which seems somehow even more real than the everyday world. One may feel exalted, fascinated, perhaps horrified or threatened, or powerfully impelled to action, but in any case, involved. One's feelings fuse with the symbols and images which carry the feeling in communication and sustain it over time. One is psychologically taken into a psychodramatic fantasy world, in which others in the group are also involved. Then one is attached also to those other members.[5]

My argument is that these moments happen not only in individual reactions to works of art, or in a small group's chaining out a fantasy theme, but also in larger groups hearing a public speech. The dramatizations which catch on and chain out in small groups are worked into public speeches and into the mass media and, in turn, spread out across larger publics, serve to sustain the members'

---

[5]*Ibid.*, p. 152.

sense of community, to impel them strongly to action (which raises the question of motivation), and to provide them with a social reality filled with heroes, villains, emotions, and attitudes.

The composite dramas which catch up large groups of people in a symbolic reality, I call a "rhetorical vision." Just as fantasy themes chain out in the group to create a unique group culture, so do the fantasy dramas of a successful persuasive campaign chain out in public audiences to form a rhetorical vision.

A rhetorical vision is constructed from fantasy themes that chain out in face-to-face interacting groups, in speaker-audience transactions, in viewers of television broadcasts, in listeners to radio programs, and in all the diverse settings for public and intimate communication in a given society. Once such a rhetorical vision emerges it contains dramatis personae and typical plot lines that can be alluded to in all communication contexts and spark a response reminiscent of the original emotional chain. The same dramas can be developed in detail when the occasion demands, to generate emotional response.

The relationship between a rhetorical vision and a specific fantasy theme within a message explains why so much "persuasive" communication simply repeats what the audience already knows.[6] Balance theories explain attitude and behavior change on the basis of dissonance or imbalance, and yet many strikingly successful speakers have not created dissonances but have rather given voice to what the listener already knows or feels and accepts.[7] One perceptive commentator on Hitler noted, for instance, that

> one scarcely need ask with what arts he [Hitler] conquered the masses; he did not conquer them, he portrayed and represented them. His speeches are day-dreams of this mass soul; they are chaotic, full of contradictions, if their words are taken literally, often senseless, as dreams are, and yet charged with deeper meaning. . . . The speeches begin always with deep pessimism and end in overjoyed redemption, a triumphant happy ending; often they can be refuted by reason, but they follow the far mightier logic of the subconscious, which no refutation can touch. Hitler has given speech to the speechless terror of the modern mass, and to the nameless fear he has given a name. That makes him the greatest mass orator of the mass age.[8]

The explanatory power of the fantasy chain analysis lies in its ability to account for the development, evolution, and decay of dramas that catch up groups of people and change their behavior. A rhetorical movement contains small group fantasy chains, public fantasy events, and a rhetorical vision in a complex and reciprocal set of relationships. The subsystems fit into a larger communication system as follows: A small group of people with similar individual psychodynamics meet to discuss a common preoccupation or problem. A member dramatizes a theme that catches the group and causes it to chain out because it hits a common psychodynamic chord or a hidden agenda item or their common difficulties vis-a-vis the natural environment, the socio-political systems, or the

[6]See for example A. J. M. Sykes, "Myth in Communication," *The Journal of Communication,* 20 (Mar. 1970), 17–31 and A. J. M. Sykes, "Myth and Attitude Change," *Human Relations,* 18 (Nov. 1965), 323–337.

[7]Exposition of typical balance theories can be found in Theodore M. Newcomb, *The Acquaintance Process* (New York: Holt, Rinehart, 1961) and Fritz Heider, *The Psychology of Interpersonal Relations* (New York: Wiley, 1958).

[8]Konrad Heiden, *Der Fuehrer: Hitler's Rise to Power,* trans. Ralph Manheim (Boston: Houghton Mifflin, 1944), p. 106.

economic structures. The group grows excited, involved, more dramas chain out to create a common symbolic reality filled with heroes and villains. If the group's fantasy themes contain motives to "go public" and gain converts to their position they often begin artistically to create messages for the mass media for public speeches and so forth. When they need to develop a message for a specific context they often find themselves shaping the drama that excited them in their original discussions into suitable form for a different public.

Some of the dramas of their public rhetoric now catch members of the audience in the situation which Bales called, "individual responses to works of art, when one is 'transported' to a world which seems somehow even more real than the everyday world." Those so transported take up the dramas in small groups of acquaintances, and some of these derivative dramas again chain out as fantasy themes in the new groups; thus the rhetorical vision is propagated to a larger public until a rhetorical movement emerges.[9]

Individuals in rhetorical transactions create subjective worlds of common expectations and meanings. Against the panorama of large events and seemingly unchangeable forces of society at large or of nature the individual often feels lost and hopeless. One coping mechanism is to dream an individual fantasy which provides a sense of meaning and significance for the individual and helps protect him from the pressures of natural calamity and social disaster. The rhetorical vision serves much the same coping function for those who participate in the drama and often with much more force because of the supportive warmth of like-minded companions.

In most instances a viable rhetorical vision accounts plausibly for the evidence of the senses, so those who pick up the dramatic actions and find it personally satisfying are not troubled by contradictory evidence from commonsense experience. On occasion, however, small, highly dedicated groups of people generate and sustain rhetorical visions so out of joint with the common-sense and everyday experience of the majority of a community that their appeal is very limited. The analogy of the more bizarre rhetorical visions with pathological states in individuals caused one observer, Richard Hofstadter, to refer to the former as paranoid.[10]

What answer can be given, then, to the question of the relation between public fantasies and "reality" or action or substance? Writers in General Semantics often argue that the word is not the thing.[11] Scholars in many disciplines often go on to assume that since the word is not the thing any discrepancy between

---

[9]A study that traces the conscious attempts of some participants to chain out group fantasies that individuate a rhetorical vision to radicalize the uncommitted is James W. Chesebro, John F. Cragan, and Patricia McCullough, "The Small Group Techniques of the Radical-Revolutionary: A Synthetic Study of Consciousness Raising," *Speech Monographs*, 41 (June 1973), 136–146. The investigators discovered that in the opening phases of the consciousness raising sessions members dramatized events and characters prominent in the national rhetorical vision of Gay Liberation. After the dramatization of the national vision had formed a common bond the participants turned to dramatizing personal experience narratives.

[10]Richard Hofstadter, *The Paranoid Style in American Politics and Other Essays* (New York: Knopf, 1965).

[11]See Wendell Johnson, *People in Quandaries: The Semantics of Personal Adjustment* (New York: Harper and Row, 1946) and S. I. Hayakawa, *Language in Thought and Action* (New York: Harcourt, Brace and World, 1964).

words and things must necessarily be resolved by assigning the greater importance to things, and the words are, therefore, to be discounted as misleading or unimportant.

One line of historical analysis, for example, suggests that although the abolitionists often argued from theological grounds that slavery was a sin and that to save their eternal souls all persons must work for its elimination, the "real" reason the abolitionists fought with zeal to free the slaves was because they were members of a displaced social elite caught in a status crisis. The words of the abolitionists are discounted as being unimportant to the historical reality of the situations.[12]

Sociological analysis often starts from the premise that the words are generated out of social context rather than that the words *are the social context*. Duncan laments the common view: "American sociologists simply do not believe that how we communicate determines how we relate as social beings. Most sociologists really think of symbols as photographs of some kind of reality that is 'behind' symbols. . . . Class *exists* and *then* is expressed, it does not arise *in* expression."[13]

When a critic makes a rhetorical analysis he or she should start from the assumption that when there is a discrepancy between the word and the thing the most important cultural artifact for understanding the events may not be the things or "reality" but the words or the symbols. Indeed, in many vital instances the words, that is, the rhetoric, are the social reality and to try to distinguish one symbolic reality from another is a fallacy widespread in historical and sociological scholarship which the rhetorical critic can do much to dispel.[14]

A critic can take the social reality contained in a rhetorical vision which he has constructed from the concrete dramas developed in a body of discourse and examine the social relationships, the motives, the qualitative impact of that symbolic world as though it were the substance of social reality for those people who participated in the vision. If the critic can illuminate how people who participated in the rhetorical vision related to one another, how they arranged themselves into social hierarchies, how they acted to achieve the goals embedded in their dreams, and how they were aroused by the dramatic action and the dramatis personae within the manifest content of their rhetoric, his insights will make a useful contribution to understanding the movement and its adherents.

How might the critic making a fantasy theme analysis proceed? There is not space to describe the technique in detail, but I shall raise some of the more

---

[12]For a quick survey of some representative historical accounts of the Abolitionists see "Introduction" in Richard O. Curry, ed., *The Abolitionists: Reformers or Fanatics?* (New York: Holt, Rinehart, 1965), pp. 1–9. See also David Donald, "Abolition Leadership: A Displaced Social Elite," *ibid.*, pp. 42–48.

[13]"The Search for a Social Theory of Communication in American Sociology," Frank E. X. Dance, ed., *Human Communication Theory: Original Essays* (New York: Holt, Rinehart, 1967), p. 237.

[14]Not all social scientists start from the assumption that rhetoric differs from social reality. Hugh Dalziel Duncan's work is illustrative of one who viewed symbolic forms as social reality. A group of sociologists exploring what they often referred to as the sociology of knowledge also assumed that social reality was symbolic. See, for example, Peter L. Burger and Thomas Luckmann, *The Social Construction of Reality: A Treatise in the Sociology of Knowledge* (1966: rpt. Garden City, N.Y.: Doubleday Anchor Books, 1967). See also Wallace J. Thies, "Public Address and the Sociology of Knowledge," *Journal of the Wisconsin Speech Communication Association*, 1 (1971), 28–41.

general questions that a critic might choose to investigate. The critic begins by collecting evidence related to the manifest content of the communication, using video or audio tapes, manuscripts, recollections of participants, or his own direct observations. He discovers and describes the narrative and dramatic materials that have chained out for those who participate in the rhetorical vision. When a critic has gathered a number of dramatic incidents he can look for patterns of characterizations (do the same people keep cropping up as villains?) of dramatic situations and actions (are the same stories repeated?) and of setting (where is the sacred ground and where the profane?). The critic must then creatively reconstruct the rhetorical vision from the representative fantasy chains much as a scholar would delineate a school of drama on the basis of a number of different plays.

Once the critic has constructed the manifest content of the rhetorical vision he can ask more specific questions relating to elements of the dramas. Who are the dramatis personae? Does some abstraction personified as a character provide the ultimate legitimatization of the drama? God? The People? The Young? (What are young people really trying to tell us?) Who are the heroes and the villains? How concrete and detailed are the characterizations? Motives attributed? How are the members of the rhetorical community characterized? For what are the insiders praised, the outsiders or enemies castigated? What values are inherent in the praiseworthy characters?

Where are the dramas set? In the wilderness? In the countryside? In the urban ghetto? Is the setting given supernatural sanction?

What are the typical scenarios? What acts are performed by the ultimate legitimatizer? The neutral people? The enemy? Which are sanctioned and praised; which censored? What life-styles are exemplified as praiseworthy?

What meanings are inherent in the dramas? Where does the insider fit into the great chain of being? How does the movement fit into the scheme of history? What emotional evocations dominate the dramas? Does hate dominate? Pity? Love? Indignation? Resignation? What motives are embedded in the vision? Would the committed work for or resist legal action? Violence? Would they resign this life to get ready for an afterlife?

How does the fantasy theme work to attract the unconverted? How does it generate a sense of community and cohesion from the insider?

How artistic is the development of the fantasy theme? How skillful the characterization? How artistic the use of language? How rich the total panorama of the vision? How capable is the drama to arouse and interpret emotions?

A critic need not, of course, raise all of such questions for a given piece of criticism but for some in-depth critiques of a single message the critic might ask more questions and search for more details. A brief analysis of one important rhetorical vision from American history illustrates the way a critic might proceed.

The point relating to the way fantasy themes help people transcend the everyday and provide meaning for an audience is made graphically by the rhetorical vision embedded in the preaching of Puritan ministers to their small congregations huddled in unheated, crude, and undecorated meeting houses in the wilderness in the early years of the Massachusetts Bay Colony. The daily routine of the people was one of backbreaking drudgery. The niceties of life were almost nonexistent; music, the arts, decoration of home or clothing, largely unavailable. A discursive description of the emigration and the daily externals of life would be very grim. But the Puritans of Colonial New England led an internal fantasy life of mighty grandeur and complexity. They participated in a rhetorical vision that saw the migration to the new world as a holy exodus of God's chosen people. The Biblical drama that supported their vision was that of the journey of the Jews from Egypt into Canaan. John Cotton's sermon delivered when Winthrop's company was leaving for Massachusetts was on the text, "Moreover I will appoint a place for my People Israell, [sic] and I will plant them, that they may dwell in a place of their own, and move no more."[15]

The Puritan rhetorical vision saw them as conquering new territories for God, saving the souls of the natives, and, most importantly, as setting up in the wilderness a model religious community, a new Israel, patterned after the true meaning of the scriptures to light the way for the reformation still to be accomplished in old England and in all of Europe.

Such a vision gave to every social and political action a sense of importance. Every intrusion of nature or of other communities upon their inner reality also was given added significance. A time of troubles such as a drought or an Indian raid became evidence of God's displeasure and served as a motive to drive the Puritans to higher effort and greater striving to please God.

The Puritan vision also gave meaning to each individual with the movement. The scenario places each member of the audience firmly in the role of protagonist. Cotton Mather wrote to students preparing to be ministers that, "the *Gaining* of one Soul to GOD by your Ministry, will be of more Account with you than any *Gain* of this World; than all the *Wealth* in the World."[16]

In creating fantasy themes for specific sermons the minister would use all his art of assertion, imperatives, and descriptive language to search out the hiding places and bring each member of the congregation center stage to play out the drama of salvation or damnation. Turn and dodge as the listener might, the skillful minister kept driving the auditors to the recognition of their personal spiritual dramas. The odds against success were enormous, the fruits of victory unbelievably sweet, the results of defeat incredibly awesome and terrifying. Thomas Hooker, a first generation minister, does an excellent job of presenting the Puritan rhetorical vision in the following fantasy theme:

> Imagine thou sawest the Lord Jesus coming in the clouds, and heardest the last trump blow, *Arise ye dead, and come to judgment:* Imagine thou sawest the Judg [sic] of all the World sitting upon the Throne, thousands of Angels before him, and ten thousand ministring unto him, the Sheep standing on his right hand, and the Goats at the left: Suppose thou heardest that dreadful Sentence, and final Doom pass from the Lord of Life (whose Word made Heaven and Earth, and will shake both) *Depart from me ye cursed;* How would thy heart shake and sink, and die within thee in the thought thereof, were thou really perswaded it was thy portion? Know, that by thy dayly continuance in sin, thou dost to the utmost of thy power execute that Sentence upon thy soul: It's thy life, thy labor, the desire of thy heart, and thy dayly practice to depart away from the God of all Grace and Peace, and turn the Tombstone of everlasting destruction upon thine own soul.[17]

[15]John Cotton, "God's Promise to His Plantations," *Old South Leaflets,* Vol. 3, No. 53.

[16]Cotton Mather, *Manductuo ad Ministerium: Directions for a Candidate of the Ministry* (1726; rpt. New York: Published for the Facsimile Text Society by Columbia Univ. Press, 1938), p. 114.

[17]Perry Miller and Thomas H. Johnson, eds., *The Puritans,* I (1938; rpt. New York: Harper Torchbooks, 1963), p. 298.

For the members of the community who participated in the Puritan rhetorical vision the events in the meeting house were significant far beyond the crude externals of their living conditions. In their private prayers and in public worship they participated in a social reality resonant with high drama and rich symbolism

An audience observing the drama from the outside might find it lacking in suspense, find it inartistic because the basic assumption upon which it rested was the deus ex machina. Man was completely dependent upon God for election to sainthood. The plot was similar to the pattern of the classical Greek plays. Reading the sermons today, we find the action static, the protagonist an insect squirming helplessly in the hands of an all-powerful Diety. But for the listener who chained out on the fantasy and imaginatively took the central role, the suspense might well become unbearable. Each hour might bring eternal salvation or eternal death. In his famous revival sermon Jonathan Edwards said, "And it would be no wonder if some persons, that now sit here, in some seats of this meetinghouse, in health, quiet and secure, should be there [in hell] before tomorrow morning."[18]

The predominant emotion which the Puritan vision evoked was that of awe. The focus is upon an afterlife with high potential for ecstasy or terror, almost beyond the power of the ministers to fantasize. The rhetoric contained powerful pragmatic motivations. The preoccupation with time, the fear of death before God's call to election, impelled the participant in the fantasy to do as much as soon as possible to put herself or himself in the proper posture for election to sainthood. The minutes wasted might be those very ones when his time had come.

One basic action line contained the motive power for much of the Puritan's tough and unrelenting effort to do good and to make good in the material world, namely that a time of troubles was God's punishment for the evil ways of an individual or a community, but that out of punishment would arise an understanding of guilt and a rebirth and regeneration so that the punishment would really serve as a means to salvation. By a zealous striving in the new direction, the guilt of their sins revealed by God's punishment would be propitiated. Insofar as they were cleansed by the experience in the sight of God, the new venture would increase and prosper. When they began again to fall from God's grace they could anticipate more hardships. To some extent, therefore, since in their view nothing happened by chance, the prospering of worldly affairs was evidence of their ability to please God. (Without this dramatic line one might well expect that a vision that emphasized the afterlife would result in contemplative inaction in this life).

The fantasy themes in which good Puritans took each setback and difficulty as a sign from God and made good use of them to become better persons contained strong motives for action and reform.[19] Contemplation, inactivity, impracticality, and apathy were undesirable in the context of the scenario. Working, striving,

[18]Wayland Maxfield Parrish and Marie Hochmuth, eds., *American Speeches* (New York: Longmans, Green, 1954), p. 88.

[19]Cotton Mather's advice to stammerers is typical of the Puritan vision which saw each affliction as an opportunity to improve in God's eyes. The stutterer should "*fetch Good out of Evil . . .* and make a very *pious Improvement* of your very *humbling Chastisement* which a sovereign GOD has laid upon you," quoted in Ernest G. Bormann, "Ephphatha, or, Some Advice to Stammerers," *Journal of Speech and Hearing Research*, 12 (Sept. 1969), 457.

acting in a hard-headed way, involvement, were all positive values. The drama began with a rite of self-abasement which loaded the participant with a high charge of guilt and turned to a plan of action which was providentially the path to salvation furnished by God. By working hard and doing the right thing they released the charge of guilt, and success became the final evidence that their conscience need no longer be troubled. The rhetoric used failure as evidence that they had not tried hard enough, or been good enough and must therefore work even harder and be even better.

Two common fantasy themes expressed the Puritan rhetorical vision. The first was the pilgrim making his slow, painful, and holy way, beset by many troubles and temptations. The second was the Christian soldier fighting God's battles and overcoming all adversaries in order to establish the true church. The first emphasized the abasement, sacrifice, and dedication of the Puritans to things of the other world, the second emphasized their militancy. Those who participated in the rhetorical vision exhibited an active and if need be, violent, bloody temper. When they could not convert the Indians they fought them and they fought, as well, their fellow Englishmen in the old country for the true faith.

The motivations embedded in the Puritan rhetorical vision, therefore, required great energy and overt activity. Morison, writing a history of Harvard, noted that Emmanuel College, Cambridge was a Puritan stronghold and produced many of the early leaders who emigrated to Massachusetts. Emmanuel College also had an active group of Cambridge neo-Platonists. Morison regrets that "the tolerant and generous philosophy of these men . . . could not have set the tone of Harvard College." But even as he regrets it, he recognized that "Harvard must have been puritan, or not have existed. A neo-Platonist could not be a man of action, a pioneer, an emigrant, any more than a Hindu. The kingdom of God was within him, not in Massachusetts Bay."[20]

Of course to do justice to a fantasy theme analysis of the rhetorical vision of the Puritans would require a monograph. However, even this sketch can point to some of the insights that a fantasy theme analysis could provide. If we view the Puritans as organisms grubbing away in the wilderness to keep alive or create material wealth or to achieve status or to reach self-actualization we find the enterprise relatively mean and trivial. However, if we examine the internal fantasy of the community as revealed in the sermons of their ministers, we discover the characters of the drama, their emotional values, their actions, and their relationship to an over-reaching supernatural power. We come to a new understanding of the grubbing in the wilderness and we have an opportunity to be in possession of much more of the Puritan experience.

Of course, nature does intrude upon our fantasies. Factual descriptions of our common-sense perceptions of the world are also part of the manifest content of rhetorical discourse. A total rhetoric consists of both discursive material and fantasy themes. Cassirer provides the rhetorical critic with an approach to the relationship between discursive material and fantasy themes when he writes, " . . . myth, art, language and science appear as symbols; not in the sense of mere figures which refer to some given reality by means of suggestion and allegorical renderings, but in the sense of forces each of which produces and posits

[20]Samuel Eliot Morison, *The Founding of Harvard College* (Cambridge: Harvard Univ. Press, 1935), pp. 99–100.

a world of its own."[21] In Langer's words Cassirer was helped, "by a stroke of insight: the realization that *language,* man's prime instrument of reason, reflects his mythmaking tendency more than his rationalizing tendency. Language, the symbolization of thought, exhibits two entirely different modes of thought. Yet in both modes the mind is powerful and creative. It expresses itself in different forms, *one of which is discursive logic, the other creative imagination.*"[22]

When the authentic record of events is clear and widely understood, the competing visions must take it into account. If two teams play a game and team A beats team B by 5 to 4, the two teams may chain out different fantasies about the game. Team A may participate in a drama to the effect that justice has been done and the best team has won by superior play. Team B may fantasize that they did not really lose and that the game was stolen from them by an inept official or by dirty play on the part of their opponents. However, the outcome of the game as represented in the authentic record by a score of 5 to 4 is accounted for and incorporated into the explanatory system of both fantasies.

Whenever occasions are so chaotic and indiscriminate that the community has no clear observational impression of the facts, people are given free rein to fantasize within the assumptions of their rhetorical vision without inhibition. On such occasions fantasy themes become the main explanatory systems for the events. Rumors are illustrations of the principle in action.[23]

The conventional wisdom of communication theorists that "meanings are in people, not messages" is much too simple for the critic who wishes to study the rhetorical vision of a movement, an organization, or a community.[24] In a very important way meanings *are* in messages. When the members of a group chain out a fantasy they emerge from the meeting with new meanings, that may not have existed before, else how can we account for novelty and innovation? The new meanings are embedded in the messages created during the meeting. The members have appropriated them by sharing in their creation through public dramatization. (One might as well say the meanings associated with *Hamlet* are in the people who know the play rather than in the productions or the manuscripts. The trouble with that view, of course, is that until the first production of *Hamlet* very few people had the meanings. Unless the meanings relating to *Hamlet* are to some extent in the communication transactions associated with a performance of the play, the new meanings could never have been created.)

The emotions associated with the meanings are, also, partly in the message as well as in the people participating in a fantasy chain. The rhetorical vision provides its participants with an emotional evocation. Thus, the critical analysis of emotional appeals is illuminated by the process of fantasy theme analysis.

[21]Ernest Cassirer, *Language and Myth,* trans. Susanne K. Langer (New York: Harper, 1946), p. 8.

[22]Cassirer, pp. viii–ix.

[23]See, for example, Tamotsu Shibutani, *Improvised News: A Sociological Study of Rumor* (Indianapolis: Bobbs-Merrill, 1966).

[24]A seminar in organizational communication at the University of Minnesota taught by Professor David Smith in 1972 analyzed organizational myths (rhetorical visions) of all or part of four organizations in the Metropolitan Twin Cities area. Included in the study was a religious organization, a division of a major computer facility, a small family-owned business supply company, and a station of the University of Minnesota hospitals. The investigators used interviews to elicit narratives about the organizations and then submitted the resulting dramas to fantasy theme analysis.

Physiological studies of emotions reveal that changes in blood chemistry, heart rate, endocrine secretion, palm sweat, and so forth vary little from emotion to emotion.[25] Whether an individual's aroused physiological state is interpreted as hate, fear, anger, joy, or love is partly determined by the drama that accompanies the emotional state.

Finally, and most importantly, motives are in the messages. The rhetorical vision of a group of people contains their drives to action. People who generate, legitimatize and participate in a public fantasy are, in Bales' words, "powerfully impelled to action" by that process. Motives do not exist to be expressed in communication but rather arise in the expression itself and come to be embedded in the drama of the fantasy themes that generated and serve to sustain them. Motives are thus available for direct interpretation by a community of scholars engaged in rhetorical criticism.[26]

When an actor assumes a role in a drama he gains with the part constraining forces (the dramatic action of the unfolding plot) which impel him to do and to say certain things. When a person appropriates a rhetorical vision he gains with the supporting dramas constraining forces which impel him to adopt a life style and to take certain action. The born-again Christian is baptized and adopts a life style and behavior modeled after the heroes of the dramas that sustain that vision. The devout Puritan in Massachusetts was driven by his vision. Likewise the convert to one of the countercultures in the 1960s would let his hair and beard grow, change his style of dress, and his method of work, and so forth. Concurrently a person might participate in a number of narrower visions related to such issues as foreign policy, taxation, civil rights, and women's rights.

One widespread explanation of human motivation posits a fixed schedule of motives that most people have within them. When one uses a schedule of motives as a check-list in preparing persuasive discourse or in critically analyzing it, several shortcomings become apparent. While the schedule is fixed, human behavior is not; thus, accounting for action by attributing a motive to the actor tends to work only after the fact. For instance, when a person chooses a martyr's death the notion that the most fundamental of human motives is self-preservation does not predict the behavior. After the fact the critic can select some other motive from the schedule and argue that it has clearly become more compelling for the martyr than self-preservation.

When a critic begins instead with the approach that each rhetorical vision contains as part of its substance the motive that will impel the people caught up in it, then he can anticipate the behavior of the converts. If the critic discovers that

[25]For a representative analysis of emotions by a psychologist see Norman L. Munn, *Psychology: The Fundamentals of Human Adjustment*, 5th ed. (Boston: Houghton Mifflin, 1966), pp. 189–221.

[26]My notion is not the same as Kenneth Burke's concept as interpreted by Richard E. Crable and John J. Makay, "Kenneth Burke's Concept of Motives in Rhetorical Theory," *Today's Speech*, 20 (Win. 1972), 11–18. Crable and Makay present a survey of various commentaries on Burke's view of motives in rhetorical theory and provide an interpretation of their own. Much closer to my view of motivation is that developed by Karlyn Kohrs Campbell, "The Ontological Foundations of Rhetorical Theory," *Philosophy and Rhetoric*, 3 (Spr. 1970), 97–108. She writes, for instance, of theorists who "contend that human motivation is distinct from that of other beings because the interaction between men and his language profoundly transforms his physical, biological, and animal needs, drives and desires. . . . In addition, the interaction between man and language is viewed as a process which destroys all purely 'animal' or 'biological' motives." (p. 104)

a person faced with the choice of martyrdom participates in a rhetorical vision that includes the fantasy of persons assuring themselves eternal salvation by dying for God's purposes, he can anticipate the act itself.

The notion that motives are hidden within individuals makes them difficult to study in a critical way, and that same inaccessibility makes it possible for people involved in argument and conflict to attribute motives to their friends and enemies. Indeed, a person who tries to get a fantasy to chain out often uses the technique of attributing motives to characters in a dream. A speaker can characterize a hero by attributing praiseworthy motivation, or create a bad image by suggesting unsavory motives. Almost every major evangelist in American history has become a central character in several rhetorical visions, which alternately portray him as a villain seeking money, power, and notoriety, or as a selfless hero trying to better the human condition and do God's will. Those whose rhetorical vision in the 1960s contained the draft resister as hero saw him motivated by a high moral commitment to do good for humanity and those whose fantasy saw him as a villain often attributed to him a cowardly motive to save his own skin. For the scholar, at any rate, to view motives as embedded in the rhetorical vision rather than hidden in the skulls and viscera of people makes it possible to check the critic's insights by going directly to the rhetoric rather than relying on inferences about psychological entities unavailable for analysis.

Not only does the fantasy analysis of rhetorical visions provide at least as great if not greater power of prediction than the fixed-schedule-of-motives approach but, more importantly, once we participate in the rhetorical vision of a community or movement, even if we keep an aesthetic distance, we have come vicariously to experience a way of life that would otherwise be less accessible to us, we have enlarged our awareness, we have become more fully human. Certainly the discovery and appreciation of rhetorical visions should be one possible function of criticism.

RELATIONSHIP STYLES IN POPULAR ROMANCE NOVELS, 1950 TO 1983

Rita C. Hubbard

Romance fiction is a publishing phenomenon. While the total number of paperback books sold in the United States in a given year exceeds 575 million, romance novels account for 40% of this total. Inexpensive "brand name" novels, published monthly, with author identification minimized, constitute the largest category of these romance novels. From 1950 to 1979, Harlequin Books was the sole publisher of such novels. In 1979, they sold over 168 million copies in a world-wide market—an average of five books every second—making their line of fiction the most successful ever published. That same year, Simon and Schuster provided competition in the U.S. with Silhouette Books, and since that time new lines have been introduced by various publishers, six of these launched in 1983. More than 100 new category romances, written almost exclusively by women, are published each month.

The American readers of these books, estimated to be 99% female, number in the multi-millions. Marketing researchers report that romances of all types are the first choice of non-college educated women and the second choice among the college-educated.

These romance novels offer dramatic visions of male/female interactions which lead to satisfying and enduring love commitments. Readers do, in fact, read these novels consistently, with the average romance reader buying six per month. For them, the novels provide a way of looking at the world, interpretations of gender roles, a set of expectations, and implied guidelines for romantic success.

This study examines the rhetorical visions of male/female relationship styles in category romances over 33 years, tracing the development of particular fantasy themes and focusing on contemporary attitudes in four specific time periods. Two questions influence choices affecting its development:

1) How are females and males defined in these romances?
2) Have the romances changed their view of male/female relationship styles over a 33-year period?

The analysis is designed to emphasize the definitions of femininity and masculinity and ultimately to identify the rhetorical visions which control such definitions. Femininity and masculinity are cast as variables which can be socially constructed, and they become the factors which signify the changes which have occurred in relationship styles exhibited in the novels.

The novel has traditionally been cast as an artistic form of entertainment, and analyses have centered on the poetic rather than the rhetorical nature of the form. But this conventional critical assumption has been challenged recently.

From *Communication Quarterly* 33 (Spring 1985): 113–125. Reprinted by permission of the author and the Eastern Speech Communication Association (ECA).

Rita C. Hubbard is an associate professor of speech communication and chairperson of the Department of Arts and Communication at Christopher Newport College, Newport News, Virginia. A shorter report on this study was presented at the joint convention of the American Culture Association and the Popular Culture Association in Toronto, Canada on April 29, 1984.

Booth (1961) contends that authors of fiction are ever-presently constructing realities and establishing values and attitudes. Chesebro and Hamsher argue: "We may repeatedly observe that entertainment and persuasion are not exclusive dimensions; entertainment may be persuasive; persuasion may be entertaining" (1975, p. 590). Besides dissolving the traditional distinction between persuasion and entertainment, various critics have suggested that many other types of communication traditionally reviewed as non-persuasive may, in fact, function predominantly and essentially as rhetoric. Even the discourse of scientists has been cast as rhetoric, and some have argued that other informative modes have persuasive dimensions, such as network news, investigative reporting, information briefings, sociological studies, and even medical analyses. Accordingly, it seems appropriate to consider the rhetorical potential of novels.

Women have read romance novels for centuries, and it is generally assumed that they have recognized the heroines as representations of actual women with whom they can identify. There is something seductive about such identification as the reader contemplates the idea of becoming a heroine because in so doing she may not only seek the heroine's romantic success and derived happiness from a permanent love commitment, but she may also accept the interaction rules which govern the heroine's and the hero's behaviors. The purpose and effect of romances can be conceived in several ways. They are apparently popular escape novels written to entertain and transport readers from their own humdrum worlds to exciting fictional worlds. Yet they can also recommend and validate specific social orders.

The Critical Method

The rhetorical critical method used is fantasy theme analysis. Bormann (1972) has argued that any time discourse adopts a dramatic frame of reference in which protagonist and antagonist play out a plot along particular themes, a rhetorical vision is constructed, and that such a vision can be adopted by one group and passed on to an increasingly larger number of groups, ultimately dominating an entire cultural system or sub-system. Subscribing to the belief that people construct a social reality that differs from the mere existence of phenomena, he has advanced a dramatistic theory of rhetorical visions in which composite dramas can catch up large groups of people in a common symbolic reality.

These dramas are composed of particular fantasy themes which are created by the interrelations of four major concepts: 1)the *dramatis personae*, i.e. heroes, villains, and supporting players; 2) the *plotline* or action of the drama which expresses ideological positions; 3) the *scene;* and 4) the *sanctioning agent* or source of justification for the creation, acceptance, and promotion of a particular vision. A sanctioning agent might be peace, the fatherland, justice, God, love, democracy, or some other ideal concept. These four particular elements converge to create each fantasy theme, a complete scenario or dramatistic statement of socially constructed reality. One fantasy theme may embody a complete rhetorical vision or it may be one of several fantasies which together create a full rhetorical vision. Bormann contends that the analysis of fantasy themes can manifest the meanings, emotions, and motives of rhetoric and can lead to explanations of human events and actions as well as to predictions of future events and actions.

This method has been used successfully in approximately 50 studies to date. Among those which have dealt with relationship styles are studies by Kidd (1975), Doyle (1978), and Koester (1982).

Primary Sources

Forty-five novels were chosen for analysis.[1] Since Harlequin Romances were the only existing category romances from 1950 to 1979, they were chosen for the first part of this study which was undertaken in 1980.

The population of Harlequin Romances was defined by three lists of available novels provided by Harlequin Books in September, October, and November of 1980. These lists were used to define the population of Harlequin Romances because: 1) they provide an arbitrary selection of past novels which the readers of these novels are exposed to; 2) Harlequin Books claim approximately equal sales of all novels so that any lists used become acceptable to secure a sample of the population of novels; 3) each list gives roughly equal attention to all three decades.

A random sample of *all* Harlequin Romances was not used because: 1) readers are not exposed to such random choices, and therefore a method was devised which reflected books to which the reader is exposed; 2) not all novels are currently available; 3) no cooperation from the publisher could be obtained to secure a random sample of all books because Harlequin Books reprints on a rotation basis and does not maintain all books as current choices.

Thirty Harlequin Romances were selected randomly from the three lists: ten from the 1950s, ten from the 1960s, and ten from the 1970s. Other publishing houses entered the category romance field beginning in 1979; therefore, 15 novels with 1983 publication dates were selected for the second part of this study undertaken in 1983. These novels were randomly drawn from Walden Books' 1983 display of category romance novels, namely Harlequin American Romance, Second Chance at Love, Silhouette Desire, Silhouette Intimate Moments, Loveswept, Candlelight Ecstasy Supreme.

Descriptions of Rhetorical Visions

Vision I of the 1950s: Cinderella as Virgin Earth Mother and the Prince as Benign Dictator   Harlequin Romances of the 1950s extol in their fantasy themes the assumed virtues of the virginal earth mother and the benign male dictator, creating a rhetorical vision of the rigid male/female complementarity which has dominated relations between the sexes in Western culture. In this vision, sexual conservatism is recommended, leading to predefined modes of feeling and action, and the system works to perfection for the instrumental heroes and the expressive heroines.

Without exception, the hero is masterful, tall, handsome, passionate and powerful, educated, and engaged in a successful career. Thus he can deliver to his chosen heroine all the benefits expected of the ambitious male. His chosen heroine, who fully accepts dominance, is young, small, isolated from family and friends, modestly educated, and low in self-esteem. But she is both

---

[1]Interested readers are encouraged to contact the author for a complete list of romances analyzed for this study.

willing and able to meet the hero's needs for support, admiration, nurturance, purity, and devotion.

Both find comfort, safety, and a sense of worth in the blending of what are assumed to be their natural competencies. Their arrangement includes divisions of opportunity, responsibility, and privilege. He has a monopoly on formal, overt power, and he assumes his right to rule. She gladly gives obedience in exchange for upward mobility, protection, and enduring love.

At no time in the novels of the 1950s do the heroes and heroines challenge the prevailing symbiosis between men and women. Their posture is accepting and their method of coping with interpersonal problems is to fit themselves neatly into the societally ordained stereotypes of the decade; their misgivings and reservations are harmlessly ventilated as they grow more and more accepting of their roles which lead them eventually to conjugal happiness.

Love is the sanctioning agent which justifies their motives and actions. It transforms the faults of the hero—moodiness, arrogance, and occasional cruelty—into expressions of caring. Love permits the hero to view the heroine's weakness, ignorance, and capriciousness as endearing qualities. She can accept his past sexual experience and his right to awaken her, knowing that he is dependent on her to control his passionate nature. He can accept her lack of achievement, realizing that his is the role of the risk-taker and doer.

Thus the rhetorical vision of the 1950s offers the traditional prescription for a successful male/female relationship style. Woman's role is that of the supportive "Other." Her ultimate security and happiness are to be found in romance, marriage, and the family. Man's role is to rule by his achievement; he is incomplete, however, without the nurturing female to complement him and teach him in the affective domain.

Sweet Waters (Brett, 1955) is a typical novel. A plain heroine who is alone in the world is hired by an affluent landowner in Capetown, Africa to care for an orphan boy living with him temporarily. She finds her employer to be cold, sharp, arrogant, and chauvinistic. He orders her about, demands strict obedience, and refuses to teach her or any woman to drive because of assumed female incompetence. Yet she falls in love with him, arguing to herself that, "He's perfectly horrid, devastatingly frank and uncaring about other people's feelings, yet there's a charm about him that somehow makes it worthwhile putting up with the brutally calm arrogance" (p. 49). He calls her a doormat, silences her with a raised finger, accepts no "backchat," and declares that "one of these days I'm going to give you all the punishment you deserve" (p. 136).

But love, the agent of forgiveness and understanding, infuses their lives. He finds her tenderness and temerity irresistible and she glories in his masterfulness. In the final pages, he proposes marriage. "I shall be a demanding husband, and I'll never let you forget you're mine" (p. 191). "She thought tremulously that she would never quite believe the miracle of belonging to Nicholas, and for the rest of her life she would strive to deserve it" (p. 191). The plain Cinderella finds validation in the love of a male she considers superior, and he has been assured during the novel of her admiration, acquiescence, nurturance, and purity.

Vision II of the 1960s: Cinderella as Feisty Female and the Prince as Subduer

Of the ten 1960s novels examined, two are similar in vision to those of the 1950s. Eight, however, while they contain a rhetorical vision resembling that of the 1950s books, introduce three new fantasy themes: female rebellion, struggle, and final acquiescence.

The newer heroine has become aware of the social inequality of the sexes and offers feisty but tentative resistance to domination. She challenges the hero principally in discourse and occasionally by her actions. She may choose from among various methods to declare her independence: insult the hero as despicable and arrogant, declare that nature intended her to be more than a docile showpiece, seek a traditional male career, exhibit fearlessness in the face of a gun, venture into the jungle alone, steal a trawler to prove her capability in handling a ship.

Her independence is short-lived, however, because failure is built into the scenario. She is a young woman alone without support systems and, if working at all, receives low wages because of her lack of higher education or developed skills. By contrast, the hero against whom she struggles is physically strong, socially and economically secure, and determined to command. He is articulate in argumentation against what he considers her foolish ideas and actions, and he is fully capable of rescuing her from dangers.

The heroine's quest for independence, while it fails, brings her unexpected romantic success because she does not carry her rebellion beyond the bounds of propriety. The hero finds that her spirit excites him and once he has learned to control that spirit, he offers her a lifetime of passionate love, marriage, safety and security, sometimes promising to wrap her in cotton wadding or to treat her like a fragile glass bird. His reward, after having aggressively tested her self-control, is assurance that his bride-to-be is both pure and awakened by him. He is secure once she has declared that next to being his wife nothing else in the world is of any importance.

In the new plotlines, gender-related values are no longer assumed. The tensions and ambiguities that arose from the new thrust of sexual equality that began in the decade of the 1960s are present, but these tensions and ambiguities are resolved as their heroines come to realize that their challenge for equality can and will be rebuffed at every level by dominant and desirable males, and that the rewards for submissiveness are great. Thus, the novels assimilate in their formulas changes in values, and they likewise offer dramatic evaluations of the new thrust for equality between the sexes which they categorize in their plots as dangerous to female security. Finally in their imaginary worlds, they affirm the interests and attitudes of a majority of society in the 1960s when only a small percentage of women, principally the highly educated, exhibited a strong interest in the new feminism.

In *House of the Winds* (Lane, 1968), we can observe the newer heroine, in this case a small, young orphan who admits that she would have gotten a fuller education if she had the brains for it. She tricks a big game hunter in Tanzania into taking her on safari into the African bush so that she can photograph wild animals and gain stature in her career. He becomes angry and abusive because he is set against taking women on such dangerous trips, and he scoffs at her ambitions. Unlike heroines of the 1950s, this one can drive a car, speak her mind, and brave dangers. As the plot unfolds in the African bush, however, her courage and ambition diminish as the strong, gruff hero rescues her six times from wild animals, the elements, and other threats to her life, each time offering insults as he grabs her roughly out of danger. Finally, he adds to the later rescues his hard kisses which kindle frightening sparks in him and in her. They almost "go too far," but she proves her virtue. She abandons camera and career, promises to be his obedient wife, and to follow him to Nymbaya, even though she does not know what their life will be like there. He promises eternal love, to care for her, and to give her children, as they walk hand in hand toward the "whispering waves."

Vision III of the 1970s: Cinderella as Virgin Temptress and the Prince as Warrior   If equality between the sexes was not possible in the 1970s real world, nevertheless some women made significant strides toward that goal, and many men and women were converted to equalitarianism in concept if not in action. In Harlequin Romances of the 1970s, this new feminism intrudes significantly into the fictional world creating a third rhetorical vision with fantasy themes of acknowledged female sexuality, female militancy, and counter exhibitions of male power. There, is, however, in this vision no affirmation of equality as a legitimate goal. In fact, the heroine's militant demands are cast as threats to her own and the hero's happiness and security, and she is confronted and humbled repeatedly until she sees the error of her ways and embraces traditional male/female complementarity as a relationship style.

The heroine of the 1970s has increased confidence in her own abilities and exhibits knowingly a powerful sexuality to tempt the hero. But she is led gradually and forcefully by him to the realization that her attempts to assume power and to enjoy sexual freedom will bring about her own ruin. In the end, she not only accepts his domination but rejoices in it. Thus, she reaffirms the old ways dramatically because she has tested equality, even beyond the limits set for the 1960s heroines, and found it frightening.

In Harlequin Romances of all three decades, the hero is cast as superior to the heroine in wealth, position, and education. In the 1970s novels he must use these advantages to battle the new feminism and to preserve the old ways. As the militant heroine tests his mettle, he resorts to exhibitions of power. Earlier heroes frequently subdued heroines physically when in the grips of passion, often bruising flesh, and occasionally spanking lightly. The 1970s hero, however, goes further; in his frustrations he may shake the heroine, jerk her out of a seat, threaten to strike her, and even drive his truck within inches of her body. And along with these physical displays, he also educates the heroine with insults, exasperation, and argumentation until she recants. Thus he provides a counterstatement, both verbal and nonverbal, to her liberation rhetoric.

At times he must also preserve her virginity when she is ready to submit to his advances. Although he may be sexually experienced, he has no respect for a permissive woman and holds onto his requirement that his bride be virginal.

The rhetorical vision of the 1970s is one which reflects women's thrust for equality, labels it dangerous, and promises happiness for those who accept the complementary relationship style. It differs significantly from Visions I and II in that the heroines in this vision are permitted to exhibit a strong militancy, to acknowledge their sexuality, and to test the male almost beyond his powers of endurance. As in previous novels, love is the sanctioning agent which transforms behaviors formerly perceived as faults into virtues. The heroine's strong spirit is accepted by the hero once he has channeled it toward his goals. His former threats and abuse are seen finally by the heroine as the results of her not trusting him and his consequent frustration and injured pride.

The Crescent Moon (Hunter, 1974) illustrates the changes. A young shorthand-typist meets a famous, wealthy university professor, and though she feels the strong stirrings of passion she cannot accept his chauvinistic attitude. She asserts that she believes in complete equality. And so the sparring begins and continues as he presses his points. "There is no such thing as equality between us" (p. 71). "I don't like ambitious females" (p. 41). "Wouldn't you rather be the chattel of a man that the equal of a mouse" (p. 126)? "You'll find yourself a better follower than a leader when we finally do come to terms" (p. 120). And he is right. As he takes an "unhurried toll of her lips" and proposes marriage, she recants.

> In any argument between them he would always win hands down. They both knew that physically he could dominate her any time he chose. If he stopped to ask her, the result would be just the same; he would demand and she would submit and would delight in her own weakness. You could call it chemistry, or the way things were meant to be, but she wouldn't like it at all if it were the other way about (p. 186).

Vision IV of the Early 1980s: The Liberated Heroine with Her Man as Equal Partner   Vision IV of the early 1980s bears little resemblance to the rhetorical visions of the prior three decades except that love continues to be the sanctioning agent. While Visions II and III were evolutions, with variations, out of Vision I, Vision IV has a new base of fantasy themes drawn from the feminist perspective: female control, male acceptance of equality between the sexes, and negotiation of relationship terms.

The nature of the heroine shows the most striking changes. She is no longer the standard Cinderella. Instead, she represents many women, all of whom can be heroines. She may be a young woman or as old as 45. She may be small or nearly six feet in height. She may struggle with hardships like divorce, a child born out of wedlock, a troubled husband, but she is not weak or ordinary. She is most often highly skilled, artistic or well-educated, occasionally holding a graduate degree. She may be a concert pianist, head of a construction business, owner of a dance studio, a big animal trainer, president of her own corporation, or independently wealthy. Her energies are devoted to her career and her independence, and she maintains healthy self-esteem. She is situationally nurturing but is not agreeable to the encompassing self-sacrifice of former heroines. She may live alone, but she is not isolated from family and friends. She might be a virgin, but most often she is fully aware of her own sexual needs and, while she is not promiscuous, she is sexually active when she and her hero establish a love commitment. Further, she does not readily accept a marriage proposal until she is sure that she and her hero can negotiate terms.

Likewise, the 1980s hero is a new man. He might be, like earlier heroes, tall and handsome, affluent, and successful, but these characteristics are not essential. He has become closer in life-size to the men with whom women normally interact. And his situation might even call for a reversal of the Cinderella scenario as he depends on the heroine to help him reach his full potential. However, he has characteristics which were not present in earlier heroes. He is articulate and sensitive in matters of human relations, respecting the ambitions and desires of the heroine and accepting her as an equal partner. He is strong but not overpowering, and he is as caring of the relationship as the heroine is. The arrogant, power-bent hero has disappeared from the 1980s romances.

With this new balance of power, the plotlines of the novels show marked changes as the modern heroine is consciously selective in her choices. Does she want a career first and love later? Is love without marriage a better choice? How can she handle a long-distance relationship? Does she dare to love again after a painful divorce? Will the new man in her life be suitable as a father for her children?

The novels' scenes, therefore, shift from the worlds of the heroes into which earlier heroines gained entry to the multi-dimensional worlds of heroines who act, pursuing careers, establishing friendships, dealing with a world in which not only love but success is important to them.

Finally even love which continues to be at the core of these novels has changed character. The earlier love was an erotic one that fastened on the beauty and perfection of the beloved and changed flaws into virtues. The 1980s novels are sensual and sexual in thrust, and yet erotic love is tempered by pragmatic considerations about whether a permanent relationship will work, whether the parties are compatible, and whether the needs and desires of both participants can be satisfied.

Calculated Risk (Chase, 1983) features the newer heroine who must be convinced by an ardent suitor that there is room in her life for a relationship. She is tall and assertive, in her thirties, the self-disciplined president of one of Nashville's most prestigious talent management firms. She drives a blue diesel Mercedes, carries a leather attaché case, and has a male secretary. When the hero tries to enter her life, she resists the intrusion and must be persuaded to accept his offer of marriage. In the novel, she acts more than she is acted upon, taking the initiative in working out problems with her suitor's son, setting the conditions of her new relationship, and enjoying a sexual and love commitment without sacrificing hard-won career success. A permanent relationship enriches her life, but it does not change its other dimensions.

Assessment of Rhetorical Visions

The four rhetorical visions of category romances bear certain similarities coming out of the very nature of the genre, yet each creates distinct gender definitions which lead to different roles and rules for males and females in each period. They are similar in the set of expectations they provide, expectations consistent with the ideology of heterosexual romantic love which has its roots in the courtly tradition of the Middle Ages. Love between the sexes is an overwhelming passion, inspired by the beauty and character of the loved one, and leading to bliss or misery. Love strikes the hero and heroine almost instantly; often upon merely seeing each other there is a bonding that forecasts a permanent union in which the heroine finds validation for her uniqueness by being singled out from among many women by the hero, and he finds through her the missing key to his happiness.

The outstanding characteristics of this love are magic and transformation. Magic works to solve all problems; neither intellectual activity, the passage of time, frequent interactions, nor hard work are required for the development of a healthy relationship and the blending of personalities. Any problems of character, misunderstanding, or incompatible goals evaporate rapidly in the fire of love over a period of days, weeks, or months. And there are no problems beyond the relational. Economic, political, racial, sociological, or philosophical considerations do not intrude. Romance evolves in a white, heterosexual, middle- or upper-class world.[2]

Love also transforms. A plain heroine can become shining and beautiful when it touches her. A moody, punishing hero can become tender. And love fills them up, permitting them to deny the isolation natural to the human condition because the fusion of their two beings is perfectly accomplished, whether that fusion brings about a complementary relationship as in the first three visions or a symmetrical one as in the fourth vision. So the ultimate promise is sexual and affectional fulfillment in a permanent relationship resulting in happiness-ever-after, even though such promise is incompatible with the facts of human existence.

The distinct gender definitions in each vision, however, lead to different implicit recommendations for relationship styles and relate to changes historically occurring outside the dramas. In Vision I both the female and male are incomplete as individuals. They have different characteristics, separate roles to play, and their complementary relationship is promoted as both natural and good. Dominance is placed at the root of masculinity and nurturance at the core of femininity. While this vision undergoes changes in later category romances, it has continued unchanged in other romance types, among them the novels of Barbara Cartland who has promoted romantic fantasy for over 50 years. According to Doyle (1978), Cartland consistently defines woman's primary job as providing romance and beauty for men through purity, charm and total devotion to their needs.

The feelings and actions of this vision are not unlike those that predominated in the 1950s. An indication that the particular gender types of these romances and the behaviors which the novels implicitly recommend were standard ideals of the 1950s can be found in Kidd's (1975) study of advice articles on interpersonal relations appearing in popular magazines. In these articles, aimed principally at female readers, the rhetorical vision which dominated in the 1950s and early 1960s found virtue in those who made others happy, promoted togetherness, and declared conflict an indication of serious relationship problems. "Females and males were expected to behave according to traditional patterns, and when one did not do so, it was not the pattern but the individual's sexuality that was at fault" (p. 33). Career women were faulted for causing their husbands and children psychological damage. Men were described as having a greater sex drive and as needing to have a fragile male ego reinforced with approval and admiration even if this meant, for example, deceiving them during sexual intercourse in order to make them feel kinship with the gods. The meanings of interactions in these articles then were interpreted on a value scale like that in romances of the same period that promoted female nurturance and sacrifice for the good of the relationship and placed men in assertive dominant positions.

But all activity is contextual and all contexts can be broken. There is changeability in social structures as well as in assumptions about gender. Vision II changes somewhat as conflict over gender roles enters the scenarios. The heroine continues to be tender and nurturing, but not to the same extent as her 1950s counterpart who seemed to be constantly in the service of children and adults. She has also become articulate and feisty in rebellion. This articulateness and

---

[2]Although a few ethnic and homosexual romances have been published, they did not sell well and a recent inquiry indicates that no known publisher has plans for further market experimentation with these.

occasional action to assert her independence causes the hero, still superior in strength, status and education, to subdue her, though his job is relatively easy. Her rebellion is cast as a temporary aberration. Thus, the complementary relationship style is only temporarily jarred. Eventual female acquiescence is structured into the novels because the heroine is defined as incapable of independence.

Yet the novels' minor changes introduce some of the tensions and ambiguities arising from the new feminism of the late 1960s and suggest female dissatisfaction with the unequal state. This same change was noted by Kidd in the vision of interpersonal relationship styles that began to emerge in the advice articles of the 1960s and 1970s. "Change" became the key word and "standard preconceived meaning could no longer adequately be applied to human interaction" (p. 35). Meaning became negotiable. Specialists began to examine the model marriage as myth and declare that universal conventions could not be applied to all relationships. Advice was given on self-fulfillment and talking through conflict. The world of this vision, like that of romances, was not the safe, predictable world of the past but a world which must accommodate change.

This same female quest for self-fulfillment intensifies in Vision III, as in the 1970s real world, and so gender definitions and interaction styles change. The female grows in strength and issues militant demands for equality, engaging the hero in a symbolic war. Her consciousness has been raised, her demands are explicit, and her resolve strong. But again, her conviction is not sturdy enough and her capabilities not developed enough to win the war, for the male is defined with even greater strength and he unleashes his full powers of intellect and physical strength to "educate" her and cause her to recant. Thus the novels are tragicomedies reflecting a social structure in which the female continues to be defined as incapable of the self-determination she desires; therefore, she fails to gain independence but is nevertheless rewarded with fiction's romantic happiness-ever-after when she accepts her inabilities.

Vision IV changes gender definitions radically and promotes a significantly different relationship style that confronts the twin dangers of the human condition, isolation from others and domination by others. Both sexes share certain traits formerly considered gender specific to become equally instrumental and expressive. They reflect feminist ideals of the 1980s as the woman achieves independence and the male accepts sexual equality. There is, however, a special female control fantasy in this vision because the novels concentrate on the heroine's decision-making. She contemplates the male's proposal for a permanent relationship, evaluates the chances of its success, and negotiates its terms just as she negotiated her own career success. She is in total control of her life and fully responsible for all of its dimensions.

This new fantasy theme mirrors to some extent the control fantasy prominent in recent popular self-help books giving advice to women on achieving success as managers. Koester (1982) found that most writers depicting the female manager vision show the woman at the doorway or already present in the organization. "In the stock scenarios of the vision the locus of control for the outcome of the scene is placed squarely on the shoulders of the female" (p. 167). Success is possible if she knows how to manipulate events and relationships; the presence of forces and occurrences beyond her control are not considered. So the reversal is complete; the definition of woman has moved from woman incapable to woman in total control.

Over 33 years, the four rhetorical visions in category romances have reflected the on-going changes in social structures and the gradual movement from patriarchy toward equality of the sexes. They have indicated that in fiction as well as in reality conceptual and social frameworks are open to revision, gender definitions are not universally given nor relationship styles unchangeable. But the visions are obviously not authentic reproductions of the real world. By omission and deception they deny the complexity of human relationships and promote impossible dreams. Yet these dreams are so seductive that millions of modern women have made romances a publishing phenomenon.

We cannot assess accurately the degree to which these women accept the social structures and myths portrayed, but we can note that the novels contain potentially powerful rhetorical messages related to the nature of the sexes and the recommended repertoire of behaviors which theoretically lead to happiness-ever after. While romances are generally considered escape entertainments, they can also recommend and validate specific social orders for those caught up in their visions.

References

Booth, W. C. (1961). *The rhetoric of fiction*. Chicago: Univ. of Chicago Press.

Bormann, E. G. (1972). Fantasy and rhetorical vision: The rhetorical criticism of social reality. *Quarterly Journal of Speech, 58*, 396–407.

Brett, R. (1955). *Sweet waters*. London: Mills and Boon Limited.

Chase, E. R. (1983). *Calculated risk*. New York: Simon & Schuster, Inc.

Chesebro, J. W., & Hamsher, C. W. (1975). Communication, values, and popular television series. *Journal of Popular Culture, 8*, 589–602.

Doyle, M. V. (1978). *The rhetoric of romance fiction: A fantasy theme analysis of Barbara Cartland novels*. Unpublished master's thesis, University of Minnesota.

Hunter, E. (1974). *The crescent moon*. London: Mills and Boon Limited.

Kidd, V. V. (1975). Happily ever after and other relationship styles: Advice on interpersonal relations in popular magazines, 1951–1972. *Quarterly Journal of Speech, 61*, 31–39.

Koester, J. (1982). The Machiavellian princess: Rhetorical dramas for women managers. *Communication Quarterly, 30*, 165–172.

Lane, R. (1968). *House of the winds*. London: Mills and Boon Limited.

THE NARRATIVE APPROACH

THE NARRATIVE PARADIGM: AN ELABORATION

Walter R. Fisher

In presenting the narrative paradigm in the March, 1984, issue of this journal, I expressed the hope that it would elicit serious attention. It has, and for that I am grateful. Of the questions raised by the presentation, the most frequent and fundamental are two: (1) How does the narrative paradigm relate to traditional theories in the social sciences and the humanities? (2) How may the narrative paradigm be employed in an interpretation and assessment of a text in which there are claims to knowledge, truth, or reality? This essay explores answers to these questions. The text chosen for analysis is the exchange between Socrates and Callicles in Plato's *Gorgias* (Plato, 1973a).

Before embarking on the exploration, two points of clarification about the nature and functions of the narrative paradigm are essential. First, the narrative paradigm is misconstrued if it is considered as a representation of practices that characterize inquiry in a specific discipline—as a "sociological" paradigm—or as a precise model of or for such practices—as an "artifact . . . construct" paradigm. It is, as indicated in the original essay, a "metaparadigm" (Masterman, 1970, p. 65; see also Laudan, 1984, pp. 68–69). The narrative paradigm is meant to reflect an existing set of ideas shared in whole or in part by scholars from diverse disciplines, particularly those whose work is informed by, or centers on, narrativity. Second, the narrative paradigm does not necessarily impinge upon the existence or desirability of particular genres of discourse (Fisher, 1970). It does, however, directly bear on how they are to be interpreted and assessed. The narrative paradigm does not deny the utility of drawing distinctions regarding macroforms of discourse—philosophy, rhetoric, poetic, and so on—or microforms of discourse—myths, metaphors, arguments, and so on. It insists, though, that any instance of discourse is always more than the individuated forms that may compose it. The central point here is that there is no genre, including technical communication, that is not an episode in the story of life (a

From *Communication Monographs* 52 (December 1985): 347–67. Used by permission of author and the Speech Communication Association.

Walter R. Fisher is professor of communication arts and sciences, University of Southern California. He wishes to thank Professors Wayne Brockriede, John Angus Campbell, Thomas S. Frentz, Randall A. Lake, Calvin O. Schrag, and John R. Stewart for their constructive readings of early drafts. He is especially grateful to Michael Calvin McGee, whose critiques enabled him to transform an immature text into the admittedly imperfect but finished piece.

part of the "conversation") and is not itself constituted by *logos* and *mythos* (see MacCormac, 1976). Put another way: Technical discourse is imbued with myth and metaphor, and aesthetic discourse has cognitive capacity and import. The narrative paradigm is designed, in part, to draw attention to these facts and provide a way of thinking that fully takes them into account.

Relationships to Other Theories

By organizing this section into how the narrative paradigm relates to social scientific and humanistic theories, I risk suggesting that absolute boundaries can be drawn between the assumptions and methods of those who identify themselves in one or the other of these disciplines. I may also encourage the idea that narrativity does not inform or constitute the primary interest of investigations by representatives of these disciplines. The following discussion should dispel these notions. For now, however, it is worthy of note that work in conversational analysis focusing on narrativity clearly crosses these disciplines (see Beach, 1983; Nofsinger, 1983), and that there is a "third world of inquiry" (Brockriede, 1985). Its title is "human sciences," and its practitioners include researchers who employ empirical, historical, linguistic, hermeneutical, ethnomethodological, and philosophical methods of investigation. What unites them, I believe, is their rejection of, or resistance to, what Richard Bernstein calls the "Cartesian Anxiety": "With a chilling clarity Descartes leads us with an apparent and ineluctable necessity to a grand and seductive Either/Or. *Either* there is some support for our being, a fixed foundation for our knowledge, *or* we cannot escape the forces of darkness that envelope us with madness, with intellectual and moral chaos" (1983, p. 18). The narrative paradigm is a place beyond this. It is a ground where human scientists can and do meet, however they may pursue their individual projects.

Social Scientific Theories and the Narrative Paradigm   The theories chosen for mention here are representative, basic to communication inquiry, and illustrative of constructs that are not controlled by Cartesianism (See Daniels & Frandsen, 1984). I have in mind attribution theory (Heider, 1958; Kelley, 1971), balance theory (Heider, 1946; Newcomb, 1953), constructivism (Delia, 1977), social convergence theory (Bormann, 1983), reinforcement theory (Hovland, Janis & Kelley, 1953), social exchange theory (Thibaut & Kelley, 1959), and symbolic interactionism (Blumer, 1969; Mead, 1934). By and large, these theories are inspirited by the dream of Cartesianism: descriptive, explanatory, and predictive knowledge. In practice, however, they are, or at least can be interpreted as, various ways to account for *how* people come to adopt stories that guide behavior. In this, and in their ultimate non-positivism, they are related to the narrative paradigm, for it, too, seeks to account for *how* people come to adopt stories that guide behavior. It, too, is productive of description, explanation, and even prediction—in the sense that if one's character can be determined and if one's story in regard to a particular issue can be ascertained, it is possible to predict a person's probable actions, which is the best that social scientific theories can offer. (For an example, see Barber, 1972).

Where the narrative paradigm goes beyond these theories is in providing a "logic" for assessing stories, for determining whether or not one *should* adhere to the stories one is encouraged to endorse or to accept as the basis for decisions and actions. For the most part, social scientific theories ignore the role of values or they deny the possibility of developing rational schemes for their assessment. They thereby disregard the ultimate questions of good and evil—of the good life, which is the very topic of the Socrates-Callicles exchange. And this principle applies as well to any critical theory that, like Descartes's, denies room for values. This is not to say, of course, that social scientists do not have values or that they have no concern for humane relations. It is that their theories—by their nature—do not take the *assessment* of values into consideration.

On the other hand, their theories are characteristically normative, presuming such goods as appropriate meanings, psychological equilibrium, co-orientation, consensus, mutual benefit, and unity of mind and action. Balance theory and Burke's concept of identification (Burke, 1955), which is central to symbolic interactionism, are cases in point. Neither balance theory nor dramatism is tied to a rational system for assessing the stories one *should* adopt to achieve psychological equilibrium or to achieve consubstantiality in order to resolve human conflicts. The norm that marks many models in social scientific constructs is "efficacy," the power or capacity to strategically control one's environment.

Erving Goffman's theory of interpersonal interaction is illustrative. While he takes a "storytelling" approach in his studies of human relations, his focus is on the presentation of self and impression management (Goffman, 1959, 1969). "The goal of the Goffmanesque role player," as Alasdair MacIntyre observes, is "effectiveness and success" and success is "nothing but what passes for success" (MacIntyre, 1981, pp. 108–109). The epistemology that underlies the model is inherited from Francis Bacon—Knowledge is power over things—but it is implicitly extended in Goffman's social scientific theory to Knowledge is also power over people.

The precise way in which the narrative paradigm goes beyond traditional social scientific theories is in the concept of narrative rationality, which provides principles—probability and fidelity—and considerations for judging the merits of stories, whether one's own or another's. (The concept will be reviewed later.) No guarantee exists that one who uses narrative rationality will not adopt "bad" stories, rationalizations, but it does mitigate this tendency. Its use engenders critical self-awareness and conscious choice.

An example should clarify the distinction I am trying to make between the narrative paradigm and traditional social science theories. Balance theory predicts that a person will manifest balance-restoring behavior when he or she experiences psychological disequilibrium. Someone tries out for a track team or a play, or runs for office and is not successful. To restore balance, the person searches for a story that will justify his or her effort. Such stories may be positive or negative: I wasn't chosen but I had a great experience. I made new friends, learned valuable skills, and had lots of fun. Or, I wasn't chosen because I just wasn't prepared for the contest. Besides, some of the other contestants cheated and I wasn't treated fairly. For the person involved, these stories would satisfy the need for equilibrium and the demands of narrative probability and fidelity—or at least they could be defended by using these principles. It may be, however, that another observer would think otherwise, that the involved person was rationalizing. In any event, it is precisely in this sort of situation that narrative rationality is relevant as a system for determining whether or not one *should* accept a story, whether or not a story is indeed trustworthy and reliable as a guide to belief and action.

Narrative Rationality Revisited Before moving to the relationships of the narrative paradigm to humanistic theories, it might be well to review the concept of narrative rationality in some detail. Narrative probability refers to formal features of a story conceived as a discrete sequence of thought and/or action in life or literature (any recorded or written form of discourse); i.e., it concerns the question of whether or not a story coheres or "hangs together," whether or not the story is free of contradictions.[1]

Narrative fidelity concerns the "truth qualities" of the story, the degree to which it accords with the logic of good reasons: the soundness of its reasoning and the value of its values. To test soundness, one may, *when relevant*, employ standards from formal or informal logic. Thus, one must be attentive to facts, particular patterns of inference and implicature, and issues—conceived as the traditional questions arising in forensic (fact, definition, justification, and procedure) or deliberative (the nature of a problem and the desirability of proposed solutions) practices. However, the narrative paradigm envisions reasons as being expressed by elements of human communication that are not always clear-cut inferential or implicative forms. Any individuated form of human communication may constitute a "good reason" if it is taken as a *"warrant for accepting or adhering to the advice fostered"* by that communication (Fisher 1978, p. 378). To weigh the values, one considers questions of fact, relevance, consequence, consistency, and transcendent issue. The questions involve determination of what the values are; discernment of their pertinence to the story or case at hand; appraisal of their impact, if adopted, on one's concept of self, one's relationship with others, and the process of rhetorical transaction; ascertainment of their confirmation or disconfirmation in one's life, the lives of those whom one admires, and the best life that one can conceive; and evaluation of their effects on the quality of life generally (Fisher, 1978). Narrative rationality, as I suggested elsewhere (Fisher, 1980), is an attempt to recapture Aristotle's concept of *phronesis*, "practical wisdom." (The second part of this essay should further clarify the nature and utility of narrative rationality.)

Humanistic Theories and the Narrative Paradigm Though it should have been clear in the original essay (Fisher, 1984), I did not mean to suggest that the proposal marked the beginning of serious study of narrativity or that it was the only developed view of the subject. As the following discussion will show, narrativity has been of primary interest to diverse scholars for a long period of time. Again, I will attempt to situate the narrative paradigm by pointing out similarities and differences. At the same time, however, I hope to give force to the idea that there is a community which sees narrativity as a legitimate and useful way to interpret and understand human relations.

The theories to be examined include structuralism/post-structuralism, critical theory, analytic/post-analytic philosophy, and hermeneutics. Obviously, I cannot reconstruct these theories historically or in all of their permutations. Except for analytic philosophy, all of them are compatible with or constitutive of the narrative paradigm. A primary consideration in examining them will be how each orientation responds to the question: How and to what do symbols refer? I believe it is in respect to answers to this question that the various schools of

---

[1]The concept of coherence has been elaborated in chapter 2 to include material coherence and characterological coherence. Fisher, *Human Communication as Narrative*, pp. 47–48.

thought may be differentiated (relevant works on reference include: Gombrich, 1984; Krieger, 1984; Ricoeur, 1984; Thompson, 1983; White, 1984). Another consideration will be whether or not the theory offers a scheme for critique. If it does, what is the scheme and how does it relate to narrative rationality? Finally, I want to observe an important way that hermeneutics enriches the conception of human communication in the narrative paradigm.

One of the most significant lines of inquiry into narrativity has been structuralism, post-structuralism, and semiotics. These studies have made a major contribution to the interpretation of texts. Because the narrative paradigm is concerned with the pragmatic effects of texts as well as interpretation, there are some important differences between the orientations. Whether of the classical, semiotic, or deconstructionist schools, structuralist thinkers tend to regard narrative synchronically, as a form or genre, and not as a way of understanding lived, as well as imagined, stories. Narratology (Andrews, 1982), for instance, the "scientific" study of narrative discourse, which was advanced by such writers as J. Greimas, Tzvetvan Todorov, Gerard Genette, and Roland Barthes, took as given that:

> Narrative does not show, does not imitate; the passion which may excite us in reading a novel is not that of a "vision" (in actual fact, we do not "see" anything). Rather it is that of a meaning, that of a higher order or relation which also has its emotions, its hopes, its dangers, its triumphs. "What takes place" in a narrative is from the referential (reality) point of view literally *nothing;* "what happens" is language alone, the adventure of language, the unceasing celebration of its coming (Barthes, 1977, p. 124; Barthes's statement is in response to Mallarme's *Crayonne au theatre, OEuvres completes,* p. 296; see also Genette, 1980, p. 27; Todorov, 1977, pp. 19–28).

In short, structuralism approaches narrative formally; the narrative paradigm approaches it, along with other genres, rhetorically, as a mode of social influence.

Second, as indicated in Barthes's observation, structuralists, at least of the classical school, deny the relevance of reference in their studies. A poststructuralist exponent of this position is Paolo Valesio, a student of Roman Jakobson who has been a pivotal figure in the structuralist movement. Valesio argues that *"every discourse in its functional aspect is based on a relatively limited set of mechanisms—whose structure remains essentially the same from text to text, from language to language, from historical period to historical period—that reduce every referential choice to formal choice"* (1980, p. 21). He also insists that "All facts are accessible to us only as linguistic constructions" (p. 113). Thus, in viewing narration or any other kind of discourse only in terms of making meanings and in restricting an understanding of praxis to linguistic constructions, structuralism neglects two of the most basic features of the narrative paradigm.

As already indicated, the narrative paradigm is a paradigm in the sense of a philosophical view of human communication; it is not a model of discourse as such. The primary function of the paradigm is to offer a way of interpreting and assessing human communication that leads to critique, a determination of whether or not a given instance of discourse provides a reliable, trustworthy, and desirable guide to thought and action in the world. It predicates that all normal human discourse is meaningful and is subject to the tests of narrative rationality.

Contrary to structuralist thinking, it holds that meaning is a matter of history, culture, and character as well as linguistic convention and interanimation.

In taking this position, I invite Derrida's now famous (or infamous) charge of "logocentrism." However, I do not privilege oral over written communication or adhere to a positivist view of the world. I would agree that symbols are indeed "indeterminant"—if one pushes them far enough—that an author's name (or presence) is irrelevant for understanding many mundane forms of communication, and that one of the pervasive functions of language is to foster ideology. Meaning, for Derrida, is a matter of use rather than reference to people and things in the world. The purpose of critique, according to Derrida, is to reveal this fact in a Nietzschian fashion and to deform the basis of "Western metaphysics," which includes everyday thought and language as well as the philosophical tradition. His method is well illustrated in his essay on Plato's *Phaedrus*, "Pharmacia" (Derrida, 1981). It is clear what Derrida seeks to subvert (Derrida, 1982, p. 67); it is unclear what he seeks to affirm (for another view of Derrida's project, see Rorty, 1984). Epistemological skepticism can lead anywhere, as evidenced by the uses to which Nietzsche's thought has been put in the twentieth century.

Critical theory, on the other hand, has an historic direction—"liberation," "emancipation," or a "rational society"—and, until now, a consistent method of critique—dialectic. Departing from the Frankfurt School's early focus on "consciousness," then "instrumental reason," Jürgen Habermas has turned his attention to a theory of communicative action (1984; see also Habermas, 1979). The shift has entailed a move from a concern about "cognitive-instrumental rationality" to "communicative rationality" (Habermas, 1984). Like Karl-Otto Apel (1977), Habermas conceives rationality as grounded in the presuppositions of speech, specifically, argumentative interactions. Rationality is determined by "whether, if necessary," persons could, "*under suitable circumstances,* provide reasons for their expressions" (Habermas, 1984, p. 17). Thus, he reserves rationality for argumentation, "that type of speech in which participants thematize contested validity claims and attempt to vindicate or criticize them through arguments. An argument contains reasons or grounds that are connected in a systematic way with the *validity claim* of a problematic expression" (p. 18).

Validity claims may concern truth in terms of the objective world; the rightness, appropriateness, or legitimacy of speech acts; or the sincerity or authenticity of intentions or feelings. The nature of validity claims relates clearly to his conception of the nature of communicative functions: *teleological,* which is manifest in monologic communication; *normative,* which is featured in interpersonal (cultural) communication; and dramaturgical, which is evidenced in self-presentational communication. (Habermas relies on Goffman for his understanding of dramaturgy instead of Kenneth Burke; this reliance accounts, I suspect, for some of the differences in his theory and mine.) Habermas maintains that his view of language encompasses all three functions and that his "communicative model of action" is in the traditions of "Mead's symbolic interactionism, Wittgenstein's concept of language games, Austin's theory of speech acts, and Gadamer's hermeneutics" (p. 95).

The end of communication, Habermas holds, is understanding, by which he means "valid agreement" (p. 392). In order for understanding to be achieved rationally, a communicative interaction must not only include arguers, it must also be symmetrical and non-coercive. Such communicative encounters would be exhibited in an "ideal speech situation." There would be equal opportunity to participate, to criticize, to express personal aims and attitudes, and to perform these acts without regard to power or ideology. These requirements are parallel with the conditions I presuppose as necessities of human communication: "Beyond the physical requirements of communicants who share some commonality in symbol systems, human communication relies on some degree of trust, a willingness to participate in the process, a belief in the desirability of the interaction, and an interest in (or expectation of) the attainment and/or advancement of truth" (Fisher, 1978, p. 382). These necessities can be formed as norms and then can serve as standards for the evaluation of communication interaction, like the requirements of the "ideal speech situation." However, two features of these requirements/necessities should be noted. First, Habermas's requirements are "counterfactual"; the necessities are empirical. Second, neither the requirements nor the necessities speak to the soundness of the reasoning that occurs in a communication interaction. This function can only be accomplished through some scheme such as that provided by narrative rationality.

Thus, while critical theory anticipated themes developed in the narrative paradigm and there are common objectives in Habermas's project and mine, there are also some differences. Habermas posits persons as arguers; I see them, including arguers, as storytellers. He conceives reasons as warrants tied to claims of validity; I conceive reasons as warrants that are to entail values (good reasons). His interest is argumentation; mine is all forms of human communication. His concept of the end of communication is understanding; my concept of the end of communication is practical wisdom and humane action. In sum, our differences primarily concern the nature and functions of human communication. Ordinary discourse, in my view, is not inherently "distorted," and there are many forms of human communication beyond argumentation and the specific individuated units we call arguments.

Except for Alasdair MacIntyre (1981), analytic and post-analytic philosophers neglect the idea of narrative. The concept of narrative rationality is specifically denied by analytic philosophers, such as A. J. Ayer, Donald Davidson, Hilary Putnam, and Gilbert Ryle, who hold strongly to an epistemological position generally referred to as "foundationalism." This is the position that insists that only certain forms of discourse can lay claim to knowledge and that there are absolute grounds or methods that can assure such claims. Post-analytic philosophers regard this position with skepticism or outright rejection. Among them, Rorty (1984) argues, are John Dewey, Ludwig Wittgenstein, Martin Heidegger, and himself. It is obviously beyond the scope of this discussion to review the arguments that characterize each camp. One can get an excellent overview of them from *The Linguistic Turn* (Rorty, 1967; see also Schrag, 1985), *Philosophy and the Mirror of Nature* (Rorty, 1979), and *Beyond Objectivism and Relativism* (Bernstein, 1983). My own position is indicated by my heavy reliance on MacIntyre's *After Virtue* (1981); this dependence puts me on the side of the post-analytic philosophers. The narrative paradigm stresses ontology rather than epistemology, which is not to say that knowledge does not exist but that it does not have an absolute foundation in ordinary discourse. The subject of such discourse is symbolic action that creates social reality.

MacIntyre is explicit in supporting the narrative view of human decision-making and action. As reported in the original essay, he holds that the essential genre "for the characterisation of human actions" (p. 194) is "enacted dramatic narrative" (p. 200). Rorty does not mention narration but he does subscribe to a view of conversation that is compatible with the narrative paradigm (Fisher, 1984). He writes, "If we see knowing not as having an essence, to be described by scientists or philosophers, but as a right, by current standards, to believe, then we are well on the way to seeing *conversation* as the ultimate context within which knowledge is to be understood" (Rorty, 1979, p. 389). While I concur with the substance of the statement and its implication for how persons should relate to one another, I do not wholly accept Rorty's pragmatism. There are two problems with the position, as I see it: First, it suggests that whatever keeps the "conversation going" (p. 377) is good; second, it ignores criteria for determining whether what is said in the conversation is worthy of belief and action. I believe, as indicated by the concept of narrative rationality, that there are rational criteria for distinguishing the reliability, trustworthiness, and desirability of statements made in the conversation of life.

Before moving to the relationship of the narrative paradigm to hermeneutic thought, one more point seems important. Bernstein, whom I would include among the post-analytic philosophers, characterizes the modern state of intellectual thought as a need to get beyond objectivism and relativism (Bernstein, 1983). The solution to this problem, he argues, cannot be a "typical modern response . . . the idea that we can make, engineer, impose our collective will to form" communities marked by intersubjective practices, freedom, "a willingness to talk and to listen, mutual debate, and a commitment to rational persuasion" (p. 226). The solution, he proposes, is "to try again and again to foster and nurture those forms of communal life in which dialogue, conversation, *phronesis*, practical discourse, and judgment are concretely embodied in our everyday practices" (p. 229). He find ideas conducive to this effort in the visions of Gadamer, Habermas, Rorty, and Arendt.

My point is that this aim is an historic feature of classic conceptions of rhetoric. It is evident in Aristotle's view of *phronesis*, which recognizes a contingent world, the particularities of practical existence and the possibility of wisdom—a virtue that involves an interest in matters that transcend immediate circumstances. It is present in Kenneth Burke's concept of "permanence and change" and in his idea of identification, which may move dialectically from the particular to the universal. It is also a significant part of Perelman's theory of rhetoric, specifically, his distinction between particular and universal audiences, a distinction that is never absolute. And, it is an intended constituent of the narrative paradigm. Good reasons are an expression of practical wisdom; they are, in their highest expression, an encompassment of what is relative and objective in situations. They function to resolve exigencies by locating and activating values that go beyond the moment, making it possible that principles of decision or action can be generalized.

Except for dramatism, the narrative paradigm is most compatible with the themes of the later Heidegger, Gadamer, and Ricoeur, the leading contemporary figures in hermeneutics. Particularly helpful to me in Heidegger's work is his view that "man is a *thinking*, that is, a *meditating* being" (1966, p. 47). The concept was put forth as an antithesis to the idea that man is, or should be always, a "calculative thinker, a person who 'computes' "—weighs, measures, and counts— possibilities, benefits, and outcomes but does not "contemplate the meaning which reigns in everything that is" (p. 46). The operation of narrative rationality presupposes (synthesizes) both notions but lays stress on the meditative as the foundation. In another essay, Heidegger celebrates a line from a poem by Hölderlin: "Poetically Man Dwells" (1971). I would alter the line slightly: "Narratively Persons Dwell" (see Hyde, 1983; Schrag, 1985).

There are a number of themes in Gadamer's work that enrich the narrative paradigm. I share his ontological perspective on human action; his concept of language: "Language is not just one of man's possessions in the world, but on it depends the fact that man has a world at all" (Gadamer, 1982, p. 401, see also Gadamer, 1981); his view of the constitutive nature of communication: "The process of communication is not mere action, a purposeful activity, a setting-up of signs, through which I transmit my will to others. . . . It is a living process in which a community of life is lived out" (p. 404); his stance on reason: "Reason exists for us only in concrete, historical terms, i.e. it is not its own master, but remains constantly dependent on the given circumstances in which it operates" (p. 245); his emphasis on *phronesis* (pp. 20ff, 278ff, and 376ff); his interpretation of aesthetic and scientific forms: the object of aesthetic awareness "is a part of the essential process of representation" (p. 104), and "all scientific research has the form of literature, insofar as it is essentially bound to language. If words can be written down, then they are literature, in the widest sense" (p. 144); and his position on conversation (within the conversation of life) as dialogue: "Thus it is characteristic of every true conversation that each opens himself to the other person, truly accepts his point of view as worthy of consideration and gets inside the other to such an extent that he understands not a particular individual, but what he says" (p. 347).

This last point relates to something I alluded to earlier—that the hermeneutic conception adds an important dimension to the narrative paradigm. The paradigm advances the idea that good communication is good by virtue of its satisfying the requirements of narrative rationality, that it offers a reliable, trustworthy, and desirable guide to belief and action. Gadamer suggests that communication is good, along with whatever truth it may advance, if it honors the dignity and worth of the participants. (The standard is also suggested by Habermas, Rorty, Arendt, and Bernstein.) This is the thesis of Martin Buber's *I and Thou* (1970) and the premise of John Stewart's approach to interpersonal communication (1980; see also Stewart, 1978). I fully endorse the standard as it is a primary feature of the praxis supported by the narrative paradigm (Fisher, 1984, pp. 9–10).

The narrative paradigm diverges from Gadamerian thought exactly at the point where hermeneutics and rhetoric diverge. Gadamer holds that "hermeneutics is a kind of inversion of rhetoric and poetic" (p. 166). Hermeneutics seeks understanding; rhetoric and poetic seek to project understanding into the world. Put another way: Hermeneutics is concerned with the recovery or an appropriation of truth in texts, and rhetoric and poetic are modes of expressing truth; they provide texts. But rhetoric is more than form of discourse; it is also theory and offers the basis of critique, which is the purpose of the concept of narrative rationality. Calvin O. Schrag makes the case for hermeneutic critique in his book, *Communicative Praxis and the Space of Subjectivity* (1986; see also Schrag, 1980). He cites the narrative paradigm and narrative rationality, in particular, as useful in moving hermeneutics to a critical stance.

Paul Ricoeur's recent writings inform and reinforce the narrative paradigm. In his essay, "The Narrative Function" (1983), for instance, he maintains that "the form of life to which narrative discourse belongs is our historical condition itself" (p. 288); he asserts that "all narrative makes, in a certain sense, a referential claim'' (p. 289); he argues that "history is both a literary *artefact* (and in this sense a fiction) and a representation of *reality*" (p. 291; see also White, 1984); he contends that "all symbolic systems make and remake reality" (p. 293); and he concludes, in part, that *"the world of fiction leads us to the heart of the real world of action"* (p. 296). These are all ideas that I endorse, but I do not think they go quite far enough.

While Ricoeur (1977) sees the concept of "test" as being relevant to the interpretation of human action, it is clear that he views narration as a distinct form. I do not deny that narration is a distinct form, as argument is a form or explication is a form. And I agree that narration as a form reveals or unfolds a world that is a "temporal world" (Fisher, 1984, p. 4). I am particularly indebted to him for his discussion of metaphor (1979, pp. 216–256) and *mimesis* (1979, pp. 31ff, 1984, pp. 45ff). The poetic function of language, he writes in the preface to *Time and Narrative,* "is not limited to the celebration of language for its own sake, at the expense of the referential function, which is predominant in descriptive language" (1984, p. x). He goes on to observe that "whereas metaphorical redescription reigns in the field of sensory, emotional, aesthetic, and axiological values, which make the world a habitable world, the mimetic function of plots takes place by preference in the field of action and its temporal values" (p. xi). The narrative paradigm is, in a sense, a radicalization of these ideas, an extension of Ricoeur's logic to its own conclusion; it adds to them a conception of rationality and praxis. It posits, furthermore, that even scientific (technical) discourse, which is a form of literature, is informed by metaphor (and myth), contains "plots," and is time-bound.

There is, in other words, no form of human communication that is purely descriptive. Hence, works such as Charles Darwin's *Origin of the Species,* and Einstein's *Relativity: The Special and the General Theory,* are as usefully interpreted and assessed through the narrative paradigm as the President's last speech or the latest popular film. The criteria for assessment of the texts would certainly vary, as the form of good reasons varies in each of the forms of communication, but the principles of coherence and fidelity would apply to all. In short, I believe that the structural elements that Ricoeur attributes to narrative form are relevant and instructive in understanding non-fiction as well as fiction, the texts of life as well as learned and unlearned discourse.

Michel Foucault poses a special problem in this exploration of the relationship of the narrative paradigm to humanistic thought. He is not exactly a structuralist, a deconstructionist, a critical theorist, a professional philosopher, or a follower of hermeneutics, but there are elements of each of these orientations in his work. It has even been alleged that his work is "anti-humanist" (Lemert & Gillan, 1982). There is *prima facie* evidence for this claim in a series of Foucault's studies (1965, 1970, 1973, 1977, 1978) in which "subjects" are reduced to "role players" controlled by existing *epistemes,* or discourse formations (1972). The claim is also supported by Foucault's wanting to dismiss not only subjects, but also tradition, influence, development and evolution, spirit, genre, book and oeuvre (1972). Equally troubling is his view of truth. By truth, he writes, "I do not mean 'the ensemble of truths which are to be discovered and accepted,' but rather 'the ensemble of rules according to which the true and the false are separated and specific effects of power are attached to the true' "(1980, p. 132). One may, in addition, see an anti-humanistic bias in his genealogical method, "a form of history which can account for the constitution of knowledges, discourses, domains of subjects etc., without having to make reference to a subject which is either transcendental in relation to the field of events or runs in its empty sameness throughout the course of history" (1980, p. 117). Whether one accepts or rejects the claim, it seems to me, depends on whether or not one sees humanistic value in Foucault's aim: "to question our will to truth; to re-store its character as event; to abolish the sovereignty of the signifier" (1969, p. 229). Later, I will suggest that the historical problem of politics is not the will to truth in and of itself, but the will to truth tied to a will to power. I ap-plaud the demystification of practices that oppress or repress persons, but I can-not endorse subversion without affirmation. And I am sure where Foucault is uncertain about narration. He writes: "I suppose, though I am not altogether sure, there is barely a society without its major narratives; told, retold and varied" (1972, p. 220).

The final theorist to be mentioned in this exploration is Perelman, whose the-ory of rhetoric is to be counted with Kenneth Burke's as one of the most signif-icant of the twentieth century. I have delineated the relationship of the narrative paradigm to "the New Rhetoric" in a chapter (Fisher, 1987).[2] Suffice it to say here that our differences stem from differences in our views of human beings—arguers/storytellers—and in our conceptions of rationality—*an argument is as good as the audience that would ahere to it*/an argument (good reason) is as good as it can withstand the tests of narrative rationality. There is overlap in our views in that the narrative paradigm assumes that arguers tell stories and story-tellers argue.

To the first question posed by this essay—how does the narrative paradigm relate to leading social scientific and humanistic theories?—I offer this summary answer: The narrative paradigm is a fabric woven of threads of thought from both the social sciences and humanities. It seeks, like any other theory of human action, to account for how persons come to believe and to behave. It differs from social scientific and humanistic theories in that it projects narration not as an art, genre, or activity, but as a paradigm. It goes beyond these theories in pro-viding a "new" logic, the concept of narrative rationality, which is applicable to all forms of human communication. Finally, it is, not uniquely, a response to the exigence of our time identified by Gadamer: "In the age of science, is there any way of preserving and validating the great heritage of knowledge and wisdom?" (1981, p. 159). That way is to formulate a theory of human communication that recognizes permanence and change, culture and character, reason and value, and the practical wisdom of all persons.

Application of the Narrative Paradigm to the Stories of Socrates and Callicles

The second question posed by this essay—how may the narrative paradigm be em-ployed in an interpretation and assessment of a text in which there are claims to knowledge, truth, or reality?—is appropriate in this essay for three reasons. (It should be noted that there is no serious discourse that does not make such claims.) First, any construct is only as good as it can be applied and provide con-vincing and useful understanding of actual texts, of real experience. Second, an answer to this question will clarify further the differences between the

[2]See "Judging the Quality of Audiences and Narrative Rationality," in *Practical Rea-soning in Human Affairs*, ed. J. L. Golden and J. J. Pilotta (D. Reidel, 1986), 85–103.

narrative paradigm and the theories surveyed in the previous section. And third, the exploration will complement the interpretations offered earlier of *Death of a Salesman* and *The Great Gatsby* (Fisher & Filloy, 1982), the nuclear controversy, and *The Epic of Gilgamesh* (Fisher, 1984).

While the narrative paradigm as a worldview of human communication does not provide a specific method of analysis, it does propose a precise perspective for critically reading texts. Regardless of its genre, a text is viewed as composed of good reasons, elements that give warrants for believing or acting in accord with the message fostered by that text. Good reasons may be expressed by any individuated form of discourse or performance: "argument," metaphor, myth, gesture, and so on. The perspective focuses on the message, the individuated forms that constitute it, and the reliability, trustworthiness, and desirability of the message as determined by the tests of narrative rationality. Throughout the interpretation and assessment, values are taken as the principal ingredient of the individuated forms and the message. Thus, one may adhere to the narrative paradigm and approach a text respecting its genre and conduct the analysis in a variety of ways. The criteria for assessing a scientific text will surely differ from those used in criticizing a popular film. But, this holds true insofar as the scientific text is viewed technically (epistemologically) and not in terms of its ontological implications for ordinary life. Once this consideration is made, the principles of coherence and fidelity are clearly relevant. I would argue that they are also relevant in technical assessment, because, as I have already indicated, I believe that technical discourse is as imbued with myths, metaphors, and strategic design as nontechnical discourse. In what follows, I will focus on themes, values, and the behavior of the storytellers.

One other note is necessary before moving to the stories told by Socrates and Callicles. The narrative perspective entails an analysis of stories: discrete sequences of symbolic actions. It insists, however, on the recognition that no text is devoid of context; that is, relationship to other texts. The meaning and value of a story are always a matter of how it stands with or against other stories. There is no story that is not embedded in other stories.

The story told by Socrates in the *Gorgias* is a case in point. It appears in several of Plato's dialogues, especially the *Protagoras,* the *Apology,* and the *Republic.* It can also be found in the *Phaedrus,* where he elaborates the story further in connection with rhetoric. While the story concerns choosing the life of philosophy, as exemplified in the life of Socrates, over the life of political hedonism, as represented by Callicles, it would be a mistake to see this choice as a purely philosophical one; it is eminently and fundamentally a practical choice, a decision that affects the mode of one's personal and public behavior, the way education, politics, and communication are to be conceived and practiced. As it appears in the *Gorgias,* the story is, as E. R. Dodds observes: "more than an *apologia* for Socrates; it is at the same time Plato's *apologia pro vita sua*" (1959, p. 31). A basic theme of the story and Socrates' life is that "the man and woman who are noble and good" are "happy, but the 'evil and base' are wretched" (Plato, 1973a, 470e). There was but one way that the good life could be achieved—living by Socrates' idealism.

The strongest rival of this form of life was and is the life represented by Callicles, a political hedonism. The key theme of this life was and is that the powerful person determines what is happy and just and that happiness and justice are realized by the exercise of one's own proclivities.

The conflict between Socrates and Callicles begins when Callicles enters the ongoing conversation about the nature and functions of rhetoric, the point at which he asks: "Tell me, Chaerephon, is Socrates in earnest or joking?" (Plato, 1973a, 481b). That Socrates is serious is demonstrated by several statements: philosophy is his "love" (his life); she is never capricious. He would rather "that the majority of mankind should disagree with and oppose me" than he "should be out of tune with and contradict" himself (482b, c); "and do not take what I say as if I were merely playing, for you see the subject of our discussion—and on what subject should even a man of slight intelligence be more serious?—namely, what kind of life one should live, the life to which you invite me, that of a 'real man,' speaking in the assembly and practicing rhetoric and playing the politician according to your present fashion, or the life spent in philosophy, and how one differs from the other" (500c). His seriousness is also evident in his tone and his willingness to forego the elenchos, his method of cross examination, in order to persuade Callicles (507ff). That Callicles is equally serious may be seen in his willingness to enter the conversation, his fervent manner, and his persistent questioning of Socrates' seriousness.

The themes of Socrates' story are these: "every man is his own master" (491d); pleasure is not synonymous with the good; pain is not synonymous with evil; "all our actions should be done for the sake of the good" (499e); a true art must be grounded on a conception of the good (as medicine is founded on the conception of health); rhetoric is not an art; it is an irrational knack tied to an irrational conception of politics (justice); true virtue is marked by harmony and order; a true rhetorician should be occupied with "how justice may be implanted in the souls of the citizens and injustice banished, how temperance may be implanted and indiscipline banished, and how goodness in general may be engendered and wickedness depart" (504e); such a rhetorician has never existed; a happy life is a temperate life; an unhappy life is an intemperate life; "if injustice is the greatest of evils to the wrongdoer . . . , it is an even greater evil, if that be possible, to escape punishment when one does wrong" (599b): "For to arrive in the other world with a soul surcharged with many wicked deeds is the worst of all evils" (522d). The message of the dialogue is that one should choose to live as Socrates lived or at least by the values he celebrated. He is the "enactment," the living proof, of his philosophy (Kaufman, 1979; see also Campbell & Jamieson, n.d.; Rendall, 1977; Spitzer, 1975). Perhaps the capstone of his view is this: "I renounce the honors sought by most men, and pursuing the truth I shall endeavor both to live and, when death comes, to die, as good a man as I possibly can" (Plato, 1973a, 526e). He also asserts: "I think that I am one of the very few Athenians, not to say the only one, engaged in the true political art, and that of the men of today I alone practice statesmanship" (521d).

Socrates' story is informed by the values of truth, the good, beauty, health, wisdom, courage, temperance, justice, harmony, order, communion, friendship, and a oneness with the Cosmos. These are the values that humankind has historically professed and aspired to. They are compatible, for instance, with the values of the moralistic myth of the American Dream: "tolerance, charity, compassion, and true regard for the dignity and worth of each and every individual" (Fisher, 1973, p. 161).

The appeal of Socrates' story resides in his character, his commitment to his philosophy to the point of martyrdom, and the coherence of his position. There can be no question of the coherence of Socrates' story. One can, of course, show that Socrates is a "logic-chopper," but that misses the point. Logic, as we know it, was not in existence until Aristotle "invented" it. Plato's dialectic is based on ontology and is structured by definitional moves, not formal logic. The only recourse in opposing his philosophy is to propose an alternative one, such as that advanced by Plato's pupil, Aristotle. Callicles offers an alternative philosophy, political hedonism, but it is an easy mark for an idealist, especially since it is grounded on relativism. There is no way to reconcile the philosophies of Socrates and Callicles.

The good reasons that constitute Socrates' story are arguments and myths centered on the meaning and implications of his values, particularly the good, the true, and the just. To the question why Socrates should resort to myths, one can suggest several answers: Frustration is one. His move to myth is not, however, as some would argue, because his dialectical argument has failed (Kaufman, 1979). There is no approach to persuasion that will not fail if an audience refuses to attend to a message. Another answer is that myths were still a generally accepted mode of communication; *logos* had not yet supplanted *mythos,* so Socrates was trying to speak in a form that was appropriate for his audience. A third answer is that the myths are the most efficacious means of communicating a sense of transcendental truth, in this case, of the afterlife. As Dodds (1959) notes, "the *Gorgias* myth (the one at the end of the dialogue) is called λόγος because it expresses in imaginative terms a 'truth of religion' " (p. 377; see also Dodds, 1951; Friedlander, 1928). In other words, Plato's conception of mind (*nous*) is in regard to "the imaginative vision of truth" (Randall, 1960, 1970). Myth, at least Plato's version of it, not only offers support for dialectical argument, it is also a mode of discourse in which a vision of truth is made manifest.

The problem that arises with Socrates' story is in respect to its fidelity to the world, the world we know from ordinary experience. No matter how deeply one may want to emulate the life of Socrates, to adhere to his ideals, one knows the frustrations and possible martyrdom that can result from doing so. One may well admire Socrates, but one also realizes the "ring of truth" in Callicles' representation of the way people and things actually are. As Randall observes, "Man cannot live without ideals, but equally man cannot live by ideals alone" (1970, p. 149). More will be said on this matter later in the discussion of the appeal of Callicles' story.

At this point, it is important to recognize that the values espoused by Socrates can be used to justify (or mystify) elitist systems of governance. Indeed, they are the grounds of Plato's *Republic,* which is structured as an aristocracy of talent. They are also celebrated by the USSR. The differences between these systems are in where "truth" is to be found, in the noumenal or phenomenal world, and in their "religious" orientations. Plato would please the "gods;" in the USSR, there is no "god," only the Presidium. In both systems, public and social knowledge are denied and rhetoric is relegated to a purely instrumental role. There is another difference worthy of note: While Plato was not a friend of democracy (Popper, 1971), the *Republic* is an imagined society, a utopia meant to contrast with current society and serve as a basis of critique. Plato should not be held accountable for the Soviet system or any other nation state.

The themes of Callicles' story are these: Nature rather than convention is the guide to life (Plato 1973a, 484c); philosophy is a study for youth; when a man who is "growing older still studies philosophy, the situation becomes ridiculous" (485b); philosophy leaves a person defenseless in the political arena

(486b); natural justice is realized in the circumstance in which "the better and wiser should rule over and have more than the inferior" (490a); "anyone who is to live aright should suffer his appetites to grow to the greatest extent and not check them, and through courage and intelligence should be competent to minister to them at their greatest and to satisfy every appetite with what it craves" (492a); the truth is this: "Luxury and intemperance and license, when they have sufficient backing, are virtue and happiness and all the rest is tinsel, the unnatural catchwords of mankind, mere nonsense and of no account" (492c); conventional justice and equality are values fostered by the weak to control the strong; there are some rhetoricians who were good men—Themistocles, Cimon, Miltiades, and Pericles (503c); and one should live "to serve and minister" to the polis (521b). In sum, Callicles' story celebrates hedonism, relativism, and power politics—the "survival of the fittest"—which are justified on the basis that this is the way nature itself dictates that things should be.

Callicles' position is informed by the values of pleasure, expediency, self-aggrandizement, courage, strength, political acumen and success, and the will to power. Just as Socrates' values correspond with the values of the moralistic myth of the American Dream, so do Callicles' values accord with the values of the materialistic myth of the American Dream: "effort, persistence, 'playing the game,' initiative, self-reliance, achievement and success" (Fisher, 1973 p. 161).

It would be a mistake, however, to see the materialistic myth of Callicles as being without moral dimension. The materialistic myth is tied to the Calvinist ethos and Callicles, who obviously was not a Calvinist, "does not deny the significance of ethical-judgments, but like Nietzsche he 'transvalues' them. . . . " Callicles believed that "might really is *right*" (Dodds, 1959, pp. 15, 314; Friedlander, p. 261). Friedlander characterizes Callicles' ethics in this way: "There is a morality by nature, genuine, original, and founded upon true being—a morality of powerful men to whom suffering wrong is not only worse, but more disgraceful than doing wrong" (p. 260). If Callicles had not held such a position, one with philosophical grounding, he would not have been such an attractive opponent for Socrates. His orientation to the "good life" made him an idea foil for Plato, who as a youth shared many of the inclinations of Callicles. In the *Seventh Letter*, Plato wrote, "Once upon a time in my youth I cherished like many another the hope of entering upon a political career as soon as I came of age" (Plato, 1973b). Dodds notes, "We may even conjecture, with Festugière (387) and Jaeger (*Paideia*, ii, 138), that 'in his character Plato had so much of that unruly will to power to find, and fight, part of himself in Callicles;' or with Alain (*Idees*, 17) that 'Plato paints *himself* here as he might have been, as he feared to be' " (1959, p. 267).

The appeal of Callicles' story derives from its narrative probability and its fidelity with the way politics are often practiced—whether democratic, republican, feudal, fascist, or socialistic. The good reasons that constitute his story are inevitably circular; they are expressed in the idea that "might makes right" (right is might). While Callicles' overall philosophy is coherent (tautological), Socrates shows, on many counts, that elements of his story are inconsistent. On a central theme of their dispute—whether it is better to suffer wrong than to do it—for instance, Socrates demonstrated that Callicles' position, that it is better to do wrong than suffer it, is incompatible with his admission that the good is not the same as pleasure (Plato, 1973a, 500a). Socrates' own position, for which he was ready to die, was that "we should be more on guard against doing than suffering wrong" (527b). Callicles may have died because of his beliefs, or his actions based on them (Dodds, 1959), but he does not express a willingness to do so, as Socrates does. Callicles' "God" was the polis and his commandments were the standards by which one would serve as its leader.

The problems in Callicles' story arise in consideration of how it evades the values of truth, universal good, equality, harmony, order, communion, friendship, and a oneness with the Cosmos. (That one cannot, unless one is a Socrates, totally live by these values is not a denial of their desirabilty as standards of conduct.) It also poses difficulties in consideration of what life would be like if everyone believed and behaved as Callicles advises. This criticism is appropriate because any ethical stipulation regarding how one ought to live is subject to generalization: One cannot argue that one can live one way and claim that others cannot (Perelman, 1979; Singer, 1971). "To the extent that the seeking of pleasure and the avoidance of suffering and death could be made the basis of ethics," Perelman (1981, p. 319) observes, "there would be no further need for rhetoric. One needs rhetoric only to overcome fear or suffering, in order not to give in to temptation." Neither Callicles nor Nietzsche should be held accountable for the tyrannies the world has suffered throughout history. But the motive they espoused—the will to power—must be seen as not only the source of much of humankind's material progress, but also of many of its social and political ills. As suggested earlier, it is not the will to power in and of itself that leads to expansionist and totalitarian systems; it is, in the modern age, the will to power tied to a presumption of truth, as demonstrated by the practices of nations led by Hitler, Mussolini, and Stalin. No doubt there have been nations (and persons) that have exercised power for power's sake, for conquest or plunder, but mindless violence may be overcome by superior force. Fanaticism in the exercise of power is another thing; it must be met by rival ideology and more power. Finally, it must be said of Callicles that, while his ethics are in sharp contrast with those of classical rhetoricians, such as Isocrates and Cicero, his position does make rhetoric a vital force in civic affairs.

One further note should be made here regarding Callicles' refusal to continue the conversation at 505c. As already suggested, no story can be persuasive if one closes oneself from its possible truth. Hans-Georg Gadamer expresses the idea this way: "there is no means of compelling someone to see the truth who does not want to see it" (1980, p. 116). In order for any form of discourse to work, whether dialogue (dialectic), argumentation, narrative, and so on, participants in the transaction must be open and reflective, not approach life as a series of habits only for survival and success. From this, one may hazard the view that unless communicants admit the possibility of truth and goodness, they have no rational basis for rejecting evil, even as a way of life. Such a life was that of Adolf Eichmann, who rendered evil a "banality" (Arendt, 1965; Berger, 1969).

Choosing between Socrates and Callicles   That the Western world, at least, has celebrated the values that mark the story of Socrates is, I believe, beyond question. Along with other martyrs to truth—Jesus, Gandhi, and Lincoln—Socrates' story is preferred to that of Callicles in principle, if not always in practice, in the same way that Milton's *Areopagitica* is preferred to Machiavelli's *The Prince* and John Stuart Mill's *On Liberty* to Nietzsche's *The Will to Power.*

Though persons seem to prefer idealistic stories, a modern reader of *Gorgias*, Randall believes, "is apt to sympathize with the Romantic ideal of Callicles. There is much in the modern temper," he writes, "that wants to live to the full, to get a thrill out of it, rather than live with Socratic wisdom" (1970, p. 91). I think this is a correct judgment if one considers how people live rather than how they may celebrate virtue. The suggestion here is that *good stories function in two ways: to justify (or mystify) decisions or actions already made or performed and to determine future decisions or actions.* Be this as it may, the narrative perspective leads to the conclusion that idealistic stories, Socrates' story being an exemplar, generate adherence because they are coherent and "ring true" to life as we would like to live it. Such stories involve us in a choice of characters in competition with other characters, leading us to choose our "heroes" and our "villains"; the choice is existential.

The appeal of idealistic stories resides in presuming the best in people and activating it. As noted in the original essay, "Any story, any form of rhetorical communication, not only says something about the world, it also implies an audience, persons who conceive of themselves in very specific ways" (Fisher, 1984, p. 14). It would appear that there is a public, an actual community existing over time that believes in the values of truth, the good, beauty, health, wisdom, courage, temperance, justice, harmony, order, communion, friendship, and a oneness with the Cosmos—as variously as these values may be defined or practiced in "real" life. In terms of the logic of good reasons, persons have found them *relevant* to the good life, *consequential* in advancing moral obligation and civilized relations, *consistent* with their highest experiences, with the testimony of leaders in thought and action, and with the demands of the best audience one might conceive, and satisfying in regard to the *transcendental issue:* "the ideal basis for human conduct" (Fisher, 1978, p. 380).

On the other hand, there is a public, an actual community existing over time, that practices, even if it does not celebrate, the values of pleasure, expediency, self-aggrandizement, courage, strength, political acumen and success, and the will to power as the ultimate constituents of the ideal life. Persons have found these values *relevant* to their material lives, *consequential* in determining their survival and well-being, *consistent* with statements made by those who subscribe to the "rags to riches" myth and the example of those who succeed by following it, and, in some instances, satisfying as ideal standards for human conduct. I suspect, however, that if confronted by a Socrates, or the better part of themselves, even these persons would admit that while Callicles' philosophy has some fidelity with the way they must live their lives, it is not entirely coherent or true to their whole lives, or the life that they would most like to live. It is, finally, a rationalization for a power-oriented, hedonistic life style, not a representation of the "ideal" life.

Earlier I noted that there is no way to reconcile the philosophies of Socrates and Callicles. This is not quite true in that the values they espouse can and do inform one another in praxis, for instance, in the lived experience of the American Dream. Trying to live according to the moralistic and materialistic myths of the American experiment can, however, lead to a kind of "schizophrenia." "When one of the myths tends to dominate, whether in the culture or in an individual, the other myth is always hauntingly there in the background" (Fisher, 1973, p. 163).

This concludes the narrative interpretation and assessment of the exchange between Socrates and Callicles. It is, in effect, an answer to the second question posed by this essay. It is not the only answer possible, as earlier analyses of *Death of a Salesman, The Great Gatsby,* the nuclear controversy, and *The Epic of*

Gilgamesh indicate and as future studies will show. The present reading contrasts with other readings of Plato's *Gorgias* in several ways: It is not analytical, philological, historical, or aesthetic—except tangentially. It does not privilege "argument" over myth, or myth over "argument." It considers not the truth *per se* of the stories told by Socrates and Callicles, but the consequences of accepting them as truth after a determination of their truth qualities as assessed by the tests of narrative rationality.

As for the "worth" of the reading, beyond its adequacy in demonstrating the narrative paradigm at work and how it differs from other interpretative schemes, one may consider its import in regard to the dispute on Plato's stance toward rhetoric. Whether rhetoric is the "real theme" of the *Gorgias* or not, the life represented by Callicles requires rhetoric for its being and the life urged by Socrates necessitates dialectic and Plato's metaphysical position. There can be no doubt that Plato's concern about rhetoric was pervasive—how it distorted education, corrupted politics, and failed as philosophy and a way of life. The interpretation presented here supports the conclusion that he does not relent in the *Phaedrus* from the view in the *Gorgias*. It is not the case that "Plato opposed only a particular view of rhetoric unsuccessfully defended in the dialogue by Gorgias, Polus, and Callicles, and probably defended by leading Sophists and rhetoricians of Plato's time" (Black, 1958, p. 367). Plato's position, as brought to life in the character of Socrates, is an ontological one. It was not a view he could have changed without rejecting his metaphysical beliefs.

The "art" of discourse outlined at the end of the *Phaedrus* is not an art concerned with contingent matters; it is a "science" parallel with medicine. It would make a rhetorician a physician to the soul of the body politic. "Those who see in the *Phaedrus* a 'correction' of the uncompromising views of the *Gorgias* (Pohlenz, p. 343)," Dodds writes, "or a 'new stage in Plato's developing attitudes towards rhetoric' (Jaeger, *Paideia*, iii, p. 185) seem to overlook the present passage (503a). The two dialogues differ widely in emotional tone . . . , but the implication of both is that the only true ῥήτωρ is Socrates himself" (521d, Dodds, 1959, p. 330; see also Conley, 1981). At 503a, Socrates says of rhetoric:

> For even if there are two sides to this, yet one part of it, I suppose, would be flattery and shameful mob appeal, while the other is something fine—the effort to perfect as far as possible the souls of the citizens and the struggle to say always what is best, whether it be welcome or unwelcome to the hearers. But you yourself have never seen rhetoric of this kind, or if you can mention any such orator, why do you not tell me his name at once? (Plato, 1973a)

As noted earlier, Socrates rejects the candidates proposed by Callicles. From the narrative perspective, Plato's version of the good life, personal and public, could not include rhetoric so long as it was the art of probable, practical discourse.

Conclusion

My purpose has been to advance the narrative paradigm beyond the point reached in my earlier essay (Fisher, 1984). In this analysis, I hope to have situated it clearly in regard to major social scientific and humanistic theories and to have demonstrated its usefulness in interpreting and assessing philosophical discourse. I have also proposed that a significant feature of compelling stories is that they provide a rationale for decision and action. As such, they not only constrain behavior, they may also determine it. There is no doubt that the stories we tell, in private and in public, can be, perhaps often are, "mystifications." The only way to determine whether or not a story is a mask for ulterior motives is to test it against the principles of narrative probability and fidelity, as done in this essay with the stories of Socrates and Callicles. It is clear, however, that neither Socrates nor Callicles sought to hide their true beliefs or their intended courses of action. Further applications of narrative rationality should concern less straightforward discourse. A case in point would be the stories regarding our actions in Grenada; were they justifiably described as a "rescue" or an "invasion?"

Further investigations should also be informed by another point that emerges from this study. As indicated before, formal features of narrative probability concern coherence, consistency, and noncontradiction. It appears that they also depend on a comparison and contrast with prior, accepted stories. Thus, Socrates and Callicles found each other's stories to lack narrative probability not only because they seemed contradictory but also because they were not coherent with the stories (the truths) already held by them. Narrative probability, therefore, should be viewed as including material as well as formal features. Such a view is necessary to any interpretation and assessment of stories, especially those told to "mystify" an audience.

References

Andrews, J. D. (1982). The structuralist study of narrative: Its history, use, and limits. In P. Hernadi (Ed.), *The horizon of literature* (pp. 99–124). Lincoln, NE: The University of Nebraska Press.

Apel, K-O. (1977). The *a priori* of communication and the foundation of the humanities. In F. R. Dallmayr & T. A. McCarthy (Eds.), *Understanding and social inquiry* (pp. 292–315). Notre Dame, IN: University of Notre Dame Press.

Arendt, H. (1965). *Eichmann in Jerusalem: A report on the banality of evil.* New York: Viking Press.

Barber, J. D. (1972). *The presidential character: Predicting performance in the White House.* Englewood Cliffs, NJ: Prentice-Hall.

Barthes, R. (1977). Introduction to the structural analysis of narratives. In S. Heath (Ed.), *Image-music-text* (pp. 79–124). New York: Hill and Wang.

Beach, Wayne A. (1983). Background understanding and the situated accomplishment of conversational telling-explanations. In R. T. Craig & K. Tracy (Eds.), *Conversational coherence: Form, structure, and strategy* (pp. 196–221). Beverly Hills, CA: Sage Publications.

Berger, P. L. (1969). *A rumor of angels: Modern society and the rediscovery of the supernatural.* Garden City, NY: Doubleday.

Bernstein, R. (1983). *Beyond objectivism and relativism: Science, hermeneutics, and praxis.* Philadelphia: University of Pennsylvania Press.

Black, E. (1958). Plato's view of rhetoric. *Quarterly Journal of Speech, 44,* 361–374.

Blumer, H. (1969). *Symbolic interactionism: Perspective and method.* Englewood Cliffs, NJ: Prentice-Hall.

Bormann, E. (1983). Fantasy theme analysis. In J. L. Golden, G. F. Berquist & W. E. Coleman (Eds.), *The rhetoric of Western thought* (3rd ed., pp. 433–449). Dubuque, IA: Kendall/Hunt.

Brockriede, W. (1985). Constructs, experience, and argument. *Quarterly Journal of Speech, 71,* 151–163.

Buber, M. (1970). *I and thou* (W. Kaufman, Trans.). New York: Scribner.

Burke, K. (1955). *A rhetoric of motives.* New York: George Braziller.

Campbell, K. K., & Jamieson, K. (n.d.). Form and genre in rhetorical criticism. An introduction. In K. K. Campbell & K. Jamieson (Eds.), *Forms and genre: Shaping rhetorical action* (pp. 9–12). Falls Church, VA: Speech Communication Association.

Conley, T. (1981). Phaedrus 259ff. *Rhetoric Society Quarterly, 11,* 11–15.

Daniels, T. D., & Frandsen, K. D. (1984). Conventional social science inquiry in human communication. Theory and practice. *Quarterly Journal of Speech, 70,* 223–240.

Delia, J. G. (1977). Constructivism and the study of communication. *Quarterly Journal of Speech, 63,* 66–83.

Derrida, J. (1981). *Dissemination* (B. Johnson, Trans.). Chicago: The University of Chicago Press.

Derrida, J. (1982). *Margins of philosophy* (A. Bass, Trans.). Chicago: The University of Chicago Press.

Dodds, E. R. (1951). *The Greeks and the irrational.* Berkeley, CA: University of California Press.

Dodds, F. R. (1959). *Gorgias.* Oxford: Oxford University Press.

Fisher, W. R. (1970). A motive view of communication. *Quarterly Journal of Speech, 56,* 131–139.

Fisher, W. R. (1973). Reaffirmation and the subversion of the American dream. *Quarterly Journal of Speech, 59,* 160–169.

Fisher, W. R. (1978). Toward a logic of good reasons. *Quarterly Journal of Speech, 64,* 376–384.

Fisher, W. R. (1980). Rationality and the logic of good reasons. *Philosophy and Rhetoric, 13,* 121–130.

Fisher, W. R. (1981). Good reasons: Fields and genre. In G. Ziegelmueller & J. Rhodes (Eds.), *Dimensions of argument: Proceedings of the second summer conference on argumentation* (pp. 114–125). Annandale, VA: Speech Communication Association.

Fisher, W. R., & Filloy, R. A. (1982). Argument in drama and literature: An exploration. In J. R. Cox & C. A. Willard (Eds.), *Advances in argumentation theory and research* (pp. 343–362). Carbondale, IL: Southern Illinois University Press.

Fisher, W R. (1984). Narration as a human communication paradigm: The case of public moral argument. *Communication Monographs, 51,* 1–22.

Fisher, W. R. (1987). Judging the quality of audiences and narrative rationality. In J. L. Golden & J. J. Pilotta (Eds.), *Studies in honor of Chaïm Perelman.* Boston: D. Reidel.

Foucault, M. (1965). *Madness and civilization: A history of sanity in the age of reason* (R. Howard, Trans.). New York: Vintage Books.

Foucault, M. (1969). *The order of things. An archaeology of the human sciences* New York: Pantheon Books.

Foucault, M. (1972). *The archaeology of knowledge and the discourse on language.* (A. M. S. Smith, Trans.). New York: Pantheon Books.

Foucault, M. (1973). *The birth of the clinic: An archaeology of medical perception.* New York: Vintage Books.

Foucault, M. (1977). *Discipline and punish: The birth of the prison* (A. Sheridan, Trans.). New York: Pantheon Books.

Foucault, M. (1978). *The history of sexuality, part I* (R. Hurley, Trans.). New York: Pantheon Books.

Foucault, M. (1980). *Power/knowledge: Selected interviews and other writings* (C. Gordon, Ed., C. Gordon, L. Marshall, J. Mepham & K. Soper, Trans.). New York: Pantheon Books.

Friedlander, P. (1928). *Plato: The dialogues, first period* (H. Myerhoff, Trans.). New York: Bollingen Series LIX, Pantheon Books.

Gadamer, H-G. (1980). *Dialogue and dialectic: Eight hermeneutic studies on Plato* (P. C. Smith, Trans.). New Haven, CT: Yale University Press.

Gadamer, H-G. (1981). *Reason in the age of science* (F. G. Lawrence, Trans.). Cambridge, MA: The MIT Press.

Gadamer, H-G. (1982). *Truth and method.* New York: Crossword Publishing.

Genette, G. (1980). *Narrative discourse: An essay in method* (J. E. Lewin, Trans.). Ithaca, NY: Cornell University Press.

Goffman, E. (1959). *The presentation of self in everyday life.* Garden City, NY: Doubleday.

Goffman, E. (1967). *Interaction ritual: Essays on face-to-face behavior.* Garden City, NY: Doubleday.

Gombrich, E. H. (1984). Representation and misrepresentation. *Critical Inquiry, 11,* 195–218.

Grube, G. M. A. (1964). *Plato's thought.* Boston: Beacon Press.

Habermas, J. (1979). *Communication and the evolution of society* (T. A. McCarthy, Trans.). Boston: Beacon Press.

Habermas, J. (1984). *The theory of communicative action: Reason and the rationalization of society* (T. A. McCarthy, Trans.). Boston: Beacon Press.

Heidegger, M. (1966). *Discourse on thinking: A translation of gelassenheit* (J. M. Anderson & E. H. Freund, Trans.). New York: Harper & Row.

Heidegger, M. (1971). *Poetry, language, and thought.* (A. Hofstadter, Trans.). New York: Harper & Row.

Heider, F. (1946). Attitudes and cognitive organization. *Journal of Psychology, 21,* 107–112.

Heider, F. (1958). *The psychology of interpersonal relations.* New York: John Wiley.

Hovland, C., Janis, I., & Kelley, H. (1953). *Communication and persuasion.* New Haven, CT: Yale University Press.

Hyde, M. (1983). Rhetorically man dwells: On the making known function of discourse. *Communication, 7,* 201–220.

Kaufman, C. (1979). Enactment as argument in the *Gorgias, Philosophy and Rhetoric, 12,* 114–129.

Kelley, H. (1971). Attribution in social interaction. In E. E. Jones, D. E. Kanouse, H. H. Kelley, R. E. Nisbett, S. Valins & B. Weiner (Eds.), *Attribution: Perceiving the causes of behavior* (pp. 1–26). Morristown, NJ: General Learning Press.

Krieger, M. (1984). The ambiguities of representation and illusion: An E. H. Gombrich retrospective. *Critical Inquiry, 11,* 181–194.

Laudan, L. (1984). *Science and values: The aims of science and their role in scientific debates.* Berkeley, CA: University of California Press.

Lemert, C. C., & Gillan, G. (1982). *Michel Foucault: Social theory and transgression.* New York: Columbia University Press.

MacCormac, E. R. (1976). *Metaphor and myth in science and religion.* Durham, NC: Duke University Press.

MacIntyre, A. (1981). *After virtue: A study in moral theory* (2nd ed.). Notre Dame, IN: University of Notre Dame Press.

Masterman, M. (1970). The nature of a paradigm. In I. Lakatos & A. Musgrove (Eds.), *Criticism and the growth of knowledge* (pp. 59–89). London: Cambridge University Press.

Mead, G. H. (1934). *Mind, self, and society: From the standpoint of a social behaviorist* (C. W. W. Morris, Ed.). Chicago: The University of Chicago Press.

Newcomb, T. (1953). An approach to the study of communicative acts. *Psychological Review, 60,* 393–404.

Nofsinger, R. E. (1983). Tactical coherence in courtroom conversation. In R. T. Craig & K. Tracy (Eds.), *Conversational coherence: Form, structure, and strategy* (pp. 243–258). Beverly Hills, CA: Sage Publications.

Perelman, C., & Olbrechts-Tyteca, L. (1969). The rational and the reasonable. In *The new rhetoric and the humanities: Essays on rhetorical and its applications* (pp. 117–123). Boston: D. Reidel.

Perelman, C. (1981). The rhetorical point of view in ethics: A program (D. R. Tourville, Trans.). *Communication, 6,* 315–320.

Plato. (1973a). *Gorgias* (W. D. Woodhead, Trans.). In E. Hamilton & H. Cairns, (Eds.), *Plato: The collected dialogues, including the letters* (pp. 229–307). Princeton, NJ: Bollingen Series LXXI, Princeton University Press.

Plato. (1973b). *Letters* (L. A. Post, Trans.). *Plato: The collected dialogues, including the letters* (pp. 1560–1598). Princeton, NJ: Bollingen Series LXXI, Princeton University Press.

Popper, K. R. (1971). *The open society and its enemies: The spell of Plato* (Vol. 1). Princeton, NJ: Princeton University Press.

Randall, J. H., Jr. (1960). *Aristotle.* New York: Columbia University Press.

Randall, J. H., Jr. (1970). *Plato: Dramatist of the life of reason.* New York: Columbia University Press.

Rendell, S. (1977). Dialogue, philosophy, and rhetoric: The example of Plato's *Gorgias*. *Philosophy and Rhetoric, 10*, 165–179.

Ricoeur, P. (1977). The model of the text: Meaningful action considered as text. In F. R. Dallmayr & T. A. McCarthy (Eds.), *Understanding and social inquiry* (pp. 316–334). Notre Dame, IN: University of Notre Dame Press.

Ricoeur, P. (1983). The narrative function. In J. B. Thompson (Ed.), *Paul Ricoeur, hermeneutics and the human sciences: Essays on language, action, and interpretation* (pp. 274–296). Cambridge: Cambridge University Press.

Ricoeur, P. (1984). *Time and narrative* (Vol. 1, K. McLaughlin & D. Pellaur, Trans.). Chicago: The University of Chicago Press.

Rorty, R. (1967). (Ed.). *The linguistic turn: Recent essays in philosophical method*. Chicago: The University of Chicago Press.

Rorty, R. (1979). *Philosophy and the mirror of nature*. Princeton, NJ: Princeton University Press.

Rorty, R. (1984) Deconstruction and circumvention. *Critical Inquiry, 11*, 1–23.

Schrag, C. O. (1980). *Radical reflection and the origins of the human sciences*. West Lafayette, IN: Purdue University Press.

Schrag, C. O. (1985). Rhetoric situated at the end of philosophy. *Quarterly Journal of Speech, 71*, 164–174.

Schrag, C. O. (1986). *Communicative praxis and the space of subjectivity*. Bloomington, IN: Indiana University Press.

Singer, M. G. (1971) *Generalization in ethics. An essay in the logic of ethics, with the rudiments of a system of moral philosophy*. New York: Atheneum.

Spitzer, A. (1975). The self-reference of the *Gorgias. Philosophy and Rhetoric, 8*, 1–22.

Stewart, J. R. (1978). Foundations of dialogic communication. *The Quarterly Journal of Speech, 64*, 183–201.

Stewart, J. R., & D'Angelo, G. (1980). *Together: Communicating interpersonally* (2nd ed.). Reading, MA: Addison-Wesley.

Thompson, J. B. (1983). Problems in the theory of reference and truth. In *Critical hermeneutics: A study in the thought of Paul Ricoeur and Jürgen Habermas* (pp. 182–218). Cambridge: Cambridge University Press.

Thibaut, J. W., & Kelley, H. (1959). *The social psychology of groups*. New York: John Wiley.

Todorov, T. (1977). *The poetics of prose* (R. Howard, Trans.). Ithaca, NY: Cornell University Press.

Valesio, P. (1980). *Novantiqua: Rhetorics as a contemporary theory*. Bloomington, IN: Indiana University Press.

White, H. (1984). The question of narrative in contemporary historical theory. *History and Theory, 23*, 1–33.

NARRATIVE FORM AND MORAL FORCE: THE REALIZATION OF INNOCENCE AND GUILT THROUGH INVESTIGATIVE JOURNALISM

James S. Ettema and Theodore L. Glasser

That news stories are just that—stories—is now a commonplace. It is an observation sometimes made by those who have been struck by the similarities of "news," particularly television news, and "entertainment" and who apparently suppose this similarity to be a debasement of journalistic tradition (e.g., 7, 15). The analysis of news-as-narrative, however, should begin not with television but with the origins of news itself. It might begin as early as sixteenth-century London with "broadside ballads," unabashedly vulgar renditions of the day's rumor and gossip (16). Or it might begin in nineteenth-century America with the penny press and the advent of what today is called the "human interest story." This form of news stood in contrast to the "raw intelligence" of the mercantile press and marked the beginning of one of U.S. journalism's most enduring suppositions: that the "common man," as Robert Park (18, p. xiii) put it, "would rather be entertained than edified." Park's point, unlike that of some other commentators, was not that journalists had abandoned edification for entertainment but that they had come to appreciate the importance of story as well as fact.

To appreciate news-as-narrative is not to deny the value of news but to understand, in Tuchman's (21, p. 97) terms, that news ia a "selective reality" with "its own internal validity." Further, to appreciate news-as-narrative is to understand that this selective reality can be distinguished both by its recurring themes and its peculiar forms (e.g., 3, 6, 14, 23). Indeed, form is a theme, perhaps even *the* theme, of the news story. Schudson puts the point elegantly:

> The power of the media lies not only (and not even primarily) in its power to declare things to be true, but in its power to provide the forms in which the declarations appear. News in a newspaper or on television has a relationship to the "real world," not only in content but in form: that is, in the way the world is incorporated into unquestioned and unnoticed conventions of narration, and then transfigured, no longer a subject for discussion but a premise of any conversation at all (20, p. 98).

In the news stories about the State of the Union Address analyzed by Schudson, for example, these premises concern the proper location of power and the proper conduct of politics within the American polity. Thus, concludes Schudson, the conventions of journalistic narrative function less to increase or decrease the truth value of messages than to shape and narrow the kinds of truths that can be told.

From *Journal of Communication* 38 (Summer 1988): 8–26. © 1988 *Journal of Communication*. Reprinted by permission of *Journal of Communication* and authors.

James S. Ettema is associate professor of communication studies, Northwestern University. Theodore L. Glasser is associate professor of journalism and mass communication, University of Minnesota. The research reported in this article was supported by the Gannett Foundation; the Institute for Modern Communication and the Center of Urban Affairs and Policy Research, both of Northwestern University; and the Graduate School of the University of Minnesota.

Schudson's arguments about narrative in news echo those made about narrative in other modes of "discourse of the real," particularly history. Although there are those who argue that the narrative form is merely a way to "write up" the results of historical inquiry, others have sought to investigate what the narrative form itself brings to the meaning of the facts that are written up. Mink and White, for example, both begin with the proposition that the events of the world do not provide a true but untold story that awaits the coming of the historian who will tell it. "There can in fact be no untold stories at all just as there can be no unknown knowledge," argues Mink (17, p. 147). "There can only be past facts not yet described in a context of narrative form."

In making events of the world into well-formed, coherent stories, authors of narrative history employ "an apparatus for the *production of meaning*, rather than . . . a vehicle for the transmission of information about an extrinsic referent," argues White (27, p. 19), making a point familiar to critics of journalism (cf. 13). "As thus envisaged, the 'content' of the discourse consists as much of its form as it does of whatever information might be extracted from a reading of it." White goes on to examine the sorts of meaning that can be produced by narrative form:

> In historical discourse, the narrative serves to transform a list of historical events that would otherwise be only a chronicle into a story. In order to effect this transformation, the events, agents, and agencies represented in the chronicle must be encoded as "story-elements". . . . When the reader recognizes the story being told in an historical narrative as a specific kind of story, for example, as an epic, romance, tragedy, or farce, he can be said to have "comprehended" the "meaning" produced by the discourse. This "comprehension" is nothing other than the recognition of the "form" of the narrative (27, p. 20).

One important implication of this argument about the relationship between historical narratives and the historical facts that presumably constitute them is that the coherence which the story provides to the facts is "achieved only by a tailoring of the 'facts' to the requirements of story form" (24, p. 91). Facts are selected to fit the story but, more than that, fact and story are mutually constituted, though not necessarily consciously, by the historian. "This means that the *shape* of the *relationships* which will appear to be inherent in the objects inhabiting the field will in reality have been imposed on the field by the investigator in the very *act of identifying and describing* the objects he finds there," argues White (24, p. 95, emphases in original). "The implication is that historians *constitute* their subjects as possible objects of narrative representation by the very language they use to *describe* them." If historical narrative seems to have been "found" or to "speak itself," it is because story elements are introduced implicitly in the historian's attempt to comprehend and describe the facts or events.[1]

For Mink, narrative form is a means, though a fundamentally flawed means, for comprehending historical reality. Narrative is an "instrument" of comprehension or cognition. For White, however, narrative may be that, but it is

---

[1] Although he differs from both Mink and White on many issues, Ricoeur makes much the same point: "Not only does the historian's inquiry raise the [documentary] trace to the dignity of a meaningful document, but it also raises the past itself to the dignity of a historical fact. The document was not a document before the historian came to ask it as question" (19, p. 23).

something else as well. Narrative is an instrument for the assertion of moral authority. The historian is called upon for an authoritative account of what happened only because alternative accounts of what happened are possible. In attempting to provide such an account the historian will invoke the authority of reality itself; but, White argues, reality does not provide a storylike account. What does provide such an account is an essentially moral vision of events. Indeed, it is the moral force of a story that provides the semblance of reality:

> The events that are actually recorded in the narrative appear "real" precisely insofar as they belong to an order of moral existence, just as they derive their meaning from their placement in this order. It is because the events described conduce to the establishment of social order or fail to do so that they find a place in the narrative attesting to their reality (25, p. 22).

Historical narrative is, then, a "summons . . . to participation in a moral universe" (25, p. 20). But, unlike the medieval narrative that serves as a point of departure for White's analysis, the contemporary narrative does not commence with an invocation of the authority of God or king, nor conclude with a jeremiad that calls for a new moral order in which the just are delivered and the wicked are punished. Any such overt display of moral force would, of course, be dismissed as an outrageous breach of objectivity. Nevertheless, asks White (25, p. 22), how else could *any* account of real events be brought to conclusion except through a "passage from one moral order to another"? It is the "moralizing impulse" that endows facts with relevance and stories with closure and coherence—the very features we use to judge the value and the truth of the stories we hear and tell (cf. 9, 10, 11).

Narrative form, concludes White, is fundamentally metaphorical. As metaphor, "it functions as a symbol, rather than as a sign: which is to say that it does not give us either a *description* or an *icon* of the thing it represents, but *tells us* what images to look for in our culturally encoded experience in order to determine how we *should feel* about the thing represented" (24, p. 91, emphases in original). The point here is not to dissolve the distinction between the discourse of the real and the discourse of the imaginary or, following Lacan, the discourse of desire. Rather, the point is to highlight the extent to which narrative transforms the real into an object of desire through a formal coherence and a moral order that the real lacks. Historical narratives are not, then, false and not without value. Indeed, the value of narrative is precisely this transformational potential: because the same set of facts do lend themselves to alternative story forms, whether tragedy, comedy, romance, or farce, the wise selection of story form provides the opportunity "to teach what it means to be *moral* beings" and "to judge the moral significance of human projects." And yet, as White hastens to remind us, story forms "permit us to judge [such projects] even while we pretend to be merely describing them" (26, p. 253). The moral vision of the contemporary historian—and, as we will argue, the investigative journalist—is, then, more covert and ambiguous than that of the ancient narrator unencumbered by modern conceptions of objectivity. The messages of these modern tales are essentially moral nonetheless.

Investigative journalism defends traditional virtue by telling stories of terrible vice.   The value of justice, for example, is affirmed in stories of outrageous injustice.[2] Like a number of other story forms, investigative journalism maintains and sometimes updates consensual interpretations of right and wrong, innocence and guilt, by applying them to the case at hand, though it seldom analyzes or critiques such interpretations. The moral vision of investigative journalism is, then, a conservative vision in the most fundamental sense (12). But to argue that investigative journalism is fundamentally conservative is not to argue that contemporary investigative reporters have lost the reformist spirit of their muckraking predecessors. The moralizing impulse of investigative reporters, at least the highly accomplished reporters we have chosen for analysis, is not typically activated by an isolated wrong or an individual wrongdoer. Rather, in interview after interview, these reporters mention "system-wide," usually governmental, problems as their concern:

> I guess what really interests me is showing a system-wide problem, finding out everything you can possibly know about it and making a picture clear that has just been really fuzzy before. . . . The best stories are when you see situations where people are being abused or their rights are really being trod upon.

If these stories do not usually challenge public morality, they can, as another reporter said, "amalgamate it and vocalize it." This reporter subjects story ideas to a "moral indignation test" (8) and, like many of his colleagues, speaks often of "moral outrage" or "outrageous behavior" as necessary to a worthwhile story. These reporters are, then, the intellectual successors not only to muckrakers but to Jeremiah himself. Their moral task is to evoke outrage at the violation of dearly held values in the conduct of public affairs and implicitly invite, if not explicitly demand, a return to those values. Their venue is a kind of demonstrative discourse, as Aristotle might have described it, designed to distinguish between the honorable and the dishonorable.

With it understood that reality must be made into narrative and that this can be accomplished only within the compass of an essentially moral vision, our project is to understand how masters of a particular narrative form accomplish this task. Our interest is not in average or typical narratives and narrators but rather in those most worthy of attention: the best stories by the best reporters, at least as identified by the admittedly imperfect criteria of journalism prizes and peer nomination. Our method is to collect and interpret the text of these narratives along with the text created by interviews with the narrators. The commentary reported here is drawn from in-depth interviews that we conducted with each journalist. These interviews—or, more accurately, conversations—typically lasted for the better part of a workday and ranged broadly across epistemological and ethical issues of the craft. The journalists were consistently asked to exemplify their issue positions with their own best work. It is this best thinking about the best work that we reproduce here.

We have selected for analysis two reports that have won the Pulitzer Prize: "Rape in the County Jail: Prince George's Hidden Horror" by Loretta Tofani of the *Washington Post,* which concerns sexual assaults in the Prince George's

---

[2]In this, investigative journalism bears a strong resemblance to what Cawelti calls the social melodrama genre of popular fiction: "Melodrama moves from a sense of injustice and disorder to an affirmation of a benevolent moral order in the universe. It is a highly popular form because it affirms some conventional moral or philosophical principle as the inherent basis of cosmic order by illustrating this principle at work in the lives of good and wicked characters" (5, p. 262).

County, Maryland, Detention Center, and "The K-9 Cases" by William Marimow of the *Philadelphia Inquirer*, which concerns unwarranted police dog attacks on citizens of Philadelphia. To complement the work of these newspaper reporters we have selected a report that has won both the du Pont-Columbia and George Foster Peabody Awards for broadcast journalism: "Killing Crime: A Police Cop-out" by Pam Zekman of WBBM-TV in Chicago, concerning the suppression or "killing" of crime reports by the Chicago Police Department.

In each of these reports, we focus on the accomplishment of two specific moral tasks: the realization, through narrative, of innocence and of guilt. The narrative strategies employed to meet these tasks are strikingly similar in these reports but, of course, we claim to have found neither the essential features of all narrative nor the formula for success in this particular genre of narrative. We seek only to appreciate how narrative has been, and can be, used as a moral force in the life of the community.

The moral force brought to bear through each of these reports is, in large measure, the result of skillfully crafted stories of victimization.   These reports do not merely identify individuals who apparently have been wronged but rather define them as victims who are innocent—innocent enough, at least, to make their victimization by "the system" a moral outrage. This definitional process, in turn, helps frame the central action of each story not merely as a social problem but as a terrible injustice.[3] As we will see, the task of defining victims provides a good example of the complex interdependence of fact, value, and narrative, because the "simple fact" that innocent people have been victimized turns out to be not so simple after all. Innocence must be painstakingly *made real* through narrative.

The investigation of rapes in the Prince George's County Detention Center began as the reporter sat in court covering her regular beat assignment. The reporter recalls of that moment:

> The lawyer is telling the judge that her client, who can't be over 18 years old, has been gang raped in the county jail. . . . Although I knew theoretically that men get raped in jail, it was the first time I was ever really confronted with it and it did really bother me. So I then talked to the judge and found out that it happened all the time.

Although the reporter thought that this was a good story, her editors were indifferent, suggesting, in effect, that the situation did not strike them, in the reporter's words, "as such a big wrong." And, in any case, there were other stories that demanded attention. At this point the reporter was unable to defend the story to her superiors because she had not yet properly defined the victims in the story:

> At the time I did not know that these men were often acquitted of crimes and were innocent. . . . I had the impression at the time these guys were being convicted of crimes . . . You know, it's not as great a story to say that a bunch of guys who have committed highest crimes are being raped in jail.

---

[3]Based on his analysis of courtroom storytelling, Bennett (1, 2) argues that a "story strategy underlying a case is executed through an ongoing series of tactical moves that index evidence within the developing story structure" (2, p. 312). One such tactic is to *define* items of evidence in a way that is consistent with, and contributes to, the desired framing of the central action of the case.

The reporter, however, did not give up the story idea. She found time to interview rape victims and medical personnel who worked in the jail. And as the reporter gained enough information to begin "writing the story in the air"—talking through the findings with others—she was continually drawn to the cases in which the victim had been arrested for a relatively minor offense, had not yet been tried, or was later acquitted:

> I would find myself repeating these things: "This guy was in for shoplifting and this guy was acquitted. These are the most important elements. These are the ones that I want to put up front. These are the ones that I want to dramatize."

Thus it became clear to the reporter and then to her superiors that the central action—jail rape— had little meaning until the victims had been properly defined. And so, in the series of articles produced at the conclusion of the nine-month investigation, the fact of innocence was indeed "put up front" and "dramatized." This drama was achieved through presentation of twelve carefully selected victims in brief case studies that masterfully employed two narrative strategies to evoke outrage at their plight: highlighting cruelly ironic details of the victim's experience, and privileging the victim's own account of that experience. These strategies are immediately clear in the first paragraphs of the first article in the series:

> Kevin Parrish, a 20-year-old student from Upper Marlboro, was arrested on a drunk driving charge at 3 a.m., Feb. 20 and taken to the Prince George's County Detention Center. He was to wait there for a few hours, until his mother could arrive with $50 to bail him out.
> But his mother came too late.

This case was followed by others in which the victim was always employed and always charged with a relatively minor crime—an 18-year-old waiter who was later acquitted of malicious destruction of property, a 26-year-old cook who later pleaded guilty to malicious destruction or property, a 26-year-old repairman who had not yet gone to trial for theft when the story was written, a 31-year-old air force lieutenant who developed mental problems after leading "rescue workers in the gruesome six-day-long job of sifting through [aircraft] wreckage and identifying the 21 dead."

But there was also a 32-year-old salesman who had been jailed without bond after stabbing someone who merely sat on his motorcycle. The case of the salesman is of particular interest because it required the most work to maintain the definition of the victim as innocent. The reporter begins the task immediately in the first and second paragraph of the case study by pointing out that this man, who had never been arrested before, suddenly found himself in a cellblock with about 30 inmates charged with, or convicted of, murder. At this point the salesman is allowed to tell of the nightmare into which he was soon plunged:

> I lit up a cigarette and someone said I had to go into a cell if I wanted to smoke. So I went into a side cell and sat down on a bunk to smoke. Then four or five of them came up to me and hit me in the face with fists. They told me to roll over. I yelled for the guard and they started kicking me. They banged my head against the wall, tore my clothes off and all of them raped me. It went on for about half an hour.

Later paragraphs reveal that the salesman underwent surgery for a punctured lung and spent nine days in the hospital. The charge against him was later reduced from assault with intent to commit murder to malicious stabbing, and after pleading guilty he was sentenced to five years' probation. "Today," this story concludes, "he thinks of his real sentence as the rape rather than the probation." If not entirely innocent, this victim, like the others, suffered far more than he deserved.

And so it was for the victims of police dog attacks on the streets of Philadelphia.   The investigation into their plight began with a tip that certain K-9 unit officers and their dogs were conducting "target practice" on the streets. It soon became clear to the reporter that attack cases came in "all shades of gray." A few cases were clearly accidental attacks on "innocent citizens," though many others were quite ambiguous. Some attacks, for example, occurred on subway platforms or outside of bars very late at night after the police had been called to the scene. The victims were sometimes young men who provoked the responding officers. But it also became clear to the reporter that innocence was an essential theme of the story:

> I think the more factually innocent a person is who has suffered one of these attacks the more compelling, the more important it is that these things don't happen again. . . . It makes a situation where this could happen to you, a good citizen.

As in the jail rape story, the reporter here had definitional work to do and, as in that story, the strategy was use of ironic detail and control of point of view. The first story in this series begins:

> It was nearly 1 o'clock in the morning last June 1 when an exuberant Matthew Horace bounded up the subway staircase on the east side of City Hall.
>   Like thousands of others, Horace had come to Center City to celebrate the Sixers' sweep in the NBA Championship Series. He was looking for a good time. He never found it.

And so another innocent victim is drawn to his fate.

Once again, the most interesting examples of the reporter's narrative craft are the cases in which innocence is most problematic. The narration of one such case begins not from the point of view of the victim but from that of witnesses. A young couple, both lawyers, walking home after a long day at the office see a swirl of activity across the street:

> Still on the south side of the street, across from the police, Sarah Solmssen said she saw several officers "throwing a person against a brick wall. I saw the nightsticks, and then I started running."
>   By the time she had broken free of her husband's grip and crossed Spruce Street, she said she could see a K-9 dog biting the leg of a young man who was lying inert, in a semi-fetal position, on the sidewalk in front of the Engineers' Club.
>   "I saw the dog's jaws moving up and down three or four times," she recalled. "No officer was attempting to get that dog off the boy. He was just lying there motionless."
>   Peter Solmssen, who is 29, was slightly behind his wife, but with his height, 6-foot-2, he could see the boy on the ground, his hands cuffed behind his back, unmoving.

With an image of the attack in place, "the boy" is revealed to be a 220-pound, 17-year-old who is so drunk that later he could not clearly recall the events. It is clear, however, that he had been fighting inside the bar and that, when hauled out of the bar by relatives, as his aunt reported, "he was cussing very bad." He may or may not have tried to throw a punch at either his aunt or the officer who had responded to the report of a brawl. He was handcuffed by the officer but then, suddenly, the dog was on top of him.

Of the nine cases reviewed in the story, the reporter singled out this one as the best example of his commitment to reporting "all possible points of view" and revealing "all of the foibles of the victims" so that readers could make up their own minds about what happened:

> I spoke to [the victim's] aunt who'd been at the scene. I spoke to one of her friends . . . who'd been at the scene. I got the reports of the officers even though they wouldn't talk to me. And in publishing my account I stressed that [the victim] had been profane. He'd been drunk. He'd been obnoxious and even his aunt and [her friend] said that the police would have been totally justified in arresting him for disorderly conduct and that they exercised remarkable restraint. I put that in there because I'd come to the conclusion that [the victim] should have been arrested but what happened afterwards, once he'd been knocked to the ground and hand-cuffed, was not justifiable.

Nevertheless, in privileging the account of the Solmssens, who had come onto the scene just as the victim was being bitten by the dog, the reporter had defined the target of the dog attack not as a drunken and violent teenager but as "the boy" handcuffed and in a "semi-fetal position."

It is important to note here that the reporter does not characterize the privileging of the Solmssens' account as a persuasive tactic. Indeed, he denies over attempting to persuade the reader of anything. Rather, he characterizes his reliance upon their account as the use of the best available evidence, the evidence provided by those witnesses "who have nothing to protect." And yet it is important to note that the Solmssens' account also earns its place in the story—and thus its reality—from its place in "an order of moral existence" in which innocence and guilt are principal concerns and indignation the only proper response. It can be no surprise, then, that these witnesses serve not only to define the target of the attack as "the boy" but also to vocalize indignation in the report:

> Horrified by what they had seen, the Solmssens walked directly home to their town-house on Juniper Street, less than a block from the Engineers' Club. Peter Solmssen said he wanted "something done about" what he and his wife had just witnessed.

In the investigation of the suppression of crime reports, the victims were unequiv-ocally innocent in their encounter with the police.   Nevertheless, the reporter uses the now-familiar narrative strategies to evoke the full measure of moral outrage that is due the plight of these victims, people who reported a crime to the Chicago police but who had their report discounted or "unfounded" in violation of FBI guidelines. In each case reviewed in the series, the victim—whether of rape, robbery, or burglary—is allowed to recreate the emotional response to the crime as well as the response to the unfounding of the crime report.

The second segment of the four-part "mini-documentary" series, for example, begins by evoking the terror and humiliation of rape:

> Victim 1 (taped interview): I thought he was going to kill me. He raped me and I thought he was going to just leave me in the alley.

Reporter (voice over): This woman was raped at knifepoint and this teenager was raped repeatedly by two men who grabbed her as she walked home.
Victim 2: They were laughing at me 'cuz I was bleeding. I was hurt. I started crying. They were laughing at me.

And near the end of the segment a sobbing victim responds to the unfounding of her report:

Victim 1: I was raped, I should know. Ask them. What they say there is not true. How could they say that? How? I was raped. And that is a filthy word—rape. Because if it happened to me, it could happen to anyone. To me, when I think about the police, you know, they don't give a damn. They throw my case in the garbage.

These emotionally charged accounts serve to underscore the master irony of this story—the double victimization of these innocents, once by the criminal and once again by the police. The reporter understands very well that in a few seconds of videotape she has not only established the credibility of the victim's story but has amalgamated and vocalized the moral indignation appropriate to these events:

I've had more comment about that than almost any interview I've done. It really got people angry, I mean, they believed her. . . . There's a conflict constantly in that kind of an interview. You feel like you're intruding on something very private you shouldn't be intruding on. On the other hand, she's willing to do it and you know it will help make people care about the subject—care enough, perhaps, to start doing something about it. And, in fact, that story is one of the few stories that we've done where the newspapers picked up the story and started doing editorials and reaction stories. I think that the combination of television plus the newspapers together was what forced the police department to do something that they might have ordinarily ignored.

The facts of these victims' experiences are thus emplotted as stories most akin to tragedy: stories in which ironic turns of event lead inexorably to terrible suffering for the innocent.

In the moral universe mapped by these stories, the matter of innocence cannot exist without the antimatter of guilt.   And just as the full reality of innocence must be constructed within and through narrative, so must the reality of guilt. All three of these reports will, of course, find responsibility for the plight of the victims in a failure of "the system" (i.e., the performance and policies of senior officials) to properly dispense criminal justice. Toward this end, the reports will portray attackers (i.e., jail rapists) and low-level employees of the system (i.e., jail guards and police officers) as themselves victims of the system. Any culpability of these individuals will not, then, be allowed to mitigate the culpability of the system. And, finally, these stories will show the system to be not merely responsible for failure to properly dispense criminal justice but guilty of a callous indifference to that failure. These stories do not simply identify responsibility; they allocate guilt.

In the course of the jail rape investigation, for example, the reporter became very clear on the need to properly allocate guilt:

Here you have these men, presumably of free will, violating another man's dignity and security and yet the focus of the story is not the evil rapists but rather the flaws in the system. . . . I feel as though those rapes would have been prevented, or many of them could have been prevented, if the jail had done its job. . . . They are officials who we have entrusted to take care of these people and they have failed and these effects are devastating to people.

The reporter's extensive interviews with the rapists allow her to present a theory about the causes of jail rape which, in turn, allows her to direct responsibility away from the attackers toward the system. These rapes, she argues in the report, are motivated much more by a desire for security and respect than a need for sexual release. "In jail you're not a homosexual if you're the aggressor," one of the rapists told the reporter. "You're more of a man, if anything." From these interviews the reporter does attempt to reconstruct some of the complexity of the motivations of the rapists, but at the same time the interviews build toward a central theme—the rapes are a response to the conditions of jail and, in particular, to the conditions of *this* jail. Here in condensed form is how a particularly eloquent rapist helps the reporter accomplish this task:

Francis Harper, a convicted armed robber, decided to teach a lesson to the inmate who switched the television channel in the county jail. Harper decided to rape him. . . .

"The basic thing was to keep fear in the air to keep that respect," Harper said. "I was aggressive because I was afraid. I took the fear I had and reversed it. I was afraid of getting killed. . . . "

His belief was based on certain observations. He was in a small, crowded cell block in the "upper right" section of the jail with 10 men who were charged with or convicted of armed robbery or murder. The men, who were tense and angry about being in jail, frequently got into fights or threatened each other with rape. A guard was rarely present. . . .

Looking back on the rape, Harper believes that he was motivated not only by fear for his safety but also by feelings of anger and frustration over being in jail. And the poor conditions of the Upper Marlboro jail—including extreme overcrowding, toilets that are frequently stopped up and recreation often limited to one hour of gym a week—made those feelings even more intense, according to Harper. . . .

"I feel a lot of remorse about it," he says, referring to the rape. "I wasn't strong enough to withstand the influence of my environment. They helped me to be an animal in that jail and I submitted to it."

The reporter thus grants moral immunity to the rapist in return for his testimony against the system.

The role of the jail guards in the stories told by the victims and their attackers is typically ambiguous. The guards did not stop the attacks and yet it is not clear that they were performing their duties improperly. The guards' reluctance to speak openly and the reporter's inability to locate specific guards involved in particular rape cases limits the ability of the reporter to narrativize the guards' experiences. Nevertheless, the reporter is able to use her interviews with guards to contain their culpability in the report:

Guards say they are unable to protect inmates from rapes because the poorly designed jail makes it impossible for guards to see into most cells from their watch posts. The guards say they could minimize that by patrolling the cells more often than once every eight hours, but that there aren't enough of them to do that. . . . The guards, who work alone, say that even when they are aware of rapes in progress they cannot protect the victims because they are afraid for their own safety.

The guards too, it seems, are victims of the inadequate facilities and resources.

Near the end of the series of stories the reporter brings together the interviews with inmates and guards into a powerful indictment of jail administration and policy:

> Interviews with about 10 guards and 60 inmates show that the jail routinely places those most likely to rape with those particularly vulnerable. . . . In addition, those who are raped are often no better off once they've reported the rape. They are locked in a small cell with several other inmates—the same tactic jail officials use to punish unruly inmates. Sometimes, as in the mechanic's case, those other inmates are the original rapists.
>
> During an interview two weeks ago at the jail, Gaston [the jail director] defended the jail's placement of inmates charged with misdemeanors in the same sections with those charged with violent crimes. "These people [men charged with violent crimes] are charged with, not convicted of, certain acts," Gaston said. "Under the law; they're technically innocent."

And so one last terrible irony—victims jailed with their attackers—is brought together with a display of smugly legalistic indifference on the part of the jailer. Altogether, then, this system is not merely responsible for a failure to protect jail inmates but guilty of a disgusting disregard for common decency.

Like the rapists, the officers in the dog attack investigation are shown to be caught up in a pernicious environment that they are not strong enough to withstand.   The reporter is confronted by what he calls in the report "a hard core of errant K-9 officers and their dogs [that] is out of control." Unlike the jail rapists, these police officers are not absolved of responsibility in the report; indeed, the worst offenders are singled out for close scrutiny. But according to the report these officers are part of a system that has no guidelines spelling out when to attack, has no procedures for monitoring performance, and has not even trained the dogs properly.

Although the rapists did talk about their victimization by the system, these police officers would not talk. The reporter thus begins the process of allocating guilt to the system by using interviews with Anthony Taff, a dog trainer who was contracted to found the K-9 corps, and another former K-9 transit officer:

> That officer, who declined to be named, says the dogs are trained to hold on indefinitely in this manner: "they have a burlap bag tied to a rope and suspended from a tree on a pulley system. The dog is taught to hang on to that bag while the trainer raises it higher and higher. . . . "
>
> Taff is appalled by such techniques. "That [the pulley exercise] was positively taboo when I was in charge," he says. "The whole emphasis on this long bite and hold is entirely unnecessary. . . . "
>
> It is the combination of "macho" police officers and unreliable dogs that leads to unwarranted attacks, says the former officer. "It's like, 'I've got the dog and I'm going to show you what he can do.' We all do that to a certain extent because we're all guys' guys."

The behavior of the dogs and, more important, the behavior of the officers in charge of the dogs is, it seems, a natural response to the failure of the police department to properly train and monitor the K-9 unit. Dogs will be dogs, after all, and guys will be guys.

Perhaps because the K-9 unit officers refused to talk, the reporter did not pursue the idea that some attacks were demonstrations of "macho" or the allegation from at least one source that some attacks were racially motivated. The motives of officers thus remain suspect but ambiguous. This ambiguity facilitates rather than hinders the point of the story, however, because it allows the reporter to include as part of the same pattern both accidental attacks in which the dog was out of control and more ambiguous attacks in which the officer may have been out of control. The point is that, whatever the motives of individual officers, the system has definitely failed.

In this investigation, as compared to the jail rape investigation, the reporter had little interview material that could be used to show a callous disregard for victims. The police department simply denied that a problem existed and did not respond further to the reporter's inquiries. But this ritual denial, which journalistic convention demands be included in the story, is put to strategic use as the introduction to the indictment of the system:

> For the record, the Police Department says there is no problem. John J. McKees, the department's spokesman, said the department had no way of responding to *The Inquirer's* request for a list of bites inflicted by K-9 dogs in each of the last three years.
>
> Many law enforcement officials strongly advocate the use of the dogs for crowd control . . . the detection of narcotics and explosives, the discovery of missing persons and the apprehension of fleeing suspects.
>
> But, the *Inquirer* study found, too often the dogs' use is not restricted to those purposes. Instead:
>
> The police K-9 dogs have repeatedly attacked and bitten unarmed men and women with no criminal records.
>
> Contrary to accepted standards in other K-9 units, the Philadelphia dogs are not trained to release victims quickly. . . .
>
> The resulting dog bites have left deep and disfiguring wounds and have mangled limbs. . . .
>
> Police officers themselves attempting to make arrests or apprehensions have been bitten by police dogs. . . .

The Police Department's denial of the problem thus provides the petard upon which it is hoisted. Here, then, is another system that is not merely responsible for a failure to protect citizens but guilty of a maddening refusal to "come clean" even when confronted with the evidence.

In the crime report investigation, once again, there were police officers whose responsibility was problematic.   In this investigation, however, the reporter decided not to single out individual officers for blame:

> The story was about a pervasive problem—a scandal—in the police department that was not necessarily the doing of one individual policeman but a systemic pressure being felt from the top. . . . To single out an individual policeman would make it look like individual policemen were guilty and [that] there were just a few rotten apples.

In this report, as in the others, the reporter uses interviews to establish the systemic nature of the problem. Here is one officer's explanation of how the pressure to "kill crime" flows down the chain of command:

Patrolman Jerry Crawley: The pressure is tremendous. You have to go along to get along.

Reporter: Jerry Crawley hasn't always gone along in his 5 years on the force. He told us about the time he stood up to a sergeant who wanted him to downgrade the robbery of a newspaper boy.

Crawley: He suggested that I make it a battery, and this is a quote, I was told to "make it a battery and do not mention the money." When I asked him then, "Sarge, isn't this in effect submitting a false official report?" I was physically threatened and told to get the hell out of the station because I refused to reclassify that particular incident.

The interview with Jerry Crawley, much like the interviews with the rapist Francis Harper and the dog trainer Anthony Taff, directs responsibility away from the individual and toward the system. Killing crime, according to Crawley and other officers, is "S.O.P.—Standard Operating Procedure" in the police department. Further, the city not only lies about its crime rate but boasts about it:

Reporter: Jerry Crawley is one of a dozen policemen who told us that falsifying reports has allowed a string of police chiefs to claim Chicago's crime rate is going down, while the rest of the nation's is going up. . . . Richard Brzeczek, Mayor Byrne's appointee, has continued the tradition.

Supt. Brzeczek: Among the 57 largest cities in the U.S., only three have a lower per capita crime rate than the city of Chicago.

Once again, it is not merely responsibility for systemic failure but blame for systemic indifference and hypocrisy that is realized within and through these stories.

In this investigation, much as in the others, the facts of system performance are emplotted as stories most akin to farce. Innocent victims are caged with their attackers and the jailer points out that, technically, everyone is innocent. Uncontrolled police dogs attack not only innocent citizens but their handlers as well, and officials have "no way" of providing information on these attacks. Police officers are pressured to "kill crime" so that their superiors can brag about their success in controlling it. This is indeed farce, but of a particularly cruel sort: farce that provokes righteous indignation, farce that demands a turn in the moral order. Although the conventions of journalistic objectivity discourage an explicit recognition of a turn in the moral order as the only proper conclusion to a narrative, those conventions cannot completely silence the voice of Jeremiah:

Reporter: Police Superintendent Brzeczek denied there is a policy to cover up crimes, but said he will investigate the pattern of abuses exposed in our series.

Supt. Brzeczek: If there are sufficient examples of what you are describing, and it seems to be that the problem is systemic rather than isolated, then we will have to make some systemic changes. No question about that.

Reporter: We'll be watching for those changes and reporting on the progress of Brzeczek's investigation. As to the reaction so far, dozens of policemen have called to tell us their own stories of killing crime, and the pressures they feel. But those cops are worried that an investigation will overlook the top brass, and make them a scapegoat.

And, indeed, this story did end only with the fall of the wicked and a turn in the political—if not moral—order in the city of Chicago. The reporter continued to watch and report on the situation until the incumbent mayor was defeated, precipitating the resignation of the police superintendent. The reporter recalls with satisfaction the conclusion to her story:

> Brzeczek got up at his last press conference before he resigned and announced that his audit had not only confirmed our findings but more. . . . It was the first time in my entire career that a public official had gotten up and admitted that everything we said—and more—was true. They completely changed the whole reporting system in the police department.

The innocence of victims, and the blame for their plight, are neither fictions created by the reporter nor simply "out there"; they are fully realized only through a skillful definition of the victims as innocent and a careful allocation of guilt.   This realization of innocence and guilt through narrative is at once a cognitive and moral enterprise. Events on city streets and in county jails are not merely represented but rather made compellingly real because they are shown to belong to an order of moral existence that renders them meaningful.

In this argument we clearly diverge from the reporters' own understanding of their intellectual enterprise. These reporters do acknowledge that their stories do not "speak themselves," but they maintain that their narrative skills are employed strictly in the service of cognition. "I'm creating the story," says the reporter of the crime report stories. "I'm putting together a series of information in a certain order that I think is understandable." For this reporter, the selection and sequence of facts is determined by a "logical progression," not, of course, by any moral order.

Similarly, the reporter of the dog attack stories argues that every story is a "simplification, an effort at understanding." This reporter at first denies that good reporters impose any sort of created coherence, but then he seems to equivocate:

> Life isn't, per se, organized, coherent and lucid but in an effort to come to grips with it, you can make it more coherent. This is really a philosophical question.

The attempt to resolve the question leads the reporter eventually to deny the role of narrator. "I guess usually I don't consider myself a storyteller," he concludes. "I consider myself a gatherer of facts." The reporter of the jail rape stories, on the other hand, acknowledges that storytelling technique is critical to good reporting and that it is used "to impose order":

> There were a lot of ways to tell a story about the fact that rapes occurred in the county jail but there were only a couple of ways to tell it in a way that would be meaningful to people. That day I first became aware of the problem . . . I could have written a story that day. I could have said, "This young man was raped in the jail and the judge in the case says that rapes in the jail happen all the time. The jail warden (whom I would have called afterwards) denied the charges." And so we have on-the-one-hand and on-the-other-hand and people would have said, "So what?"

This reporter wants to transcend the limits of conventional journalistic objectivity but, she concludes, this means merely that her stories must be told "in a more complete way." Even for this reporter, who is perhaps least certain that there is an immutable reality "out there," narrative is only a cognitive instrument that motivates the reader and promotes understanding of the facts. There is no acknowledgment that it is only within an encompassing moral order that facts can be "complete."

Notwithstanding our considerable respect for the accomplishments of these reporters, our argument is that the development, selection, and assembly of facts into a story serves the moral task at hand. That task, as the reporters themselves obliquely acknowledge, is the evocation of righteous indignation—indignation at the plight of victims who are, if not entirely innocent by the standards of white middle-class newspaper readers, at least innocent enough to make what happened to them an outrageous injustice, and also indignation at the demeanor of officials who are, if not guilty of criminal behavior, at least guilty of indifference and hypocrisy. The task is accomplished by cueing the audience's response to these characters through the emplotting of events as recognizably moralistic stories and, more specifically, through the skillful use of such story elements as point of view, ironic detail, and ritual denial. Innocence and guilt thus emerge from these stories as we are instructed which "images to look for in our culturally encoded experience in order to determine how we *should feel* about the thing represented" (24, p. 91). And so it is that these stories permit us to "judge the moral significance of human projects . . . even while we pretend to be merely describing them" (26, p. 253).

These stories do, then, issue a compelling summons to participate in a moral universe, a summons to confront very real and terrible injustices. With Peter Solmssen, these stories cry out for *something* to be done. But what? The answer is not clear because the story form of the summons shapes and narrows, as Schudson (20) argues, the kinds of truths that can be told. For example, several themes of public import—the otherwise-unwarranted release of prisoners who are vulnerable to jail rape, the civil liability for injuries suffered by dog attack victims, the misallocation of police resources due to faulty crime statistics—are mentioned but not developed in much detail. Even in these stories of "system-wide problems," the individual experience is emphasized while the social issue is marginalized. Similarly, assessments of what exactly has gone wrong with the system are not developed in much detail. We have too little information to judge how the inaction of guards, inadequacy of jail resources, and malfeasance of jail officials each contribute to the jail rapes; how police officer racism, poor police dog training, and lax control of the unit each contributes to the dog attacks; or where the pressure to kill crime actually begins. In these stories, the details of individual suffering become high drama; the details of system operation would be anticlimactic.

Finally, analyses of basic moral issues—what ought to be the responsibilities of the individual and institution, how ought we to hold them accountable—are sidestepped. These stories provide an embodiment and reaffirmation of what we commonly take to be innocence and guilt, but they do not provide a forum for examination of those commonsensical concepts. These stories rely upon our understanding of, and emotional reaction to, such concepts to accomplish their moral task and they do not—indeed, cannot—critique their own premises. Thus, although the reality of innocence and guilt in particular cases *emerges* from these stories, the meaning of innocence and guilt as moral terms *submerges* into them. The summons to participate in a moral universe issued by these stories is only that—a summons. It is neither an examination of the moral forces that uphold that universe nor a guide to moral action within it.

This propensity to demonstrate rather than explicate innocence and guilt locates these reports within the third of Aristotle's three traditional forms of rhetoric. These reports are, in Burke's (4, p. 70) terms, among the "sturdiest modern variant[s] of epideictic rhetoric." There are, of course, fragments of the other forms: the forensic or judicial form, concerned with establishment of the evidentiary record, and the deliberative or political form, concerned with the assessment of alternative actions. And yet it is the epideictic or demonstrative form, "concerned with public occasions of praise and blame, with celebrating or condemning," as Ziff (28, p. 113) puts it, that is the privileged form. These stories *are* more than mere exercises in pity and blame, but they do underscore Weaver's (22, p. 38) contention that news is a "moralizing" form of discourse that organizes and presents the world in a way that "is logically inimical to the deliberative discourse" often demanded of journalism by its critics. At the least, these stories are testament to both the powers and the limits of narrative and to the need for modes of public communication that can not only issue a summons to moral condemnation but provide a forum for deliberation upon moral action.

References

1. Bennett, W. L. "Storytelling in Criminal Trials: A Model of Social Judgment." *Quarterly Journal of Speech* 64, 1978, pp. 1–22.
2. Bennett, W. L. "Rhetorical Transformation of Evidence in Criminal Trials: Creating Grounds for Legal Judgment." *Quarterly Journal of Speech* 65, 1979, pp. 311–323.
3. Bennett, W. L. and M. Edelman. "Toward a New Political Narrative." *Journal of Communication* 35 (4), Autumn 1985, pp. 156–171.
4. Burke, K. *A Rhetoric of Motives*. Berkeley: University of California Press, 1969.
5. Cawelti, J. G. *Adventure, Mystery, and Romance*. Chicago: University of Chicago Press, 1976.
6. Darnton, R. "Writing News and Telling Stories." *Daedalus* 104 (2), 1975, pp. 175–194.
7. Epstein, E. J. *News from Nowhere*. New York: Vintage Books, 1974.
8. Ettema, J. S. and T. L. Glasser. "On the Epistemology of Investigative Journalism." In M. Gurevitch and M. R. Levy (Eds.), *Mass Communication Review Yearbook* 6. Newbury Park, Cal.: Sage, 1987.
9. Fisher, W. R. "Narration as Human Communication Paradigm: The Case of Public Moral Argument." *Communication Monographs* 51, 1984, pp. 1–22.
10. Fisher, W. R. "The Narrative Paradigm: An Elaboration." *Communication Monographs* 52, 1985, pp. 347–367.
11. Fisher, W. R. "The Narrative Paradigm: In the Beginning." *Journal of Communication* 35 (4), Autumn 1985, pp. 74–89.
12. Glasser, T. L. and J. S. Ettema. "Investigative Journalism and the Legitimation of Moral Order." Paper presented to the Qualitative Studies Division of the Association for Education in Journalism and Mass Communication, San Antonio, Texas, 1987.
13. Hackett, R. A. "Decline of a Paradigm? Bias and Objectivity in News Media Studies." *Critical Studies in Mass Communication* 1, 1984, pp. 229–259.
14. Hallin, D. C. and P. Mancini. "Speaking of the President: Political Structure and Representational Form in U.S. and Italian Television News." *Theory and Society* 13, 1984, pp. 829–850.
15. Henry, W. A. "News as Entertainment: The Search for Dramatic Unity." In E. Abel (Ed.), *What's News: The Media in American Society*. San Francisco: Institute for Contemporary Studies, 1981.
16. Hughes, H. M. *News and the Human Interest Story*. Chicago: University of Chicago Press, 1940.
17. Mink, L. O. "Narrative Form as a Cognitive Instrument." In R. H. Canary and H. Kozicki (Eds.), *The Writing of History*. Madison: University of Wisconsin Press, 1978.

18. Park, R. E. "Introduction" to H. M. Hughes, *News and the Human Interest Story.* Chicago: University of Chicago Press, 1940.
19. Ricoeur, P. *History and Truth.* Translated by C. A. Kelbley. Evanston, Ill.: Northwestern University Press, 1965.
20. Schudson, M. "The Politics of Narrative Form: The Emergence of News Conventions in Print and Television." *Daedalus* 111 (4), 1982, pp. 97–112.
21. Tuchman, G. "Telling Stories." *Journal of Communication* 26 (4), Autumn 1976, pp. 93–97.
22. Weaver, P. H. "Remarks." In G. Will (Ed.), *Press, Politics and Popular Government.* Washington, D.C.: American Enterprise Institute, 1972.
23. Weaver, P. H. "Newspaper News and Television News." In D. Cater (Ed.), *Television as a Social Force.* New York: Praeger, 1975.
24. White, H. *The Tropics of Discourse: Essays in Cultural Criticism.* Baltimore: Johns Hopkins University Press, 1978.
25. White, H. "The Value of Narrativity in the Representation of Reality." In W. J. T. Mitchell (Ed.), *On Narrative.* Chicago: University of Chicago Press, 1981, pp. 1–23.
26. White, H. "The Narrativization of Real Events." In W. J. T. Mitchell (Ed.), *On Narrative.* Chicago: University of Chicago Press, 1981, pp. 249–254.
27. White, H. "The Question of Narrative in Contemporary Historical Theory." *History and Theory* 23, 1984, pp. 1–33.
28. Ziff, H. "The Uses of Rhetoric: On Rereading Aristotle." *Critical Studies in Mass Communication* 3, 1986, pp. 111–114.

5

THE SOCIOLOGICAL PERSPECTIVE

Rhetorical critics have often reasoned that the structures, institutions, and processes of society itself are central to who communicates, what communicators say, and when, how, and why people communicate as they do. In this view, a social system is a vital and causal entity, possessing a particular identity that can influence individual choices and behaviors as well as the human communication process. For some, including many rhetorical critics, these societal forces are so significant that they deserve to be treated as the focal point of any analysis of human activity. When adopted as a perspective for explaining communicative exchanges, rhetorical critics have frequently sought to identify the relationships between human communication and society itself and to offer critical assessments of these relationships.

While any number of labels might usefully identify this orientation, we have opted to label the perspective *sociological*. Following the lead of rhetorical critics employing this perspective, we find the term especially appropriate as a descriptor.[1] At its broadest level, the word *sociological* connotes a concern for "social needs and problems," while in a narrower framework isolates an emphasis on "collective relationships rather than individual psychology."[2] At the same time, *sociological* is aptly linked to the discipline of sociology and its mode of inquiry. Sociology has been described as "the systematic study of the development, structure, and function of human groups conceived as processes of interaction or as organized patterns of collective behavior." Or, more simply, sociology posits an "analysis of a social institution as a functioning whole," emphasizing the "exposition of the socially significant traits of a specific group, class or social milieu."[3]

The Sociological Perspective in Rhetorical Criticism

For several decades, several major rhetorical critics have focused upon the patterns of interaction which exist between society and communication. This concentration has generated a body of criticism that possesses a viewpoint and configuration of critical factors not readily associated with the traditional, experiential, and dramaturgical rhetorical critics we examined earlier.

[1]In addition to the rhetorical critics surveyed in the section of this chapter entitled The Sociological Perspective in Rhetorical Criticism, who explicitly use the term *sociological* to describe their own work, also see, e.g., William R. Burch, Jr., "Nature and Society—Seeking the Ghost in the Sociological Machine," *Communication Quarterly* 32, 1 (Winter 1984): 9–19; Claus Mueller, *The Politics of Communication: A Study in the Political Sociology of Language, Socialization, and Legitimation* (New York: Oxford University Press, 1973); Hugh Dalziel Duncan, *Symbols in Society* (New York: Oxford University Press, 1968); and Erving Goffman, *The Presentation of Self in Everyday Life* (Garden City, NY: Doubleday Anchor, 1959).

[2]*Webster's Third New International Dictionary of the English Language Unabridged*, vol. 3 (Chicago, IL: Encyclopaedia Britannica, 1986), 2163.

[3]*Webster's Third New International Dictionary*, vol. 3, 2163.

As a point of departure, a brief historical sketch of the evolution of the sociological perspective in rhetorical criticism should be useful. In criticism we find the sociological perspective appearing as early as the late 1940s, with major advocates arguing for the utility of this perspective throughout the 1950s, 1960s, and 1970s. To illustrate the concerns of these advocates, we have selected what we believe is a representative advocate from each of these early decades.

One of the earliest exponents of the sociological perspective was S. Judson Crandell.[4] Writing in 1947, Crandell argued that greater attention should be paid "in the postwar period" to the evolution of society itself, with "the role of public address in such social reform movements as temperance, abolition, woman suffrage, and labor" deserving special "exploration."[5] While recognizing that "the public speaking activities of a movement" involves an historical perspective,[6] Crandell particularly argued that "sociology" and "social psychology" be given attention,[7] with the primary direction of the discipline pointed toward the development of "a methodology for social control."[8] Using social movements as the most meaningful indication of the evolution of society, Crandell viewed the contributions of specific sociologists as "the most helpful for the rhetorical critic." He particularly argued that "sociologists, in their consideration of social movements, are fairly well agreed that such movements tend to follow a definite pattern." Accordingly, Crandell referred to sociologists for his definition, classification, and characteristics of social movements. In addition, Crandell held that the existing societal system was the foundation for assessing rhetorical effectiveness. He posited that the success or failure of a social movement should be assessed in terms of the "criteria of effectiveness" specified by the existing "institutional ideology." Thus, the leader of social movement was viewed as "the head of the organization" and of a "hierarchy," and a leader was to be judged, according to Crandell, by his or her ability to influence "the immediate membership" of the movement and "the audience being propagandized." Accordingly, "one would not be concerned with the minutiae of stylistic criticism"; rather, Crandell stated, "the analysis of speeches should employ a subject outline with a parallel rhetorical outline stressing techniques of social control." Crandell concluded that "the methodology suggested here" is "adapted from sound and accepted works on social psychology and sociology and should provide form and delimitation to social control studies in public address."

In the mid-1950s, Thomas R. Nilsen extended Crandell's position.[9] Nilsen initially noted that the traditional perspective had been concerned with the study

---

[4]S. Judson Crandell, "The Beginning of a Methodology for Social Control Studies in Public Address," *Quarterly Journal of Speech* 33, 1 (February 1947): 36–39.

[5]Crandell, 36.

[6]Crandell, 36: "The historical methods which have been employed in the past do not warrant discussion here."

[7]Crandell (p. 36), maintains that "distinctions between the fields of sociology and social psychology" are "tenuous at best for purposes of social control studies."

[8]Crandell, 36. For the balance of our discussion regarding Crandell's essay, see p. 36–39.

[9]See, e.g., Thomas R. Nilsen, "Criticism and Social Consequences," *Quarterly Journal of Speech* 42, 2 (April 1956): 173–78; and Thomas R. Nilsen, "Interpretive Function of the Critic," *Western Journal of Speech Communication* 21, 2 (Spring 1957): 70–76 also in *Essays on Rhetorical Criticism*, ed. Thomas R. Nilsen [New York: Random House, 1968] 86–97.

of "results," but "primarily with the results the speaker intended to achieve. From the standpoint of the speaker these are, to be sure, the most important. From the standpoint of the society upon which the speech has its impact they may not be the most important and probably often are not."[10] In Nilsen's view, the decision to view a social act "so predominantly from the point of view of the individual—the speaker and his purposes—rather than from the point of view of society and it purposes" had led "to much of the conflict and confusion about effects as an object of criticism."[11] Accordingly, Nilsen proposed that the focus of the traditional perspective be reversed and that a societal perspective of effects dominate the rhetorical critic: *"The evaluation of effect should be a judgment about the contribution the speech makes to, or the influence it exerts in further-ing, the purposes of the society upon which it has its impact."*[12] Nilsen particu-larly proposed that the "judgment" about "the contribution of a speech to the purposes of society" should "be based on the extent to which the speech" af-fects the "ultimate goals of society" and "social consequences, direct and indi-rect" on the society.[13] Concluding that the "rhetorician" must be "sociologist enough to appraise an audience," Nilsen argued that *"if criticism is to be so-cially as well as intellectually responsible it must continually relate speeches to their social consequences through the application of principles that reflect the values society seeks to realize."*[14]

In the 1960s, in a series of related publications,[15] Anthony Hillbruner argued that "the ultimate function of criticism" was "to evaluate all or any factors dealing with the public speaking process" in "its relation to any facet of current

[10]Nilsen 1956, 175.

[11]Nilsen 1956, 175.

[12]Nilsen 1956, 176. Emphasis in the original.

[13]Nilsen 1956, 177. Nilsen's emphasis on societal values has come to be called an "ax-iological" approach: see, e.g., Ralph T. Eubanks and Virgil Baker, "Toward an Axiology of Rhetoric," *Quarterly Journal of Speech* 48, 2 (April 1962): 157–68; and Craig R. Smith and Howard Streifford, "An Axiological Adjunct to Rhetorical Criticism," *Central States Speech Journal* 27, 1 (Spring 1976): 15–21. Of related interest are the attempts to describe an axiological approach to rhetorical criticism and a U.S. axiology: see, e.g., Edward D. Steele, "Social Values, the Enthymeme, and Speech Criticism," *Western Journal of Speech Communication* 26, 2 (Spring 1962): 70–75; Edward D. Steele and W. Charles Redding, "The American Value System: Premises for Persuasion," *Western Journal of Speech Communication* 26, 2 (Spring 1962): 83–91; James R. Andrews, "Reflections on the National Character in American Rhetoric," *Quarterly Journal of Speech* 57, 3 (October 1971): 316–24; Mary G. McEdwards, "American Values: Circa 1920–1970," *Quarterly Journal of Speech* 57, 2 (April 1971): 173–80. Criticisms employing the basic parameters of an axiological approach include Parke G. Burgess, "The Rhetoric of Black Power: A Moral Demand?" *Quarterly Journal of Speech* 54, 2 (April 1968): 122–33; and James W. Chesebro, "Cultures in Conflict—A Generic and Axiological Approach," *Communication Quarterly* 21, 2 (Spring 1973): 11–20.

[14]Nilsen 1956, 178. Emphasis in the original.

[15]Anthony Hillbruner, "Creativity and Contemporary Criticism," *Western Journal of Speech Communication* 24, 1 (Winter 1960): 5–11; Anthony Hillbruner, *Critical Dimen-sions: The Art of Public Address Criticism* (New York: Random House, 1966); Anthony Hillbruner, "Speech Criticism and American Culture," *Western Journal of Speech Com-munication* 32, 3 (Summer 1968): 162–67; Anthony Hillbruner, "Rhetoric, Region, and Social Science," *Central States Speech Journal* 21, 3 (Fall 1970): 167–74). For an example of a more philosophical approach to the sociological approach during this period, see James G. Backes, "Rhetorical Criticism: Yet Another Emphasis," *Western Journal of Communication* 26, 3 (Summer 1962): 164–67.

society."[16] In particular, Hillbruner recommended that a critical analysis begin with an assessment of "extrinsic factors," such as the "times," "audience and occasion," a biography of the communicator, and a description and analysis of the "effects of speeches." Bearing a striking resemblance to the kind of demographic analysis recommended by sociologists, Hillbruner specifically recommended that rhetorical critics focus on the relationship between a speech and "its relation to current intellectual, scientific, religious, political, philosophical, educational or artistic problems."[17] In a subsequent essay, Hillbruner outlined his conception of the intimate relationship between rhetorical criticism and a sociological perspective:

> The sociological route to the broad highway starts with the conviction that the relationship of speech to society is vitally important. It continues by asserting that an investigation of these relationships may deepen one's response to a work of rhetoric. The rhetorical critic who makes use of sociological criticism is primarily interested in the social milieu and the manner in which the speaker responds to it Determining these relationships is not a simple task, because the ties between rhetoric and society are reciprocal. Speechmaking is not only the effect of social causes; it is also the cause of social effects as anyone can see who examines the speaking of a statesman, in the first instance, and of an agitator, in the second. Thus an objective juxtaposition of the work of rhetoric and social theory, be it capitalism, socialism or communism, can strike sparks that are genuinely illuminating.[18]

Two years later, the "sociological point of view"[19] was again an explicit component of the method of rhetorical criticism outlined by Hillbruner. He argued that a variable such as regional origin or family income "leaves an indelible stamp upon" the speaker. In his view, "there is a kind of environmental determinism here which cannot be escaped."[20]

In the 1970s, the most explicit use of the sociological perspective was to be found in the critical analyses provided by Herbert W. Simons.[21] In his

---

[16]Hillbruner 1960, 7.

[17]Hillbruner 1966, 4.

[18]Hillbruner 1968, 165. We recognize that Hillbruner explicitly recommended an interdisciplinary approach to rhetorical criticism. In our view, however, a careful reading of Hillbruner's essays provides a foundation for noting that Hillbruner's point of departure was decidedly and consistently sociological. Moreover, in our view, Hillbruner held the sociological perspective to be the governing principle for integrating the contributions other disciplines might make to his approach to rhetorical criticism.

[19]Hillbruner 1970, 168.

[20]Hillbruner 1970, 167.

[21]Herbert W. Simons, "Requirements, Problems, and Strategies: A Theory of Persuasion for Social Movements," *Quarterly Journal of Speech* 56, 1 (February 1970): 1–11; Herbert W. Simons, "Persuasion in Social Conflicts: A Critique of Prevailing Conceptions and a Framework for Future Research," *Speech Monographs* 39, 4 (November 1972): 227–47; Herbert W. Simons, "'Genre-alizing' about Rhetoric: A Scientific Approach," in *Form and Genre: Shaping Rhetorical Action*, ed. Karlyn Kohrs Campbell and Kathleen Hall Jamieson (Falls Church, VA: Speech Communication Association, 1978), 33–50; and Herbert W. Simons, "Genres, Rules, and Collective Rhetorics: Applying the Requirements-Problems-Strategies Approach," *Communication Monographs* 30, 3 (Summer 1982): 181–88.

1970 "theory of persuasion for social movements," Simons noted that his "leader-centered conception of persuasion in social movements" was "rooted in sociological theory."[22] Accordingly, Simons maintained that "the rhetoric of a movement" does not emerge from the unique characteristics of the members of a movement but "must *follow*, in a general way, from the very nature of social movements."[23] The leaders of social movements are therefore viewed, by analogy, as "the heads of private corporations or government agencies," and Simons maintained that these leaders *"must attract, maintain, and mold workers (i.e., followers) into an efficient organized unit."*[24] Likewise, the structure, institutions, and processes of the larger society function as the object of change for the leaders of social movements: *"They must secure adoption of their product by the larger structure* (i.e., the external system, the established order)."[25] Similarly, in an essay two years later, the sociological perspective once again guided Simons as he argued that "social conflict may be roughly classified as either 'actor-oriented' or 'system-oriented.' "[26] Likewise, in a 1978 essay calling for a "scientific" approach to the study of forms and genres, Simons proposed "research norms" grounded in the conceptions offered in Karl Popper's "The Sociology of Knowledge."[27] And in 1982, Simons sought to "illustrate the possibility of integrating humanistic and social-scientific constructs and concerns so as to produce a 'sociology of rhetorical choices.' "[28]

As this extremely brief historical survey of the sociological perspective in rhetorical criticism from the 1940s through the 1970s has clearly demonstrated, sociological rhetorical critics can describe their approach to rhetorical criticism with very different terminologies. Yet in our view, the points of agreement these diverse terminologies conceal are more than the differences they apparently reflect. There are ways in which these rhetorical critics commonly deal with criticism.

Methodological Choices

A wide range of choices are certainly available to rhetorical critics employing a sociological perspective. Indeed, sociological rhetorical critics often differ dramatically in the principal objects they select for analysis, the demographic variables they examine, and the societal relationships they seek to describe, interpret, and evaluate. Some focus specifically on the relationships that exist between language use and societal norms. Others seek to explain how an established societal system deals with the kinds of radical changes proposed in movements. For others, societal conventions, such as rhetorical forms and genres, constitute their primary object of analysis. Other rhetorical critics focus on more traditional demographic variables such as the relationships between gender and persuasion.

[22]Simons 1970, 2.
[23]Simons 1970, 2. Emphasis in the original.
[24]Simons 1970, 3. Emphasis in the original.
[25]Simons 1970, 3–4.
[26]Simons 1972, 228.
[27]Simons 1978, 34 and 45 (n. 8).
[28]Simons 1982, 181.

. Despite the rich diversity that can characterize this perspective, sociological rhetorical critics employ certain standardized procedures when doing rhetorical criticism. The methodological choices they make ultimately reflect and define how they perceive their object of study, society, as well as their explanations of how society functions, adjusts to change, and controls decision-making processes. For example, one of the most fundamental of these methodological choices is to attribute power to society itself, casting society as an active force in human relationships. A series of such procedural decisions or methodological choices permeate the works of sociological rhetorical critics. These fundamental procedural choices provide a base for describing the perspective, objects of study, and specific tactics and strategies of those employing a sociological perspective to rhetorical criticism.[29] Based in part on an analysis provided by sociologist Pierre van den Berghe,[30] we believe that seven propositions capture the essential methodological choices of rhetorical critics employing a sociological perspective.

1. A society is composed of interrelated parts that can be understood to function holistically as one organic unit. The interrelated parts of a society can be described in any number of ways, but regardless of how societal parts are described, they must be capable of being perceived as related to one another in some fashion. Thus, the population of a society might be described demographically to allow (theoretically, at least) a statistical analysis in which each member of a society could be compared, grouped, and contrasted with others in some systematic fashion. For example, all members of a society can be conceived in terms of their age, race, income (levels of indebtedness to zero income to high income), education level (from no formal education through grade school to high school to college to advanced degree), religion (from one of the established religions to cult affiliation to atheist or to agnostic) and gender. If sufficiently operational, demographic groupings may even allow members of a society to be described in terms of size, density, distribution, and their relationship to other demographic characteristics. Thus, a demographic analysis should allow a critic to characterize a society as "young," "middle-aged," or "older" with clarity but also to link these age groups to other demographic variables such as income, generating an observation such as "income level increases as age increases." But a demographic analysis is but one way of treating a society as a holistic unit. A critic might also wish to characterize a society in terms of its primary institutions. Jack Dennis has argued, for example, that family, school, and mass media are the most critical agencies of political socialization.[31] Regardless of how the parts of a society are characterized, the parts must be capable of being

[29]Beyond van den Berghe's analysis, we are also indebted to the theoretical contributions of several different sociologists for these axioms, including Talcott Parsons, "Some Considerations on the Theory of Social Change," *Rural Sociology* 26, 3 (1961): 219–39; Ralf Dahrendor, "Toward a Theory of Social Conflict," *Journal of Conflict Resolution* 11, 2 (1958): 170–83; Pierre Bourdieu, "Structuralism and Theory of Sociological Knowledge," *Sociological Research* 35, 1 (Winter 1968): 681–706; Walter Buckley, George A. Huaco, and Arthur L. Stinchcombe, "On Equitable Inequality," *American Sociological Review* 28, 5 (October 1963): 799–808; and Andrew Gunder Frank, "Functionalism, Dialectics, and Synthetics," *Science and Society* 30, 2 (Spring 1966): 136–48.

[30]Pierre van den Berghe, "Dialectic and Functionalism: Toward a Theoretical Synthesis," *American Sociological Review* 28, 5 (October 1963): 695–705.

[31]Jack Dennis, ed., *Socialization to Politics: A Reader* (New York: John Wiley & Sons), 321–409.

treated as interrelated and of producing generalizations that treat the society itself as an organic unit.

2. Causal explanations within a sociological perspective are multiple and reciprocal. Rather than assuming that one element within a societal system can unidirectionally account for the existence or characteristics of another element (one-way causation) or that two interacting elements account for the kind of relationship characterizing two interacting elements (two-way causation), a sociological perspective presumes that all elements within a society exert varying degrees of influence upon all other elements of the society simultaneously and constantly (multiple and reciprocal causation).[32]

3. Societies employ adjustment and control mechanisms to regulate stability and change. Van den Berghe has noted, "Although integration is never perfect, social systems are fundamentally in a state of dynamic equilibrium, i.e., adjustive responses to outside changes tend to minimize the final amount of change within the system. The dominant theory is thus towards stability and inertia, as maintained through built-in mechanisms of adjustment and social control."[33]

4. Radical changes, tensions, deviations, and dysfunctions exist within societal systems, but channels or mechanisms are ultimately developed to "institutionalize" these forces. For example, Elizabeth W. Mechling has examined the evolution of the free clinics that emerged during counterculture movement of the 1960s. While brought into existence by a radical ideology, she has reported that these clinics quickly organized along traditional health care lines and were absorbed into the medical mainstream of society. She has explained, "Put simply, while the service function is a component of the anti-institutional stance, the anti-institutional stance is not necessary to the service function."[34]

5. Societies typically experience moderate, gradual, and adjustive change, not sudden and revolutionary changes. Van den Berghe has reported, "Changes which appear to be drastic, in fact affect mostly the social superstructure while leaving the core elements of the social and cultural structure largely unchanged."[35] For example, in "A Movement Perspective on the 1972 Presidential Election," Herbert W. Simons, James W. Chesebro, and C. Jack Orr did report that the "forceful, articulate, and resolute" style of the movement speakers of the 1960s constituted a rhetorical advantage, but they also reported that underlying values of the social and cultural structure remained unchanged: "Of whites agreeing that the Vietnam War was a mistake and favoring an immediate pullout of troops, only one out of eight supported peace demonstrators, a clear majority rated peace demonstrators negatively, 23% reacted against peace demonstrators with extremely hostility, and 70% rejected the suggestion that the police had used too much force in Chicago in 1968."[36]

6. Change is a function of societal adaptation. As van den Berghe has put it, "Change comes from basically three sources: adjustment of the system to

---

[32]For a more extended treatment of causation in a communication context, see Joe A. Munshaw, "The Structures of History: Dividing Phenomena for Rhetorical Understanding," *Central States Speech Journal* 24, 1 (Spring 1973): 29–42.

[33]van den Berghe, 696.

[34]Summarized and quoted in Simons 1982, 184.

[35]van den Berghe, 696.

[36]Herbert W. Simons, James W. Chesebro, and C. Jack Orr, "A Movement Perspective on the 1972 Presidential Election," *Quarterly Journal of Speech* 59, 2 (April 1973): 168–79, esp. 170 (n. 8).

exogenous (or extra-systemic) change; growth through structural and functional differentiation; and inventions or innovations by members or groups within society."[37]

7. Societal stability is a function of value consensus. Van den Berghe has noted, "The most important and basic factor making for social intergration is value consensus, i.e., underlying the whole social and cultural structure, there are broad aims or principles which most members of a given social system consider desirable and agree on. Not only is the value system (or ethos) the deepest and most important source of integration, but it is also the stablest element of socio-cultural systems."[38]

Thus, to make the claim that a society functions as a crucial element affecting human communication, there must be reasonable ways to characterize the society as an organic and functional unit while also accounting for the enduring and innovative nature of the ways in which people interact. While one may wish to take issue with any one of these methodological decisions, we do think they adequately account for the choices made by rhetorical critics employing the sociological perspective.

Rhetoric and the Sociological Perspective

The sociological perspective highlights and attributes certain characteristics to the human symbol-using process. These attributes are both conceptual and functional. They reflect the belief that human issues are best understood as the creation of societal systems and are most adequately resolved through societal frameworks. This governing perspective generates particular ways of thinking and talking about human communication. While variations are certainly possible, we find a relatively consistent view of communication implicit in the sociological perspective.

Designed to reflect the web unifying society, critics employing the sociological perspective understandably posit and focus upon a "national rhetoric," with subcultural modes of communication examined insofar as they reinforce and detract from the dominant national rhetoric. The degree of change or stability a societal system is undergoing determines how universal, meaningful, cohesive, and effective a society's national modes of communication will be as well as how effective subcultural modes of communication will be in altering the national rhetoric. In this context, effective communication is a function of the use of the proper managerial techniques as defined by the societal structure, its institutions, and processes. In all, then, communication systems are a reflection of the value system regulating a societal system.

In this scheme, profound conflicts are and should be resolved by appealing to commonly shared aims and principles of society. The most effective advocates of change will seek to regulate the rate, scope, and intensity of change in terms of the mechanisms established by society for change. Ultimately conservative in their basic assumption, the most effective advocates of change propose innovations through the societal mechanisms designed to deal with invention.

For rhetorical critics employing the sociological perspective, communication is a product and reflection of the governing societal system. At the same time,

[37]van den Berghe, 696.
[38]van den Berghe, 696.

communication is one of the webs unifying a societal system. It is one of the institutions and processes that create the unity of a societal system. To change the nature of communication is to change the societal system. Likewise, a change in a societal system will alter the communication process. Society and communication are, for sociological rhetorical critics, intimately related forces that mutually define each other.

Sociological Rhetorical Approaches[39]

Using *sociological* as the titular term governing *perspective,* we would suggest that four major approaches to rhetorical criticism can be reasonably viewed as related extensions of a sociological worldview. These include the "sociolinguistic," "generic," "social movements," and "feminist" approaches to rhetorical criticism.

The Sociolinguistics Approach   As conceived by R. A. Hudson, sociolinguistics is *"the study of language in relationship to society."*[40] In this view, language is one of the components creating, defining, and sustaining society. For example, Hudson has argued, language "is an instrument of socialisation—the process whereby children are turned into fully competent members of their society."[41]

Yet the precise relationship between language and society remains elusive. Part of the problem stems, Hudson has reported, from the fact that "as we might expect, gross differences can be found in the role that speech is allowed to play in socialisation between cultures."[42] Accordingly, various conceptions of the relationship between language and society can exist. Nonetheless, at a minimum, the language-society relationship implies that some sort of *speech community* exists in which people experience part of their sense of belonging to a society because they share a common language.[43]

The precise relationship between language and society is also difficult to pin down because sociolinguistics is closely related to the study of the *sociology of language.* While admitting that "there is a very large area of overlap between

---

[39]Rather than discuss a sociological perspective in the second edition of this volume, we identified a concern for metatheory (theory about theory) and discussed two methods—the generic and social movement approaches—that cut across the traditional, experiential, and dramaturgical perspectives. We continue to believe that a method can share characteristics with more than one perspective. This transcendent tendency reduces even further the discrete nature of these categories and demonstrates the arbitrary nature of most systems of classification, but this system of perspectives does reflect the current practice of rhetorical criticism.

Yet we also think that approaches such as the generic and social movement can be more usefully understood if placed within their own perspective and if the relationships among these two approaches and related approaches are explicitly articulated. We believe the sociological perspective provides a clearer conceptual foundation for a more systematic accounting of the approaches to rhetorical criticism that have gained prominence since 1980.

[40]R. A. Hudson, *Sociolinguistics* (London: Cambridge University Press, 1980), 1. Emphasis in the original.

[41]Hudson, 99.

[42]Hudson, 101.

[43]For a convenient survey of several different definitions that have been used to define the *speech community,* see Hudson, 25–30.

the two," Hudson has noted that "the difference between sociolinguistics and the sociology of language is very much one of emphasis, according to whether the investigator is more interested in language or society, and also according to whether he has more skill in analysing linguistic or social structures."[44]

Some rhetorical critics have been attracted to the sociology-of-language emphasis and have found the works of authors such as Fishman[45] and Inglehart and Woodward[46] useful. But for the most part, rhetorical critics have found the works of sociolinguists such as Dell Hymes[47] and William Labov[48] more relevant to the focus on language that has traditionally characterized rhetorical scholarship. From this rhetorical perspective, Gronbeck has maintained that "the sociolinguistic process" presumes that the human beings are "symbol-using (symbolmaking, symbol-misusing) animals," that "symbols—and the society which invents, promulgates, and sanctions them—are determinative of any individual's perception or apprehension of the world, attitudes, values, and behaviors," and that "humans are born into, nurtured by, and in large measure controlled through a series of symbolic environments."[49] Thus, the sociolinguistic emphasis that has intrigued rhetorical critics is typically context- and time-specific, focuses upon language as its point of departure and primary object of study, and examines the energizing force of language upon societal structures. Our interest resides with the body of critical discourses created by rhetoricians who have used a sociolinguistic emphasis.

In the first and second editions of this book we hesitated to use the term *sociolinguistics* for the language-oriented approach to sociological rhetorical criticism because most of the work done under this label was not conducted in departments of speech communication but in departments of English or linguistics. We use this term today because we feel interdisciplinary work has increased dramatically in the last ten years. Within the sociolinguistic approach we bring theorists such as I. A. Richards and the General Semanticists together with English department stylists like Richard Ohmann, Martin Steinmann, Jr., and W. Ross Winterowd. This approach also includes the work of linguists such as

---

[44]Hudson, 5.

[45]J. A. Fishman, *The Sociology of Language: An Interdisciplinary Social Science Approach to Language in Society* (Rowley: Newbury House, 1972); and J. A. Fishman, *Advances in the Sociology of Language,* vol. 2, *Selected Studies and Applications* (The Hague: Mouton, 1972).

[46]See, e.g., R. F. Inglehart and M. Woodward, "Language Conflicts and Political Community," *Comparative Studies in Society and History* 10, (October 1967): 27–45.

[47]See, e.g., Dell Hymes, *Foundations in Sociolinguistics: An Ethnographic Approach* (Philadelphia: University of Pennsylvania Press, 1974); D. Hymes, "Toward Ethnographies of Communication: The Analysis of Communicative Events," in *Language and Social Context,* ed. Pier Paolo Giglioli (Baltimore, MD: Penguin Books, 1972), 21–44; and D. H. Hymes, "On Communicative Competence," in *Sociolinguistics: Selected Readings,* ed. J. B. Pride and Janet Holmes (Baltimore, MD: Penguin Books, 1972), 269–93.

[48]See, e.g., W. Labov, "The Study of Language in Its Social Context," in *Sociolinguistics: Selected Readings,* ed. J. B. Pride and Janet Holmes (Baltimore, MD: Penguin Books, 1972), 180–202; William Labov, *Sociolinguistic Patterns* (Philadelphia: University of Pennsylvania Press, 1973); and William Labov, *Language in the Inner City* (Philadelphia: University of Pennsylvania Press, 1973).

[49]Bruce E. Gronbeck, "The Rhetoric of Political Corruption: Sociolinguistic, Dialectical, and Ceremonial Processes," *Quarterly Journal of Speech* 64, 2 (April 1978): 155–72, esp. 157–58.

W. Labov and Dell H. Hymes as well as language philosophers such as J. L. Austin and John Searle.[50]

One of the first explicit explorations of the relationships between language and society began in 1933. Alfred Korzybski launched the General Semantics movement; and throughout the 1930s and 1940s his followers became a vocal group within speech communication.[51] Korzybski was concerned with the relationships among what we say, what we think, and what we perceive in our environment. He initially argued that "it is of utmost importance" that people "not confuse the verbal level with the objective level."[52] As he saw it, "the objective level is *not* words, can *not* be reached by words alone, and has nothing to do with 'good' or 'bad.'"[53] Korzybski proposed that our thoughts or "semantic reactions" could, through a process of "training," respond to external events "on purely objective and familiar grounds," "avoiding unnecessary psycho-logical difficulties."[54] Holding that the "special *structure* of language we acquire is due to environment and copying," Korzybski maintained that human thought processes or semantic reactions could be "trained" to avoid "delusional values" and reflect the "objective level" or reality as it was.[55]

An early statement by Irving J. Lee, "Four Ways of Looking at a Speech," attempted to establish General Semantics (along with rhetoric, logic, and semantics) as a viable method of speech criticism.[56] In a further effort to make General Semantics readily available as an instrument of speech criticism, Lee reviewed the academic progress of the movement a decade later in his "General Semantics[1952]."[57] The concepts and tools developed by the General Semanticists were presented in a highly popular form by S. I. Hayakawa in his book *Language in Thought and Action.*[58]

The relationship between words and things, or—probably better—among the three elements what we say, what we think, and what we perceive in our environments, is a problem that has long been both troublesome and fascinating. Immediately predating the General Semanticists, C. K. Ogden and I. A. Richards,

---

[50]See, e.g., L. J. Austin, *How To Do Things with Words* (Oxford: Oxford University Press, 1962); and John R. Searle, *Speech Acts: An Essay in the Philosophy of Language* (Cambridge: Cambridge University Press, 1976). Among rhetoricians who have discussed speech acts and their uses of theories stemming from such analyses are Karl R. Wallace, *Understanding Discourse: The Speech Act and Rhetorical Action* (Baton Rouge: Louisiana State University Press, 1970; Robert E. Sanders, "Utterances, Actions, and Rhetorical Inquiry," *Philosophy and Rhetoric* 9, 2 (Spring 1978): 114–33; and Paul Newell Campbell, "A Rhetorical View of Locutionary, Illocutionary, and Perlocutionary Acts," *Quarterly Journal of Speech* 59, 3 (October 1973): 284–96.

[51]Alfred Korzybski, *Science and Sanity* (Lakewood, CT: Institute of General Semantics, 1933).

[52]Alfred Korzybski, *Selections from Science and Sanity: An Introduction to Non-Aristotelian Systems and General Semantics* (Lakeville, CT: International Non-Aristotelian Library, 1948), 27.

[53]Korzybski, *Selections,* 28.

[54]Korzybski, *Selections,* 27.

[55]Korzybski, *Selections,* 27–30.

[56]Irving J. Lee, "Four Ways of Looking at a Speech," *Quarterly Journal of Speech* 28, 2 (April 1942): 148–55.

[57]Irving J. Lee, "General Semantics[1952]," *Quarterly Journal of Speech* 38, 1 (February 1952): 1–12.

[58]S. I. Hayakawa, *Language in Thought and Action* (New York: Harcourt, Brace & World, 1964).

in *The Meaning of Meaning*, struggled to clarify what they believed it meant to "refer" to something.[59] Their formalization of the problem has been stimulating on a broad front and seems to underlie much of what is now called "sociolinguistics," though most sociolinguists would reject the passivity involved in the notion of reference to fixed meaning. I. A. Richards himself worked toward a much more active—that is, interpretative—sense of language in *The Philosophy of Rhetoric*, where he emphasized the essential role of metaphor in creating meaning.[60]

In contrast with the General Semanticists' positivist belief that language should conform as closely as possible to an external reality, Richard Weaver took the idealist stance that "true rhetoric involves choices among values and courses of action; it aims at showing men 'better versions of themselves' and better visions of a ultimate Good."[61] Weaver presented much of his philosophy in *Ideas Have Consequences* and extended his thinking explicitly to rhetoric and criticism in *The Ethics of Rhetoric* and in his often-cited essay, "Language Is Sermonic."[62] While shifting from the basic premises of General Semantics and offering a more dynamic view of language, Weaver did not offer the kind of comprehensive examination of the relationship between language and society that sociolinguistics has sought.

Since the 1970s language-centered research and criticism in the field of speech communication has been quite diverse. John R. Stewart, in "Concepts of Language and Meaning: A Comparative Study," reviewed studies of language in speech-communication and encouraged scholars to use ordinary language methods.[63] Arguing that "language has the nature of an open-ended social institution," Stanley Deetz recommended approaching language as constitutive rather than simply referential; that is, proceeding "from the lived experience prior to conceptualization," the perceiver actively forms meanings in a social milieu. Deetz's title indicates the break this sort of thinking makes with older word-thought-thing representations: "Words without Things: Toward a Social Phenomenology of Language."[64] In terms of the goals sought by sociolinguistics, Deetz's conception provided a critical step in explaining how individual experiences constituted a component in the dynamic relationship between language and society.

An active interest in metaphor has also long marked rhetorical criticism, and the shift in what we are calling the sociolinguistic approach resides in moving

[59]C. K. Ogden and I. A. Richards, *The Meaning of Meaning* (London: Routledge & Kegan Paul, 1923).

[60]I. A. Richards, *The Philosophy of Rhetoric* (New York: Oxford University Press, 1936).

[61]Quoted in Richard L. Johannesen, Rennard Strickland, and Ralph T. Eubanks, eds., *Language Is Sermonic: Richard M. Weaver on the Nature of Rhetoric* (Baton Rouge, LA: Louisiana State University Press, 1970), 30.

[62]Richard M. Weaver, *Ideas Have Consequences* (Chicago, IL: University of Chicago Press, 1948); Richard M. Weaver, *The Ethics of Rhetoric* (Chicago, IL: Henry Regnery, 1965); and Richard M. Weaver, "Language Is Sermonic," in *Dimensions of Rhetorical Scholarship*, ed. by Roger E. Nebergall (Norman: University of Oklahoma Department of Speech, 1963).

[63]John R. Stewart, "Concepts of Language and Meaning: A Comparative Study," *Quarterly Journal of Speech* 58, 2 (April 1972): 123–33.

[64]Stanley L. Deetz, "Words without Things: Toward a Social Phenomenology of Language," *Quarterly Journal of Speech* 59, 1 (February 1973): 50.

from metaphor as decoration or elaboration to metaphor as indigenous to meaning. The works of Michael Osborn, beginning with his fine essay with Douglas Ehninger in 1962, "The Metaphor in Public Address," and continuing through his case studies of what he calls "archetypal metaphor" is especially vital.[65] Thomas S. Frentz conducted behavioral tests on three psychological models of metaphor and discovered support for the generative semantics approach to linguistics, as contrasted to the classical theory.[66] Paul Newell Campbell, in "Metaphor in Linguistic Theory," argued that "dictionaries have little hope of compassing the varying meanings of words when metaphor can, at the same time, so forcibly question the distinction between the two."[67]

The sociolinguistic approach is based on the assumption that the rhetorical critic should begin analysis with the speaker's or writer's use of language. As Thomas S. Frentz and Thomas B. Farrell strive to demonstrate, "a language-action paradigm for human communication" that "reaffirms the centrality of language (i.e., both verbal and nonverbal code systems) to communication [and rhetorical] theory" is vital to a full understanding of discourse.[68] Frentz followed up this essential statement with "Rhetorical Conversation, Time, and Moral Action,"[69] and Dorothy Lenk Krueger applied language-action analysis to marital decision making.[70]

Typically, sociolinguistic critics make either qualitative or quantitative textual analyses in an effort to establish language patterns that will increase the understanding of the rhetorical act. For example, Richard Ohmann in *Shaw, the Style and the Man* uses Roman Jakobson's theory of arrangement to analyze Shaw's "modes of expression," "habitual patterns of thought," and "lines of connection between rhetoric and conceptual schemes."[71] Quite different from Ohmann's adaptation of a linguistic frame of analysis, John Sommerville's "Language and the Cold War" adapts a General Semantics approach to argue for a cross-cultural semantic analysis to end the Cold War.[72] The versatility of the method was also

[65]See, e.g., Michael M. Osborn and Douglas Ehninger, "The Metaphor in Public Address," *Speech Monographs* 29, 3 (August 1962): 223–34; Michael M. Osborn, "Archetypal Metaphor in Rhetoric: The Light-Dark Family," *Quarterly Journal of Speech* 53, 2 (April 1967): 115–26; Michael M. Osborn, "The Evolution of the Archetypal Sea in Rhetoric and Poetic," *Quarterly Journal of Speech* 63, 4 (December 1977): 347–63; John Waite Bowers and Michael M. Osborn, "Attitudinal Effects of Selected Types of Concluding Metaphors in Persuasive Speeches," *Speech Monographs* 33: 2 (June 1966): 147–55; and Michael M. Osborn, "The Evolution of the Theory of Metaphor in Rhetoric," *Western Journal of Speech Communication* 31, 2 (Spring 1967): 121–31.

[66]Thomas S. Frentz, "Toward a Resolution of the Generative Semantics/Classical Theory Controversy: A Psycholinguistic Analysis of Metaphor," *Quarterly Journal of Speech* 60, 2 (April 1974): 125–33.

[67]Paul Newell Campbell, "Metaphor in Linguistic Theory," *Quarterly Journal of Speech* 61, 1 (February 1975): 12.

[68]Thomas S. Frentz and Thomas B. Farrell, "Language-Action: A Paradigm for Communication," *Quarterly Journal of Speech* 62, 4 (December 1976): 333–49, esp. 347. Frentz and Farrell do not use the term "paradigm" in the Kuhnian sense.

[69]Thomas S. Frentz, "Rhetorical Conversation, Time, and Moral Action," *Quarterly Journal of Speech* 71, 1 (February 1985): 1–18.

[70]Dorothy Lenk Krueger, "Marital Decision Making: A Language-Action Analysis," *Quarterly Journal of Speech* 68, 3 (August 1982): 273–87.

[71]Richard Ohmann, *Shaw, the Style and the Man* (Middlebury, CT: Wesleyan University Press, 1962).

[72]John Sommerville, "Language and the Cold War," *A Review of General Semantics* 23, 4 (December 1966): 425–34.

demonstrated by Darryl Hattenhauer in "The Rhetoric of Architecture: A Semiotic Approach."[73]

We classify all of these works as falling within the broad range of the sociolinguistic approach. As our examples indicate, many competing theories under different labels are relevant and current. We would classify any critical application as sociolinguistic if (1) it examines the relationship between language and society; (2) the stress falls on the language itself as the starting point of analysis; and (3) the critic sees language as embodying action, not simply reflecting, presenting, or pointing toward action.

We have chosen Thomas S. Frentz and Thomas B. Farrell's essay, "Language-Action: A Paradigm for Communication" to illustrate how a critic can construct theory within the sociolinguistics frame. We have already discussed the significance of this article and noted their claim regarding the centrality of language to communication. To illustrate the application of the sociolinguistic approach, we have chosen Martha Solomon's "Jimmy Carter and *Playboy:* A Sociolinguistic Perspective on Style."[74] Solomon contends that Carter's final remarks in his *Playboy* interview reflect an ineffective sociolinguistic code shift to a stylistic level inappropriate to Carter as a public personality and as a presidential candidate.

The Generic Approach   Genres, by definition, are convenient ways of grouping or classifying discourses sharing common characteristics. Reflecting societal conventions and norms, genres are intended to reflect how language is used in society. Indeed, J. A. Cuddon has noted that "from the Renaissance and until well on into the 18th century, the *genres* were carefully distinguished, and writers were expected to follow the rules prescribed for them."[75] M. H. Abrams has reported that genres "were widely thought to be fixed in the natural order of things, like biological species"; although he has also noted that "at present genres are most frequently held to be convenient rather than arbitrary ways to classify."[76] While no longer prescriptions for communicators, because genres continue to be designed to reflect societal conventions, we believe it is particularly appropriate to view it as one of several sociological perspectives of rhetoric.

The term *genre* is a classification traditionally associated with literary criticism. Since 1965, with the impetus of Edwin Black's influential book, *Rhetorical Criticism,* the term has gained a marked currency in the discipline of speech communication.[77] Even though Black did not present a detailed definition of *genre,* he used it to describe congregations of rhetorical discourses that shared similar strategies, situations, and effects.[78] So generic criticism transcends a

---

[73]Darryl Hattenhauer, "The Rhetoric of Architecture: A Semiotic Approach," *Communication Quarterly* 32, 1 (Winter 1984): 71–77.

[74]Martha Solomon, "Jimmy Carter and *Playboy:* A Sociolinguistic Perspective on Style," *Quarterly Journal of Speech* 64, 2 (April 1978): 173–82.

[75]J. A. Cuddon, *A Dictionary of Literary Terms,* rev. ed. (Garden City, NY: Doubleday, 1976), 285.

[76]M. H. Abrams, *A Glossary of Literary Terms* (New York: Holt, Rinehart & Winston, 1957), 40.

[77]Edwin Black, *Rhetorical Criticism: A Study in Method* (New York: Macmillan, 1965; repr. Madison: University of Wisconsin Press, 1978).

[78]Black, 132–35.

specific rhetorical act and establishes a type or class of rhetorical discourse. Black discussed the genres of exhortation and argumentation, but his concern was for these types of discourse themselves rather than for generic criticism itself.

Lawrence Rosenfield's "A Case Study in Speech Criticism: The Nixon-Truman Analog" (see chap. 3) carried generic criticism one step further. Still assuming, rather than demonstrating, the existence of genre, Rosenfield compared two speeches of the same type or genre. We should note that Rosenfield's classification of Nixon's and Truman's speeches as forms of the "mass-media apologia" is a contemporary adaptation of a traditional category. Nonetheless, this genre encouraged the use of both traditional and contemporary forms as the basis for generic criticism. Further, critics quickly moved from a comparison of two speeches to an analysis of numerous acts of a given type.[79]

Generic criticism received further impetus when one of the elements noted by Black—the situation—was defined rhetorically by Lloyd F. Bitzer as "a complex of persons, events, objects, and relations presenting an actual or potential exigence which can be completely or partially removed if discourse, introduced into the situation, can so constrain human decision or action as to bring about the significant modification of the exigence."[80] Bitzer's definition shifted critics' attention away from the traditional speaker orientation toward rhetoric as a response to a situation. Of course, other theorists disagreed with Bitzer's definition of the rhetorical situation,[81] but the impact of his analysis was to ground generic criticism in the situation, influencing critics to define rhetorical forms based on responses to various situations.

Bitzer's situational grounding of generic criticism was reinforced by Kathleen M. Hall Jamieson in her article "Generic Constraints and the Rhetorical Situation" when she extended situation to include "antecedent rhetorical forms."[82] Jamieson was the first critic to tie Bitzer's "rhetorical situation" overtly to generic criticism; but as she did, she made *genre* the dominant term.

A major step in the evolution of generic criticism occurred in 1976 when the Speech Communication Association sponsored a conference, "Significant Form" in Rhetorical Criticism. The request for papers linked *form* and *genre* together: "The phrase 'significant form' is intended to refer to recurring patterns in discourse or action including, among others, the repeated use of images, metaphors, arguments, structural arrangements, configurations of language or a combination of such elements into what critics have termed 'genres' or 'rhetorics.' "[83] The outcome of the conference was the book *Form and Genre:*

[79]James W. Pratt, "An Analysis of Three Crisis Speeches," *Western Speech* 34, 3 (Summer 1970): 194–202.

[80]Lloyd F. Bitzer, "The Rhetorical Situation," *Philosophy and Rhetoric* 1, 1 (January 1968): 6.

[81]See, e.g., Richard E. Vatz, "The Myth of the Rhetorical Situation," *Philosophy and Rhetoric* 6, 3 (Summer 1973): 154–61; and Scott Consigny, "Rhetoric and Its Situations," *Philosophy and Rhetoric* 7, 3 (Summer 1974): 175–86.

[82]See, e.g., Kathleen M. Hall Jamieson, "Generic Constraints and the Rhetorical Situation," *Philosophy and Rhetoric* 6, 3 (Summer 1973): 162–70. Also see Kathleen Jamieson, "Interpretation of Natural Law in the Conflict over *Humanae Vitae*," *Quarterly Journal of Speech* 60, 2 (April 1974): 201–11; and Kathleen M. Jamieson, "Antecedent Genre as Rhetorical Constraint," *Quarterly Journal of Speech* 61, 4 (December 1975): 406–15.

[83]Karlyn Kohrs Campbell and Kathleen Hall Jamieson, eds., *Form and Genre: Shaping Rhetorical Action* (Falls Church, VA: Speech Communication Association, 1978), 3.

Shaping Rhetorical Action, edited by Karlyn Kohrs Campbell and Kathleen Hall Jamieson, who in their introduction, traced the evolution of generic criticism and established a general definition for genre—"a classification based on the fusion and interrelationship of elements in such a way that a unique kind of rhetorical act is created."[84] *Form and Genre* reflects the diversity of generic criticism. It includes Herbert W. Simons's "scientific approach" as well as Ernest Bormann's "humanistic approach."[85]

The diversity of generic criticism is further reflected in the types of studies conducted in its name. Genres such as apology,[86] death,[87] premillennial apocalyptic,[88] and radical strategies[89] have been studied. Also, in examining the "rhetoric" of black power, desecration, confrontation, the New Left, and the radical right[90] critics have highlighted important genres.

The genre that has been most fully studied is that of "apology." In the second edition of this book, it was highlighted with Jackson Harrell and Wil A. Linkugel's article, "On Rhetorical Genre: An Organizing Perspective"[91] and B. L. Ware and Wil A. Linkugel's "They Spoke in Defense of Themselves: On the Generic Criticism of Apologia."[92] These articles still merit study along with Noreen Wales Kruse's "The Scope of Apologetic Discourse: Establishing Generic Parameters"[93] and Robert A. Vartabedian's "Nixon's Vietnam Rhetoric: A Case Study of Apologia as Generic Paradox."[94] Finally, Halford Ross Ryan has edited *Oratorical Encounters: Selected Studies and Sources of Twentieth-Century Political Accusations and Apologies*[95] that presents criticisms of the major

[84]Campbell and Jamieson, 25.

[85]Herbert W. Simons, "'Genre alizing' about Rhetoric: A Scientific Approach," 35–50, and Ernest Bormann, "Rhetorical Criticism and Significant Form: A Humanistic Approach," 165–87, both in *Form and Genre*.

[86]See, e.g., Robert A. Vartabedian, "Nixon's Vietnam Rhetoric: A Case Study of Apologia as Generic Paradox," *Southern States Communication Journal* 50, 4 (Summer 1985): 366–81.

[87]See, e.g., Charles Carlton, "The Rhetoric of Death: Scaffold Confessions in Early Modern England," *Southern Speech Communication Journal* 49, 1 (Fall 1983): 66–79.

[88]Barry Brummett, "Premillennial Apocalyptic as a Rhetorical Genre," *Central States Speech Journal* 35, 2 (Summer 1984): 84–93.

[89]James W. Chesebro, "Rhetorical Strategies of Radicals," *Today's Speech* 21, 2 (Winter 1972): 37–48.

[90]Parke Burgess, "The Rhetoric of Black Power: A Moral Demand," *Quarterly Journal of Speech* 54, 2 (April 1968): 122–33; Richard J. Goodman and William I. Gordon, "The Rhetoric of Desecration," *Quarterly Journal of Speech* 57, 1 (February 1971): 23–31; Robert L. Scott and Donald K. Smith, "The Rhetoric of Confrontation," *Quarterly Journal of Speech* 55, 1 (February 1969): 1–8; Leland M. Griffin, "The Rhetorical Structure of the 'New Left' Movement: Part I," *Quarterly Journal of Speech* 50, 2 (April 1964): 113–35; Barnet Baskerville, "The Cross and the Flag: Evangelists of the Far Right," *Western Speech* 27, 4 (Fall 1963): 197–206; and Dale G. Leathers, "Fundamentalism of the Radical Right," *Southern Speech Communication Journal* 33, 4 (Summer 1968): 245–58.

[91]Jackson Harrell and Wil A. Linkugel, "On Rhetorical Genre: An Organizing Perspective," *Philosophy and Rhetoric* 2, 4 (Fall 1978): 262–81.

[92]B. L. Ware and Wil A. Linkugel, "They Spoke in Defense of Themselves: On the Generic Criticism of Apologia," *Quarterly Journal of Speech* 59, 3 (April 1973): 273–83.

[93]Noreen Wales Kruse, "The Scope of Apologetic Discourse: Establishing Generic Parameters," *Southern Speech Communication Journal* 46, 3 (Spring 1981): 278–91.

[94]Robert A. Vartabedian, "Nixon's Vietnam Rhetoric: A Case Study of Apologiaas Generic Paradox," *Southern Speech Communication Journal* 50, 4 (Summer 1985): 366–81.

[95]Halford Ross Ryan, ed., *Oratorical Encounters: Selected Studies and Sources of Twentieth-Century Political Accusations and Apologies* (New York: Greenwood, 1988).

contemporary apologetic encounters. These and related sources[96] provide an exhaustive study of the theory and application of the genre of apology.

Critics have also explored the limits of generic criticism. Kathleen Hall Jamieson and Karlyn Kohrs Campbell examined "rhetorical hybrids."[97] Herbert W. Simons considered leadership and collective rhetoric.[98] Carlyn R. Miller offered "Genre as Social Action."[99] Finally, Walter R. Fisher's "Genre: Concepts and Applications in Rhetorical Criticism" provided an overview of the work done.[100]

Both the diverse and transcendent nature of generic criticism is reflected in the fact that generic studies have employed methods from all three previously discussed perspectives. Leff and Mohrmann, who presented a traditional neo-Aristotelian criticism of Lincoln's Cooper Union address, see genre theory as strengthening traditional criticism because it can serve "as a corrective to some defeats in the neo-Aristotelian mode,"[101] and Thomas M. Conley tied the generic approach to ancient rhetoric.[102] Two very different examples of experiential generic studies are Rosenfield's "Nixon-Truman Analog"[103] and Hermann Stelzner's analysis of Richard Nixon's Vietnam address as a "quest."[104] And a good example of a dramaturgical study is Robert L. Ivie's "Presidential Motives for War."[105] The diverse nature of this approach is further reflected in a special issue of the *Southern Speech Communication Journal* devoted to generic criticism ten years after the conference on form and genre. The editors, Karlyn Kohrs Campbell and Kathleen Hall Jamieson, acknowledge a mixed record for generic criticism but then offer essays "discussing the rhetorical practices of sophists in ancient Greece" to "examining the genres that came to be part of nineteenth-century American pedagogy" as "a body of work that we believe contributes to our knowledge of rhetorical action and to our understanding of the concept of genre."[106]

[96]Also see, e.g., Rosenfield's "Nixon-Truman Analog" (in part 3 of this volume); and Sherry Devereau Butler, "The Apologia, 1971 Genre," *Southern Speech Communication Journal* 37, 2 (Spring 1972): 281–89.

[97]Kathleen Hall Jamieson and Karlyn Kohrs Campbell, "Rhetorical Hybrids: Fusions of Generic Elements," *Quarterly Journal of Speech* 68, 2 (May 1982): 146–57.

[98]Herbert W. Simons, "Genres, Rules, and Collective Rhetorics: Applying the Requirements-Problems-Strategies Approach," *Communication Quarterly* 30, 3 (Summer 1982): 181–88.

[99]Carolyn R. Miller, "Genre as Social Action," *Quarterly Journal of Speech* 70, 2 (May 1984): 151–67.

[100]Walter R. Fisher, "Genre: Concepts and Applications in Rhetorical Criticism," *Western Journal of Speech Communication* 44, 4 (Fall 1980): 288–99.

[101]Michael C. Leff and G. P. Mohrmann, "Lincoln at Cooper Union: A Rhetorical Analysis of the Text," *Quarterly Journal of Speech* 60, 3 (October 1974): 346–58. Also see G. P. Mohrmann and Michael C. Leff, "Lincoln at Cooper Union: A Rationale for Neoclassical Criticism," *Quarterly Journal of Speech* 60, 4 (December 1974): 459.

[102]Thomas M. Conley, "Ancient Rhetoric and Modern Genre Criticism," *Communication Quarterly* 37, 4 (Fall 1979): 47–53.

[103]See chap. 3.

[104]Hermann G. Stelzner, "The Quest Story and Nixon's November 3, 1969 Address," *Quarterly Journal of Speech* 57, 2 (April 1971): 163–72.

[105]Robert L. Ivie, "Presidential Motives for War," *Quarterly Journal of Speech* 60, 3 (October 1974): 337–45.

[106]Karlyn Kohrs Campbell and Kathleen Hall Jamieson, introduction to "Special Issue on Genre Criticism," *Southern Speech Communication Journal* 51, 4 (Summer 1986): 297–99.

We find little surprising at the fact that some critics have employed methods generally associated with the traditional, experiential, and dramaturgical perspectives to fashion generic analyses. But to apply an approach from another perspective requires a kind of conceptual and methodological "stretching." The method itself must be adapted in major ways and applied in ways it was never intended to serve. When applied to a fundamentally societal issue, a method designed to deal with a single speaker, a critic's unique experience, or a particular dramatization begins to undergo essential transformations, ultimately altering the procedures originally defining the basic structure of the method. Thus, we continue to believe that the generic approach is most appropriately understood as sociological. Genres become conventional and normative, because they reflect sociological relationships. Accordingly, from a critic's perspective, to attain conceptual power, generic formulations must likewise reflect societal conventions and norms.

We have chosen two articles by Karlyn Kohrs Campbell and Kathleen Hall Jamieson to illustrate both the theory and an application of the generic approach to rhetorical criticism. The theoretical essay is extracted from Campbell and Jamieson's introduction to *Form and Genre: Shaping Rhetorical Action,* which seeks to define, establish the significance of, and suggest guidelines for, generic criticism.[107] Campbell and Jamieson's essay, "Inaugurating the Presidency," functions as an application of the generic approach. In this article, they transcend individual addresses to establish "the special character of presidential inaugural addresses."[108]

The Social Movements Approach   A third sociological approach accounts for societal change and stability in terms of "social movements." As we noted at the outset of this chapter, social movements have traditionally been defined in terms of their relationship to the larger established societal system. Indeed, as early as 1930, sociologists argued that "every social movement tends to traverse a cycle of change."[109] While this cycle can be described in various ways, "if the movement is successful it becomes institutionalized—becomes the pattern of majority, and group controls set in. Any one who does not conform to the new pattern code is disciplined."[110] Accordingly, at its inception, during its period of confrontation,[111] and at its conclusion, a movement is defined by its relationship to the larger established societal system. Thus, in our view, a sociological perspective provides the foundation for defining social movement and accounting for their strategic choices and for the outcomes of their efforts.

When rhetorical critics initially began to study social movements, they studied a single speech or an individual orator; and at times this speaker orientation

---

[107]Karlyn Kohrs Campbell and Kathleen Hall Jamieson, "Form and Genre in Rhetorical Criticism: An Introduction," in *Form and Genre: Shaping Rhetorical Action,* ed. Karlyn Kohrs Campbell and Kathleen Hall Jamieson (Falls Church, VA: Speech Communication Association, 1978), 9–32.

[108]Karlyn Kohrs Campbell and Kathleen Hall Jamieson, "Inaugurating the Presidency," in *Form, Genre, and the Study of Political Discourse,* ed. Herbert W. Simons and Aram A. Aghazarian (Columbia: University of South Carolina Press, 1986), 203–25.

[109]Jerome Davis, *Contemporary Social Movements* (New York: Century, 1930), 8–9.

[110]Davis, 9. Also see Simons, n. 21 above.

[111]See, e.g., Scott and Smith in n. 89 above.

would be extended to include a group of speakers over a period of time. In such studies, the period of history was highly significant, so the historical approach usually was dominant, with neo-Aristotelian language woven into the description at appropriate times. The first volume of *A History and Criticism of American Public Address* illustrates this tendency. As a context for a study of the "leaders in American Public Address," five studies developed "The Historical Background of American Public Address." All were period studies in which the historical method dominated, with one study, "Women's Introduction to the American Platform,"[112] clustering a group of speakers together within a period.

Breaking from this traditional perspective, Leland M. Griffin launched movement studies with his article, "The Rhetoric of Historical Movements." Raising and answering questions, Griffin described the focus, scope, process of analysis, evaluation, and synthesis of reports on movements. Griffin indicated that the primary objective was "to discover . . . the rhetorical pattern inherent in the movement selected for investigation." But he also saw a larger purpose because he indicated that when movement studies became "a discrete field for research," broader rhetorical patterns might be identified.[113]

In establishing a new approach to rhetorical criticism, Griffin's departure—his rejection of a speaker orientation—was not radical because he maintained a historical orientation; he recommended isolating "the rhetorical movement within the matrix of the historical movement."[114] Yet his shift in emphasis to conceive histories "in terms of movements rather than of individuals" is significant and led to what has become a major effort of rhetorical criticism in the 1960s, 1970s, and 1980s.

Not only did Griffin initiate theoretical and methodological probes for movement studies, he was also the first to apply these methods. His two earliest studies, "The Rhetorical Structure of the Antimasonic Movement" and "The Rhetorical Structure of the 'New Left' Movement, Part I," for years served as models for movement studies. In tracing the Antimasonic movement, Griffin was able to describe both *aggressor* and *defendant* rhetoricians through the periods of *inception, rhetorical crisis,* and *consummation,* so that eventually he was able to arrive at a judgment about the movement.[115] In contrast, Griffin was only able to consider the inception period for the "New Left," making it more difficult to perceive a pattern for the movement and draw conclusions about it.[116]

Leland Griffin's next contribution to movement studies, "A Dramatistic Theory of the Rhetoric of Movements," represented a more radical shift from the traditional perspective. Instead of a historical orientation, Griffin adopted a Burkeian dramaturgical approach in developing "a dramatistic model, or abstraction, of the structure of a movement's rhetoric."[117] Griffin's new model

[112]W. Norwood Brigance, ed., *A History and Criticism of American Public Address,* vol. 1 (New York: McGraw-Hill, 1943).

[113]Griffin, 188.

[114]Griffin, 185.

[115]In *The Rhetorical Idiom,* ed. Donald C. Bryant (New York: Russell & Russell, 1966), 145–60.

[116]Leland M. Griffin, "The Rhetorical Structure of the 'New Left' Movement, Part I," *Quarterly Journal of Speech* 50, 2 (April 1964): 113–35.

[117]Leland M. Griffin, "A Dramatistic Theory of the Rhetoric of Movements," in *Critical Responses to Kenneth Burke,* ed. William H. Rueckert (Minneapolis: University of Minnesota Press, 1969), 456.

retained the important elements of his initial article but replaced the historical context with Burke's "dramatistic" process, demonstrating how movement studies critically transcend and often cut across the three perspectives we have discussed.

Acknowledging Griffin's contribution to movement studies and attempting to provide a direction for future studies, Herbert W. Simons drew on sociological theory to present a "broad framework within which persuasion in social movements, particularly reformist and revolutionary movements, may be analyzed."[118] Simons' framework took a leader-centered approach toward rhetorical requirements, problems, and strategies. It is interesting that Simons recommended a return to a focus upon individuals (leaders) even though the orientation would be sociological rather than neo-Aristotelian or historical.

Robert S. Cathcart, also responding to a variety of approaches to the study of movements, argued that a rhetorical, not an historical or social-psychological, definition of movements was required because the definition would determine the theory and methods for studying movements. Referring to Griffin's presentation of a Burkeian "dramatistic" approach to movements, Cathcart identified the essential attribute of a movement—"*a dialectical tension growing out of moral conflict.*"[119] This attribute, then, was his starting point for a definition: "It is this *reciprocity or dialectical enjoinment in the moral arena* which defines movements and distinguishes them from other dramatistic forms."

After Griffin separated movement studies from the traditional perspective and after Simons recommended the use of sociological theory, it was not surprising that other critics attempted to bring movements back into the traditional mode again. Dan F. Hahn and Ruth M. Gonchar, in "Studying Social Movements: A Rhetorical Methodology," described how the Aristotelian concepts of ethos, logos, pathos, and style could be adapted to study movements[120] and later argued that movement theory itself was a dead end.[121]

Beyond Hahn and Gonchar's efforts to moderate the concept of social movements, other critics argued that social movements could gradually lose their "radical" function and become increasingly institutionalized. Herbert W. Simons, James W. Chesebro, and C. Jack Orr took a social movement perspective on the 1972 presidential campaign;[122] Ralph Smith and Russell Windes suggested that movements were not always confrontational but could be innovative;[123] and Christine Oravec examined the rhetoric of preservationism.[124] So a complete consensus has never developed for Cathcart's definition of social movements

[118]Herbert W. Simons, "Requirements, Problems, and Strategies: A Theory of Persuasion for Social Movements," *Quarterly Journal of Speech* 56, 1 (February 1970): 11.

[119]Robert S. Cathcart, "New Approaches to the Study of Movements: Defining Movements Rhetorically," *Western Speech* 36, 2 (Spring 1972): 87. Emphasis in the original.

[120]Dan F. Hahn and Ruth M. Gonchar, "Studying Social Movements: A Rhetorical Methodology," *Speech Teacher* 20, 1 (January 1971): 44–52.

[121]Dan F. Hahn and Ruth M. Gonchar, "Social Movement Theory: A Dead End," *Communication Quarterly* 28, 1 (Winter 1980): 60–64.

[122]Herbert W. Simons, James W. Chesebro, and C. Jack Orr, "A Movement Perspective on the 1972 Presidential Campaign," *Quarterly Journal of Speech* 59, 2 (April 1973): 168–79.

[123]Ralph R. Smith and Russell R. Windes, "The Innovational Movement: A Rhetorical Theory," *Quarterly Journal of Speech* 61, 2 (April 1975): 140–53.

[124]Christine Oravec, "John Muir, Yosemite, and the Sublime Response: A Study in the Rhetoric of Preservationism," *Quarterly Journal of Speech* 67, 3 (August 1981): 245–58.

as confrontational or politically extreme even though this is the most common approach.

Having traced the evolution of the theories and methods affecting movement studies, applications of this approach deserve mention. The turmoil of the 1960s resulted in numerous studies focusing on the goals of movements—civil rights, human rights, student rights, black power, Chicano, antiwar, women's liberation, and sexual liberation. [125] Most of these movements are in some way related to the "New Left." In contrast, other critics studied what might be called "right-wing" rhetoric in groups like the proslavery, Nazis, the radical right, Stop ERA, pro-life, and militant deism. [126] Other critics approached movements by studying the strategies used to attain their ends. [127] Certainly, periods of value conflict like the 1960s encourage social movements, as opposed to periods of consensus like the 1950s and early 1980s.

We have selected two essays to illustrate the theory and application of movements criticism. Robert S. Cathcart in "Movements: Confrontation as Rhetorical Form" extends his article defining movements rhetorically argues that "movements are a kind of ritual conflict whose most distinguishing form is confrontation." The concern for confrontation is clearly embodied in Celeste Condit Railsback's "The Contemporary American Abortion Controversy: Stages in the Argument." In this essay, she examines the interaction between pro-choice and

[125]See, e.g., David M. Jabusch, "The Rhetoric of Civil Rights," *Western Speech* 30, 3 (Summer 1966): 176–84; Martin J. Medhurst, "The First Amendment vs. Human Rights: A Case Study in Community Sentiment and Argument from Definition," *Western Journal of Speech Communication* 46, 1 (Winter 1982): 1–19; Burgess, "Black Power"; Robert L. Scott and Wayne Brockriede, *The Rhetoric of Black Power* (New York: Harper & Row, 1969); Arthur L. Smith, *The Rhetoric of Black Revolution* (Boston: Allyn & Bacon, 1969); James R. Andrews, "Confrontation at Columbia: A Case Study in Coercive Rhetoric," *Quarterly Journal of Speech* 55, 1 (February 1969): 9–16; James F. Klumpp, "Challenge of Radical Rhetoric: Radicalization at Columbia," *Western Speech* 37, 3 (Summer 1973): 146–56; J. Robert Cox, "Perspectives on Rhetorical Criticism of Movements: Antiwar Dissent, 1964–1970," *Western Speech* 38, 4 (Fall 1974): 254–68; Lloyd D. Powers, "Chicano Rhetoric: Some Basic Concepts," *Southern Speech Communication Journal* 38, 4 (Summer 1973): 340–46; Jeff D. Bass, "The Rhetorical Opposition to Controversial Wars: Rhetorical Timing as a Generic Consideration," *Western Journal of Speech Communication* 43, 3 (Summer 1979): 180–91; Brenda Robinson Hancock, "Affirmation by Negation in the Women's Liberation Movement," *Quarterly Journal of Speech* 58, 3 (October 1972): 264–271; and James W. Chesebro and Caroline D. Hamsher [Caroline Drummond-Ecroyd], *Orientations to Public Communication* (Chicago, IL: Science Research Association, 1976), 17–29.

[126]See, e.g., Philip C. Wander, "The Savage Child: The Image of the Negro in the Pro-Slavery Movement," *Southern Speech Communication Journal* 37, 4 (Summer 1972): 335–60; Bruce T. Zortman, "The Theatre of Ideology in Nazi Germany," *Quarterly Journal of Speech* 57, 2 (April 1979): 153–61; Michael McGuire, "Mythic Rhetoric in *Mein Kampf*: A Structuralist Critique," *Quarterly Journal of Speech* 63, 1 (February 1977): 1–13; Barnet Baskerville, "The Cross and the Flag Evangelists of the Far Right," *Western Speech* 27, 4 (Fall 1963): 197–206; Dale G. Leathers, "Fundamentalism of the Radical Right," *Southern Speech Communication Journal* 33, 4 (Summer 1968): 245–58; Martha Solomon, "The Rhetoric of STOP ERA: Fatalistic Reaffirmation," *Southern Speech Communication Journal* 44, 1 (Fall 1978): 42–59; Martha Solomon, "Redemptive Rhetoric: The Continuity Motif in the Rhetoric of the Right to Life," *Central States Speech Journal* 31, 1 (Spring 1980): 52–62; and Richard S. Rogers, "The Rhetoric of Militant Deism," *Quarterly Journal of Speech* 54, 3 (October 1968): 247–51.

[127]See, e.g., Franklyn S. Haiman, "The Rhetoric of the Streets: Some Legal and Ethical Considerations," *Quarterly Journal of Speech* 54, 3 (October 1968): 247–51.

pro-life rhetoric between 1960 and 1980. She discovers a rhetorical shift from narrative to a series of ideographs—"life," "discrimination," and "choice"—into normalization and stalemate.

Feminist Approach   From a sociological perspective gender, or sex-related, differences have been consistently viewed as one of the most meaningful and stable demographic variables for explaining societal structures and processes, especially when correlated with societal institutions such as the family, marriage and divorce, and, more recently, labor market participation.[128] Prior to the full impact of the contemporary women's movement, gender differences were consistently treated as a foundation for distinguishing societal classes, particularly when explaining the political system and dominant-subordinate power structures, relationships and processes.[129] For example, writing in 1959, Robert E. Lane reported in *Political Life: Why and How People Get Involved in Politics,* that "women should vote less than men has become a fact so familiar now that it has been taken for granted."[130] Similarly, in 1961, Fred I. Greenstein reported that "sex-related political differences" could be detected in the "degree of involvement" in politics: "At the mass level, women are less likely than men to engage in the whole range of activities available to the politically interested citizen."[131] For some, these gender-political correlations constituted a base for enduring relationships in sociological thought. For example, Claus Mueller argued that "social class" is "the determinant of political communication."[132] For others, while gender remains the base for a societal class, cultural conditioning explains sex-related differences in politics. As Lane has concluded, "The culture emphasizes moral, dependent, and politically less competent images of women which reduce their partisanship and sense of political effectiveness and define a less active political role for them."[133] Regardless of how one might respond to these issues, it remains clear that gender has consistently been treated as a class or demographic variable in traditional sociological analyses and more recently in communication research.[134]

With the advent of women's movement in the mid-1960s, many of the generalizations regarding relationships between gender and society began to undergo dramatic changes. And a relationship between feminism and criticism was asserted shortly thereafter. Writing in *The New Feminist Criticism,* Elaine

[128]See, e.g., Peter L. Berger and Brigitte Berger, *Sociology: A Biographical Approach* (New York: Basic Books, 1972), esp. 76–99.

[129]See, e.g., Fred J. Greenstein, "Sex-related Political Differences in Childhood," in *Socialization to Politics: A Reader,* ed. Jack Dennis (New York: John Wiley & Sons, 1973), 269–86.

[130]Robert E. Lane, *Political Life: Why and How People Get Involved in Politics* (New York: Free Press, 1959), 213.

[131]Greenstein, 271.

[132]Claus Mueller (see n. 1 above), 43–85.

[133]Lane, 215.

[134]See, e.g., Barbara Westbrook Eakins and R. Gene Eakins, *Sex Differences in Human Communication* (Boston, MA: Houghton Mifflin Company, 1978); Judy Cornelia Pearson, *Gender and Communication* (Dubuque, IA: Wm. C. Brown, 1985); Lea P. Stewart, Pamela J. Cooper, and Sheryl A. Friedley, *Commuication between the Sexes: Sex Differences and Sex-Role Stereotypes* (Scottsdale, AZ: Gorsuch Scarisbrick, 1986); and a special section of the *Journal of Communication* 24, 2 (Spring 1974): 103–55 entitled, "Women: Nine Reports on Role, Image, and Message."

Showalter[135] has reported that Kate Millett's *Sexual Politics*[136] in 1970 was "the first major book of feminist criticism" in the United States, and she has specifically noted that subsequent "feminist criticism has established gender" as "a fundamental category" of "analysis."

We are particularly concerned about how the feminist movement has altered the study of communication, especially rhetorical theories and methods. Certainly, feminism is recognized by some as an emerging approach to criticism. Nancy Fraser and Linda Nicholson have reported that feminists have "sought to develop new pardigms of social criticism which do not rely on traditional philosophical underpinnings."[137] And after editing a special issue of *Communication,* "Feminist Critiques of Popular Culture," Paula A. Treichler and Ellen Wartella have reported that "feminist theory derives from the feminist movement" and concluded that "feminist theory and U.S. communication studies can fruitfully inform each other."[138] From what we have read and considered, we find the prospect of a feminist approach to rhetorical criticism particularly worthy of attention.

In rhetorical criticism the discourse of members of the women's movement was initially perceived only as a topic or object of study. However, as this discourse was examined, it increasingly revealed a foundation for theoretical explanations of the communication process itself and ultimately a basis for a rhetorical method for analyzing all discourse. Accordingly, of the major changes that have emerged from the women's movement, one has been to create a new method in rhetorical criticism that we have identified as the *feminist approach.* We think a brief historical sketch of the evolution of feminist research in communication demonstrates our point.

Critical analyses of feminist discourse do not appear in any substantial way in the discipline of communication until the early 1970s.[139] Yet three earlier studies are worthy of attention as a base for comparing the analyses of feminist discourse that appeared in the 1970s and 1980s.[140] In 1937, Doris G. Yoakam examined "pioneer women orators of America."[141] Yoakam concluded, "these

---

[135]Elaine Showalter, introduction to *The New Feminist Criticism: Essays on Women, Literature, and Theory,* ed. Elaine Showalter (New York: Pantheon Books, 1985), 5 and 1.

[136]Kate Millett, *Sexual Politics* (Garden City, NY: Doubleday, 1970).

[137]Nancy Fraser and Linda Nicholson, "Social Criticism without Philosophy: An Encounter between Feminism and Postmodernism," *Communication* 10, 3–4 (1988): 345–66, esp. 353.

[138]Paula A. Treichler and Ellen Wartella, "Interventions: Feminist Theory and Communication Studies," *Communication* 9, 1 (1986) 12 and 1.

[139]For years, the classic reference in the discipline was the three-volume history of rhetorical criticism. See William N. Brigance, ed., *A History and Criticism of American Public Address,* vols. 1–2 (New York: McGraw-Hill, 1943); and Marie Hochmuth Nichols, ed., *A History and Criticism of American Public Address,* vol. 3 (London: Longmans, Green, 1955). Of the 38 chapters devoted to individual speakers in these three volumes, only one examines a woman speaker; see Doris Yoakam Twiachell, "Susan B. Anthony," in Nichols, vol. 3, 97–132. Beyond this single essay, women speakers are only considered in "Woman's Introduction to the American Platform," in Brigance, vol. 1, 153–92.

[140]Women communicators have systematically been ignored within the discipline of communication, see, e.g., Carol Spitzack and Kathryn Carter, "Women in Communication Studies: A Typology for Revision," *Quarterly Journal of Speech* 73, 4 (November 1987): 401–23, esp. 402–5.

[141]Doris G. Yoakam, "Pioneer Women Orators of America," *Quarterly Journal of Speech* 23, 2 (April 1937): 251–59.

women were versatile extemporaneous persuaders with inspiring messages and fine voices" who "helped mightily in toppling oratory off its rhetorical stilts, and in guiding it toward a more natural, straightforward and conversational means of communication," ultimately making it "possible for oratory to enjoy the conversational comraderie and warm psychological persuasion it possesses today."[142] Similarly, in 1951, Alice Donaldson examined women who had emerged as "political speakers."[143] Donaldson's most frequent standard for the rhetorical effectiveness of those women speakers was the performance of male speakers.[144] And in 1958, employing Ernest J. Wrage's social and intellectual historical method, Anthony Hillbruner assessed the discourse of Frances Wright, "egalitarian reformer."[145] Hillbruner maintained that although Frances Wright's "views wielded only a modicum of impact upon her times, they are part of an interesting chapter in American intellectual and social history."[146]

These three pre-1970 studies are particularly important. Beyond their rich and detailed descriptive emphases, they treat a source of communication that had previously been neglected.[147] Yet the critical standards of evaluation for assessing these speakers are not derived from an analysis of their societal roles and messages. Their effectiveness is instead assessed in terms of the tradition established by males to assess male speakers. While perhaps a stimulus for examining women communicators, these three early analyses do not provide a foundation for a feminist approach to rhetorical criticism. To identify the origins of this approach, we must examine critical analyses that appeared in the 1970s and 1980s.

In the first half of the 1970s, rhetorical analyses of feminist discourse predominantly focused on the content and style of members of the women's movement, using traditional critical techniques. For example, in 1970, Martha Thomson Barclay compared the campaign techniques of the presidential candidates' wives from June 15 to November 1 for 1964 and 1968. Barclay assessed the rhetorical contribution of each wife to her husband's political campaign and concluded that the wives were "important" to their husbands' image and "aroused interest and contributed to his campaign process." Barclay concluded by asking if the parties will continue to "cling to the traditional image" of the candidate's wife as "devoted wife and mother" or if they would "present a candidate's wife as an acknowledged political professional whose value and appeal lie separate from, but equal to, that of her husband."[148] Barclay assumed that women would continue to function as "distaff" counterparts to men's active political roles and that traditional standards for measuring the effectiveness of candidate's wives were appropriate. Similarly, Brenda Robinson Hancock examined the rhetoric of "the women's liberation movement" in terms of Leland M. Griffin's dramatistic

[142]Yoakam, 258–59.

[143]Alice Donaldson, "Women Emerge as Political Speakers," *Speech Monographs* 18, 1 (March 1951): 54–61.

[144]Donaldson, 58–61.

[145]Anthony Hillbruner, "Frances Wright: Egalitarian Reformer," *Southern Speech Communication Journal* 23, 4 (Summer 1958) 193–203.

[146]Hillbruner, 193.

[147]For an analysis of the rhetorical techniques intended to prevent women from communicating, see Kathleen Hall Jamieson, *Eloquence in an Electronic Age: The Transformation of Political Speechmaking* (New York: Oxford University Press, 1988), 67–89.

[148]Martha Thomson Barclay, "Distaff Campaigning in the 1964 and 1968 Presidential Elections," *Central States Speech Journal* 21, 2 (Summer 1970): 117–22, esp. 122.

theory of the rhetoric of movements. While she concluded that the "pro-woman line that developed was instrumental in giving women a new identity and sense of political strength," she found no reason to suggest that the rhetorical situation women encountered required new standards or procedures for assessing the discourse of women communicators.[149] The same conclusion can be drawn for the analyses that focused upon Emmeline Pankhurst,[150] Mary Baker Eddy,[151] Frances Wright,[152] Abigail S. Duniway,[153] calls for and assessments of research on women orators,[154] the internal and external assessments of the communication techniques of the women's liberation movement,[155] comparisons of women's movement and black movement techniques,[156] and assessments of the nineteenth-century women's movement.[157]

However, three rhetorical analyses of the women's movement appearing in the first half of the 1970s do provide a foundation for viewing feminism as a critical approach to rhetoric. The first of these essays, "The Rhetoric of Women's Liberation: An Oxymoron" by Karlyn Kohrs Campbell, cast the rhetoric of women's liberation as a distinct genre of rhetoric, isolated its unique substantive and stylistic features, and concluded that "traditional or familiar definitions of persuasion do not satisfactorily account for rhetoric of women's liberation."[158] We find Campbell's arguments for this position compelling and have included this essay as an example of an application of the feminist approach to rhetorical criticism.

[149]Brenda Robinson Hancock, "Affirmation by Negation in the Women's Liberation Movement," *Quarterly Journal of Speech* 58, 3 (October 1972): 264–71.

[150]John C. Zacharis, "Emmeline Pankhurst: An English Suffragette Influences America," *Speech Monographs* 38, 3 (August 1971): 198–206.

[151]Gage William Chapel, "Christian Science and the Nineteenth Century Women's Movement," *Central States Speech Journal* 26, 2 (Summer 1975): 142–49.

[152]Kathleen Edgerton Kendall and Jeanne Y. Fisher, "Frances Wright on Women's Rights: Eloquence versus Ethos," *Quarterly Journal of Speech* 60, 1 (February 1974): 58–68. The authors do recognize the inconsistency between the requirements for effective persuasion and the role of women, but rather than argue for a new standard for assessing women speakers, the authors conclude that Wright was an ineffective speaker: "Eloquence without extrinsic ethos produces museum pieces of oratory, not catalytic compositions that influence the course of history. Her one real accomplishment was to be remembered as an early pioneer in the history of the American women's movement" (p. 68).

[153]Dorothy M. Mansfield, "Abigail S. Duniway: Suffragette with Not-so-common Sense," *Western Journal* 35, 1 (Winter 1971): 24–29.

[154]Robert J. Brake, "Women Orators: More Research?" *Communication Quarterly* 15, 4 (November 1967): 20–22; and Robert J. Brake and Robert D. Neuleib, "Famous Women Orators: An Opinion Survey," *Communication Quarterly* 21, 4 (Fall 1973): 33–37.

[155]See, e.g., Marie J. Rosenwasser, "Rhetoric and the Progress of the Women's Liberation Movement," *Communication Quarterly* 20, 3 (Summer 1972): 45–56; Louise McPherson, "Communication Techniques of the Women's Liberation Front," *Communication Quarterly* 21, 2 (Spring 1973): 33–38; and Judith Anderson, "Sexual Politics: Chauvinism and Backlash?" *Communication Quarterly* 21, 4 (Fall 1973): 11–16.

[156]Diana Schaich Hope, "Redefinition of Self: A Comparison of the Rhetoric of Women's Liberation and Black Liberation Movements," *Communication Quarterly* 23, 1 (Winter 1975): 17–25.

[157]Elizabeth Myette Coughlin and Charles Edward Coughlin, "Convention in Petticoats: The Seneca Falls Declaration of Women's Rights," *Communication Quarterly* 21, 4 (Fall 1973); and Haig A. Bosmajian, "The Abrogation of the Suffragists' First Amendment Rights," *Western Speech* 38, 4 (Fall 1974): 218–232.

[158]Karlyn Kohrs Campbell, "The Rhetoric of Women's Liberation: An Oxymoron," *Quarterly Journal of Speech* 59, 1 (February 1973): 74–86, esp. 84.

A second essay also recognized and addressed the same issue in the early 1970s. In her assessment, "Women's Speech: Separate but Unequal?" Cheris Kramer noted that "women as speakers have been largely ignored in communication research" and that "there is a sizable amount of information that can be called folk-view: how people think women speak and how people think women should speak." Kramer concluded by calling for an alternative framework for assessing women communicators, arguing that "researchers interested in studying the speech of women as women" should not assume that they can be assessed as "part of the category termed 'man'—said to be an inclusive term but all too often actually meaning 'male.'" Recommending the use of "'open-ended exploratory questions' about males and females in our society," Kramer suggested that the gender, socioeconomic status, origin, race, age, and religion of "women speakers might be important factors which bring diversity into the larger category of 'women's speech.'"[159]

Similarly, in her final assessment of Abigail Adams's correspondence with the John Adams on the topic of women's rights, Judy C. Pearson has noted that the requirements for effective persuasion were inconsistent with the role assigned women in 1775. As Pearson put it, "In Adams' case the conflict was between two roles. As a wife and an advocate, Adams found herself pulled in two directions. She had an obligation to her husband, but she also felt compelled to further the cause of women. In addition, these two duties ran counter to each other—satisfying one resulted in a reduction in the other." Pearson concluded that "this glimpse of an American woman demonstrates that the concepts of cognitive dissonance and conflicting demands are as applicable to historical figures as they are to contemporary persons." For the study of women as communicators, the issue was clear to Pearson: "the rhetoric of women" is "a relatively unexplored area of research for critics of communication."[160]

In the latter half of the 1970s, the contradictions between women's societally assigned role and the standards for effective persuasion in society were even more vividly articulated. In her 1976 essay, Sandra E. Purnell argued that rhetoric and rape could be intimately connected for women, for any effort by women to initiate communication could be perceived by males as an inducement to assault.[161] In a similar vein, but using the Equal Rights Amendment as her primary example, Sonja K. Foss argued that the conflict between pro- and anti-ERA forces could not be explained through the traditional "argumentative perspective" of rhetorical criticism; for "this argumentative approach does not explain the vehemence with which the debate is conducted and the emotional response elicited by the amendment, and it appears to ignore some rhetorical factors that affect the controversy and that perhaps are more significant than the arguments themselves."[162] To deal with the two forces involved, Foss finally constructed two different symbolic worldviews. She concluded,

[159]Cheris Kramer, "Women's Speech: Separate but Unequal?" *Quarterly Journal of Speech* 60, 1 (February 1974): 14–24.

[160]Judy C. Pearson, "Conflicting Demands in Correspondence: Abigail Adams on Women's Rights," *Today's Speech* 23, 4 (Fall 1975): 29–33, esp. 33.

[161]Sandra E. Purnell, "Rhetoric/Rape: Communication as Inducement to Assault," *ACA Bulletin* 16, 1 (April 1976): 20–21.

[162]Sonja K. Foss, "Equal Rights Amendment Controversy: Two Worlds in Conflict," *Quarterly Journal of Speech* 65, 3 (October 1979): 275.

The creation of two conflicting rhetorical worlds by the proponents and opponents of the ERA leaves little or no common ground on which argumentation can occur or through which an understanding of the opposing viewpoint can be reached. Each side's rhetoric is not only a threat to the other's way of making sense of the world, but also is a reason to defend strongly their particular world. Once the two sides in a controversy have developed worlds that are in total conflict—with different notions of the settings, characters, and acts in these worlds—the traditional modes of argumentation and persuasion are not likely to be effective in dissuading participants from their worlds.[163]

In two related essays dealings with the ERA, Martha Solomon extended the analysis provided by Foss, suggesting that opposition to the ERA was part of a profoundly mythical and fatalistic view of reality.[164]

In the 1980s, the volume of published feminist essays tripled what had previously been written on this subject. Communication journals provided special issues such as "Women and Communication: An Introduction to the Issues,"[165] "Intersections of Power: Criticism-Television-Gender,"[166] "Feminist Critiques of Popular Culture,"[167] and "Postmodernism/Marxism/Feminism."[168] Individual essays regarding historical and contemporary feminist issues also dramatically increased.[169] Many of these essays were likewise profoundly self-conscious of the potential of feminism as a method of analysis employed to examine rhetoric. Indeed, Carole Spitzack and Kathryn Carter's survey of published feminist essays has provided a systematic scheme for examining the theoretical and methodological choices organizing feminist criticism. We have included Spitzack and Carter's essay, "Women in Communication Studies: A Typology for Revision,"[170] in this volume as the theoretical foundation for viewing feminism as an approach to rhetorical criticism.

---

[163]Foss, 288.

[164]Martha Solomon, "The 'Positive Woman's' Journey: A Mythic Analysis of the Rhetoric of STOP ERA," *Quarterly Journal of Speech* 65, 3 (October 1979): 262–74; and Martha Solomon, "The Rhetoric of STOP ERA: Fatalistic Reaffirmation," *Southern Speech Communication Journal* 44, 1 (Fall 1978): 42–59.

[165]*Communication Quarterly* 31, 2 (Spring 1983).

[166]*Communication* 9, 3–4 (1987).

[167]*Communication* 9, 1 (1986).

[168]*Communication* 10, 3–4 (1988).

[169]See, e.g., Karlyn Kohrs Campbell, "Stanton's 'The Solitude of Self': A Rationale for Feminism," *Quarterly Journal of Speech* 66, 3 (October 1980): 304–12; Karlyn Kohrs Campbell, "Style and Content in the Rhetoric of Early Afro-American Feminists," *Quarterly Journal of Speech* 72, 4 (November 1986): 434–45; Charles Conrad, "Agon and Rhetorical Form: The Essence of 'Old Feminist' Rhetoric," *Central States Speech Journal* 32, 1 (Spring 1981); 45–53; Charles Conrad, "The Transformation of the 'Old Feminist' Movement," *Quarterly Journal of Speech* 67, 3 (August 1981): 284–97; Ellen Reid Gold, "The Grimke Sisters and the Emergence of the Women's Rights Movement," *Southern Speech Communication Journal* 46, 4 (Summer 1981): 341–60; Carol J. Jablonski, "Rhetoric, Paradox, and the Movement for Women's Ordination in the Roman Catholic Church," *Quarterly Journal of Speech* 74, 2 (May 1988): 164–83; Phyllis M. Japp, "Ester of Isaiah? The Abolitionist-Feminist Rhetoric of Angelina Grimke," *Quarterly Journal of Speech* 71, 3 (August 1985): 335–48; Lana F. Rakow, "Gendered Technology, Gendered Practice," *Critical Studies in Mass Communication* 5, 1 (March 1988): 57–70; H. Leslie Steeves, "Feminist Theories and Media Studies," *Critical Studies in Mass Communication* 4, 2 (June 1987): 95–135; Julia T. Wood and Charles Conrad, "Paradox in the Experiences of Professional Women," *Western Speech* 47, 4 (Fall 1983): 305–22.

[170]Carole Spitzack and Kathryn Carter, "Women in Communication Studies: A Typology for Revision," *Quarterly Journal of Speech* 73, 4 (November 1987): 401–23.

While a uniform consensus cannot be expected among so many different critics, we do detect certain central principles and procedures that define feminism
as a unique rhetorical method. One of the most striking of the initial perspectives
shaping the feminist approach to rhetorical criticism is the claim that all communication is genderized. Within this framework, a rhetorical critic seeks to identify sex-related biases and their societal implications. Moreover, criticism
itself—as one type of communication—is likewise viewed as genderized, reflecting sex-related biases. Thus, the claim is cast as universal and therefore
potentially constitutes the foundation for a theoretical position.[171]

The existence of genderized communication has also led to a further postulate
that genderized communication reflects and fosters a gender-based class relationship among men and women. The analysis of the paradox faced by women
speakers, particularly the tension between the traditional definitions of effective
persuasion and the traditional role assigned to women, has functioned as a foundation for identifying class characteristics faced by women but not men.[172] In
this regard, a related method has been to maintain, describe, interpret, and evaluate the power differentials distinguishing male and female communicators as
class entities.[173]

Beyond these descriptive and interpretative procedures, the feminist approach
has also spawned alternative standards for assessing rhetorical effectiveness.
While communicators' strategies are often assessed in managerial terms, or in
how effectively they change and control the attitudes, beliefs, and actions of
respondents, feminist criticism has frequently invoked a qualifying principle
holding that societal or role constraints may make persuasion, in any traditional
sense, impossible. Accordingly, rather detailed procedures have been employed
to establish the role constraints that preclude persuasive effectiveness.[174] Many
feminist critics have adopted even more radical postures, which seek to shift the
assessment of communicative exchanges from a linear and competitive model to
a transactional and cooperative framework in which communication is valued if
it promotes openness, trust, risk taking, individuality, and pluralism.[175] While
challenging a host of preconceived traditions among rhetorical critics,[176] this
kind of standard for effective communication underscores our belief that feminism warrants consideration as a distinct method for rhetorical criticism.

Characteristics of the Sociological Perspective   As with the traditional, experiential, and dramaturgical perspectives, the essential characteristics of the sociological perspective are appropriately isolated. Abstractions of this nature always

---

[171]See, e.g., Fraser and Nicholson, 353; and Treichler and Wartella, 12 and 1.

[172]See our earlier summaries in this section of the works by Campbell, Kramer, and
Pearson on this issue.

[173]Beyond the measures commonly employed to describe the power relationships between men and women, such as earned income in equivalent jobs, the gender-based power
relationship between men and women as classes in communication has also been described. See, e.g., Spitzack and Carter, 411, but this class-based power struggle in communication has been a subject of extended discussion; see, e.g., the reference cited in n.
141 immediately above.

[174]See, e.g., Campbell, "Oxymoron," 86.

[175]See, e.g., Spitzack and Carter, 411.

[176]For an exploration of "feminized" power as an established and effective rhetorical
conception and standard, see Michael Calvin McGee, "The Origins of 'Liberty': A Feminization of Power," *Communication Monographs* 47, 1 (March 1980): 23–45.

involve overgeneralizations, yet the generalizations provide a foundation isolating the central tendencies of the sociological perspective as compared to the other perspectives examined earlier.

1. *Orientation.* The structure, institutions, and processes of society and communicative exchanges are viewed as continuously interacting and mutually defining systems.

2. *Assumptions*
   a. Societies develop built-in adjustment and control mechanisms that minimize change and promote stability and inertia.
   b. The values and consensus mechanisms of societies establish the parameters for the study of communication.
   c. The symbolic frameworks unifying and regulating society determine the psychology of individuals and the range of feasible rhetorical options available to individuals in rhetorical situations.
   d. The word-thought-thing relationship is directly regulated by the structure, institutions, and processes of society.

3. *Consensus.* Responding potentially to a multitude of extremely different socialization variables, a wide diversity of theories is likely to emerge from the sociological perspective to rhetorical criticism. In this sense, as a collective unit, the understandings generated by this perspective are probably best viewed as a "polytheoretical," for the objects of these rhetorical analyses and the communicative patterns identified are more than likely to be extremely different. Yet a unified rhetorical perspective does bind these rhetorical critics, for they commonly extract their theoretical understandings by examining society as a whole providing the foundation for the study of rhetoric and criticism.

As often conceived, the sociological perspective presumes that social issues and solutions are a product of societal structures, institutions, and processes. Shifting attention from the individual to society, this perspective reflects the common sense belief that issues such as pollution, AIDS, national defense, illiteracy, and poverty are to be defined and understood in societal, not personal, terminologies. Likewise, if resolutions to these problems are to be found, societal policies and programs, not personal actions, are necessary. To achieve such ends, the essential parameters of society must be preserved and conserved. Change must be directed and channeled through society's established control and adjustment mechanisms. In these senses, both radical and reactionary political objectives must be "institutionalized" to become part of the policies and programs of society. In this context, the sociological perspective has been perceived by some as emphasizing security rather than innovation.

For the rhetorical critic, the sociological perspective offers at least two fundamental choices. The perspective can be employed to sustain the structure, institutions, processes, and values of the established societal system. Or a sociological perspective can be employed as a context and vantage point from which rhetorical criticism is initiated to change the existing societal system. The choice selected, we believe, turns on the critic who is responsible for both the means and the ends that shape the analysis defining rhetorical criticism.

THE SOCIOLINGUISTICS APPROACH

LANGUAGE-ACTION:
A PARADIGM FOR COMMUNICATION

Thomas S. Frentz and Thomas B. Farrell

Throughout its varied history, communication has been an object of conceptual controversy.[1] Although the methods and aims of natural science treat communication as a behavioral object with human vehicles but impersonal causes,
numerous philosophical critiques have been directed at these positivist assumptions as an exclusive guide to inquiry. Recently in communication, the action-
centered studies of Hawes and Nofsinger imply a dialectical alternative to strict
behaviorism.[2]

Three characteristics of action-centered research highlight its contrasts with
positivist assumptions. First, additional research has been particularistic and
situation-specific. This orientation departs radically from the goal of maximal
theoretic generalizability. Second, actional studies have focused attention upon
the human actor—who conducts relationships with others, whose behaviors are
seen by self and others as actions, whose choices imply responsibility as well as
percentiles of significance. Finally, such research promises a renewed interest in
communicative approaches to meaning. An actional approach to meaning is in
sharp contrast to behavioral and scientistic perspectives which view "meanings"
as being in people, in messages, or in between the two.

For all its innovations, however, actional research has one overriding limitation: the conceptual structure implied by these studies has not been clearly delineated. Lacking the integration and focus a conceptual paradigm brings, the

From *Quarterly Journal of Speech* 62 (December 1976): 333–349. Used by permission
of authors and the Speech Communication Association.

Mr. Frentz is visiting associate professor of communication at the University of
Colorado. Mr. Farrell is assistant professor of communication studies at Northwestern
University.

[1]As will become clear shortly, the immediate application of our paradigm is to *interpersonal* communication. However, for stylistic reasons we shall employ the generic term
"communication" in most subsequent references.

[2]See, for example, Leonard C. Hawes, "Elements of a Model for Communication Processes," *QJS*, 59 (1973), 11–21; Leonard C. Hawes, "How Writing is Used in Talk: A
Study of Communicative Logic-In-Use," is this issue; Leonard C. Hawes, "The Naturalistic Study of Human Communication: A Naturalistic Perspective," paper presented at the
Speech Communication Association's National Convention, Houston, Texas, December
1975; Robert E. Nofsinger, "Conversational Analysis," paper presented at the Speech Com-
munication Association's National Convention, Houston, Texas, December 1975; Robert
E. Nofsinger, "On Answering Questions Indirectly: Some Rules in the Grammar," *Human
Communication Research* 2 (1976), 172–180; Robert E. Nofsinger, "The Demand Ticket:
A Conversational Device for Getting the Floor," *Speech Monographs*, 42 (1975), 1–9.

actional studies often remain unclear in implication and heuristic import.[3] And, as O'Keefe and others have noted, the reordering of theory and research in communication depends upon the development of a coherent and structured paradigm.[4]

In this essay, we (1) generate and explicate a "language-action" paradigm, (2) offer an extended example of its explanatory potential, and (3) set forth several important implications for theory and research in communication.

I

Influenced by some of the techniques of analytic philosophy,[5] our paradigm consists of three, heirarchically structured constructs. Our most general term, *context*, specifies the criteria for interpreting both the meaningfulness and propriety of any communicative event. *Episodes* are fundamental communicative sequences of action which are understandable only in terms of the contexts in which they occur. Finally, *symbolic acts* are the most elemental communicative constituents from which actors generate episodes.

Context   The "deductive" character of our paradigm necessitates our discussing context first. But since context is logically necessary and prior to the intelligibility of communication, the intelligibility of contexts, themselves, poses a serious problem of outside reference. Cryptically put, what can be the explanatory context for "context"? This traditional paradox renders our discussion of context somewhat abstract and general. Nevertheless, in communication, context is known on two hierarchical levels.

Form of life. Form of life names the broadest formal context of communication. According to Toulmin, forms of life are those partially linguistic and partially nonlinguistic constellations of activities which fix the meanings of concepts and expressions.[6] Furthermore, form of life has the following more specifiable characteristics of relevance to human communication: First, form of life is a kind of knowledge which communicators share through language. Second, form of life imposes upon communication an aesthetic pattern which trig-

---

[3]Our use of the term "paradigm" employs its ordinary meaning—namely, a conceptual structure which serves as an example from which research and theory might emanate. Our usage differs from the more fashionable Kuhnian translation, as that usage renders all social sciences preparadigmatic.

[4]Daniel J. O'Keefe, "Logical Empiricism and the Study of Human Communication," *Speech Monographs*, 42 (1975), 169–183.

[5]See in particular, R. Harré, "Some Remarks on 'Rule' as a Scientific Concept," in *Understanding Other Persons*, ed. Theodore Mischel (Oxford: Blackwell, 1974), pp. 141–184; A. R. Louch, *Explanation and Human Action* (Berkeley: Univ. of California Press, 1966), especially pp. 7–17; Charles Taylor, *The Explanation of Behaviour* (London: Humanities Press, 1964); Stephen Toulmin, "Concepts and the Explanation of Behavior," in *Human Action*, ed. Theodore Mischel (New York: Academic Press, 1969), pp. 71–104; Stephen Toulmin, "Reasons and Causes" in *Explanation in the Behavioural Sciences*, eds. Robert Borger and Frank Cioffi (Cambridge: Cambridge Univ. Press, 1970), pp. 1–26; Stephen Toulmin, "Rules and Their Relevance for Understanding Human Behavior," in *Understanding Other Persons*, pp. 85–215; Thomas P. Wilson, "Conceptions of Interaction and Forms of Sociological Explanation," *American Sociological Review*, 35 (1970), 697–709; Ludwig Wittgenstein, *Philosophical Investigations* (New York: Macmillan, 1953).

[6]Toulmin, "Concepts . . . ," pp. 73–74.

gers actor expectations. Finally, form of life exerts indirect social regulation upon communicative events. We now explore each of these three features in more detail.

The world of communication acquires form through its shared differentiation. The concept of communication itself demands a common ontology which is accessible to its participants through form.[7] This ontology includes the total conceptual, aesthetic, and cultural knowledge which a society shares and which is recreated and expressed through the overall structure of that society's language. An example from Whorf clarifies the knowledge dimension of form of life. As Whorf notes, the Hopi Indian language conceptualizes "time" as a continuous variable where discriminations are expressed through length of duration. By contrast, most Indo-European languages structure "time" as a discrete construct differentiated in terms of past, present, and future.[8] Insofar as the knowledge dimension of form of life is not shared among actors, communication will not be totally meaningful.

Form of life also imposes aesthetic dimensions upon communication. As Burke notes, the general term, "form" implies, " . . . the creation of an appetite in the mind of the audience and the adequate satisfaction of that appetite."[9] Put another way, the aesthetic dimension of form of life invests communication with a pattern, creating expectations which must be fulfilled or justified (in the case of deviations) if communication is to be completely meaningful. For example, the expectation that all communicative events have beginnings, middles, and endings, derives from this aesthetic dimension of form of life. Our knowledge that questions are logically prior to answers, problems to solutions, causes to effects, etc , enables actors to apprehend the recurring aesthetic pattern of communication.

Finally, the institutional dimension of form of life renders constraint recognizable in communication. The institutional structure of form of life can be found in rituals, ceremonies, procedures of decision-making, and so on. Durkheim offers a rich variety of apparently individual acts which acquire meaning through their conformity to institutionalized constraint.

> The system of signs I use to express my thought, the system of currency I employ to pay my debts, the instrument of credit I use in my commercial relations, the practices followed in my profession, etc. function independently of my use of them. And these statements can be repeated for each member of society. Here then are ways of acting, thinking, feeling that present the noteworthy property of existing outside the individual consciousness.[10]

Relationships among students and teachers, wives and husbands, brothers and sisters, executives and subordinates are both typified and constrained by the institutional structure found in form of life.

Encounters. If communication becomes generally meaningful through the knowledge, aesthetic, and institutional dimensions of form of life, communication

[7]Martin Holl's, "Reason and Ritual," in *The Philosophy of Social Explanation,* ed. Alan Ryan (London: Oxford Univ. Press, 1973), pp. 38–39.

[8]Benjamin L. Whorf, "Science and Linguistics," in *Psycholinguistics,* ed. Sol Saporta (New York: Holt, Rinehart and Winston, 1961), pp. 465–467.

[9]Kenneth Burke, *Counter-Statement* (Berkeley: Univ. of California Press, 1968), p. 31.

[10]Emile Durkheim, *Rules of Sociological Method* (New York: Free Press of Glencoe, 1938), p. 2.

becomes appropriate through a second level of context; namely, encounters, which particularize form of life through rules of propriety. Encounters are "points of contact" among conscious human actors. The external signs of an encounter are classrooms, bus depots, theaters, football stadiums, churches, restaurants, bars—any concrete location where actors converge.

The sufficient condition for an encounter is the acknowledgement of one another's presence. Individual actors experience this condition as an inward "psychological readiness" prior to the actual inception of communication. Intersubjectively, encounters are experienced as a specified period of time. For example, If A and B spend four hours together in a local bar, the total time spent defines the encounter for A and B—even though some of that time may not involve direct communication.

As the concrete situational dimension of context, encounters actualize form of life in several important ways. First, the immediate "here and now" character of an encounter is an undeniable counterpart to the abstraction in form of life. Encounters apply relevant form of life knowledge to each given situation. For example, although shared forms of life will probably enable two cyberneticists to communicate, it will be the encounter which determines whether they abandon their common jargon and shop talk in order to exchange, say, political views or the local sports news.

A similar point of contrast and fulfillment can be found in the aesthetic dimension of context. Whereas form of life provides persons with their conception of patterned relations in the phenomenological world (in temporal sequence, spatial relation, contrast, repetition, and so forth), encounters provide practical significance to these patterns through the communicative choices available. People do not go to parties—as in Bünuel's *Exterminating Angel*—and remain indefinitely, unable to leave. The encounter-type in which parties occur creates particular expectations of form, and also practical communicative means to fulfill those expectations.

Finally, institutional constraint is brought to fruition through the encounter. The institutional constraint in form of life generates relational meaning among actors. The institutional constraint of encounters determines the propriety of available communicative choices. During the encounter, actors will survey the probable rules of propriety and—in principle—exclude the least likely candidates. The actual application of such rules occurs in communicative forms known as episodes.

Episodes   The pivotal concept for understanding communication is a rule-conforming sequence of symbolic acts generated by two or more actors who are collectively oriented toward emergent goals. Episodes are both flexible in content and collective in creative origin; because of this, they cannot be "operationalized" in any reductionistic sense. Nevertheless, episodes display three identifiable characteristics and unfold in terms of five structural "imperatives."[11] Both the defining features and structural imperatives will be considered in some detail.

---

[11]Episodes, we maintain, can be emergent and still possess recognizable group properties. The classic conception of an emergent phenomenon simply acknowledges that the phenomenon is possessed of properties which are not reducible to the properties of its constituents. A society, a musical composition, a drama, and an episode are all examples of emergent wholes which have recognizable group features, and yet trace their particular

Three general features distinguish the construct of an episode. First, episodes are rule-conforming to the extent that actors assume responsibility for free choice within any episode. Episodes activate the rules of each encounter which specify relations of propriety between means and ends. Accordingly, the rules which constrain communicative choice in any episode do not generalize beyond the overall encounter-type in which they occur. For example, the rules which determine assessments of propriety in "Meet-the-new-boss" type encounters would explain the impropriety of A's second comment:

A: How do you do? Very nice to have you as our new department head.
B: Thanks—it's nice to be here.
A: For us too. Say, is it true you're having some problems with your wife?

If A's second comment had occurred in an encounter-type called "Therapy," in which A was the therapist and B the patient, the operative rules would render this fragment fully appropriate.

A second defining characteristic of episodes is their peculiar goal-orientation. In order for an episode to progress, actors must agree, at least tacitly, upon the complementarity of goals they are pursuing. Even in those extremely asymmetrical episodes involving conflict, actors must agree to discuss divergencies in their goals or the episode will literally "break down." Since the congruence of episodic goals depends upon consensual agreement by actors, they are generated and will fluctuate as a function of actor choice. Suppose A initiates an episode with a business associate whom he has not seen for some time. A reasonable initial goal might be to share information concerning the progress of their respective careers. If, however, A's associate eventually discloses his recent divorce, it is likely that A will acquiesce and reorient the goal to one of shared sympathy and concern. Without necessarily making a conscious strategic choice, A's associate has tacitly invited A to redefine the goal of their episode. This offer, of course, need not be accepted by A. If A were to reply with *Yeah, well this seems to be the year for those things. Listen, I've got this new language-action paradigm. . . ."* no goal redefinition would occur. In all likelihood, the actors, if still speaking, would resort to the original goal or collectively seek a new, less threatening goal (for A).

The final and most important characteristic of episodes is the explanatory significance of their developmental structure. The centrality of episodes represents a conscious departure from those conceptions of communication which have elevated "rapid eye movements," head-nodding, even singular utterances and expressions to the status of central communication constructs and in so doing have left the meaning of those constructs in question. It is only the encompassing form of an episode which allows for the meaningful explanation of more particularistic communicative acts. Individuated acts and expressions have conventional reference; but these isolated references are seldom germane to the act's communicative meaning in an episode. For example, consider B's remark in insolation:

---

manifestations to the free, creative choice of one or more individuals. For analysis of issues related to emergence, see Robert Brown's "Comment" on J. O. Wisdom, "Situational Individualism and the Emergent Group-Properties," in *Explanation in the Behavioural Sciences*, pp. 297–305.

B: How the hell should I know?!

What communicative meaning can we attribute to this comment independent of an episode? Clearly, the act is a question probably uttered with at least a trace of anger. But suppose we "place" this act in the episodic fragment from which it was originally extracted.

A: Hey Tom, where are my car keys?
B: How the hell should I know?!
A: Because, cypherhead, you borrowed them thirty minutes ago to open the shed lock!

It could be argued that the structure of this fragment is what enables our attribution of communicative significance to occur. The problem with that interpretation is that A's final comment calls B's attention to a prior event outside the immediate fragment. It is, in other words, the total episodic structure in which this fragment occurred which determines its communicative significance. Lacking the explanatory force supplied by episodic structure, communication would simply be one more thing that individuals "do." And if this were true, communication would be reducible to perceptions, motives, or even the physiological movements.

Episodic form defines the structure of communication. This structure is composed not of surface stylistic variations, but rather of a recurrent analytic base. We now offer the workings of this analytic base—a series of structural imperatives to guide the developmental sequence of episodes. While these imperatives are fulfilled in different ways (ranging from explicit statement to implicit consent) their commonality admits rigor to the explanation of episodes.[12]

Episodes typically begin with an *initiation* imperative, wherein actors acknowledge one another's presence and their willingness to enact an episode. The optimal explicit form of this imperative is a greeting plus the expressed intention to consume time through communication. Consider the following phone conversation as an illustration:

A: Hi Tom.
B: Hi, what's up?
A: You busy?
B: Yeah, as a matter of fact I am, why?

In this episodic fragment, the greeting is present, but the expressed intent to engage in an episode is not mutual. The initiation imperative need not be explicitly uttered, but because of its logical necessity, it must be acknowledged.

A second imperative in episodic sequencing is *definition*. If actors have acknowledged a willingness to partake in an episode, they must next consensually agree upon what general type of episode will be enacted. If definitional agreement does not occur, some utterances may still be expressed, but they will appear cryptic and disconnected. Consider the following:

[12]Our structural imperatives define an "ideal type" episode. As such, they will not describe with empirical precision all possible episodic variations. For example, overheard conversations, misunderstood injunctions or attributions, the often confusing claims of unconscious discourse are among the atypical variations not highlighted by the imperatives. Structural imperatives function as norms from which these atypical deviations become understandable.

> A: Well, if an episode is a series of symbolic acts, the actual sequence of these acts must be specified, don't you think?
>
> B: Huh? Oh—I'm sorry—hang on a minute. Fisk is up and the score is tied in the 10th.

B's failure to agree immediately on the definitional character of the episode as suggested by A results in temporary confusion. Before the episode can proceed, A and B must somehow agree on the definition of their episode.

In the definitional imperative, three general types of episodes may be activated. Some episodes may be defined as *structurally* dominant. In these episodes, the formulary quality of the action defines the character of the episode, as in the case of formal introductions, turn-taking procedures, and the vast array of interpersonal rituals we enact daily. Second, episodes may be *informationally* dominant; in these instances, the disclosure of knowledge to accomplish purposes will distinguish the episode. Examples include lecture giving, essay-writing, bomb-defusing, and so on. Finally, there are *relationally* dominant episodes, in which the formation, confirmation, or undermining of personal relationships characterizes the episode. Examples here are intimacy and disclosure acts, demonstrations of power, distance, and the servicing of exclusively personal needs. While analytically distinct, it is quite possible for some composite of the above types to be defined and for the resultant interchange to run smoothly.

After initiating and defining an episode, a transitional phase of *rule-confirmation* occurs. The rule-confirmation imperative is loosely analogous to a group of acquaintances who sit down for a poker game. Before play begins, the participants will normally determine the typical house rules. Actors may assume that they share all important encounter-activated rules of propriety, they may experiment with alternative rules, or they may overtly confirm such sharing as an explicit part of the episode. The following example depicts one such process:

> A: You see, we could introduce this thing with a quote from McBowis and . . .
>
> B: McBowis! Are you crazy? I refuse to be associated with that turkey!
>
> A: Hey! Why don't you let me finish?
>
> B: Sorry. Go ahead. It's just that you have to draw the line somewhere.

In this example, A and B have stumbled upon a rule of appropriateness for turn-taking. Notice that initially A assumed that rule was shared by B, but B's interruptive *McBowis! Are you crazy?* alerted A to the fact that this rule was not shared. B's eventual acknowledgement of A's rule—namely, each actor should complete a thought, in informational episodes, before the other acts—allows this episode to continue.

Perhaps the central imperative of any episodic sequence involves *strategic development*. In this imperative, actors make communicative choices which are guided by the collective emergent goal(s) of each episode. This imperative is similar to the developmental phase of chess wherein choices in each game will generate a pattern constraining subsequent choice. The analogy is not exact, of course, because the terminal goals in chess are mutually exclusive, whereas most communication episodes orient actors to mutually compatible goals.

The understanding of strategic choice in episodes depends upon both chosen acts and unchosen alternatives. For each actor, the appropriate alternative moves the episode through structural imperatives toward the consensual goal. For the communication scholar, any adequate explanation of episodes will—as Harré notes—entail knowledge of *both* actual and potential choices.

The action possibilities being envisaged in the course of the cognitive process by which the actions of the episode are generated, are nearly always much richer than the behavioral sequence being produced, so that a good many possible actions in a situation of a given definition are discarded, and a good many opening moves aborted. For this reason alone, any theory which restricts itself to those behavioral concepts derived from observation of overt behavior of the action is clearly adequate, even if the action is properly understood in terms of its social meaning.[13]

The strategic development imperative, then, will both direct actors to the mutual fulfillment of emergent goals and alert scholars to the often ignored significance of strategic choice in communication.

The final episodic imperative is called *termination*. Termination occurs whenever the goal dominating the previous imperative is either accomplished, abandoned, or redefined. The definitive act of termination is to leave one another's presence. Yet this act—and it is a communicative choice—does not conform to the rules of propriety which permeate most encounters. The more typical conclusion of an episode signals the actors' mutual desire to conclude the episode, expresses satisfaction with the accomplishment of goals, and proposes the enactment of another episode at a future designated time. The following is an example of termination choices:

A: Well, I think we're finally locked in on these structural imperatives.
B: Yeah, they're getting better, but I'm so punchy I don't know whether to tie my shoe or go to the john.
A: Next week?
B: Sounds good. Why don't you tinker with the introduction and I'll wrestle with the Watergate example?
A: OK.

One final characteristic of the termination imperative is that it is not necessarily final. That is, the termination imperative may simply function as a transition to a new episode in the total encounter time-span the actors share together. When this occurs, the termination phase may simultaneously constitute the initiation phase of a new episode still to be defined.

Symbolic Acts Thus far, we have maintained that episodes—as rule-conforming, goal-oriented, patterns of communicative action—comprise the fundamental units of human communication. Further, as emergent constructs, episodes show no signs of being reducible to a "lower common denominator." Yet this irreducibility does not impede finer discriminations among episodic components. In fact, while the properties of more specific components are not sufficient to account for episodes in the sense of genetic or causal explanation, these components—symbolic acts—do perform important functions in the development of episodic structure.

Symbolic acts are verbal and/or non-verbal utterances which express intentionality. Three properties of symbolic acts clarify their recognizable features. First, symbolic acts possess *propositional* force. That is, such acts are recognized to have a certain sense and reference which is approximately equivalent to formal semantic meaning (e.g., *Tom is drunk.*) Second, symbolic acts manifest an

[13]Harré, p. 152.

expressive force in the act of performing them. Expressive force is an asituational function such as promising, threatening, commanding, asserting, questioning, which each act performs. A's symbolic act, *Go see if Tom is drunk,* adds a command to the propositional clause, *Tom is drunk.* Finally, symbolic acts exhibit *consequential* force, which is the effect the act has on another actor. Thus, the consequential force of A's, *Go see if Tom is drunk,* might be, *See for yourself, I'm busy.*

As characterized above, the forces of symbolic acts (i.e., propositional, expressive, and consequential forces) seem to parallel the Speech Act vocabulary of Austin and Searle (i.e., locutionary, illocutionary, and prelocutionary forces).[14] We depart from the Speech Act constructs because the approach they represent is insufficient as an explanation of communication. Specifically, Speech Act philosophy attempts to explain symbolic acts independent of the episodes in which they occur. The neglect of episodes has caused two problems in analysis. First, the expressive force of a symbolic act in isolation is not identical to the force of that act as it occurs in an episodic sequence. Second, the consequential force of an act often cannot be deduced from the expressive force of that act without the explanatory context of an episode.

A communicative understanding of symbolic acts demands an explanation of how such acts function in an episodic context. When placed in the context of an episode, symbolic acts acquire a fourth feature—namely, *episodic* force. Episodic force completes the explanation of symbolic acts by specifying the communicative function of acts within the overall sequential structure of an episode. The structure of our paradigm clearly implies that communicative meaning is not inherent in individual symbolic acts. Rather, the overall form of an episode determines the overall meaning of a symbolic act. An illustration will clarify this linkage.

> A: Could I have a drink of water?
> B: Mark, it's bedtime.
> A: But I'm thirsty.
> B: Really?
> A: Yes.
> B: Just a second, I'll get it.

In terms of its encounter-context, A is the senior author's son, B is the senior author, and it is 8:30 any evening, which is A's bedtime.

When placed in its encounter-context, two general rules emerge: the first is clearly a rule of propriety, while the second formalizes a tactical use of that propriety rule.

> R-1: Given question/requests for basic need fulfillment, it is not only polite, but obligatory as institutionally defined responsibility that parents fulfill such requests for their children.
> R-2: Given the recurrent fulfillment of expectations of institutional responsibility, the strategic option emerges of using R-1 as a means of achieving extrinsic goals.

---

[14]See, for example, J. L. Austin, *How To Do Things with Words* (Oxford: Oxford Univ. Press, 1962); John Searle, *Speech Acts: An Essay in the Philosophy of Language* (Cambridge: Cambridge Univ. Press, 1969).

Consider the first two symbolic acts in this episodic fragment. Clearly, the "explicit." expressive force of *Could I have a drink of water?* is a question/request. But notice that the consequential force of that act results in B's failure to acknowledge the request. Rather, B's subsequent act—*Mark, it is bedtime*—appears to be unrelated to *Could I have a drink of water?* Only if those first two symbolic acts are seen in terms of the larger episode in which they occur does the logical relationship between them emerge. *Mark, it's bedtime* follows logically from *Could I have a drink of water?* if and only if B construes the episodic force of *Could I have a drink of water?* to be roughly analogous to *I don't want to go to sleep yet*. In terms of the episode, then the "implicit," episodic force of *Could I have a drink of water?* is the assertion *I don't want to go to sleep yet*, while the "explicit" expressive force is a question/request. Moreover, the *I-don't-want-to-go-to-sleep-yet* interpretation seems non-idiosyncratic and known to all actors who are aware of the regulatory rules in this encounter-type.

We can specify more clearly how episodic force links symbolic acts to episodes. The consequential force of any symbolic act occurring in an episode follows logically from the episodic force of that act. In cases where the episodic force and the expressive force of an act are identical, the consequential force can be inferred directly. In cases where they are different—e.g., the "Indirect Delay Episode" above—the consequential force and the expressive force of an act becomes utterance "clues," and are pivotal to identifying the implicit, episodic force of the act. Such identification necessitates placing the act within the episode in which it is used. No amount of linguistic trickery can extract—independent of an episode—*I don't want to go to sleep yet* from *Could I have a drink of water?*

Episodic force applies not only to individual utterances, but also to the totality of an actor's communication at any given point in an episode. Thus, single sentences can have episodic force; several sentences and gestures by the same actor can have episodic force; even extended narratives by a given actor can exhibit such force. It is not the quantity or quality of symbolic acts which is important to the recovery of episodic force, but rather the function of the acts in an episodic sequence.

We have now presented a three part paradigm for explaining communication as language-action. We began by discussing contexts which functioned as vehicles for explanation. Contexts are composed of forms of life which define general criteria for meaningfulness and encounters which coorient actors and activate specific rules of propriety. We then argued that communication becomes manifest as episodes—strategically generated sequences of communicative action whose goals and form are conjointly created by two or more actors. Finally, symbolic acts were presented as the most elemental utterances from which actors direct episodes. Symbolic acts manifest propositional, expressive, and consequential force and acquire communicative meaning through episodic force.

II

We demonstrate the explanatory potential of the language-action paradigm by examining a portion of the Watergate transcripts. There are two reasons for this choice. First, the Watergate transcripts provide a complex set of "real" conversations—i.e., they were not constructed in order to be explained through our paradigm. Second, the transcripts provide a particularly difficult challenge insofar as they have been "explained" exhaustively by countless social critics. If our paradigm can shed new meaning on communicative events which are subtle and complex, and have already been overburdened with analysis, the usefulness of the language-action approach is illustrated.

The transcripts of Richard Nixon's less-than-finest hours have proved the major vehicle for public understanding and assessment of elite responsibility in the Watergate apocalypse. Moral and legal culpability of the nation's highest elected official has come to rest upon the meaning of his recorded communicative utterances. The transcripts have received a computer content analysis (to trace Nixon's changing psyche),[15] a dramatic analysis by a major playwright (to assess Nixon's personal authenticity),[16] an organizational decision-making critique (to determine management errors),[17] and—of course—the usual degree of moral indignation.[18] But paradoxically, the only persons analyzing the transcripts as communication are those people untrained as communication scholars; namely, journalists and congressional representatives. Their reading of the transcripts—and, in particular, Dean's relationship with Nixon—has become social knowledge. Not surprisingly, this knowledge is grounded in a purely narrative reading. Specifically, the March 21, 1973 conversation is seen as one more fragment in a chain of events—wherein Dean questions the viability of the containment strategy but remains ostensibly loyal to its execution.

The central difficulty with narrative readings is their lack of a conceptual framework sufficient to explain the meaning and propriety of the communication. Previous readings were forced to assume that the meaning of choices was "conventional," cumulative, or sentence-specific. By either assuming a conventional form of life, or ignoring this dimension, the differential meaning of the action could not be understood. Lack of acquaintance with encounter-sensitive rules of propriety prohibits the understanding of alternative communicative possibilities. By failing to consult the developmental structure of episodes, narrative readings ignore the episodic force of symbolic acts. Finally, the traditional interpretations, lacking the normative implications of the language-action paradigm, cannot offer ethical judgments as a logical outcome of analysis, and are left with ad hoc or a priori indignation.

Our own analysis unfolds in four phases. First, from the overall form of life and encounters which informed each episode, we extract the operative rules of propriety. Second, these rules underscore two episodic fragments which assume critical importance in explaining the transcripts. Third, we examine Dean and Nixon's strategic choices through their developing episodic form. Finally, we offer a normative assessment of the primary actors—Nixon and Dean.

If the transcripts are meaningful communication, the actors must acknowledge a recurrently fulfilling form of life, which—in turn—constrains potential communicative choice. Form of life is first of all knowledge. We assume that the actors in Watergate conversations shared knowledge of a differential social world characterized by (1) hierarchy as fact, (2) a personal relationship to power, and (3) structural definitions of self. Such attributions cannot be proved through discrete

[15]Geoffrey Stokes, "A Computer Analysis of the Watergate Tapes," Harpers, Oct. 1974, p. 6.

[16]Arthur Miller, "The Limited Hang-out; A Drama of Nixon as Anti-Hero," Harpers, September, 1974, p. 13.

[17]Dennis S. Gouran, "The Watergate Coverup: Its Dynamics and Its Implications," Speech Monographs 43 (1976), 176–187.

[18]See, for instance, the commentary of journalists, Bob Woodward, Carl Bernstein, Haynes Johnson, and Lawrence Meyer in The Presidential Transcripts, in conjunction with the staff of The Washington Post (New York: Dell, 1974).

instances of discourse (since they inform the interpretation of each instance). But if our assumption is consistent with an insightful reading, the shared knowledge of a differential social world will structure each important conversation. Consider, for example, the three attributes of social knowledge implied in the following:[19]

> D. The resources that have been put against this whole investigation to date are really incredible. It is truly a larger investigation than was conducted against the after inquiry of the JFK assassination.
> P. Oh.
> D. Good statistics supporting the finding.
> H. Isn't that ridiculous—this silly thing.
> P. Yes (*expletive deleted*). Goldwater put it in context when he said "(*expletive deleted*) everybody bugs everybody else. You know that."
> D. That was priceless.
> P. It happens to be totally true. . . .[20]

In this conversation, Dean, Haldeman, and the president, while acknowledging the empirical significance of the Watergate inquiry, dismiss this significance because of their personal relationship to a hierarchically structured social world.

Form of life's second dimension—its aesthetics—reveals a communication pattern of problem-reassurance. Furthermore, this pattern is both expected and fulfilled by actors in most major episodes. Consider the following array of typical examples:

> P. (*on phone to Mitchell*). This thing is just one of those side issues and a month later everybody looks back and wonders what all the shooting was about.[21]

One episode later:

> P. We are all in it together. This is a war. We take a few shots and it will be over. We will give them a few shots and it will be over. Don't worry. I wouldn't want to be on the other side right now. Would you?[22]

On March 13, 1973:

> D. Well one thing, the saturation level of the American People on this story is cracking. The saturation level in this city is getting pretty high now, and they can't take too much more of this stuff.
> P. Think not?
> D. There is nothing really new coming out.
> P. I talked with some kid and he said I don't think that anybody incidently would care about anybody infiltrating the peace movement that was demonstrating against the President, particularly on the war in Vietnam. Do you think so?
> D. No![23]

---

[19]Consistent with *The Washington Post*'s notations, subsequent references were codified as follows: John Dean (D); Richard Nixon (P); John Erlichman (E); and John Haldeman (H).

[20]*The Presidential Transcripts,* p. 33.

[21]Ibid., p. 36.

[22]Ibid., p. 37.

[23]Ibid., p. 79.

Finally, form of life exerts institutional constraint through a decision-making *praxis* in which roles are differentiated, and the chief role—that of executive—remains "above the battle." Consider the following instance:

> P. It will be somewhat serious but the main thing, of course, is also the isolation of the President.
>
> D. Absolutely! Totally true![24]

This institutional dimension of form of life suggests that there is a particular hierarchy of meaningfulness shared only by heads of state. Since the role of chief executive is asituational, all occupants are protected as well as governed by its exclusivity of meaning. Consider, as a provocative exemplar, Nixon's peculiar loyalty to Lyndon Johnson:

> H. I have some stuff too—on the bombing incident and too in the bombing halt stay.
>
> P. The difficulty with using it, of course, is it reflects on Johnson. It it weren't for that, I would use it. Is there any way we could use it without using his name?[25]

Since actors cannot share all of their world at once, form of life is actualized within concrete encounters. This actualization takes the form of regulatory encounter rules. From the overall context of meaning generated by placing the transcripts within their form of life, we now explicate the rules of propriety implicit in each prospective encounter.

We identify three central rules. Encounter rules determine that portion of form of life knowledge which is appropriate to explicit communication. In the Watergate transcripts, the rule is:

> R-1: P, as a cooperative actor on a crisis management team, must be presumed to share the same knowledge as other institutional actors. But the knowledge P is presumed to have can never be explicity articulated; for to do so would legally implicate him.[26]

The aesthetic dimension of form of life generates a recurring pattern of expectations. Within the Watergate conversations, this aesthetic pattern yields a rule of problem-reassurance.

> R-2: Information-sharing episodes in crisis management must produce strategic choices which (a) generate practical solutions and (b) reaffirm the eventual solubility of the problem.

From the institutional dimension of form of life, the rule is:

---

[24]Ibid., p. 63.

[25]Ibid., p. 34.

[26]No method could determine—beyond a reasonable doubt—that the President and his aides committed crimes. It could be argued that the assumption of legal culpability does not derive from our method. However, it is not our purpose to determine guilt or innocence; that is for the courts and history to decide. We are able to deduce that certain knowledge, whatever its character is continually and cooperatively withheld from the President. And this discovery prompts any serious observer to search for an explanation—including that of legal culpability.

R-3: Because of his defined leadership role, P must make, and assume responsibility for, all final decisions regarding solutions.

These three rules define the norms of propriety tacitly accepted by all actors in the Watergate episodes. The wary reader will detect, within these rules, an important paradox. According to R-3, Nixon must legitimate all final decisions concerning solutions to the problems emerging from Watergate. Yet, according to R-1, the knowledge which must be presumed in order to generate effective solutions may never be specifically articulated in Nixon's presence.

These rules explain important episodes. More specifically, they accentuate entire episodes or more specific symbolic acts within episodes which reflect a significant departure from the rules. For if a departure occurs, it will logically point to an important shift in the communicative action.

On March 21, 1973, John Dean performed an unusual series of acts; cumulatively, he violated R-1 and R-2, redefining the episode from one of information-sharing to an explicit power relationship, and—most important (because it has never been acknowledged)—he violated implicitly R-3. The following text encapsulates Dean's tour de force performance:

> D. The reason that I thought we ought to talk this morning is because in our conversations, I have the impression that you don't know everything I know and it makes it very difficult for you to make judgments that only you can make on some of these things and I thought that—
> P. In other words, I have to know why you feel that we shouldn't unravel something.
> D. Let me give you my overall first.
> P. In other words, your judgment as to where it stands, and where it will go.
> D. I think that there is no doubt about the seriousness of the problem we've got. We have a cancer within, close to the Presidency, that is growing. . . .[27]

Dean took knowledge which was an implicit part of Nixon's form of life, and then explicitly articulated it, thus violating the understood sanction of R-1 to keep that knowledge tacit. With respect to R-2, Dean violated the aesthetic episodic expectation that actors be reassured as to the solubility of problems. Certainly, Dean's last comment has defined the problem as terminal through his famous cancer metaphor. And, from the language-action perspective, once Dean has violated R-1 and R-2, he must logically violate R-3. Nixon cannot be expected to exercise a leadership position of objectivity—he cannot remain above the battle—once he has been legally implicated in criminal acts. Since Dean has just legally implicated him, Nixon's own ability to make executive decision (i.e., decisions which do something more than simply protect the individual within the role) is exposed to serious question.

The clinical ingenuity of Dean's tactical choices is apparent. In his first statement, Dean has used the very inconsistency between R-1 and R-3 as rationale for this episode: *I have the impression that you don't know everything I know and it makes it very difficult for you to make judgments that only you can make.* Now Nixon (as he acknowledges elsewhere in another connection) is "not dumb." His responses to Dean are very guarded—understandably so—since he wishes the knowledge to remain tacit and unexpressed. Dean simply sidesteps the first comment (*Let me give you my overall first*) and consciously ignores Nixon's last poignant attempt to preserve ambiguity, only to launch his celebrated diagnosis.

[27]*The Presidential Transcripts,* pp. 98–99.

A little-noticed dimension of this exchange is that Dean, by violating all three rules, has irretrievably broken with the institutional form of life and elevated himself to a position of considerable power. Previously, when Dean reassured Nixon (R-2) as to the solubility of Watergate problems, Nixon necessarily maintained control over the decision-making process. Now, by violating all three rules and rendering Nixon's position partisan, Dean has taken the power initiative and can himself define—if not the cure for the cancer—at least the time span for remedial care.

With these rule violations and episodic redefinitions in mind, a less dramatic fragment of the transcripts assumes greater clarity.

> D. Well, I see in this conversation what I have talked about before. They do not ultimately solve what I see as a grave problem of a cancer growing around the Presidency. This creates another problem. It does not clean the problem out.
>
> P. Well,
>
> E. But doesn't it permit the President to clean it out at such time as it does come up? By saying, "Indeed, I relied on it. And now this later thing turns up and I don't condone that. And if I had known that before, obviously I would have run it down."
>
> P. Here's what John is to do. You really think you've got to clean the cancer out now, right?
>
> D. Yes sir.
>
> P. How would you do that? Do you see another way? Without breaking down our executive privilege.
>
> D. I see a couple of ways to do it.
>
> P. You certainly don't want to do it at the Senate, do you?
>
> D. No sir. I think that would be an added trap.
>
> P. That's the worst thing. Right. We've got to do it. We aren't asked to do it.
>
> D. You've got to do it, to get credit for it. That gets you above it. As I see it, naturally you'll get hurt and I hope we can find the answer to that problem.[28]

Dean's first series of acts affirm his position of power as well as his announced intentions to share information which will implicate Nixon. Dean says specifically that what he is about to say he has said before. In response to Erlichman's attempt to reconfirm R-1 (by now, an impossibility), Dean's final acts—particularly, *You've got to do it, to get credit for it,* and *. . . naturally you'll get hurt and I hope we can find the answer to that problem*—perform a dual strategic function. First, Dean is clearly acknowledging the contradiction between rules; and second, he is extending the implications of this contradiction. Nixon will be unable to solve this problem without knowledge which can only implicate him. For Nixon's part, he seems reduced to expressive questions which function episodically as weak commands—commands of someone who has lost power in a relationship—e.g., *You certainly don't want to do it at the Senate, do you?*[29]

The strategic subtlety of Dean's communication is worthy of some attention. Consider the indirection with which Dean implicates Nixon. In the presence of others, Dean does not use explicit information. He continues superficially to honor R-1 (which he has violated in principle) by using metaphor (e.g., *cancer*) and the indirect pronoun *it*. Hence, while Dean has violated the sense of R-1, his

---

[28]Ibid., pp. 147–148.

[29]Of course, Nixon made the final decision to authorize protection payments to Watergate conspirators thereby recording his awesome responsibility for the outcome. However, the ability to determine the consequences of *any* subsequent decisions rested with Dean; in this sense, he had gained a power initiative.

strategic action is to honor the form of the rule by implicating Nixon through the same indirect means as have always been used in the Watergate episodes.

If the March 21 conversation marks an irretrievable departure from the rules governing executive decision-making, then some assessment of responsibility is in order. No actor emerges as a moral giant from the Watergate episodes. What distinguishes the other actors from Dean, however, is their strict adherence to encounter rules which are—in principle—contradictory.[30] Furthermore, these rules would not be opposed were it not for the moral and legal incrimination of knowledge presupposed in R-1. Whatever his real motives, then, the actual communicative choices of Dean did render manifest a latent contradiction in encounter rules, thus forcing a decision of momentous ethical import.

Applying the language-action paradigm to the Watergate transcripts, we have discovered both the active form of life and encounter-sensitive rules of propriety. More important, the rules were found to be self-contradictory, rendering communicative decision-making increasingly difficult. John Dean, by violating the operable rules, at once sealed the ultimate fate of the Watergate episodes and at the same time defined himself as the actor with the controlling power. This explanation was not directly apprehensible without the language-action paradigm.

III

We have set forth a language-action paradigm for human communication and demonstrated its explanatory potential with the Watergate transcripts. We conclude by discussing several implications—theoretical and methodological— which follow from our perspective. These implications are already being implemented by communication scholars.[31]

The language-action paradigm reaffirms the centrality of language (i.e., both verbal and nonverbal code systems) to communication theory. This centrality has long been noted by communication scholars, but rarely have the notations been translated into meaningful theory.[32] In part, this is because linguists have been more interested in the grammatical structure of language than in its communicative function.[33]

[30]Jürgen Habermas, *Legitimation Crisis* (Boston: Beacon Press, 1975), p. 27.

[31]In addition to Hawes and Hofsinger, see Donald Cushman and Gordon C. Whiting, "An Approach to Communication Theory: Toward Consensus on Rules," *The Journal of Communication,* 22 (1972), 217–238; Lawrence W. Rosenfield, "A Game Model of Human Communication," Minnesota Symposium in Speech Communication, 1968; Lawrence W. Rosenfield, Laurie S. Hayes, and Thomas S. Frentz, *The Communication Experience* (Boston: Allyn & Bacon, 1976); Robert E. Sanders, "The Question of a Paradigm for the Study of Speech-using Behavior," *OJS* 59 (1973), 1–10. Varying implications of our language-action paradigm are debated by Hawes and Grossman/O'Keefe in Colloquy." *OJS,* 61 (1975), 195–219. From our perspective, this exchange can best be understood as both an information sharing and power relationship episode.

[32]One of the clearest expressions of the centrality of language comes from the Report of the New Orleans Conference on Research and Instructional Development. The initial recommendation of the conference was that "Spoken symbolic interaction is the central force of study in the speech-communication area." *Conceptual Frontiers in Speech-Communication,* eds. Robert J. Kibler and Larry L. Barker (New York: Speech Association of America, 1969), p. 18.

[33]For a penetrating analysis of the conceptual inadequacy of even the grammatical approaches, see Jerry L. Morgan, "Some Remarks on the Nature of Sentences," in *Papers from the Parasession on Functionalism* (Chicago: Univ. of Chicago Press, 1975), pp. 433–447.

However, if communication is viewed as language-action, a central facet of language structure emerges as an analogous feature of language function—namely, a duality of level. For some time, linguists have noted that the "surface" grammar of a sentence rarely reflects the "underlying" grammar from which sentence meaning is derived.[34] These two levels of grammatical structure explain the phenomena of both synonymy (multiple surface forms, one underlying meaning) and ambiguity (one surface form, multiple underlying meanings). When language is viewed through the expressive and episodic force of symbolic acts, an analogous duality of level arises. We have argued, for instance, that the "explicit," expressive force of a symbolic act is often modified and changed by the "implicit," episodic force of that act in an episodic sequence. And if this is true, then the concepts of synonymy and ambiguity should have special import viewed communicatively rather than linguistically. We might ask, for example, what episodic conditions must hold for a given symbolic act to be communicatively ambiguous—or synonymous with another act?

Several research strategies follow from this regenerated centrality of language. Initially, it is essential to identify and formalize the language-action rules which link the expressive force of a symbolic act to the episodic force of that act. Methods of formalization have already been suggested by linguists examining language in context.[35] Moreover, since the pattern of any episode is a sequence of logically related symbolic acts, specific formalization of that patterning seems to be another problem for language-action research. Our structural imperatives, for example, while providing a first approximation of episodic patterning, need refinement and specificity.[36]

Also, the language-action paradigm invites a participant/observation methodology.[37] If actors' decisions regarding strategies as well as the reasons supplied in justification of the actual choices are an essential part of explaining communication, then, the communication scholar must gain access to these "data." Harré provides both evidence for this alternative as well as a warning of the consequences should the point be lost.

[34]See for example Noam Chomsky, "Problems in Linguistics," in *Explanation in the Behavioural Sciences*, pp. 425–451. Although certain modifications have occurred since Chomsky's initial formulations, his distinctions typify the contrast we are discussing here.

[35]See David Gordon and George Lakoff, "Conversational Postulates," in *Papers From the Seventh Regional Meeting, Chicago Linguistics Society* (Chicago: Univ. of Chicago Press, 1971), pp. 63–84; Robin Lakoff, "Language in Context," *Language*, 48 (1972), 907–927; Robin Lakoff, "The Logic of Politeness," in *Papers from the Ninth Regional Meeting, Chicago Linguistics Society* (Chicago: Univ. of Chicago Press, 1973), pp. 292–305; Ann Weiser, "How To Not Answer a Question: Purposive Devices in Conversational Strategy," in *Papers from the Eleventh Regional Meeting, Chicago Linguistics Society* (Chicago: Univ. of Chicago Press, 1975), pp. 649–660.

[36]For a discussion of the rules which generate different episodic types, see Thomas S. Frentz, "A Generative Approach to Episodic Structure," unpublished manuscript, University of Southern California, 1976.

[37]For both a description and justification of this method, see Severyn T. Bruyn, "The Methodology of Participant Observation," *Human Organization*, 21 (1963), 224–235; William Filstead, *Qualitative Methodology; Firsthand Involvement with the Social World* (Chicago: Markham, 1970); Janice Rushing, "Participant Observation: A Neglected Method for Small Groups Research," paper presented at the Western Speech Communication Association's Regional Convention, Newport Beach, California, November 1974; Wilson.

> How then is human behavior generated, particularly that behavior that can be given meaning as social action? Is it a series of conditioned responses to the state of controlling variables? This idea is both factually false and methodologically disastrous. We all know that in fact what happens in certain paradigm cases is something like this: people consider various alternative actions and examine their consequences by an imaginative rehearsal of episodes. In light of this rehearsal and their intuitions about the propriety of each form the episode might take, a particular social action is chosen. The effects of the action are carefully monitored, and rapid modifications of the plan are usually made as the action of the episode unfolds.[38]

Since there are no valid a priori means of tapping actors' pre-action rehearsals, it is imperative that the researcher experience this rehearsal so that its import can become part of the explanation.

How does a participant/observation methodology affect the communication scholar? Initially, the approach eschews the usual forms of behavioral control. As Wilson notes,

> If social action is taken to be an interpretive process, such explanations cannot be reconstructed meaningfully in deductive form but rather must be viewed as imputations of purposes and circumstances to actors that render their actions intelligible to the observer.[39]

Wilson's message is that social researchers must begin *being* subjects as well as *treating* objects; they must both experience and reflect upon the communicative events to be explained. In addition, the communication scholar must develop an entirely new attitude concerning research. Objectivity must be subordinated to a synthesis of sensitive experience and thoughtful reflection as the basis for an adequate theory of communication.[40]

Finally, our language-action paradigm allows the judgment of communication as a necessary complement to explanation. Judgment in communication has traditionally been the domain of rhetorical criticism. However, as our discussion of the Watergate transcripts indicates, the language-action paradigm provides a critical perspective for both explaining and judging interpersonal communication as well. For if communication is essentially normative action, then any complete explanation of such action must include at least a prudential assessment of an actor's choices. And that critical assessment will depend on the scholar/critic's own norms. Put somewhat differently, the language-action perspective enables the theorist to discuss values and the contingency of moral choice within the usual context of description and explanation.

Adding judgment to theory construction creates an important new priority in communication. The communication scholar must wrestle with the synthesis between the scientific (observable action) and aesthetic (strategic choice) dimensions of communication. Although particularistic language-action studies imply this synthesis, our paradigm imparts its urgency. For to focus on one of these dimensions to the exclusion of the other would not only be highly unfortunate; it would be logically incomplete as well.

[38]Harré, p. 151.
[39]Wilson, pp. 705–706.
[40]Rosenfield, Hayes, and Frentz, pp. 7–11.

JIMMY CARTER AND *PLAYBOY:* A SOCIOLINGUISTIC PERSPECTIVE ON STYLE

Martha Solomon

No single incident in the 1976 presidential campaign seemed to draw more attention or excite more comment than Jimmy Carter's interview with Robert Scheer for *Playboy.* Particularly troublesome for Carter were his comments about lustful meditations and his blunt remarks about President Lyndon Johnson's deceit. Yet, despite the concrete evidence that Carter's rhetoric had gone awry and despite the guesses hazarded by commentators on the impact of the statements, no thorough attempt has been made to examine the interview as a whole and to explain why the remarks generated so much controversy.

The goal of the present study is to analyze and explain Carter's remarks within the context of the interview to isolate the factors which made his comments unsettling to so many people. Essentially, the article will contend that the remarks (1) represented a striking stylistic contrast to the rest of the interview and, thus, are an example of stylistic variation (code-switching) in the context of the interview; (2) involved the use of a stylistic level felt by many to violate norms of linguistic behavior appropriate both for a presidential candidate and for the personal image Carter sought to convey; and (3) were a response to a complex rhetorical situation marked by several conflicting elements. The consideration of style here will focus on the analysis of grammar, vocabulary, and syntax.

Style and Appropriateness

Stylistic decorum has always been viewed as an essential ingredient in successful communication. In classical rhetoric appropriateness of style to the audience, topic, situation, and speaker was one key consideration. Aristotle, for example, listed appropriateness as one virtue of style. Cicero in *Orator* not only outlined three levels of style but also emphasized that the style of a speech should be apt for audience, speaker, and object.[1] However, classical rhetoricians were interested in style only in the context of formal oral presentation and focused on stylistic variation primarily as ornamentation.

Modern sociolinguistics, in contrast, concentrates on the social implications of stylistic variation. From this viewpoint, style—in the sense of choices about diction, syntax, tone, and even content—is an important ingredient in discourse of

From *Quarterly Journal of Speech* 64 (April 1978): 173–82. Used by permission of author and the Speech Communication Association.

Ms. Solomon is assistant professor of speech communication, Auburn University.

[1]Aristotle, *Rhetoric,* Book III: chs. 2 and 3; Cicero, *Orator,* v. 20–vi, 21; xx, 69–xxiii, 75. Cf., also, Cicero, *De Oratore,* Book III.

all levels, and stylistic variation is crucial in signalling, maintaining, and changing the social relationships which exist between the participants.[2] Each individual possesses a linguistic repertoire from which to choose the level of style best suited to a particular situation.[3] As Hymes notes, "No normal person, and no normal community, is limited in repertoire to a single variety of code, to an unchanging motonony which would preclude the possibility of indicating respect, insolence, mock-seriousness, humor, role-distance, etc. by switching from one code variety to another."[4] When individuals within a speech community change the style of their discourse in different situations or with different companions, they are "code-switching," which may involve alternation between two distinct languages, two dialects of the same language, or simply different levels of style in the same dialect.[5] One's "communicative competence," which is acquired quite early, dictates the choice and variation of different codes to suit various contexts.[6] There are two basic varieties of code-switching; metaphorical alternations, which are used for emphasis with a conversation and which do not indicate a change in the relationship between participants, and situational variations, which signal a change in social relationships.[7] For example, at a faculty cocktail party among a group of friends one might switch to a French accent to accentuate a point in telling a story (a metaphorical code switch), but when the dean joins the group all participants may use a more formal style (a situational switch). Situational code switching will be the focus of this study.

The decision about which code from a repertoire an individual should use is determined by that person's relationships with the other participants and by the situation itself. In particular, the type of group in which the individual is involved is one important situational factor in determining code choice. Sociological theory suggests two basic types of groups, differing in both physical and social characteristics, which embody distinctive relationships and, thus, mandate the use of different linguistic styles. Each person belongs to several groups of both types and varies linguistic style to suit the group context. The chart below

[2]Pier Paolo Giglioli, "Introduction," in *Language and Social Context,* ed. Pier Paolo Giglioli (Middlesex, Eng.: Penguin Books, 1972), pp. 8–17; H. A. Gleason, Jr., *Linguistics and English Grammar* (New York: Holt, Rinehart and Winston, 1965), pp. 356–61. Moreover, Howard Giles and Peter F. Powesland have proposed that individuals through speech sometimes modify or disguise their personae to make themselves more acceptable to the individual addressed. *Speech Style and Social Evaluation* (London: Academic Press, 1975), pp. 154–66.

[3]Cf. Basil Bernstein, *Class, Codes and Control: Theoretical Studies towards a Sociology of Language* (London: Routledge & Kegan Paul, 1971), I, 76–94. Although beyond the scope of this article, Bernstein's analysis of elaborated and restricted codes and his discussion of the linguistic dimensions of socialization are important elements in modern sociolinguistic theory. Also, see Basil Bernstein, "A Sociolinguistic Approach to Socialization; with some Reference to Educability," in *Directions in Sociolinguistics: The Ethnography of Communication,* ed. John J. Gumperz and Dell Hymes (New York: Holt, Rinehart and Winston, 1972), pp. 465–97, for a brief treatment of this question.

[4]Dell Hymes, "Models of the Interaction of Language and Social Setting," *Journal of Social Issues,* 23, No. 2 (1967), 9.

[5]Dell Hymes, *Foundations in Sociolinguistics: An Ethnographic Approach* (Philadelphia: Univ. of Pennsylvania Press, 1974), p. 103.

[6]Giglioli, "Introduction," pp. 15–16. "Linguistic competence," in contrast, involves only knowledge about the rules of the code itself and does not include notions about alternation between codes or stylistic levels.

[7]J. A. Fishman, "The Sociology of Language," in Giglioli, pp. 48–51.

	Characteristics		Examples
	Physical	*Social*	
Primary Group	Proximity Smallness Long in duration	Common goals Intrinsic valuations Extensive knowledge of participants Freedom Informal controls Essential solidarity	Friendships Family
Secondary Group	Distance Large size Short duration	Disparate goals Extrinsic valuation Partial knowledge about participants Constraints Formal controls Essential power	Officer-subordinate Employer-employee Performer-spectator

summarizes the distinctions.[8] Applying these concepts to speech acts, Gumperz notes that in primary groups participants engage in *personal linguistic interactions,* which display an informal style in which each participant relates to each other as an individual. In secondary groups, by contrast, participants are involved in *transactional linguistic interactions,* which require a more formal style since each participant reacts in terms of role and status instead of individual personality. In transactional linguistic interaction the participants "in a sense suspend their individuality and act by virtue of their status . . . as salesmen, customers, bank tellers, physicians, rather than as Tom Hansen or Inger Stensen. Each society has definite norms of behavioral and linguistic etiquette which attach to these statuses. Regardless of their individual personalities, occupants of such statuses are expected to conform to these norms. . . . To deviate from the expected behavior . . . would be to risk defeating the goals of the interaction."[9]

Joos more explicitly outlines five levels of style which reflect different degrees of social intimacy and range from close personal contact to quite detached and formal interactions. He concentrates his analysis of speech on the features of

Type of Interaction	Level of Style	Personal Relationship
Personal	Intimate Casual	Extremely close Friendly, relaxed
Personal-Transactional	Consultative	Cordial, somewhat restrained
Transactional	Deliberative Oratorical	Detached, little personal interaction Formal, no personal interaction

[8]Adapted from Kingsley Davis, *Human Society* (New York: Macmillan, 1948 and 1949), p. 306.

[9]John J. Gumperz, "On the Ethnology of Linguistic Change," in *Sociolinguistics: Proceedings of the UCLA Sociolinguistics Conference, 1964,* ed. William Bright (The Hague: Mouton, 1966), p. 35, Gumperz' article concerns interaction in a Scandinavian community, but the concepts are applicable outside that context.

grammar, vocabulary, and syntax which distinguish each level.[10] The two "informal" levels outlined by Joos involve personal linguistic interactions, while the two most "formal" levels embody transactional linguistic exchanges. The middle category, the consultative level, mixes elements of both. The chart immediately above summarizes these concepts.

In essence, modern sociolinguistic theory broadens and deepens traditional concepts of stylistic variation. It suggests that each individual has a repertoire of stylistic codes and that choice and use of a particular level of style signals the nature of the relationship between and among the participants and reflects the nature of the situation in which they are communicating. Appropriateness, thus, is defined in terms of context and relationships. The use of a particular level of style or code-switching from one level to another is appropriate (or decorous) if both (all) parties feel comfortable with the choice. If, however, one person chooses a level of style which is perceived as too formal or too casual by the other participant(s), the result is divisive for the relationship, and the ethos of the speaker making the inappropriate linguistic choice is weakened. Moreover, movement from one code or level to another is effective and desirable only if it mirrors accurately the relationship between or among the participants and suits the roles through which they are relating to each other.

Stylistic Variation Within the Interview

To understand the impact of Carter's most publicized *Playboy* remarks, one must see them in the context of the interview as a whole.[11] The comments were, in fact, addenda to the interview proper and were made after the formal session ended as Carter was leaving the room. The remainder of the interview has all the characteristics of the consultative style and seems to exemplify a transactional linguistic interaction between interviewer and respondent. Carter's diction, for example, revealed care and precision. Phrases and words such as "contrivances and subterfuges" (64), "simplistic answers" (64), "quizzical" (66), and "inexorable" (71) suggest a rather formal tone in which the speaker was paying considerable attention to his language. Moreover, the topic choices, which focused largely on the influence of Carter's background and philosophy on policy decisions, also indicated a professional orientation rather than a personal one. Carter seemed to respond as a candidate rather than as a private individual.

Even the personal remarks, which were sprinkled throughout, were actually nonintimate. They expressed almost stock feelings and reactions which, though apparently genuine, entailed no embarrassment for the discloser. For example, he spoke openly of his relationship with his family and acknowledged unhesitatingly and with unruffled calm his strong religious bent (66, 68, 84). One feels he had practiced these responses before and that what he conveyed in his answers showed only one side of his personality, the side which he intended for media consumption. For example, in response to a question about whether he prayed twenty-five times a day, Carter adroitly managed to down-play the emotional

[10]Martin Joos, *The Five Clocks* (New York: Harcourt, Brace & World, 1961, 1962, 1967), pp. 3–41.

[11]To simplify citations, numbers in parentheses refer to pages in Robert Scheer, "Playboy Interview: Jimmy Carter," *Playboy,* Nov. 1976, pp. 63–86, or to Scheer's article "Jimmy, We Hardly Know Y'all," in the same issue, pp. 91–98, 186–94.

overtones and admitted that when something was "a little disconcerting," if he felt "trepidation," he said "a brief silent prayer" that he might be able to understand the other person's feelings. It was not, he admitted, "conscious or formal. It's just a part of my life" (66). When asked if he and his wife had the usual trouble in adjusting to marriage, Carter agreed that initially they did but had managed to cope. His last statement in that response revealed the rather pat nature of his personal disclosures: "So, to summarize, years ago we had a lot of quarrels—none serious, particularly—but now we don't" (84).

In essence, the reader, learning little about Carter's thoughts and feelings, begins to sense a lack of spontaneity. Scheer hinted at this controlled tone when he noted that one remark made by Carter as the interview began *"was a flattering opening shot, but probably more canny and less casual than it sounded."* (64). Throughout his article "Jimmy, We Hardly Know Ya'll," which followed the interview and conveyed his personal impression of Carter, Scheer emphasized the controlled tone of Carter's campaign. He termed Carter "the most guarded presidential candidate in decades" (91), and added, "The problem is that one's judgments about Carter are necessarily fragmented, because we have no sense of the depth of the man. . . . Carter's people are good at their business, so good that they've managed to cover the hard and interesting edges of the man. What we see is the packaging"(92). Carter, himself, revealed how wary he was in response to a question by Scheer about how he felt the media were covering the issues of the campaign: "Issues? The local media are interested all right, but the national news media have absolutely no interest in issues *at all.* . . . But the traveling press have zero interest in any issue unless it's a matter of making a mistake. What they're looking for is a 47-second argument between me and another candidate or something like that. There's nobody in the back of this plane who would ask an issue question unless he thought he could trick me into some crazy statement" (66). In essence, the initial part of the interview mirrored Carter's suspicion of the media. His guarded responses indicated an awareness not only of the image he was trying to build but also of the possible misinterpretation of his personality by the press. He reacted as a respondent to an interviewer in a transactional interaction, employing largely the consultative level of style.

The last section of the interview had a distinctly different tone. Carter obviously switched codes to a more personal and informal style. The code switch evident here was a situational alternation in response to a different social relationship between the two participants.[12] Carter moved from a detached, deliberate tone to a more intimate self-disclosing mode. Scheer characterized the difference succinctly when he labeled the final segment *"an open and revealing monolog that occurred because we happened to ask him one last question on a topic about which he'd become impatient and frustrated"* (64). Scheer also noted that the monologue *"grew in intensity as he made his final points"* (86). Both the diction and personal content are evidence of a code switch to a more informal style. In contrast to his earlier rather formal language, Carter moved to colloquial expressions: "screws," "shacks up with," "lying, cheating and distorting the truth" (86). Interestingly, earlier in the interview Carter had spoken of these

---

[12]Cf. Jan-Petter Blom and John J. Gumperz, "Social Meaning in Linguistic Structure; Code-Switching in Norway," ed. Gumperz and Hymes, pp. 424–26, for a full discussion of situational vs. metaphorical code-switching. Interestingly, Carter used a metaphorical code switch in the interview to characterize his opponents' stereotyped picture of him (77).

same matters but with more cautious language, a point which will be more fully developed below. Moreover, his choice of an example also revealed the movement to a more personal style, for his remarks about lust provided an intimate insight into his personality and thoughts (86). For once Carter seemed to respond as an individual rather than simply as a candidate being interviewed. Since Scheer's perceptions and a brief look at Carter's language and content suggested that the final segment of the interview had a different tone and involved a switching of stylistic level from the earlier part, one must question whether the shift was appropriate in terms of Carter's rhetorical goals.

Code-Switching and Rhetorical Appropriateness

Two separate standards are used to judge the linguistic decorum of a public figure: (1) the standards of expectations the public has about behavior for the role the person is seeking to fill, and (2) the expectations the public develops about the personal image the individual is trying to project. Thus, we expect significantly different types of rhetorical behavior from a Supreme Court Justice than we do from a local justice of the peace. We expect the language used and the ways the issues are addressed by a Supreme Court Justice to reflect greater sophistication and broader knowledge than we anticipate from a local political figure. Similarly, we evaluate rhetoric in terms of the political image the person hopes to convey. Bella Abzug's image, therefore, mandates a different rhetorical stance than would Margaret Chase Smith's because each seeks to project a unique picture of herself to the public. Carter's rhetoric in the final section of his interview seems indecorous in the light of each of these standards.

Carter's remark about Johnson is interesting rhetorically because it offended party-line Democrats, who would normally react positively to statements of the party nominee. Instead of identifying himself with one of the party's past major leaders, Carter alienated himself from that image. "But I don't think I would *ever* take on the same frame of mind that Nixon or Johnson did—lying, cheating, and distorting the truth"(86). Earlier in the interview Carter had made substantially the same statement, but the wording was more discreet. In reference to lying he had said, "it's just a matter that evolved as a habit over several administrations. There was a governmental consciousness to deal in secrecy, to exclude the American people, to mislead them with false statements and sometimes outright lies. Had the American people been told the facts from the beginning by Eisenhower, Kennedy, MacNamara, Johnson, Kissinger and Nixon, I think there would have been different decisions made in our Government" (70). The blunter remark at the conclusion of the interview offended party regulars' sense of acceptable political rhetoric, while the earlier statement was less objectionable for several reasons. First, in the later statement Johnson was charged personally with lying, while in the earlier remark the lying was a governmental "habit." Also, in the earlier remark Johnson's name was included in a list of people who should have "told the facts" to the American people, a notably different phrase from alleging that Johnson personally was "lying, cheating and distorting the truth." Finally, Johnson's name was linked in a series with Nixon's in the later excerpt, a juxtaposition which, in the light of past events, reflected heightened discredit on Johnson. In essence, the earlier remark was discreet—it defined a mistake in administrative policy; the concluding remark was a personal charge made in unflattering terms. Party members were not offended by the rhetoric of the first statement because it was not a direct attack on past Democratic leaders; it distributed blame broadly and impersonally. The final comment, however, offended the standard of rhetorical decorum appropriate for a political nominee, because it ignored the political rule which prohibits unfavorable remarks about former party leaders. Thus, Carter's remark did not fit the desired *party* image of a candidate, who gives at least lip service to the great party tradition.

Carter's remarks about Johnson also were evidence of the rhetorical tightrope he was forced to walk in the campaign. Part of the personal image he hoped to project was that of the outsider who was removed from the corruption and taint of Washington politics. Moreover, he sought to convey an image of rectitude in contrast to the deceit of the past. Handling the issue of the Johnson administration was, thus, a delicate problem; to defend that administrator's actions would imply involvement with the ingroup politics from which Carter hoped to be divorced, but to attack Johnson's behavior would be potentially divisive for the party. In the early part of the interview Carter handled the difficulty quite skillfully by carefully phrasing his responses and mixing ample praise for Johnson with his criticisms (70–71). But his final remarks, although they may have enhanced Carter's personal image with those unsympathetic to Johnson, disappointed many loyalists' expectations about rhetoric prosper for a Democratic nominee.

Carter's comments about sex were even more problematical in his campaign. In explaining his belief that one should not feel superior to another because of less obvious sin, Carter admitted, "I've looked on a lot of women with lust. I've committed adultery in my heart many times. . . . But that doesn't mean that I condemn someone who not only looks on a woman with lust but who leaves his wife and shacks up with somebody out of wedlock. Christ says, Don't consider yourself better than someone else because one guy screws a whole bunch of women while the other guy is loyal to his wife" (86). This passage evoked much criticism.

Without considering the forum of the interview, one can conclude that the remarks themselves violated the rhetorical decorum many voters associate with the role of president. Although most people are familiar with the terms "screws" and "shacks up with," the objections arose because these words did not seem appropriate to the *public* vocabulary of a president. In contrast, the synonymous word "fornicating," which he had used earlier (70), was acceptable—perhaps because of its biblical usage. Carter's word choice, then, was one critical factor. Beyond that, Carter's choice of the example to illustrate his belief, particularly since it was volunteered rather than in response to a direct question by the interviewer, seemed indecorous in view of his political aspirations. Had he used "theft" or "disrespect for parents" to illustrate his point, his remarks would almost certainly have received far less notice. Carter's choice of adultery as an example probably reflected in part his concern with an earlier series of questions about his personal beliefs on sexual behavior (68–70). Another factor, which probably influenced Scheer's earlier questions as well, is the nature and audience of the magazine itself. Since one tailors one's rhetoric to the audience at hand, sexual promiscuity or permissiveness is a predictable choice for developing both questions and examples for *Playboy*'s readership. Unfortunately for Carter, the example, while perhaps appropriate for the *Playboy* readers, was not suitable for the larger public's image of presidential behavior. In addition, by referring to himself and lust in his own heart, rather than discussing secret sins abstractly, Carter was too open, too familiar. The concept of sinning in one's heart is not offensive, but Carter's confession of it was; it violated the detachment many voters feel desirable between a public figure and the public figure's private life. Instead of creating a feeling of identification between himself and the electorate, which might have been his goal, Carter's remarks disturbed many voters. Although the public realizes rationally that political figures do have normal emotional reactions and personal doubts and problems, these are not expected to intrude on public images. Thus, for example, Edmund Muskie's outrage and emotional response to reports about his wife in the 1972 campaign, though understandable in personal terms, were unacceptable intrusions of the private man into the public arena.[13] Carter's remark about lust in his heart was likewise a disquieting intrusion of private matters into the public spotlight. Carter's case represented, then, an especially interesting conflict between the natural urge of voters to identify with candidates and the delicate process of image making, through which voters evaluate how well each candidate meets their role expectations for a particular office. Although many voters undoubtedly shared Carter's views, and, thus, might well have identified with him, his remarks violated their expectations of public behavior appropriate for a president.

Two more elements, however, further complicated this particular event. Some voters who were not distressed by the remarks themselves were upset by their appearance in *Playboy*. *Playboy* though expensively produced, retains some of the taint of being a "girly" magazine. Such a magazine seemed to many voters an improper forum for a presidential candidate. Despite the fact that numerous other prominent figures have given interviews to or written for *Playboy*, as Walter Mondale mentioned in the vice-presidential debates, the entire interview would probably have received less negative comment had it appeared in *Ladies' Home Journal* or *The Christian Science Monitor*. In fact, Republican campaign officials immediately made it known that Gerald Ford, their candidate, had refused to be interviewed by *Playboy*, but had given an interview to be published that same month to *Ladies' Home Journal*.

Finally, Carter's remarks violated the rhetorical expectations of his audience in another way. Throughout his campaign Carter had characterized himself as a "born-again" Southern Baptist. Thus, aside from their expectations about behavior proper for a presidential candidate, voters also had an image of behavior appropriate for a man of Carter's religious views. The context, the choice of topics, and the diction all violated these expectations for some voters. Earlier in the interview Carter expressed his concern about the public's tendency to see him as a stereotype. He remarked: "I'm a human being. I'm not a packaged article that you can put in a little box and say, 'Here's a Southern Baptist, an ignorant Georgia peanut farmer' . . . You know, that's the sort of stereotype people tend to assume, and I hope it doesn't apply to me" (77). He also attempted to indicate the weakness in the Southern Baptist stereotype by noting that former President Harry Truman was also a Baptist (69). Despite the truth of Carter's protestations about stereotypes, the public does tend to react strongly in terms of them. In this light, Carter's remarks were rhetorically indecorous for the stereotype the public has of a "born-again" Christian.

[13]James M. Naughton, "Muskie Denies an Ethnic Slur," *New York Times*, 27 Feb. 1972, p. 54.

Conclusion

The crux of Carter's problem in the final phase of the interview was that he moved from a stylistic level which met the expectations of voters for his role and image to a more personal and informal level of style which disappointed their expectations; he switched from a style appropriate for a transactional linguistic interaction to one suitable to a personal interaction. Although he did have the requisite personal relationship with Scheer to make the change acceptable in an immediate context, he did not have the close contact with the public as a whole to make such a personal tone appropriate. In discussing such shifts from transactional to personal styles, Gumperz emphasizes that a personal relationship must exist for the change to be effective. He adds, prophetically for Carter, "If this personal relationship does not in fact exist, he risks misunderstanding."[14] Carter's remarks provide evidence to support Gumperz' claim.

If Carter's switch to an informal code did seem inappropriate for his personal image and his political aspirations, the remarks must also be seen in the light of the rhetorical situation within which they developed. This context was rhetorically complex in three important ways. First, the entire interview grew out of a perceived need to allay the doubts about Carter held by such voters as read *Playboy.* Such voters were believed to be uneasy about Carter's image as a religiously conservative person. As Hamilton Jordan expressed it in a private conversation with one of the interviewers, "*We wouldn't do it* [the interview] *if it weren't in our interest. It's your readers who are probably predisposed toward Jimmy—but they may not vote at all if they feel uneasy about him*" (64). But as Carter adjusted his image to appear more tolerant and liberal for *Playboy* readers, he also risked alienating the conservative religious groups who approved of what they initially perceived to be his religious views. Thus, once the wire services, the television networks, and the news magazines publicized his remarks out of their context for the *Playboy* readership, Carter was judged in terms of rhetorical expectations which conflicted with those he had deemed appropriate to his original audience.

Second, Carter also seemed consciously to be trying to project two, at times conflicting, personal images. On the one hand he chose to emphasize his candor and straightforwardness; on the other he hoped to project a picture of himself as a competent and cool-headed executive. Carter seemed to hope for public appreciation both in his role as a private individual and as a potential leader. However, his eagerness to appear open with the public conflicted with the electorate's desire to maintain some sense of distance between the candidate and the crowd.

Finally, the interview situation itself created mixed demands on the participants. It embodied characteristics of both primary and secondary social groups and mixed elements of both transactional and personal linguistic interactions. Scheer suggested that, having spent many hours with Carter in a variety of situations, he developed strong personal feelings about the candidate (63, 91, 194). In fact, Scheer logged more hours with Carter prior to the publication of the interview than any other media person (63). Thus, the relationship between Scheer and Carter evolved on two levels—the transactional confrontation between interviewer and interviewee and the personal interaction between two men who have come to know each other well over a period of three months (63).

[14]Gumperz, "Ethnology of Linguistic Change," p. 36.

Moreover, in the final session, Carter was talking with Scheer on a one-to-one basis in his home in Plains, Georgia, although the ultimate audience was both more extensive and more distant. Carter had, in reality, two audiences—Scheer, whom he knew, and the general public, which was not physically present. The tone of the first segment of the interview suggested a keen awareness on Carter's part of the impact of his comments on the larger public and was clearly a transactional interaction. But the tone of the final section, although inappropriate for the broad readership, was perfectly acceptable in a personal exchange between two adult males. The problem of maintaining social distance throughout a long private exchange and of gearing remarks to both audiences was substantial.

Taken together these three factors—allaying doubts of one audience without disturbing another, combining two images which at times conflict, and the dual nature of the interview format—created a rhetorically difficult situation for any respondent. Thus Carter's final remarks in the interview represented an inappropriate shift in style for both his image as a presidential candidate and as a "born-again" Christian. Moreover, those comments were in striking contrast to the carefully controlled style and tone of the earlier interview responses. Growing out of a complex rhetorical situation, the comments represented an unfortunate choice of stylistic levels by Carter and were indecorous for him. The comments offended some voters, not entirely because they were offensive in themselves, but because they violated those voters' unstated but sensed norms of rhetorical appropriateness.

THE GENERIC APPROACH

INTRODUCTION TO *FORM AND GENRE*

Karlyn Kohrs Campbell and Kathleen Hall Jamieson

Generic Criticisms

[In the late 1960s], a small number of essays began to appear which made explicit claims that genres existed, genres as varied as the diatribe, the papal encyclical, doctrinal rhetoric, and contemporary women's rights rhetoric. Once these appeared, theoretical questions were inevitable: Just what is a genre? How does one justify a generic claim? Why do generic criticism? How does generic criticism differ from other kinds of rhetorical criticism? . . . Here, we shall examine the answers given by critics in selected generic criticisms.

In 1950, Harold Zyskind, a scholar in the field of English, published a generic analysis of Lincoln's Gettysburg Address.[1] He presented his analysis as an example of generic criticism that would enable others to see its value as a method for treating texts in undergraduate courses. His approach to genres was deductive: the measurement of the text against a preexisting model. After justifying his view of the Address as rhetoric (rather than as history or political philosophy), Zyskind attempted to determine whether the address was best viewed as epideictic or deliberative rhetoric. He justified this classical, even traditional, approach to genre on the grounds that it requires the student to scrutinize the text in a systematic manner. The value of generic classification should be tested by asking, "Are the meaning and purpose of the Address—in its uniqueness—in any illuminated by an analysis of it as belonging to that genre?"[2] The bulk of his critique develops a case for concluding that the epideictic elements in the Address are subordinate to its deliberative purpose. This is done through an analysis of structure, imagery, diction, the role of the listener, and the relationship between the audience and the "we" of the Address. The criticism produces not only a generic placement but a statement of the unique qualities of this particular act:

From *Form and Genre: Shaping Rhetorical Action,* edited by Karlyn Kohrs Campbell and Kathleen Hall Jamieson (Falls Church, VA., Speech Communication Association), 16–32. Used by permission of authors and the Speech Communication Association.

Professor Campbell is at the University of Minnesota; Professor Jamieson is at the University of Texas.

[1]Harold Zyskind, "A Rhetorical Analysis of the Gettysburg Address," *Journal of General Education,* 4 (April 1950), 202–212.

[2]Zyskind, p. 202.

> Thus the deliberative aim of the Address is not to persuade the listeners of the truth of the idea that the Union must be reborn. In a logical sense the truth of the general idea that future action is needed is largely taken for granted. The aim rather is to take this accepted general idea and sink it deeply into the feelings of the audience, fix it as an emotional experience so powerful that each listener will, at any crucial time, do what he can specifically for the future of the nation to which he is here dedicated.[3]

If Zyskind's essay is taken as the model he intends it to be, generic criticism is an orderly means of close textual analysis. It unifies the questions the critic asks about various formal and substantive elements. Generic analysis is justified if and only if the meaning and the purpose of the work are illuminated by struggling with the evidence to determine the work's best classification. Finally, Zyskind reminds us that each of the classical genres was an amalgam of elements drawn from the situation, the issue, the lines of argument, the audience, and the appropriate diction. As he notes in this case, an address may have some elements of one genre (epideictic) and still be an exemplar of another (deliberative).

Like Zyskind, Windt's method is deductive, at least in part[4]. He develops a model of the diatribe from the practices of the ancient Cynics, a model which is then applied to the practices of contemporary Yippies to establish a recurrent mode of symbolic action. Like Zyskind, Windt develops a genre which synthesizes situational, substantive, and stylistic elements, and he justifies his classification in terms of the illumination it provides of the behaviors of apparently self-defeating persuaders of both ancient and contemporary times.

Unlike Zyskind and Windt, Hart proceeds inductively to survey a variety of discourses to see if there are clusters of similar symbolic acts[5]. Out of these tests, he cautiously posits a genre of doctrinal rhetoric. Like Zyskind, this cluster of acts reflects not only substantive and stylistic features but the relationship between the speaker and the audience. Since this is the most systematically developed inductive genre, the points of similarity to Zyskind are of particular interest.

Jamieson also proceeds inductively but within a more limited body of discourses, papal encyclicals.[6] However, she does not presume a genre; she examines these discourses to determine if one exists. Like Zyskind, her motive is illumination—she wishes to understand the forces which constrain *Humanae Vitae* so that it cannot adapt to its times and its audience. Her work adds an additional insight for the generic critic: the power of conventions, traditions, prior rhetoric, to mold and constrain subsequent rhetorical action. She reminds us most strongly that rhetorical acts are born into a symbolic/rhetorical context as well as into an historical/political milieu. Once again, the genre which emerges is a complex of elements—a constellation of substantive, stylistic and situational characteristics.

---

[3]Zyskind, p. 212.

[4]Theodore Otto Windt, Jr., "The Diatribe: Last Resort for Protest," *Quarterly Journal of Speech*, 58 (February 1972), 1–14

[5]Roderick P. Hart, "The Rhetoric of the True Believer," *Speech Monographs*, 38 (November 1971), 249.

[6]Kathleen M. Hall Jamieson, "Generic Constraints and the Rhetorical Situation," *Philosophy & Rhetoric*, 6 (Summer 1973), 162–170. See also "Interpretation of Natural Law in the Conflict over *Humanae Vitae*," *Quarterly Journal of Speech*, 60 (April 1974), 201–211.

Like Hart, Campbell's approach to contemporary women's rights rhetoric is inductive.[7] No prior model is assumed; a genre must emerge from, or be discerned in, the discourses themselves. Yet the concept of genre remains constant—it is formed out of substantive and stylistic elements and out of the unique situation of a female audience in 20th century America. And, like all the others, the justification for a generic claim is the understanding it produces rather than the ordered universe it creates.

These are only a few of the available generic criticisms. Since these first essays appeared, many have followed. But as a sample, they will do. Despite their variety, there are certain noteworthy constants: 1) Classification is justified only by the critical illumination it produces, not by the neatness of a classificatory schema; 2) Generic criticism is taken as a means toward systematic, close textual analysis; 3) A genre is a complex, an amalgam, a constellation of substantive, situational, and stylistic elements; 4) Generic analysis reveals both the conventions and affinities that a work shares with others; it uncovers the unique elements in the rhetorical act, the particular means by which a genre is individuated in a given case.

Ideally, theory develops out of and is tested by criticism. Whether or not that is true of generic concepts, these and other criticisms have raised the questions which have become so exigent in contemporary rhetorical criticism.

Form and Genre

Northrop Frye, the most eminent critic to comment on generic criticism, wrote in his *Anatomy* that "the study of genres is based on analogies in form."[8] He called these forms "typical recurring images," "associative clusters," and "complex variables"; he compared them to the *topoi* or rhetorical commonplaces; and he described them as "communicable units," i.e., the forms through which experience and feeling can be made intelligible to others. In other words, formal similarities establish genres, and the forms relevant to genres are complex forms present in all discourse. If the forms from which genres are constituted have the characteristics indicated by Frye, they will be the kinds of forms that rhetoricians ordinarily call "strategies"—substantive and stylistic forms chosen to respond to situational requirements. For example, refutation may be described as a strategy in which one states an opposing position and responds to it by offering an alternative conclusion or by demonstrating the inadequacy of evidence or premises. As a strategy, refutation implies a situation in which there are competing positions and persuaders that must be taken into account. The power of such rhetorical forms is evident in this paragraph from John F. Kennedy's speech, *"Ich bin ein Berliner"*:

> There are many people in the world who really don't understand, or say they don't, what is the great issue between the free world and the Communist world. Let them come to Berlin. And there are some who say that communism is the wave of the future. Let them come to Berlin. And there are some who say in Europe and

[7]Karlyn Kohrs Campbell, "The Rhetoric of Women's Liberation," *Quarterly Journal of Speech*, 59 (February 1973), 74–86.

[8]Northrop Frye, *Anatomy of Criticism: Four Essays* (Princeton University Press, 1957), 99. See also pp. 95–115.

> elsewhere we can work with the Communists. Let them come to Berlin. And there are even a few who say that it is true that communism is an evil system, but it permits us to make economic progress. *Lass'sie nach Berlin kommen.* Let them come to Berlin.[9]

The most evident form is *repetition,* a strategy implying a situation in which a key idea must be established and emphasized. In this case the refrain not only repeats the theme, it also functions as *refutation.* The repeated sentence is a condensed, even *enthymematic,* answer to the four opposing positions. Sheer repetition produces yet another form. When the passage is read aloud, it is nearly impossible to repeat the refrain, "let them come to Berlin," with identical emphasis. Rather, each repetition tends to become more emphatic and intense, creating a *crescendo.* The situation is perceived and described by the speaker as a conflict, and the refrain becomes a climactic sequence dramatizing the conflict. There is still another form of critical interest. John Kennedy delivered this speech in the city of Berlin. The refrain is reflexive, a dramatic *enactment* which says, in effect, "Do as I did—come to Berlin." This form is of particular importance because it is reinforced by the title and by the rest of the speech in which Kennedy says that not only is he, symbolically, a citizen of Berlin, but all of "us" (as opposed to "them") should become symbolic citizens of this beleaguered city which stands for the struggle between the "free" and the "Communist" worlds.

As this analysis illustrates, rhetorical forms do not occur in isolation. In addition, it should be apparent that these forms are phenomena—syntheses of material that exists objectively in the rhetorical act and of perceptions in the mind of a critic, a member of the audience, or a future rhetor. The phenomenal character of forms is reflected in Kenneth Burke's reference to the "psychology of forms" and in his remark that "form is the creation of an appetite in the mind of the auditor, and the adequate satisfying of that appetite."[10] That forms are phenomena has persuasive and critical significance because, as a result, forms can induce participation by others. This is never more evident than in the quintessentially rhetorical form, the enthymeme, whose force is explained by the fact that auditors participate in the construction of the arguments by which they are persuaded.[11]

It should now be apparent that the rhetorical forms that establish genres are stylistic and substantive responses to perceived situational demands. In addition, forms are central to all types of criticism because they define the unique qualities of any rhetorical act, and because they are the means through which we come to understand how an act works to achieve its ends.[12]

From earliest antiquity, rhetoricians have been interested in forms. Analyses of recurrent lines of argument, such as those done by Measell and Carpenter . . . , resemble the ancient study of the *topoi* or commonplaces.[13] The concept of *stasis*

---

[9]*American Short Speeches,* eds. Bower Aly and Lucile Folse Aly (N.Y.: Macmillan, 1968), 132–133.

[10]Kenneth Burke, *Counter-Statement* (University of Chicago Press, 1931; rpt. 1957), 31.

[11]Lloyd F. Bitzer, "Aristotle's Enthymeme Revisited," *Quarterly Journal of Speech,* 45 (December 1959), 408.

[12]Kenneth Burke, *A Grammar of Motives* and *A Rhetoric of Motives,* 581–582.

[13]John F. Wilson and Carroll C. Arnold, *Public Speaking as a Liberal Art,* 3rd ed. (Boston: Allyn & Bacon, 1973).

(or *status*) expressed a judgment that there were only a limited number of issues (being, quantity, quality, procedure) over which clash could occur.[14] Halloran's analysis of the issues in the public proceeding . . . falls in this tradition. To Aristotle, the most important rhetorical form was the enthymeme, the form of deductive argument found in rhetoric. . . . Carpenter's interest in the interpretations of readers who filled in premises or drew inferences from relatively factual material reflects this tradition. . . . The canons and modes of proof can be used as a basis for formal analysis. Finally, from classical to contemporary times, the important role of literary forms has been acknowledged. . . . Herbert Wichelns recognized the role of literary tools in rhetorical criticism: Hoyt Hudson refers to poetic expression as *"an indispensable means"* to instrumental ends,[15] and Northrop Frye assumes that "most of the features characteristic of literary form, such as rhyme, alliteration, metre, antithetical balance, the use of exempla, are also rhetorical schemata"[16]

If the recurrence of similar forms establishes a genre, then genres are groups of discourses which share substantive, stylistic, and situational characteristics. Or, put differently, in the discourses that form a genre, similar substantive and stylistic strategies are used to encompass situations perceived as similar by the responding rhetors. A genre is a group of acts unified by a constellation of forms that recurs in each of its members. These forms, *in isolation*, appear in other discourses. What is distinctive about the acts in a genre is the recurrence of the forms *together* in constellation.

The eulogy is illustrative. The eulogy responds to a situation in which a community is ruptured by death. In this situation, persons must alter their relationship with the deceased and also confront their own morality. The very act of eulogizing acknowledges the death. In so doing, it necessitates a juxtaposition of past and present tense which recasts the relationship to the deceased to one of memory. The assurance that the deceased, hence the audience, survives, at least in memory, eases confrontation with mortality. Thus the assertion of persistent life is intrinsic to the eulogy. That conviction is expressed in claims that the deceased survives in memory—in deeds, family or history. Metaphors of rebirth articulate this eulogistic claim.

The act of eulogizing is, in another important respect, performative. By uniting the bereaved in a rhetorical act, the eulogy affirms that the community will survive the death. Typically, eulogies reknit the sundered community through rhetorical devices which appeal to the audience to carry on the works, to embody the virtues, or to live as the deceased would have wished. These are the situational requirements, strategic responses, and stylistic choices that, taken together, form the eulogy. These characteristics do not co-exist by chance. They exist in a reciprocal, dynamic relationship.

External factors, including human needs and exposure to antecedent rhetorical forms, create expectations which constrain rhetorical responses. But the internal dynamic of fused elements also creates expectations which testify to its constraining force. Generic exemplars have an internal consistency. For example, the papal encyclical presupposes truths of natural law known by God's vicar on earth who interprets and explicates the law. This premise dictates a deductively struc-

[14]Otto Alvin Loeb Dieter, "Stasis," *Speech Monographs*, 17 (November 1950), 345–369
[15]Hoyt H. Hudson, "Rhetoric and Poetry," *Quarterly Journal of Speech Education*, 10 (April 1924), 146.
[16]Northrop Frye, *Anatomy of Criticism*, 245.

tured document which employs a formal and authoritative tone that is consistent with dogmatic statement. It also entails the use of absolutistic, categorical vocabulary. Encyclicals assume print form because the sort of doctrinal matters addressed require a careful, prepared, precise form of communicating God's will. (Clarification of truth and of doctrine are serious and exacting matters. An oral form is transitory in a way a print form is not.) Each of these elements implies the others. The rhetoric of dogma, for example, cannot be structured inductively without undermining the dogmatic tone and the sense of authority pivotal to the document. One might even argue that the concept of papal authority on certain doctrinal matters entails the form of address which is the encyclical.

In other words, a genre does not consist merely of a series of acts in which certain rhetorical forms recur; for example, it is conceivable that parallelism and antithesis might recur jointly without establishing a generic similarity. Instead, a genre is composed of a constellation of recognizable forms bound together by an internal dynamic.

When a generic claim is made, the critical situation alters significantly because the critic is now arguing that a group of disclosures has a synthetic core in which certain significant rhetorical elements, e.g., a system of belief, lines of argument, stylistic choices, and the perception of the situation, are fused into an indivisible whole. The significance of this fusion of forms for the critic is that it provides an angle of vision, a window, that reveals the tension among these elements, the dynamic within the rhetorical acts of human beings, in different times and places, responding in similar ways as they attempt to encompass certain rhetorical problems—the death of a member of the community, an accusation to which no forensic defense is adequate, and the like.

Because a genre is a constellation of elements, the appearance of the same forms in different genres poses no critical problem; a genre is given its character by a fusion of forms not by its individual elements. Thus the argument that Aristotle's genres are not useful because epideictic elements are found in deliberative and forensic addresses, deliberative elements in epideictic and forensic works, etc., is irrelevant; Aristotle's schema is weak generically only if the constellation of elements forming epideictic works does not permit the critic to distinguish the epideictic clustering from the constellations which form the other Aristotelian genres.

The concept of an internal dynamic fusing substantive, stylistic, and situational characteristics permits the critic to determine the generic significance of recurring elements. For example, Rosenfield identifies the clustering of facts in one section of the mass media apologia as a generic characteristic.[17] To test whether the characteristic has generic significance, one must ask: Why would such an element occur in the apology? What is its necessary relationship to other elements in the apology? What substantive, stylistic or situational constraints might require the inclusion of this element and its particular positioning in the structure?

Generic claims are difficult to sustain because constellations of elements rarely fuse into unique and indivisible wholes of the sort described. In addition, generic claims are difficult because of the nature of the processes by which genres may be established.

Some genres, probably most, are established deductively from a model or touchstone. For instance, Socrates' *Apology* is taken as a paradigm and acts

---

[17] Lawrence W. Rosenfield, "A Case Study in Speech Criticism: The Nixon-Truman Analog," *Speech Monographs* 35 (November, 1968), 441–442.

which resemble it in essential ways are said to form a genre; similar procedures are followed with the rhetoric of Jeremiah or the rhetoric of the Old Testament prophets, and so on. There are at least two major pitfalls in this method: 1) the critic may fail to delineate the essential characteristics of the model so that the basis for comparison is faulty, or 2) a generic "fit" is asserted although certain essential characteristics are absent or significant dissimilarities exist. The first problem can be eliminated if the critic analyzes the original and refuses to accept "received wisdom" about classic works. The second can be eliminated only if the critic makes the goal in analogic or comparative criticism that of delineating similarities *and differences* and proffers a generic claim only when the evidence *requires* such a claim.

Some genres are established inductively. One can look at a vast number of discourses delivered in response to the death of a member of the community and discover that, at least in Western cultures, they seem to evince essential similarities.[18] One can examine the papal encyclicals and establish a generic resemblance. One can examine all available samples of contemporary rhetoric demanding women's rights in the U.S. and make a case that they form a coherent whole which can be distinguished from the acts of other protest groups. Each of these is an enormous project and each claim is difficult to justify. In most cases, the results of inductive efforts will be disappointing, and a generic claim will not be warranted by the evidence. The problems with this approach are those inherent in any procedure that draws inductive generalizations. Until now, conscientious rhetorical critics have tested their claims about inductively derived genres by selecting specimens from dissimilar eras and/or rhetors to minimize the possibility that the characteristics of an age or a class of persons would be mistaken for generic qualities. Thus a student who generalized from a sample of 19th century eulogies to the conclusion that eulogies are stylistically florid would be told that a characteristic of 19th century rhetoric had been mistaken for a generic characteristic and would be urged to sample eulogies from different periods. This approach was based on the scientific notion that random sampling would minimize critical error. A deeper understanding of the nature of genres provides other rhetorical-critical tests: Why should a eulogy be characterized by a florid style? What is the necessary relationship between such a style and the substantive and situational elements which comprise the eulogy?

The confusion of deductive and inductive approaches to genres can also create difficulties. In a number of cases, critics have assumed, *a priori,* that a genre already exists and is known and defined—e.g., the sermon,[19] the presidential inaugural,[20] the apology,[21] among others—and an inductive procedure, content analysis in some cases, is applied to parse its elements. Such studies are suspect because the *a priori* definition of a genre and identification of its members generates a circular argument: an essential and preliminary procedure defining the generic

[18]See James O. Payne, "The American Eulogy: A Study in Generic Criticism," (M.A. Thesis, University of Kansas, 1975). We are indebted to Charley Conrad, a graduate student at the University of Kansas, for the concept of inductive and deductive approaches to the formation of genres.

[19]Thomas Clark, "An Analysis of Generic Aspects of Contemporary American Sermons." Paper presented at the Central States Speech Association Convention (April 1976).

[20]Donald Wolfarth, "John F. Kennedy in the Tradition of Inaugural Speeches," *Quarterly Journal of Speech,* 47 (April 1961), 124–132.

[21]B. L. Ware and Wil A. Linkugel, "They Spoke in Defense of Themselves: On the Generic Criticism of Apologia," *Quarterly Journal of Speech,* 59 (October 1973), 273–283.

characteristics has been omitted. Generic critics need to recognize explicitly the assumptions they are making and the procedures required to establish their claims.

An understanding of the genre as a fusion of elements, formed from a constellation of forms, permits one to distinguish between classification and generic analysis. There are some troublesome pieces of rhetoric, such as presidential inaugurals, in which a series of rhetorical elements recur. For example, the inaugurals establish the philosophy and tone of new administrations. Because they follow the divisive rhetoric of a campaign, they employ unifying appeals and articulate superordinate goals. In an attempt to overcome the fear that the incoming president is an incipient despot, each places the country in the hands of a higher power and acknowledges humility in the face of future tasks. The tone is dignified. Yet Lincoln's second inaugural and Washington's first are basically dissimilar. There are several possible explanations: 1) What have been isolated as inaugural elements are, in fact, elements inherent in a broader genre, rehearsal rhetoric; a hierarchical error, as Simons would call it, has been made; 2) A genre, the inaugural, does exist, but critics have failed to isolate the generic elements and the dynamic which binds them. Hence we cannot see the fundamental similarity between Lincoln's and Washington's addresses; 3) The evidence at hand would suggest that although it is possible that a genre properly termed "inaugural" does exist, it is not necessarily evoked in the situation created by the swearing-in of a President, as the inability to locate dynamic interrelationships among the elements of the inaugural and the inability to distinguish it from other rehearsal rhetoric testify.

The concept of a genre as a constellation of fused elements refines the notion that, in a genre, the significant rhetorical similarities outweigh the significant rhetorical differences. In its earlier form, generic "significance" resided in the mind of the critic, and any generic claim seemed vulnerable to a charge of subjectivism. Testing a generic claim on the grounds that "significant similarities will permit prediction of the form of an address not yet conceived or delivered" was problematic. The test does not assure that the critic is dealing with genre. For example, it is possible to predict certain characteristics of an inaugural address although there is general scholarly agreement that the claim that inaugurals form a genre has yet to be established. Unless the elements cohere in a necessary and significant relationship, in a dynamic fusion, the ability to predict that certain characteristics will appear in an act on a certain occasion does not assure that a genre has been located. If an element is generically significant, it is so fused to the other elements that its absence would alter the character of the address.

Critics have assumed that genres are bodies of discourses that, as distinctive symbolic acts, recur in different times and places. Conversely, Black has argued that a genre may have a single identifiable member and illustrated his view with Chapman's Coatesville Address, a piece of rhetoric that functions as a morality play.[22] The view of genre described here, as a dynamic constellation of forms, focuses not only on what has recurred but on what may recur. In this sense, a constellation of elements bound together dynamically need only exist in a single instance to establish a genre or a generic potential. Clearly, the dynamic of the

[22]Black, 79–91.

constellation and the fusion of its forms are more easily recognized when their recurrence is observed, but it is now possible both to isolate the constellation and its dynamic without comparing multiple specimens of the genre.

Similarly, this definition helps to explain the perseveration of rhetorical forms which the critic judges to be inappropriate to the demands of the situation. Jamieson has argued that the papal encyclical, at least as a form illustrated by *Humanae Vitae,* is a perseverative rhetorical form. An internal dynamic combines the elements in an encyclical, and the internal dynamic accounts, at least in part, for its perseveration as a genre. One cannot abandon elements of a genre which are dynamically fused without undermining the genre itself. For example, classical Latin with its rigorous controlling verbs complements the deductive structure of the papal encyclical, and that structure itself is dictated by, and consonant with, the concept of papal authority on matters of dogma.

The definition emphasizes the interrelationships among generic elements. Genres often exist in dynamic responsiveness to situational demands—e.g., an encyclical appears in order to affirm papal authority. Those instances in which a dynamic is sustaining a genre in the absence of, or counter to, situational demands invite the label "degenerative." The critic labelling a form "degenerative" risks the charge that ideological bias has colored the critical act. In the context developed here, the "degenerative" nature of the diagnosed genre can be subjected to a test of evidence. Does an internal dynamic exist? Is it consonant with perceived demands of the situation? If not, the genre is rhetorically degenerate because the audience and other germane situational variables are being ignored—and also degenerative in a literal sense; that is, a genre which fails to achieve its purpose—e.g., reknit a community ruptured by death or affirm papal authority—is more likely to "degenerate" and ultimately to disappear than is a genre consonant with perceived situational demands.

The concept of genre may be illustrated by analogy. Biologists speak of the genetic code inherent in the germ plasm of each species. Although there will be variations, that code is the internal dynamic which determines the biological form of the individual member of the species. The internal dynamic of a genre is similar. It is the determinant of the generic form of the rhetorical utterance although like individual members of species, individual rhetorical acts—although part of a common genre—will show some individual variation. What is significant about the concept of genre is the fusion of elements and the critical insight the fusion provides.

The term "constellation" suggests another metaphorical insight. The stars forming a constellation are individuals but they are influenced by each other and by external elements; consequently they move together and remain in a similar relation to each other despite their varying positions over time. Like genres, constellations are perceived patterns with significance and usefulness—they enable us to see the movements of a group of individual stars and they enable us to understand the interrelated forces in celestial space.

Both metaphors and the very concept of the internal dynamic suggest the difference between classification or creating a taxonomy on the one hand, and critical analysis on the other. A "genre" is a classification based on the fusion and interrelation of elements in such a way that a unique kind of rhetorical act is created. Approaching such acts generically gives the critic and unusual opportunity to penetrate their internal workings and to appreciate the interacting forces that create them.

Genre and Criticism

"Genre" is not the key term in a philosophy of rhetoric; it is an important concept in one kind of criticism. The theory underlying the concept of genre is critical theory, theory about the enterprise of criticism. It is no accident that Frye is a major source for material on genre, as his *Anatomy* is a study of criticism as an autonomous enterprise. Frye argues strongly for a pluralistic approach to criticism, and he justifies his view by showing that all discourse is polysemous, i.e., that it has many levels of meaning or means in different ways. These different levels or kinds of meaning require different critical perspectives. Because all works are not only unique but also resemble other works, generic criticism is essential. Frye notes that part of the meaning of a work is derived from the tradition of which it is a part, from the conventions it observes. The conventions found in a discourse indicate the tradition to which it belongs and the works to which it has close affinities. Consequently, he says that

> when he [Milton] uses the convention of invocation, thus bringing the poem [*Paradise Lost*] into the genre of the spoken word, the significance of the convention is to indicate what tradition his work primarily belongs to and what its closest affinities are with. The purpose of criticism by genres is not so much to classify as to clarify such traditions and affinities, thereby bringing out a large number of literary relationships that would not be noticed as long as there were no context established for them.[23]

What Frye is describing is a *generic perspective* toward criticism, not a crusading search to find genres. The generic perspective recognizes that while there may be few clearly distinguishable genres, all rhetoric is influenced by prior rhetoric, all rhetorical acts resemble other rhetorical acts. Such a critical perspective emphasizes the symbolic and rhetorical contexts in which rhetorical acts are created.

Some elements of a generic perspective are intrinsic in all criticism because classification and comparison are integral parts of the critical process. As a critic, one is perpetually classifying and labelling—e.g., this is an introduction, this is an example, this is high style, this is satirical, this is a eulogy. Inherent in each classification are two comparative standards—the comparison of like to like, the comparison of like to unlike. The first comparison arises out of definition. To label some part of a discourse as an introduction is to have a definition that contains essential attributes and, implicitly, suggests an ideal or model. Such classifications are the basis of evaluative comparisons—this is better, this is more fully realized, and the like. The second, comparison or contrast, differentiates introductions and conclusions, one form of support from another, distinguishes styles, tones, and ultimately, between classifications by type or genre. These contrasts compel re-definitions and form the basis for strategic evaluations—e.g., this style was chosen, but an alternative style would have been preferable because of its ability to accomplish "x" objective. No one who recognizes the role of comparison and contrast in interpreting and evaluating rhetorical discourse is likely to ignore the traditions which have generated or shaped discourse and the relationships among discourses which extend the critic's capacity to make comparative judgments.

[23]Frye, 247–248.

Because rhetoric is of the public life, because rhetorical acts are concerned with ideas and processes rooted in the here and now of social and political life, rhetoric develops in time and through time. Ironically, the traditional emphasis on individual speeches and speakers as rooted historically in a particular time and place is, in an important sense, anti-historical, because it fails to recognize the impact of rhetorical acts on other rhetorical acts, and it fails to recognize the powerful human forces which fuse recurrent forms into genres which, in an important sense, transcend a specific time and place. The critic who classifies a rhetorical artifact as generically akin to a class of similar artifacts has identified an undercurrent of history rather than comprehended an act isolated in time. Recurrence of a combination of forms into a generically identifiable form over time suggests that certain constants in human action are manifest rhetorically. One may argue that recurrence arises out of comparable rhetorical situations, out of the influence of conventions on the responses of rhetors, out of universal and cultural archetypes ingrained in human consciousness, out of fundamental human needs, or out of a finite number of rhetorical options or commonplaces. Whatever the explanation, the existence of the recurrent provides insight into the human condition.

A generic approach to rhetorical criticism would culminate in a developmental history of rhetoric that would permit the critic to generalize beyond the individual event which is constrained by time and place to affinities and traditions across time. It would move from the study of rhetors and acts in isolation to the study of recurrent rhetorical action. It would produce a critical history exploring the ways in which rhetorical acts influence each other. Such a "genealogy" would trace the imprint of form on form, style on style, genre on genre. It would, for example, trace imperial forms of address from the Roman emperor's decree to the papal encyclical in order to discern imperial tendencies in papal address, trace the form of the State of the Union address from the form of the King's speech to Parliament in order to account for monarchical qualities in early State of the Union speeches. It would trace the Congressional speeches in reply to State of the Union addresses back to the echoing speeches of Parliament in order to account for the curiously subservient tone of early Congressional responses. It would root the Presidential Inaugural in the theocratic addresses of Puritan leaders in order to explain the supplicative elements in early inaugurals.

It is now manifest that a concern with form and genre does not prescribe a critical methodology. Mohrmann and Leff have argued for a synthesis of neo-Aristotelian and generic perspectives[24] Bitzer suggests a situational basis for generic study; Hart proceeds inductively using content analysis and other quantitative and non-quantitative methods; Campbell relies on dramatistic concepts.[25] In short, generic analysis is an available critical option regardless of the critical perspective that one cherishes.

However, a generic perspective does make some demands on the critic. It is a critical approach that requires careful textual analysis, for instance. It also

---

[24]G. P. Mohrmann and Michael C. Leff "Lincoln at Cooper Union: A Rationale for Neo-classical Criticism," *Quarterly Journal of Speech,* 60 (December 1974), 459–467.

[25]Karlyn Kohrs Campbell, "The Rhetoric of Radical Black Nationalism: A Case Study in Self-conscious Criticism," *Central States Speech Journal,* 22 (Fall 1971), 151–160; "An Exercise in the Rhetoric of Poetic Injustice," in *Critiques of Contemporary Rhetoric,* (Belmont, California; Wadsworth, 1972), pp. 142–151; "The Rhetoric of Women's Liberation: An Oxymoron."

heightens an awareness of the interrelationship between substantive and stylistic elements in discourse.

A generic perspective is intensely historical, but in a sense somewhat different from most prior efforts. It does not seek detailed recreation of the original encounter between author and audience; rather it seeks to recreate the symbolic context in which the act emerged so that criticism can teach us about the nature of human communicative response and about the ways in which rhetoric is shaped by prior rhetoric, by verbal conventions in a culture, and by past formulations of ideas and issues.

It can be argued that generic placement and comparison to an ideal type—touchstone criticism—are both familiar forms of rhetorical criticism. We have noted their classical origins and we note a contemporary, Walter Fisher, who writes that rhetorical criticism "says how and in what ways a rhetorical transaction fits, falls short of, or transcends other examples of its kind."[26] This essay amends that statement to emphasize the role of formal analysis in the process of generic placement. One's capacity to clarify and reveal a rhetorical act is based on one's ability to see it clearly, to understand its nature, to select the most apt characterization of it. It matters greatly, as Zyskind indicates, whether one calls Lincoln's Gettysburg Address an epideictic eulogy or labels it a deliberative act designed to urge the audience toward the actions it should follow if the Union was to be preserved. Similarly, Barnet Baskerville's critique of Nixon's "Checkers Speech" treats the address as forensic and demonstrates persuasively that it did not serve to answer the charges that had been made.[27] But if the speech is more properly classified as an apologia, such a "failure" is inevitable—the apologia is a speech in which one responds to forensic charges in a non-forensic way—by transcending them to present one's life and character to one's judges.

[26]Barnet Baskerville, "The Illusion of Proof," *Western Speech*, 25 (Fall 1961), 236–242.

[27]Walter R. Fisher, "Rhetorical Criticism as Criticism," *Western Speech*, 38 (Spring 1974), 76.

INAUGURATING THE PRESIDENCY

Karlyn Kohrs Campbell and Kathleen Hall Jamieson

The presidential inaugural address is a discourse whose significance all recognize but few praise. Arthur Schlesinger, Jr., for example, acknowledges that, during inaugural addresses, "the nation listens for a moment as one people to the words of the man they have chosen for the highest office in the land,"[1] but he finds little merit in such speeches: "Even in the field of political oratory, the inaugural address is an inferior art form. It is rarely an occasion for original thought or stimulating reflection. The platitude quotient tends to be high, the rhetoric stately and self-serving, the ritual obsessive, and the surprises few."[2]

Conceivably, inaugurals mirror the alleged mediocrity of American presidents. In our view, presidential inaugurals are maligned because their symbolic function is misunderstood. Resolving this misunderstanding requires us to address several issues in the criticism of political rhetoric: Can inaugural addresses be treated as a group? Are they a distinct type, a rhetorical genre?[3] If so, what predetermines their characteristics?

Conventional wisdom and ordinary language treat inaugural addresses as a class. Critics have intuitively taken them to belong to a distinct rhetorical type, but generalizing about them has been difficult. Despite apparent dissimilarities among them, we hold that presidential inaugural addresses form a genre, and in this essay we attempt to identify the shared qualities that render them distinctive. In that process, we shall account for the recurrent and the variable in these speeches, explain the unique functions of the presidential inaugural, and illuminate the power of those inaugural addresses widely regarded as eloquent.

U.S. presidential inaugurals are a subspecies of the kind of discourse that Aristotle called epideictic, a form of rhetoric that praises or blames on ceremonial occasions,[4] addresses an audience that evaluates the rhetor's skill (*Rhetoric*

From *Form, Genre and the Study of Political Discourse,* edited by Herbert W. Simons and Aram A. Aghazarian (Columbia: University of South Carolina Press, 1986), 203–25. Used by permission of the authors, University of South Carolina Press, and *Presidential Studies Quarterly.*

Professor Campbell is at the University of Minnesota; Professor Jamieson is at the University of Texas.

[1]Arthur Schlesinger, Jr., Introduction to *The Chief Executive: Inaugural Addresses of the Presidents of the United States from George Washington to Lyndon B. Johnson* (New York: Crown Publishers, 1965), p. vi.

[2]Ibid., p. vii, Generally, the literary quality of presidential discourse is not high. For example, in announcing that Thomas Jefferson's autobiographical writings and public papers would be included in the Library of America series, Daniel Aaron, president of the selection committee, commented that the works of only a few additional presidents—Lincoln, Grant, Wilson, and both Roosevelts—were likely to be included. The criteria for selection are literary, not political, and, in Aaron's words, "Some could write well, others were wooden," (Cited by Herbert Mitgang, "Jefferson's Prose Joins Library of America Series," *New York Times,* May 28 1984, p. 15Y.)

[3]We are concerned here exclusively with addresses delivered every four years, following presidential elections. For an analysis of speeches by ascendant vice presidents, see Kathleen Hall Jamieson and Karlyn Kohrs Campbell, "Rhetorical Hybrids: Fusions of Generic Elements," *Quarterly Journal of Speech* 68 (May 1982):146–57.

[4]Aristotle, *Rhetoric,* trans. W. Rhys Roberts (New York: Modern Library, 1954), 1358b.12. Subsequent citations from the *Rhetoric* are identified in parenthesis in the text.

1354b.2–4), recalls the past and speculates about the future while focusing on the present (1358b.18–20), employs a noble, dignified, literary style (1414a.15), and amplifies or rehearses admitted facts (1368a.27).

In a recent work on rhetoric in the Catholic Church, John O'Malley noted that epideictic rhetoric presents speakers with a unique problem of invention—a problem in discovering and developing appropriate lines of argument. Unlike forensic (courtroom) or deliberative (legislative) speeches that deal "with more immediate and pressing issues" for which "classical theory proposed *topoi* or commonplaces, . . . the occasional or ceremonial nature of epideictic often deprived it of obviously immediate issues."[5] As a result, *memoria*, or recollection of a shared past, becomes an exceptionally important resource for epideictic speeches, O'Malley also called attention to the distinctively contemplative character of this genre. He remarked: "Epideictic wants as far as possible to present us with works and deeds, . . . not for metaphysical analysis but quite literally for viewing . . . 'to look,' to 'view,' to 'gaze upon,' and to 'contemplate.' . . . "[6] Harry Caplan added that in epideictic discourse a speaker tries, by means of his art, "to impress his ideas upon [the audience], without action as a goal."[7]

Using these criteria one can see that presidential inaugurals are epideictic rhetoric because they are delivered on ceremonial occasions, fuse past and future in present contemplation, affirm or praise the shared principles that will guide the incoming administration, ask the audience to "gaze upon" traditional values, employ elegant, literary language, and rely on "heightening of effect" by amplification and reaffirmation of what is already known and believed.

The special character of presidential inaugural addresses is defined by these general epideictic features and by the nature of the inauguration ceremony. Inauguration is a rite of passage, a ritual of transition in which the newly elected President is invested with the office of the Presidency.[8] The fusion of epideictic features with the requirements of this rite of investiture creates the distinctive rhetorical type that is the U.S. presidential inaugural address.

Investiture necessitates participation in a formal ceremony in which a duly constituted authority, before appropriate witnesses, confers the right to play a certain role or to take a certain position. The ceremony usually involves a demonstration by the candidate for investiture of her or his suitability for such elevation. In the inauguration ceremony, the President must swear an oath specified by the Constitution,[9] before "the people" as witnesses, and demonstrate by rhetorical enactment his worthiness, his capacity to be the President. More specifically, the President must show that he understands the principles of a

---

[5]John W. O'Malley, *Praise and Blame in Renaissance Rome: Rhetoric, Doctrine, and Reform in the Sacred Orators of the Papal Court, c. 1450–1521* (Durham, N.C.: Duke University Press, 1979, p. 40.

[6]Ibid., p. 63.

[7]Harry Caplan, Introduction to *Rhetorica ad herennium* (Cambridge, Mass.: Harvard University Press, 1954), p. 173.

[8]James L. Hoban, Jr., "Rhetorical Rituals of Rebirth," *Quarterly Journal of Speech* 66 (October 1980):282–83.

[9]According to historian John McCollister in his book *So Help Me God* (Minneapolis, Minn.: Landmark Books, 1982), George Washington ad-libbed the additional words "so help me God" in taking the oath of office, although these words are not part of the oath specified in the Constitution. His addition has become part of the convention of the ceremony. (Cited by Francis X. Clines, "Presidents and Churchgoing, a Sensitive Subject," *New York Times*, March 23, 1982, p. 12Y).

democratic-republican form of government and the limits it imposes on executive power, and he must manifest rhetorically his ability to lead and to be the symbolic head of state, who is President of all the people. All of these are culturally evolved expectations that specify the "appropriate" features of a presidential inaugural address.

The general qualities of epideictic rhetoric, modified by the nature of presidential investiture, generate a constellation of four interrelated elements that constitute the essential presidential inaugural address and differentiate it from other types of epideictic rhetoric.[10] The presidential inaugural (1) unifies the audience by reconstituting its members as "the people" who can witness and ratify the ceremony; (2) rehearses communal values drawn from the past; (3) sets for the political principles that will govern the new administration; and (4) demonstrates that the President appreciates the requirements and limitations of the executive functions. Each of these ends must be achieved through means appropriate to epideictic address, i.e., while urging contemplation not action, focusing on the present while incorporating past and future, and praising the institution of the Presidency and the values and the form of the government of which it is a part.

The special "timelessness" of epideictic discourse is the key to fusing the elements of the dynamic that symbolically constitutes the presidential inaugural. The time of epideictic rhetoric, including inaugurals, is the eternal present, the mythic time that Mircea Eliade calls *illud tempus,* time out of time. Eliade writes: "Every ritual has the character of happening *now,* at this very moment. The time of the event that the ritual commemorates or re-enacts is made *present,* 're-presented' so to speak, however far back it may have been in ordinary reckoning.[11] This "time out of time" has two distinguishing features: (1) in it one experiences a universe of eternal relationships; in the case of inauguration, the relationship between the ruler and the ruled; and (2) it has the potential to be reenacted, made present once again, at any moment. This special sense of the present is central to the generic character of the inaugural because the address is about an institution and a form of government fashioned to transcend any given historical moment. The timelessness of an inaugural address affirms and ensures the continuity of the constitutional system and the immortality of the Presidency as an institution, and timelessness is reflected in its contemplative tone and by the absence of calls to specific and immediate action.

In order to transcend the historical present, inaugurals need to reconstitute an existing community, rehearse the past, affirm traditional values, and articulate timely and timeless principles that will govern the administration of the incoming President. Inaugurals bespeak their locus in the eternal present in a "high" style that heightens experience, invites contemplation, and speaks to "the people" through time. The quality of epideictic timelessness to which inaugurals

---

[10] The idea of a rhetorical genre as a constellation of elements governed by a dynamic principle is developed in Karlyn Kohrs Campbell and Kathleen Hall Jamieson, "Form and Genre in Rhetorical Criticism: An Introduction," in Karlyn Kohrs Campbell and Kathleen Hall Jamieson, eds., *Form and Genre: Shaping Rhetorical Action* (Falls Church, Va.: Speech Communication Association, 1978), pp. 9–32.

[11] Mircea Eliade, *Patterns in Comparative Religion,* trans. Rosemary Sheed (Cleveland, Ohio: World Publishing Co., 1970), p. 392; cited in David Cole, *The Theatrical Event: A Mythos, a Vocabulary, a Perspective* (Middletown, Conn.: Wesleyan University Press, 1975), p. 8.

aspire was captured by Franklin Roosevelt in his 1941 address: "To us there has come a time, in the midst of swift happenings, to pause for a moment and take stock—to recall what our place in history has been, and to rediscover what we are and what we may be. . . . "[12]

Reconstituting "the People"

Before an audience can witness and ratify an ascent to power, the audience must be unified and reconstituted as "the people." John Adams illustrated the reconstituting power of historical reenactment when he rehearsed the founding of the nation in 1797: "In this dangerous crisis [under the Articles of Confederation] the people of America were not abandoned by their usual good sense, presence of mind, resolution, or integrity. Measures were pursued to concern a plan to form a more perfect union . . . " (p. 10). Jefferson sought to create a single people out of partisan division when he said: "We have called by different names brethren of the same principles. We are all republicans. We are all federalists" (p. 16).[13] More recently, after a close election and a divisive campaign, John F. Kennedy in 1961 began: "We observe today not a victory of party, but a celebration of freedom . . . " (p. 269). As one would expect, explicit appeals for unity are most common in addresses that follow divisive campaigns or contested electoral outcomes.[14]

Partisan politicking is not the only source of division. Occasionally a major crisis or a war creates disharmony that must be set aside if a President is to govern all the people. Acknowledging the disunity created by the Civil War, McKinley in 1901 declared: "We are reunited. Sectionalism has disappeared. Division on public questions can no longer be traced by the war maps of 1861" (p. 180). In 1917, in the face of U.S. entry into World War I, Wilson affirmed the importance of unity: "It is imperative that we should stand together. We are being forged into a new unity amidst the fires that now blaze throughout the world" (p. 205).

Once the audience has been united as "the people," it can perform its role in the inaugural ceremony. Inaugural addresses themselves attest to the witnessing role of "the people." For example, in 1889, Benjamin Harrison said:

> There is no constitutional or legal requirement that the president shall take the oath of office in the presence of the people, but there is so manifest an appropriateness

[12]Davis Newton Lott, *The Presidents Speak: The Inaugural Addresses of the American Presidents from Washington to Nixon* (rev. ed.; New York: Holt, Rinehart & Winston, 1969), p. 243. Subsequent citations from inaugurals delivered through 1969 are from this source and are identified by page numbers in parentheses in the text and in subsequent notes.

[13]Dumas Malone, *Jefferson and His Time*, vol. 4, *Jefferson the President: First Term, 1801–1805*, 4 vols. (Boston: Little, Brown, 1970), p. 20. Malone comments that Jefferson did not capitalize these key words and turn them into party names. (Cited in Gregg Phifer, "Two Inaugurals: A Second Look," *Southern Speech Communication Journal* 48 [Supper 1983] 385).

[14]See *e.g.,* Buchanan's 1857 address, which followed an election held during the conflict between pro- and anti-slavery forces in "bloody Kansas" (p. 111); Hayes's inaugural of 1877 (pp. 140–41); Cleveland's inaugural of 1885 (p. 151); Benjamin Harrison's address in 1889 (p. 162); Cleveland's speech in 1893 (p. 168); and Nixon's address in 1969 (p. 280), in addition to those cited in the text.

in the public induction to office of the chief executive of the nation that from the beginning of the Government the people, to whose service the official oath consecrates the officer, have been called to witness the solemn ceremonial [p.155].

Similar statements appear in many others. John Quincy Adams said: "I appear, my fellow citizens, in your presence and in that of heaven to bind myself . . . " (p. 51). "In the presence of this vast assemblage of my countrymen," said Cleveland, "I am about to supplement and seal by the oath which I have taken the manifestation of the will of a great and free people" (p. 151). "I, too, am a witness," noted Eisenhower, "today testifying in your name to the principles and purposes to which we, as a people, are pledged" (p. 263).[15]

Without the presence of "the people," the rite of presidential investiture cannot be completed. The people ratify the President's formal ascent to power by acknowledging his oath, witnessing his enactment of his role, and accepting the principles he lays down to guide his administration. Benjamin Harrison recognized the interdependence of the President and the people in this inaugural act:

The oath taken in the presence of the people becomes a mutual covenant. . . . My promise is spoken; yours unspoken, but not the less real and solemn. The people of every State have here their representatives. Surely I do not misinterpret the spirit of the occasion when I assume that the whole body of the people covenant with me and with each other today to support and defend the Constitution of the Union of the States, to yield willing obedience to all the laws and each to every other citizen his equal civil and political rights [p. 155].

That an inaugural address is an adjunct to or an extension of the oath of office is demonstrated dramatically in the shortest address, Washington's second. After describing himself as "called upon by the voice of my country" to "this distinguished honor," Washington said:

Previous to the execution of any official act of the President, the Constitution requires an oath of office. This oath I am now about to take, and in your presence: That if it shall be found during my administration of the Government I have in any instance violated willingly or knowingly the injunctions thereof, I may (besides incurring constitutional punishment) be subjected to the upbraidings of all who are now witnesses of the present solemn ceremony [p. 7].

Although it consists entirely of a presidential reavowal of the constitutional oath, this inaugural also recognized the witnessing role of the audience in the rite of investiture.

That an inaugural address is an extension of the oath of office is certified by many of these speeches.[16] However, one of the more eloquent addresses derived its power in part from its construction as an extension of the oath of office and

---

[15]See, among others, Lincoln's first (p. 117) and McKinley's first (p. 171).

[16]Van Buren spoke of "an avowal of the principles that will guide me . . . " (p. 65); Buchanan repeated the oath at the beginning of his address (p. 111); Cleveland referred to his speech as a supplement to the oath of office (p. 151); Eisenhower said: "We are called as a people to give testimony in the sight of the world to our faith that the future shall belong to the free" (p. 257); Lyndon Johnson said: "The oath I have taken before you and before God is not mine alone, but ours together" (p. 275).

For discussion of another rhetorical covenant pertinent to presidential discourse, see Roderick P. Hart, *The Political Pulpit* (West Lafayette, Ind.: Purdue University Press, 1977), pp. 43–65.

as an invitation to participate in a mutual covenant. In 1961 each assertion or promise articulated by Kennedy was phrased as a pledge jointly made by leader and people. His litany of mutual pledges culminated in the claim: "In your hands, my fellow citizens, more than mine, will rest the final success or failure of our course" (p. 271). Finally, he explicitly invited audience participation by asking: "Will you join in that historic effort?" (p. 271). By casting his speech as an extension of the oath of office and by inviting the audience to join him in these avowals, Kennedy underscored the ritualistic nature of the occasion.

The force of Lincoln's first inaugural also derived, in part, from his call for audience participation. Lincoln's speech made listeners peculiarly aware that contemplation is a precursor of action.[17] After offering his interpretation of constitutional principles, and defining his audience as those "who really love the Union," Lincoln said:

> Before entering upon so grave a matter as the destruction of our national fabric, with all its benefits, its memories, and its hope, would it not be wise to ascertain precisely why we do it? Will you hazard so desperate a step while there is a possibility that any of the ills you fly from have no real existence? Will you, while the certain ills you fly to are greater than all the real ones you fly from, will you risk the commission of so fearful a mistake? [p. 120].

His conclusion drew participation from contemplation: "My countrymen, one and all, think calmly and *well* upon this whole subject" (p. 122), and, in the line paraphrased by Kennedy, he said: "In *your* hands, my dissatisfied fellow-countrymen, and not in *mine,* is the momentous issue of civil war" (p. 122). One reason that Lincoln's first inaugural is a great address is that the audience was asked to participate actively in contemplating the meaning of the constitutional principles Lincoln laid down and in judging whether these principles warranted secession.[18]

Each of the elements forming a presidential inaugural ought to facilitate the President's task of reconstituting his listeners as "the people." The traditional values rehearsed by the President need to be selected and framed in ways that unify the audience. Thus, for example, following a campaign replete with charges that he was an atheist, Jefferson's speech assured former adversaries that he recognized the power of the deity, "acknowledging and adoring an overruling Providence . . . , that Infinite Power which rules the destinies of the

---

[17]For a discussion of this dimension of epideictic rhetoric, see Chaim Perelman and L. Olbrechts-Tyteca, *The New Rhetoric: A Treatise on Argumentation,* trans. John Wilkinson and Purcell Weaver (Notre Dame, Ind.: University of Notre Dame Press, 1969), pp. 49–51.

[18]Garfield made a moving plea that echoed Lincoln's first inaugural. In 1881 he said: "My countrymen, we do not now differ in our judgment concerning the controversies of past generations, and fifty years hence our children will not be divided in their opinions concerning our controversies. They will surely bless their fathers and their fathers' God that the Union was preserved, that slavery was overthrown, and that both races were made equal before the law. We may hasten or we may retard, but we can not prevent, the final reconciliation. Is it not possible for us now to make a truce with time by anticipating and accepting its inevitable verdict?" (p. 146).

In a footnote to his analysis of Nixon's first inaugural, Robert L. Scott called attention to Nixon's excessive use of the pronoun "I." Such personal references, discussed below, not only violate the presidential persona that the speaker should assume but, as Scott noted, they also tend to preclude the joint action through which the President and the people covenant together. (See "Rhetoric That Postures: An Intrinsic Reading of Richard M. Nixon's Inaugural Address," *Western Speech* 34 [Winter 1970], p. 47.)

universe . . . " (pp. 16–17). Similarly, the founders were eulogized in early inaugurals but disappeared as the Civil War approached. Since Garrison and other abolitionists had widely publicized the founders' slaveholding, public veneration of them would ally a President with those who favored slavery and invite the enmity of its opponents. Van Buren's exceptional reference in 1837 to Washington and the other founders can be explained by his explicitly pro-slavery position.[19] The point to be noted is that when an appeal that was once a unifying recollection of past heroes interferes with the process of reconstituting the audience as a unified people, it is abandoned.

Just as recollection of the past and rehearsal of traditional values need to be non-controversial and unifying, so recommitment to constitutional principles unifies by assuring those who did not vote for this President that he will, nevertheless, scrupulously protect their rights. The same needs to unify the audience and to speak in the epideictic present also influence the language in which Presidents articulate the principles that will govern their administrations.

Rehearsing Traditional Values

To demonstrate his qualifications for the office, the President must venerate the past and show that the traditions of the institution continue unbroken in him. He must affirm that he will transmit the institution intact to his successors. Consequently, the language of conservation, preservation, maintenance, and renewal pervades these speeches. What we conserve and renew is often sanctified as our "creed," our "faith," and our "sacred trust." Cleveland's statement in 1885 is illustrative: "On this auspicious occasion we may well renew the pledge of our devotion to the Constitution, which, launched by the founders of the republic and consecrated by their prayers and patriotic devotion, has for almost a century borne the hopes and aspirations of a great people through prosperity and peace and through the shock of foreign conflicts and the perils of domestic strife and vicissitudes" (p. 151).

Presidential use of the principles, policies, and presidencies of the past suggests that, in the inaugural address, *memoria* or shared recollection is a key source of *inventio*, the development of lines of argument. Lincoln's final appeal in his first inaugural illustrates the rhetorical power and resources of the past: "The mystic chords of memory, stretching from every battlefield and patriot grave to every living heart and hearthstone all over this broad land, will yet swell the chorus of the Union, when again touched, as surely they will be, by the better angels of our nature" (p. 123). Coolidge put it more simply: "We cannot continue these brilliant successes in the future, unless we continue to learn from the past" (p. 215). Such use of the past is also consistent with the ritualistic process of representing beginnings, origins, and universal relationships.

The past is conserved by honoring past Presidents. Washington was praised by John and John Quincy Adams, Jefferson, Taylor, and Van Buren; Monroe and

---

[19] The extent to which the founders, including George Washington, were identified with pro-slavery positions was illustrated by John C. Calhoun, speaking in the Senate on March 4, 1850. He said: "Nor can the Union be saved by invoking the name of the illustrious Southerner whose mortal remains repose on the western bank of the Potomac. He was one of us—a slaveholder and a planter. We have studied his history, and find nothing in it to justify submission to be wrong." (Text as in A. Craig Baird, ed., *American Public Addresses, 1740–1952* [New York: McGraw-Hill, 1956], p. 83.)

Jackson referred to their illustrious predecessors; Lincoln spoke of the distinguished citizens who had administered the executive branch. The past is also conserved by reaffirming the wisdom of past policies. Cleveland, for example, praised policies of Washington, Jefferson and Monroe (p. 152); McKinley praised the policy of "keeping ourselves free from entanglement, either as allies or foes" (p. 17).

The past is also used analogically to affirm that just as we overcame difficulties in the past, so will we now; the venerated past assures us that the nation has a future. Thus, in 1932, in the face of severe economic problems, Franklin Roosevelt said: "Compared with the perils which our forefathers conquered because they believed and were not afraid, we have still much to be thankful for" (p. 232), and in 1941 he reminded his audience of the difficult tasks that confronted Washington and Lincoln (p. 243).

In the world of inaugural addresses, we have inherited our character as a people; accordingly, veneration of the past not only unifies the audience but warrants present and future action, as recurring references to "no entangling alliances" have illustrated. A more recent example is found in the 1981 inaugural in which Reagan paraphrased a statement Jefferson made in 1801. Jefferson said: "Sometimes it is said that man cannot be trusted with the government of himself. Can he, then, be trusted with the government of others?" (p. 16). Reagan said: "But if no one among us is capable of governing himself, then who among us has the capacity to govern someone else?"[20]

As Reagan's use of Jefferson illustrated, a President must go beyond the rehearsal of traditional values and veneration of the past to enunciate a political philosophy that will inform the incoming administration. Because rhetorical scholars have focused on the specific political principles laid down in individual inaugurals, they have often failed to note that although these principles vary from inaugural to inaugural, all inaugurals not only lay down political principles but present and develop such principles in predictable ways.

Enunciating Political Principles

In many inaugurals, presidents indicate that they feel obliged to set forth the principles that will govern their tenure in office. Jefferson's explicit 1801 statement exemplified this: "About to enter, my fellow-citizens, on the exercise of duties which comprehend everything dear and valuable to you, it is proper you should understand what I deem the essential principles of our Government, and consequently those which ought to shape its Administration . . . " (p.16). In keeping with the epideictic character of inaugurals, however, specific policies are proposed for contemplation, not action. Proposals are not an end in themselves but illustrations of the political philosophy of the speaker. This contemplative, expository function differentiates policy proposals embedded in inaugurals from those in State of the Union addresses, where there is a call to immediate action.[21]

[20]Ronald Reagan, "Inaugural Address," *Vital Speeches of the Day* 47 (Feb. 15, 1981):258–59. Bert E. Bradley, "Jefferson and Reagan: The Rhetoric of Two Inaugurals," *Southern Speech Communication Journal* 48 (Winter 1983):119–36, is an extended comparison of the inaugural addresses of 1801 and 1981.

[21]Kathleen Hall Jamieson, *Critical Anthology of Public Speeches* (Chicago: Science Research Associates, 1978), pp. 28–30.

So, for instance, in a relatively detailed statement of his political views, Polk discussed "our revenue laws and the levy of taxes," but this discussion was an *illustration* of the principle that "no more money shall be collected than the necessities of an economical administration shall require" (p. 93). Similarly, he aired his position on the national debt to *illustrate* the principle that "melancholy is the condition of that people whose government can be sustained only by a system which periodically transfers large amounts from the labor of the many to the coffers of the few. Such a system is incompatible with the ends for which our Republican Government was instituted" (p. 93).

Because Taft conceived the inaugural address as a vehicle of articulating relatively specific policy, his speech provides a rigorous test of the claim that inaugurals deal with principles rather than practices. Taft said: "The office of an inaugural address is to give a summary outline of the main policies of the new administration, so far as they can be anticipated" (p. 189), but his tedious list of recommendations functions not as a call for specific, immediate action, but as evidence of continuity and of loyalty to the Constitution. He said, for example: "I have had the honor to be one of the advisers of my distinguished predecessor, and as such, to hold up his hands in the reforms he has initiated. . . . To render such reforms lasting, however, . . . further legislative and executive action are needed" (p. 189). Such reforms ("the suppression of the lawlessness and abuses of power of the great combinations of capital invested in railroads and in industrial enterprises carrying on interstate commerce") were defined as means of maintaining the democratic character of the government. Again, they became illustrations of following broad principles.

The rite of investiture demands that the President do more than rehearse traditional values and enunciate a political philosophy. He must also enact his presidential role.

Enacting the Presidency

The audience, unified as "the people," witnesses the investiture of the President. To complete and ratify the President's ascent to power, the inaugural address demonstrates rhetorically that this person can function as a leader within the constitutionally established limits of executive power and that he can perform the public, symbolic role as President of all the people.

The inaugural address is thus performative. It evinces presidential leadership by the very fact of its delivery. As President, the speaker appropriates the country's history and assumes the right to say what that history means; as President, the speaker asserts that some principles are more salient than others at this moment; as President, the speaker constitutes hearers as "the people"; and as President, the speaker asks "the people" to join in a mutual covenant to commit themselves to the political philosophy enunciated in the address.

Franklin Roosevelt's first inaugural dramatically underscored his role as a leader and the special importance of executive action. He spoke of "a leadership of frankness and vigor" and said: "I am convinced that you will again give the support to leadership in these critical days" (p. 231). "This Nation asks for action, and action now" (p. 232), and "With this pledge taken, I assume unhesitatingly the leadership of this great army of our people . . . " (p. 233). However, Roosevelt was aware that he was pressing the limits of executive power. He said:

It is to be hoped that the normal balance of executive and legislative authority may be wholly adequate to meet the unprecedented tasks before us. But it may be that an unprecedented demand and need for undelayed action may call for temporary departure from that normal balance of public procedure, I am prepared under my constitutional duty to recommend the measures that a stricken nation . . . may require. . . . I shall ask Congress for the one remaining instrument to meet the crisis—broad Executive power to wage a war against the emergency, as great as the power that would be given to me if we were in fact invaded by a foreign foe [p. 234].

What is crucial here is that Roosevelt portrayed his leadership as constitutional. Special powers would be conferred by Congress, and those powers would be analogous to the extraordinary powers exercised by previous Presidents in similarly extreme circumstances.

An abiding fear of the misuse of executive power pervades our national history. Washington's opponents accused him of wanting to be king; Jackson was called King Andrew and Van Buren, King Martin; Teddy Roosevelt was attacked in cartoons captioned "Theodore Roosevelt for ever and ever"; Lincoln's abolition of habeas corpus and Franklin Roosevelt's use of executive power as well as his pursuit of a third and fourth term were damned as monarchical, or worse, as despotic.[22] The American Revolution was fought, the Declaration of Independence reminds us, in response to "repeated injuries and usurpations, all having in direct object the establishment of an absolute Tyranny over these States. . . ." To allay fears of incipient tyranny, the incoming President must assure the citizenry that he does not covet power for its own sake and that he recognizes and respects constitutional limits on his authority.

There is a paradox in the demand that a President demonstrate rhetorically a capacity for effective leadership while carefully acknowledging constitutional limitations. To the extent that the speaker promises strong leadership, there is a risk of being seen as an incipient tyrant. By contrast, should the President emphasize the limits on executive power, there is a risk of being seen as an inept or enfeebled leader. Eloquent Presidents have walked this tightrope with agility, as Lincoln did in his first inaugural when he responded to the fear that he would use executive power to abolish slavery: "I have no purpose, directly or indirectly, to interfere with the institution of slavery in the States where it exists" (p. 117). He attested that this was a consistent position for him by citing statements from his campaign speeches and a plank from the Republican party platform. This material he characterized as "the most conclusive evidence of which the case is susceptible" (pp. 117–18). Addressing abolitionist revulsion against the fugitive slave law, he quoted Article 4 of the Constitution and averred that the law was merely an extension of that article, a part of the Constitution he had just sworn to uphold. He added: "I take the official oath to-day with no mental reservations and with no purpose to construe the Constitution or laws by any hypercritical rules" (p. 118).

In recognizing the limits on presidential power, inaugurals not only affirm the balance of power and locate executive initiatives in the mandate of the people, they also offer evidence of humility. The new President humbly acknowledges deficiencies, humbly accepts the burdens of office, and humbly invokes God's

[22]Marcus Cunliffe, *American Presidents and the Presidency* (New York: American Heritage Press, 1968), pp. 149, 152, 154–55, 158, 163, 172.

blessings. The precedent for evincing humility was set in the first inaugural when Washington said: "The magnitude and difficult of the trust to which the voice of my country called me, being sufficient to awaken in the wisest and most experienced of her citizens a distrustful scrutiny into his qualifications, could not but overwhelm with despondence one who ought to be peculiarly conscious of his own deficiencies . . . " (p. 3). Washington's attitude was echoed in Carter's less felicitous comment in 1977: "Your strength can compensate for my weakness, and your wisdom can help to minimize my mistakes."[23]

Inaugurals typically place the President and the nation under God, and this, too, is part of the process of acknowledging limits. By calling upon God, the President subordinates himself to a higher power. References to God are not perfunctory. The God of the inaugurals is a personal God who is actively involved in affairs of state, an "Almighty Being whose power regulates the destiny of nations," in the words of Madison (p. 27), a God "who led our fathers," in the words of Jefferson (p. 22), a God who protects us, according to Monroe (p. 38), a God revealed in our history, according to Cleveland (p. 153), and a God who punishes us, according to Lincoln: "He gives to both North and South this terrible war as the woe due to those by whom the offense came . . . " (p. 126). The President enacts the presidential role by placing himself and the nation in God's hands. We should note, however, that it is only when the President is fully invested in office that he has claimed the authority to place the nation "under God." For this reason, perhaps, prayers or prayerlike statements have usually occurred near or at the end of inaugurals. This can explain why Eisenhower called the prayer he delivered prior to his first inaugural "a private prayer." Although he had taken the oath of office, he was not yet fully invested as the President and until he had performed further rhetorical acts of acceptance, he sensed that he lacked the authority to represent the nation before God.

The placement of prayers or prayerlike statements is a subtle indication that the inaugural address is an integral part of the rite of investiture. Some inaugurals have articulated the notion that the President becomes the President *through* delivering the inaugural address. For example, William Henry Harrison concluded his 1841 speech this way: "Fellow citizens, being fully invested with that high office to which the partiality of my countrymen has called me, I now take affectionate leave of you" (p. 86).[24]

If an inaugural address is to function performatively as part of the investiture, the President must speak in his public role as the President. An inaugural would not fulfill this function if the address pressed forward the personality or personal history of the incoming President.[25] When evidence is drawn from the President's personal past, it must reveal something about the presidency or about the people or the nation. Personal narrative is inappropriate in a rhetorical genre designed for the formal display of the President as the President. The functions of personal material in an inaugural are clearly different from the functions of

---

[23]Carter's statement calls attention to the risks involved in confessing limitations. This remark could be taken as evidence of inability to lead forcefully.

[24]In 1877 Rutherford B. Hayes expressed similar sentiments as he began his address: "We have assembled to repeat the public ceremonial, begun by Washington, observed by all my predecessors, and now a time-honored custom, which marks the commencement of a new term of the Presidential office" (p. 137).

[25]See material from Scott cited in n. 18, above.

like material in campaign oratory where a high level of self-disclosure and self-aggrandizement is not only appropriate but expected. The functions of self-references also distinguish the inaugural address from other presidential rhetoric.[26]

A dramatic example of inappropriate personal material appeared in the final paragraph of Grant's second inaugural. He concluded: "Throughout the war, and from my candidacy for my present office in 1868 to the close of the last Presidential campaign, I have been the object of abuse and slander scarcely ever equalled in political history, which to-day I feel that I can afford to disregard in view of your verdict, which I gratefully accept as my vindication" (p. 135). The statements speak of Grant, the person, not of the presidency or of Grant, the President. In so doing, the statement called into question Grant's ability to fulfill the symbolic role of President of all the people.

By contrast, Franklin Roosevelt used his personal past effectively. In his fourth inaugural in 1945, he said: "I remember that my old schoolmaster, Dr. Peabody, said, in days that seemed to us then to be secure and untroubled: 'Things in life will not always run smoothly. Sometimes we will be rising toward the heights—then all will seem to reverse itself and start downward. The great fact to remember is that the trend of civilization itself is forever upward; that a line drawn through the peaks and valleys of the centuries always has an upward trend' " (p. 247). It was wartime; this statement brought hope out of tribulation and became the basis for Roosevelt's claim that although the Constitution is a firm foundation, it is still a document open to improvement. The lesson of his mentor allowed Roosevelt to say something he could not have asserted himself as effectively.

More recently, Carter's use of a statement by a former teacher illustrates a potential pitfall in using personal material. Immediately after thanking Gerald Ford for all he had done to heal the divisions in the nation, Carter said: "In this outward and physical ceremony, we attest once again to the inner and spiritual strength of our Nation. As my high school teacher, Miss Julia Coleman, used to say, 'We must adjust to changing times and still hold to unchanging principles.' "[27] As we have argued, the first duty of the President in an inaugural is to reconstitute his audience as "the people." Carter was attempting to forge an American community out of his listeners. However, only certain people have the standing to do that, and Miss Julia Coleman, however able she may have been as a high school teacher, was not one of them. Had Carter made her the voice of the people expressing a timeless truth, Coleman's aphorism might have been appropriate later in the inaugural. Despite Coleman's lack of authority, her adage might have served had it been an unusual, penetrating, immediately intelligible,

---

[26]Roderick P. Hart's computerized analysis of 380 presidential speeches generated by 8.01 level of self-reference (all first-person pronouns were counted). By contrast, the nine inaugurals in this sample generate a 1.12 level of self-reference. (See *Verbal Style and the Presidency* [Orlando, Fla.: Academic Press, 1984], pp. 273, 279.) A further refinement of self-referencing has been made by Dan Hahn, who noted that in 1977 Carter used "we" forty-three times, "our" thirty-six times, but "I" only six times in his inaugural. (See "The Power of Rhetorical Form," a paper presented at the Fourth Annual Conference on Discourse Analysis, Temple University, March 1983, p. 6.)

[27]Jimmy Carter, "Inaugural Address," *Public Papers of the Presidents of the United States,* Jimmy Carter, 1977, Book I (Washington, D.C.: U.S. Government Printing Office, 1977), p. 1.

vivid statement of the relationship between change and continuity. However, even such a claim is questionable. In Carter's statement we have the rhetorical equivalent of what would have occurred had Kennedy said, "To paraphrase my old headmaster, 'Ask not what your country can do for you. . . .' " [28]

A presidential inaugural address is part of the process by which the President is invested in office. As a result, the audience expects the presidential role to be enacted: a demonstration of ability to lead, to recognize the limits of executive power, to speak and act in a presidential, rather than a personal, role. A President, as President, can unify the audience as "the people" and lay down the principles that will guide the coming administration. Finally, the President must demonstrate his understanding of the epideictic demands of a ritualistic event.

Fulfilling Epideictic Requirements

The qualities Aristotle ascribes to epideictic discourse are qualities appropriate to ritualistic or ceremonial events. All U.S. presidential inaugurals are speeches of display inviting the audience to evaluate the rhetor's skill in enacting his role. Like other epideictic discourse, they praise or blame, affirm traditional values, heighten what is known and believed, use elegant language, and focus on the eternal present. Great inaugurals express the nuances of the relationship between the people and the President and respond to situational exigencies in a more subtle fashion than their more pedestrian peers. Inaugurals frequently praised include Washington's first, Jefferson's first, Lincoln's first and second, Franklin Roosevelt's first, and Kennedy's. Some add Theodore Roosevelt's first, Wilson's first, and Franklin Roosevelt's second. [29] These especially admired inaugurals share certain characteristics: (1) they reinvigorate as well as rehearse traditional values; (2) they create memorable phrases that sum up who we are as a people and what the presidency is as an institution; (3) they involve us actively in redefining the nation as embodied in the principles guiding the incoming administration; and (4) they address timely questions timelessly, or, in the words of William Faulkner, their "griefs grieve on universal bones." [30]

Great inaugurals capture complex, situationally resonant ideas in memorable phrases. We still recall Jefferson's "peace, commerce, and honest friendship with all nations, entangling alliances with none" (p. 17) and Lincoln's "With malice toward none, with charity for all, with firmness in the right as God gives us to see the right, let us strive to finish the work we are in, to bind up the nation's wounds, to care for him who shall have borne the battle and for his widow and his orphan, to do all which may achieve and cherish a just and lasting peace among ourselves and with all nations" (p. 126). We remember Franklin Roosevelt's "So, first of all, let me assert my firm belief that the only thing we have to fear is fear itself" (p. 231) and Kennedy's "And so, my fellow Americans, ask not what your country can do for you: Ask what you can do for

[28]The Rev. George St. John, headmaster of Choate, the preparatory school in Wallingford, Conn., attended by John F. Kennedy, used to say to his students, "Ask not what your school can do for you; ask what you can do for your school" ("Walter Scott's Personality Parade," *Parade*, Dec. 15, 1968, p. 2).

[29]Schlesinger, *The Chief Executive*, p. vii.

[30]William Faulkner, "Nobel Prize Speech," in Stewart H. Benedict, ed., *Famous American Speeches* (New York: Dell, 1967), p. 223.

your country" (p. 271). Such phrases illustrate special rhetorical skill in reinvigorating traditional values; in them familiar ideas become fresh and take on new meaning.

Stylistically and structurally, great presidential inaugurals are suited to contemplation. Through the use of parallelism, for example, Kennedy revived our traditional commitment to the defense of freedom when he said: "We shall pay any price, bear any burden, meet any hardship, support any friend, oppose any foe, in order to assure the survival and success of liberty" (p. 269). The memorable antithesis, "Let us never negotiate out of fear. But let us never fear to negotiate" (p. 270), was a vivid restatement of our modern tradition of relationship to foreign nations. Kennedy's more famous antithesis asked citizens to contemplate a redefinition of who they were as a people, a redefinition based on sacrifice. through the use of assonance, Kennedy underscored the nuclear peril when he spoke of "the steady spread of the deadly atom" (p. 270). By arresting attention, such literary devices invite listeners and readers to ponder these ideas, ideas less suited to contemplation when started in more mundane language.

Inaugurals enable us to consider who and what we are as a people; great inaugurals invite us to see ourselves in new lights, to constitute ourselves as a people in new ways. In 1913, for example, Wilson said: "We have been proud of our industrial achievements, but we have not hitherto stopped thoughtfully enough to count the human cost. . . . We have come now to the sober second thought" (p. 200). In 1865, Lincoln compelled listeners to consider God's view of the conflict between the North and the South when he said: "Both read the same Bible and pray to the same God, and each invokes His aid against the other. . . . The prayers of both could not be answered. That of neither has been answered fully. The Almighty has His own purposes" (pp. 125–26). In 1961, Kennedy spoke of "a call to bear the burden of a long twilight struggle, year in, and year out . . . " (p. 271), a call that suggested *Götterdämmerung* and denied easy victory or inevitable triumph.[31]

In a special and significant sense, the great inaugurals are timeless. They articulate a perspective that transcends the situation that parented them and for this reason they retain their rhetorical force. For instance, although Lincoln's first inaugural encompassed the situation of a nation poised on the brink of civil war, Lincoln's message speaks to all situations in which the rights of constituent units are seen to clash with the powers of a central body. Similarly, the eloquent conclusion of Lincoln's second inaugural might be applied today to the wounds that remain in the nation from the conflict over the war in Vietnam. Although Franklin Roosevelt's first inaugural assured his hearers that they, as a people led by Roosevelt, could surmount that economic crisis, it also assures us that Americans can surmount all material problems. Kennedy's inaugural reflected the history of the cold war, but it also expressed the resoluteness required under any circumstances to sustain a struggle against a menacing ideology. Finally, George Washington's inaugural not only spoke to the immediate crisis but articulated what Arthur Schlesinger calls "a great strand that binds them [the inaugurals] together."[32] Washington said: "The preservation of the sacred fire of liberty and the destiny of the republican model of government are justly considered,

---

[31]A number of other inaugurals include admonitions. See, e.g., the addresses of Eisenhower in 1957 (p. 264), Truman (p. 252), and Harding (p. 211).

[32]Schlesinger, *The Chief Executive*, p. vii.

perhaps, as *deeply*, as *finally* staked on the experiment intrusted to the hands of the American people" (pp. 4–5).

The great inaugurals not only re-present this fundamental idea, they reenact the process by which the President and the people "form a more perfect union." In recreating this mutual covenant, great inaugurals both reconstitute the audience as "the people," they constitute us as a people in some new way: as those entrusted with the success or failure of the democratic experiment (Washington I), as members of a perpetual Union (Lincoln I), as a people whose spiritual strength can overcome material difficulties (Franklin Roosevelt I), as a people willing to sacrifice for an ideal (Kennedy), as a people capable of counting the costs of industrial development (Wilson I), as members of an international community (Wilson II), as limited by the purposes of the Almighty (Lincoln II), as a people able to transcend political differences (Washington I, Jefferson I). Notably, the great inaugurals dramatically illustrate the processes of change within a continuous tradition. In them, the resources of epideictic rituals are yoked to political renewal.

We have identified four major elements that constitute the American presidential inaugural as a genre. Our analysis suggests the processes by which a distinctive kind of epideictic rhetoric comes into being. Its broadest parameters are set by the general characteristics of epideictic discourse. A specific kind of ceremony and occasion refines the genre further. In this case, the presidential inaugural is part of a rite of passage, of investiture, a rite that establishes a special relationship between speaker and audience. The demands of investiture require a mutual covenant, a rehearsal of fundamental political values, an enunciation of political principles, and the enactment of the presidential persona.

The conventions of this rhetorical type also emerge because the Presidents we elect know the tradition and tend to study past inaugurals before formulating their own. So, for example, in 1809 in the sixth inaugural, Madison said: "Unwilling to depart from examples of the most revered authority, I avail myself of the occasion now presented to express the profound impression made on me by the call of my country" (p. 25).[33] Over time, earlier presidential inaugurals have frequently been quoted, especially those of Washington, Jefferson, Lincoln, and Franklin Roosevelt. This process of rhetorical introversion illuminates some remarkable coincidences. Harding and Carter, for example, quoted the same verse from Micah. Franklin Roosevelt and Carter quoted a former teacher; Franklin Roosevelt and Kennedy had a rendezvous with destiny, Reagan paraphrased Jefferson, Nixon paraphrased Kennedy, Kennedy echoed Lincoln, Polk rephrased Jackson, Reagan echoed Kennedy. In other words, Presidents recognize, capitalize on, and are constrained by the inaugurals of their predecessors which, taken together, form a tradition.

As we have said, presidential inaugurals are shaped by their epideictic character, by inauguration as a rite of investiture, and by the inaugural tradition. However, presidential inaugurals vary. What makes the U.S. presidential inaugural a

---

[33]Eight years later, in 1817, Monroe said: "In commencing the duties of the chief executive office it has been the practice of the distinguished men who have gone before me to explain the principles which would govern them in their respective Administrations. In following their venerated example my attention is naturally drawn to the great causes which have contributed in a principal degree to produce the present happy condition of the United States" (p. 33).

genre is that the variation is of a certain sort. Circumstances vary as do the personalities of the presidents, but the variation among inaugurals is predictable.

Inaugural addresses vary substantively because presidents choose to rehearse aspects of our tradition that are consistent with the party or political philosophy they represent. Such selective emphasis is illustrated in Franklin Roosevelt's second inaugural address, in which he said:

> Instinctively we recognize a deeper need—the need to find through government the instrument of our united purpose to solve for the individual the ever-rising problems of a complex civilization . . . In this we Americans were discovering no wholly new truth; we were writing a new chapter in our book of self-government. . . . The essential democracy of our Nation and the safety of our people depend not upon the absence of power, but upon lodging it with those whom the people can change or continue at stated intervals through an honest and free system of elections. . . . We have made the exercise of all power more democratic; for we have begun to bring private autocratic powers into their proper subordination to the people's government . . . [pp. 237–38].

Later, he added: "Today we reconsecrate our country to long-cherished ideals in a suddenly changed civilization" (p. 240). Similarly, in 1981 Ronald Reagan chose to emphasize facets of the system in order to affirm values consistent with his conservative political philosophy. He said: "Our government has no power except that granted it by the people. It is time to check and reverse the growth of government which shows signs of having grown beyond the consent of the governed."[34]

A major variation occurs in inaugurals delivered by incumbent Presidents. Because a covenant already exists between a reelected President and "the people," the need to reconstitute the community is less urgent. Because the country is familiar with a sitting President's political philosophy, the requirement of stating one's philosophy is also muted. Reelected Presidents tend to recommit themselves to principles articulated in their prior inaugurals or to highlight only those principles relevant to the agenda for the coming term. In this respect, subsequent inaugurals by the same President tend to be extensions, not replications, of earlier inaugurals.

The inaugural addresses themselves articulate the reason for this generic variation. For instance, although he was a President in the midst of the most serious of crises, Lincoln said:

> At this second appearing to take the oath of the Presidential office there is less occasion for an extended address that there was at the first. Then a statement somewhat in detail of the course to be pursued seemed fitting and proper. Now, at the expiration of four years, during which public declarations have been constantly called forth on every point and phase of the great contest which still absorbs the attention and engrosses the energies of the nation, little that is new could be presented [p. 125].[35]

---

[34]Reagan, "Inaugural Address," p. 259.

[35]In 1805 Jefferson reported that his conscience told him he had lived up to the principles he had espoused four years earlier (p. 19). In 1821 Monroe said: "If the person thus elected has served the preceding term, an opportunity is afforded him to review its principal occurrences and to give the explanation respecting them as in his judgment may be useful to his constituents" (p. 41).

Some Presidents have used a subsequent inaugural to review the trials and successes of their earlier terms. In so doing, they have rehearsed the immediate past, a move rarely made in first inaugurals. When subsequent inaugurals develop specific policies, these are usually described as continuations of policies initiated in the previous term, continuations presumably endorsed by the President's reelection.

Special conditions faced by some Presidents have caused some subsequent inaugurals to resemble first inaugurals. For example, in 1917 Wilson said: "This is not the time for retrospect. It is time rather to speak our thoughts and purposes concerning the present and the immediate future" (p. 203). In the face of the events of World War I: "We are provincials no longer. The tragic events of the thirty months of vital turmoil through which we have just passed have made us citizens of the world. There can be no turning back. Our own fortunes as a nation are involved whether we would have it so or not" (p. 204). The war prompted Wilson to constitute "the people" in a new way, as citizens of the world. Similarly, the events leading to World War II affected Franklin Roosevelt's choices in 1941. He said: "In this day the task of the people is to save the Nation and its institutions from disruptions from without" (p. 243). That statement of "the task" diverged sharply from the principles emphasized in 1933 and 1937.

Conclusion

Variability in inaugural addresses is evidence of an identifiable cluster of elements that fuse to form the *essential* inaugural act. Each apparent variation is an emphasis on or a development of one or more of the key elements we have described. Washington's second inaugural address underscored the role of the audience as witnesses and the address as an extension of the oath of office. Jefferson's first address was a call to unity through the enunciation of political principles; Lincoln's first inaugural was a dramatic appeal to the audience to join in the mutual covenant between the President and the people; his second was an exploration of what it means to say that this nation is "under God." Theodore Roosevelt explored the meaning of our "sacred trust" as it applied to a people with an international role; Franklin Roosevelt's first address explored the nature of executive leadership and the limits of executive power, whereas his second constituted the audience as a caring people; Wilson's first inaugural explored the meaning of U.S. industrial development. Finally, Kennedy's address exploited the possibilities of the noble, dignified, literary language characteristic of the epideictic to such an extent that his address is sometimes attacked for stylistic excess.[36]

The U.S. presidential inaugural as a genre, then, must reconstitute "the people" as an audience that can witness the rite of investiture. The inaugural must

---

[36]E.g., Garry Wills wrote: "The famous antitheses and alliterations of John Kennedy's rhetoric sound tinny now" (*The Kennedy Imprisonment: A Meditation on Power* [New York: Pocket Books, 1982], p. 312).

More detailed treatments of the style of John Kennedy's inaugural address include Edward P. J. Corbett, "Analysis of the Style of John F. Kennedy's Inaugural Address," *Classical Rhetoric for the Modern Student* (2nd ed.; New York: Oxford University Press, 1971), pp. 554–65; and Sam Meyer, "The John F. Kennedy Inauguration Speech: Function and Importance of Its 'Address System,' " *Rhetoric Society Quarterly* 12 (1982):239–50.

rehearse communal values from the past, set forth the political principles that will guide the new administration, and demonstrate that the President can enact the presidential persona appropriately. Still more generally, the presidential inaugural address in an epideictic ritual that is formal, unifying, abstract, and eloquent; at the core of this ritual lies epideictic timelessness—the fusion of the past and future of the nation in an eternal present in which were affirm what Franklin Roosevelt called "our covenant with ourselves" (p. 247); a covenant between the executive and the nation that is the essence of democratic government.

THE SOCIAL MOVEMENTS APPROACH

MOVEMENTS: CONFRONTATION AS RHETORICAL FORM

Robert S. Cathcart

"Every movement . . . has form. It is a progress from *pathema* through *poiema* to *mathema:* from a 'suffering, misfortune, passive condition, state of mind,' through 'a deed, doing, action, act,' to an 'adequate idea; the thing learned.' . . . To study a movement is to study a drama, an act of transformation, an act that ends in transcendence, the achievement of salvation. . . . And hence to study a movement is to study its form."[1]

This statement will serve as a beginning point for the contentions I advance. I assume that few would quarrel with the notion that a movement has form, and most rhetorical scholars accept the idea that a movement is primarily a symbolic or rhetorical act.[2] But, having said that movements are rhetorical acts, I have not said much more than the sociologists who say that movements are collective acts seeking social change. To understand movements as rhetorical acts constrained by a particular rhetorical form requires that we know something about how this form is exhibited, what are the forces that shape it and in turn are shaped by it, how it does its work, and the reasons for its existence as form.

From the *Southern Speech Communication Journal*, 43, 3 (Spring 1978): 223–47. Used by permission of the Southern Speech Communication Association and Robert S. Cathcart.

Dr. Cathcart is professor of speech at Queens College, New York.

[1]Leland M. Griffin, "A Dramatistic Theory of the Rhetoric of Movements," *Critical Responses to Kenneth Burke*, ed. William H. Rueckert (Minneapolis: University of Minnesota Press, 1969), 461–62. Within this statement Griffin is quoting from Kenneth Burke's *A Grammar of Motives*, pp. x–xvi, 38–43, 376; *Counter Statement*, pp. 48, 128, 213–14; and *The Philosophy of Literary Form*, p. 76.

[2]See Leland M. Griffin, "The Rhetoric of Historical Movements," *Quarterly Journal of Speech*, 38 (1952), 181–85; Edwin Black, *Rhetorical Criticism* (New York: The Macmillan Co., 1965); Herbert Simons, "Requirements, Problems and Strategies: A Theory of Persuasion for Social Movements," *Quarterly Journal of Speech*, 56 (1970), 1–11; Dan F. Hahn and Ruth Gonchar, "Studying Social Movements: A Rhetorical Methodology," *The Speech Teacher*, 20 (1971), 44–52; Charles A. Wilkinson, "A Rhetorical Definition of Movements," *The Central States Speech Journal*, 27 (1976), 88–94; Ralph R. Smith and Russell R. Windes, "The Rhetoric of Mobilization. Implications for the Study of Movements," *The Southern Speech Communication Journal*, 42 (1976), 1–19.

In an earlier essay I argued that "movements are carried forward through language, both verbal and non-verbal, in strategic [ways] that bring about identification of the individual with the movement. . . . Movement is a form related to a rationale and a purpose . . . one which gives substance to its rationale and purpose."[3]

It was my purpose then to establish the notion that movements are essentially rhetorical transactions of a *special type,* distinguishable by the peculiar reciprocal rhetorical acts set off between the movement on the one hand and the established system or controlling agency on the other. I argued, "It is this *reciprocity* or *dialectical enjoinment in the moral arena* which defines movements and distinguishes them from other dramatistic forms."[4] I concluded, this "particular dialectic . . . becomes the necessary *ingredient* which produces the rhetorical form that we have come to recognize as a political or social movement."[5]

Since the appearance of that essay a number of articles on the rhetoric of movements have expressed disagreement with my position. The disagreements have centered mainly around the contentions that either my definition was incomplete, or too narrow and restrictive to be of practical use to rhetoricians studying movements.[6] That it was incomplete must be granted. That it was too narrow depends on whether one seeks definitions which will cast the widest net, allowing a multitude of acts to be claimed as movements, or definitions that will so focus our vision that we can more exactly distinguish amongst various similar appearing rhetorical acts. I for one think there is much merit in pursuing definitions which allow us to sort out rhetorical transactions that in the general sociopolitical milieu appear to be quite similar but which have at base a particular rhetorical form which brings forth a unique set of rhetorical strategies.

With that in mind, I will argue that a movement can be identified by its *confrontational form.* More specifically, I will argue that movements are a kind of ritual conflict whose most distinguishing form is *confrontation.* Unfortunately, the word "confrontation" is loosely applied to a wide variety of acts and enactments such as "confronting the morning newspaper" or "confronting the elements," as well as "confronting the police" or "confronting the system." Also, when applied in socio-political conflict it carries the notion of violence and the negation of reason. Despite such common usage and mis-usage, I find the concept *confrontation* to have a symbolic significance which, when traced to its conceptual underpinnings, is quite revealing of those collective behaviors referred to as "movements."

In this essay I will use confrontation to mean that form of human behavior labeled "agonistics," i.e., pertaining to ritual conflicts. Confrontation is

[3]Robert S. Cathcart, "New Approaches to the Study of Movements: Defining Movements Rhetorically," *Western Speech,* 36 (Spring 1972), 86. This point is supported in part by William Bruce Cameron, *Modern Social Movements* (New York: Random House, 1966), p. 174.

[4]Cathcart, "New Approaches to the Study of Movements: Defining Movements Rhetorically," p. 87.

[5]Cathcart, "New Approaches to the Study of Movements: Defining Movements Rhetorically, p. 88.

[6]Wilkinson (p. 90) states, "Unfortunately, Cathcart's article, though quite intentionally, ends where it should begin." And, Smith and Windes (p. 142) observe, "Change to a more restricted usage can have negative consequences." Also, Ralph R. Smith and Russel R. Windes in "The Innovational Movement: A Rhetorical Theory," *Quarterly Journal of Speech,* 61 (1975), 142, state, "While Cathcart properly limits the definition of rhetorical movements to the features of discourse, his approach does not distinguish between movements and other classes of rhetorical acts."

symbolic display acted out when one is in the throes of agony. It is a highly dramatistic form; for every ritual has a moral aspect, expressing, mobilizing social relationships, confining or altering relationships, maintaining a reciprocal and mutual balancing system. Agnostic ritual is redressive. It is a means of reaffirming loyalties, testing and changing them or offering new ones to replace old loyalties, always expressed in a kind of muted symbolic display designed to elicit a symbolic response which changes attitudes and values without major and unlimited conflict. Confrontation as an agonistic ritual is not a prelude to revolution or warfare but is a ritual enactment that dramatizes the symbolic separation of the individual from the existing order.[7]

I note that others in the field of rhetoric like Scott, Burgess, Simons, Andrews, and Bailey have found "confrontation" to be worthy of examination in its own right, or at least as an adjunct to communication.[8] They have pointed out that, contrary to popular notions, confrontation is not anti-communication but rather is an extension of communication in situations where confronters have exhausted the normal (i.e., accepted) means of communication with those in power.[9] Further, they consider confrontation to be a communicative form directly associated with movements. Their examination of confrontation has, however, been limited to its *instrumental role*—to its use as a tactic for gaining an audience or opening channels to carry the primary message.[10] In addition, some of these studies have implied that confrontation is a somewhat questionable or exceedingly desperate form of communication.[11]

Without denying confrontation's widespread and important instrumental function, I wish to present confrontation as a *consummatory form essential to a movement*. To do so it is necessary first to re-examine the question, What is it we are seeing and describing when we talk about *a movement?* Most rhetorical

[7]H. L. Nieburg, "Agonistics Rituals of Conflict," *The Annals of the American Academy of Political and Social Science*, 391 (1970), 56–73.

[8]Robert L. Scott and Donald K. Smith, "The Rhetoric of Confrontation," *Quarterly Journal of Speech*, 55 (1969), 1–8; James R. Andrews, "Confrontation at Columbia: A Case Study in Coercive Rhetoric," *Quarterly Journal of Speech*, 55 (1969), 9–16; Herbert W. Simons, "Confrontation as a Pattern of Persuasion in University Settings" (Unpublished paper, Temple University, 1969); Harry A. Bailey, Jr., "Confrontation as an Extension of Communication," *Militancy and Anti-Communication*, ed. Donn W. Parson and Wil A. Linkugel (Lawrence, Kansas: House of Usher, 1969), pp. 11–26; and Parke G. Burgess, "The Rhetoric of Moral Conflict: Two Critical Dimensions," *Quarterly Journal of Speech*, 56 (1970), 120–30.

[9]See, for example, Bailey, "Confrontation as an Extension of Communication" (p. 24): "It [confrontation] is generally a signal that the usual and established methods of securing policy are not sufficient."

[10]See Bailey (p. 24): "Confrontation . . . is that which is designed to bring about non-negotiable demands." See also, Andrews (p. 16): "It may be that in an examination of the means of protest and not necessarily in an inherent worthiness of their goals . . . the rhetorical critic could reach judgments concerning the essential nature of confrontation." Scott and Smith (p. 7), however, treat confrontation as both instrumental and consummatory: "One should observe the possible use of confrontation as a tactic for achieving attention and an importance not readily attainable through decorum." And, "Without doubt, for many the act of confrontation itself, the march, the sit-in, or altercation with police is enough. It is consummatory."

[11]An example is the statement by William Bruce Cameron, "Some Causes and Effects of Campus Confrontations," in *Militancy and Anti-Communication (p. 35):* "Confrontation precludes disproof because it does not permit a rational examination of the issues. Often the very people who claim to be most concerned about examining the issues stage confrontations in such a way that no serious examination could possibly take place."

scholars have answered this in part by using sociological descriptions; for example, the object referred to as a movement is "an uninstitutionalized collectivity that mobilizes for action to implement a program for the reconstitution of social norms and values."[12] In addition, there has been a general acceptance of the idea that there are various or distinctive types of movements such as reform movements, radical movements, etc. This view of movements as types has also been drawn from the literature of the sociologists of collective behavior. Accordingly, what we seem to be seeing when we observe a movement is a group of people, not identified by institutional membership, who act together to produce change; and this "acting together" can be distinguished by how militantly or aggressively the group performs, and by whether the goal of the group is change in social norms, hierarchical change, or a reordering of values. It generally is argued that, depending on the group's goals and methods, there will be produced a distinctive *form* of rhetoric.

I find it difficult to accept such a construct or definition of movements, not because I want to be a purist about the word "movement" but because such a definition fails, in my opinion, to help us distinguish between two fundamentally different forms of rhetoric—one which I shall call *managerial* and the other I shall call *confrontational*. To put it another way, it can be very useful to our understanding of socio-political activities if we can distinguish between those rhetorical acts which by their form uphold and re-enforce the established order or system and those which reject the system, its hierarchy and its values. Needless to say, the great bulk of communication in any society must of necessity fall into the former category. As Scott, Bevilacqua and others have pointed out, almost all Aristotelian rhetorics are *managerial* in form.[13] They are designed to keep the existing system viable: they do not question underlying epistemology and group ethic. On the other hand, *confrontational* rhetoric occurs only in special and limited circumstances, such as periods of societal breakdown or when moral underpinnings are called into question.

It is this confrontational aspect—the questioning of the basic values and societal norms—that makes true movements a real threat that cannot be explained away as a temporary malfunction of the system or as the conspiratorial work of a handful of fanatics. Though some individuals may have felt threatened when former Black Panther leader Bobby Seale ran for the office of Mayor of Oakland, California, many more felt a great sense of relief. And, rightly so, because no matter how radical his campaign platform, the form of his rhetoric as *office seeker* was supportive of the system. It was an overt act of faith in the legitimacy of the established order. On the other hand, no member of the established order could mistake the threat to the whole system when Seale and other Black Panthers confronted the Oakland police and the California State Assembly with rifles and shotguns in hand, for the Panthers were saying symbolically that they rejected the laws and codes of the "white establishment" and were placing themselves outside or apart from the existing white racist hierarchy. To know that the latter was confrontational and not managerial communication, one has only to examine the reciprocating rhetorical acts which came forth from all levels

---

[12]Simons, p.3

[13]Robert L. Scott, "A Synoptic View of Systems of Western Rhetoric," *Quarterly Journal of Speech,* 61 (1975), 445–46; Vincent Bevilacqua, "Philosophical Origins of George Campbell's Philosophy of Rhetoric," *Speech Monographs,* 32 (1965), 7.

of the existing system. Almost all, including many blacks, condemned the act as a step toward anarchy or toward a suicidal racial war perpetuated by black devils of destruction. In other words, almost all perceived of it as a rhetorical act emanating from *outside the system.*

Using this notion of confrontational rhetoric as the counterpart of managerial rhetoric, I find that many of the so-called "types" of movements described in recent literature do not appear to be movements at all, but rather adjustments to the existing order. A closer look at those activities labeled "reform" movements reveals a rhetorical form which is managerial rather than confrontational. Their rhetoric is primarily concerned with adjusting the existing order, not rejecting it. The reformist campaign stays inside the value structures of its existing order and speaks with the same vocabularies of motive as do the conservation elements in the order. The reform must not seem to be a threat to the very existence of the established order, or the reformers may be forced out of the common value system. The reform movement uses a managerial rhetoric because to some degree it must have a *modus vivendi* with those in power if it is to exist.

To place reform movements on a continuum with radical movements by the claim that they are inherently the same kind of act—just less militant or aggressive—is to misconstrue the uses of "identification" and "consubstantiation" in a rhetorical setting.[14] I find Griffin to be instructive on how to recognize the managerial form of identification and consubstantiation underlying reform movement rhetoric: "Though men, in any system, are inevitably divided, 'identification is compensatory to division.' And through identification with a common condition or 'substance,' men achieve an understanding (a sense of unity, identity, or consubstantiality). Any system that endures implies an adequate understanding, a dynamic understanding. . . . It is the understanding essential to the ultimate achievement of integration. . . . For it provides the basis for communication. . . . Men agree on meaning, value, and desire; and hence they gladly submit to a code of control, obey the commandments."[15] What we see when a "reform" movement or "status" movement, etc., is viewed through the Burkean prism is a rhetorical form which recognizes the division but accepts "the common substance." Such movements produce a rhetoric that embraces the values of the system, accepts that the order has a code of control which must not be destroyed, while at the same time striving to gain acceptance of that which will perfect (or restore to perfection) the system. Such a rhetoric is essentially managerial.

Furthermore, I believe that those who would have an activity that seeks corrective change in the system labeled "a movement" make the mistake of assuming that either there will be no alienation or agitation within a well-ordered system, or that movements are the only means of redress or alteration in the established order. As I pointed out in my earlier essay,

> We must be aware that when we talk of society, or the establishment, or the system, we are talking about a dynamic, everchanging collection of groups. In one sense every group activity within society is a movement but in another and more important

---

[14]For an explanation of "identification" and "consubstantiation" as ingratiation see Kenneth Burke, *A Rhetoric of Motives* (New York: George Braziller, Inc., 1955), pp. 19–29, and Kenneth Burke, "Rhetoric—Old and New," *The Journal of General Education*, 5 (1951), 203.

[15]Griffin, *Critical Responses to Kenneth Burke*, p. 458.

sense the ever-evolving, changing society is the status quo. What the rhetorical critic of movements must be concerned with then is not definitions [of movements] . . . which describe the dynamic status quo, i.e., the [activities] which give it its dynamism, but definitions which describe those collective behaviors which cannot be accommodated within the normal [motion] of the status quo.[16]

What most so-called reform movements have in common is the basic acceptance of the system as *the* system, along with its moral imperatives and ethical code. The rhetorical form produced by such groups is characterized by consubstantiating motives which are ground for the strategies for improving or perfecting the order. Examples of this are the Populist call for more direct representation in government and more control over (and therefore more rightful rewards for) one's own labors, and the Civil Rights call of the 1960s for "Freedom Now," meaning the wider distribution and more even application of the justice and equality basic to the established system. Even so-called "status" or "transcendent" movements, with their striving for the moral improvement of individuals, are at base claiming that more perfected individuals will improve the existing order and make it function better morally.

Further, I believe that a careful examination of the rhetoric of such collectives, reform movements and the like, will reveal that their strategies of identification and consubstantiation are formed out of what Burke calls "the mystery" or the "keeping of the secret." It is Burke's position that "mystery arises at that point where different kinds of beings are in communication."[17] In any good rightful system men accept the mystery and strive to keep the secret; that is, preserve the hierarchy.[18] Within such rhetoric, identification with agency and purpose is always present. It is necessarily so because what we have is the rhetoric of piety, the essence of which is to establish what properly goes with what. To Burke, the rhetoric of piety is "a system builder, a desire to round things out, to fit experience together as a unified whole."[19] It is the rhetoric of piety—the keeping of the secret—that is characteristic of most reform activities, and it is that which keeps the rhetoric in bounds—that which limits its agitation and dictates it strategies. This keeping of the secret governs also the *counter rhetoric* produced, which *defines the acts of the group seeking change as "reforms" rather than revolution.*

There is, I believe, another kind of collective behavior which is perceived of (or reacted to) as "radical" or "revolutionary." Its form is *confrontational.* It contains the rhetoric of "corrosion" and "impiety."[20] The dramatic enactment of this rhetoric reveals persons who have become so alienated that they reject "the mystery" and cease to identify with the prevailing hierarchy. They find themselves in a scene of confrontation where they stand alone, divided from the existing order; and inevitably they dream of a new order where there will be salvation and redemption. Once again, Griffin's description of this act is informative. He says such persons are "moved by an impious dream of a mythic new

[16]Cathcart, pp. 85–86.
[17]Burke, *A Rhetoric of Motives,* p. 115
[18]Griffin, *Critical Responses to Kenneth Burke,* p. 458.
[19]Burke, *Permanence and Change* (Rev. ed., Los Altos, California: Hermes Publications, 1954), 69–75.
[20]Burke, *The Rhetoric of Religion* (Berkeley: University of California Press, 1970), pp. 215–22.

Order—inspired with a new purpose . . . they are moved to act: moved . . . to rise up and cry *No* to the existing order—and prophesy the coming of the new. And thus movements begin."[21]

This confrontation I consider to be "consummatory"—the essential form of a movement, *because up to the point of confrontation it is impossible to know that a radical or true movement exists.* That is, without confrontation the movement rhetoric cannot be distinguished from the rhetoric of the collective seeking change and improvement, but not replacement of the existing order. It is the confrontation form that *produces dialectial enjoinment in the moral area.* For, in every political order there are those who are alienated and who seek change within the hierarchy, and there will always be those who seek power and control over events and groups—those who want a greater "share of the pie" and those who want to improve the existing order for its own sake. Inevitably these persons will form collectives and utilize a rhetoric that petitions, that recruits, that even threatens dire consequences. What distinguishes these collectives from radical or true movements is that *they do not confront the system.* Rather, they maintain the mystery; i.e., keep the secret that the existing order is a true order, one that is in continual movement toward perfection and in which communication through identification and consubstantiation is possible. No matter how contentious the change seekers may become, there is an understood code of control—an identity, a consubstantiality which places limits on the kinds of rhetorical acts that may be performed. In short, there is a dramatization at this level that is rhetorically different from the dramatic enactment of those who confront the system.

For a movement to be perceived as something other than the evolving status quo or the legitimate action of system change agents, there must be created a drama or agonistic ritual which forces a response from the establishment commensurate with the moral evil perceived by movement members. The confrontation ritual is enacted by the juxtaposing of two human forces or two agents, one standing for the erroneous or evil system and the other upholding the new or perfect order. These two agents must be brought into ritual conflict through confrontation in order for both to recognize that this is no ordinary reform or realignment of the established order.

The rhetoric of a movement is a rhetoric of re-ordering rather than of re-forming. As Burke points out, every order implies hierarchy—what goes with what, what is more, what is less, what is necessary, etc. Hierarchy includes what is *not* proper, *not* useful, *not* valuable; thus, "the negative." Man, the seeker after perfection, recognizes the negative and becomes aware of his own guilt. And to remove guilt he must seek redemption either through striving to perfect the hierarchy (i.e., established order) or by recognizing the evil of the erroneous system, confessing to his own victimage (mortification) and confronting the evil system with a new, more perfect order (redemption).

Through confrontation the seekers of change (the victims) experience a conversion wherein they recognize their own guilt, transcend the faulty order and acquire a new perspective. This "symbolic rejection of the existing order is a purgative act of transformation and transcendence. It affirms the commitment of the converted to the movement—to the new understanding . . . and hence it endows

[21]Griffin, *Critical Responses to Kenneth Burke,* p. 460.

them with a new condition 'substance'—with a new identity, a new unity, a new motive.''[22]

The enactment of confrontation gives a movement its identity, its substance and its form. No movement for radical change can be taken seriously without acts of confrontation. The system co-opts all actions which do not question the basic order, and transforms them into system messages. Confrontational rhetoric shouts "Stop!" at the system, saying, "You cannot go on assuming you are the true and correct order; you must see yourself as the evil thing you are."

An excellent example of the rhetoric of confrontation can be found in the act of the "Catonsville 9" wherein nine Catholic priests and lay workers use napalm to burn the selective service files at Catonsville, Maryland, in 1968. According to Charles Wilkinson, who has made a rhetorical study of this incident as part of the Catholic Anti-War Movement in the United States,[23] "The rhetoric of guilt is employed by nine 'American Citizens' and 'Catholic Christians' burdened with a collective sense of guilt for their country as a war-waging empire and for the church as an accomplice in those wars. Here, the rhetoric is clearly directed to themselves as well as to the masses which comprise the status quo of both church and state. . . . Most immediately it addressed the Nine themselves since they also required the rhetorics of its languaging process to enable them to act as they did."[24] The words of the Nine in their mimeographed press release reveal the nature of the confrontation—the rejection of the mystery, the victimage, and the dream of a new order:

> We, American citizens, have worked with the poor in the ghetto and abroad. In the course of our Christian ministry we have watched our country produce more victims than an army of us could console or restore. . . . All of us identify with the victims of American oppression all over the world. We use napalm on these records because napalm has burned people to death in Vietnam, Guatemala and Peru; and because it may be used on America's ghettos. We destroy these draft records not only because they exploit our young men, but because these records represent misplaced power, concentrated in the ruling class of America. . . . We are Catholic Christians who take the Gospel of our Faith seriously. . . . We confront the Catholic Church, other Christian bodies and the synagogues of America with their silence and cowardice in the face of our country's crimes.[25]

The incident at Catonsville was a confrontation, and as such it forced a dialectical enjoinment in the moral arena between the perpetrators and the established order.

No individual can be *of* the movement without an act which recognizes one's own guilt or complicity with the system and which commits the individual to the *new* order. As Scott and Smith point out in their study of the rhetoric of confrontation, confrontation symbolizes the rite of the kill: "The situation [confrontation] shrieks kill-or-be-killed. . . . The blighted self must be killed in striking

[22]Griffin, *Critical Responses to Kenneth Burke*, p. 465.

[23]Charles Wilkinson, "The Rhetoric of Movements: Definition and Methodological Approach, Applied to the Catholic Anti-War Movement in the United States," Dissertation, Northwestern University, 1974.

[24]Charles Wilkinson, "The Rhetorical Criticism of Movements: A Process Analysis of the Catonsville Nine Incident" (Unpublished paper, Northwestern University, 1977), p. 9.

[25]Charles Wilkinson, "The Rhetorical Criticism of Movements: A Process Analysis of the Catonsville Nine Incident," p. 16.

the enemy. By the act of overcoming his enemy, he who supplants demonstrates his own worthiness, effacing the mark, whatever it may be—immaturity, weakness, sub-humanity—that his enemy has set upon his brow. . . . To satisfy the rite that destroys the evil self in the act of destroying the enemy that has made the self evil, the radical may work out the rite of the kill symbolically."[26]

Brenda Hancock Robinson demonstrates how this act of confrontation as guilt and redemption is essential to the Women's Liberation Movement. In her article, "Affirmation by Negation in the Women's Liberation Movement," she points out that, "lashing out at the enemy can serve to release women's own guilt feelings in a liberating catharsis. A frequent refrain in feminist rhetoric is that no revolution can occur unless women recognize their oppressed status; such recognition implies they have somehow participated in the oppression, at least by submitting to it. Many women have actually prided themselves on their duplicity—their ability to play at ignorance and helplessness, for example. Guilt from recognizing one's own acquiescent role in the oppression must be turned outward toward the oppressor."[27]

Robinson provides an analysis of an essay by Robin Morgan, "Goodbye to All That," which she considers exemplary of this aspect of the movement, and she finds that "Morgan's statement rings with the eloquence of all the previous no's combined, with a spirit not tentative but angry and final. The enemy is established. The victimage is complete. There is no entreaty to denounce male chauvinism; she rejects it outright." She concludes: "Morgan's essay illustrates that the process of negating the existing order and naming the enemy is important not only in isolating the movement's victim, but also in giving women identity as the *antithesis* of men."[28]

Here we see the use of confrontational rhetoric as a "totalistic strategy," to use the words of Scott and Smith.[29] The members of the movement through confrontation draw the line that excludes themselves from the existing order and creates their total dependence on the movement. It is the point from which there is no turning back. Confrontation is a proclamation. It proclaims through the movement, "We are already dead but we are reborn." It says, "We are united in the movement and we understand you for what you are, and you know that we understand."

Confrontation as rhetoric is not an act of violence per se; nor is it a method of warfare. Rather, it is a symbolic enactment which dramatizes the complete alienation of the confronter. As a rhetorical act it is more consummatory than instrumental. It takes a form which prevents the receiver from construing its meaning as an expression of personal dissatisfaction or as a prod toward more rapid response to grievances. Confrontation demands a response that goes beyond the actions of the confrontation itself. It is a dramatization created by the forced juxtaposing of two agents, one standing for the evil, erroneous system and the other upholding the new or "perfect" order. These two agents must be brought into conflict through confrontation in order for both to recognize that what is

---

[26]Scott and Smith, p. 4. In this passage the authors draw upon the ideas of Franz Fanon as expressed in *The Wretched of the Earth*.

[27]Brenda Robinson Hancock, "Affirmation by Negation in the Women's Liberation Movement," *Quarterly Journal of Speech*, 58 (1972), 266.

[28]Hancock, p. 267.

[29]Scott and Smith, p. 6.

called for is a moral response appropriate to the moral accusation communicated by the act of confrontation.

It is the act of confrontation that causes the establishment to reveal itself for what it is. The establishment, when confronted, must respond not to the particular enactment but to the challenge to its legitimacy. If it responds with full fury and might to crush the confronters, it violates the mystery and reveals the secret that it maintains power, not through moral righteousness but through its power to kill, actually or symbolically, those who challenge it. Invariably, the response of the establishment spokesmen will reveal whether or not there has been an actual confrontation. The response to confrontation is always characterized by polarization and radical division. Grievances are not recognized as such in confrontation; they are portrayed as trumped-up charges to fool the public and hide the conspiracy. The leadership of the movement is not recognized, for it has no legitimacy, and to confer with it would be tantamount to doing business with the devil. The response of the establishment to confronters is to treat them as moral lepers: to isolate them and pin the anarchist label on them. Such response fuels the confrontation and points the way for the movement. Now the secret has been revealed—the mystery violated—and the struggle can be seen as a true moral battle for power and for the legitimate right to define the true order.

Confrontation serves, also, to identify the membership of the movement. Movements are rag-tag organizations at best, continually plagued by problems of organization, recruitment and mobilization. Acts of confrontation demand a personal commitment beyond simply agreeing with the goals of the movement or recognizing that there are wrongs to be righted. To engage in confrontation requires that the individual admit complicity with the oppressors and to publicly confess guilt, while at the same time redeeming oneself. Many a follower of a movement stops short of confrontation, hoping to keep up a protest without either denying the system or the self. Witness, for example, the role of many liberals during the Vietnam antiwar movement. Acts of confrontation, however, are acts of acting together. They are public statements of conversion which, when coupled with the establishment response, formally commit the individual to the movement, making such individuals dependent on the movement for whatever legitimacy they are to have. Without the act of confrontation a movement would not be able to identify its true believers.

There remains much to be discovered about confrontation and the rhetoric of movements. Confrontation as a rhetorical act may be as important in its own way as the rhetorical act of identification. I believe a Burkean philosophy of rhetoric allows for, even requires, a rhetoric of confrontation if we are to fully understand the role of man as symbol maker and user.

THE CONTEMPORARY AMERICAN ABORTION CONTROVERSY: STAGES IN THE ARGUMENT

Celeste Condit Railsback

Most Americans are tired of hearing about the painful and apparently irresolvable issue of abortion.[1] They feel that they have heard all the arguments, have seen all the ghastly pictures, and have been offered no happy answers. The current public debate about abortion seems to be stalemated, but this is a relatively recent stage in the controversy. A tracing of arguments about abortion during the crucial decades of the sixties and seventies shows major changes in the public arguments used to discuss the topic.[2] The controversy has evolved through seven identifiable stages, from emotional narrative to squabbling implementation and stalemate.

A close examination of these stages accomplishes several objectives.[3] It helps to explain how and why the current American assessments of abortion have come to be as they are. It also fills research gaps cited by Robert S. Cathcart, James R. Andrews, and Leland Griffin, because it provides a "social movement" study that is detailed, that focuses on language strategies rather on events and actors, and that takes into account the interaction between "movement" and

From *Quarterly Journal of Speech* 70 (November 1984): 410–24. Used by permission of the author and Speech Communication Association.

Dr. Railsback is an assistant professor of speech communication, University of Illinois. The author wishes to thank Professors Bruce E. Gronbeck, Michael Calvin McGee, and John R. Lyne for their help with the dissertation upon which this essay is based (University of Iowa, 1982).

[1]See, for example, Robert N. Lynch, "Abortion and 1976 Politics," *America*, 6 March 1976, p. 177. The exhaustion of the issue was also noted in the legislature; see, Susan Fraker et al., "Abortion under Attack," *Reader's Digest*, September 1978, p. 42. Since there can be no "neutral position" on a moral issue such as abortion, I wish to admit my biases from the outset. I believe that abortion, especially after the first eight weeks of pregnancy, is highly undesirable because it takes the life of a potential human and submits a woman to an unpleasant (or worse) medical procedure. I do not believe, however, that the most effective means to reduce the number of abortions (especially late-term abortions) is to outlaw all abortions.

[2]This analysis is based on a systematic reading of all the articles indexed under the heading "abortion" in the *Reader's Guide to Periodical Literature* from 1960 to 1980. In addition, a non-systematic analysis was made of newspaper articles and editorials, pamphlets, books, and broadcast items. The major differences between the magazine sample and the other sources are these: the newspapers are more particularized, dealing with specific subsets of issues; the broadcast media tend to be vastly abbreviated, except in Public Broadcast debates, and pamphlets tend to be extremist.

[3]The method involved counting and analyzing what some theorists consider to be the two main elements of argumentative discourse—the ideographs and the pentadic elements. An ideograph is a condensed social normative term which serves as a warrant for public behavior (e.g. "liberty"). See Michael Calvin McGee, "The 'Ideograph': A Link between Rhetoric and Ideology," *Quarterly Journal of Speech*, 66 (1980), 1–17. A "pentadic analysis" charts the grammar of the motive structure in a discourse. The grammar consists of the relationships among the agents, acts, agencies, scenes, and purposes which are "characterized" concretely by the rhetors. See Kenneth Burke, *A Grammar of Motives* (1945; rpt. Berkeley: University of California Press, 1969).

"counter-movement," rather than viewing a movement in isolation.[4] Finally, the study also provides more general hypotheses about patterns of rhetoric in the process of social change.

Prelude—Professional Arguments

When the argument over abortion became public in the early sixties, it was not the first time. In the 19th century, a similar violent and vigorous argument over abortion had raged.[5] This argument was settled when the various state legislatures outlawed almost all abortions. Gradually, a dominant ideology solidified which held that abortion constituted the taking of human life and was an assault on the primary social values of "family" and "motherhood." As described by Barbara Plant, however, that settlement did not provide a congenial solution for all, and it produced small-scale, but persistent resistance.[6] Advocates in the sixties made little reference to these earlier arguments. Indeed, most of them seemed oblivious to the existence of such argumentation.[7]

Of more direct importance to the eventual formulation of the public argument in the sixties were the abortion arguments in the professional fields that occurred in the fifties.[8] Professionals gave focus to the early public arguments and also recruited abortion reform advocates—many from the ranks of the physicians. Thus, the first stage of the contemporary American abortion controversy was the professional stage.

The professional debate appeared in scholarly forums.[9] The controversy involved psychiatrists, doctors, social workers, population analysts, and lawyers who were faced with ever-increasing tensions because their roles required them to provide assistance of various kinds to women who desired abortions and who

[4]See Robert S. Cathcart, "Defining Social Movements by Their Rhetorical Form," *Central States Speech Journal*, 31 (1980), 267, and in the same number, James R. Andrews, "History and Theory in the Study of the Rhetoric of Social Movements," 274–81; and Leland Griffin, "On Studying Movements," 226; see also Leland Griffin, "The Rhetoric of Historical Movements," *Quarterly Journal of Speech*, 38 (1952), 184–88.

[5]James C. Mohr, *Abortion in America: "The Origins and Evolution of National Policy, 1800–1900* (New York: Oxford Union Press, 1978).

[6]Barbara Plant, "Abortion as a Secondary Birth Control Measure: A Funcational Approach," M.A. Thesis, University of Windsor, April 1971.

[7]Authors may cite pre-18th-century roots of abortion policy, but they pay little attention to later periods, especially to the 20th century. See John T. Noonan, Jr., *The Morality of Abortion: Legal and Historical Perspectives* (Cambridge, Massachusetts: Harvard University Press, 1970), pp. xi–xvii; Lawrence Lader, *Abortion II: Making the Revolution* (Boston: Beacon Press, 1973), p. xi; for a slight exception, see Betty Sarvis and Hyman Rodman, *The Abortion Controversy* (New York: Columbia University Press, 1974).

[8]I borrow the distinction among "fields" of argument from Stephen Toulmin, *The Uses of Argument* (Cambridge: The University Press, 1958). For elaborations of the concept, see Bruce E. Gronbeck, "Sociocultural Notions of Argument Fields: A Primer," in *Dimensions of Argument: Proceedings of the Second Summer Conference on Argumentation*, ed. George Ziegelmueller and Jack Rhodes (Annandale, Va: Speech Communication Association, 1981), pp. 1–21. In the same volume, see also David Zarefsky, " 'Reasonableness' in Public Policy Argument: Fields as Institutions," pp. 88–100, and "Historical Reason: Field as Consciousness," pp. 101–13, and Walter R. Fisher, "Good Reasons: Fields and Genre," pp. 114–26.

[9]See, for example, Harold Rosen, ed., *Therapeutic Abortion* (New York: Julian Press, 1964). For a discussion of early conferences, see Sarvis and Rodman.

often sought illegal abortions.[10] The issues of their arguments were narrow and related primarily to the specific concerns of the various professions. For example, one of the first "solutions" to the abortion "problem" was the decision among physicians to create hospital committees to decide which women could have "legal" abortions. This solution eased only the emotional burden felt by individual physicians.[11] The growing pressures that had led professionals to experience a "problem" with abortion, however, soon led nonprofessionals to similar experiences.[12] Once nonprofessionals became involved, the professionally oriented and limited issues were rapidly found to be inadequate; they did not cover the full range of concerns in vocabulary appropriate to the public.

The Early Sixties

Public argument in the early sixties centered on legal reforms and consisted largely of the retelling of the tale of illegal abortion. The second stage of the argument, therefore, was dominated by a narrative form. The tale consisted of powerful descriptions of the traumas many women faced when having illegal abortions. In these mini-dramas, the rhetors described the agents, purposes, scenes, and agencies in "typical" illegal abortions.

The women in these dramatic horror stories were depicted quite sympathetically. For example, Marguerite Clark referred to the "wan nervous girl [who] could see only one way out of her dilemma."[13] Later, Sherri Finkbine, who had unknowingly taken thalidomide and had gone to Sweden to abort a deformed fetus, was portrayed as "a healthy and happily married Arizona woman, mother of four" and host of *Romper Room*.[14]

The reasons cited for these abortions were also dramatic. The women were emotionally ill, they had been raped, they carried deformed fetuses, or they were young girls of fourteen or fifteen who had been seduced by older men (even their fathers) and had been deserted.[15] Even the stories that cited

[10]I am making no attempt to speculate on the "causes" of this alteration in pressure. It does not matter whether the increased tension was caused by an increase in the numbers of illegal abortions, the number of legal abortions sought, or merely changes in attitudes. The rhetorical effect was "tension" among the physicians and they expressed that through discourse and behavior changes. Doctors with opinions ranging from Guttmacher's liberalism to Nathanson's eventual conservativism on the issue testified to these "tensions." See Bernard Nathanson with Richard Ostling, *Aborting America* (Garden City, New York: Doubleday and Company, Inc., 1979); Alan Guttmacher, *The Case for Legalized Abortion Now* (Berkeley: Diablo Press, 1967).

[11]See Lawrence Lader, *Abortion* (Boston: Beacon Press, 1966), pp. 24–41, for a Pro-choice view. Throughout, I use the terms "Pro-reform," "Pro-life," and "Pro-choice" as indications of what the advocates call themselves, not as labels of endorsement.

[12]It also led some professionals to enter the public arena as well (e.g. Guttmacher and Nathanson).

[13]Marguerite Clark, "Abortion Racket, What Should Be Done?" *Newsweek*, 15 August 1960, pp. 50–2, or Muriel Davidson, "Deadly Favor," *Ladies Home Journal*, November 1963, pp. 53–7. When citing arguments, I will generally refer to only one or two representative examples. It would be too unwieldy to list all of the articles that use a particular argument.

[14]"Abortion and the Law," *Time*. 3 August 1962, p. 30.

[15]For example, Marguerite Clark; James Ridgeway, "One Million Abortions," *New Republic*, 9 February 1963, pp. 14–17; "Why Did You Do It? France's Biggest Postwar Mass Abortion Trial," *Newsweek*, 10 June 1963, p. 54.

socio-economic reasons portrayed the most drastic possible cases of destitu-
tion—women who were "unwilling and unable to face a future with another
mouth to feed."[16]

The portrayals of the means used in these illegal abortions were often ghastly.
In contrast to references to "safe and simple" legal operations in which the
doctor simply "scrapes the products of conception out of the uterus,"[17] the articles graphically detailed the instruments of illegal abortions. One author indicated that the "bizarre items doctors have found include turkey quills, knitting
needles, hairpins, rattail combs, plastic bottles and even elastic bandages," as
well as "the most favored 'instrument' of the amateur"—"a straightened out
wire coat hanger inserted into a catheter" used for a "pack job."[18]

Recountings of these instruments were often accompanied by gory descriptions of the techniques of an entire abortion. One story of a young woman, who
had an engineering student abort her, told that

> he bought an ordinary flashlight, removed the batteries and cut the bottom off with
> a can opener. He used the flashlight as a speculum. . . . through this "speculum"
> he pushed a catheter into which he had threaded a wire. He then forced air through
> the contraption, which, unknown to him, had penetrated a blood vessel in the girl's
> womb. An air bubble entered the blood stream and in seconds reached her brain.
> Today this young woman is totally paralyzed.[19]

Other grisly methods—falling down stairs or injecting caustic soap solutions
into the womb—were also frequently described, and the most shocking details
possible were included. One such story told of an abortionist who thought he did
not have all the fetal matter out and ended up pulling out a woman's intestines.[20]
These horrific descriptions of the methods used in illegal abortions added great
impact to the emotional rejection of illegal abortion sought by the Pro-reform
authors.

As Kenneth Burke has noted, the container and the thing contained must suit
each other, and in this case, the arguers generally provided a suitable scene for
the grotesque operations.[21] The "back alley" became the common term for the
illegal abortion scene, but detailed depictions of dirty kitchens (some even with
photographs) or back car seats were also plentiful in this period.[22] In addition,
the involvement of the "underworld" was related in stories of women who met
strangers on street corners or in front of sleazy hotels, to be blindfolded and
driven to temporary, hidden destinations. Direct references to other "rackets,"
such as prostitution and gambling, were also included.[23]

[16]Clark, p. 51; Allan F. Guttmacher, "Law That Doctors Often Break," *Reader's Digest,*
January 1960, pp. 51–4.

[17]John Bartlow Martin, "Abortion," *Saturday Evening Post,* 20 May 1961, pp. 19–21;
"Abortion Facts Reported," p. 86; Faye Marley, "Legal Abortion Safer," *Science News
Letter,* 2 March 1963, p. 134.

[18]Davidson, pp. 53–4.

[19]Davidson.

[20]Martin, p. 21.

[21]Burke, p. 3.

[22]Martin, pp. 19–20; Walter Goodman, "Abortion and Sterilization: The Search for the
Answers," *Redbook,* October, 1965, pp. 70–1; Jack Starr, "Growing Tragedy of Illegal
Abortion," *Look,* 19 October 1962, pp. 52–3.

[23]Martin, pp. 19–20; Lader, *Abortion,* pp. 65–6.

Restatements of such stories aroused strong emotion, but they did not present a case for the desirability of abortion, only for the undesirability of illegal abortion.[24] Moreover, the audience, as well as many of the advocates themselves, believed that abortion was murder and a challenge both to God and patriarchal authority.[25] Consequently, activists urged only that abortions be permitted in limited and extreme circumstances. When five states modified their laws in the mid-sixties, the reforms reflected these limitations: abortions were legalized in the special cases of rape, incest, fetal deformity, or threat to the pregnant woman's physical or mental health.[26]

Resistance to these changes can be discovered in anti-reform arguments, which were infrequent. In contrast to the Pro-reform argument, which would eventually go through several significant ideographic shifts, the anti-legalization argument remained focused on one ideograph throughout—"life." Pro-life advocates stated simply that abortion was the taking of life, and hence *all* abortions had to remain illegal.[27] Pro-life advocates also argued for positive alternatives to abortion, such as adoptions or more rigid sexual standards.[28] This strategy allowed the dominant ideology to maintain its key values intact, while still responding to the tale of illegal abortion.

Thus, in the early sixties, the argument about abortion did not present a direct challenge to the prevailing beliefs about abortion, family, and motherhood. Instead, through an emotionally powerful narrative, it argued for minor concessions for extreme circumstances. Advocates of the dominant ideology answered that such exceptions could not be made because they would amount to murder. Both sides gained many adherents, but the Pro-reform side gained ground, because, for the first time in roughly a century, legal abortions were sanctioned in situations beyond the protection of the pregnant woman's life.

[24]Other arguments were also widely used in this period. The most important of these was the largely anti-Catholic argument that no religion should be allowed to impose its morality on others. In addition, physicians made the argument that they should be able to assess their patients' treatment based on medical expertise. A wide array of specific, refutative arguments were also used; for example, there were charges and counter-charges with regard to the Finkbine thalidomide case. Throughout, I will make generalizations about the major strands of argument in each period, but when I claim that an argument was made in a certain period, I mean it was most dominant then, not that the argument was not made at any other time or that no other arguments were made at that time.

[25]This ideology was expressed most vocally in the Catholic magazines during the early period. Other magazines did not carry the Pro-life argument until the late sixties (even conservative magazines like the *National Review*). For more elaboration, see Celeste Condit Railsback, "The Contemporary American Abortion Controversy: A Study of Public Argumentation," Diss., University of Iowa, 1982. This ideology and interest was not, of course, exclusively Catholic, but they were the most vocal group. This changed later in the controversy as conservative and fundamentalist organizations became involved. In the early sixties, the argument was based on God's gift of life. In later periods it was based on other foundations for "life" and on the importance of the family.

[26]Legal changes occurred in 1967, as Colorado, North Carolina, and California all modified their statues more or less after the American Legal Institute's Model Code. In 1968 Georgia and Maryland also made changes. In 1969, Kansas, Delaware, Arkansas, New Mexico, and Oregon modified their laws. A list of the dates of reform and repeal bills can be found in Sarvis and Rodman, pp. 30–33.

[27]See "Is Abortion Ever Justified? Two Church Views," *U.S. News and World Report,* 3 September 1962, p. 89; "Candle in a Dark World: West German Protestant Consultation Centers to Check Abortions," *America,* 19 October 1963, p. 445; R. A. McCormick, "Abortion," *America,* 19 June 1965, pp. 1241–44.

[28]"Candle in a Dark World," and McCormick.

The Late Sixties

It was unlikely that the abortion argument would rest at this point, however. Advocates of reform had, intentionally or not, made a forceful emotional claim against the horrors of all illegal abortions.[29] If knitting needles and back alleys were repugnant for "good women with good reasons," they were also gruesome for women with more "selfish" purposes. Moreover, the increased expectations of access to abortions outran the increased availability of abortions. Few additional abortions were performed under the new laws.[30] More central perhaps, the continued repetition of the tale of illegal abortion, and the Pro-life advocates' response to it, put a great deal of pressure on the narrative. If there were contradictions in the ideology and social conditions the tale abridged, the narrative would reveal them. The contradictions disclosed by the tale were many.[31]

The most blatant inconsistencies appear in the depictions of the agents involved—both the women having abortions and the men (frequently) performing the abortions. On the one hand, the women so vividly and fully characterized as aborters were generally young, single "victims." On the other hand, the pro-reform advocates noted in passing that illegal abortion really affected married women more frequently: "not the wanton teenager . . . not the naive girl in the big city . . . but the young (between 21 and 25 years) married woman is most likely to undergo an abortion," they warned.[32] A Pro-reform article might describe two or three "typical cases" of young victims, often having already declared that such cases were not typical at all.[33]

This contradiction arose because of the need to appeal to two ideological components. In the first instance, the tale worked best to generate sympathy within the "old" ideology if it told of the unfortunates who, through no fault of their own, were forced into an abortion. The entrenched ideology held that the only women who should have sex were those who were married, and if sex in marriage resulted in pregnancy, then every wife would want to carry through that pregnancy to enact or reenact the joys of motherhood.[34] Women were held generally responsible for their pregnancies and only youth, rape, or catastrophe could excuse them.

---

[29]From early in the sixties, advocates publicly argued for total repeal of abortion laws. Their views were generally not given much public and legislative attention until the late sixties. Other advocates argued only for reform.

[30]"Abortion and the Law," Newsweek, 2 December 1968; Lawrence Lader, "First Exclusive Survey of Non-Hospital Abortions," Look, 21 January 1969, pp. 63–65.

[31]To indicate that the narratives contained contradictions is not to indict them. The contradictions are a result of the rhetorical situation, not the ineptitude or error of the speakers.

[32]Clark, "Abortion Racket: What Should Be Done?" p. 51.

[33]Clark; Goodman, pp. 70–1.

[34]For example, Richard P. Vaughn notes that "the immature side of her nature rebels against the prospect of being a mother," but at another level she craves "the experience of fulfillment and creativity that accompanies motherhood," in "Psychotherapeutic Abortion: Bill under Consideration in California," America, 16 October 1965, pp. 436–8. See also, "Abortion by Consent?" Christian Century, 1 February 1967, p. 132 which seems to view abortion as a temporary whim. The dramatic "fetus talking to its mother" articles draw on these stereotypes as well; "Slaughter of the Innocent," trans. L. F. Chrobot, America, 2 June 1962, p. 39. In addition, the contrast between articles about women who desperately want children but miscarry and the women who desperately want abortions speaks to the tensions here.

Despite the rhetorical strength of this tale of illegal abortion, the motivating forces that led to many illegal abortions were quite different—the desire or economic need to control one's family, life style, and status through abortion.[35] Yet, because the women's liberation ideology had not been fully and publicly articulated, there were no salient arguments readily available to express the need or desire for abortion as a demand, and no advocates expressed the political "rights" of women.[36] Therefore, until the late sixties, the reality remained incongruously juxtaposed against the tale built by the arguers.[37]

A contradiction also existed in the descriptions of the abortionists. On the one hand, abortionists were described as "hacks" and "incompetents." They were men who

> lead disorganized lives—numerous divorces, alcoholism, drifting from job to job and place to place. Police sometimes find pornographic literature in their possession. Sometimes abortionists have sexual relations with their patients before aborting them.[38]

However, the reformers emphasize that, in fact, "90% of all the illegal abortions are performed by physicians using sterile procedures."[39] Sympathetic portraits described "a genial, graying family doctor who had served them [the community] for thirty years . . . founder of the Grove Public Library, former city councilman and the PTA's choice for Father of the Year in 1960."[40]

This contradiction arose from two sources. At the surface level, two different arguments for liberalizing abortion laws conflicted. The fear of disease and death from illegal abortion was a major impetus for reform, and painting a dirty and incompetent abortionist was necessary to generate that fear. Simultaneously, however, to placate the reigning ideology, advocates wished to argue that changing abortion laws would not bring about a change in the moral climate, and would not lead to more abortions. Therefore, they argued that legal changes would only legalize existing practices; illegal operations already conducted by physicians would merely become legal.

More importantly, there was a dramatic difference between the types of abortionists available to different classes. Upper middle class women were often able to get safe abortions from competent physicians. They had long been travelling to Cuba, Mexico and Puerto Rico for abortions that might not have been

---

[35]The actual number of illegal abortions is uncertain. Most estimates range from 200,000 to two million. In any case, the number had to be substantial (especially given 350,000 hospital admissions for complications from abortion). For "real causes," see Walter Goodman, and also, "Abortion Sought Abroad," *Science News Letter,* 24 July 1965, p. 63; *Health,* April, 1965, pp. 24–25.

[36]I refer here to the date the "women's movement" was brought into the public consciousness, not the academic or aesthetic circles. Gallup polls and popular magazine coverage indicate that this did not occur until the late sixties.

[37]This is, of course, a reflexive relationship; the material conditions surrounding the act of abortion help to generate the ideographs, but then are affected by interpretations produced by the ideology once it is developed.

[38]Martin, p. 52.

[39]Estimates range from "many" to 75% to 90%. "Abortion Facts Reported," *Science News Letter,* André E. Hellegers, "Law and the Common Good," *Commonweal,* 30 June 1967, p. 418 ff.; Ridgeway, p. 14.

[40]"Doc Henrie's Farewell," *Newsweek,* 30 June 1962, pp. 22 ff.

completely legal, but they were fairly routine.[41] More frequently, perhaps, their close contact with a private physician allowed them to get abortions at home as well. Poorer women turned to the abortionist quack.

Again, however, the ideological structure that would allow the clear expression of this discrepancy was not firmly in place in the early sixties. It was not until the later sixties that the term "discrimination" became general enough to be applied to abortion and the third stage of the argument, the ideographic stage, occurred.

By the late sixties, the Civil Rights movement's key terms—"freedom," "equality" (or "discrimination"), and "rights"—had gained strong salience.[42] The broad exposure and general acceptance of these terms provided a way to explain publicly the contradictions in the tale of illegal abortion.[43] The ideographs sorted out the confusion between tales of married and single women, competent physicians and incompetent hacks, by arguing that illegal abortion resulted from "discrimination." Affluent, married women were able to flaunt the poorly enforced law and gain safe abortions from well-qualified doctors. Their abortions constituted the statistics. The horror stories were created by the poor, single women who received "hatchet jobs" from untrained criminals.[44] The poor were being treated "unequally" and their "rights" violated. The heightened salience of the ideographs thus allowed advocates to do more than lament the sad stories of illegal abortion; the ideographs allowed the expressions of a legal and social demand.

This shift from narrative toward ideographic argument also required that a new policy be offered. If existing laws were objectionable because they caused discrimination, the inequity could not be remedied by changes in laws to allow a few of the more pitiable abortions, but only by elimination of the entire discriminatory system. Instead of arguing for reform laws, the new demand was for repeal of virtually all abortion laws.

During the late sixties, arguments about abortion also became tied with another growing "discrimination" issue, that of women's rights in general. If women were "free to choose" not to have children, their lifestyles would be quite different than if their only role was a "mother." Consequently, "control of our own bodies" began, in this period to become a major claim about "rights" in support of legalization of all abortions.[45] This line was not yet firmly instantiated as an ideographic argument for "choice," but clearly the foundations of that claim were laid at this point.

[41]Goodman, p. 71; Lader, *Abortion,* pp. 56–7; Davidson, p. 54.

[42]I am not arguing that changes in economics or social structure had taken place, merely that the terms were prevalent in popular discourse at the time. Even the somewhat negative polls showing that "racial harmony" was a major concern in the presidential elections of the period establish this point. See "Most Important Problems during Election Campaigns," *Gallup Opinion Index,* No. 181, September 1980, p. 11.

[43]A shift in attitudes can be traced, for example, in the desirability of black neighbors to whites. From 1958 to 1963 the primary position changes towards equality occurred in the South. From 1963 to 1965 there were also important attitude changes of about ten percent in the North. George H. Gallup, *Public Opinion: 1935–1971* (New York: Random House, 1972), pp. 1572–73, 1824, 1941.

[44]See as examples, Lader, *Abortion*; P. Kerby, "Abortion: Laws and Attitudes," *Nation,* 12 June 1967, pp. 754–56; "Abortion and the Law," *Newsweek,* 2 December 1968, pp. 82–83.

[45]See as examples, "Protecting Civil Liberties: The Right To Have an Abortion," *Current,* May 1968, pp. 26–28, or Robert E. Hall in *Saturday Review,* 7 December 1968, pp. 78–9.

The appearance of this argument was the first major challenge to the dominant ideology. Although the auxiliary ideograph "discrimination" made total legalization of abortion necessary,[46] that argument still worked within the key value terms of the status quo (e.g., "equality"). In contrast, the claim for "control of our own bodies," and the consequent implied repudiation of the role of "motherhood," would, in the seventies, come to represent a major challenge to the dominant ideology, which portrayed woman's highest (and virtually sole) calling as that of bearing children.[47] That break would generate the feminist stage of the argument and result in the key ideograph of the movement—"choice."

One final argument was of major importance in the late sixties—concern about "the unwanted child."[48] Before the 1960's, advocates had used eugenic arguments to condemn abortion. Eugenicists had argued that abortion led to the decrease of the upper classes and the increase of the lower classes.[49] This argument was reversed in a benign form in the "no unwanted children" argument in the later 1960's. Especially in 1967, Pro-reform advocates contended that unwanted children were a serious social problem. They linked unwanted children to delinquency and the cycle of poverty and child abuse. Abortion, they argued, was preferable to bearing a child who would be unwanted, for the sake both of the child and the society.[50]

The late sixties thus saw major shifts from narrative based argument to ideographic argument, from a reform argument to a repeal argument, and from an argument based on the dominant ideology to a feminist argument which would challenge the dominant ideology.

The Early Seventies

Some temporary legislative successes for the advocates of repeal signalled that America at least was tempted by these new arguments to endorse legalized abortion and to accept a more tolerant general understanding of abortion.[51] New York, for example, legalized virtually all abortions in 1970, and the number of

[46]Discrimination, the argument went, was caused by the rich having the resources to circumvent a law that was not supported by public experience, whereas the poor did not have such resources. Reform laws did not ameliorate that discrepancy.

[47]See n. 34. The concept "choice" arose as much from this demand to have motherhood be an option, as from any other source.

[48]"Desperate Dilemma of Abortion," Time, 13 October 1967, pp. 32–3, "Coping with Abortion: Panel Discussion," Mademoiselle, October 1967, pp. 211–212. Further reflections of the argument can be found in Carl Reiterman, ed., Abortion and the Unwanted Child (New York: Springer Publishing Co., 1971). This issue was also tied to the argument over the population "explosion" and the role of abortion in containing that growth.

[49]Mohr, p. 167.

[50]"Coping with Abortion."

[51]Alaska and Hawaii adopted very liberal laws, and New York adopted a virtual repeal law. However, in 1971 and 1972 there was a strong counter-reaction as referenda in North Dakota and Michigan were vigorously rejected and New York's repeal law was almost overturned, while Pennsylvania, Connecticut, and even the federal courts rejected abortion repeal. Actual changes in attitudes are difficult to document. Judith Blake, in "The Abortion Decisions: Judicial Review and Public Opinion," in Edward Manier, William Liu and David Solomon, eds., Abortion: New Directions for Policy Studies (Notre Dame, Indiana: University of Notre Dame Press, 1977), pp. 51–81, concluded that there was relatively little change from 1964 to 1971. At that time, the laws were merely "catching up" with public attitudes. However, there was a fair amount of change reported after this period by Eric M. Ulsaner and Ronald E. Weber in "Public Support for Pro-Choice Abortion Poli-

abortions performed there sky-rocketed.[52] The success of the reform laws and the resultant demand for repeal, however, were correlated with other changes as well. Reform advocacy was not conducted in a vacuum, and during this period there were major changes in the argument against legalized abortion which were advanced by those who called themselves "Pro-life." Those opposed to liberal abortion laws consistently had argued from the dominant ideology that the fetus must be protected as a human life.[53] In the late sixties they seemed to realize that the ideograph "life" was not protecting the fetus because the public did not unconditionally characterize a fetus as a human life. Then, and increasingly in the early seventies, they began to mobilize and to advance strong arguments linking the fetus and "life."

Several material grounds were available to establish this discursive link. First, scientific references to genetic development were frequently cited.[54] Second, the distribution of photographs of fetuses seemed to have the effect of representing the fetus as human.[55] Third, the liberalizing of abortion laws by some states added highly visible, material grounds for this linkage; there were a few highly-publicized late-term abortions where the fetus struggle to survive for a pathetically short period. These added force to characterizations of the fetus as human.[56] Finally, reform and repeal laws allowed massive numbers of legal abortions for wide-ranging purposes in the repeal states.[57] These conditions were widely successful in challenging the Pro-reform narrative, which had suggested that women sought abortions only for "good" reasons.

Overall, the reaffirmation of the fetus as human seemed to make great headway in undermining the "choice" ideology. Both a stronger voter reaction and a shift in tone in the popular magazines signalled rejection of repeal laws in 1971 and 1972.[58]

---

cies in the Nation and States: Changes and Stability after the Roe and Doe Decisions," in Carl E. Schneider and Maris A. Vinovskis, eds., *The Law and Politics of Abortion* (Lexington, Massachusetts: D.C. Heath and Company, 1980), pp. 206–23.

[52]Over 200,000 abortions were performed in New York in a single year; see Lader, *Abortion II*, pp. 166–67.

[53]See as examples, Norman St. John-Stevas, "Abortion, Catholics, and the Law," *Catholic World*, January 1968, pp. 149–52; Eunice Kennedy Shriver, "When Pregnancy Means Heartbreak: Is Abortion the Answer?" *McCalls*, April 1968, p. 139.

[54]Brenton F. Brown, "Criminal Abortion," *Vital Speeches of the Day*, 1 July 1970, pp. 549–53; Harold B. Kuhn, "Now Generation Churchmen and the Unborn," *Christianity Today*, 29 January 1971, p. 38; Virgil C. Blum, "Public Policy Making: Why the Churches Strike Out," *America*, 6 March 1971, pp. 224–28; Rev. James Fisher, letter to the editor, *National Review*, 9 February 1971, p. 116.

[55]Kirk, p. 1407; "Twisted Logic: Propositions to Legalize Abortion," *Christianity Today*, 22 December 1972, pp. 24–5. In addition to the testimony of these Pro-life sources, it is telling evidence to the effectiveness of the picture campaigns that Lader is silent about the defeat of the referenda on abortion in Michigan. He indicates a good bit of organization and effort by Pro-choice forces in Michigan, and does not attempt to account for the loss. Lader, *Abortion II*, pp. 182–84.

[56]Blum; Irene Fischl, "Why Are Nurses Shook Up over Abortion?" *Look*, 9 February 1971, p. 66. J. O. Douglas, "Abortion Problems in Britain," *Christianity Today*, 17 March 1972, p. 47.

[57]Lader, *Abortion II*; Paul Marx, "On Not Changing Womb into Tomb," *Catholic World*, January 1972, p. 218.

[58]On the counter-reaction, see Russell Kirk, "The Sudden Death of Feticide," *National Review*, 22 December 1972, p. 1407 or "Twisted Logic: Propositions to Legalize Abortion," *Christianity Today*, 22 December 1972, pp. 24–5.

Meanwhile, the rationale for supporting legal abortion was also evolving. The focus on "discrimination" led to a belief in the "right" to abortion. This belief interacted with the earlier depictions of illegal abortions to produce a new ideographic argument. A combination of the ideograph "right" and the narrative depiction of the disastrous consequences of a lack of "choice" resulted in the generation of the ideograph "choice." The term gradually gained strength from the late sixties into the mid-seventies.[59] It was not until the seventies, however, that the "Pro-choice" argument became dominant and replaced the ideograph "discrimination."

Development of this fourth stage of the argument was tightly interwoven with the rise of the feminist movement. The abortion controversy both fueled the development of the feminist ideology and fed on feminism's development. The ideograph "choice" had particularly important implications for the woman's role in the traditional family. It was a crucial factor in the right to select non-traditional lifestyles for women. The right to choice and new concepts of "family" eventually were accepted by many.[60] It was at this fourth stage, the feminist stage, that the argument from the legal arena impinged on the public controversy.

In its January 1973 ruling on *Roe* v. *Wade*, the Supreme Court avoided resolving the issues in the abortion controversy at an ideographic level.[61] The Court accepted the Pro-choice characterization of motherhood as an occasionally negative state, accepted the Pro-life characterization of the fetus as human potential, but it rejected both the claim to absolute choice and the claim for the absolute humanity of the fetus.[62] Although the policy implications outlined by the Court were more extreme than any the public consciousness might then have felt comfortable with, the general characterization of abortion as an occasionally necessary, if distasteful, element of community and legal life was quite consistent with the evolving popular opinion, according to the polls.[63]

Pro-life reaction to this decision was virulent. Pro-life advocates always had characterized legalized abortion as a journey down a "slippery slope" to destruction.[64] When the Supreme Court rendered its decision on *Roe* v. *Wade*, the lamentations were vehement. At that point, the Pro-life advocates believed that they had established undeniably the full humanity of the fetus. Therefore,

[59]Ramifications of the still-developing ideograph "choice" have not yet been fully appreciated. Applications to euthanasia, the draft, suicide, work, and even travel become increasingly important as the persuasive power of the term grows. Examples of the "choice" rhetoric can be seen in John D. Rockefeller III, "No Retreat on Abortion," *Newsweek*, 21 June 1976, p. 11 and Francis Baudry and Alfred Wiener, "Women's Choice: Pregnancy or Abortion," *Mademoiselle*, April 1974, p. 34.

[60]Gallup poll data show that a majority of the people adopted the ideographs of the "women's movement" while maintaining the concrete characterizations of the dominant ideology. For a more detailed analysis, see Railsback, pp. 113–18.

[61]Roe v. Wade, 410 U.S. 113 (October 1972), 70–1B, pp. 154, 163.

[62]Roe v. Wade, pp. 153, 163.

[63] To describe public opinion adequately would require more space than is available. I have argued, however, that Judith Blake's interpretation is oversimplified. The public accepted the ideographs of both sets of advocates, but viewed their application as a weighting based on two factors: stage of fetal development and goodness of purpose as defined by the dominant ideology. See Railsback, pp. 167–75.

[64]Robert M. Byrn, "Goodbye to the Judeo-Christian Era in Law," *America*, 2 June 1973, p. 511; Eunice Kennedy Shriver, "When Pregnancy Means Heartbreak: Is Abortion the Answer?" *McCalls*, April 1968, p. 139.

they viewed the Supreme Court's ruling not as a rejection of the humanity of the fetus, but as a rejection of the principle of human life in general. Such a rejection produced a major reaction, apocalyptic in tone.[65] Legal abortion was now a fact, however, and that made a major difference in the discussion of abortion in the public arena.

The Mid-Seventies

The fifth stage of the debate, the normalization struggle, was characterized by two competing tendencies: (1) attempts to normalize abortion by working it into the daily understandings of Americans and (2) an escalation of the opposition to such normalization, focusing on a constitutional amendment. In addition to relatively minor issues, such as the propriety of television portrayals of abortion, fetal research, and the beliefs of church members, the major questions of fetal viability and funding for abortions provided the battle grounds for this struggle.[66]

The fetal viability issue was pointed up by the manslaughter trial of Dr. Kenneth Edelin. This sensational trial, arising from Edelin's performance of an abortion by hysterotomy, revealed the inadequacies of the Supreme Court's decision; in actual cases, "choice" and "life" were brought into bloody conflict. But the Court had not ranked one ideograph over the other; consequently, public understanding of abortion remained confused. Individuals such as Marla Pitchford and Drs. Edelin and William Waddill were caught in these definitional conflicts.[67]

The issue of public funding of abortions was equally tortuous. At the narrative level, public funding of abortions was as desirable for preventing back alley abortions as had been legalizing abortions in the first place. However, on this issue the Pro-choice advocates faced their own ideology as a limiting condition. Disputants who opposed public funding of abortions used the Pro-choice group's own ideograph, "choice," as an argument against requiring those who believed

[65]Bryn; Russell Shaw, "Alienation of American Catholics," *America*, 8 September 1973, pp. 138–40; John A. Miles, Jr., "Wife of Onan and the Sons of Cain," *National Review*, 17 August 1973, pp. 891–94; Timothy O'Connell, "For American Catholics: End of an Illusion," *America*, 2 June 1973, p. 514; John T. Noonan, Jr., "Right to Life: Raw Judicial Power," *National Review*, 2 March 1973, pp. 16–64.

[66]Mrs. Theodore Wedel, "Maude Case: Pressure or Persuasion," *America*, 15 December 1973, p. 465; "That's Entertainment," *Time*, 27 August 1973, p. 630; Robert R. Beusse and Russell Shaw, "Maude's Abortion: Spontaneous or Induced?" *America*, 3 November 1973; "When to Baptise . . . When to Dismiss," *America*, 21 September 1974, p. 123; Tony Fuller, "Baptism of Ire," *Newsweek*, 2 September 1974, p. 75; "Fight Over Fetuses," *Time*, 31 March 1975, p. 82; J. Robert Nelson, "New Protection for the Unborn Child," *Christian Century*, 20 August 1975, p. 725.

[67] Dr. Kenneth Edelin was tried and convicted for killing a fetus when he conducted a second term abortion, but his conviction was eventually overturned. Dr. William Waddill was brought to trial three times in a similar case that bridged the abortion-murder linguistic ambiguity. Marla Pitchford was tried for attempting to abort herself when she was unable to obtain a late-term medical abortion from legal sources. David M. Alpern, "Abortion and the Law," *Newsweek*, 3 March 1975, pp. 18–29; Carol Altekruse Berger and Patrick F. Berger, "The Edelin Decision," *Commonweal*, 25 August 1975, p. 77; "Abortion: The Edelin Shock Wave," *Time*, 3 March 1975, p. 54; Eileen Keerdoja and Ying Yilng Wu, "Dr. Wadill: Triple Jeopardy?" *Newsweek*, 7 January 1980, p. 10; "The Scarlet A," *Time*, 11 September 1978, p. 22.

abortion to be immoral to pay for abortions through their taxes.[68] Congressional adoption of the Hyde Amendment, which cut off most federal funds for abortions, the Court's support of that amendment, and the general tenor of public advocacy all indicated that the limitation of public abortion funding on grounds of "choice" was the view most popularly held at that time.[69]

During the seventies, therefore, the rhetorical process of working the new ideographs, narratives, and characterizations of abortion into the public ideology went forward in piecemeal fashion. Although abortion was legal, and although the tale of illegal abortion was widely recognized, the fundamental conflict between the ideographs "life" and "choice" was not resolved and a continuing adherence to a positive characterization of the family and motherhood was not disturbed.[70] In addition, Pro-life advocates maintained a steady effort to limit the times, places, finances, and conditions under which an abortion could be performed. Thus, by 1977, the sixth stage of the argument, the stalemate, had occurred.

The Late Seventies

New argumentative strategies based on comparison arose from the standoff. Advocates on both sides attempted to assert a superior claim to their opponents' ideographs, narratives, and characterizations. For example, Pro-choice advocates claimed legal abortions protected "life"—the lives of adult women. Meanwhile, Pro-life advocates claimed that "choice" was exercised in the decision to have sexual intercourse, and that one did not have a right to choose to kill.[71]

---

[68]"Abortion and the Poor," *America,* 2 February 1980, p. 73; "Hyde Amendment," *America,* 8 March 1980, p. 181; Peter Steinfels, "Politics of Abortion," *Commonweal,* 22 July 1977, p. 45.

[69]The Hyde Amendment withdrew government funding of abortion through sources such as Medicaid. Other amendments eliminated funding for military and other government personnel. In the legislature, the most frequent argument for elimination of government funding remained the claim that abortion was the murder of the unborn. However, this was not the most effective argument because it appealed primarily to the solid anti-abortion constituency. The argument that federal funding of abortions was a "choice" and that it took away the choice of some taxpayers was more crucial because it appealed to the "swing vote." Although no polls of legislators are available to indicate the reasons for their choices (and such polls would probably be inaccurate), the fact that the argument for "taxpayers choice" gradually gained in frequency of presentation throughout the several years of hearings indicates that it came to be viewed as one of the most persuasive arguments. See Rep. (Mrs.) Lloyd, *Congressional Record,* 124, pt 13, 13 June 1978, (Washington, D.C.: The U.S. Government Printing Office), p. 17261. See also Mr. Quie of Minn. same publication, vol. 122, pt 2, 10 August 1976, p. 26788, or Mr. Guyer, 24 June, 1976 p. 20411.

[70] The acceptance of these disparate factors is evident in poll data which show that majorities favored positions which gave women the choice in abortion, but, when asked about which abortions should be legal, they were most lenient with the "hard case" abortions and scaled their leniency to the stage of pregnancy and whether or not birth control had been used. Poll data also support continued reliance on traditional sex role stereotypes. See Railsback, pp. 114–18, 167–72.

[71]As examples see Thomas A. Prentice, "Letters from Readers," *Progressive,* December 1980, p. 37; James Jason Kilpatrick, "A Comment," *National Review,* 25 May 1979, p. 679; "Fight Over Abortions," *US News and World Report,* 19 December 1977, p. 68. For a more detailed discussion, see Railsback, pp. 237–44.

This stalemate was actually the first step in a public reconciliation of the two ideographic clusters. The standoff led to a reaching for new audiences. Pro-life advocates attempted to convert liberals on the humanistic, ideographic grounds of "life." Pro-choice advocates attempted to convert conservatives on the practical and ideographic grounds of costs and "no government interference."[72]

These attempts to gain new adherents led rapidly, in the late seventies, to a seventh stage, fragmentation. As the ideologies became less and less univocal, the Pro-life argument took three major forms.[73] First, Catholics and liberals argued on the basis of the ideographs "life" and "humanity."[74] Second, fundamentalists and the Right argued from the ideograph "family" and from characterizations of women, home, and children.[75] Finally, all parties used the argument based on "love," which asked for sacrifice for the sake of the fetus.[76]

The Pro-choice ideology also showed some signs of differentiation.[77] A demand for "control" and rejection of male "oppression" remained, but it was not complete. The request for "control" was rooted in a negative characterization of the traditional family. That was generally effective as a demand for eliminating the old order, but because "choice" and "individual freedom" were the bases of the new order, there were no concrete narratives and no clear, positive characterizations supplied by the Pro-choice advocates to indicate what should replace the old order. It seemed that any image or characterization that was suggested to fill the void might imply a denial of the freedom to choose an alternative image or characterization.

In addition, fundamental disagreements and uncertainties existed among the advocates.[78] Some wished to celebrate motherhood as a special feminine strength; others wished to deny uniqueness to motherhood.[79] One possibility in rejecting the old order of female second-class status was to promote the female

[72]As examples of such "reaching out" arguments, see Richard John Neuhaus, "Hyde and Hysteria," *Christian Century,* September 10–17, 1980, p. 852; Susan Fraker, "Abortion Under Attack," *Newsweek,* 5 June 1978, pp. 36–7; "Unborn and the Born Again," *New Republic,* 2 July 1977, p. 5.

[73]Compare the leftist tone of Juli Loesch, "Pro-Life, Pro-ERA," *America,* 9 December 1978, p. 435 to the conservative tone of Basile J. Uddo, "Inquiry on Abortion: View of J. T. Noonan," *America,* 7 July 1979, p. 14. For further detail, see Railsback, pp. 259–71.

[74]For examples of such rhetoric, see Mary Meehan, "Abortion: the Left Has Betrayed the Sanctity of Life," *Progressive,* September 1980, p. 34; Juli Loesch, "Pro-Life, Pro-ERA," *America,* 9 December 1978, p. 435; Anne Bernard, "Born and the Unborn Alike," *America,* 26 March 1977, p. 272; Francis X. Meehan, "Social Justice and Abortion," *America,* 17 June 1978, p. 478.

[75]For example, see Basil J. Uddo, "Inquiry on Abortion: View of J. T. Noonan," *America,* 7 July 1979, p. 14; Dale Vree, "Bourgeois Abortions," *National Review,* 27 October 1978, p. 1351; John Warwick Montgomery, "Abortion: Courting Severe Judgment," *Christianity Today,* 25 January 1980, p. 54.

[76]Thomas Ashford, "Countdown to an Abortion," *America,* 12 February 1977, p. 128; Peter Steinfels, "Politics of Abortion," *Commonweal,* 22 July 1977, p. 45.

[77]Compare Gloria Steinem, "Update: Abortion Alert," *Ms.,* November 1977, p. 118 and Ellen Willis, "Abortion Backlash: Women Lose," *Rolling Stone,* 3 November 1977, p. 65 to Linda Birde Francke, quoted by Elaine Fein, "The Facts about Abortion," *Harper's Bazaar,* May 1980, p. 76. See also, Railsback, pp. 271–280.

[78]See the ambivalence indicated in Alice Lake, "Abortion Repeaters," *McCalls,* September 1980, p. 58.

[79]Compare Mary Scott Welch and Dorothy Hermann, "Why Miscarriage Is So Misunderstood," *MS.,* February 1980, p. 14, to Gloria Steinem, "Nazi Connection," *Ms.,* November 1980, p. 14; October 1980, pp. 88–90.

to first-class status ahead of males. To many, however, that sounded too much like the Phyllis Schlafly-style claim that women already were "put on a pedestal."[80] Moreover, the previous emphasis on equal rights from the Civil Rights movement led to a focus on equal treatment of women and men. Even the equality solution was problematic. Whether because of natural causes or socialization, many women did not want to give up the positive values of childbearing, motherhood, and customs of deference to males. Thus, although the Pro-choice advocates generally agreed that they wanted to replace the "traditional" family, many wanted to celebrate a new concept of "family," and others rejected family altogether.

This stage of fragmentation signalled a form of public reconciliation. In spite of continued vociferous argument from advocates on all sides, the poll data, legislative outcomes, and public characterizations of abortion indicate that the public had begun to accept key values from both sides. This does not mean that "public agreement" of any permanent and clear form had been achieved. Nonetheless, the controversy had reoriented our national understanding of abortion in a manner that more fully recognized both the undesirability and desirability of abortion for its roles in protecting women, fetal life, and social family structures.[81] In other words, the material forces of the various sides had been balanced precariously through a long and difficult rhetorical process.

The material forces involved (working women, churches, doctors, patriarchs, etc.) could not "negotiate" with each other directly. An individual woman could only have or not have an abortion. She could only be forced or not forced into motherhood. However, on the social level, rhetoric could mediate these material forces to engender a social consensus about abortion which expressed all of the relevant forces. Such a consensus allowed the continued existence of these social forces in some form or another, and determined the nature of the *experience* of abortion for all Americans.[82]

Even in a callously quantitative way, in fact, a compromise had been reached. Many abortions were conducted legally each year, but social attitudes against abortion and in favor of nurturing had been retained, so that abortion had not generally become the birth control method of choice (as it had in Eastern countries where no such public mediation of values took place every time abortion policy was altered).[83] The rhetorical balance thus materially protected women from hundreds of thousands of dangerous illegal abortions, while discouraging

[80]These are the same arguments described in feminist philosophy; see Alison Jagger, "Political Philosophies of Women's Liberation," in *Feminism and Philosophy*, ed. Mary Vetterling-Braggin, Frederick A. Elliston, and Jane English (Totowa, NJ: Littlefield, Adams, and Company, 1981).

[81]This does not rule out further legal change. However, major shifts in attitudes and experience seem unlikely, and even further legal change will probably provide exceptions for some legal abortions.

[82]This is not to suggest that serious legal and material conflicts or "irrationalities" do not remain. For example, the current number of late-term abortions, current funding conditions, and squabbles over "informed consent" laws show important residual problem areas that desperately need further negotiation.

[83]Henry P. David, ed., *Abortion Research: International Experience* (Lexington, Massachusetts: Lexington Books, 1974); Daniel Callahan, *Abortion: Law, Choice, and Morality* (New York: The MacMillan Co., 1970), pp. 219–66. Lader, *Abortion*, pp. 116–131; Robert Blumstock, "Hungary," *Attitudes in Eastern Europe and the Soviet Union*, ed. William A. Welsh (New York: Pergamon Press, 1981), 330–31.

many hundreds of thousands of preventable fetus killings. It did not satisfy all participants, but it met some of the needs of all.

After twenty years of vitriolic debate an important plateau in the public argument about abortion was reached in 1980. The argument had passed through seven identifiable stages. First, a *professional* stage of argument conducted in non-public arenas had shaped and encouraged a public argument. Then, the early public argument began with a *narrative* phase, in which stories of the horrors of illegal abortion were recounted. Third, in interaction with the Civil Rights issue and as a result of weaknesses in the narrative argument, the *auxiliary ideographic* stage focusing on "discrimination" developed. Fourth, feminist concerns spurred the stage of *intrinsic ideographic* argument, as the ideograph "choice" became central. Then, in the mid-seventies came the complicated stage of *normalization* following legal intervention. Some parties attempted to work out the details of legal abortion, while others escalated the arguments against it. In the sixth stage came the *stalemate;* two mature ideological components presented themselves to the public and compared their values and practices to each other. Finally, the arguments on each side began to reach out for new audiences, and in so doing, to fracture, becoming multi-vocal. The seventh stage, *fragmentation,* signalled that elements of a new ideological structure had become widely accepted by the public—abortion was legal, a majority favored a "woman's choice," and millions of women were exercising the option of legal abortion. However, this structure was tightly hedged by other values, and "choice" was thus limited by "life" and "family."[84]

The American process of public argument led to a reaffirmation of the core of each of these values and interests by broadening the vocabulary and altering legal and medical conditions. Even though the rhetorical war had been vicious and even violent at times, the resulting stasis was exactly what the heralds of public argument (Milton, Locke, Mill, etc.) proclaimed open public argument would bring—a rational moderation (though not an ideal or necessarily equitable one) of the conflicting interests of arguing groups.

Implications

This study indicates the need for several lines of further research. For example, the relationship between the patterns described here and Aileen Kraditor's distinction between arguments from "expediency" and from "justice" in the suffrage movement need to be explored.[85] A fuller explanation of the relationship between the arguments of the women's movement and the abortion controversy is also worthy of examination.[86] On the theoretical level, the seven-stage pattern of argument that arose in the abortion argument may prove to underlie, at least in part, some set of social movements. An investigation of the generalizability of the pattern seems desirable.

---

[84]As described in notes 60 and 63, the polls provide proof of such an interpretation. In addition, admission by Pro-choice advocates of the negative aspects of abortion, and continued rejection of those who used abortion as their primary birth control method, further suggested the hedgings around the legalization of abortion. See Railsback, pp. 278–79.

[85]Aileen S. Kraditor, *Ideas of the Woman Suffrage Movement, 1890–1920* (New York: Columbia University Press, 1965), pp. 43–74).

[86]Jagger.

Finally, this essay demonstrates a viable method for rhetorical analyses of social change. First, it indicates the value of diachronic, rather than synchronic investigation. Too many movement studies treat the rhetoric of an organization as one static unit, rather than as a responsive, developing set of arguments.[87] Second, instead of focusing on the advocacy of only one side of a controversy, it analyzes the social text created by the advocates of various sides of the controversy, interacting with each other and the public.[88] Third, in contrast to Burkean and other studies, which prescribe a pattern to be found in discourse (e.g. order, guilt, victimage, or inception, crisis, and consummation), this study argues that if we purposefully and systematically follow specific units of discourse throughout the course of a movement, we may discover a variety of patterns and relationships.[89] We may note ideographs, narratives, and characterizations; or fantasy themes, personae, and scenarios; or metaphors, culturetypes, and images. A systematic tracing of a specific set of features can tell us a good deal about both the content and structure of the movement. In the process of collecting several such systematic, diachronic studies of the discourse produced in our "social text," we may add significantly to our theoretical understanding of the fascinating processes of human social change.

[87]For an argument in favor of the historical approach, see Andrews. For a good example of his method, see James R. Andrews, "Piety and Pragmatism: Rhetorical Aspects of the Early British Peace Movement," *Communication Monographs,* 34 (1967), 423–36.

[88]See Griffin and compare to Simons, who describes first, reform strategies, and then status quo strategies without viewing the interaction of the two. See Herbert Simons, Elizabeth Mechling, and Howard N. Schrier, "Mobilizing for Collective Action from the Bottom Up. The Rhetoric of Social Movements," *Handbook of Rhetoric and Communication,* ed. John W. Bowers and Carroll C. Arnold, 1984.

[89]Leland Griffin, "A Dramatistic Theory of the Rhetoric of Movements," *Critical Responses to Kenneth Burke,* ed. William H. Rueckert, (Minneapolis, Minnesota: University of Minnesota Press, 1969). Other patterns are described in Ralph Turner and Lewis Killian, *Collective Behavior* (Englewood Cliffs, NJ: Prentice-Hall, Inc., 1972). They note two phase sets—mass excitement, popular involvement, formal phase and institutional phase, and the problem, proposal, policy, program, and appraisal phases.

THE FEMINIST APPROACH

THE RHETORIC OF WOMEN'S LIBERATION: AN OXYMORON

Karlyn Kohrs Campbell

Whatever the phrase "women's liberation" means, it cannot, as yet, be used to refer to a cohesive historical-political movement. No clearly defined program or set of policies unifies the small, frequently transitory groups that compose it, nor is there much evidence of organizational unity and cooperation.[1] At this point in time, it has produced only minor changes in American society,[2] although it has made the issues with which it is associated major topics of concern and controversy. As some liberation advocates admit, it is a "state of mind" rather

From *Quarterly Journal of Speech* 59 (February 1973): 74–86. Used by permission of the author and Speech Communication Association.

Dr. Campbell is a professor of speech communication at the University of Minnesota.

[1]A partial list of the numerous groups involved in women's liberation and an analysis of them is available in Julie Ellis, *Revolt of the Second Sex* (New York: Lancer Books, 1970), pp. 21–81. A similar list and an analysis emphasizing disunity, leadership problems, and policy conflicts is found in Edythe Cudlipp, *Understanding Women's Liberation* (New York: Paperback Library, 1971), pp. 129–170, 214–220. As she indicates, more radical groups have expelled members for the tendency to attract personal media attention, used "counters" to prevent domination of meetings by more articulate members, and rejected programs, specific policies, and coherent group action (pp. 146–147, 166, 214–215). The most optimistic estimate of the size of the movement is made by Charlotte Bunch-Weeks who says there are "perhaps 100,000 women in over 400 cities." ("A Broom of One's Own: Notes on the Women's Liberation Program," *The New Women*, ed. Joanne Cooke, Charlotte Bunch-Weeks and Robin Morgan [1970; rpt. Greenwich, Conn.: Fawcett Publications, 1971], p. 186.) Even if true, this compares unfavorably with the conservative League of Women Voters with 160,000 members (Cudlipp, p.42) and the National Council of Women representing organizations with some 23 million members whose leadership has taken an extremely anti-liberationist stance. (See Lacey Fesburgh, "Traditional Groups Prefer To Ignore Women's Lib," *New York Times*, 26 Aug. 1970, p. 44.)

[2]Ti-Grace Atkinson said: "There is no movement. Movement means going some place, and the movement is not going anywhere. It hasn't accomplished anything." Gloria Steinem concurred: "In terms of real power—economic and political—we are still just beginning. But the consciousness, the awareness—that will never be the same." ("Women's Liberation Revisited," *Time*, 20 Mar. 1972, pp. 30, 31.) Polls do not seem to indicate marked attitude changes among American women. (See, for example, *Good Housekeeping*, Mar. 1971, pp. 34–38, and Carol Tavris, "Woman and Man," *Psychology Today*, Mar. 1972, pp. 57–64, 82–85.)

than a movement. Its major manifestation has been rhetorical, and as such, it merits rhetorical analysis.

Because any attempt to define a rhetorical movement or genre is beset by difficulties, and because of the unusual status of women's liberation I have briefly described, I wish to state explicitly two presuppositions informing what follows. First, I reject historical and sociopsychological definitions of movements as the basis for rhetorical criticism on the grounds that they do not, in fact, isolate a genre of *rhetoric* or a distinctive body of *rhetorical* acts.[3] The criteria defining a rhetorical movement must be rhetorical; in Aristotelian terminology, such criteria might arise from the relatively distinctive use or interpretation of the canons and modes of proof. However, rather than employing any codified critical scheme, I propose to treat two general categories—substance and style. In my judgment, the rhetoric of women's liberation (or any other body of discourses) merits *separate* critical treatment if, and only if, the symbolic acts of which it is composed can be shown to be distinctive on both substantive and stylistic grounds. Second, I presume that the style and substance of a genre of rhetoric are interdependent.[4] Stylistic choices are deeply influenced by subject-matter and context,[5] and issues are formulated and shaped by stylistic strategies.[6] The central argument of this essay is that the rhetoric of women's liberation is a distinctive genre because it evinces unique *rhetorical* qualities that are a fusion of substantive and stylistic features.

Distinctive Substantive Features

At first glance, demands for legal, economic, and social equality for women would seem to be a reiteration, in a slightly modified form, of arguments already familiar from the protest rhetoric of students and blacks. However, on closer examination, the fact that equality is being demanded *for women* alters the rhetorical picture drastically. Feminist advocacy unearths tensions woven deep into the fabric of our society and provokes an unusually intense and profound "rhetoric of moral conflict."[7] The sex role requirements for women contradict the dominant values of American culture— self-reliance, achievement, and independence.[8] Unlike most other groups, the social status of women is defined primarily by

[3] An excellent critique of both historical and socio-psychological definition of movements as the basis for rhetorical criticism has been made by Robert S. Cathcart in "New Approaches to the Study of Movements: Defining Movements Rhetorically," *Western Speech*, 36 (Spr. 1972), 82–88.

[4] A particularly apt illustration of this point of view is Richard Hofstadter's "The Paranoid Style in American Politics," *The Paranoid Style in American Politics and Other Essays* (New York: Knopf, 1965), pp. 3–40. Similarly, the exhortative and argumentative genres developed by Edwin Black are defined on both substantive and stylistic grounds in *Rhetorical Criticism: A Study in Method* (New York: Macmillan, 1965), pp. 132–177.

[5] The interrelationship of moral demands and strategic choices is argued by Parke G. Burgess in "The Rhetoric of Moral Conflict: Two Critical Dimensions," *QJS*, 56 (Apr. 1970), 120–130.

[6] The notion that style is a token of ideology is the central concept in Edwin Black's "The Second *Persona*," *QJS*, 56 (Apr. 1970), 109–119.

[7] See Burgess, op. cit. and "The Rhetoric of Black Power: A Moral Demand?" *QJS*, 54 (Apr. 1968), 122–133.

[8] See Matina S. Horner, "Femininity and Successful Achievement: A Basic Inconsistency," *Roles Women Play: Readings toward Women's Liberation*, ed. Michele Hoffnung Garskof (Belmont, Calif.: Brooks/Cole, 1971), pp. 105–108.

birth, and their social position is at odds with fundamental democratic values.[9] In fact, insofar as the role of rhetor entails qualities of self-reliance, self-confidence, and independence, *its very assumption is a violation of the female role.* Consequently, feminist rhetoric is substantively unique by definition, because no matter how traditional its argumentation, how justificatory its form, how discursive its method, or how scholarly its style, it attacks the entire psychosocial reality, the most fundamental values, of the cultural context in which it occurs. As illustration, consider the apparently moderate, reformist demands by feminists for legal, economic, and social equality—demands ostensibly based on the shared value of equality. (As presented here, each of these demands is a condensed version of arguments from highly traditional discourses by contemporary liberationists.)

The demand for legal equality arises out of a conflict in values. Women are not equal to men in the sight of the law. In 1874, the Supreme Court ruled that "some citizens could be denied rights which others had," specifically, that "the 'equal protection' clause of the Fourteenth Amendment did not give women equal rights with men," and reaffirmed this decision in 1961, stating that "the Fourteenth Amendment prohibits any arbitrary class legislation, except that based on sex."[10] The legal inferiority of women is most apparent in marriage laws. The core of these laws is that spouses have reciprocal—not equal—rights and duties. The husband must maintain the wife and children, but the amount of support beyond subsistence is at his discretion. In return, the wife is legally required to do the domestic chores, provide marital companionship, and sexual consortium but has no claim for direct compensation for any of the services rendered. Fundamentally, marriage is a property relationship. In the nine community property states, the husband is considered the head of the "community," and so long as he is capable of managing it, the wife, acting alone, cannot contract debts chargeable to it. In Texas and Nevada, the husband can even dispose of the property without his wife's consent, property that includes the income of a working wife. The forty-one common law states do not recognize the economic contribution of a wife who works only in the home. She has no right to an allowance, wages, or income of any sort, nor can she claim joint ownership upon divorce. In addition, every married woman's surname is legally that of her husband, and no court will uphold her right to go by another name.[11]

It seems to me that any audience of such argumentation confronts a moral dilemma. The listener must either admit that this is not a society based on the

[9]"Women's role, looked at from this point of view, is archaic. This is not necessarily a bad thing, but it does make women's position rather peculiar: it is a survival. In the old world, where one was born into a class and a region and often into an occupation, the fact that one was also sex-typed simply added one more attribute to those which every child learned he or she possessed. Now to be told, in Erik Erikson's words, that one is 'never not-a-woman' comes as rather more of a shock. This is especially true for American women because of the way in which the American ethos has honored the ideas of liberty and individual choice . . . woman's traditional role *in itself* is opposed to a significant aspect of our culture. It is more than restricting, because it involves women in the kind of conflict with their surroundings that no decision and no action open to them can be trusted to resolve." (Elizabeth Janeway, *Man's World; Woman's Place: A Study in Social Mythology* [New York: William Morrow, 1971], p. 99.)

[10]Jo Freeman, "The Building of the Gilded Cage," *The Second Wave*, 1 (Spr. 1971), 33.

[11]Ibid., 8–9.

value of equality or make the overt assertion that women are special or inferior beings who merit discriminatory treatment.[12]

The argument for economic equality follows a similar pattern. Based on median income, it is a greater economic disadvantage to be female than to be black or poorly educated (of course, any combination of these spells economic disaster). Although half of the states have equal pay laws, dual pay scales are the rule. These cannot be justified economically because, married or single, the majority of women who work do so out of economic necessity, and some forty percent of families with incomes below the poverty level are headed by women. Occupationally, women are proportionately more disadvantaged today than they were in 1940, and the gap between male and female income steadily increases.[13] It might seem that these data merely indicate a discrepancy between law and practice—at least the value is embodied in some laws—although separating values and behavior is somewhat problematic. However, both law and practice have made women economically unequal. For example, so long as the law, as well as common practice, gives the husband a right to the domestic services of his wife, a woman must perform the equivalent of two jobs in order to hold one outside the home.[14] Once again, the audience of such argumentation confronts a moral dilemma.

The most overt challenge to cultural values appears in the demand for social or sexual equality, that we dispense forever with the notion that "men are male *humans* whereas women are human *females*,"[15] a notion enshrined in the familiar phrase, "I now pronounce you *man* and wife." An obvious reason for abolishing such distinctions is that they lead to cultural values for men as men and women as wives. Success for men is defined as instrumental, productive labor in the outside world whereas "wives" are confined to "woman's place"—child care and domestic labor in the home.[16] As long as these concepts determine "masculinity" and "femininity," the woman who strives for the kind of success defined as exclusive domain of the male is inhibited by norms prescribing her

[12]Judicial opinions upholding discriminatory legislation make this quite evident. "That woman's physical structure and the performance of maternal functions place her at a disadvantage in the struggle for subsistence is obvious . . . the physical well-being of woman becomes an object of public interest and care in order to preserve the strength and vigor of the race . . . looking at it from the viewpoint of the effort to maintain an independent position in life, she is not upon an equality . . . she is properly placed in a class by herself. . . . The reason . . . rests in the inherent difference between the two sexes, and in the different functions in life which they perform." (Muller v. Oregon, 208 U.S. 412 [1908], at 421–423.) This and similar judicial opinions are cited by Diane B. Schulder, "Does the Law Oppress Women?" *Sisterhood Is Powerful*, ed. Robin Morgan (New York: Vintage Books, 1970), pp. 139 157.

[13]Ellis, pp. 103–111. See also Caroline Bird, with Sara Welles Briller, *Born Female: The High Cost of Keeping Women Down* (1968; rpt. New York: Pocket Books, 1971), particularly pp. 61–83.

[14]"The Chase Manhattan Bank estimated a U.S. woman's hours spent at housework at 99.6 per week." (Juliet Mitchell, "Women: The Longest Revolution [excerpt]," *Liberation Now!* ed. Deborah Babcox and Madeline Belkin [New York: Dell, 1971], p. 250.) See also Ann Crittenden Scott, "The Value of Housework," *Ms.*, July 1972, pp. 56–59.

[15]Aileen S. Kraditor, *Up from the Pedestal: Selected Writings in the History of American Feminism* (Chicago: Quadrange Books, 1968), p. 24.

[16]The concepts underlying "woman's place" serve to explain the position that women hold outside the home in the economic sphere: "Are there any principles that explain the meanderings of the sex boundaries? One is the idea that women should work inside and

"role" and must pay a heavy price for her deviance. Those who have done research on achievement motivation in women conclude that "even when legal and
educational barriers to achievement are removed, the motive to avoid success
will continue to inhibit women from doing 'too well'—thereby risking the possibility of being socially rejected as 'unfeminine' or 'castrating' "[17] and "the
girl who maintains qualities of independence and active striving (achievement-
orientation) necessary for intellectual mastery defies the conventions of sex-
appropriate behavior and must pay a price, *a price in anxiety.*"[18] As long as
education and socialization cause women to be "unsexed" by success whereas
men are "unsexed" by failure, women cannot compete on equal terms or develop their individual potentials. No values, however, are more deeply engrained
than those defining "masculinity" and "femininity." The fundamental conflict
in values is evident.

Once their consequences and implications are understood, these apparently
moderate, reformist demands are rightly seen as revolutionary and radical in the
extreme. They threaten the institutions of marriage and the family and norms
governing child-rearing and male-female roles. To meet them would require major, even revolutionary, social change.[19] It should be emphasized, however, that
these arguments are drawn from discourses that could not be termed confrontative, alienating, or radical in any ordinary sense. In form, style, structure, and
supporting materials, they would meet the demands of the strictest Aristotelian
critic. Yet they are substantively unique, inevitably radical, because they attack
the fundamental values underlying this culture. The option to be moderate and
reformist is simply not available to women's liberation advocates.

Distinctive Stylistic Features

As a rhetoric of intense moral conflict, it would be surprising indeed if distinctive stylistic features did not appear as strategic adaptations to a difficult rhetorical situation.[20] I propose to treat "stylistic features" rather broadly, electing

---

men outside. Another earmarks service work for women and profit-making for men. Other
rules reserve work with machinery, work carrying prestige, and the top job to men. Most
sex boundaries can be explained on the basis of one or another of these three rules." (Bird,
p. 72.)

[17]Horner, p. 121.

[18]From E. E. Maccoby, "Woman's Intellect," *The Potential of Women,* ed. S. M. Far-
ber and R. H. L. Wilson (New York: McGraw-Hill, 1963), pp. 24–39; cited in Horner,
p. 106.

[19]In the economic sphere alone, such changes would be far-reaching. "Equal access to
jobs outside the home, while one of the pre-conditions for women's liberation, will not in
itself be sufficient to give equality for women. . . . Society must begin to take responsibility for children; the economic dependence of women and children on the husband-father
must be ended. The other work that goes on in the home must also be changed—communal eating places and laundries for example. When such work is moved into the public
sector, then the material basis for discrimination against women will be gone." (Margaret
Benston, "The Political Economy of Women's Liberation," *Roles Women Play,* pp. 200–
201.)

[20] The individual elements described here did not originate with women's liberation.
Consciousness raising has its roots in the "witnessing" of American revivalism and was an
important persuasive strategy in the revolution on mainland China. Both the ancient Cynics
and the modern Yippies have used violations of the reality structure as persuasive techniques (see Theodore Otto Windt, Jr., "The Diatribe: Last Resort for Protest," *QJS,* 58

to view women's liberation as a persuasive campaign. In addition to the linguistic features usually considered, the stylistic features of a persuasive campaign include, in by view, characteristic modes of rhetorical interaction, typical ways of structuring the relationships among participants in a rhetorical transaction, and emphasis on particular forms of argument, proof, and evidence. The rhetoric of women's liberation is distinctive stylistically in rejecting certain traditional concepts of the rhetorical process—as persuasion of the many by an expert or leader, as adjustment or adaptation to audience norms, and as directed toward inducing acceptance of a specific program or a commitment to group action. This rather "anti-rhetorical" style is chosen on substantive grounds because rhetorical transactions with these features encourage submissiveness and passivity in the audience[21]—qualities at odds with a fundamental goal of feminist advocacy—self-determination. The paradigm that highlights the distinctive stylistic features of women's liberation is "consciousness raising," a mode of interaction or a type of rhetorical transaction uniquely adapted to the rhetorical problem of feminist advocacy.

The rhetorical problem may be summarized as follows: women are divided from one another by almost all the usual sources of identification age, education, income, ethnic origin, even geography. In addition, counter-persuasive forces are pervasive and potent—nearly all spend their lives in close proximity to, and under the control of, males—fathers, husbands, employers, etc. Women also have very negative self-concepts, so negative, in fact, that it is difficult to view them as an audience, i.e., persons who see themselves as potential agents of change. When asked to select adjectives to describe themselves, they select such terms as "uncertain, anxious, nervous, hasty, careless, fearful, dull, childish, helpless, sorry, timid, clumsy, stupid, silly, and domestic . . . understanding, tender, sympathetic, pure, generous, affectionate, loving, moral, kind, grateful, and patient."[22] If a persuasive campaign directed to this audience is to be effective, it must transcend alienation to create "sisterhood," modify self-concepts to create a sense of autonomy, and speak to women in terms of private, concrete, individual experience, because women have little, if any, publicly shared experience. The substantive problem of the absence of shared values remains: when women become part of an audience for liberation rhetoric, they violate the norms governing sex-appropriate behavior.

In its paradigmatic form, "consciousness raising" involves meetings of small, leaderless groups in which each person is encouraged to express her personal feelings and experiences. There is no leader, rhetor, or expert. All participate and lead; all are considered expert. The goal is to make the personal political: to

---

[Feb. 1972], 1–14), and this notion is central to the purposes of agit-prop theatre, demonstrations, and acts of civil disobedience. Concept of leaderless persuasion appear in Yippie documents and in the unstructured character of sensitivity groups. Finally, the idea that contradiction and alienation lead to altered consciousness and revolution has it origins in Marxian theory. It is the combination of these elements in women's liberation that is distinctive stylistically. As in a metaphor, the separate elements may be familiar; it is the fusion that is original.

[21]The most explicit statement of the notion that audiences are "feminine" and rhetors or orators are "masculine" appears in the rhetorical theory of Adolf Hitler and the National Socialist Party in Germany. See Kenneth Burke, "The Rhetoric of Hitler's 'Battle,' " *The Philosophy of Literary Form* (1941; rpt. New York: Vintage Books, 1957), p. 167.

[22]Jo Freeman, "The Social Construction of the Second Sex," *Roles Women Play,* p. 124.

create awareness (through shared experiences) that what were thought to be personal deficiencies and individual problems are common and shared, a result of their position as women. The participants seek to understand and interpret their lives as women, but there is no "message," no "party line." Individuals are encouraged to dissent, to find their own truths. If action is suggested, no group commitment is made; each must decide whether, and if so which, action is suitable for her.[23] The stylistic features heightened in this kind of transaction are characteristic of the rhetoric as a whole: affirmation of the affective, of the validity of personal experience, of the necessity for self-exposure and self-criticism, of the value of dialogue, and of the goal of autonomous, individual decision making. These stylistic features are very similar to those Maurice Natanson has described as characteristic of genuine argumentation":

> What is at issue, really, in the risking of the self in genuine argument is the immediacy of the self's world of feeling, attitude, and the total subtle range of its affective and conative sensibility. . . . I open myself to the viable possibility that the consequence of an argument may be to make me *see* something of the structure of my immediate world . . . the personal and immediate domain of individual experience. . . .
> . . . Feeling is a way of meaning as much as thinking is a way of formulating. Privacy is a means of establishing a world, and what genuine argument to persuade does is to publicize that privacy. The metaphor leads us to suggest that risking the self in argument is inviting a stranger to the interior familiarity of our home.[24]

Even a cursory reading of the numerous anthologies of women's liberation rhetoric will serve to confirm that the stylistic features I have indicated are characteristic. Particularly salient examples include Elizabeth Janeway's *Man's World; Woman's Place,* "The Demise of the Dancing Dog,"[25] "The Politics of Housework,"[26] *A Room of One's Own,*[27] and "Cutting Loose,"[28] The conclusion of the last essay cited will serve as a model:

> The true dramatic conclusion of this narrative should be the dissolution of my marriage; there is a part of me which believes that you cannot fight a sexist system while acknowledging your need for the love of a man. . . . But in the end my husband and I did not divorce. . . . Instead I raged against him for many months and joined the Woman's Liberation Movement, and thought a great deal about myself, and about whether my problems were truly all women's problems, and decided

---

[23] The nature of consciousness raising is described in Susan Brownmiller, "Sisterhood Is Powerful" and June Arnold, "Consciousness-Raising," *Women's Liberation: Blueprint for the Future,* ed. Stookie Stambler (New York: Ace Books, 1970), pp. 141–161; Charlotte Bunch-Weeks, pp. 185–197; Carole Hanisch, "The Personal Is Political," Kathie Sarachild, "A Program for Feminist 'Consciousness Raising,' " Irene Peslikis, "Resistances to Consciousness," Jennifer Gardner, "False Consciousness," and Pamela Kearon, "Man-Hating," in *Notes from the Second Year: Women's Liberation, Major Writings of the Radical Feminists,* ed. Shulamith Firestone and Anne Koedt (New York: By the Editors, 1970), pp. 76–86.

[24] Maurice Natanson, "The Claims of Immediacy," *Philosophy, Rhetoric and Argumentation,* ed. Maurice Natanson and Henry W. Johnstone, Jr. (University Park: Pennsylvania State Univ. Press, 1965), pp. 15, 16.

[25] Cynthia Ozick, "The Demise of the Dancing Dog," *The New Women,* pp. 23–42.

[26] Redstockings, "The Politics of Housework," *Liberation Now!,* pp. 110–115. Note that in this, as in other cases, authorship is assigned to a group rather than an individual.

[27] Virginia Woolf, *A Room of One's Own* (New York: Harbinger, 1929).

[28] Sally Kempton, "Cutting Loose," *Liberation Now!,* pp. 39–55. This essay was originally published in *Esquire,* July 1970, pp. 53–57.

that some of them were and that some of them were not. My sexual rage was the most powerful single emotion of my life, and the feminist analysis has become for me, as I think it will for most women of my generation, as significant an intellectual tool as Marxism was for generations of radicals. But it does not answer every question. . . . I would be lying if I said that my anger had taught me how to live. But my life has changed because of it. I think I am becoming in many small ways a woman who takes no shit. I am no longer submissive, no longer seductive. . . .

My husband and I have to some degree worked out our differences. . . . But my hatred lies within me and between us, not wholly a personal hatred, but not entirely political either. And I wonder always whether it is possible to define myself as a feminist revolutionary and still remain in any sense a wife. There are moments when I still worry that he will leave me, that he will come to need a woman less preoccupied with her own rights, and when I worry about that I also fear that no man will ever love me again, that no man could ever love a woman who is angry. And that fear is a great source of trouble to me, for it means that in certain fundamental ways I have not changed at all.

I would like to be cold and clear and selfish, to demand satisfaction for my needs, to compel respect rather than affection. And yet there are moments, and perhaps there always will be, when I fall back upon the old cop-outs. . . . Why should I work when my husband can support me, why should I be a human being when I can get away with being a child?

Women's liberation is finally only personal. It is hard to fight an enemy who has outposts in your head.[29]

This essay, the other works I have cited here, and the bulk of women's liberation rhetoric stand at the farthest remove from traditional models of rhetorical discourse, judged by the stylistic features I have discussed. This author, Sally Kempton, invites us into the interiority of her self, disclosing the inner dynamics of her feelings and the specific form that the problem of liberation takes in her life. In a rhetorically atypical fashion, she honors her feelings of fear, anger, hatred, and need for love and admits both her own ambivalence and the limits of her own experience as a norm for others. She is self-conscious and self-critical, cognizant of the inconsistencies in her life and of the temptation to "cop out," aware of both the psychic security and the psychic destruction inherent in the female role. She is tentatively describing and affirming the beginnings of a new identity and, in so doing, sets up a dialogue with other women in a similar position that permits the essay to perform the ego-functions that Richard Gregg has described.[30] The essay asks for the participation of the reader, not only in sharing the author's life as an example of the problems of growing up female in this society, but in a general process of self-scrutiny in which each person looks at the dynamics of the problems of liberation in her own life. The goal of the work is a process, not a particular belief or policy; she explicitly states that her problems are not those of all women and that a feminist analysis is not a blueprint for living. Most importantly, however, the essay exemplifies "risking the self" in its most poignant sense. The Sally Kempton we meet in the essay has been masochistic, manipulative, an exploiter of the female role and of men, weak, murderous, vengeful and castrating, lazy and selfish. The risk involved in such brutal honesty is that she will be rejected as neurotic, bitchy, crazy, in

---

[29]Ibid., pp. 54–55.

[30]Richard B. Gregg, "The Ego-Function of the Rhetoric of Protest," *Philosophy & Rhetoric*, 4 (Spr. 1971), 71–91. The essay is discussed specifically on pp. 80–81.

short, as not being a "good" woman, and more importantly, as *not like us*. The risk may lead to alienation or to sisterhood. By example, she asks other women to confront themselves, recognize their own ambivalence, and face their own participation and collaboration in the roles and processes that have such devastating effects on both men and women. Although an essay, this work has all the distinctive stylistic features of the "consciousness raising" paradigm.

Although the distinctive stylistic features of women's liberation are most apparent in the small group processes of consciousness raising, they are not confined to small group interactions. The features I have listed are equally present in essays, speeches, and other discourses completely divorced from the small group setting. In addition, I would argue that although these stylistic features show certain affinities for qualities associated with psychotherapeutic interaction, they are rhetorical rather than expressive and public and political rather than private and personal. The presumption of most psychotherapy is that the origins of and solutions to one's problems are personal;[31] the feminist analysis presumes that it is the social structure and the definition of the female role that generate the problems that individual women experience in their personal lives. As a consequence, solutions must be structural, not merely personal, and analysis must move from personal experience and feeling to illuminate a common condition that all women experience and share.

Finally, women's liberation rhetoric is characterized by the use of confrontative, non-adjustive strategies designed to "violate the reality structure."[32] These strategies not only attack the psycho-social reality of the culture, but violate the norms of decorum, morality, and "femininity" of the women addressed. Essays on frigidity and orgasm,[33] essays by prostitutes and lesbians,[34] personal accounts of promiscuity and masochism,[35] and essays attacking romantic love and urging

---

[31]Granted, there are humanistic or existential psychological theorists who argue that social or outer reality must be changed fully as often as psychic or inner reality. See, for example, Thomas S. Szasz, *The Myth of Mental Illness* (1961; rpt. New York: Dell, 1961), R. D. Laing and A. Esterson, *Sanity, Madness, and the Family* (1964; rpt. New York: Basic Books, 1971), and William H. Grier and Price M. Cobbs, *Black Rage* (New York: Basic Books, 1968). However, the vast majority of psychological approaches assumes that the social order is, at least relatively, unalterable and that it is the personal realm that must be changed. See, for example, Sigmund Freud, *A General Introduction to Psychoanalysis*, trans. Joan Riviere (1924; rpt. New York: Washington Square Press, 1960), Wilhelm Stekel, *Technique of Analytical Psychotherapy*, trans. Eden and Cedar Paul (London: William Brown, 1950), Carl A. Whitaker and Thomas P. Malone, *The Roots of Psychotherapy* (New York: Blakiston, 1953), and Carl R. Rogers, *Client-centered Therapy* (Boston: Houghton Mifflin, 1951).

[32]This phrase originates with the loose coalition of radical groups called the Female Liberation Movement (Ellis, p. 55). See also Pamela Kearon, "Power as a Function of the Group," *Notes from the Second Year*, pp. 108–110.

[33]See, for example, Anne Koedt, "The Myth of the Vaginal Orgasm," *Liberation Now!*, pp. 311–320; Susan Lydon, "The Politics of Orgasm," and Mary Jane Sherfey, M.D., "A Theory on Female Sexuality," *Sisterhood Is Powerful*, pp. 197–205, 220–230.

[34]See, for example, Radicalesbians, "The Woman-identified Woman," *Liberation Now!*, pp. 287–293; Ellen Strong, "The Hooker," Gene Damon, "The Least of These: The Minority Whose Screams Haven't Yet Been Heard," and Martha Shelley, "Notes of a Radical Lesbian," *Sisterhood Is Powerful*, pp. 289–311; Del Martin and Phyllis Lyon, "The Realities of Lesbianism," *The New Women*, pp. 99–109.

[35]Sally Kempton's essay is perhaps the most vivid example of this type. See also Judith Ann, "The Secretarial Proletariat," and Zoe Moss, "It Hurts To Be Alive and Obsolete: The Ageing Woman," *Sisterhood Is Powerful*, pp. 86–100, 170–175.

man-hating as a necessary stage in liberation[36] "violate the reality structure" by
close analysis of tabooed subjects, by treating "social outcasts" as "sisters" and
credible sources, and by attacking areas of belief with great mythic power. Two
specific linguistic techniques, "attack metaphors" and symbolic reversals, also
seem to be characteristic. "Attack metaphors" mix matrices in order to reveal
the "nonconscious ideology"[37] of sexism in language and belief, or they attempt
to shock through a kind of "perspective by incongruity."[38] Some examples
are "Was Lurleen Wallace *Governess* of Alabama?" a drawing of Rodin's
"Thinker" as a female, and "Trust in God; She will provide."[39] "Prostitutes are
the only honest women because they charge for their services, rather than submitting to a marriage contract which forces them to work for life without pay."[40]
"If you think you are emancipated, you might consider the idea of tasting your
menstrual blood—if it makes you sick you've got a long way to go, baby."[41] Or
this analogy.

> Suppose that a white male college student decided to room or set up a bachelor
> apartment with a black male friend. Surely the typical white student would not
> blithely assume that his black roommate was to handle all the domestic chores. Nor
> would his conscience allow him to do so even in the unlikely event that his room-
> mate would say: "No, that's okay. I like doing housework. I'd be happy to do
> it. . . . " But change this hypothetical black roommate to a female marriage part-
> ner, and somehow the student's conscience goes to sleep.[42]

Symbolic reversals transform devil terms society has applied to women into god
terms and always exploit the power and fear lurking in these terms as potential
sources of strength. "The Bitch Manifesto" argues that liberated women are
bitches—aggressive, confident, strong.[43] W.I.T.C.H., the Women's International
Terrorist Conspiracy from Hell, says, in effect, "You think we're dangerous,
creatures of the devil, witches? You're right! And we're going to hex you!"[44]
Some feminists have argued that the lesbian is the paradigm of the liberated
female;[45] others have described an androgynous role.[46] This type of reversal has,

[36]See Shulamith Firestone, "Love," and Pamela Kearon, "Man-Hating," *Notes from the Second Year*, pp. 16–27, 83–86.

[37]This term originates with Sandra L. Bem and Daryl J. Bem, "Training the Woman to Know Her Place: The Power of a Nonconscious Ideology," *Roles Women Play*, pp. 84–96.

[38]This phrase originates with Kenneth Burke and is the title of Part II of *Permanence and Change*, 2nd rev. ed. (Indianapolis: Bobbs-Merrill, 1965).

[39]Emmeline G. Pankhurst, cited by Ellis, p. 19.

[40] Ti-Grace Atkinson, cited by Charles Winick and Paul M. Kinsie, "Prostitutes," *Psychology Today*, Feb. 1972, p. 57.

[41]Germaine Greer, *The Female Eunuch* (New York: McGraw-Hill, 1970), p. 42.

[42]Bem and Bem, pp. 94–95.

[43]Joreen, "The Bitch Manifesto," *Notes from the Second Year*, pp. 5–9.

[44]"WITCH Documents," *Sisterhood Is Powerful*, pp. 538–553.

[45]See, for example, Martha Shelley, "Notes of a Radical Lesbian," *Sisterhood Is Powerful*, pp. 306–311, Paralleling this are the negative views of some radical groups toward heterosexual love and marriage. See "The Feminists: A Political Organization To Annihilate Sex Roles," *Notes from the Second Year*, pp. 114–118.

[46]See, for example, Caroline Bird, "On Being Born Female," *Vital Speeches of the Day*, 15 Nov. 1968, pp. 88–91. This argument is also made negatively by denying that, as yet, there is any satisfactory basis for determining what differences, if any, there are between males and females. See, for example, Naomi Weisstein, "Psychology Constructs the Female, or the Fantasy Life of the Male Psychologist," *Roles Women Play*, pp. 68–83.

of course, appeared in other protest rhetorics, particularly in the affirmation that "black is beautiful!" But systematic reversals of traditional female roles, given the mystique associated with concepts of wife, mother, and loving sex partner, make these reversals especially disturbing and poignant. Quite evidently, they are attempts at the radical affirmation of new identities for women.[47]

The distinctive stylistic features of women's liberation rhetoric are a result of strategic adaptation to an acute rhetorical problem. Women's liberation is characterized by rhetorical interactions that emphasize affective proofs and personal testimony, participation and dialogue, self-revelation and self-criticism, the goal of autonomous decision making through self-persuasion, and the strategic use of techniques for "violating the reality structure." I conclude that, on stylistic grounds, women's liberation is a separate genre of rhetoric.

The Interdependence of Substantive and Stylistic Features

The rhetorical acts I have treated in the preceding section, particularly as illustrated by the excerpt from an essay by Sally Kempton, may seem to be a far cry from the works cited earlier demanding legal, economic, and social equality. However, I believe that all of these rhetorical acts are integral parts of a single genre, a conclusion I shall defend by examining the interdependent character of the substantive and stylistic features of the various discourses already discussed.

Essays such as that of Sally Kempton are the necessary counterparts of works articulating demands for equality. In fact, such discourses spell out the meaning and consequences of present conditions of inequity and the implications of equality in concrete, personal, affective terms. They complete the genre and are essential to its success as a persuasive campaign. In the first section, I argued that demands for equality for women "attack the entire psycho-social reality." That phrase may conceal the fact that such an attack is an attack on the *self* and on the roles and relationships in which women, and men too, have found their identities traditionally. The effect of such an argument is described by Natanson: "When an argument hurts me, cuts me, or cleanses and liberates me it is not because a particular stratum or segment of my world view is shaken up or jarred free but because *I* am wounded or enlivened—*I* in my particularity, and that means in my existential immediacy: feelings, pride, love, and sullenness, the world of my actuality as I live it."[48] The only effective response to the sensation of being threatened existentially is a rhetorical act that treats the personal, emotional, and concrete directly and explicitly, that is dialogic and participatory, that speaks from personal experience to personal experience. Consequently, the rhetoric of women's liberation includes numerous essays discussing the personal experiences of women in many differing circumstances—black women, welfare mothers, older women, factory workers, high school girls, journalists, unwed mothers,

---

[47]Elizabeth Janeway makes a very telling critique of many of these attempts. She argues that the roles of shrew, witch, and bitch are simple reversals of the positively valued and socially accepted roles of women. The shrew is the negative counterpart of the public role of the wife whose function is to charm and to evince honor and respect for her husband before others; the witch is the negative role of the good mother—capricious, unresponsive, and threatening; the bitch is the reversal of the private role of wife—instead of being comforting, loving, and serious, she is selfish, teasing, emasculating. The point she is making is that these are not new, creative roles, merely reversals of existing, socially defined roles. (Pp. 119–123, 126–127, 199–201.)

[48]Natanson, pp. 15–16.

lawyers, secretaries, and so forth. Each attempts to describe concretely the personal experience of inequality in a particular situation and/or what liberation might mean in a particular case. Rhetorically, these essays function to translate public demands into personal experience and to treat threats and fears in concrete, affective terms.

Conversely, more traditional discourses arguing for equality are an essential counterpart to these more personal statements. As a process, consciousness raising requires that the personal be transcended by moving toward the structural, that the individual be transcended by moving toward the political. The works treating legal, economic, and social inequality provide the structural analyses and empirical data that permit women to generalize from their individual experiences to the conditions of women in this society. Unless such transcendence occurs, there is no persuasive campaign, no rhetoric in any public sense, only the very limited realm of therapeutic, small group interaction.

The interrelationship between the personal and the political is central to a conception of women's liberation as a genre of rhetoric. All of the issues of women's liberation are simultaneously personal and political. Ultimately, this interrelationship rests on the caste status of women, the basis of the moral conflict this rhetoric generates and intensifies. Feminists believe that sharing personal experience is liberating, i.e., raises consciousness, because all women, whatever their differences in age, education, income, etc., share a common condition, a radical form of "consubstantiality" that is the genesis of the peculiar kind of identification they call "sisterhood." Some unusual rhetorical transactions seem to confirm this analysis. "Speak-outs" on rape, abortion, and orgasm are mass meetings in which women share extremely personal and very negatively valued experiences. These events are difficult to explain without postulating a radical form of identification that permits such painful self-revelation. Similarly, "self-help clinics" in which women learn how to examine their cervixes and look at the cervixes of other women for purposes of comparison seem to require extreme identification and trust. Feminists would argue that "sisterhood is powerful" because is grows out of the recognition of pervasive, common experience of special caste status, the most radical and profound basis for cooperation and identification.

This feminist analysis also serves to explain the persuasive intent in "violating the reality structure." From this point of view, women in American society are always in a vortex of contradiction and paradox. On the one hand, they have been, for the most part, effectively socialized into traditional roles and values, as research into their achievement motivation and self-images confirms. On the other hand, "femininity" is in direct conflict with the most fundamental values of this society—a fact which makes women extremely vulnerable to attacks on the "reality structure." Hence, they argue, violations of norms may shock initially, but ultimately they will be recognized as articulating the contradictions inherent in "the female role." The violation of these norms is obvious in discourses such as that of Sally Kempton; it is merely less obvious in seemingly traditional and moderate works.

Conclusion

I conclude, then, that women's liberation is a unified, separate genre of rhetoric with distinctive substantive-stylistic features. Perhaps it is the only genuinely *radical* rhetoric on the contemporary American scene. Only the oxymoron, the figure of paradox and contradiction, can be its metaphor. Never is the paradoxical character of women's liberation more apparent than when it is compared to conventional or familiar definitions of rhetoric, analyses of rhetorical situations, and descriptions of rhetorical movements.

Traditional or familiar definitions of persuasion do not satisfactorily account for the rhetoric of women's liberation. In relation to such definitions, feminist advocacy wavers between the rhetorical and the non-rhetorical, the persuasive and the non-persuasive. Rhetoric is usually defined as dealing with public issues, structural analyses, and social action, yet women's liberation emphasizes acts concerned with personal exigences and private, concrete experience, and its goal is frequently limited to particular, autonomous action by individuals. The view that persuasion is an enthymematic adaptation to audience norms and values is confounded by rhetoric which seeks to persuade by "violating the reality structure" of those toward whom it is directed.

Nor are available analyses of rhetorical situations satisfactory when applied to the rhetoric of women's liberation. Parke Burgess' valuable and provocative discussion of certain rhetorical situations as consisting of two or more sets of conflicting moral demands[49] and Thomas Olbricht's insightful distinction between rhetorical acts occurring in the context of a shared value and those occurring in its absence[50] do not adequately explicate the situation in which feminists find themselves. And the reason is simply that the rhetoric of women's liberation appeals to *what are said to be* shared moral values, but forces recognition that those values are *not* shared, thereby creating the most intense of moral conflicts. Lloyd Bitzer's more specific analysis of the rhetorical situation as consisting of "one controlling exigence which functions as the organizing principle" (an exigence being "an imperfection marked by urgency" that "is capable of positive modification"), an audience made up "only of those persons who are capable of being influenced by discourse and of being mediators of change," and of constraints that can limit "decision and action needed to modify the exigence"[51]—this more specific analysis is also unsatisfactory. In women's liberation there are dual and conflicting exigences not solely of the public sort, and thus women's liberation rhetoric is a dialectic between discourses that deal with public, structural problems and the particularly significant statements of personal experience and feeling which extend beyond the traditional boundaries of rhetorical acts. A public exigence is, of course, present, but what is unavoidable and characteristic of this rhetoric is the accompanying and conflicting personal exigence. The concept of the audience does not account for a situation in which the audience must be *created under the special conditions* surrounding women's liberation. Lastly, the notion of constraints seems inadequate to a genre in which to act as a mediator of change, either as rhetor or audience member, is itself the most significant constraint inhibiting decision or action—a constraint that requires the violation of cultural norms and risks alienation no matter how traditional or reformist the rhetorical appeal may be.

And, similarly, nearly all descriptions of rhetorical movements prove unsatisfactory. Leland Griffin's early essay on the rhetoric of historical movements creates

---

[49]Parke G. Burgess, "The Rhetoric of Moral Conflict: Two Critical Dimensions."

[50] Thomas H. Olbricht, "The Self as a Philosophical Ground of Rhetoric," *Pennsylvania Speech Annual*, (Sept. 1964), 28–36.

[51]Lloyd F. Bitzer, "The Rhetorical Situation," *Philosophy & Rhetoric*, 1 (Jan. 1968), 6–8.

three important problems: he defines movements as occurring "at some time in the past"; he says members of movements "make efforts to alter their environment"; and he advises the student of rhetoric to focus on "the pattern of public discussion."[52] The first problem is that the critic is prevented from examining a contemporary movement and is forced to make sharp chronological distinctions between earlier efforts for liberation and contemporary feminist advocacy; the second problem is that once again the critic's attention is diverted from efforts to change the self, highly significant in the liberation movement, and shifted toward efforts to change the environment; and the third is a related deflection of critical concern from personal, consciousness-raising processes to public discussion. Herbert Simons' view of "a leader-centered conception of persuasion in social movements" defines a movement "as an uninstitutionalized collectivity that mobilizes for action to implement a program for the reconstitution of social norms or values."[53] As I have pointed out, leader-centered theories cannot be applied profitably to the feminist movement. Further, women's liberation is not characterized by a *program* that mobilizes feminist advocates to reconstitute social norms and values. Dan Hahn and Ruth Gonchar's idea of a movement as "socially shared activities and beliefs directed toward the demand for change in some aspect of the social order"[54] is unsuitable because it overlooks the extremely important elements of the personal exigence that require change in the self. There are, however, two recent statements describing rhetorical movements that are appropriate for women's liberation. Griffin's later essay describing a dramatistic framework for the development of movements has been applied insightfully to the inception period of contemporary women's liberation.[55] What makes this description applicable is that it recognizes a variety of symbolic acts, the role of drama and conflict, and the essentially moral or value-related character of rhetorical movements.[56] Also, Robert Cathcart's formulation, again a dramatistic one, is appropriate because it emphasizes "*dialectical enjoinment in the moral arena*" and the "*dialectical tension growing out of moral conflict.*"[57]

And so I choose the oxymoron as a label, a metaphor, for the rhetoric of women's liberation. It is a genre without a rhetor, a rhetoric in search of an audience, that transforms traditional argumentation into confrontation, that "persuades" by "violating the reality structure" but that presumes a consubstantiality so radical that it permits the most intimate of identifications. It is a "movement" than eschews leadership, organizational cohesion, and the transactions typical of mass persuasion. Finally, of course, women's liberation is baffling because it has no program, because there is no clear answer to the recurring question, "What do women want?" On one level, the answer is

---

[52]Leland M. Griffin, "The Rhetoric of Historical Movements," *QJS*, 38 (Apr. 1952), 184–185.

[53]Herbert W. Simons, "Requirements, Problems, and Strategies: A Theory of Persuasion for Social Movements," *QJS*, 56 (Feb. 1970), 3.

[54]Dan F. Hahn and Ruth M. Gonchar, "Studying Social Movements: A Rhetorical Methodology," *Speech Teacher*, 20 (Jan. 1971), 44, cited from Joseph R. Gusfield, ed., *Protest, Reform, and Revolt: A Reader in Social Movements* (New York: Wiley, 1970), p. 2.

[55]Brenda Robinson Hancock, "Affirmation by Negation in the Women's Liberation Movement," *QJS*, 58 (Oct. 1972), 264–271.

[56]Leland M. Griffin, "A Dramatistic Theory of the Rhetoric of Movements," *Critical Responses to Kenneth Burke*, ed. William H. Rueckert (Minneapolis: Univ. of Minnesota Press, 1969), p. 456.

[57]Robert S. Cathcart, p. 87.

simple; they want what every person wants—dignity, respect, the right to self-determination, to develop their potentials as individuals. But on another level, there is no answer—not even in feminist rhetoric. While there are legal and legislative changes on which most feminists agree (although the hierarchy of priorities differs), whatever liberation is, it will be something different for each woman as liberty is something different for each person. What each woman shares, however, is the paradox of having "to fight an enemy who has outposts in your head."

WOMEN IN COMMUNICATION STUDIES: A TYPOLOGY FOR REVISION

Carole Spitzack and Kathryn Carter

Studies by and about women are gaining increased visibility in the communication discipline. Courses in gender and communication are being added to departmental curricula, the number of women in professional organizations is growing, articles by women appear regularly in communication publications, and in recent years scholars have formed caucuses and journals that are devoted explicitly to the study of women's communication.[1] Although female visibility and diversity *may* contribute to a knowledge of women's communication, the suggestion that mere presence or strength in numbers signals understanding may be overly optimistic. Unless investigations of women serve to challenge and complicate depictions of human communication, the insights gained by gender and feminist scholars are easily placed back into the pre-established frameworks that have been found to distort women's communication. Improved understanding becomes possible when taken for granted assumptions concerning the questions asked and the strategies employed by researchers are critically examined. Such analysis not only demands attention to *women's* communication, but in the process of critique, dominant assumptive bases in communication research must come under scrutiny. Within dominant paradigms and sex-role imagery female experience is restricted and excluded. Critical reflection on these paradigms challenges male *and* female researchers to design truly inclusive strategies.

Our aim is to describe five conceptualizations of women that are present in communication research: Womanless Communication; Great Women Communicators; Woman as Other; The Politics of Woman as Other; Women as Communicators. Each conceptualization assumes a particular picture of women's "place" in communication studies, and more generally, in socio-cultural practices. By making assumptions and gender imagery explicit, we encourage self-consciousness regarding research choices, ultimately leading to the pluralism advocated by communication scholars.

From *Quarterly Journal of Speech* 73 (November 1987): 401–23. Used by permission of the authors and Speech Communication Association.

Carole Spitzack is assistant professor of communication at Tulane University. Kathy Carter is associate professor of communication at Wayne State College.

[1]For an overview of the past and present status of communication research on women, see Karen A. Foss and Sonja K. Foss, "The Status of Research on Women and Communication," *Communication Quarterly* 31 (1983): 195–204. See also, Barrie Thorne, Cheris Kramarae, and Nancy Henley, eds., "Language, Gender and Society: Opening a Second Decade of Research," in *Language, Gender and Society* (Rowley, MA: Newbury House, 1983), 7–24. Organizations such as the Women's Caucus of the Speech Communication Association; the Society for the Study of Language, Gender, and Communication; and the Organization for Research on Women's Communication add to female visibility in communication studies. In addition, *Women's Studies in Communication* is a journal devoted explicitly to analyses of female communication behavior and gender issues.

Our typology is based in an adaptation of the model proposed by Peggy McIntosh in "Interactive Phases of Curriculum Re-Vision: A Feminist Perspective."[2] McIntosh uses the discipline of History to describe each phase in her model: Womanless History; Women in History; Women as Problem, Anomaly, or Absence in History; Woman as History; History Redefined or Reconstructed to Include Us All.[3] The model is subsequently applied by McIntosh to English, Biology, and Art History. Although McIntosh focuses specifically on curriculum development in areas other than communication, her phase model challenges all academicians to examine the relation between perceptions of women and research practices within their own disciplines. In the analysis to follow, the term *types* replaces McIntosh's *phases*, however, because earlier phases of communication research do not dissolve into later research. Each type is an important component in contemporary disciplinary definition. The final section, Women as Communicators, highlights the interrelation of the five conceptualizations of women by examining the concept of leadership as it might be approached within each type of communication research. We use research on leadership as the exemplar because it is an area of study within rhetoric, interpersonal communication, and small group communication, whether the methods are those of rhetorical criticism or empirical studies.

Womanless Communication

Womanless communication research simply leaves women out of its account of human communication. The lives and experiences of women are omitted implicitly from such accounts because, McIntosh observes, scholarly attention is focused on "those who had most public power and whose lives were involved with laws, wars, acquisition of territory, and management of power."[4] Historically, by comparison to the influence of men, women have enjoyed only marginal participation in public realms. That womanless communication has for a long time been the academic norm is evident, for example, in a survey of 45 speech anthologies, where, among thousands of speeches, Karlyn Campbell found only 52 speeches or speech excerpts by women.[5] Similarly, Karen Foss and Sonja Foss reveal that in major publication outlets for communication scholars,

[2]Peggy McIntosh, "Interactive Phases of Curriculum Re-Vision: A Feminist Perspective," Working Paper No. 124, Wellesly College Center for Research on Women (1983); reprinted as "Interactive Phases of Curricular Re-Vision," in *Toward a Balanced Curriculum*, eds. Bonnie Spanier, Alexander Bloom, and Darlene Boroviak (Cambridge: Schenkman, 1984), 25–34.

[3]McIntosh, 3–23.

[4]McIntosh, 7.

[5]During a 1985 lecture titled, "Women Speaking: A Feminist Analysis of Rhetoric," given at Tulane University in New Orleans, Louisiana, Campbell presented the results from her survey of 45 speech anthologies with copyright dates of 1896–1981. No speeches by women appeared, for example, in books with the following titles: *Speeches in English; American Public Address, 1740–1952; Famous American Speeches; Speeches for Illustration and Example; Famous Speeches of American History; British and American Eloquence; The Library of Universal Literature, Vols. I and II; American Speeches; Contemporary Forms of American Speeches;* and *Twentieth Century Issues.* There were no speeches by Lucy Stone, Angelina Grimke, Anna Howard Shaw, or Lucretia Mott. Only incomplete versions of speeches by Elizabeth Cady Stanton appeared, along with one speech by Susan B. Anthony that was actually a congressional hearing.

there is a disproportionately low number of female authored articles and studies about women.[6] These observations, along with insights gained from numerous feminist communication scholars, help to frame two important questions: despite the appearance of increased female participation in recent years, why and in what sense has the study of communication remained *womanless?*

George Kennedy's comprehensive analysis of rhetoric warns that history documents a perspective since most of the world's population does not appear in records that describe cultural progress.[7] Kennedy's observation, combined with our field's focus on public communicative contexts, leads to the tendency to omit large numbers of people, both male and female, from historical records. Until recently, neither minority groups nor women held visibly powerful positions, for example, in political office, media, corporations, or academia.[8] Hence, to continue to use the public and the political as criteria for scholarly interest is to continue to exclude most people from cultural records.

In addition to exclusion as one of the general cultural omissions of minority groups, female stereotypes establish a double barrier for women. Presumptions regarding the role and/or nature of women are inconsistent with public power. Traditionally, femininity is associated with private domains such as home and family, while masculinity is at home in the public areas of politics and commerce.[9] Moreover, as Lea Stewart, Pamela Cooper, and Sheryl Friedley point out, "traditional sex roles have labeled males as aggressive, assertive, active, and independent and have labeled females as subjective, noncompetitive, and dependent."[10] Insofar as public career aspirations involving individual advancement and competitive instincts are thought to be secondary to, and perhaps even incompatible with, femininity, the publicly visible woman becomes a contradiction in terms.

Even a woman who attains social visibility in a respected domain, such as Geraldine Ferraro in her bid for the 1984 vice presidency, finds much public attention centered on personal relationships, family, and appearance; in short, her ability to occupy a male role is questioned implicitly by highlighting her *female* obligations. The mere presence of a woman in a traditionally male domain complicates even routine communicative acts, evidenced, for example, in the controversy surrounding the greeting gestures of Ferraro and Mondale: should they kiss or shake hands? The public female figure who does not display

---

[6]Karen A. Foss and Sonja K.Foss, "Incorporating the Feminist Perspective in Communication Research," in *Doing Research on Women's Communication: Alternative Perspectives in Theory and Method*, eds. Kathryn Carter and Carole Spitzack (Norwood, NJ: Ablex, 1988).

[7]George A. Kennedy, *Classical Rhetoric and Its Christian and Secular Tradition from Ancient to Modern Times* (Chapel Hill: University of North Carolina Press, 1980), 3–17.

[8]See, for example, Jo Freeman, ed., *Women: A Feminist Perspective*, 3rd ed. (Palo Alto, CA: Mayfield Publishing Co., 1984); Gerda Lerner, ed., *Black Women in White America* (New York: Vintage Books, 1972); Clyde W. Franklin, II, *The Changing Definitions of Masculinity* (New York: Plenum Press, 1984).

[9]For comprehensive analyses of the feminine role in cultural practices and rituals, see Susan Brownmiller, *Feminity* (New York: Fawcett Columbine Press, 1984); Rosalind Coward, *Female Desires: How They Are Sought, Bought and Packaged* (New York: Grove Press, 1985).

[10]Lea P. Stewart, Pamela J. Cooper, and Sheryl A. Friedly, *Communication between the Sexes: Sex Differences and Sex-Role Stereotypes* (Scottsdale, AZ: Gorsuch Scarisbrick, 1986), 27.

feminine characteristics and concerns is suspect because within the confines of role prescriptions, she is deemed "unnatural"; at the same time her "natural" female qualities render her unsuitable for the public realm.[11]

Women are omitted from present communication studies when the field sets criteria that exclude critical comment because cultural stereotypes define women as poor communicators. The devaluation of women's communication rarely evolves by way of explicit sanctions against female participation. Rather, the logic that informs dominant world views assumes a basis in neutrality, providing claims of *human* truths which, in fact, reflect the interests and predispositions of privileged groups—namely men. Communication scholars contribute to female invisibility by the particular definitions of humanism and free speech. Here, tension exists between the demand for pluralism and the potentially exclusionary way in which pluralism has been defined. For example, Roderick Hart identifies communication practitioners as "liberals of the first order," persons who "accept all comers into the world of human discourse," humanists who "think about the resources of language as well as how to utter words."[12] He suggests that all individuals should have opportunities to achieve recognition through communicative competence because, "We are a pull-yourself-up-by-the-bootstraps profession."[13] To the extent that he emphasizes the need for diversity, Hart's portrayal is consistent with the works of numerous communication scholars who argue that knowledge is most accurate and valuable when multiple perspectives are considered.[14]

Although admirable in many respects, the call for diversity can be used to justify the *exclusion* of women. Because women may not *want* to pull themselves up to the place defined as "communicative competence" by the "liberals," they are excluded for a failure to meet the "objective" criteria. Mary Ann Fitzpatrick addresses a similar problem by observing that most empirical studies, in the quest for "objective" results, treat all persons identically, failing to account for variation based in gender socialization.[15] The unwillingness to recognize gender variables and the particular perspective that underlies investigation presents a distorted picture of homogeneity and impartiality that Fitzpatrick calls "communication science fiction." In essence, if all persons are accepted according to global definitions of competence which are in fact *particular* definitions, excluded social members are valued only when and if they display the characteristics of dominant culture.

Embedded in the bootstraps characterization of communication is a world view entrenched in values of individual strength, competition, and distinction. McIntosh argues that within social hierarchies, those who have not achieved

---

[11]Brownmiller observes, "Femininity always demands more. It must constantly reassure its audience by a willing demonstration of difference, even if one does not exist in nature. . . . To fail at the feminine difference is to appear not to care about men, and to risk the loss of their attention and approval." *Femininity*, 15.

[12]Roderick P. Hart, "The Politics of Communication Studies: An Address to Undergraduates," *Communication Education* 34 (1985): 164.

[13]Hart, 164.

[14]Cf. Wayne C. Booth, *Critical Understanding: The Powers and Limits of Pluralism* (Chicago: University of Chicago Press, 1979); Richard Cherwitz and James W. Hikins, "Rhetorical Perspectivism," *Quarterly Journal of Speech* 69 (1983): 249–266.

[15]Mary Ann Fitzpatrick, "Effective Interpersonal Communication for Women in the Corporation: Think Like a Man, Talk Like a Lady," in *Women in Organizations: Barriers and Breakthroughs*, ed. Joseph J. Pilotta (Prospect Heights, IL: Waveland Press, 1983), 73.

individual recognition are "construed as not worth studying in a serious and sustained way."[16] Here, cultural organization can be viewed as a pyramidal structure in which a few persons occupy the uppermost areas or peaks, while the majority exists in the relatively immense and stratified base. The correlation between gender and social position is clearly defined by Ann Oakley: "Power is unequally distributed in most societies, and depends not only on personal qualities of the individual but on social position. Different people occupy different social positions and men occupy a different position in society from women: class inequality and gender inequality coexist."[17] The experience of persons who are dependent and powerless by societal standards is beneath the serious intellectual pursuits of those who occupy the peaks. By virtue of their base status, women have not demonstrated climbing capabilities and have thus failed as competitors. Even authors who tacitly promote female characteristics in depictions of humane and ethical communication, potentially revaluing women's experience, often take male figures as exemplars.[18] The very qualities that discount women are admirable in men who have managed to gain recognition in competitive cultures for their commitments to pacifism, community, and equality.

When the position of dominant culture is clothed in neutrality, the experience of those at the pyramidal base is named, evaluated, and dehistoricized within dominant codes. When pointing out, for example, that women have contributed to historical progress and thus their experience should be included in research and pedagogy, one is often asked to provide evidence for female contribution. If women have truly accomplished important tasks, the argument goes, they will gain the attention of researchers. But because the activism of muted group members is thought to be secondary and opposed to the feminine role centered on child care and family maintenance, their speech has often not been preserved in cultural records.[19] A case of the failure to preserve women's speech is found in Phyllis Japp's analysis of Angelina Grimke's feminist rhetoric, where the author notes that "only incomplete texts of two of Angelina's speeches remain extant."[20] The dynamics of this process are central to what Dale Spender calls "constructing women's silence."[21] Here, the historical chain of female influence is broken repeatedly "so that each new generation [has] to begin afresh to create

[16]McIntosh, 7.

[17]Ann Oakley, *Subject Women* (New York: Pantheon, 1981), 281.

[18]See Ronald C. Arnett, *Dwell in Peace: Applying Nonviolence to Everyday Relationships* (Elgin, IL: The Brethren Press, 1980). In a chapter titled, "The Dialogue of Peace," Arnett outlines the views of Martin Buber and Mahatma Gandhi to exemplify nonviolent resolutions to conflict, 125–126. See also, John Stewart, ed. *Bridges Not Walls: A Book about Interpersonal Communication*, 4th ed. (New York: Random House, 1986). In describing four central views of humanistic communication, Stewart presents exemplary essays by Leo Buscaglia, Carl R. Rogers, Erich Fromm, and Martin Buber, 337–392.

[19]See Ann Crittenden Scott, "The Value of Housework," in *Feminist Frameworks: Alternative Theoretical Accounts of the Relations between Women and Men*, 3rd ed., eds. Alison M. Jaggar and Paula Rothenberg Struhl (New York: McGraw-Hill, 1978), 227–231. In the *Dictionary of Occupational Titles*, observes Scott, "Each occupation is rated on a skill scale from a high of 1 to to a low of 887. Listed at the 878 level are home-makers, foster mothers, child-care attendants, home health aids, nursery school teachers, and practical nurses," 229. This publication is compiled by the United States Department of Labor.

[20]Phyllis M. Japp, "Esther or Isiah? The Abolitionist-Feminist Rhetoric of Angeline Grimke," *Quarterly Journal of Speech* 71 (1985): 336.

[21]Dale Spender, *Man Made Language*, 2nd ed. (London: Routledge and Kegan-Paul, 1985), 52–75.

its meanings, unaware of what had gone before."[22] A sustained history of female contribution is interrupted so that, according to Adrienne Rich, each wave of interest in women's lives is "received as if it emerged from nowhere: as if each of us had lived, thought and worked without any historical past or contextual present. This is one of the ways in which women's work and thinking has been made to seem sporadic, erratic, orphaned of any tradition of its own."[23] According to Spender, the likelihood of preservation is directly proportional to parity with the dominant culture: "Where the meanings of women have been discontinuous with the male version of reality they have not been retained."[24]

In womanless communication, strategies and styles of human interaction are made and reported by those who occupy cultural peaks. The base population in social ordering is labeled so that it is not only inferior, but has no means of escaping inferior status because the logic of inquiry has the privilege of discounting or marginalizing all that is essentially *different*. In so doing, McIntosh argues, the privilege enjoyed by dominant groups entails the ability to discount "types of power and versions of knowledge which this privileged class of men does not share."[25] If as a discipline we encourage diverse perspectives without simultaneously questioning the value or presumed validity of concepts such a neutrality and competition in the context of gender arrangements, the result is censorship of the very perspectives that could lead to enriched accounts of *human* communication.

Great Women Speakers

The second type of communication research shifts to a specific mode of female visibility. Because significant communication is often presumed to occur in public contexts, the women analyzed are characterized as *great women speakers.*[26] Here, women comprise part of our sociopolitical history and are thought to be influential. In communication studies, analyses of great women are most readily found in the area of rhetoric. Knowledge about women and their speaking activities lends richness and balance to research practices. Rather than excluding women as objects of study, these studies depict women as conscious actors who influence society. In addition to an identification of the barriers confronted by women speakers, rhetorical analyses reveal and clarify the history, style, and themes in public address by women.[27] The hostility encountered by female speakers, since they were entering a domain typically reserved for men,

---

[22]Spender, 53.

[23]Cited in Spender, 53.

[24]Spender, 53.

[25]McIntosh, 7.

[26]See, for example, Kathleen Edgerton Kendall and Jeanne Y. Fisher, "Francis Wright on Women's Rights: Eloquence versus Ethos," *Quarterly Journal of Speech* 60 (1974); 58–68; Anthony Hillbruner, "Francis Wright: Egalitarian Reformer," *Southern Speech Communication Journal* 23 (1958): 193–205; Karlyn Kohrs Campbell, "Stanton's 'The Solitude of Self': A Rationale for Feminism," *Quarterly Journal of Speech* 66 (1980): 304–312.

[27]See, for example, Karlyn Kohrs Campbell, "The Rhetoric of Women's Liberation: An Oxymoron," *Quarterly Journal of Speech* 59 (1973): 74–86; Brenda Robinson Hancock, "Affirmation by Negation in the Women's Liberation Movement," *Quarterly Journal of Speech* 58 (1972): 264–271.

necessitated alternative rhetorical strategies.[28] Sustained investigations recognize the many women orators active in social and political causes. Thus, analyses of influential women serve two important purposes: a recognition of female influence in public domains and a reevaluation of taken for granted speaking domains and styles.

The study of women speakers is unquestionably valuable, but because of its capacity to focus attention on women's experience in a male-dominated area, caution is also necessary. Investigations of women who overcame obstacles in order to have a public voice, thus making their way into historical records and academic publications, do much to dismantle the assumption that only men are capable of greatness. Yet, the appearance of a few great women can easily support the presumption that the *majority* of women cannot rival male accomplishments. Great women are presumed to be atypical, and simultaneously they are thought to represent the concerns and styles of women. The addition of a few speeches by women to anthologies, journals, classrooms, "pretends to show us 'women' but really shows us only a famous few, or makes a place for a newly-declared or newly-resurrected famous few."[29] The very concept of greatness is exclusionary and to this extent, warns Mary Daly, it implies that women's speaking is motivated by a "desire to parallel the record of men's achievements."[30] The women who are not famous, exceptional, or great by male standards remain invisible. This is not to suggest that women as public orators should be ignored simply because a vast majority of women are unrepresented, nor do we suggest that great women speakers are ineffective. Rather, the very concept of greatness needs to be reevaluated, for such an assessment is often defined according to insidious criteria that often remain invisible.

Traditional rhetorical paradigms, observes Campbell, contain narrowly defined criteria for determining who and what is heard and studied.[31] The power wielded by particular institutions such as religion and politics, typically populated by men, is central in definitions of influence, significance, and timeliness. Great speeches, recorded and preserved with care, often focus on historical turning points, significant political or activist change, and economic issues.[32] Such topic areas or speeches are not problematical in principle, but because of concomitant assumptions concerning female domains of expertise, women are presumed to have no experiential credibility in political or social matters. In contemporary politics, women who advocate rights for women are viewed as a special interest group, since issues such as reproductive freedom are not deemed significant for the general populace. Conversely, spokespersons who rise above special interests and focus on the "real" issues of our times—war, the arms race, advances in high-powered weaponry—are seen to address the concerns of humanity at large.

[28]Until recently there were numerous prohibitions against women speaking in public. Speakers such as Wright and Stanton encountered hostility because conventional norms held that women's place was in the home and not in the public sphere, particularly the speaking platform. See Campbell, "Women Speaking." Kendall and Fisher point out that Wright's "failure to meet societal expectations" greatly diminished her ethos, 58.

[29]McIntosh, 7.

[30]Mary Daly, *Gyn-Ecology: The Meta-Ethics of Radical Feminism* (Boston: Beacon Press, 1978), 24.

[31]Campbell, "Women Speaking."

[32]Examples include Nixon's "Checkers" speech; Martin Luther King, Jr.'s "I Have a Dream" speech; Reagan's 1982 speech in which a balanced budget was proposed.

Female speaking is complicated by assigning to women the task of sustaining cultural moral values and preserving social order through duties involving support, nurturance, relationship maintenance, and procreative responsibility. Sanctions imposed against female speakers by clergy, for example, are grounded precisely in morality-related concerns.[33] Although women hold a vested interest in social issues, for instance in controversy surrounding temperance, abolition, and voting rights, their views are often placed in the category of special interest and thus easily dismissed as non-issues.

Many great-speaker paradigms support the devaluation of women because when assessing greatness, critical vision is trained to see what has already been deemed effective. For example, in a study of Francis Wright's oratory, Kathleen Kendall and Jeanne Fisher use Aristotelian categories in judging Wright's extrinsic ethos and conclude by noting, "Eloquence without extrinsic ethos produces museum pieces of oratory, not catalytic compositions that influence the course of history. Her one real accomplishment was to be remembered as an early pioneer in the history of the American women's movement."[34] Wright's "failure" as an important social influence is explained as a "failure to meet societal expectations," which in turn "lowered her ethos and thereby mitigated her effectiveness."[35] Kendall and Fisher's treatment of Wright's speaking, which could have led to a radical questioning of applicability between Aristotelian criteria and women's speech, instead finds Wright to be ineffective. Analyses of greatness are clothed in presumptions that complicate female participation by linking rhetorical effectiveness to overarching criteria and distinctive individuals. As Campbell asserts, "The questions have not been 'what is rhetoric'? or 'what speeches really illustrate great rhetorical inventions'? but rather who our political leaders were and what they said on certain kinds of political occasions."[36] So long as women's speaking is judged according to criteria that exclude women, it will be deemed inconsequential, specialized, or lacking in persuasive appeal.

The investigation of female speakers requires a shift in the process of critical inquiry. We offer two possible alternatives to the great speaker paradigm. First, the rhetorical activities, strategies, and styles of women can be examined according to generative criteria that do not establish hierarchies of greatness. That is, the concept of greatness can be redefined with criteria that do not privilege male speakers. Second, we suggest that rhetorical competency need not define influence solely in the context of individual speakers and social institutions. Analysis of historical movements that concern the lives and choices of ordinary women, such as Celeste Condit Railsback's work on abortion, are valuable because they call attention to the means by which female identity is constructed in sociorhetorical discourse.[37] From here, questions asked concerning effectiveness can move beyond singularity, focusing on female collectivities such as the comtemporary women's movement. An analysis of women's groups does not abandon the individual altogether, but recognizes that individuals are enmeshed in, and defined by, everyday social and relationship networks. As Campbell argues, for

[33]Campbell, "Women Speaking."
[34]Kendall and Fisher, 68.
[35]Kendall and Fisher, 58.
[36]Campbell, "Women Speaking."
[37]Celeste Condit Railsback, "The Contemporary American Abortion Controversy: Stages in the Argument," *Quarterly Journal of Speech* 70 (1984): 410–424.

example, the rhetoric of women's liberation merits study as a distinct genre because it evinces a fusion of substantive and stylistic features. Here, women's speaking

> is distinctive stylistically in rejecting certain traditional concepts of the rhetorical process. . . . Traditional or familiar definitions of persuasion do not satisfactorily account for the rhetoric of women's liberation. In relation to such definitions, feminist advocacy wavers between the rhetorical and the non-rhetorical, the persuasive and the non-persuasive. Rhetoric is usually defined as dealing with public issues, structural analyses, and social action, yet women's liberation emphasizes acts concerned with personal exigencies and private, concrete experience, and its goal is frequently limited to particular, autonomous action by individuals.[38]

Rules for speaking and determinations of significance become truly inclusive through a reassessment of the rhetorical tradition. Additionally, the inventiveness of female speakers offers an enriched understanding of rhetorical strategies and relevant historical issues. The challenge in not one of creating a place for women in an already existing framework of great speakers. As Gerda Lerner observes, an uncritical assimilation of women into intact social structures is limited because it "deals with women in male-defined society and tries to fit them into categories and value systems which consider man the measure of significance."[39] As McIntosh suggests, rhetoric can be studied not by asking *if* women say anything important, or *if* there are any great women speakers, but by asking, what women say, how women use the public platform, how women speak.[40] If, however, women's concerns and styles are granted no place in cultural discourse, they will retain the *mistaken* status of academic "museum pieces"—interesting to observe but where essential function is missed.

Woman as Other

The third type of research, comprised predominantly of empirical studies, expands the parameters of the great women speaker's domain by focusing on gender as a variable in public contexts, small group settings, organizational cultures, and interpersonal relationships. Female existence is here thought to be "other" than its male counterpart, and so researchers are obliged to examine both the dynamics of this otherness and the comparative relation between two differing realities. The precedent for male/female opposition in communication studies is set by a more general cultural view of the relation between masculine and feminine, culture and nature. Michael Zimmerman notes that "man's conception of himself as essentially cultural, non-female, non-natural, immortal, and transcendent, as opposed to the essentially natural, non-cultural, mortal woman, has continued in various guises for several thousands of years."[41] The oppositions between masculine and feminine, culture and nature, frame difference in a mutually exclusive and hierarchical manner, constituting a major barrier for women attempting cultural inclusion.

---

[38]Campbell, "The Rhetoric of Women's Liberation," 78, 84–85.

[39]Cited in Ellen Carole Dubois, et al., *Feminist Scholarship: Kindling in the Groves of Academe* (Urbana: University of Illinois Press, 1985), 55.

[40]McIntosh, 17.

[41]Michael Zimmerman, "Feminism, Deep Ecology, and Environmental Ethics," *Environmental Ethics* 9 (Spring 1987): 25.

Early studies in the area of male/female differences moved from biological to psychological arguments. In many respects, biological findings were translated into the domains of psychology and anthropology. Lionel Tiger's research on friendship is exemplary in this respect.[42] Because men are physically larger and stronger than women, he argued, they are better prepared to suffer "an array of humiliations, discomforts, fears and other oppressions," sealing the bonds of loyalty and camaraderie.[43] Because of the questionable nature of such conclusions, primarily the confusion of cause and effect which led to reliability problems, researchers turned almost completely to theories of psychological sex and sex-role orientation for explanations of male/female differences. Sandra Bem's investigation of androgyny and the Bem Sex-Role Inventory led to studies centered on psychological sex differences as manifested in communication situations.[44] A host of male/female psychological differences emerged, derived largely from experimental and observational techniques, suggesting that women are characterized by passivity, verbal ability, compliance, fear, dependence, and attentiveness, while men exhibit behaviors associated with aggressiveness, analytic or mathematical ability, high levels of activity, rebelliousness, and independence.[45]

The study of sex differences in communication behavior, often owing to the findings of psychologists, constitutes a rich body of research.[46] The most pervasive area of inquiry is comprised of language behavior analyses that address the syntactic and semantic disparities in male and female speech. Three distinct yet related issues in research of this type can be identified.

The first issue, framing the largest body of findings, locates sex differences by noting variance in phonology, pitch, intonation, lexicon, and meaning.[47] A

---

[42]A detailed analysis of Tiger's research is provided in Robert R. Bell, *Worlds of Friendship* (Beverly Hills: Sage Publications, 1981), 75–94.

[43]Cited in Bell, 76.

[44]See, for example, Sandra L. Bem, "The Measurement of Psychological Androgyny," *Journal of Consulting and Clinical Psychology* 42 (1974): 155–162; Sandra L. Bem, "Sex-Role Adaptability: One Consequence of Psychological Androgyny," *Journal of Personality and Social Psychology* 31 (1975): 634–643; Donald G. Ellis and Linda McCallister, "Relational Control in Sex-typed and Androgynous Groups," *Western Journal of Speech Communication* 44 (1980): 35–49; Lynda Greenblatt, James E. Haswnauer, and Vicki S. Freimuth, "Psychological Sex Type and Androgyny in the Study of Communication Variables: Self-Disclosure and Communication Apprehension," *Human Communication Research* 6 (1980): 117–129; Charles L. Montgomery and Michael Burgoon, "An Experimental Study of the Interactive Effectives of Sex and Androgyny on Attitude Change," *Communication Monographs* 44 (1977): 130–135; Mary A. Talley, Richmond Talley, and Virginia Peck, "The Relationship between Psychological Gender Orientation and Communication Style," *Human Communication Research* 6 (1980): 326–339.

[45]Stewart, Cooper, and Friedley, 24–26.

[46]For a comprehensive bibliography on sex differences research in communication, see Susan B. Shimanoff, "Sex as a Variable in Communication Research 1970–1976: An Annotated Bibliography," *Women's Studies in Communication* 1 (1977): 8–20. For a survey and summary of research on women, gender, and sex differences published in communication journals, see Foss and Foss, "The Status of Research on Women." See also, Judith C. Pearson, *Gender and Communication* (Dubuque, IA: Wm. C. Brown Publishers, 1985) for an extensive bibliography on sex differences and gender research.

[47]For bibliographies on linguistic studies in sex differences, see Nancy Henley and Barrie Thorne, "Sex Differences in Language, Speech, and Nonverbal Communication: An Annotated Bibliography," in *Language and Sex: Difference and Dominance*, eds. Barrie Thorne and Nancy Henley (Rowley, MA: Newbury House, 1975), 204–305. See also

second issue concerns the relation between perception and role expectation; in particular, researchers analyze the extent to which language behavior is perceived as "masculine" or "feminine."[48] When a woman uses profanity and shouts in anger, for example, her actions contradict the stereotypically feminine characteristics of passivity, politeness, and compliance. A final issue concerns an assessment of communicative competence based on gender differences in language use.[49] Identical communication behaviors, such as the use of tag questions, often lead to different competence evaluations depending on speaker sex. For example, when a woman says, "It's a nice day, isn't it?" she is thought to lack authority, thereby reducing her competence; when a man makes the same utterance, he is perceived as an open and congenial conversation partner, thus elevating his level of competence.

Studies focused on sex differences have recently come under attack by a number of scholars.[50] Criticism centers on the labeling process whereby women's language and communication behaviors are found to be deviant or deficient. As Barrie Thorne, Cheris Kramarae, and Nancy Henley suggest, gender scholars are now beginning to realize that early reliance on the findings of influential male linguists such as Jesperson is problematic because, in the very questions asked about sex differences, female deficiency is already presumed:

> Do women have a more limited vocabulary than men do, or do they use more—or different—adjectives and adverbs? Are women more apt to leave their sentences unfinished? Do they enunciate more properly? Do they use lots of "superficial" words? Are their sentences longer or shorter, than men's? Do they use more questioning, or uncertain notation?[51]

Arguably, not all of these questions suggest female inferiority, but in each case, male speech is the standard against which female or "other" speech is judged. The project of finding difference is highly contingent on more general assumptions that in many ways pre-establish relations between cultural members. Indeed, Joseph Pillota states, "To recognize differences it is necessary either to assume one of the cultures as a base and interpret others in terms of it or to assume common features across various cultures on the basis of which the variations are comprehensible."[52] Female difference, then, is comprehensible and judged to be deficient within the context of male communication behavior.

studies cited in a section titled "Phonetic Variants," in Nancy Henley and Barrie Thorne, *She Said/He Said* (Pittsburgh: Know, Inc., 1975). *She Said/He Said* is a reprint of Henley and Thorne's original work.

[48]These studies fall under the general heading of "attribution." For a bibliography of attribution studies, see "Attribution," in Foss, and Foss, 1983. 198.

[49]See studies cited under "Evaluation" in Foss and Foss, 1983, 198.

[50]See, for example, Spender; Linda L. Putnam, "In Search of Gender: A Critique of Communication and Sex Roles Research," *Women's Studies in Communication* 5 (1982): 1–9; Cheris Kramer, Barrie Thorne, and Nancy Henley, "Perspectives on Language and Communication," *Signs* 3 (1978): 638–651; *Women's Studies in Communication* 7 (1984), a special issue on papers selected from those prepared for the 1984 Conference on Gender and Communication Research, The Pennsylvania State University, University Park, Pennsylvania.

[51]Thorne, Kramarae, and Henley, "Opening a Second Decade," 12.

[52]Joseph J. Pilotta, ed., *Interpersonal Communication: Essays in Phenomenology and Hermeneutics* (Washington, DC: Center for Advanced Research in Phenomenology and the University Press of America, 1982), 49.

The female difference is viewed as a handicap when compared to a standard that finds deviation in all that is non-standard male usage. In Robin Lakoff's work, women are found to lack authority and seriousness in speaking, hence reducing their effectiveness.[53] Here, women's speech is ineffective because it is laden with weak expletives, trivializing particles, intensifiers and polite forms, tag questions, and hedges; in short, Lakoff finds women's language behavior to be tentative, uncertain, and indecisive. Dale Spender criticizes Lakoff's work by noting that the observations made, like those in Jesperson's work, are grounded in an implicit acceptance of masculine speech as the norm:

> Lakoff accepts that men's language is superior and she assumes that this is a feature of their linguistic performance and not of their sex. . . . She takes male language as the norm and measures women against it, and the outcome of this procedure is to classify any difference on the part of women as "deviation." Given these practices, it is unlikely that Lakoff could have arrived at positive findings for women, for any differences revealed, whether a product of language or of sex, would be predisposed to interpretation as yet more evidence of female deficiency.[54]

As Lakoff's work exemplifies, if women's speech is thought to be deficient, it will appear deficient since she presumes that *women* speak differently, not that women and men speak differently.

Frequently, sex difference researchers suggest male usage as the solution to female deficiency.[55] If women can be taught to communicate like men, they will become equally competent. However, women who adopt male usage are often evaluated as less successful and less likable than men. Even when actual behavior is identical, it is viewed differently depending on the source. In an analysis of male/female conversational dynamics in small groups, Patricia Bradley finds that qualifying devices "diminish discussants' positive reactions to *women* in small group settings. It cannot be argued on the basis of these findings, however, that tag questions and disclaimers are inherently 'weaker' or credibility deflating since men were able to use them with virtual impunity."[56] Moreover, as Martha Solomon points out, much research involves participants in tasks and situations that, given sex-role stereotypes, render female communication behavior less salient and less effective.[57] For instance, subjects may be asked to argue for a single position, select the best solution to a problem, or influence another person—all of which are part of the male sex-typed script in American culture.[58] Studies designed with implicit male norms, combined with negative evaluations

[53]See Robin Lakoff, *Language and Women's Place* (New York: Harper and Row, 1975). See also Spender's critique of Lakoff's work, 8–9, 17, 18–19, 34–40, 86, 125.

[54]Spender, 8.

[55]For example, Pearson ends nearly every chapter in *Gender and Communication* by suggesting that women and men blend aspects of male and female communication styles, but inadvertently she accepts stereotyped sex-role characteristics. For example, women must learn to be logical and men must learn to be emotional. Given the presumed deficiency of women's communication, females must alter their communication considerably if they hope to achieve competence in social situations.

[56]Patricia Hayes Bradley, "The Folk-Linguistics of Women's Speech: An Empirical Examination," *Communication Monographs* 48 (1981): 90.

[57]Martha Solomon, "A Prolegomenon to Research on Gender Role Communication," *Women's Studies in Communication* 7 (1984): 98.

[58]Solomon, 98.

of women's speech, make it impossible for a woman to attempt to speak like a man because her female identity is taken into account in evaluations of her speaking behavior.

An additional problem occurs when researchers begin by assuming female difference. Specifically, if men and women are thought to exist in an oppositional relation, findings are likely to highlight differences rather than similarities. "Researchers may tend to presume and overreport differences rather than similarities," suggest Kramer, Throne, and Henley, "because our culture is infused with stereotypes which polarize females and males."[59] Statistical procedures may be especially problematic when used in gender studies, Fitzpatrick indicates, because such research strategies "focus on testing and finding *differences* between people and ignore similarities."[60] An example illustrates. Fitzpatrick describes an investigation in which male and female subjects were tested to determine self-perceptions of communication behavior, along with perceptions of the behavior of same- and opposite-sex friends. Approximately ten dimensions of behavior, ranging from control to nurturance, were examined. Although researchers found difference in only two dimensions, "the entire discussion section of the paper focused on the two differences discovered between males and females."[61] A failure to find male-female disparity or "significance," especially when one begins by positing its existence, often results in an unpublishable article. Unfortunately, the dilemma is typically resolved by selecting new subjects, changing variables, or altering data collection techniques so that difference can be found.

While research in the area of sex differences provides an important source of knowledge about women's communication, its implicit characterization of woman as "other" risks further sedimentation of male-female stereotypes. When studies take women's speaking to be the problem and fail to question men's speaking with equal rigor, we can expect a storehouse of information that sings the praises of differences, but does little to challenge definitions of competence, influence, and success. Simply pointing to woman as a disadvantaged other falsely implies that women are passive victims, trapped in sex-typed communication constraints with no hope of escape, when in fact they can be viewed as active agents. Valid investigations of female communication behavior require a noncomparative approach which, by implication, not only questions the normative power of male experience, but views women as self-conscious actors, as co-producers of their communicative climates.

The Politics of Woman as Other

The project of learning to value women's experience is an inherently political enterprise because it entails seeing women not as a problem but as valuable human beings.[62] Because the male/female opposition is inequitable, women are not only seen as deficient communicators, but their everyday lives are named by dominant culture. When women discuss their experiences, for example, their talk is often labeled "chit-chat," "gossip," or "girl talk"; when men do the same, they are "making a point," "stating a position," or imparting social

[59]Kramer, Thorne, and Henley, "Perspectives," 640.
[60]Fitzpatrick, 74.
[61]Fitzpatrick, 75.
[62]McIntosh, 14.

knowledge.[63] A crucial task in learning to value women's communication first involves a critical questioning of female experience as defined within an andro-centric framework, and second, a revaluing of women's experience *in its own terms*. Traumatic female experiences such as childbirth, when named within a culture that still in large measure both mandates and devalues motherhood, are either deemed unimportant in the overall scheme of scholarly interests, or if ad-dressed, are stripped of their complexity. As Spender points out, childbirth is portrayed as an event of "rapturous joy," a life-completing achievement for women.[64] On television programs we might well see a young woman enduring mildly uncomfortable labor pains, immediately and miraculously followed by mother and child in a hospital bed. Neither the physical pain involved in giving birth nor the intense ambivalence is seen by viewers. In describing her own ex-perience of birth, Rich critiques the long-standing silence concerning mother-hood:

> No one mentions the psychic crises of bearing a first child, the excitation of long-buried feelings about one's own mother, the sense of confused power and power-lessness, of being taken over on the one hand and of touching new physical and psychic potentialities on the other, a heightened sensibility which can be exhilarat-ing, bewildering, and exhausting.[65]

Within the *politics of woman as other* paradigm, researchers promote a critical female voice that speaks on behalf of its own complexity.

Sustained investigations of female experience reveal complex forms of communication, definitions of relationships, and styles of reasoning. Novel conceptions of human communication emerge from such studies. Female communication behaviors are transactional and cooperative rather than linear and competitive.[66] For example, Fern Johnson and Elizabeth Aries find that women's friendships are sustained by talk involving non-critical listening, mutual support, and enhancement of self-worth.[67] Storytelling as a conversational paradigm in women's communication serves to maintain horizontal power relationships such that closeness and inclusiveness are insured.[68] Through question-asking and af-firming utterances, women's speaking promotes understanding.[69] Rather than de-fining a conversation partner as one who alternatively listens and speaks, which

[63]See Kristin M. Langellier and Eric E. Peterson, "Spinstorying: A Communication Analysis of Women's Storytelling," Speech Communication Association Conference, Chi-cago, Illinios 1984. See also Dubois, et al., 23.

[64]Spender, 52–74.

[65]Adrienne Rich, *Of Woman Born: Motherhood as Experience and Institution* (New York; Bantam Books, 1977), 17.

[66]See, for example, Susan Kalcik, " ' . . . like Ann's gynecologist or the time I was almost raped': Personal Narrative in Women's Rap Groups," in *Women and Folklore*, ed. Claire R. Farrer (Austin: University of Texas Press, 1975), 3–11; Deborah Jones, "Gossip: Notes on Women's Oral Culture," in *The Voices and Words of Women and Men*, ed. Che-ris Kramarae (Oxford: Pergamon Press, 1980), 193–198; Lee Jenkins and Cheris Kramer, "Small Group Processes: Learning from Women," *Women's Studies International Quar-terly* 1 (1978): 67–84.

[67]Fern L. Johnson and Elizabeth J. Aries, "The Talk of Women Friends," *Women's Studies International Forum* 6 (1983): 353–361.

[68]See, for example, Carole Edelsky, "Who's Got the Floor," *Language in Society* 10 (1983): 383–421: Langellier and Peterson; Kalcik, 3–11.

[69]See Paula A. Treichler and Cheris Kramarae, "Women's Talk in the Ivory Tower," *Communication Quarterly* 31 (1983): 118–132.

often results in a two-person monologue, the topics and experiences shared *between* female partners are woven together.[70] A dissatisfying conversation is one in which a partner attempts to gain distinction from the other, which is often taken implicitly as a request for distance or separation.

The preceding research on female interaction demonstrates unique strategies. These strategies are revealed when women's communication is studied in its own terms. When female relationship behavior enters the domain of traditional research in the area of interpersonal communication, the problem of deficiency is likely to occur because the weaving together of shared issues is not amenable to strict quantification and control. The predominance of exchange models and statistical assessments of communication behavior places the study of relationships in a realm filled with economic imagery.[71] Viewing interpersonal communication as something that is exchanged and that becomes comprehensively known only by isolating and testing variables is consistent with the experience of persons for whom individual control is central. In Gerald Miller's anthology, *Explorations in Interpersonal Communication,* there is much hope expressed for ongoing relational communication research.[72] On the one hand, Miller notes a "change in emphasis from the *individual,* as the primary unit of analysis, to the *relationship,*" which may indicate a willingness to decentralize issues of individual control and distinction; on the other hand, "powerful mathematical models" for use in studying relationships, "allow the researcher to milk maximum information from the data and permit closer approximation of the processual complexities of interpersonal communication."[73] Essentially, Miller advocates statistical analyses of relationship dynamics because the *researcher* is given greater control, "a precision and parsimony not found in verbal constructions," stating almost as a tangential point, "a major outstanding question, of course, concerns the extent to which certain assumptions of these models can be met in the domain of the 'real' world."[74]

Indeed, a "counting" approach to the study of female relationship behavior, emphasizing control, power, and static precision, may be inappropriate when everyday interactional emphasis is not centered on reducing relationship strategies to their essential components but on bringing together a great many experiences, emotions, expressions, and individuals within the space of a single conversation. Rather than viewing a relationship as an entity comprised of two individuals, women leave open possibilities for a rethinking of individual identities and relationship boundaries, depending on the directions taken in conversation. We are not suggesting that women do not engage in exchange-like relationships or that women are incapable of quantifying relationship behaviors. We are suggesting, however, that such approaches reflect a masculine view of relationships. In Kathryn Carter's research on perception in relationships, for example, men describe their involvements through the use of economic metaphors, while women use

[70]See Treichler and Kramarae, 118–132.

[71]For a discussion of the problems created when an economic metaphor is used to explain social interaction, see Mercilee M. Jenkins and Cheris Kramarae, "A Thief in the House," in *Men's Studies Modified: The Impact of Feminism on the Academic Disciplines,* ed. Dale Spender (Oxford: Pergamon Press, 1981), 11–18.

[72]Gerald R. Miller, ed., *Explorations in Interpersonal Communication* (Beverly Hills, CA: Sage Publications 1976), 9–16.

[73]Miller, 14.

[74]Miller, 14.

gardening metaphors.[75] Women discuss the process of tending, nurturing, weathering storms and seasons, and growing; men describe costs, benefits, trade-offs and losses, and often "rank" or "rate" the value of a relationship.

Women's perceptions of relationships continue to remain invisible not only when research relies on exchange approaches, but also when researchers assume that relationships are based in mutuality and equality. Michael Roloff defines a relationship as a "mutual agreement, implicit or explicit, between two people in order to maximize rewards."[76] In interpersonal communication textbooks, healthy relationships are typically defined as those in which definition is mutual, respect for the other is presumed, and mutual negotiation of rules and roles takes place. Even in the case of "complementary" relational structure, where one partner has more power than the other, both partners *mutually* designate superior and subordinate roles.[77] When gender as a social organizing force is incorporated into research of this kind, the concepts of equality and mutuality must be reexamined. Although part of the feminine stereotype defines women as controlling in relationships, the realities of economic dependence, the value placed on intimacy for women and independence for men, and the general devaluation of female communication behavior, do not promote mutuality or equality.

An understanding of women's relationship dynamics requires a move away from traditional conceptions of human communication research. Not only are concepts of equality and mutuality misleading when women are involved, but female relationships are often not experienced in terms of rules and exchanges. In Carol Gilligan's study of moral development, most women are found to negotiate relationships through an ethic of care.[78] Many women attempt to generate novel and inclusive interactional strategies which preserve networks of personal and social relationships. As studies of children's game playing reveal, boys are likely to place emphasis on abiding by rules; girls are apt to stop or alter a game when rules interfere with the preservation of relationship bonds.[79] The ethic of care, problematized by rules, has consequences for the larger question of ethics in communicative choices. One of Gilligan's respondents describes an immoral decision as one in which a person attempts to "decide carelessly or quickly or on the basis of one or two factors when you know that there are other things that are important and that will be affected."[80] Respected individuals are those who "are really connected to the concrete situations in their lives."[81]

A revaluing of the female ethics of care and connection depends on an assessment of who is in a position to define societal relationships between men and women. Lana Rakow observes that "men have been in a position to 'structure

[75]Kathryn Carter, "The Experience of Relationships for Women and Men," Women's Studies Colloquia, Newcomb College Center for Research on Women, Tulane University, New Orleans, Louisiana, February, 1986.

[76]Michael E. Roloff, "Communication Strategies, Relationships, and Relational Changes," in *Explorations in Interpersonal Communication*, ed. Gerald R. Miller (Beverly Hills, CA: Sage Publications, 1976), 182.

[77]One example: Dennis R. Smith and Keith L. Williamson, *Interpersonal Communication: Roles, Rules, Strategies and Games*, 3rd ed. (Dubuque, IA: Wm. C. Brown Publishers, 1985), 88–90.

[78]Carol Gilligan, *In a Different Voice: Psychological Theory and Women's Development* (Cambridge, MA: Harvard University Press, 1982), 5–23.

[79]See Gilligan's discussion, 9–23.

[80]Gilligan, 147.

[81]Gilligan, 148.

the structures,' to make their use of metaphors and metonyms count, and to construct a symbolic system which fits and explains their experiences, creating a gendered world within which we take our gendered places.''[82] The relationship strategies of women are at once mandated and marginalized by male structures. That is, women are deemed healthy if they are nurturing and other-directed; simultaneously, male hierarchies of value equate feminine qualities with low levels of reasoning capacity and intellectual prowess. It is unlikely that *women* would have devised a gender system in which female relationship behaviors are seen as both essential and inferior. Moreover, a socially defined position of powerlessness does not give women the luxury of clothing female experience in neutrality in order to make claims about *human* experience.

The study of women's communication, because of its very lack of fit with traditional research paradigms, can serve to enrich and expand the repertory of research options found in the communication discipline. Female interaction styles, in fact, challenge scholars to reconsider the crucial issue of using methods that are appropriate to the questions asked in research studies. In Oakley's analysis of pregnancy, for example, where the goal is to understand women's experience of being pregnant and giving birth, many traditional guidelines for researcher-respondent interview interaction are found to be inadequate.[83] The intensely personal experience of pregnancy is difficult to share with a "neutral" data collector, especially if the researcher refuses to communicate with some degree of reciprocity. Studies by Carole Spitzack and Deanna Hall and Kristen Langellier, among others, reconsider the separation of researcher and respondent communication, and researchers opt instead to interact with their respondents.[84] These authors, like Oakley, conduct interviews with a particular subject area in mind, but allow respondents the freedom to reframe or refocus the direction of the interview, to ask questions and receive answers from the researcher, to introduce issues that are not part of the researcher's agenda. In short, the communication of these female researchers and female respondents matches the experience of woman-to-woman interaction that is characterized by a weaving together of experiences. In view of Gilligan's observations, we can expect a high degree of richness, complexity, and respondent involvement when such tactics are used because here the "rules of the game" can be influenced and redefined to preserve the relationship between interviewer and respondent.

An examination of the confrontation between women's communication and research practices does not suggest that women's communication is simply different or better than men's, but rather presents women's experience as valid and complex, posing the question: how can women's communication be examined so that it is seen as significant and richly competent? As Spender points out, "it is political choice on the part of feminist scholars to find in favour of women, but this is no different from non-feminist researchers who have exercised their

[82]Lana F. Rakow, "Rethinking Gender Research in Communication," *Journal of Communication* 36 (1986): 22–23.

[83]Ann Oakley, "Interviewing Women: A Contradiction in Terms," in *Doing Feminist Research*, ed. Helen Roberts (London: Routledge and Kegan Paul, 1981), 30–61.

[84]Carole Spitzack, "Body Talk: The Politics of Weight Loss and Female Identity," in *Women Communicating*, eds. Anita Taylor and Barbara Bate (Norwood, NJ: Ablex, 1988); Deanna Hall and Kristin Langellier, "Storytelling Strategies in Mother-Daughter Communication," in *Women Communicating*, eds. Anita Taylor and Barbara Bate (Norwood, NJ: Ablex, 1988).

political choice by almost always finding in favour of men."[85] The difference, Spender adds, "is that feminism acknowledges its politics."[86] Scholars who conduct studies on women's communication, like their colleagues, argue for a fit between research questions and methods. Given the social polarization of males and females, identical communication behaviors are unlikely: thus, presumably universal principles that guide inquiry are not universally applicable. The priority placed on objectivity in research practices serves dominant culture because registers of discourse "have been encoded by males for their own ends. . . . Women shall either be excluded, or made 'uncomfortable,' or serve those ends if, and when, they do participate."[87] The views and judgments contained within male registers are imposed on others who do not have male experiences. The practical side of research on women entails a focus on the everyday lives, experiences, and communication behaviors of women; the critical side calls attention to the imposition.

A number of communication scholars conduct feminist research, and current activities in our discipline suggest a gradual acceptance of women's communication as a valid area of investigation. At the 1985 Speech Communication Association Conference, participants in a seminar on women and communicative power spent considerable time discussing publication outlets for research on women. Taylor and Bate's anthology, *Women Communicating,* provides analyses of female communication behavior, including mother-daughter interaction, women and appearance, and group dynamics among female adolescents.[88] Organizations such as the Society for the Study of Language, Gender, and Communication; the Organization for Research on Women's Communication; the Women's Caucus of the Speech Communication Association; and annual gatherings such as the Annual Conference for Gender and Communication Research, all promise to establish links and support networks among feminist researchers. The potential empowerment afforded by these forms of woman-to-woman communication, which gives visibility and legitimacy to the lives of women, is dependent on a more general willingness of non-feminist or anti-feminist scholars to rethink the rules of the research game.

The awareness generated by studying women's experience in its own terms challenges all disciplines, claim Marilyn Schuster and Susan Van Dyne, for the operation of "invisible paradigms" is made explicit in the very process of research.[89] Questions remain, however, as to how a new-found understanding of women becomes practical and truly empowering. At this point, answers must be speculative because women are not yet afforded the luxury of full inclusion. The study of women's communication, even though it addresses at least half the population, is still considered a specialty area. Communication departments may offer courses in gender studies, but by implication the separation of gender from presumably mainstream area sends a strong message: the study of women is marginal and lacks import for the discipline as a whole. A reluctance on the part of

[85]Spender, 8.

[86]Spender, 8.

[87]Spender, 80.

[88]Anita Taylor and Barbara Bate, eds., *Women Communicating* (Norwood, NJ: Ablex, 1988).

[89]Marilyn R. Schuster and Susan R. Van Dyne, eds. *Women's Place in the Academy: Transforming the Liberal Arts Curriculum* (Totowa, NJ: Rowman and Allanheld, 1985), 7, 24.

communication scholars to identify and discuss sexism as a component of disciplinary practices outside the context of gender courses or gender issues also contributes to the problem of female marginality. In her examination of 55 communication textbooks with copyright dates of 1980 or later, Phyllis Randall finds that only "six confront the issue of sexism directly," and only nine mention sexist language.[90] These realities necessitate caution for researchers attempting to reposition female experience into the general framework of communication studies; before invisible paradigms can become visible, it is first necessary to have an audience that is willing to look.

A second complication in the mainstreaming of women in communication research concerns the possible co-opting of the findings derived from research on women. The concerns and speaking structures unearthed in women's communication can easily be renamed and transformed into evidence that supports female stereotypes. To suggest that women are "connected" to their everyday circumstances, for example, can support views that portray women as incapable of objective thinking. Alternatively, if experiences such as motherhood and pregnancy are examined and discussed to include contradictions and complexities, research findings can be read not only as further evidence for the "natural" female role, but also as support for labels often applied to women, such as "irrational" and "indecisive." Co-option and distortion can be diminished if women's experience is valued *within* communication studies, as an *already present* and valuable component of the discipline.

Women as Communicators

In a recent conversation we were told that the problem with feminists is a tendency to push their "in group" politics on other people even when most people on the "outside" do not share their politics. This comment indicates the extent of work yet to be done in bringing about an inclusion of women in communication studies, but in its characterization of inside vs. outside perspectives, the remark also poses a challenge to feminist communication scholars. The general belief still seems to be that feminists mix politics and research, but most people who investigate human communication do not. In describing the first four conceptualizations of women in communication research we have climbed down the pyramid envisaged by McIntosh, dismantling it piece by piece, to show that, as many feminists claim, personal choices often have political significance. This is not to suggest that researchers, by virtue of affiliation with particular political systems, intentionally exclude female experience, but rather to suggest that a complex cultural process of silencing renders it impossible for women who support women to have a voice from the "inside" of contemporary communication studies. The very term "feminist," with its negative social implication, can be taken as yet another means of discounting research about and for women. The point at which all communication scholars acknowledge the culturally sedimented presumptions contained in their views is the point at which, as a discipline, women can be seen *as* communicators.

When women are viewed as communicators, researchers examine the relationship between sedimented assumptions and the degree of female visibility

[90]Phyllis R. Randall, "Sexist Language and Speech Communication Texts: Another Case of Benign Neglect," *Communication Education* 34 (1985): 128.

afforded by particular cultural definitions of men and women. The critical collaboration of researchers in diverse areas of communication studies—for example, rhetoric, interpersonal and group, mass communication—encourages analyses of the extent to which our scholarship promotes an inclusive understanding of women's communication. For purposes of illustrating how this analysis takes place, we outline the study of leadership as it may be approached within each kind of research presented in our typology. McIntosh stresses that disciplinary inclusiveness is contingent on seeing points of divergence and convergence, consciousness regarding differing and similar assumptions in the context of issues we share.[91] Leadership is an area of study within many divisions in our field, and an area that is approached from diverse perspectives. Our aim in describing approaches to leadership is at once disciplinary and cultural; that is, leadership is understood, and is opened to critical scrutiny, when it is connected to our shared and diverse *cultural* images of men and women.

We show that assumptions contained in each type of research are "connected" to culture at large by utilizing Edwin Ardener's model of the relation between dominant and muted groups.[92] Ardener suggests that "women constitute a *muted group*, the boundaries of whose culture and reality overlap, but are not wholly contained by, the *dominant (male) group.*"[93] The markers that separate the two groups are clear yet penetrable, indicating the possible vacillation by women between dominant and muted groups. Originally designed to depict the range of possible relationships between dominant and muted groups with particular cultures, Ardener's model is often adopted by feminist scholars to explain the places occupied by women in patriarchal cultures. "Women," Elaine Showalter explains, can then be seen not as persons who are "inside and outside the male tradition; they are inside two traditions simultaneously."[94] The "bilingual" nature of women's communication is called upon in differing contexts and in various degrees, depending, in the case of leadership, on the extent to which women's experiences are given a voice.

In *womanless communication,* the qualities of leadership are gender neutral. Researchers are careful to point out that an "ideal" leader does not exist, and to this extent, leadership is said to be situationally dependent. The shift from "leader" to "leadership," Robert Cathcart and Larry Samovar suggest, signals a growing awareness that "leadership is a function of group process rather than a series of traits residing in an individual."[95] While the focus appears to move away from individual leaders, leadership is often defined in the context of influence and personal power. Moreover, leadership is always something done by an individual, as is evident in the many arguments against shared or absent leadership positions. Leadership is often contrasted to followership, which assumes an inequitable division between the leader and the led. As Robert Tannenbaum, Irving Wechsler, and Fred Massarik observe, "Leadership always involves attempts on the part of a *leader* (influencer) to affect (influence) the behavior of a

[91]See McIntosh's discussion of plurality in curriculum development, 20–33.

[92]Ardener's model is presented in Elaine Showalter, "Feminist Criticism in the Wilderness," *Critical Inquiry* 8 (1983): 197–205.

[93]Showalter, 199.

[94]Showalter, 202.

[95]Robert S. Cathcart and Larry A. Samovar, eds., *Small Group Communication: A Reader,* 4th ed. (Dubuque, IA: Wm. C. Brown Publishers, 1984), 368.

follower (influenced) or followers in a *situation.*"[96] The role of leader *or* follower will in all likelihood depend on status and power, given the presumption of inequity. Stuart Tubbs points out, for example, that "higher status tends to result in greater personal power or ability to influence others. Increased power, in turn, tends to elevate an individual's status level. Power and status go hand in hand, reciprocally influencing each other."[97] In assessing the qualities of good leadership, then, researchers turn to individuals who demonstrate a capacity for influence or compliance gaining.

Given the positioning of persons within cultural heirarchies, the qualities of model leadership are epitomized by men. Leader effectiveness is often contingent on characteristics that are thought to be at variance with female socialization. Most women are not likely to wield individual influence or power as defined within culture; thus, female traits may well appear in definitions of poor leadership. James Kinder, for example, compares four types of leaders by combining four behavioral traits: dominance, submission, warmth, and hostility.[98] The traits are combined in order to present four styles of leadership, followed by evaluations of effectiveness. Leaders who are both dominant and warm are maximally effective because they show commitment to tasks and people. The submissive-warm leader, by contrast, fails because he is "a kindly soul who puts happy relationships above all other considerations. . . . He strives to create a warm, pleasant, social atmosphere where an easygoing work tempo may be maintained."[99] Given the socialization of women, which gives much attention to nurturing, preserving relationships at the cost of rules, and creating horizontal bonds between people, women may be viewed as ineffective leaders.

Leadership from a *great women speakers* paradigm begins by asking, "Who are the great leaders in history?" Here, the spheres of men and women cross to a negligible degree with the realization that some successful leaders are women, thus the following question, "Who are the great female leaders?" A small percentage of women gain access to dominant leadership studies. Membership is composed of privileged women who are acceptable by male standards, women whose leadership skills match those of their male counterparts. Geraldine Ferraro may exist in the privileged realm because, in running for the second-highest office in American politics, she proved to be an "exceptional" woman.

Yet, the model also explains the failure of greatness as it pertains to women. The extraordinary female, because of physiology and socialization, is grouped simultaneously with her muted counterparts. Her behavior is interpreted with gender in mind so that even the title that affirms dominant membership, "Great Women," provides assurance that most women are unqualified for greatness. Moreover, regardless of leadership capabilities, gender remains a salient feature of leadership evaluations. A woman's role and temperament, as seen in depictions of greatness in *womanless communication*, is thought to be incompatible with leadership. For example, when Ferraro called attention to Bush's partronage

[96]Robert Tannenbaum, Irving B. Wechsler, and Fred Massarik, "Leadership: A Frame of Reference," in *Small Group Communication: A Reader*, 4th ed., eds. Robert S. Cathcart and Larry A. Samovar, 371.

[97]Stewart L. Tubbs, *A Systems Approach to Small Group Communication*, 2nd ed. (Reading, MA: Addison-Wesley Publishing, 1984), 154.

[98]See James F. Kinder, "Styles of Leadership," in *Small Group Communication*, 4th ed., eds. Robert S. Cathcart and Larry A. Samovar, 400–406.

[99]Kinder, 404.

in the 1984 vice-presidential debate by saying, "Don't patronize me," critics remarked on the emotional and uncontrolled character of her response. The practical problem, as argued by Schuster and Van Dyne, is that within the dominant realm, "most women's histories . . . will not measure up to the prominent male model: as writers, their production will seem minor in form or scope; as political activists, their participation in the sweep of history will appear sporadic."[100] The greatness paradigm, then, provides a relatively stable vision of male history; the few women deemed extraordinary must set themselves apart from, and identify with, the vast majority of invisible women.

If woman is defined as an *other,* male definitions of competent leadership are adopted and female leadership styles are compared to them. Research questions ask: How does female leadership differ from male leadership? Are women as competent as men in commanding roles? Do people respond more favorably to male or female leaders? The muted group is compared to the dominant group, but the reverse, which asks, "Are men as competent as women in leadership roles?" seldom occurs. Here, the muted status of women remains constant. Research activity centers on the elaboration of differences between the two spheres, with the dominant group serving a normative function. Assumptions concerning effectiveness are grounded in male sex-role stereotypes; thus good leaders are found to be aggressive, competitive, task-oriented, analytic, and logical.[101] Because leadership has been defined in public and corporate spheres, Fitzpatrick argues, the behavioral "script" required for leader competence is often perceived to be consistent with male socialization.[102] In fact, studies report that female leaders are generally found to be less effective, less competent, and less successful than their male counterparts.[103] Moreover, women who *do* follow the dictates of professional competence in leadership roles are often viewed as pushy, bitchy, hostile, overly-ambitious.[104] The great leader paradigm and the notion of women leaders as "others" are similar insofar as neither equalizes the status of dominant and muted groups. Rather, both implicitly presume universality based on male experience. Female leadership, then, appears deficient.

When scholars work to uncover the dynamics of female leadership without adopting the dominant paradigm, research questions and presumptions are

---

[100]Schuster and Van Dyne, 19.

[101]See, for example, Gerald M. Phillips, Douglas J. Pedersen, and Julia T. Wood, *Group Discussion: A Practical Guide to Participation and Leadership* (Boston: Houghton Mifflin, 1979); Steven A. Beebe and John T. Masterson, *Communicating in Small Groups: Principles and Practices,* 2nd ed. (Glenview, IL: Scott, Foresman, 1986).

[102]Fitzpatrick, 74–78.

[103]See, for example, B. Bass, J. Krusell, and R. Alexander, "Male Managers' Attitudes towards Working Women," *American Behavioral Scientists* 15 (1971): 221–236; V. E. Schein, "The Relationship between Sex Role Stereotypes and Requisite Management Characteristics," *Journal of Applied Psychology* 57 (1973): 95–100; V. E. Schein, "Relationships between Sex Role Stereotypes and Requisite Management Characteristics among Female Managers," *Journal of Applied Psychology* 60 (1975): 340–344. For a review of male-female differences in small group communication, see also John E. Baird, "Sex Differences in Group Communication: A Review of Relevant Research," *Quarterly Journal of Speech* 62 (1976): 179–192.

[104]See, for example, K. Deaux, "Self-Evaluations of Male and Female Managers," *Sex Roles* 5 (1979): 571–580; B. Rosen and T. H. Jerdee, "Influence of Sex-Role Stereotypes on Personnel Decisions," *Journal of Applied Psychology* 39 (1974): 9–14; K. Deaux and J. Taynor, "Evaluation of Male and Female Ability: Bias Works Two Ways," *Psychological Reports* 32 (1973): 261–262; D. M. Siegler and R. S. Siegler, "Stereotypes of Males' and Females' Speech," *Psychological Reports* 39 (1976): 167–170.

radically altered. The study of leadership is simultaneously a critical analysis because competency assessments account for the *politics of woman as other*. Women's experience is validated and named such that it is seen to comprise half the world's history. Scholars focus on the female sphere, working to unearth richness and diversity among individual women. Inquiries are framed inclusively: How do women experience leadership? How do women define successful leadership? How are corporate and personal relationships affected when women lead? How do women work together? Addressing these questions may involve analyses of homemakers, teachers, managers, secretaries, and students. In general, women who have a capacity to direct and influence the course of daily events, either collectively or individually, are potential sources of data. Conceptions of leadership expand to include the everyday lives of women, incorporating such qualities as compassion, sensitivity, and trust. Fidelity to women's communication behavior allows researchers to describe ambiguities in female leadership, such as an ability to occupy both leader and led roles simultaneously. The circle of mutation becomes larger as women's styles of communication are found to be strong, effective, and valid.

When women are viewed *as* communicators, rather than as a deviant or mysterious subculture, disciplinary conceptions of men *and* women are found to have a basis in cultural practices. Showalter explains,

> Both muted and dominant groups generate beliefs or ordering of social reality at the unconscious level, but dominant groups control the forms or structures in which consciousness can be articulated. Thus muted groups must mediate their beliefs through the allowable forms of dominant structures. Another way of putting this would be to say that all language is the language of the dominant, and women, if they speak at all, must speak through it. [105]

The experience of muted groups is rich in critical potential because women are typically placed in a relation of exteriority with respect to dominant culture. By living as "outsiders" *within* culture, women are able to see the exclusive character of many claims about *human* behavior. They may find their communication behavior described in portrayals of ineffective leadership, for example, and conclude that they are ill-suited for leadership roles. However, the same observation can be used to point out the exclusionary nature of such seemingly "neutral" definitions. From here, women can begin to question the qualities proposed for leadership and conduct investigations which do not begin by assuming that female behaviors impede group progress. Female leadership may, in fact, *promote* cohesiveness, openness, trust, and commitment.

The study of women as communicators can expand the knowledge base of the communication discipline, providing men and women with both behavioral and research alternatives. An excellent example of the critical insight made possible when women are studied within culture is provided in Gillian Michell's investigation of Grice's conversational maxims. [106] Grice's maxims are supposedly general, widely cited rules for conversations, which make the implicit assumption that conversational participants are rational and equal. Michell analyzes each maxim and notes that women do not follow Grice's rules when conversing with men because there are social constraints present, limiting women's choices and

---

[105]Showalter, 200.
[106]Gillian Michell, "Women and Lying: A Pragmatic and Semantic Analysis of 'Telling It Slant,' " *Women's Studies International Forum* 7/5 (1984): 373–383.

positioning women hierarchically with respect to a male partner. It is only by *violating* Grice's maxims that women can achieve the maximally effective exchanges of information. Michell observes that women must "tell it slant" in order to converse in a sexist society. That is, they must "follow the rules" of dominant culture, *and* understand that the rules are not applicable to their own conversational vantagepoint.

The inclusion of women in communication studies is counter-productive if one form of exclusion is simply replaced with another. The proposal for a normative shift from male to female communication behaviors is based in a view which is both hierarchical and linear. Nor is it enough to simply acknowledge women's experience through the use of gendered examples and mixed-gender pronouns. These "add women and stir" solutions are often cosmetic, having no effect on the research process. Rather, we argue that female inclusion is dependent on a global disciplinary awareness of assumptions that exclude and devalue female communication. Female inclusion requires not only an understanding of women within the parameters of communication studies, but includes analyses of gender as an organizing force in social interaction.[107] Such inclusion may well involve an investigation of *researcher* communication, as evidenced in publications, classrooms, and everyday interaction, along with studies centered on the communication of others, because researchers, too, exist within socially defined gender arrangements.

The inclusion of women in communication studies is dependent on collaboration within our discipline. We endorse the view of Susan Bellrichard, who argues that socially excluded persons are "heard" through a formulation of "counter-discourse from the inside."[108] We do not suggest that a "counter-discourse" requires researchers to surrender tarditional investigative approaches. Strategies designed to comprehend male versions of reality play an important role in disciplinary definition, as does our pluralistic tradition. We do, however, call for a specification of the presumptions contained in strategies that purport to be objective, along with concomitant assumptions that give the label of "subjective" or "soft" to alternative procedures. The challenge then involves more than conducting studies on women. The task is to analyze embedded assumptions concerning the objects of study, the methods of data collection, and the questions guiding research.[109] In so doing, portrayals of human communication are not found to be definitively right or wrong, but to reflect gendered and therefore *political* presumptions. The net gains resulting from self-reflexive criticism are substantial. First, as women become empowered as active agents in communication studies, possibilities for growth and disciplinary change are uncovered. Second, researchers will be better able to match research methods to the particularities of their research questions. Third, novel theories, investigative strategies and topic areas emerge when the perspectival nature of taken for granted assumptions comes under scrutiny. And perhaps most importantly, the critical activity we endorse promotes a *truly* pluralistic view of human communication.

[107]Dubois et. al., 47. See also Jenkins and Kramarae, "A Thief in the House."

[108]Susan Bellrichard, "Voices from the Margin," *Canadian Journal of Political and Social Theory* 10 (1986): 1.

[109]Dubois et al., 16.

6

THE POSTMODERN PERSPECTIVE

Growing in popularity throughout the 1980s, postmodernism, or poststructuralism, now represents a significant critical approach to rhetorical scholarship in the United States. Extended attention has been devoted to major postmodern theorists such as Michel Foucault,[1] Jurgen Habermas,[2] Jacques Derrida,[3] Hans-Georg Gadamer,[4] Paul de Man,[5] Ernesto Grassi,[6] Jean Baudrillard,[7] and Pierre Bourdieu.[8] Postmodern critical analyses have likewise become a central component of rhetorical scholarship in the United States, with particular attention devoted to the mass media,[9] feminism,[10] Marxism,[11] U.S. communication research

[1]See, e.g., Sonja K. Foss and Ann Gill, "Michel Foucault's Theory of Rhetoric as Epistemic," Western Journal of Speech Communication 51, 4 (Fall 1987): 384–401; Carole Blair, "The Statement: Foundation of Foucault's Historical Criticism," Western Journal of Speech Communication 51, 4 (Fall 1987): 364–383; and Sonja K. Foss, Karen A. Foss, and Robert Trapp, "Michel Foucault," in Contemporary Perspective on Rhetoric (Prospect Heights, IL: Waveland, 1985), 189–211.

[2]See, e.g., Brant R. Burleson and Susan L. Kline, "Habermas' Theory of Communication: A Critical Explication," Quarterly Journal of Speech 65, 4 (December 1979): 412–428; Sonja K. Foss, Karen A. Foss, and Robert Trapp, "Jurgen Habermas," Comtemporary Perspectives on Rhetoric (Prospect Heights, IL: Waveland, 1985), 213–239; and Kyle A. Pasework, "Communicative Irrationality and Political Discourse in Jurgen Habermas: A Theoretical Experiment," in Communication Yearbook 9, ed. Margaret L. McLaughlin (Beverly Hills: Sage, 1986), 741–755.

[3]See, e.g., Walter J. Ong, Orality and Literacy: The Technologizing of the Word (New York: Methuen, 1982), 156–179; Jonathan Culler, "Jacques Derrida," in Structuralism and Since, ed. John Sturrock (New York: Oxford University Press, 1979), 154–180.

[4]See, e.g., John Angus Campbell, "Hans-Georg Gadamer's Truth and Method," Quarterly Journal of Speech 64 1 (February 1978), 101–110; and Kuan-hsing Chen, "Beyond Truth and Method: On Misreading Gadamer's Praxical Hermeneutics," Quarterly Journal of Speech 73, 2 (May 1987): 183–199.

[5]See, e.g., Dilip Parameshwar Gaonkar, "Deconstruction and Rhetorical Analysis: The Case of Paul de Man," Quarterly Journal of Speech 73, 4 (November 1987): 482–528. Following his death in December of 1984, de Man was identified as a writer for a anti-Semitic, pro-Nazi Belgium newspaper during World War II: "Yale Scholar Wrote for Pro-Nazi Newspaper," New York Times, December 1, 1987, pp. B1, B6; Scott Heller, "Scholars Grapple with Literary Critic's Early Writings for Pro-Nazi Periodical," Chronicle of Higher Education, May 11, 1988, pp. A1, A6; James Atlas, "The Case of Paul de Man," New York Times Magazine, August 28, 1988, sect. 6, pp. 36–37, 60, 66, 68–69. The December 1, 1987 New York Times particularly concluded that "critics of Professor de Man have labeled deconstructionism a nihilistic philosophy that makes moral or political beliefs impossible" (p. B6).

[6]See, e.g., Sonja K. Foss, Karen A. Foss, and Robert Trapp, "Ernesto Grassi," in Contemporary Perspectives on Rhetoric (Prospect Heights, IL: Waveland, 1985), 125–151.

[7]See, e.g., Kuan-hsing Chen, "Mass Media and Postmodernity: The Cultural Politics of Silencing in Jean Baudrillard," in Communication Yearbook 10, ed. Margaret L. McLaughlin (Newbury Park, CA: Sage, 1987), 666–683.

[8]See, e.g., Mary S. Mander, "Bourdieu, the Sociology of Culture and Cultural Studies: A Critique," European Journal of Communication 2, 4 (December 1987): 427–453.

[9]See, e.g., David Barker, "Television Production Techniques as Communication," Critical Studies in Mass Communication 2, 3 (September 1985): 234–246; John Fiske, "Television: Polysemy and Popularity," Critical Studies in Mass Communication 3, 4 (December 1986): 391–408; Henry Jenkins III, "Star Trek Rerun, Reread, Rewritten: Fan

as a symbolic construction[12] and with special issues of journals such as "Postmodernism/Marxism/Feminism,"[13] "Intersections of Power: Criticism-Television-Gender,"[14] and "Stuart Hall."[15] While perhaps still tentative in its formulations, the basic principles and methodologies of postmodern rhetorical criticism have also been articulated.[16]

Historically, the seeds for this approach to criticism emerged in the mid-1960s in the essays of several U.S. and Western European critics.[17] While lacking a coherent or unifying set of principles at its inception, nonetheless a series of critical terminologies such as *postmodernism, poststructuralism, text,* and *deconstruction* began to be used in rather unusual ways yet with definite regularity. These critical terminologies were fashioned and proposed by advocates who were not generally considered rhetoricians.

Writing as Textual Poaching," *Critical Studies in Mass Communication* 5, 2 (June 1988) 85–107; Eileen R. Meehan, "Conceptualizing Culture as Commodity: The Problem of Television," *Critical Studies in Mass Communication* 3, 4 (December 1986): 448–457; Scott R. Olson, "Meta-television: Popular Postmodernism," *Critical Studies in Mass Communication* 4, 3 (September 1987): 284–300; Eric E. Peterson, "Media Consumption and Girls Who Want To Have Fun," *Critical Studies in Mass Communication* 4, 1 (March 1987): 37–50; Stuart J. Sigman and Donald L. Fry, "Differential Ideology and Language Use: Readers' Reconstructions and Descriptions of News Events," *Critical Studies in Mass Communication* 2, 4 (December 1985): 307–322.

[10]See, e.g., Anne Balsamo, "Unwrapping the Postmodern: A Feminist Glance," *Journal of Communication Inquiry* 11, 1 (1987): 64–72; Lana F. Rakow, "Gendered Technology, Gendered Practice," *Critical Studies in Mass Communication* 5, 1 (March 1988): 57–70; H. Leslie Steeves, "Feminist Theories and Media Studies," *Critical Studies in Mass Communication* 4, 2 (June 1987): 95–135; and Linda Steiner, "Oppositional Decoding as an Act of Resistance," *Critical Studies in Mass Communication* 5, 1 (March 1988): 1–15.

[11]See, e.g., Lawrence Grossberg, "Strategies of Marxist Cultural Interpretation," *Critical Studies in Mass Communication* 1, 4 (December 1984): 392–421; and Stuart Hall, "Signification, Representation, Ideology: Althusser and the Post-Structuralist Debates," *Critical Studies in Mass Communication* 2, 2 (June 1985): 91–114.

[12]See, e.g., Lawrence Grossberg, "Critical Theory and the Politics of Empirical Research," *Mass Communication Review Yearbook*, vol. 6, ed. Michael Gurevitch and Mark R. Levy, (Newbury Park, CA: Sage, 1987), 86–106; Hanno Hardt, "Comparative Media Research: The World According to America," *Critical Studies in Mass Communication* 5, 2 (June 1988): 129–146; and Michael Schudson, "The New Validation of Popular Culture: Sense and Sentimentality in Academia," *Critical Studies in Mass Communication* 4, 1 (March 1987): 51–68.

[13]*Communication* 10, 3–4 (1988).

[14]*Communication* 9, 3–4 (1987).

[15]*Journal of Communication Inquiry* 10, 2 (Summer 1986).

[16]See, e.g., Briankle G. Chang, "Deconstructing the Audience: Who Are They and What Do We Know about Them?" in *Communication Yearbook 10*, ed. Margaret L. McLaughlin (Newbury Park, CA: Sage, 1987), 649–665; Stanley Deetz, "Negation and the Political Function of Rhetoric," *Quarterly Journal of Speech* 69, 4 (November 1983): 434–441; Stephen Glynn, "Beyond the Symbol: Deconstructing Social Reality," *Southern Speech Communication Journal* 51, 2 (Winter 1986): 125–141; Astrid Kersten, "Philosophical Foundations for the Construction of Critical Knowledge," *Communication Yearbook 9*, ed. Margaret L. McLaughlin (Beverly Hills, CA: Sage, 1986), 756–774; and Mary S. Strine, "Constructing 'Texts' and Making Inferences: Some Reflections on Textual Reality in Human Communication Research," *Communication Yearbook 11*, ed. James A. Anderson (Newbury Park, CA: Sage, 1988), 494–500.

[17]For a more extended view of the origin of postmodernism from Aristotle through Jakobson, by a postmodernist, in terms of the evolution of theoretical conceptions of a symbol, see Tzvetan Todorov, *Theories of the Symbol*, trans. Catherine Porter (Ithaca, NY: Cornell University Press, 1983).

Without question, these new advocates have intended that their terminologies be perceived as part of an alternative approach to the critical perspectives and methods that have dominated the post–World War II criticism. Indeed, by the end of the 1960s and in the early 1970s, among literary critics, the distinction between "modernity" and "postmodernity" was common. *New Literary History: A Journal of Theory and Interpretation* devoted its Autumn 1971 issue solely to an exploration of "modernism and postmodernism" and included such essays as "Modernism and History," "Politics and Modernity: The Strategies of Desperation," and even "The Death of Literature."[18]

Certainly, by the end of the 1970s and in the early 1980s, a pointed break from prior critical traditions was evident in how these new postmodern critics discussed their critical endeavors. Emphasizing an evolution in critical conceptions, in 1979 John Sturrock collected the writings of several of the new critics in a book entitled *Structuralism and Since: From Lévi-Strauss to Derrida*. Sturrock maintained that these essays represented "a new philosophy" that integrated "ideas hitherto dispersed and seemingly heterogeneous" into "a coherent whole."[19] In a very similar vein, in September of 1980, Jurgen Habermas declared that a new historical-cultural era in criticism had emerged. In sharp contrast to those who "considered themselves modern," Habermas held that a new "emotional current of our times" had emerged "which had penetrated all spheres of intellectual life." "It has," argued Habermas, "placed on the agenda theories of postenlightenment, postmodernity, even of posthistory."[20]

Postmodernism has exerted a corresponding influence on rhetorical theory and method. The influence is conveniently illustrated in Foss, Foss, and Trapp's survey of "different perspectives on rhetoric" that have dominated the twentieth-century "contemporary" rhetorical "period."[21] While experiential, dramaturgical, and sociological rhetorical critics such as I. A. Richards, Richard Weaver, Stephen Toulmin, Chaim Perelman, and Kenneth Burke are represented in their survey, the postmodern critics clearly constitute a dominant force in their view of the contemporary rhetorical period; for over one-third of their attention is devoted to Ernesto Grassi, Michel Foucault, and Jurgen Habermas. Such an emphasis reflects, rather than distorts, the emerging and growing attention that has been devoted to postmodern critics in the discipline of communication by both rhetorical critics and social scientists.

At the same time, it is easy to overstate the influence and impact of the postmodern perspective among rhetorical critics. The new terminologies and meanings of the postmodern critics have frequently lacked a historical context placing its concepts within a framework immediately useful to rhetorical critics trained in other perspectives. Likewise, the massive output of the postmodern critics has often overshadowed the effort to provide a concise and carefully delineated philosophy. In addition, more clearly than other rhetorical perspectives, the perspective's politics has often detracted from the view of rhetoric that guides it. In

[18]*New Literary History: A Journal of Theory and Interpretation* 3, 1 (Autumn 1971).

[19]John Sturrock, ed., *Structualism and Since: From Lévi-Strauss to Derrida* (Oxford: Oxford University Press, 1979), 2.

[20]Jurgen Habermas, "Modernity—An Incomplete Project," in *The Anti-Aesthetic: Essays on Postmodern Culture*, ed. Hal Foster (Port Townsend, WA: Bay Press, 1983), 3.

[21]Sonja K. Foss, Karen A. Foss, and Robert Trapp, *Contemporary Perspectives on Rhetoric* (Prospect Heights, IL: Waveland, 1985).

sum, we do not think it is unfair to note that the postmodern rhetorical perspective has generated a kind of "culture shock" within the discipline.

Given the apparent shock created by the postmodern rhetorical perspective, it is appropriate to underscore some of the fundamental perceptions and philosophical elements guiding postmodern criticism. Accordingly, this introduction to postmodern rhetorical theory and criticism is governed by five objectives. First, it seeks to identify the factors or influences within the discipline of communication that have spawned an interest in postmodern criticism. Second, as a preliminary effort to define the essential features of postmodern criticism, the worldview of postmodern critics requires attention. Particularly, as distinguished by postmodern critics, the meaning of the terms *modern* and *postmodern* as sociocultural eras are examined. Third, rhetoric and criticism are explicitly reassessed from a postmodern perspective. Fourth, the two dominant methods constituting postmodern rhetorical criticism are identified and examined. Fifth and finally, the assumptions of the postmodern criticism are overtly articulated in a manner that allows it to be compared and contrasted to the traditional, experiential, dramaturgical, and sociological perspectives considered earlier.

Early Influences

The reasons why a new view of rhetoric and criticism emerge are always complex, but perhaps we can identify a few of the interrelated causes for the growing interest among rhetoricians in postmodern criticism.

First, critics change because rhetoric changes. Since World War II, an increasing quantity of rhetorical efforts have shifted from face-to-face encounters to mediated experiences. The medium itself has increasingly been recognized as a decisive variable in understanding what the rhetorical process is. Rather than viewed as neutral conduits that merely transmit a message, media systems themselves are more frequently viewed as critical factors affecting apprehension.[22] The production techniques employed to create a television program may, for example, have a tremendous impact on what a viewer understands a persuasive message to be.[23] In a larger view, technology itself has increasingly defined how a messge is to be constructed and ultimately understood. Accordingly, these systems have received far greater attention by rhetorical critics, and many rhetorical critics sought a new set of terminologies to capture the influence of high technology upon rhetorical transactions. In many respects, the introduction of the journal *Critical Studies in Mass Communication* and the publication of a volume such as Martin J. Medhurst and Thomas W. Benson's *Rhetorical Dimensions in Media: A Critical Casebook*,[24] both in 1984, provided a formal recognition of the need to explore many of the relationships now existing among rhetoric, criticism, and media systems. The media orientation of many of the postmodern

[22]See, e.g., Walter J. Ong. *Orality and Literacy: The Technologizing of the Word* (London: Methuen, 1982).

[23]See, e.g., Scott R. Olsen, "Meta-Television: Popular Postmodernism," *Critical Studies in Mass Communication* 4, 3 (September 1987), 284–300.

[24]Martin J. Medhurst and Thomas W. Benson, eds., *Rhetorical Dimensions in Media: A Critical Casebook* (Dubuque, IA: Kendall/Hunt, 1984).

critics has provided an extremely convenient reference for adapting to the changing nature of rhetoric.[25]

Second, the provincial relationship that has traditionally existed between U.S. and Western European critics has dissolved. The global structure of post–World War II information systems and the ever-increasing quantity of communication journals have contributed to the decline of provincial regional orientations in rhetorical criticism. The writings of Western European critics such as Jacques Derrida and Roland Barthes are no longer restricted by geographic boundaries. Likewise, the simultaneous introduction in 1984 of the *European Journal of Communication* and *Telematics and Informatics: An International Journal* to both U.S. and European scholars formally signaled the decline of the provincial regionalism that had previously governed rhetorical criticism.

Third, while initially a response to the movement politics of the 1960s,[26] rhetorical critics have paid increasing attention to the ideological component of persuasive messages and, with increasing self-consciousness, to the ideological dimension of criticism itself. Feminism constitutes an excellent example of how the ideological has become a feature of rhetorical criticism. Certainly, the discourse of feminists has increasingly constituted an object of study for rhetorical critics. And feminist discourse, like other forms of discourse, is, among other things, decidedly ideological. But, more profoundly, feminism has also emerged as an approach to rhetorical criticism. The critics of feminist discourse have increasingly been women who have handled their objects of study as both critics and women. Accordingly, the ideological dimension of such criticism is explicit, but the insightfulness and power of this ideological perspective has also been virtually impossible to deny. This ideological feature of rhetorical criticism has also been formally recognized within the literature by rhetoricians such as Philip Wander[27] and Michael Calvin McGee.[28] The explicit attention given to the social and contextual, if not ideological, nature of criticism by the postmodern critics has served to make postmodern critics a potential model for refashioning the conception of rhetorical criticism.[29]

Fourth, the changing conception of knowledge in rhetorical criticism has required that the nature of rhetorical criticism be reconsidered. All human message systems have been increasingly recognized as epistemic, socially created, or

[25]See, e.g., Roland Barthes, *The Responsibility of Form: Critical Essays on Music, Art, and Representation* (New York: Hill and Wang/Farrar, Straus, and Giroux, 1985).

[26]See e.g., Robert L. Scott and Donald K. Smith, "The Rhetoric of Confrontation," *Quarterly Journal of Speech* 55, 1 (February 1969). 1–8.

[27]See, e.g., Philip Wander, "The Ideological Turn in Modern Criticism," *Central States Speech Journal* 34, 1 (Spring 1983): 1–18.

[28]See, e.g., Michael Calvin McGee, "The Ideograph: A Link between Rhetoric and Ideology," *Quarterly Journal of Speech* 66, 1 (February 1980): 1–16. Of special interest to the analysis being developed here, also see the following by Michael Calvin McGee: "The Origins of Liberty: A Feminization of Power," *Communication Monographs* 47, 1 (March 1980): 23–44; "Another Philippic: Notes on the Ideological Turn in Criticism," *Central States Speech Journal* 35, 1 (Spring 1984): 43–50; "On Feminized Power," Van Zelst Lecture in Communication, (Northwestern University School, 1985); and "Power to the [People]," *Critical Studies in Mass Communication* 4, 4 (December 1987): 432–437.

[29]See e.g., Jonathan Culler, *On Deconstruction: Theory and Criticism after Structuralism* (Ithaca, NY: Cornell University Press, 1982), esp. 43–83.

rhetorical.[30] Two of the consequences of the epistemic viewpoint for the rhetorical critic deserve special attention. First, it is no longer clear how the persuasive message and the critical analysis of a persuasive message differ. In many respects, both the persuasive message and the critical analysis of the persuasive message share common characteristics. Indeed, for many, criticism is now viewed as a form of persuasion. Second, the traditional distinction in criticism between *description* and *interpretation* as separate stages in a critical analysis seems not to hold. Given the complexity of any single event, many now hold that any description of an event must necessarily reflect the orientation, perspective, or interpretation of a critic. Likewise, any interpretation of an event must necessarily reflect a highly selective description of the causal elements creating a particular conception of an event. In all, the epistemic theory of human understanding has blurred the distinction between persuasion and criticism and between description and interpretation. New conceptions of rhetorical criticism have therefore been required, and readily available models have been offered, for some time now, by postmodern critics.[31]

These explanations or reasons for the emergence of the postmodern perspective underscore the dynamic nature of rhetorical criticism. In this context, it should also be noted that the reasons for the break from the traditional paradigm noted on pages 86–87 have also influenced the emergence of the postmodern perspective. In contrast to what we believed were accurate statements in 1971 and 1980, at this point in time we would simply note that the break from the traditional paradigm has now yielded at least four perspectives, the experiential, dramaturgical, sociological, and postmodern.

Distinguishing the Modern and Postmodern Eras

Postmodern critics believe that a dramatic shift in the nature of society has occurred, requiring that these new conditions be reflected in how messages are assessed. The most dramatic of these societal shifts is the belief that a disjuncture has occurred between individuals and the nature, structure, and processes of all societies in the developing nations throughout the world. While a host of schemes have been invoked to characterize this transformation, the *modernity-postmodernity* dichotomy has probably received the greatest attention and captures, in several respects, the most critical elements of the perspective of postmodern critics.

Defined in terms of a specific time period, postmodern critics have clearly recognized that *modern* is an ambiguous referent. Yet the diverse connotations of the concept have also been found to be useful. For example, Habermas has reported that

the word "modern" in its Latin form "modernus" was used for the first time in late 5th century in order to distinguish the present, which had become officially

---

[30]See, e.g., Robert L. Scott, "On Viewing Rhetoric as Epistemic," *Central States Speech Journal* 18, 1 (February 1967): 9–16; and Robert L. Scott, "On Viewing Rhetoric as Epistemic: Ten Years Later," *Central States Speech Journal* 27, 4 (Winter 1976): 259–266.

[31]See e.g., Michel Foucault, *Madness and Civilization: A History of Insanity in the Age of Reason* (New York: Pantheon Books, 1965).

Christian, from the Roman and pagan past. With varying content, the term "modern" again and again expresses the consciousness of an epoch that relates itself to the past of antiquity, in order to view itself as the result of a transition from the old to the new.

Some writers restrict the concept of "modernity" to the Renaissance, but this is historically too narrow. People considered themselves modern during the period of Charles the Great in the 12th century, as well as in France of the late 17th century at the time of the famous "Querelle des Anciens et des Modernes." That is to say, the term "modern" appeared and reappeared exactly during those periods in Europe when the consciousness of a new epoch formed itself through a renewed relationship to the ancients—whenever, moreover, antiquity was considered a model to be recoverd through some kind of imitation.[32]

In terms of his more specific use, Habermas has argued that modernity gained its contemporary meaning when the "ideals of the French Enlightenment" were no longer, for the "first" time, tied to classical conceptions and standards. Particularly, the "radicalized consciousness of modernity" emerged when it "freed itself from all specific historical ties." Rejecting classical idealism, nineteenth-century moderns were "inspired by modern science"; and, in Habermas' view, science and its related technologies were to provide for the contemporary modern a belief "in the infinite progress of knowledge and in the infinite advance toward social and moral betterment."[33]

Holding that "modernism is dominant but dead," Habermas particularly noted that the "project of enlightenment" offered by nineteenth-century moderns has distinguished with artificial and misleading terms science (*truth* and *cognitive-instrumental*), morality (*normative rightness* and *practical*), and art (*authenticity and beauty* and *expressive rationality*). In Habermas' view, the postmodernism of "the 20th century has shattered this optimism." In his view, a new agenda has been established for the critic in which the relationships among science, morality, and art must be reestablished: "Communication processes need a cultural tradition covering all spheres—cognitive, moral-practical and expressive." Particularly, the cult of the expert must be replaced by a system in which "the layman" becomes "an expert" and "relates aesthetic experiences to his own life problems" and in which "critical judgments" are "used to illuminate a life-historical situation and are related to life problems."[34]

Other postmodern critics have offered specific metaphors for characterizing the modern era. Noting that "every culture" cannot "sustain and absorb the shock of modern civilization" without destroying itself, Kenneth Frampton, an

[32]Jurgen Habermas, "Modernity—An Imcomplete Project," in *The Anti-Aesthetic: Essays on Postmodern Criticism,* ed. Hal Foster (Port Townsend, WA: Bay, 1983), 3. Habermas provides a philosophical extension of his discussion of modernity-postmodernity in Jurgen Habermas, *The Philosophical Discourse of Modernity: Twelve Lectures,* trans. Frederick Lawrence (Cambridge: MIT Press, 1987). For an application of the modernity-postmodernity perspective to communication, see Jurgen Habermas, *The Theory of Communicative Action,* vol. 1, *Reason and the Rationalization of Society,* trans. Thomas McCarthy (Boston, MA: Beacon, 1984); and Jurgen Habermas, *The Theory of Communicative Action: Lifeword and Systems: A Critique of Functional Reason,* Vol. 2, (Boston, MA: Beacon, 1987). Of related interest from a communication perspective is Jurgen Habermas, *Communication and the Evolution of Society,* trans. Thomas McCarthy (Boston, MA: Beacon, 1979).

[33]Habermas, 4.

[34]Habermas, 8–13.

architect, has argued that the automobile and "the freestanding high-rise and the serpentine freeway" have become the dominant symbols of the modern age, with "automotive distribution" limiting "the scope of urban design" and ultimately redefining art, entertainment, and "scenography." In Frampton's view, the concept of "the overall spectrum of world culture" must ultimately be "deconstructed" and replaced with human-centered forms of "critical regionalism."[35] Beyond urban planning, as amply illustrated in *Rhetoric of the Human Sciences: Language and Argument in Scholarship and Public Affairs*,[36] the sciences themselves have been approached from a postmodern perspective. Others have offered a similar critique and alternative visions for literature, sculpture, museums, male-female roles, consumption, and aesthetics.[37]

These postulates regarding the modern and postmodern eras provide a foundation for strikingly different conceptions of symbol using and criticism. The governing principles of the modernity-postmodernity dichotomy as extracted by us and applied to the specific case of human communication suggest at least five different conceptions as distinguishing the modern and the postmodern critic.

First, the modern and the postmodern critic hold two different views regarding what information is and how human beings process information. The modern critic assumes that information is an extrinsic phenomenon, independent of human perception, which an individual must react to and use. The postmodern critic holds that the individual is an information processing system that integrates selectively, ultimately *creating* whatever is perceived as information.

Second, the discreteness of the symbolic form and criticism distinguish the modern and the postmodern critic. The modern critic would compartmentalize, or distinguish, most symbolic forms from criticism, treating a symbolic form as an artistic product of a creativity or inventive mode and criticism as a response and assessment of a symbolic form. Accordingly, the province or world of the artist is governed by one set of standards, expertise, and study; while the province or enclave of the critic is governed by alternative standards, expertise, and study. In contrast, the postmodern critic dissolves the distinction between symbol forms and criticism, holding that both are forms of persuasion or social control, and therefore ultimately hold that both are "power texts."

Third, ontological questions of objectivity and subjectivity distinguish the modern and the postmodern critic. The modern critic holds that science, morality, and art are distinct systems of logic. The postmodern critic maintains that all views are ideological, for a description can only reflect the perceptual perspective and biases of a particular symbol user in a given place at a specific time.

Fourth, different views of society distinguish the modern and the postmodern critic. For the modern critic, the modern era is a period of ordering, structuring, and finding transcendent universals, ultimately favoring the use of experts for such ends. For the postmodern critic, social interactions must reflect a populist

[35]Kenneth Frampton, "Towards a Critical Regionalism: Six Points for an Architecture of Resistance," in *The Anti-Aesthetic: Essays on Postmodern Culture*, ed. Hal Foster (Port Townsend, WA: Bay, 1983), 16–30. It should also be noted that postmodern views of architecture are beginning to make their way into the popular media; see, e.g., Linnea Lannon, "Post-Modern," *Detroit Free Press*, Section H, pp. 1,4; and Ellen Posner, "Deconstructive Criticism," *Wall Street Journal*, July 18, 1988, p. 16.

[36]John Nelson et al., *Rhetoric of the Human Sciences: Language and Argument in Scholarship and Public Affairs* (Madison, WI: University of Wisconsin Press, 1987).

[37]See, e.g., the balance of the essays in Hal Foster, op. cit.

view and therefore presume that differences exist whenever human beings communicate, ultimately asssessing human communication as a series of contradictory orientations.

Fifth, the modern and postmodern posit distinct forms of understanding. The modern critic seeks to identify theoretical postulates to explain human patterns and ordering systems, with analysis as a critical mode for generating what is to be understood. The postmodern critic emphasizes the uniqueness of each situation and the particular nature of all circumstances—ultimately an atheoretical or antitheoretical view, in which the power texts must be deconstructed if the unique vision and identity of each community is to be preserved.

These differences between the modern and the postmodern critics generate different conceptions of rhetoric and criticism.

Rhetoric and Criticism

While modern rhetorical criticism has traditionally been viewed as the description, interpretation, and evaluation of social engineering techniques and styles, postmodern rhetorical criticism seeks to determine the ways in which the paradoxical power struggles can coexist. This postmodern view of rhetorical criticism finds its origin in the fundamental distinction between the concepts of *work* and *text* that quides postmodern rhetorical criticism.

For the postmodern critic, a *work* is a physical object, whereas a *text* is any response to or experience derived from the work. As Barthes has explained, "The work is concrete, occupying a portion of book-space (in a library, for example); the Text, on the other hand, is a methodological field. . . . In other words, *the Text is experienced only in an activity, a production.* It follows that the Text cannot stop, at the end of a library shelf, for example; the constitutive movement of Text is a *traversal (traversée):* it can cut across a work, several works." Accordingly, any experience derived from, any response to, or any use made of, a work must be understood as distinct from the original work, for the reactions to the work are a discrete text or human extension and construction that may have virtually nothing to do with the original work.

This *text-work* distinction has profound implications in defining rhetorical criticism for the postmodern critic. Three of these implications warrant our attention here for they constitute critical dimensions of the postmodern conception of rhetorical criticism.

First, rhetorical criticism functions independently of the original work, ultimately displacing the original work. As a form of textual analysis, rhetorical criticism is itself to be viewed as an original work, perhaps to be subjected to other textual analyses; but the textual analysis itself constitutes a distinct symbolic construction to be assessed as part of an ongoing sociocultural system that brought the textual analysis or rhetorical criticism into existence, of which only one part of it can be assumed to have been formed by the original work analyzed. In this sense, a text or rhetorical criticism of work necessarily displaces an original work, because the text or rhetorical criticism now occupies the attention once held by the original work. More profoundly, the rhetorical analysis inherently creates a new symbolic orientation of the original work, for it (1) links the original work with new symbolic concepts, relationships, and qualifiers not previously associated with an original work; (2) creates a new setting and context for assessing the original work; and (3) affects the ethos of the original work, for the characteristics attributed to the source of the rhetorical criticism are now linked to the original work. In addition, there is a sense in which rhetorical criticism would not have been created unless the adequacy of the original work as presented somehow required renewal, modification, amplification, or revision.

Second, all rhetorical analyses are ideological constructions. Assuming, as Genette has argued,[38] that all symbol using is arbitrary and conventional, language using has no necessary relationship to external phenomena. In the postmodern framework, language using represents the orientation, drives, and needs of the symbol user and therefore the ideological position of the symbol user. As Barthes has maintained, "*A work whose integrally symbolic nature one conceives, perceives, and receives is a text.*"[39]

Third, every rhetorical analysis inherently conveys multiple and contradictory meanings. As Culler has noted,[40] postmodern critics have denied the validity and usefulness of concepts such as the "ideal," "implied," "authorial," and "narrative" audience. For the postmodern critic, the issue turns on the "actual audience." When examining the reactions of an actual audience, the issue is not that a work can potentially generate divergent reactions, but rather that, as Marin has stated,[41] "*meaning is plural.*" Grossberg has spelled out the implications of postmodern pluralism: "No element is definable in and of itself; it exists—its identity takes shape—only in its complex relations to, its differences from, its others (and of course, there can be no single definition of the other, i.e., contradiction is itself a complex and historical relationship)."[42]

Given the critical ways in which the distinction between *work* and *text* defines rhetorical criticism from a postmodern perspective, we have included Roland Barthes's essay "From Work to Text" as the initial reading of this section. Barthes's analysis is devoted solely to the seven propositions he believes can be derived from the *work-text* dichotomy and to how this distinction defines the critical endeavor. Ultimately, as we have suggested and Barthes argues directly, the *work-text* distinction defines the essential features of rhetorical criticism as postmodern critics see them.

Postmodern Rhetorical Methods

The specific tactics, strategies, and modes of presentation of postmodern criticism have ranged from the historic[43] to the semiotic.[44] We have encountered a

---

[38]G. Gennette, "Valery and the Poetics of Language," in *Textual Strategies: Perspectives in Post-Structuralist Criticism*, ed. J. V. Harari (Ithaca, NY. Cornell University Press), 359–373.

[39]Barthes, 76.

[40]Culler, 34.

[41]L. Marin, "On the Interpretation of Ordinary Language: A Parable of Pascal," in *Textual Strategies: Perspectives in Post-Structuralist Criticism*, ed. J. V. Harari (Ithaca, NY: Cornell University Press), 239–259.

[42]Lawrence Grossberg, "Critical Theory and the Politics of Empirical Research," in *Mass Communication Review Yearbook*, vol. 6, ed. M. Gurevitch and M. R. Levy (Newbury, CA: Sage), 86–106.

[43]See, e.g., Carole Blair, "The Statement: Foundation of Foucault's Historical Criticism," *Western Journal of Speech Communication* 51, 4 (Fall 1987): 364–383.

[44]See, e.g., Roland Barthes, *Elements of Semiology* (New York: Hill and Wang/Farrar,

tremendously rich variety of specific schemes for analyzing symbol using across the wide diversity of critics who constitute postmodern criticism. As is true with any other method of rhetorical criticism, such diversity is to be expected. Yet we do find commonalities across these diverse critical endeavors.

Four basic operations appear to unify the procedures of postmodern critics:[45]

First, the strategies contained within an author's original work are identified. The work-text distinction is employed as an initial premise in this critical process. Postmodern critics rather consistently distinguish the original work to be analyzed from the critic's text or response to the original work. The work-text distinction presumes that differences exist between experiences and understandings that shaped the original work of an author and the text to be created by the critic. The work-text distinction therefore establishes the initial procedure of the critic, namely to identify strategies that highlight the differences between the viewpoints of the original author's work and the critic.

Second, the critic seeks to articulate the ideological, worldview or life-style differences reflected in the original work of an author and the text to be created by the critic. In this sense, the critical objective is to construct the view of reality and knowledge system governing the original work of an author and the text to be created by the critic. Toward this end, a critic might initially seek to identify explicitly the roles, tones, and moods as well as the dichotomies, values, attitudes, and language choices that distinguish the author of the original work and the critic. Ultimately, the distinction between the original work of an author and the text created by the critic must reflect a fundamental difference in life-style, such as "male versus female," "black versus white," "radical versus liberal," and so forth.

Third, the societal implications of the difference between the original work of an author and the position of the critic are identified. The goals, structures, and processes of society constitute the parameters for this investigation. For example, the differences in interpersonal, cultural, social, or economic policies might constitute a foundation for identifying the differences in the types of societies sought by the author of the original work and by the critic.

Fourth, the political or power relationships distinguishing the original work of an author and the text of the critic emerge. This decidedly evaluative stage posits a deconstruction of the original work of an author. The critic seeks to determine how the original work of an author would "empower" certain groups at the expense of others. Correspondingly, the critic seeks to determine how the stance adopted by the critic realigns such a power relationship, shifting the political relationship toward a system of mutual sharing, respect, and equal decision making and action.

These four procedural steps are richly illustrated in Jonathan Culler's "Reading as a Woman." Culler's statement of procedure does occur within the context

---

Straus, and Giroux, 1968); Farrell Corcoran, "Towards a Semiotic of Screen Media: Problems in the Use of Linguistic Models," *Western Journal of Speech Communication 45*, 2 *(Spring 1981): 182–193;* Darryl Hattenhauer, "The Rhetoric of Architecture: A Semiotic Approach," *Communication Quarterly 32, 1 (Winter 1984): 71–77;* John R. Lyne, "Rhetoric and Semiotic in C. S. Peirce," *Quarterly Journal of Speech 66, 2 (April 1980): 155–168; and* John R. Lyne, "Semiotics Self-Signifying: The Ongoing Constitution of Sign Studies," *Quarterly Journal of Speech 70, 1 (February 1984): 80–110.*

[45]For a discussion of specific postmodern textual analysis procedures of "strategies," see Vincent B. Leitch, *Deconstructive Criticism: An Advanced Introduction* (New York: Columbia University Press, 1983), 165–252.

of an example. He focuses on how feminists "read" the works of males who unknowingly proposed systems of thought that dominated women. Nonetheless, Culler explicitly identifies how a postmodern critic functions operationally. Accordingly, we have included this excerpt from Culler's book[46] as the second reading in this section.

While certain commonalities constitute a foundation for defining the essential elements of the methods of postmodern critics, postmodern critics have often found it useful to develop specialized procedures that serve their particular critical ends more directly. One of two basic methodologies—*constructivism* or *deconstructivism*—currently reflects the basic methodological choice of most postmodern rhetorical critic.

For the postmodern critic, the constructivist method is an essential and defining feature of postmodern rhetorical criticism because it reveals the diverse ways in which different audiences react to the same message. A basic premise of postmodern rhetorical criticism is that a single concept generates contradictory responses, and the constructionist method is the most direct method for illustrating the basic contradictory premise of symbol using.

As one might anticipate, the most effective demonstration of this thesis would be a comparative analysis in which several different audiences view the same message and report diverse understandings of the same message. We have selected Tamar Liebes's "Cultural Differences in the Retelling of Television Fiction,"[47] to illustrate the postmodern critic's use of the constructionist method. Liebes and Katz asked five different audiences to view the same television program. They found that each audience had a flagrantly different understanding of the same television program.

For the postmodern critic, the deconstructionist method constitutes an equally important feature of postmodern rhetorical criticism. Deconstruction has been viewed as a nihilistic method that debunks, without offering a compensating solution to, ongoing social problems. We have no doubt that deconstruction can function in such a fashion. At the same time, as we have already suggested, the postmodern critic holds that individuals use symbols to construct different social realities and that these different social realities generate advantages for certain groups and disadvantages for others. Insofar as the postmodern critic intervenes in social processes as a social activist, seeking to equalize power relationships and ultimately asking all to think together, but in admittedly different ways, it may frequently be necessary for the postmodern critic to illustrate the self-defeating principles governing the symbolic constructions of the powerful. This deconstructive procedure is designed to allow all to interact as equals, recognizing differences but finding ways in which all may realize their objectives without the destruction of others. We have selected Lawrence Grossberg's essay "Is There Rock after Punk?"[48] to illustrate how the deconstruction method can be used by the postmodern rhetorical critic. We find Grossberg's essay to be instructive not only because it illustrates the deconstruction method but because he is conscious of the method he uses and overtly draws attention to the critical steps and procedures he employs.

---

[46]*On Deconstruction: Theory and Criticism after Structuralism* (Ithaca, NY: Cornell University Press), 43–64.

[47]*Critical Studies in Mass Communication* 5 (December 1988): 277–292.

[48]*Critical Studies in Mass Communication* 3, 1 (March 1986): 50–74.

For pedagogical purposes, we have treated constructionism and deconstructionism as two discrete options a postmodern critic may elect to employ. Yet the two methods can be merged within a single and extended piece of rhetorical criticism. An excellent example of how these two methods complement each other is found in Michel Foucault's *The History of Sexuality,* volume 1. In this volume, Foucault identifies a series of different symbolic constructions others have employed to deal with sexual activity. Foucault maintains that each of these symbolic constructions of reality has allowed a few to gain control over others. Accordingly, as social activist, Foucault seeks to deconstruct these symbolic constructions in order to restore the mystery and excitement to sex.[49] For those wishing to examine how constructionism and deconstructionism functions as mutually defining and complementary methods of the postmodern critic, we strongly recommend Foucault's analysis of sexuality.

Characteristics of the Postmodern Perspective

As with the traditional, experiential, dramaturgical, and sociological perspectives, the essential characteristics of the postmodern perspective are appropriately isolated. Abstractions of this nature always involve overgeneralizations, yet the generalizations provide a foundation for comparing the basic assumptions of the postmodern perspective to the other perspectives examined earlier.

1. *Orientation.* The critic concentrates the diverse meanings discourse may generate and the corresponding power relationships established by these diverse meanings. Accordingly, contradiction and power become the central objects of attention for the postmodern critic. The purpose of the postmodern critic is to identify how power texts construct social realities and can be deconstructed.

2. *Assumptions*
    a. The modern industrial state creates, maintains, and uses a series of paradoxical symbolic constructions of reality as modes of social control.
    b. To understand the control systems employed by societal systems, the diverse symbolic constructions of reality must be identified by the rhetorical critic.
    c. In order to promote equality, the rhetorical critic functions as social activist, deconstructing the symbolic constructions of reality erected by political elites.
    d. The word-thought-thing relationship is directly challenged by postmodern critics. The word-thing relationship is cast as solely arbitrary and conventional, designed to create and reinforce word-thought relationships that facilitate dominant and subordinate relationships.

3. *Consensus.* Symbol using is a context-specific activity in which any understanding of a symbol reflects only the specific background, perceptions, values, and needs of those using and responding to symbols. A single generalization positing an universal understanding or meaning of a symbol must necessarily distort how human beings use symbols. In this sense, postmodern criticism is essentially antitheoretical.

[49]Random House, 1980 (originally published in 1978).

FROM WORK TO TEXT

Roland Barthes

Over the past several years, a change has been taking place in our ideas about language and, as a consequence, about the (literary) work, which owes at least its phenomenal existence to language. This change is obviously linked to current developments in, among other fields, linguistics, anthropology, Marxism, and psychoanalysis (the word "link" is used here in a deliberately neutral fashion: it implies no decision about a determination, be it multiple and dialectical). The change affecting the notion of the work does not necessarily come from the internal renewal of each of these disciplines, but proceeds, rather, from their encounter at the level of an object that traditionally depends on none of them. *Interdisciplinary* activity, valued today as an important aspect of research, cannot be accomplished by simple confrontations between various specialized branched of knowledge. Interdisciplinary work is not a peaceful operation: it begins *effectively* when the solidarity of the old disciplines breaks down—a process made more violent, perhaps, by the jolts of fashion—to the benefit of a new object and a new language, neither of which is in the domain of those branches of knowledge that one calmly sought to confront.

It is precisely this uneasiness with classification that allows for the diagnosis of a certain mutation. The mutation that seems to be taking hold of the idea of the work must not, however, be overestimated: it is part of an epistemological shift [*glissement*] rather than of a real break [*coupure*], a break of the kind which, as has often been remarked, supposedly occurred during the last century, with the appearance of Marxism and Freudianism. No new break seems to have occurred since, and it can be said that, in a way, we have been involved in repetition for the past hundred years. Today history, our history, allows only displacement, variation, going-beyond, and rejection. Just as Einsteinian science requires the inclusion of the *relativity of reference points* in the object studied, so the combined activity of Marxism, Freudianism, and structuralism requires, in the case of literature, the relativization of the *scriptor's*, the reader's, and the observer's (the critic's) relationships. In opposition to the notion of the work—a traditional notion that has long been and still is thought of in what might be called Newtonian fashion—there now arises a need for a new object, one obtained by the displacement or overturning of previous categories. This object is the *Text*. I realize that this word is fashionable and therefore suspect in certain quarters, but that is precisely why I would like to review the principle propositions at the intersection of which the Text is situated today. These propositions are to be understood as enunciations rather than arguments, as mere indications, as it were, approaches that "agree" to remain metaphoric. Here, then, are those propositions: they deal with method, genre, the sign, the plural, filiation, reading (in an active sense), and pleasure.

From *Textual Strategies: Perspectives in Post-Structuralist Criticism*, translated and edited by Josue V. Harari (Ithaca, NY: Cornell University Press, 1979): 73–81. Copyright 1979 by Cornell University. Used by permission of the author and the publisher, Cornell University Press.
Roland Barthes, who died in 1980, last taught at the College de France.

1. The Text must not be thought of as a defined object. It would be useless to attempt a material separation of works and texts. One must take particular care not to say that works are classical while texts are avant-garde. Distinguishing them is not a matter of establishing a crude list in the name of modernity and declaring certain literary productions to be "in" and others "out" on the basis of their chronological situation. A very ancient work can contain "some text," while many products of comtemporary literature are not texts at all. The difference is as follows: the work is concrete, occupying a portion of book-space (in a library, for example); the Text, on the other hand, is a methodological field.

This opposition recalls the distinction proposed by Lacan between "reality" and the "real": the one is displayed, the other demonstrated. In the same way, the work can be seen in bookstores, in card catalogues, and on course lists, while the text reveals itself, articulates itself according to or against certain rules. While the work is held in the hand, the text is held in language: it exists only as discourse. The Text is not the decomposition of the work; rather it is the work that is the Text's imaginary tail. In other words, *the Text is experienced only in an activity, a production.* It follows that the Text cannot stop, at the end of a library shelf, for example; the constitutive movement of the Text is a *traversal [traversée]:* it can cut across a work, several works.

2. Similarly, the Text does not come to a stop with (good) literature; it cannot be apprehended as part of a heirarchy or even a simple division of genres. What constitutes the Text is, on the contrary (or precisely), its subversive force with regard to old classifications. How can one classify Georges Bataille? Is this writer a novelist, a poet, an essayist, an economist, a philosopher, a mystic? The answer is so uncertain that manuals of literature generally chose to forget about Bataille: yet Bataille wrote texts—even, perhaps, always one and the same text.

If the Text raises problems of classification, that is because it always implies an experience of limits. Thibaudet used to speak (but in a very restricted sense) about limit-works (such as Chateaubriand's *Life of Rancé,* a work that today indeed seems to be a "text"): the Text is that which goes to the limit of the rules of enunciation (rationality, readability, and so on). The Text tries to situate itself exactly *behind* the limit of *doxa.* (Is not public opinion constitutive of our democratic societies and powerfully aided by mass communication—defined by its limits, its energy of exclusion, its *censorship?*) One could literally say that the Text is always *paradoxical.*

3. Whereas the Text is approached and experienced in relation to the sign, the work closes itself on a signified. Two modes of signification can be attributed to this signified: on the one hand, one can assume that it is obvious, in which case the work becomes the object of a "science of the letter" (philology); on the other hand, one can assume that the signified is secret and ultimate, in which case one must search for it, and the work then depends upon a hermeneutic, an interpretation (Marxist, psychoanalytic, thematic, for example). In brief, the work itself functions as a general sign and thus represents an institutional category of the civilization of the Sign. The Text, on the contrary, practices the infinite deferral of the signified [le recul infini du signifié]: the Text is *dilatory:* its field is that of the signifier. The signifier must not be conceived as "the first stage of meaning," its material vestibule, but rather, on the contrary, as its *aftermath* [aprés-coup]. In the same way, the signifier's *infinitude* does not refer back to some idea of the ineffable (of an unnamable signified) but to the idea of *play.* The engendering of the perpetual signifier within the field of the text

should not be identified with an organic process of maturation or a hermeneutic process of deepening, but rather with a serial movement of dislocations, overlappings, and variations. The logic that governs the Text is not comprehensive (seeking to define "what the work means") but metonymic; and the activity of associations, contiguities, and cross-references coincides with a liberation of symbolic energy. The work (in the best of cases) is moderately symbolic (its symbolism runs out, comes to a halt), but the Text is *radically* symbolic *A work whose integrally symbolic nature one conceives, perceives, and receives is a text.*

In this way the Text is restored to language: like language, it is structured but decentered, without closure (here one might note, in reply to the scornful insinuation of "faddishness" which is often directed against structuralism, that the epistemological privilege presently granted to language proceeds precisely from our discovery in language of a paradoxical idea of structure, a system without end or center).

4. The Text is plural. This does not mean just that is has several meanings, but rather that it achieves plurality of meaning, an *irreducible* plurality. The Text is not coexistence of meanings but passage, traversal; thus it answers not to an interpretation, liberal though it may be, but to an explosion, a dissemination. The Text's plurality does not depend on the ambiguity of its contents, but rather on what could be called the *stereographic plurality* of the signifiers that weave it (etymologically the text is a cloth: *textus,* from which *text* derives, means "woven").

The reader of the Text could be compared to an idle subject (a subject having relaxed his "imaginary"[1]): this fairly empty subject strolls along the side of a valley at the bottom of which runs a *wadi* (I use *wadi* here to stress a certain feeling of unfamiliarity) What he sees is multiple and irreducible; it emerges from substances and levels that are heterogeneous and disconnected: lights, colors, vegetation, heat, air, bursts of noise, high-pitched bird calls, children's cries from the other side of the valley, paths, gestures, clothing of close and distant inhabitants. All these *occurences* are partially identifiable: they proceed from known codes, but their combination is unique, founding the stroll in difference that can be repeated only as difference. This is what happens in the case of the Text: it can be itself only in its difference (which does not mean its "individuality"): its reading is semelfactive (which renders all inductive-deductive sciences of text illusory—there is no "grammar" of the text) and yet completely woven with quotations, references, and echoes. These are cultural languages (and what language is not?), past or present, that traverse the text from one end to the other in a vast stereophony.

Every text, being itself the intertext of another text, belongs to the intertextual, which must not be confused with a text's origins: to search for the "sources of" and "influence upon" a work is to satisfy the myth of filiation. The quotations from which a text is constructed are anonymous, irrecoverable, and yet *already read:* they are quotations without quotation marks. The work does not upset monistic philosophies, for which plurality is evil. Thus, when it is compared with the work, the text might well take as its motto the words of the man possessed by devils: "My name is legion, for we are many" (Mark 5:9).

---

[1]"Qui aurait détendu en lui tout imaginaire," *Imaginary* is not simply the opposite of real. Used in the Lacanian sense, it is the register, the dimension of all images, conscious or unconscious, perceived or imagined.—Trans.

The plural or demonic texture that divides text from work can carry with it profound modifications in the activity of reading and precisely in the area where monologism seems to be the law. Some of the "texts" of the Scriptures that have traditionally been recuperated by theological (historical or anagogical) monism may perhaps lend themselves to a diffraction of meaning, while the Marxist interpretation of the work, until now resolutely monistic, may be able to materialize itself even further by pluralizing itself (if, of course, Marxist "institutions" allow this).

5. The work is caught up in a process of filiation. Three things are postulated here: a *determination* or the work by the outside world (by race, then by history), a *consecution* of works among themselves, and an *allocation* of the work to its author. The author is regarded as the father and the owner of his work; literary research therefore learns to *respect* the manuscript and the author's declared intentions, while society posits the legal nature of the author's relationship with his work (these are the "author's rights," which are actually quite recent; they were not legalized in France until the Revolution).

The Text, on the other hand, is read without the father's signature. The metaphor that describes the Text is also distinct from that describing the work. The latter refers to the image of an *organism* that grows by vital expansion, by "development" (a significantly ambiguous word, both biological and rhetorical). The Text's metaphor is that of the *network:*[2] if the Text expands, it is under the effect of a *combinatorial,* a *systematics*[3] (an image which comes close to modern biology's views on the living being).

Therefore, no vital "respect" is owed to the Text: it can be broken (this is exactly what the Middle Ages did with two authoritative texts, the Scriptures and Aristotle). The Text can be read without its father's guarantee: the restitution of the intertext paradoxically abolishes the concept of filiation. It is not that the author cannot "come back" into the Text, into his text: however, he can only do so as a "guest," so to speak. If the author is a novelist, he inscribes himself in his text as one of his characters, as another figure sewn into the rug: his signature is no longer privileged and paternal, the focus of genuine truth, but rather, Tudic. He becomes a "paper author": his life is no longer the origin of his fables, but a fable that runs concurrently with his work. There is a reversal, and it is the work which affects the life, not the life which affects the work: the work of Proust and Genet allows us to read their lives as a text. The word "biography" reassumes its strong meaning, in accordance with its etymology. At the same time, the enunciation's sincerity, which has been a veritable "cross" of literary morality, becomes a false problem: the *I* that writes the text is never, itself, anything more than a paper *I*.

6. The work is ordinarily an object of consumption. I intend no demoagoguery in referring here to so-called consumer culture, but one must realize that today it is the work's "quality" (this implies, ultimately, an appreciation in terms of "taste") and not the actual process of reading that can establish differences between books. There is no structural difference between "cultured" reading and casual subway reading. The Text (if only because of its frequent

---

[2]Barthes uses here the word *réseau.* I have chosen to translate it by "network" (rather than "web," for instance) at the risk of overemphasizing the mechanical implications of the metaphor.—Trans.

[3]*Systematics* is the science (or method) of classification of living forms.—Trans.

"unreadability") decants the work from its consumption and gathers it up as play, task, production, and activity. This means that the Text requires an attempt to abolish (or at least to lessen) the distance between writing and reading, not by intensifying the readers' projection into the work, but by linking the two together in a single signifying process [*pratique signifiante*].

The distance separating writing from reading is historical: during the era of greatest social division (before the institution of democratic cultures), both reading and writing were class privileges. Rhetoric, the great literary code of those times, taught *writing* (even though speeches and not texts were generally produced). It is significant that the advent of democracy reversed the order: (secondary) school now prides itself on teaching how to *read* (well), and not how to *write*.

In fact, *reading* in the sense of *consuming* is not *playing* with the text. Here "playing" must be understood in all its polysemy. The text itself *plays* (like a door on its hinges, like a device in which there is some "play"); and the reader himself plays twice over: playing the Text as one plays a game, he searches for a practice that will re-produce the Text; but, to keep that practice from being reduced to a passive, inner mimesis (the Text being precisely what resists such a reduction), he also *plays* the Text in the musical sense of the term. The history of music (as practice, not as "art") happens to run quite parallel to the history of the Text. There was a time when "practicing" music lovers were numerous (at least within the confines of a certain class), when "playing" and "listening" constituted an almost undifferentiated activity. Then two roles appeared in succession: first, that of the *interpreter*, to whom the bourgeois public delegated its playing: second, that of the music lover who listened to music without knowing how to play it. Today, post-serial music has disrupted the role of the "interpreter" by requiring him to be, in a certain sense, the coauthor of a score which he completes rather than "interprets."

The Text is largely a score of this new type: it asks the reader for an active collaboration. This is a great innovation, because it compels us to ask "Who *executes* the work?" (a question raised by Mallarmé, who wanted the audience to *produce* the book). Today only the critic *executes* the work (in both senses). The reduction of reading to consumption is obviously responsible for the "boredom" that many people feel when confronting the modern ("unreadable") texts, or the avant-garde movie or painting: to suffer from boredom means that one cannot produce the text, play it, open it out, *make it go*.

7. This suggests one final approach to the Text, that of pleasure. I do not know if a hedonistic aesthetic ever existed, but there certainly exists a pleasure associated with the work (at least with certain works). I can enjoy reading and rereading Proust, Flaubert, Blazac, and even—why not?—Alexandre Dumas; but this pleasure as keen as it may be and even if disengaged from all prejudice, remains partly (unless there has been an exceptional critical effort) a pleasure of consumption. If I can read those authors, I also know that I cannot *rewrite* them (that today, one can no longer write "like that"); that rather depressing knowledge is enough to separate one from the production of those works at the very moment when their remoteness founds one's modernity. (For what is "being modern" but the full realization that one cannot begin to write the same works once again?) The Text, on the other hand, is linked to enjoyment [jouissance], to pleasure without separation. Order of the signifier, the Text participates in a social utopia of its own: prior to history, the Text achieves, if not the transpar-

ency of social relations, at least the transparency of language relations. It is the space in which no one language has a hold over any other, in which all languages circulate freely.

These few propositions, inevitably, do not constitute the articulation of a theory of the Text. This is not just a consequence of the presenter's insufficiencies (beside, I have in many respects only recapitulated what is being developed around me); rather, it proceeds from the fact that a theory of the Text cannot be fully satisfied by a metalinguistic exposition. The destruction of metalanguage, or at least (since it may become necessary to return to it provisionally) the questioning of it, is part of the theory itself. Discourse on the Text should itself be only "text," search, and textual toil, since the Text is that *social* space that leaves no language safe or untouched, that allows no enunciative subject to hold the position of judge, teacher, analyst, confessor, or decoder. The theory of the Text can coincide only with the activity of writing.

READING AS A WOMAN

Jonathan Culler

Suppose the informed reader of a work of literature is a woman. Might this not make a difference, for example, to "the reader's experience" of the opening chapter of *The Mayor of Casterbridge,* where the drunken Michael Henchard sells his wife and infant daughter to a sailor for five guineas at a country fair? Citing this example, Elaine Showalter quotes Irving Howe's celebration of Hardy's opening:

> To shake loose from one's wife; to discard that drooping rag of a woman, with her mute complaints and maddening passivity; to escape not by slinking abandonment but through the public sale of her body to a stranger, as horses are sold at a fair; and thus to wrest, through sheer amoral wilfulness, a second chance out of life—it is with this stroke, so insidiously attractive to male fantasy, that *The Mayor of Casterbridge* begins.

The male fantasy that finds this scene attractive may also be at work transforming Susan Henchard into a "drooping rag," passive and complaining—a portrait scarcely sustained by the text. Howe goes on to argue that in appealing to "the depths of common fantasy," the scene draws us into complicity with Henchard. Showalter comments:

> In speaking of "our common fantasies," he quietly transforms the novel into a male document. A woman's experience of this scene must be very different; indeed, there were many sensation novels of the 1870s and 1880s which presented the sale of women into marriage from the point of view of the bought wife. In Howe's reading, Hardy's novel becomes a kind of sensation-fiction, playing on the suppressed longings of its male audience, evoking sympathy for Henchard because of his crime, not in spite of it. ("The Unmanning of the Mayor of Casterbridge," pp. 102–3)

Howe is certainly not alone in assuming that "the reader" is male. "Much reading," writes Geoffrey Hartman in *The Fate of Reading,* "is indeed like girl-watching, a simple expense of spirit (p. 248). The experience of reading seems to be that of a man (a heart-man?) for whom girl-watching is the model of an expense of spirit in a waste of shame.[1] When we posit a woman reader, the result

From *On Deconstruction: Theory and Criticism after Structuralism* by Jonathan Culler (Ithaca, NY: Cornell University Press, 1982), 43–65. Copyright © 1982 by Cornell University. Used by permission of the author and publisher, Cornell University Press.

Jonathan Culler is a professor of English and comparative literature at Cornell University.

[1]This alerts one to the remarkable scenario of Hartman's recent criticism. *The Fate of Reading* offers this prognostic: most reading is like girl-watching, doubtless "perjur'd,

is an analogous appeal to experience: not to the experience of girl-watching but to the experience of being watched, seen as a ''girl,'' restricted, marginalized. A recent anthology that stresses the continuity between women's experience and the experience of women reading is appropriately entitled *The Authority of Experience: Essays in Feminist Criticism.* One contributor, Maurianne Adams, explains:

> Now that the burden of trying to pretend to a totally objective and value-free perspective has finally been lifted from our shoulders, we can all admit, in the simplest possible terms, that our literary insights and perceptions come, in part at least, from our sensitivity to the nuances of our own lives and our observations of other people's lives. Every time we rethink and reassimilate *Jane Eyre,* we bring to it a new orientation. For women critics, this orientation is likely not to focus particular attention upon the dilemmas of the male, to whom male critics have already shown themselves understandably sensitive, but rather on Jane herself and her particular circumstances. (''*Jane Eyre:* Woman's Estate,'' pp. 140–41)

''Rereading *Jane Eyre,*'' she notes, ''I am led inevitably to feminist issues, by which I mean the status and economics of female dependence in marriage, the limited options available to Jane as an outlet for her education and energies, her need to love and to be loved, to be of service and to be needed. These aspirations, the ambivalence expressed by the narrator toward them, and the conflicts among them, are all issues raised by the novel itself'' (p. 140).

An unusual version of this appeal to women's experience is an essay in the same collection by Dawn Lander that explores the literary commonplace that ''the frontier is no place for a woman,'' that women hate the primitive conditions, the absence of civilization, but must stoically endure them. Lander reports that her own experience as a woman living in the desert made her question this cliché and seek out what frontier women had written about their lives, only to discover that her ''own feelings about the wilderness were duplicated in the experience of historic and contemporary women'' (''Eve among the Indians,'' p. 197). Appealing to the authority first of her own experience and then of others' experiences, she reads the myth of women's hatred of the frontier as an attempt by men to make the frontier an escape from everything women represent to them, an escape from renunciation to a paradise of male camaraderie where sexuality can be an aggressive, forbidden commerce with nonwhite women. Here the experience of women provides leverage for exposing this literary topos as a self-serving male view of the female view.

Women's experience, many feminist critics claim, will lead them to value works differently from their male counterparts, who may regard the problems women characteristically encounter as of limited interest. An eminent male critic, commenting on *The Bostonians,* observes that ''the doctrinaire demand for equality of the sexes may well seem to promise but a wry and constricted story, a tale of mere eccentricity'' (Lionel Trilling, *The Opposing Self,* p. 109). This is no doubt what Virginia Woolf calls ''the difference of view, the difference of standard'' (*Collected Essays,* vol. 1, p. 204). Responding to a male

---

murderous, bloody, full of blame.'' The cure is a period of *Criticism in the Wilderness,* after which, chastened and purified, criticism can turn to *Saving the Text*—saving it, it turns out, from a frivolous, seductive, and ''self-involved'' deconstruction that ignores the sacred.

critic who had patronizingly reproached her for trying to "aggrandize [Charlotte] Gilman's interesting but minor story" of incarceration and madness, "The Yellow Wallpaper," by comparing it with Poe's "The Pit and the Pendulum," Annette Kolodny notes that while she finds it as skillfully crafted and tightly composed as anything in Poe, other considerations doubtless take precedence when judging whether it is "minor" or not: "what may be entering into *my* responses is the fact that, as a female reader, I find the story a chillingly symbolic evocation of realities which women daily encounter even in our own time" ("Reply to Commentaries," p. 589). Conviction that their experience as women is a source of authority for their responses as readers has encouraged feminist critics in their revaluation of celebrated and neglected works.

In this first moment of feminist criticism, the concept of a woman reader leads to the assertion of continuity between women's experience of social and familial structures and their experience as readers. Criticism founded on this postulate of continuity takes considerable interest in the situations and psychology of female characters, investigating attitudes to women or the "images of women" in the works of an author, a genre, or a period. In attending to female characters in Shakespeare, the editors of a critical anthology observe, feminist critics are "compensating for the bias in a critical tradition that has tended to emphasize male characters, male themes, and male fantasies" and drawing attention instead to the complexity of women characters and their place in the order of male values represented in the plays (Lenz et al., *The Women's Part*, p. 4). Such criticism is resolutely thematic—focused on woman as a theme in literary works— and resolute too in its appeal to the literary and nonliterary experience of readers.

> Feminist criticism of Shakespeare begins with an individual reader, usually, although not necessarily, a female reader—a student, teacher, actor—who brings to the plays her own experience, concerns, questions. Such readers trust their responses to Shakespeare even when they raise questions that challenge prevailing critical assumptions. Conclusions derived from these questions are then tested rigorously against the text, its myriad contexts, and the explorations of other critics.
> (p. 3)

Criticism based on the presumption of continuity between the reader's experience and a woman's experience and on a concern with images of women is likely to become most forceful as a critique of the phallocentric assumptions that govern literary works. This feminist critique is by now a familiar genre, authoritatively established by such works as Simone de Beauvoir's *The Second Sex*, which, while indicting familiar ways of thinking about women, provides readings of the myths of women in Montherlant, Lawrence, Claudel, Breton, and Stendhal. A similar enterprise, in which a woman reader responds critically to the visions embodied in the literature celebrated by her culture, is Kate Millett's *Sexual Politics*, which analyzes the sexual visions or ideologies of Lawrence, Miller, Mailer, and Genet. If these discussions seem exaggerated or crude, as they have seemed to male critics who find it hard to defend the sexual politics of the writers they may have admired, it is because by posing the question of the relation between sex and power and assembling relevant passages from Lawrence, Miller, and Mailer, one displays in all their crudity the aggressive phallic visions of three "counterrevolutionary sexual politicians" (p. 233). (Genet, by contrast, subjects the code of male and female roles to withering scrutiny.)

Millett's strategy in reading as a women is "to take an author's ideas seriously when, like the novelists covered in this study, they wish to be taken seriously," and to confront them directly. "Critics who disagree with Lawrence, for example, about any issue are fond of saying that his prose is awkward. . . . It strikes me as better to make a radical investigation which can demonstrate why Lawrence's analysis of a situation is inadequate, or biased, or his influence pernicious, without ever needing to imply that he is less than a great and original artist" (p. xii).

Instead of playing down, as critics are wont to do, those works whose sexual vision is most elaborately developed, Millett pursues Lawrence's sexual religion to an apotheosis where sexuality is separated from sex: the priests of "The Women Who Rode Away" are "supernatural males, who are 'beyond sex' in a pious fervor of male supremacy that disdains any genital contact with women, preferring instead to deal with her by means of a knife." This pure or ultimate maleness is, Lawrence says, "something primevally male and cruel" (p. 290). Miller's sexual ethos is much more conventional: "his most original contribution to sexual attitudes is confined to giving the first full expression to an ancient sentiment of contempt": he has "given voice to certain sentiments which masculine culture had long experienced but always rather carefully suppressed" (pp. 309, 313). As for Mailer, his defense of Miller against Millett's critique confirms Millett's analysis of Mailer himself, as "a prisoner of the virility cult" "whose powerful intellectual comprehension of what is most dangerous in the masculine sensibility is exceeded only by his attachment to the malaise" (p. 314). Here is Mailer restating, in Miller's defense, their male ideology:

> For he captured something in the sexuality of men as it had never been seen before, precisely that it was man's sense of awe before woman, his dread of her position one step closer to eternity (for in that step were her powers) which made men detest women, revile them, humiliate them, defecate symbolically on them, do everything to reduce them so one might dare to enter them and take pleasure of them. . . . Men look to destroy every quality in a woman which will give her the powers of a male, for she is in their eyes already armed with the power that she brought them forth, and that is a power beyond measure—the earliest etchings of memory go back to that woman between whose legs they were conceived, nurtured, and near strangled in the hours of birth. (*The Prisoner of Sex*, p. 116)

How does a woman read such authors? A feminist criticism confronts the problem of women as a consumer of male-produced literature.

Millett also offers, in an earlier chapter, brief discussions of other works: *Jude the Obscure, The Egoist, Villette*, and Wilde's *Salome.* Analyzing these reactions to the sexual revolution of the nineteenth century, she establishes a feminist response that has served as a point of departure for debates within feminist criticism—disagreements about whether, for example, despite his sensitive portrait of Sue Bridehead, Hardy is ultimately "troubled and confused" when it comes to the sexual revolution.[2] But the possibility of quarreling with Millett to develop

---

[2]See, for example, an early rejoinder by Mary Jacobus, who argues that what Millett calls Hardy's "confusion" is in fact "careful non-alignment": "through Sue's obscurity he probes the relationship between character and idea in such a way as to leave one's mind engaged with her as it is engaged with few women in fiction" ("Sue the Obscure," pp. 305, 325).

more subtle feminist readings should not obscure the main point. As Carolyn
Heilbrun puts it,

> Millett has undertaken a task which I find particularly worthwhile: the consider-
> ation of certain events or works of literature from an unexpected, even startling
> point of view. . . . Her aim is to wrench the reader from the vantage point he has
> long occupied, and force him to look at life and letters from a new coign. Hers is
> not meant to be the last word on any writer, but a wholly new word, little heard
> before and strange. For the first time we have been asked to look at literature as
> women; we, men, women and Ph.D's, have always read it as men. Who cannot
> point to a certain overemphasis in the way Millett reads Lawrence or Stalin or
> Euripides. What matter? We are rooted in our vantage point and require transplant-
> ing. ("Millett's *Sexual Politics:* A Year Later," p. 39)

As Heilbrun suggests, reading as a women is not necessarily what occurs
when a woman reads: women can read, and have read, as men. Feminist readings
are not produced by recording what happens in the mental life of a female reader
as she encounters the words of *The Mayor of Casterbridge,* though they do rely
heavily on the notion of the experience of the woman reader. Shoshana Felman
asks, "Is it enough to be a woman in order to speak as a woman? Is 'speaking as
a woman' determined by some biological condition or by a strategic, theoretical
position, by anatomy or by culture?" ("Women and Madness: The Critical Phallacy," p. 3). The same question applies to "reading as a woman."

To ask a woman to read as a woman is in fact a double or divided request. It
appeals to the condition of being a woman as if it were a given and simultaneously urges that this condition be created or achieved. Reading as a woman is
not simply, as Felman's disjunctions might seem to imply, a theoretical position,
for it appeals to a sexual identity defined as essential and privileges experiences
associated with that identity. Even the most sophisticated theorists make this
appeal—to a condition or experience deemed more basic than the theoretical
position it is used to justify. "As a female reader, I am haunted rather by another
question," writes Gayatri Spivak, adducing her sex as the ground for a question
("Finding Feminist Readings," p. 82). Even the most radical French theorists,
who would deny any positive or distinctive identity to woman and see *le feminin*
as any force that disrupts the symbolic structures of Western thought, always
have moments, in developing a theoretical position, when they speak as women,
when they rely on the fact that they *are* women. Feminist critics are fond of
quoting Virginia Woolf's remark that women's "inheritance," what they are
given, is "the difference of view, the difference of standard"; but the question
then becomes, what is the difference? It is never given as such but must be
produced. Difference is produced by differing. Despite the decisive and necessary appeal to the authority of women's experience and of a female reader's
experience, feminist criticism is in fact concerned, as Elaine Showalter astutely
puts it, "with the way in which the *hypothesis* of a female reader changes our
apprehension of a given text, awakening us to the significance of its sexual
codes" ("Towards a Feminist Poetics," p. 25, my italics).[3]

[3]Feminist criticism is, of course, concerned with other issues as well, particularly the
distinctiveness of women's writing and the achievements of women writers. The problems
of reading as a woman and of writing as a woman are in many respects similar, but concentration on the latter leads feminist criticism into areas that do not concern me here,

Showalter's notion of the *hypothesis* of a female reader marks the double or divided structure of "experience" in reader-oriented criticism. Much male response criticism conceals this structure—in which experience is posited as a given yet deferred as something to be achieved—by asserting that readers simply do in fact have a certain experience. This structure emerges explicitly in a good deal of feminist criticism which takes up the problem that women do not always read or have not always read as women: they have been alienated from an experience appropriate to their condition as women.[4] With the shift to the hypothesis of a female reader, we move to a second moment or level of feminist criticism's dealings with the reader. In the first moment, criticism appeals to experience as a given that can ground or justify a reading. At the second level the problem is precisely that women have not been reading as women. "What is crucial here," writes Kolodny, "is that reading is a *learned* activity which, like many other learned interpretive strategies in our society, is inevitably sex-coded and gender-inflected" ("Reply to Commentaries," p. 588). Women "are expected to identify," writes Showalter, "with a masculine experience and perspective, which is presented as the human one" ("Women and the Literary Curriculum," p. 856). They have been constituted as subjects by discourses that have not identified or promoted the possibility of reading "as a woman." In its second moment, feminist criticism undertakes, through the postulate of a woman reader, to bring about a new experience of reading and to make readers—men and women—question the literary and political assumptions on which their reading has been based.

In feminist criticism of the first sort, women readers identify with the concerns of women characters; in the second case, the problem is precisely that women are led to identify with male characters, against their own interests as women. Judith Fetterley, in a book on the woman reader and American fiction, argues that "the major works of American fiction constitute a series of designs upon the female reader." Most of this literature "insists on its universality at the same time that it defines that universality in specifically male terms" (*The Resisting Reader*, p. xii). One of the founding works of American literature, for instance, is "The Legend of Sleepy Hollow." The figure of Rip Van Winkle, writes Leslie Fiedler, "presides over the birth of the American imagination; and it is fitting that our first successful homegrown legend should memorialize, however playfully, the flight of the dreamer from the shrew" (*Love and Death in the*

---

such as the establishment of a criticism focused on women writers that parallels criticism focused on male writers. Gynocriticism, says Showalter, who has been one of the principal advocates of this activity, is concerned "with woman as the producer of textual meaning, with the history, themes, genres, and structures of literature by women. Its subjects include the psychodynamics of female creativity; linguistics and the problem of a female language; the trajectory of the individual or collective female literary career; literary history; and, of course, studies of particular writers and works" ("Towards a Feminist Poetics," p. 25). For work of this kind, see Sandra Gilbert and Susan Gubar, *The Madwoman in the Attic*, and the collection edited by Sally McConnell-Ginet, Ruth Borker, and Nelly Furman, *Women and Language in Literature and Society* (New York: Praeger, 1980).

[4]The analogy with social class is instructive: progressive political writing appeals to the proletariat's experience of oppression, but usually the problem for a political movement is precisely that the members of a class do not have the experience their situation would warrant. The most insidious oppression alienates a group from its own interests as a group and encourages it to identify with the interests of the oppressors, so that political struggles must first awaken a group to its interests and its "experience."

American Novel, p. xx). It is fitting because, ever since then, novels seen as archetypally American—investigating or articulating a distinctively American experience—have rung the changes on this basic schema, in which the protagonist struggles against constricting, civilizing, oppressive forces embodied by woman. The typical protagonist, continues Fiedler, the protagonist seen as embodying in the universal American dream, has been "a man on the run, harried into the forest and out to sea, down the river or into combat—anywhere to avoid 'civilization,' which is to say, the confrontation of a man and a woman which leads to the fall to sex, marriage, and responsibility."

Confronting such plots, the woman reader, like other readers, is powerfully impelled by the structure of the novel to identify with a hero who makes woman the enemy. In "The Legend of Sleepy Hollow," where Dame Van Winkle represents everything one might wish to escape and Rip the success of a fantasy, Fetterley argues that "what is essentially a simple act of identification when the reader of the story is male becomes a tangle of contradictions when the reader is female" (*The Resisting Reader*, p. 9). "In such fictions the female reader is co-opted into participation in an experience from which she is explicitly excluded; she is asked to identify with a selfhood that defines itself in opposition to her; she is required to identify against herself" (p. xii).

One should emphasize that Fetterley is not objecting to unflattering literary representations of women but to the way in which the dramatic structure of these stories induces women to participate in a vision of woman as the obstacle to freedom. Catherine in *A Farewell to Arms* is an appealing character, but her role is clear: her death prevents Frederic Henry from coming to feel the burdens she fears she imposes, while consolidating his investment in an idyllic love and in his vision of himself as a "victim of cosmic antagonism" (p. xvi). "If we weep at the end of the book," Fetterley concludes, "it is not for Catherine but for Frederic Henry. All our tears are ultimately for men, because in the world of *A Farewell to Arms* male life is what counts. And the message to women reading this classic love story and experiencing its image of the female ideal is clear and simple: the only good woman is a dead one, and even then there are questions" (p. 71). Whether or not the message is quite this simple, it is certainly true that the reader must adopt the perspective of Frederic Henry to enjoy the pathos of the ending.

Fetterley's account of the predicament of the woman reader—seduced and betrayed by devious male texts—is an attempt to change reading: "Feminist criticism is a political act whose aim is not simply to interpret the world but to change it by changing the consciousness of those who read and their relation to what they read" (p. viii). The first act of a feminist critic is "to become a resisting rather than an assenting reader and, by this refusal to assent, to begin the process of exorcizing the male mind that has been implanted in us" (p. xxii).

This is part of a broader struggle. Fetterley's account of the woman reader's predicament is powerfully confirmed by Dorothy Dinnerstein's analysis of the effects, on women as well as men, of human nurturing arrangements. "Woman, who introduced us to the human situation and who at the beginning seemed to us responsible for every drawback of that situation, carries for all of us a pre-rational onus of ultimately culpable responsibility forever after" (*The Mermaid and the Minotaur*, p. 234). Babies of both sexes are generally nurtured at first by the mother, on whom they are completely dependent. "The initial experience of dependence on a largely uncontrollable outside source of good is focused on a woman, and so is the earliest experience of vulnerability to disappointment and pain" (p. 28). The result is a powerful resentment of this dependency and a compensatory tendency to identify with male figures, who are perceived as distinct and independent. "Even to the daughter, the mother may never come to seem so completely an 'I' as the father, who was an 'I' when first encountered" (p. 107). This perception of the mother affects her perception of all women, including herself, and encourages her "to preserve her 'I' ness by thinking of men, not women, as her real fellow creatures"—and to become engaged as a reader in plots of escape from women and domination of women (p. 107). What feminists ignore or deny at their peril, warns Dinnerstein, "is that women share men's anti-female feelings—usually in a mitigated form, but deeply nevertheless. This fact stems partly, to be sure, from causes that other writers have already quite adequately spelled out: that we have been stepped in self-derogatory societal stereotypes, pitted against each other for the favors of the reigning sex, and so on. But it stems largely from another cause, whose effects are much harder to undo: that we, like men, had female mothers" (p. 90). Without a change in nurturing arrangements, fear and loathing of women will not disappear, but some measure of progress might come with an understanding of what women want: "What women want is to stop serving as scapegoats (their own scapegoats as well as men's and children's scapegoats) for human resentment of the human condition. They want this so painfully, and so pervasively, and until quite recently it was such a hopeless thing to want, that they have not yet been able to say out loud that they want it" (p. 234).

This passage illustrates the structure at work in the second moment of feminist criticism and shows something of its power and necessity. This persuasive writing appeals to a fundamental desire or experience of women—what women want, what women feel—but an experience posited to displace the self-mutilating experiences Dinnerstein has described. The experience appealed to is nowhere present as indubitable evidence or *point d'appui*, but the appeal to it is not factitious: what more fundamental appeal could there be than to such a possibility? This postulate empowers an attempt to alter conditions so that women will not be led to cooperate in making women scapegoats for the problems of the human condition.

The most impressive works in this struggle are doubtless books like Dinnerstein's, which analyzes our predicament in terms that make comprehensible a whole range of phenomena, from the self-estrangement of women readers to the particular cast of Mailer's sexism. In literary criticism, a powerful strategy is to produce readings that identify and situate male misreadings. Though it is difficult to work out in positive, independent terms what it might mean to read as a woman, one may confidently propose a purely differential definition: to read as a woman is to avoid reading as a man, to identify the specific defenses and distortions of male readings and provide correctives.

By these lights, feminist criticism is a critique of what Mary Ellmann, in her witty and erudite *Thinking about Women*, calls "phallic criticism." Fetterley's most impressive and effective chapter, for example, may well be her discussion of *The Bostonians*, where she documents the striking tendency of male critics to band together and take the part of Basil Ransom in his determination to win Verena away from her feminist friend, Olive Chancellor. Treating the relation between the women as perverse and unnatural, critics identify with Ransom's fear that female solidarity threatens male dominance and the male character:

"The whole generation is womanized; the masculine tone is passing out of the world; . . . The masculine character . . . that is what I want to preserve, or rather, as I may say, to recover; and I must tell you that I don't in the least care what becomes of you ladies while I make the attempt."

Rescuing Verena from Olive is part of this project, for which the critics show considerable enthusiasm. Some recognize Ransom's failings and James's precise delineation of them (others regard this complexity as an artistic error on James's part), but all seem to agree that when Ransom carries Verena off, this is a consummation devoutly to be wished. The narrator tells us in the concluding sentence of the book that Verena will have cause to shed more tears: "It is to be feared that with the union, so far from brilliant, into which she was about to enter, these were not to be the last she was destined to shed." But critics generally regard this, as one of them observes, as "a small price to pay for achieving a normal relationship." Faced with a threat to what they regard as normalcy, male critics become caught up in Ransom's crusade and outdo one another in finding reasons to disparage Olive, the character in whom James shows the greatest interest, as well as the feminist movements James criticizes. The result is a male chorus. "The criticism of *The Bostonians* is remarkable for its relentless sameness, its reliance on values outside the novel, and its cavalier dismissal of the need for textual support" (*The Resisting Reader*, p. 113).

The hypothesis of a female reader is an attempt to rectify this situation: by providing a different point of departure it brings into focus the identification of male critics with one character and permits the analysis of male misreadings. But what it does above all is to reverse the usual situation in which the perspective of a male critic is assumed to be sexually neutral, while a feminist reading is seen as a case of special pleading and an attempt to force the text into a predetermined mold. By confronting male readings with the elements of the text they neglect and showing them to be a continuation of Ransom's position rather than judicious commentary on the novel as a whole, feminist criticism puts itself in the position that phallic criticism usually attempts to occupy. The more convincing its critique of phallic criticism, the more feminist criticism comes to provide the broad and comprehensive vision, analyzing and situating the limited and interested interpretations of male critics. Indeed, at this level one can say that feminist criticism is the name that should be applied to all criticism alert to the critical ramifications of sexual oppression, just as in politics "women's issues" is the name now applied to many fundamental questions of personal freedom and social justice.

A different way of going beyond phallic criticism is Jane Tompkins's discussion of *Uncle Tom's Cabin*, a novel relegated to the trash heap of literary history by male critics and fellow travelers such as Ann Douglas, in her influential book *The Feminization of American Culture*. "The attitude Douglas expresses toward the vast quantity of literature written by women in this country between 1820 and 1870 is the one that the male-dominated scholarly tradition has always expressed—contempt. The query one hears behind every page of her indictment of feminization is: why can't a woman be more like a man?" (*"Sentimental Power,"* p. 81). Though in some respects the most important book of the century, *Uncle Tom's Cabin* is placed in a genre—the sentimental novel—written by, about, and for women, and therefore seen as trash, or at least as unworthy of serious critical consideration. If one does take this book seriously, one discovers, Tompkins argues, that it displays in exemplary fashion the features of a major American genre defined by Sacvan Bercovitch, "The American Jeremiad": "a mode of public exhortation . . . designed to join social criticism to spiritual renewal, public to private identity, the shifting 'signs of the times' to certain traditional metaphors, themes, and symbols," especially those of typological narrative (p. 93). Bercovitch's book, notes Tompkins, "provides a striking instance of how totally academic criticism has foreclosed on sentimental fiction; since, even when a sentimental novel fulfills a man's theory to perfection, he cannot see it. For him the work doesn't even exist. Despite the fact that his study takes no note of the most obvious and compelling instance of the jeremiad since the Great Awakening, Bercovitch's description in fact provides an excellent account of the combination of elements that made Stowe's novel work" (p. 93). Rewriting the Bible as the story of a Negro slave, "*Uncle Tom's Cabin* retells the culture's central myth—the story of the crucifixion—in terms of the nation's greatest political conflict—slavery—and of its most cherished social beliefs—the sanctity of motherhood and the family" (p. 89).

Here the hypothesis of a woman reader helps to identify male exclusions that forestall serious analysis, but once that analysis is undertaken it becomes possible to argue

> that the popular domestic novel of the nineteenth century represents a monumental effort to reorganize culture from the woman's point of view, that this body of work is remarkable for its intellectual complexity, ambition, and resourcefulness, and that, in certain cases, it offers a critique of American society far more devastating than any delivered by better-known critics such as Hawthorne and Melville. . . . Out of the ideological materials they had at their disposal, the sentimental novelists elaborated a myth that gave women the central position of power and authority in the culture; and of these efforts *Uncle Tom's Cabin* is the most dazzling exemplar. (pp. 81–82)

In addition to the devastating attack on slavery, reputed to have "changed the hearts" of many of its readers, the novel attempts to bring on, through the same sort of change of heart, a new social order. In the new society, envisioned in a chapter called "The Quaker Settlement," man-made institutions fade into irrelevance, and the home guided by the Christian woman becomes, not a refuge from the real order of the world, but the center of meaningful activity (p. 95). "The removal of the male from the center to the periphery of the human sphere is the most radical component of this millenarian scheme which is rooted so solidly in the most traditional values—religion, motherhood, home, and family. [In the details of this chapter,] Stowe reconceives the role of men in human history: while Negroes, children, mothers, and grandmothers do the world's primary work, men groom themselves contentedly in a corner" (p. 98).

In this sort of analysis, feminist criticism does not rely on the experience of the woman reader as it does at the first level but employs the hypothesis of a woman reader to provide leverage for displacing the dominant male critical vision and revealing its misprisions. "By 'feminist,' " suggests Peggy Kamuf, "one understands a way of reading texts that points to the masks of truth with which phallocentrism hides its fictions" ("Writing Like a Woman," p. 286). The task at this level is not to establish a woman's reading that would parallel a male reading but rather, through argument and an attempt to account for textual evidence, to produce a comprehensive perspective, a compelling reading. The conclusions reached in feminist criticism of this sort are not specific to women in the sense that one can sympathize, comprehend, and agree only if one has had certain experiences which are women's. On the contrary, these readings demonstrate the limitations of male critical interpretations in terms that male critics would purport to accept, and they seek, like all ambitious acts of criticism, to attain a generally convincing understanding—an understanding that is feminist because it is a critique of male chauvinism.

In this second moment of feminist criticism there is an appeal to the potential experience of a woman reader (which would escape the limitations of male readings) and then the attempt to make such an experience possible by developing questions and perspectives that would enable a woman to read as a woman—that is, not "as a man." Men have aligned the opposition male/female with rational/emotional, serious/frivolous, or reflective/spontaneous; and feminist criticism of the second moment works to prove itself more rational, serious, and reflective than male readings that omit and distort. But there is a third moment in which, instead of contesting the association of the male with the rational, feminist theory investigates the way our notions of the rational are tied to or in complicity with the interests of the male. One of the most striking analyses of this kind is Luce Irigaray's *Speculum, de l'autre femme,* which takes Plato's parable of the cave, with its contrast between a maternal womb and a divine paternal *logos,* as the point of departure for a demonstration that philosophical categories have been developed to relegate the feminine to a position of subordination and to reduce the radical Otherness of woman to a specular relation: woman is either ignored or seen as man's opposite. Rather than attempt to reproduce Irigaray's complex argument, one might take a single striking example adduced by Dorothy Dinnerstein, Peggy Kamuf, and others: the connection between patriarchy and the privileging of the rational, the abstract, or the intellectual.

In *Moses and Monotheism,* Freud establishes a relation between three "processes of the same character": the Mosaic prohibition against making a sensible image of God (thus, "the compulsion to worship a God whom one cannot see"), the development of speech ("the new realm of intellectuality was opened up, in which ideas, memories, and inferences became decisive in contrast to the lower psychical activity which had direct perceptions by the sense-organs as its content") and, finally, the replacement of a matriarchal social order by a patriarchal one. The last involves more than a change in juridical conventions. "This turning from the mother to the father points in addition to a victory of intellectuality over sensuality—that is, an advance of civilization, since maternity is proved by the evidence of the senses while paternity is a hypothesis, based on an inference and a premiss. Taking sides in this way with a thought-process in preference to a sense perception has proved to be a momentous step" (vol. 23, pp. 113–14). Several pages further on, Freud explains the common character of these processes:

> An advance in intellectuality consists in deciding against direct sense-perception in favour of what are known as the higher intellectual processes—that is, memories, reflections, and inferences. It consists, for instance, in deciding that paternity is more important than maternity, although it cannot, like the latter, be established by the evidence of the senses, and that for that reason the child should bear his father's name and be his heir. Or it declares that our God is the greatest and mightiest, although he is invisible like a gale of wind or like the soul. (pp. 117–18)

Freud appears to suggest that the establishment of patriarchal power is merely an instance of the general advance of intellectuality and that the preference for an invisible God is another effect of the same cause. But when we consider that the invisible, omnipotent God is God the Father, not to say God of the Patriarchs, we may well wonder whether, on the contrary, the promotion of the invisible over the visible and of thought and inference over sense perception is not a consequence or effect of the establishment of paternal authority: a consequence of the fact that the paternal relation is invisible.

If one wished to argue that the promotion of the intelligible over the sensible, meaning over form, and the invisible over the visible was an elevation of the paternal principle and paternal power over the maternal, one could draw support from the character of Freud's arguments elsewhere, since he shows that numerous enterprises are determined by unconscious interests of a sexual character. Dorothy Dinnerstein's discussions would also support the view that the intangibility and uncertainty of the paternal relation have considerable consequences. She notes that fathers, because of their lack of direct physical connection with babies, have a powerful urge to assert a relation, giving the child their name to establish genealogical links, engaging in various "initiation rites through which they symbolically and passionately affirm that it is they who have themselves created human beings, as compared with the mere flesh spawned by woman. Think also of the anxious concern that men have so widely shown for immortality through heirs, and their efforts to control the sexual life of women to make sure that the children they sponsor really do come from their own seed: the tenuousness of their physical tie to the young clearly pains men in a way that it could not pain bulls or stallions" (*The Mermaid and the Minotaur*, p. 80).

Men's powerful "impulse to affirm and tighten by cultural inventions their unsatisfactorily loose mammalian connection with children" leads them to value highly cultural inventions of a symbolic nature (pp. 80–81). One might predict an inclination to value what are generally termed metaphorical relations—relations of resemblance between separate items that can be substituted for one another, such as obtain between the father and the miniature replica with the same name, the child—over metonymical, maternal relationships based on contiguity.

Indeed, if one tried to imagine the literary criticism of a patriarchal culture, one might predict several likely concerns: (1) that the role of the author would be conceived as a paternal one and any maternal functions deemed valuable would be assimilated to paternity;[5] (2) that much would be invested in paternal authors, to whose credit everything in their textual progeny would redound; (3) that there would be great concern about which meanings were legitimate and which illegitimate (since the paternal author's role in the generation of meanings can only be inferred); and that criticism would expend great efforts to develop principles for, on the other hand, determining which meanings were truly the author's own progeny, and on the other hand, controlling intercourse with texts so as to prevent the proliferation of illegitimate interpretations. Numerous aspects of criticism, including the preference for metaphor over metonymy, the conception of the author, and the concern to distinguish legitimate from illegitimate meanings, can be seen as part of the promotion of the paternal. Phallogocentrism unites an interest in patriarchal authority, unity of meaning, and certainty of origin.

---

[5]See Gilbert and Gubar, *The Madwoman in the Attic*, pp. 3–92. Feminist critics have shown considerable interest in Harold Bloom's model of poetic creation because it makes explicit the sexual connotations of authorship and authority. This oedipal scenario, in which one becomes a poet by struggling with a poetic father for possession of the muse, indicates the problematical situation of a woman who would be a poet. What relation can she have to the tradition?

The task of feminist criticism in this third moment is to investigate whether the procedures, assumptions, and goals of current criticism are in complicity with the preservation of male authority, and to explore alternatives. It is not a question of rejecting the rational in favor of the irrational, of concentrating of metonymical relations to the exclusion of the metaphorical, or on the signifier to the exclusion of the signified, but of attempting to develop critical modes in which the concepts that are products of male authority are inscribed within a larger textual system. Feminists will try various strategies—in recent French writing "woman" has come to stand for any radical force that subverts the concepts, assumptions, and structures of traditional male discourse.[6] One might suspect, however, that attempts to produce a new feminine language will prove less effective at this stage than critiques of phallocentric criticism, which are by no means limited to the strategies of feminist criticism's second moment. There, feminist readings identify male bias by using concepts and categories that male critics purport to accept. In this third moment or mode, many of these concepts and theoretical categories—notions of realism, of rationality, of mastery, of explanation—are themselves shown to belong to phallocentric criticism.

Consider, for instance, Shoshana Felman's discussion of the text and readings of Balzac's short story "Adieu," a tale of a woman's madness, its origin in an episode of the Napoleonic wars, and her former lover's attempt to cure it. Feminist perspectives of the first and second moment bring out what was previously ignored or taken for granted, as male critics set aside women and madness to praise the "realism" of Balzac's description of war. Felman shows that critics' dealings with the text repeat the male protagonist's dealings with his former mistress, Stéphanie. "It is quite striking to observe to what extent the logic of the unsuspecting 'realistic' critic can reproduce, one after the other, all of Philippe's delusions" ("Women and Madness: The Critical Phallacy," p. 10).

Philippe thinks he can cure Stéphanie by making her recognize and name him. To restore her reason is to obliterate her otherness, which he finds so unacceptable that he is willing to kill both her and himself if he should fail in his cure. She must recognize him and recognize herself as "his Stéphanie" again. When she finally does so, as a result of Philippe's elaborate realistic reconstruction of the scene of wartime suffering where she lost her reason, she dies. The drama played out in the story reflects back on the attempt by male critics to make the story a recognizable instance of realism, and thus questions their notions of "realism" or reality, of reason, and of interpretive mastery, as instances of a male passion analogous to Philippe's. "On the critical as well as on the literary stage, the same attempt is played out to appropriate the signifier and to reduce its differential repetition; we see the same endeavor to do away with difference, the same policing of identities, the same design of mastery, of *sense-control.* . . . Along with the illusions of Philippe, the realistic critic thus repeats, in turn, his allegorical act of murder, his obliteration of the Other: the critic also, in his own way, *kills the woman,* while killing, at the same time, the question of the text and the text as question" (p. 10).

---

[6] The articles in Elaine Marks and Isabelle de Courtivron's *New French Feminisms* provide an excellent conspectus of recent strategies. See also the discussions in *Yale French Studies* 62 (1981). "Feminist Readings: French Texts/American Contexts." The relation between feminism and deconstruction is a complicated question.

Balzac's story helps to identify notions critics have employed with the male stratagems of its protagonist and thus to make possible a feminist reading that situates these concepts and describes their limitations. Insofar as the structure and details of Balzac's story provide a critical description of its male critics, exploration and exploitation of its textuality is a feminist way of reading, but a way of reading that poses rather than solves the question of how to get around or to go beyond the concepts and categories of male criticism. Felman concludes, "from this confrontation in which Balzac's text itself seems to be an ironic reading of its own future reading, the question arises: how *should* we read?" (p. 10).

This is also the question posed in feminist criticism's second moment—how should we read? what kind of reading experience can we imagine or produce? what would it be to read "as a woman"? Felman's critical mode thus leads back to the second level at which political choices are debated and where notions of what one wants animate critical practice. In this sense, the third level, which questions the framework of choice and the affiliations of critical and theoretical categories, is not more radical than the second; nor does it escape the question of "experience."

From these varied writings, a general structure emerges. In the first moment or mode, where woman's experience is treated as a firm ground for interpretation, one swiftly discovers that this experience is not the sequence of thoughts present to the reader's consciousness as she moves through the text but a reading or interpretation of "woman's experience"—her own and others'—which can be set in a vital and productive relation to the text. In the second mode, the problem is how to make it possible to read as a woman: the possibility of this fundamental experience induces an attempt to produce it. In the third mode, the appeal to experience is veiled but still there, as a reference to maternal rather than paternal relations or to woman's situation and experience of marginality, which may give rise to an altered mode of reading. The appeal to the experience of the reader provides leverage for displacing or undoing the system of concepts or procedures of male criticism, but "experience" always has this divided, duplicitous character: it has always already occurred and yet is still to be produced—an indispensable point of reference, yet never simply there.

Peggy Kamuf provides a vivid way of understanding this situation of deferral if we transpose what she says about writing as a woman to reading as a woman:

> —"a woman [reading] as a woman"—the repetition of the "identical" term splits
> that identity, making room for a slight shift, spacing out the differential meaning
> which has always been at work in the single term. And the repetition has no reason
> to stop there, no finite number of times it can be repeated until it closes itself off
> logically, with the original identity recuperated in a final term. Likewise, one can
> find only arbitrary beginnings for the series, and no term which is not already a
> repetition: " . . . a woman [reading] as a woman [reading] as a . . . " ("Writing
> Like a Woman," p. 298)

For a woman to read as a woman is not to repeat an identity or an experience that is given but to play a role she constructs with reference to her identity as a woman, which is also a construct, so that the series can continue: a woman reading as a woman reading as a woman. The noncoincidence reveals an interval, a division within woman or within any reading subject and the "experience" of that subject.

THE CONSTRUCTIONIST APPROACH

CULTURAL DIFFERENCES IN THE RETELLING OF TELEVISION FICTION

Tamar Liebes

Elihu Katz and I (n.d.) have been studying the question of how American films and television programs cross linguistic frontiers so easily. We started from the assumption that it cannot be taken for granted that everybody understands the programs in the same way or even that they are understood at all, even with dubbing or subtitling. To date, we have confirmed (1) that certain programs such as news and "best sellers" are actively viewed as individual programs and not just as "flow" or background noise;[1] (2) that such television texts, though ideologically loaded, nevertheless invite negotiation and permit different readings; (3) that the readings can be broadly classified as "referential" and "metalinguistic" depending, respectively, on viewers' inclinations to associate from the program to life, or from the program to the rules of its construction; and (4) that they are interpreted through interaction within interpretive communities, each with its own values and narrative forms. We believe that through this kind of interpersonal forum (Newcomb & Hirsch, 1983) programs infiltrate into the culture.[2]

Our study tries to address these issues by asking groups of viewers to discuss an episode, which they have just seen, of the American television serial *Dallas*. If understanding is in fact a process of negotiation between the text and the viewer, each anchored in a different culture, then retellings ought to reveal the negotiation process at work. And if the model of negotiation is correct, equal attention should be paid to what viewers bring to the program, not only how

From *Critical Studies in Mass Communication* 5 (December 1988): 277–92. Used by permission of author and the Speech Communication Association.

Ms. Liebes is lecturer in the Department of Education, Ben-Gurion University of the Negev, and research associate in the Communications Institute, Hebrew University of Jerusalem. This article is part of a project that benefits from a grant from the board of the Annenberg Schools of Communication. She is grateful to Elihu Katz for his assistance in the writing of this article.

[1]In this respect, we wish to qualify the overgeneralization of theorists like Williams (1974), Newcomb and Hirsch (1983), and Houston (1984).

[2]Confirmation of the level of attention and the shared viewing and discussion of such programs emerges from our observation of viewing groups and from individual questionnaires.

they use it or what they get from it. In this article, therefore, I examine how viewers apply their own narrative forms and their own explanatory schemes to their "editings" of the story.

This study assembled 54 groups of five to six members in Israel and the United States to view and discuss an episode of *Dallas*. As a first question, the discussion leader asked the group, collectively, "How would you retell the episode you just saw to somebody who has not seen it?" We chose *Dallas* because it was the most popular program in the world at the time and because, contrary to common belief, its meaning is not self-evident from the action; quite the contrary, it is not understandable without its words, and in some ways (kinship structure and the several strands of interwoven subplots) it is quite complex.

Groups were chosen from four widely different subcultures in Israel (Arabs, Moroccan Jews, new immigrants from Russia, second-generation Israelis living in a kibbutz) and from second-generation Americans in Los Angeles. Approximately 10 groups were assembled within each cultural community, each group consisting of three couples of like ethnicity. Age, education, and regular viewing of the program were essentially homogeneous for all participants.[3] Group members were recruited by asking a host couple to invite two more couples to meet in the living room of the host family. The hosts were recruited informally by a field supervisor and ethnic interviewers from within known ethnic neighborhoods and suburban communities around Jerusalem and Los Angeles. Obviously, we cannot make a claim of formal randomness or representativeness, but, on the other hand, we have no reason to suspect any systematic bias. Because the host typically invited others from among their circle of family, friends, and neighbors, these others were demographically alike for reasons of relatedness and propinquity.[4]

By viewing the episode off the air and in a home, we attempted to simulate the normal viewing situation as much as possible, since we had established from the questionnaire completed by each participant that the program is both viewed and later discussed with others. All groups viewed one of four consecutive episodes of *Dallas* and participated afterward in a one-hour guided discussion (Kaboolian & Gamson, 1983; Morgan & Spanish, 1984): the first half consisted of relatively open questions and the second half of more closed questions.

The ethnic communities which we chose are thought to differ widely, both in the popular image and in the social science literature (Peres, 1987), by virtue of mother tongue, media literacy, sociohistorical experience, and location in the social structure. While we did not formulate specific hypotheses concerning the differences that might be expected among the groups, we were aware of the differences between the foreign groups and the native Americans for whom the program was originally intended, between the Eastern groups (Arabs, Moroccan Jews) and the Western ones (second-generation Americans and Israelis and Russians), between those socialized in more or less collectivist ideologies (from which Russian Jews, of course, demur), and between less and more peripheral groups (Arabs in Israel and Russian newcomers vs. the others). All of these

---

[3]The Russians, on the whole, are somewhat better educated, inasmuch as many Russian immigrants in Israel tend to have had some higher education. The Arab groups also have a somewhat higher proportion of persons with some university training.

[4]We did occasionally request the hosts to limit invitations to acquaintances of like age, education, and ethnicity, and in three or four cases we disqualified discussions whose membership was too disparate.

overlapping identities might have bearing, we thought, on differences in decoding and retelling.

To mine the wealth of data generated by such focus-group discussions in a systematic way, it is necessary to return again and again to the transcripts, using different analytic schemes and different units of analysis. Thus, we began with the smallest unit, a grammatical sentence, to compare answers to the question, "Why all the fuss about babies?" (Liebes & Katz, 1989). This led us to make a fundamental distinction between "real babies" and "story babies," which was then generalized and applied to sequences of interaction among group members that could be coded as referential or metalinguistic associations from the story to life or to art (i.e., to the rules of construction of the story or its genre [Liebes & Katz, 1986]). These interactions appeared throughout the discussions and are coded wherever they appear. There is a third method that addresses a specific question but takes the response of the group as a whole as the unit of coding and analysis. This article is based on the replies of each of the 54 groups to the opening question of the questionnaire, which asks group members to retell the episode they have just seen. The unit of coding is the whole of the collective retellings (some two to five pages of typescript).

Before I propose an analysis of the different patterns of these retellings, it is important to make note of two complicating factors that have to be considered. One has to do with variation in the *definition of the situation* of the focus discussion. There appear to be cultural differences in the ways that groups of different ethnic origin perceive the intentions of the study (Tannen, 1982), as well as differences in what each group regards as discussible in public. The Russian group, for example, approached the conversation with considerable suspicion, questioning the need for a tape recorder, the motives of the interrogators, and so on. Moreover, the Russians felt superior to any discussion of *Dallas*, or perhaps to television more generally, and were reluctant to expose themselves as viewers of a program like *Dallas*. By contrast, Moroccans felt flattered at being asked (Liebes, 1984), and their eagerness to please may partially explain the details they provide in retelling the story. Thus, in analyzing the ethnic differences in the form and content of the retellings, it is necessary to be aware that these variations in the definition of the situation also play a part in what I will call "ethnicity."

A second caveat that needs to be mentioned is that our analysis of these retellings is extracted from a relatively open and multiperson discussion. Moreover, within each group it is possible to identify a range of different attempts at retelling, since the request ("Please retell the story that you have just seen. Make believe that you are telling it to a friend or somebody at work.") was addressed to the group as a whole and any or all members might attempt to answer. Our analysis, therefore, is based on a judgment about the form and content of the retelling that predominates in each of the groups. This is not an arbitrary judgment, however, since our coding decision is based on the reactions of the group members themselves to the various starts as retelling. Typically, only one of these starts "takes."[5] Of course, we could have avoided this problem by

---

[5]When, for example, Yossi, the host in a Moroccan group, tries to address the task in a supercilious manner, other members treat him as *enfant terrible;* they shut him up and pass the job to Cecile who is thought to represent the group more appropriately (see Liebes, 1984, p. 56).

working with individuals one at a time. We did not do so by design, however, because the very idea of interpretive community seems well simulated in these discussion groups where interpretation indeed arises out of conversation.

Our Retellings

Formally speaking, we proceeded as follows: One of us read through a subsample of discussions of an episode entitled "The Sweet Smell of Revenge." Each of the ethnic groups was represented in the sample. On the basis of this reading, and with Barthes' classificatory scheme (1977) in mind, three types of retellings seemed to apply, each with its own idiosyncratic form and content. We call them "linear," "segmented," and "thematic," where the linear form describes a sequential story line, the segmented form dwells on the characters, and the thematic form focuses on messages, virtually ignoring events and characters. Our linear mode corresponds to Barthes' "distributive functions" (1977), which, like Propp's functions (1968), are the units of meaning that advance the story. Barthes' "indexical functions," which operate at the level of characters, attributes, and the general atmosphere of the story, are similar to our segmented mode. However, whereas his emphasis is primarily on contribution to the story, ours is more psychological in emphasis, even if there is a straying away from the narrative. Our thematic retellings correspond to Barthes' "paradigmatic" level.[6]

Using these three rough categories, a second reader then ranked the three narrative forms according to the degree of their applicability to each of the 54 discussions in our corpus.[7] This coding was done "blind," in that the reader did not know the ethnic identity of the group (though the reader could perhaps guess) and, more important, the reader did not know the research hypotheses connecting these forms of retelling to ethnic differences.

At the same time, we went back to the script and videotape of the first of the episodes in order to retell the story for ourselves, using each of the three forms. We wanted to see how much the story lends itself to each form, or, stated otherwise, how much and what kind of "editing" needs to be done to transform the story-as-shown to the three types of story-as-retold.

Our analysis reveals that there are two main plots which run parallel and are interwoven over the four acts and some 30 scenes of the episode. The two stories deal with the two brothers (J. R. and Bobby), each of whom is trying to "produce" an heir ahead of the other: one by means of regaining a child who may or may not be his own, the other by means of adoption.[8] Their wives are punished for their efforts to act independently (Sue Ellen for leaving with the child and Pam for attempting suicide) and end up more dependent on their men than before (Swanson, 1982). In turn, both brothers move from acting, and failing, accord-

---

[6]Barthes (1977) distinguishes between the syntagmatic and the paradigmatic levels in the structure of narrative. The syntagm consists of narrative functions, defined as the smallest units of meaning out of which the story is constructed. There are two types of functions: the "distributive" ones, which are functions in Propp's sense (1968), corresponding to our linear model, and the indexical ones, which operate at the level of characters' attributes and the general atmosphere of the story. These indexes of personality and atmosphere make their appearance, repeatedly, in the segments of parallel and intersected subplots, which describe the segmented model out of which *Dallas* is constructed.

[7]We wish to thank Nahum Gelber for his coding.

[8]We have tried to compare these themes with Biblical ones (Liebes & Katz, 1988).

ing to the rules, to illegal actions: the one from the law court to kidnapping, the other from legal adoption to illegal purchase. Both brothers act to "save" their wives from themselves, that is, to rescue them from individualism and emotion and restore them to family and obligation, again revealing similarity between the "good" and the "bad" brother.[9] In addition, some five subsidiary plots are sprinkled over the 30-odd scenes of one- or two-minute duration.[10] Each scene typically consists of two people, usually a man and a woman, exchanging intimacies that are in themselves often more compelling than the plot line they serve, inasmuch as the plot is alternately predictable or reversible but always unending (Thorburn, 1987).

Linear Model   This analysis makes it clear that there is no simple linear story here. A faithful linear retelling would entail the perception that there are two stories that proceed in parallel along similar lines, one belonging to each brother. Moreover, this linearity does not proceed along the lines of Propp (1968), which requires movement from a situation of lack of a happy resolution. Rather, the two parallel stories at once conform to Propp and violate Propp, depending on who is defined as lacking. Thus, if fulfillment of women is defined as the lack, this episode moves away from fulfillment (in the sense of independence and emotion) toward deprivation, passivity, and dependence. If, however, fulfillment of familism is defined as the lack, this episode moves classically from the threat of breakup to reunion. The former violates the Propp story type where the brother-villains undermine the women as separate beings with emotional needs and overcome would-be heroes who fulfill the lack. Another way to say this is that a dilemma of modernity is involved here; there is woman's emotional fulfillment of her role as wife and mother, on the other. Heroes of the one are villains of the other and vice versa. Thus, just as there are two linear stories at work here, there are also two potential narratives within each linear story. Sue Ellen is emotionally more fulfilled as her status as wife and mother is threatened; that is, the process of overcoming one kind of lack makes the other more salient and demanding of attention. From this, it can be concluded that a single linear retelling along the lines of Propp is by no means representative of what is going on, unless the retelling brings out the dialectical tension between the two linear stories.

Segmented Model   Following Barthes, a segmented, or indexical, analysis focuses on the characters, their motivations, and their interrelations. Thus, a segmented retelling might identify a character and recount his or her interactions with different situations or with other characters in no particular sequence. The emphasis here is not on recounting a narrative but on sampling from the narrative those segments that highlight the personal attributes and motives of one or more of the characters. In other words, rather than the character playing out a

---

[9] This fits Gerbner and his colleagues' description (1979) of the diminishing difference between heroes and villains in television fiction. The good and the bad are not different in their aims or in the methods they use. The criterion, rather, is the degree of efficiency in achieving their aims. Thus, the evil J. R. can qualify as a hero more than the chaste Bobby.

[10] These plots on the side burners of the episode include crises in the marriages of other Ewing couples (that of Mitch and Lucy and that of Ray and Donna) and mounting tension in the competing dynasties (between Cliff and his mother and between Mitch and his sister Afton).

function in the story, the story serves to illuminate key aspects of the character or the dynamics of his or her personality. Retelling the story in this way, for example, might lead to a focus on the causes and consequences of the personality of J. R., explaining what made him so ruthlessly competitive and how this central attribute of character expresses itself in various situations.

Even if this form of telling seems, a priori, to fit the disjunctive form of the soap opera script, there are two complications involved in a segmental retelling of an episode of *Dallas*. One is, obviously, that the the personalities of the characters must be appraised over more than a single episode. The other, almost a contradiction of the first, is that the story writers themselves transform the personalities over time in order to stretch out the story in all its possible variations. J. R., of course, can easily switch from bad to good, but this is part of his essential personality. Not so for the others who are more fixed: Bobby, for example, is good, until somebody decides that the story would be well served if Bobby, finally, became less good. Thus, we are noting once more that a simple retelling along lines of character is not completely faithful to the story either.

Thematic Model   The third form of retelling is thematic or paradigmatic in the sense that the reader cuts through the story and the characters in search of a theme, or message, to sum up the "moral." Thus, it can be proposed, paradigmatically (as certain critics and academics have done), that the story is about the failure of women's liberation (Swanson, 1982) or that it is about the superceding of the Horatio Alger myth of American mobility by the godfather myth of corrupt, self-contained networks that hold the key to success (Mander, 1983). Newcomb (1987), taking the Texas setting seriously, reads the story as a modern western in which shoot outs take place, not in the bar on Main Street but over the telephone and in the board rooms of the *Dallas* skyscrapers.

Our own paradigmatic reading is that there is a conservative and primordial message here, going beyond what Swanson has suggested. While Swanson emphasizes the basic unity of the family as a criterion in terms of which actions are rewarded or punished by the storytellers, our reading sees the primal unit not as family but as generational continuity in the male line. It is true that there is family loyalty in *Dallas,* but, while the father-son relationship is sacrosanct, the collateral "horizontal relationship" between the brothers and between the wives and husbands is open to backstabbing and competition. While this analysis is elaborated elsewhere (Liebes & Katz, 1986), the paradigm we are proposing is of a father-son relationship that imposes competition between the sons for the father's favor, which is expressed both in business and in the demand for male children that the sons transfer to their wives. The loyalty of the women is placed in further doubt because they maintain their ties with rival dynasties. These connections are the only sources of power for *Dallas* women because they can activate them as Trojan Horses inside the Ewing compound or in the rival families. Marriage, therefore, is more of a political transaction than a romantic affair, and its success depends on the adequacy of the exchange of security and status in return for the provision of children.

Viewer Retellings

I am now in a position to ask of the viewers we studied (1) whether there is a correlation between cultural background and the choice among the forms of retelling, (2) how closely these forms of retelling correspond to our own textual analysis,[11] and (3) what can be inferred from the choice of form about the chooser's perception of the relationship of the program to real life.

The coding of the 54 discussions in terms of the three forms of retelling reveals a correlation between ethnicity and narrative form. The Arab and Moroccan groups specialized in linear retellings; in two-thirds of the groups from these communities, linear retellings were ranked first among the three forms of retelling. On the other hand, the kibbutz and American groups offered segmented retellings, emphasizing not the sequence of events but the expression of personalities over and above changing situations. For their part, the Russians put aside the story, in both linear and segmented forms, in favor of a thematic (or paradigmatic) retelling that typically concerned the moral or the message.

Thus, there is confirmation for the suggestion that readings of *Dallas* fit the three forms of retelling and that each form characterizes one or another of the ethnic groups. This does not mean, however, that the three forms, as told, correspond to our own attempt to provide an optimal fit between the story and each of the forms. Instead of the complex fittings, which seem correct to us, the discussions tend toward much simpler retellings with selective perception playing an important part. Whereas we perceive two linear strands moving parallel throughout the story, the linear retellings of Arabs and Moroccans tend to focus on only one of the two. They choose to note not Pam's suicide attempt but J. R.'s kidnapping operation, perhaps because the latter is a more obvious story of action. The story is retold in great detail, often invoking direct quotations for the high melodramatic moments:

Interviewer. First of all, I would like to ask you to retell the story of the episode you have just seen as if you were telling it to a friend who has missed it today.

William: J. R. is trying to get Sue Ellen and the child back home. So he goes off to try to get a monopoly of 25,000 barrels of oil, or maybe it is 50,000, I don't remember the exact number.

Hyan: Yes, it was 25,000 barrels.

George: To get his son back. He's trying to get a monopoly on the oil wells.

Marinett: Yes, he told him . . .

George: So he takes [control of] all the oil in order to empty all of the refineries.

William: It's in order to provoke [them] and organize an exchange. And he [Farlow?] said to him, "Others, bigger than you, weren't able to break me." After J. R.'s father was in South America on business, he [J. R.] talked to him and told him "Come back."

Hyam: Jock phones J. R. and said, "Your wife and the child will be . . . "

[11] I here make the assumption that the other three episodes of *Dallas* seen by our discussion groups are constructed along the same principles as the episode that we analyzed in detail. This must be true almost by definition (i.e., the linear story must have at least the J. R. and Bobby strands; the segmented dimension must be distorted by the writers' intentional inconsistencies of character portrayal; and, similarly, the thematic or paradigmatic must be constant across episodes). I therefore move directly to the total of all retellings of the four episodes, rather than treating each one separately.

> *William*: J. R. called his father and said to him, "When you come home next week,
> Sue Ellen and the child will be back home." (Arab group #46)

Just as the Arabs and Moroccans select between the possible linear retellings, so
the American and kibbutz groups select among the characters for their segmented retellings. It is no wonder that the most popular choice for this kind of
character-based reporting is Pam, whose story is presented as possessing deep
psychological roots. Indeed, these segmented retellers are often aware that their
focus on a character abstracted from the larger context of the story is the result
of their own psychological interests or emotional involvement.

> *Sandy*: The main thing I would tell them would be about [laugh]. . . . I'm trying to
> think of a character in the picture, Victoria Principal.
>
> *Greg*: Pam.
>
> *Others*: Pam.
>
> *Sandy*: That she was, you know, upset about a lot of things inside herself and that
> she wanted to kill herself and that her husband was trying to talk her into commit-
> ting herself to the hospital to help her. That is the main thing that got to me in this
> episode because, emotionally, that's what got to me, that she would want to kill
> herself. And that is the strongest point in this episode. (American group #3)

Within the segmented readings, there is another retelling which speaks not of
a particular character but about the interaction between two characters, who are
often connected in some primordial way. It may be the relationship between J. R.
and Sue Ellen, Bobby and Pam, Miss Ellie and J. R., and so on. For example, in
retelling the story, a kibbutz group proceeds as follows:

> *Hillel*: There was Lucy and her husband with their problems, and there was Bobby
> and Pam and their crisis, and J. R. and his son.
>
> *Orly*: There was a crisis in the marriage of Bobby and Pam. Until now, they were
> the ideal couple, and suddenly they have these problems.
>
> *Igal*: Sue Ellen is beginning to get discouraged by her what's-his-name, and with
> Pam and Bobby it simply exploded. They were always the ideal couple. They knew
> between them that it wasn't so. But at least externally. . . . But that's it. It just
> exploded. You can't bluff the whole way. (Kibbutz group #85)

But neither of these forms coincides fully with the sorts of problems that may
be said to constitute a fully segmented reading. In particular, the viewers' segmented retellings ignore nuances and changes that writers ascribe to the characters, apparently in order to make identification easier. This is not a very
"serious" misreading, of course. More serious, perhaps, is the extreme selectiv-
ity in focusing on one or two evocative characters at the expense of all the others
who make up the story. The fuller versions of the segmented retellings, those
which account for most of the characters, probably represent the best fit between
the story as presented and the story as retold. The following is an example of a
relatively full retelling in the segmented form:

> *Don*: You have Pam trying to commit suicide because of her mother. You had J. R.
> being his typical self, scheming. . . .

Beverly: Cliff Barnes, his sister, his stepsister, whatever, I think was a little upset that the mother gave him the business or gave the running of the business.

Don: Then you have the little gal and her husband split. What's her name? Oh, Charlene Tilton and her husband split up—Lucy, yeah, and him being offered a job that he really doesn't want.

Linda: Then Bobby got a picture of what's-her-name's baby, and he's got hope again.

Don: Kristen's baby. Kristen.

Beverly: Which is really his brother's.

Don: The gentleman called on the phone and said he wanted money for more information regarding the baby. (American group #7)

I wish to suggest at this point that there appears to be a correlation not only between ethnicity and forms of retelling but that this may be equally true of sex differences; indeed, it is possible that the ethnic differences themselves may be explained in the linear retellings, on the one hand, and in the segmented retellings, on the other. Thus, the Arab women are very reticent to enter the conversation; they appear to enter it when they have something "expert" to add. It is certainly true that the opening of the discussion is dominated by men. By contrast, the American and the kibbutz groups, who specialize in segmented retellings, are egalitarian; it may be that kibbutz women speak even more than the men, although this has not been studied formally. Recall in this connection the possibility, suggested by Modleski (1984) and Allen (1985), that the soap opera genre is "feminine" in the sense that it deals less in action or in one-time solutions than in words, feelings, and ad hoc management of the continuing flow of crises. If this is so, it follows that the segmented retellings that emphasize the psychology of characters and their embroilments may be attributed to the greater participation of women, whereas the linear retellings, aiming at final solutions, may reflect the greater "manliness" of the two more traditional cultures we have examined.

Unlike the ad hoc character of the segmented retellings, the linear and, even more, the thematic or paradigmatic retellings impose an organizing principle on the story as a whole that attempts to put the pieces together in a kind of cognitive map. In the case of the paradigmatic, note the way a general principle is applied deductively to construct a story. Here, for example, is the beginning of a discussion in a Russian group:

Misha: The program reflects the reality in America.

Interviewer: Let's get back to the last episode. What is it about?

Sima: The financial problem plays an important role; J. R. wants to revenge himself using his economic background. Through the oil wells. In this particular episode, the financial problem plays an important role.

Interviewer: Rosa, did you want to add something?

Rosa: That's it.

Interviewer: That's what?

Rosa: That the oil is the main theme.

Interviewer: Can you go back to the story?

Rosa: The oil is the main problem in the program. (Russian group #63)

The exchange reveals three unsuccessful attempts of the interviewer to get beyond the thematic level and into the details of the story. This refusal to get into details reflects not only a reluctance on the part of the Russians to show involvement in a television program, which is defined as trivial, but is also a statement of concern over the threat of a program like *Dallas* as capitalist propaganda. This can be seen repeatedly in numerous examples from the Russian groups, where the program is retold paradigmatically in terms of a message. Moreover, the message is not considered innocent but one that serves the hegemonic interests of the producers or of American society. The Russians, it should be recalled, are the only ones who respond in this way to the request to retell the episode.[12] Consider the following examples from three different Russian groups:

Ilona: I started to ask myself what is the secret of the popularity of the series. Why does it attract the middle class to such an extent? It is comforting for them to know that the millionaires are more miserable than themselves. Well, a poor millionaire is beautiful. Deep down, everyone would very much want a millionaire to be miserable, and, on the other hand, they themselves would like to be millionaires. In the program, they see millionaires as if they really were that way. (Russian group #62)

Hanna: The program praises the American way of life. It shows that America of the rich, and, at the same time, it shows the American middle-class viewer that our country is beautiful and rich. We have everything, and those rich people, of course, have their problems. (Russian group #67)

Misha: The program is propaganda for the American way of life. They show American characters. The program deals with the dilemma of life in America. It is actually advertising—or, more accurately, propaganda—for the American way of life. They show the average person, in an interesting way, the ideal he should be striving towards. (Russian group #63)

Thus, it may be said that the Russians are not interested in the paradigm per se but, beyond it, in the relationship among the message, the motives of the encoders, and themselves as audience. Perceived in this context, the message far overshadows the details of the narrative in its importance because it is perceived as a social and political strategy, with an ulterior and destructive aim. Like the critical theorists, the Russians who read the story paradigmatically focus on the macro level, and their analysis, therefore, is on a different level than the analysis of any episode. It is at a political level; their message, in fact, corresponds to one of the two conflicting messages that Thomas and Callahan (1982) attribute to television's high-class family drama: the message of solace for those who are not invited to move to the top.

---

[12]The Russians' inclination to get to the message of the program can also be seen in an analysis of statements which deal explicitly with the message or "moral" of the program (i.e., "What the program/the producers/the writers want to tell us is . . . "). In this analysis, the Russians are the only ones who point to messages when asked to retell the story.

Characteristics of the Forms

Each of the three patterns of retelling implies an orientation to time and different degrees of openness or inevitability. Whereas linear and thematic retellings are deterministic and closed, the segmented retellings are more open. Linear retellings are closed because they relate to a story that has mostly happened in the past, even if it is not altogether concluded, and thematic retellings are closed because they treat the continuing story as timeless repetitions of the same narrative principle. Thus, the Arabs and Moroccans, in their linear retellings, tend to tell an almost completed sequence which is presented as inevitable: J. R. has lost his baby, but he is getting him back, and the family is going to be reunited in the ancestral estate. Or, recounting an earlier episode: Sue Ellen used to be unhappy; now she has finally found a normal home for her baby and a romantic lover for herself (Moroccan group #20).[13]

By perceiving these episodes as stories with happy endings, linear tellers, ironically, blind themselves to the essence of the serial, which is that it must go on! Instead, they constantly seek to impose a scheme such as Propp's which, by definition, cannot work. The characters are thereby forced into a more stereotypical mold than suggested by the producers who keep the program going by introducing variations of personalities. For example, Sue Ellen was neither the hopeless victim that the tellers report nor will she be the happy mother and lover they foresee for her in the future. The paradigmatic retellings, for their part, treat the series, on the whole, as a constant and monolithic message, regarding any individual episode as a manifestation of the ruling principle. Any variation has to be dictated by this principle.

Put differently, it can be argued that the linear and paradigmatic forms employ inductive and deductive reasoning to attribute inevitability, or closedness, to the story. Thus, the paradigmatic story is closed because it is thought to derive from an ideological formula which is applied by the producers to the various subplots and episodes. The linear stories proceed inductively, not from a principle but from the presumed reality of the characters. Thus, the closedness of linear retellings results from it being unthinkable that the story can turn in a different direction just because the producers want the series to continue. The linear retellings, therefore, may be said to be anchored in a referential mode, while the paradigmatic retellings are rooted in a more critical mode.

It is an obvious step to the conclusion that the linear retelling, anchored, as it is, in the referential, correlates with a "hegemonic" reading in which the reality of the story is unquestioned and its message is presumably unchallenged. The paradigmatic retelling, on the other hand, is more likely to accompany an "oppositional" reading (Hall, 1980; Morley, 1980), whereby critical awareness of an overall message surely sounds an alarm that the message may be manipulative.

---

[13] This is how Cecile tells the story of the episode:

> Then she [Sue Ellen] had everything and she didn't have anything. She had a husband and she did not have a husband. She had a child at home and she did not love it, and the maid looked after it. She had everything and nothing worked. She went drinking; she tried everything. Today she doesn't drink anymore. She looks after the son. . . . She has already come to the conclusion—not money, not parties but to live a quiet, normal family life.

The narrative closedness of both the linear and the paradigmatic types leads to stereotyping. The paradigmatic stereotyping is of the producers, who are reified into single-minded propagandists. The linear stereotyping is of the characters who are made to seem more consistent. Thus, the association of the linear and the referential, invoking the reality principle, brings normative criteria with it, and the imposition of such criteria contributes, for example, to the perception of Sue Ellen as engaged in a desperate effort of self-redemption, which provides justification for what would otherwise be an unacceptable violation of the marital norm. Traditional Arab societies have put women to death for less. In other words, normative acceptability influences retellings (and, indeed, legitimates viewing itself).[14]

Unlike the linear and paradigmatic forms, the segmented retellings are more open or future oriented. Armed with the knowledge of the characters and their motivations, the segmented retellings treat the story prospectively, using what has already happened to speculate on possible continuations. Thus, rather than looking for deterministic principles in the plot, either in the lives of the characters or the ideology of the producers, the Americans and kibbutzniks (who specialize in segmented retellings) search creatively for new complications which might emerge from the temporary narrative solutions. Here are two such speculations from an American group:

Deanna: Cliff met his sister for the first time.

Jill: This sounds like it's gonna be another lead-in for another one of J. R.'s romances [laughter].

Donna: Pam's sister?

Deanna: Oh, well, one he hasn't tried yet. . . .

Jill: Just from the program and watching J. R. all the time—if it's got a skirt on, he'll get it or try. (American Group #7)

Deanna: Now it seems she [Katherine] has kind of got her eye on Bobby—and in this one episode—it had just a little bit of a hint that she might have her way.

Jill: That'll snap Pam out of her depression fast enough.

Deanna: Or put her into a worse one. (American group #7)

It is easy to see how this kind of ludic inventiveness can spill over from a discussion of the immanent machinations of the characters to taking the producer's perspective in having to decide what to do next. This explains why the segmented retellings also give attention to the real-life personalities of the actors, their traffic accidents and heart attacks, and the state of their negotiations with the producers.

The three forms of retelling also can be considered in terms of the epistemological perspectives with which they are associated. The linear retellings explain the story in sociological terms; the segmented retellings tend toward a psycho-

---

[14] The problem of the legitimacy of viewing in Arab societies was observed also when interviewers discovered that, in some villages, men and women did not view the program together. Viewing separately demands less public acknowledgement of the fact that women are also viewing.

logical or psychoanalytic explanation; and the paradigmatic patterns are mostly ideological. These epistemological perspectives help to explain why the different forms of retelling choose to focus on different subplots or characters and prefer particular forms of labeling the characters. Thus, the linear stories are told from the perspective of kinship, where the characters are motivated by social and normative considerations having to do with the hierarchical order within the family and the continuity of the dynasty. This point of view also explains the preference for the subplot that deals with J. R. and his efforts to reunite the family, rather than the subplot in the same episode that deals with Pam's troubled psyche. It also makes clear why J. R.'s plot to retrieve his child and wife is explained in terms of his commitment to his father and, in particular, why the relatively short and functionally unimportant telephone conversation with his (now dead) father is told in such great detail; recall how J. R.'s kidnapping operation is retold in direct quotations and is accorded such high dramatic value by the Arabic group.

The invocation of the sociological perspective also appears to explain the relatively frequent use of family roles when labeling characters in linear retellings. Referring to J. R. as "the older son" and to Bobby as "the younger" may be the result of lesser familiarity with the characters or their foreign names, but it is equally likely that it is due to attaching more importance to family roles than to names. Note the labeling of characters in the following example, where the story would be as applicable to Esau and Jacob or other sibling rivalries as to J. R. and Bobby:

> *Ayad*: It's a rich family, with a large inheritance. They have wealth and oil, and they have two sons. The older son is a cheat. He wanted to control by force all of the money of his father and mother. The younger wanted to share the wealth, but the older one plotted and schemed to get the money, and the two brothers fought with each other. (Arab group #49)

The segmented, character-oriented retellings focus on emotional problems in order to explain what happens on the screen. The psychological motivations and conflicts can belong either to the characters in the program or to the actors behind the scene. Thus, the actions and frustrations of the various Ewings are described as generated by unsolved internal conflicts, sometimes originating in childhood traumas or as the result of a present interpersonal crisis: Pam's problems are explained as a result of being abandoned by her mother as a baby or, alternatively, as a result of the collapse of her marriage; J. R. has to prove his worth to his parents, who are thought to have favored his two brothers during their childhood. These same developments are also explained by reference to show business. Pam's suicide attempt is the result of her wanting out of the show. Goffman's term "keyings" (1974) is helpful here: Segmented retellings may be "keyed" either to the narrative of the program or the narrative of show business.

Since psychological retellings relate to personalities, the characters are alluded to by both their on-screen and their performing names. Naturally, Americans, who are exposed to extensive gossip about the show's stars, tend to be more familiar with the stage names than the Israeli viewers.

Like the Americans, the Russians also seem to obtain a sense of control by looking behind the scenes. But, whereas the Americans are concerned with an understanding of the manipulation of the characters by the producers, the Russians see the producers being manipulated by bigger business. As has been shown, the Russian way of telling, or rather of not telling, the episode has an ideological correlate. The Russians sense an overall conspiracy intended to pacify and comfort the viewer. This concern directs their attention not to kinship roles, not to characters' names, not even to names of actors but to the names of producers and writers as manipulators of the characters and to the titles of episodes as clues to the manipulative process. That the Russians memorize these lists of credits is one of the surprises of the study.

Conclusion

In order to analyze how popular American family drama is perceived in other cultures, we asked viewers, organized in intimate focus groups, to retell an episode of *Dallas*. The viewer retellings are fit into the three levels of narrative structure deriving from Barthes' "actions," "characters," and "themes," which take forms that we call "linear," "segmented," and "paradigmatic," respectively. More generally, these types of retelling invoke "sociological," "psychological," and "ideological" perspectives.

The two more traditional groups, Arabs and Moroccan Jews, prefer linearity. They select the action-oriented subplot for attention, defining the hero's goals and adventures in trying to achieve them. They tell the story in "closed" form, as if it were an inevitable progression, and the characters they describe are rigidly stereotyped; indeed, they are often referred to by family role rather than by name. The perspective is sociological; that is, the story of the recognized reality of extended family, in an ancestral house (Lévi-Strauss, 1983), holding itself together in the face of contests of power, both within and without. The cultural proximity of these groups to the *Dallas* story may seem surprising in view of the ostensible modernity of *Dallas*. But there is considerable support for the argument that *Dallas* is, in fact, an old-fashioned family saga (Herzog, 1986; Swanson, 1982), less like the stripped-down mobile nuclear family of the West and more like the premodern clan in which economic, political, and religious functions still inhere and the division of labor by age and sex is still prescribed. A study of the reception of *Dallas* in Algeria (Stolz, 1983) gives strong support to this argument. The concern of these two ethnic groups with power and relative position in family and society may be related to their social position in Israel: the one a politically suspect minority and the other an ethnic minority with experience of status deprivation.

The Russians speak of the episode in themes or messages. They ignore the story in favor of exposing the overall principle which is repeated relentlessly and which, in their opinion, has a manipulative intent. Like the Arabs and Moroccans, their story is closed and deterministic, but the determining force is ideological rather than referential. Unlike the Arabs and Moroccans, they perceive the story as being a false picture of reality. They are also aware that their illustrations from the story are chosen, self-consciously, to highlight the potential persuasive power of the program. Their interest is in the story as a product of hegemonic control. This suspiciousness on the part of the Russians seems overdetermined; it is almost too easy to explain. Dmitri Segal (personal communication, Summer 1985) suggests that the Russians, especially Russian Jews, learn early to scan their environment for signs of where true power is hidden: they learn to read between the lines (Inkeles, 1950). Their literary training is another determining factor: unlike the Arabs or the Moroccans, Russians are steeped in a tradition of literary criticism which they apply relentlessly and with flaunted superiority to the texts and images they encounter in their new environment. What is more, these are refugees who are well trained in applying ideological criticism to other people's ideologies as well as their own. As we noted in connection with their suspiciousness of the interview situation, they are also continually alert to sources of potential danger.

If the Russians invoke ideological theory, Americans and kibbutzniks tell the story psychoanalytically. They are not concerned with the linearity of the narrative but with analyzing the problems of characters intrapersonally and interpersonally. Their retellings are "open," future oriented, and take account of the never-ending genre of the soap opera. One version of these psychological retellings relates to the business constraints and interpersonal problems on the level of actors and producers. In these keyings, the drama behind the scenes appears to be the real story of *Dallas*. Segmented retellings label the characters in terms of their on-screen or off-screen personae. Their illustrations from the story are chosen in terms of emotional effect, rather than the cognitive effects of the thematic retellings. These comparatively secure, second-generation viewers are fascinated by psychology and group dynamics and can afford the luxury of interest in the individual (i.e., in themselves). They have no illusions about the reality of the story; they allow themselves to dive into the psyches of the characters, oblivious to those aspects of the ideology, the morality, and aesthetics of the program that occupy others. Their definition of both the viewing and the retelling as liminal (Turner, 1985) permits a playful subjunctivity in their negotiations with the program, with fellow viewers, and with the discussion leaders.

References

Allen, R. (1985). *Speaking of soap opera*. Chapel Hill: University of North Carolina Press.

Barthes, R. (1977). Introduction to the structural analysis of the narrative. In *Image, music, text* (pp. 79–124). London: Hill & Wang.

Gerbner, G., Gross, L., Signorielli, N., Morgan, M., & Jackson-Beeck, M. (1979). The demonstration of power: Violence profile no. 10. *Journal of Communication, 29* (3), 177–196.

Goffman, E. (1974). *Frame analysis: An essay on the organization of experience*. Cambridge: Harvard University Press.

Hall, S. (1980). Encoding/decoding. In S. Hall, D. Hobson, A. Lowe, & P. Willis (Eds.), *Culture, media, language: Working papers in cultural studies, 1972–79* (pp. 128–138). London: Hutchinson.

Herzog-Massing, H. (1986). Decoding "Dallas." *Society, 24* (1), 74–77.

Houston, B. (1984). Viewing television: The metapsychology of endless consumption. *Quarterly Review of Film Study, 19*, 183–195.

Inkeles, A. (1950). *Public opinion in Soviet Russia*. Cambridge: Harvard University Press.

Kaboolian, E., & Gamson, W. (1983, May). *New strategies for the use of focus groups for social science and survey research*. Paper presented at an annual meeting of the American Association for Public Opinion Research, Buck Hill Falls, PA.

Katz, E., & Liebes, T. (n.d.). The export of meaning: Cross cultural readings of *Dallas*. In P. Larsen (Ed.), *The international dissemination of television drama*, Paris: UNESCO.

Lévi-Strauss, C. (1983). Histoire et ethnologie [History and ethnology]. *Annales, 38*, 1217–1231.

Liebes, T. (1984). Ethnocriticism: Israelis of Moroccan ethnicity negotiate the meaning of "Dallas." *Studies in Visual Communication, 10* (3), 46–72.

Liebes, T., & Katz, E. (1986). Patterns of involvement in television fiction: A comparative analysis. *European Journal of Communication, 1*, 151–171.

Liebes, T., & Katz, E. (1988). *Dallas* and Genesis: Primordiality and seriality in popular culture. In J. Carey (Ed.), *Media, myths, and narratives* (pp. 113–135). Newbury Park, CA: Sage.

Liebes, T., & Katz, E. (1989). On the critical abilities of television audiences. In E. Seiter, Worth, and Karautznes (Eds.), *Remote Control: TV Audiences.* London: Routledge.

Mander, M. (1983). *Dallas:* The mythology of crime and the moral occult. *Journal of Popular Culture, 17,* 44–51.

Modleski, T. (1984). *Loving with a vengeance: Mass produced fantasies for women.* London: Methuen.

Morgan, D. L., & Spanish, M. T. (1984). Focus groups: A new tool for qualitative research. *Qualitative Sociology, 7,* 253–270.

Morley, D. (1980). *The "nationwide" audience.* London: British Film Institute.

Newcomb, H. (1987). Texas: A giant state of mind. In H. Newcomb (Ed.), *Television: The critical view* (pp. 221–228). New York: Oxford University Press.

Newcomb, H., & Hirsch, P. M. (1983). Television as a cultural forum: Implications for research. *Quarterly Review of Film Studies, 8* (3), 48–55.

Peres, Y. (1987). Etsem el atsma bitsrima [The dissonant reunion of the dry bones]. *Politika, 14/15,* 20–23.

Propp, V. (1968). *Morphology of a folk tale.* Austin: University of Texas Press.

Stolz, J. (1983). Les Algériens regardent *Dallas* [Algerians view *Dallas*]. In *Les nouvelles chaines* (pp. 223–243). Paris: University of France Press.

Swanson, G. (1982). *Dallas, Framework, 14,* 32–35; *15,* 81–85.

Tannen, D. (1982). The oral/literate continuum in discourse. In R. Freedle (Ed.), *Spoken and written language: Exploring orality and literacy.* (pp. 1–16). Norwood, NJ: Ablex.

Thomas, S., & Callahan, B. (1982). Allocating happiness: TV families and social class. *Journal of Communication, 32* (3), 184–190.

Thorburn, D. (1987). Television melodrama. In H. Newcomb (Ed.), *Television: The critical view* (pp. 628–644). New York: Oxford University Press.

Turner, V. (1985). Liminality, kabbalah, and the media. *Religion, 15,* 201–203.

Williams, R. (1974). *Television: Technology and cultural form.* London: Fontana.

THE DECONSTRUCTIONIST APPROACH

IS THERE ROCK AFTER PUNK?

Lawrence Grossberg

I want to talk—sympathetically—about the current situation of rock and roll in the United States. To understand its specificity and possibilities, we must first ask how rock and roll works for its fans for, as I will argue, to call something "rock and roll"—and more than music is encompassed by that term—is to say that it works for its fans. Hence, I define "rock and roll" as a mode of functioning. I do not intend to speak either as a fan (although I am one) or as a critic (although I have been one), for, from either of these positions, one can only make judgments about the quality of the music or the appropriateness of the audience's response.

The uniqueness of the present situation is visible, subjectively, as a "crisis" for many fans, and objectively, in the changing place of rock and roll within both the larger category of popular music and the economic practices that surround the rock and roll culture. As evidence of the former, I might point to the increasingly common rhetoric of the "death of rock and roll" and to the changing tastes at both the upper and lower chronological boundaries of the potential rock and roll audience. Although these have occurred before, they are so widespread within the culture today that it seems reasonable to take them as indicating significant shifts. As evidence of the objective crisis, I can point to the decreasing sales of records (despite the industry's claim that the recession is over, the number of gold and platinum albums has significantly declined) and the decreasing attendance at live venues.

Furthermore, the industry increasingly segregates rock and roll from popular music, which contrasts sharply with the tendency of the past 25 years to collapse these categories. For example, the major format distinction in radio today sets "contemporary hits," with its flavor of fifties AM radio but with a wider range of musical sounds and styles, against "album oriented rock" which plays predominantly heavy metal and new wave. The former is described as "horizontal" because it appeals to diverse audiences (including teenage girls and parts of the

From *Critical Studies in Mass Communication* 3 (March 1986): 50–74. Used by permission of author and the Speech Communication Association.

Mr. Grossberg is associate professor of speech communication at the University of Illinois at Urbana.

"adult-contemporary audience"), while the latter defines the narrower, "vertical" appeal of rock and roll (teenage boys and college-age youth). Finally, we may point to the increasing ease and rapidity with which various styles of rock and roll have been incorporated into, and exploited by, commercial interest (e.g., network television has discovered the virtues of rock, not only in sports but in dramatic programming; and is there any product that has not tried to use breakdancing?) and reduced to harmless stereotypes.

These "facts" are neither merely symptoms of some hidden causal determination, nor the causes of the changing articulations of rock and roll. What I will offer, then, is not an exhaustive causal explanation of this situation but a description which places these "facts" in a context of mutual determination. The contemporary effects of rock and roll are inseparable from its conditions of existence, from the contradictory structure of the rock and roll culture itself, from the lines of force—the "political" tendencies and contradictions—that have displaced and redefined its effects.[1] In particular, I will point to two intersecting vectors which have deconstructed (and perhaps reconstructed) the possibility and power of rock and roll. First, punk not only opened up new musical and sociological possibilities, it also restructured the music's relation to itself and its audience. Second, the very notion of youth culture, so crucial to rock and roll, is being dismantled and undermined, partly by rock and roll itself, but also by other social and cultural discourses.

Rock and Roll as Affective Empowerment

Before describing the changes taking place in what I will call the rock and roll apparatus, we must acknowledge the surprising lack of research on it (despite its obvious economic and cultural importance).[2] This is symptomatic of the lack of any significant effort to describe the way popular culture functions in the lives of its fans. And this is due, in part, to the dictates of our paradigms, which not only place us within a dualism of textuality and sociology but increasingly reduce both domains to the category of signification.[3] The failure of contemporary communication theory to study this most visible of popular forms is based on its demands that the music speaks for itself, and that the fans define their experiences within the structures of meaning that are articulated. But music—perhaps unlike other forms—need not claim to represent, or even to signify.

Rock and roll is a cultural event which emerged at a particular moment into a particular context.[4] Part of its power is, in fact, that it has constructed its own

[1]In fact, the project of the present essay can be read as an attempt to rearticulate pop sensibilities to the political left, much as Hebdige (1979) attempted to articulate punk in England to British black culture.

[2]The best works on rock and roll are: Frith (1981); Duncan (1984); Young (1984). See also Hebdige (1979); Chambers (1981, 1985, in press); Wicke (1982); Lull (1983).

[3]For a discussion of the reductionism of contemporary communication theory, see Grossberg (1982, 1985).

[4]The argument presented here summarizes Grossberg (1983–1984, 1984a, 1984b, 1984c, 1986a, and 1986b). My use of genre terms, like "rock and roll" and "punk" unavoidably relies upon the ambiguity of such categories: they connote, simultaneously, a set of musical practices, a broader set of cultural practices and a particular affective alliance. In most cases, the context should make clear the appropriate level of abstraction. Further, I am

history through which it has maintained a unity for itself within its differences. That is, despite the changing musical, stylistic and political parameters of rock and roll and its fans, the category itself is constantly reiterated, created, albeit not quite anew, with both a changing past and a confident future ("Rock and roll will never die"). My concern is to identify what it is that constitutes this unity and opens a space within which differences function positively: what does it mean to say that rock and roll works?

Three features of rock and roll mitigate against treating it primarily within the terms of communication theory. First, and it should come as no surprise to communications researchers, whether one looks for meanings (interpretations) or uses (gratifications), one finds heterogeneity. Different people not only interpret the music differently but use it differently as well. A 13-year-old girl, a college student and a blue-collar worker may all be fans of The Police or Prince or Van Halen, but all for very different reasons. Even further, there is no necessary correspondence between the meaning someone gives a genre or text and the ways they use it. The issue is not one of individual taste because one can identify audiences, but the crucial correlations remain unexamined.

Second, in many cases, the music appears "hollow." The significance of the music is not in the music, nor in the fan. For example, the meaning may be found outside the text, in the way it marks our history. Or the meaning may be irrelevant, subservient or simply absent. As many a rock and roll fan has commented, the power of the music lies not in what it says but in what it does, in how it makes one move and feel. To find how rock functions, it is necessary to explore effects that are not necessarily signifying, that do not necessarily involve the transmission, production, structuration or even deconstruction of meaning. Rock and roll is corporeal and "invasive." For example, without the mediation of meaning, the sheer volume and repetitive rhythms of rock and roll produce a real material pleasure for its fans (at many live concerts, the vibration actually might be compared to the use of a vibrator, often focused on the genital organs) and restructure familial relations (by producing immediate outrage and rejection from its nonfans, e.g., parents). If we assume, further, that rock and roll fans are not "cultural dopes," then we must examine the contradictions and struggles that are enacted around, and in, rock and roll in various contexts. Thus, while it is often true that the "ideology" of rock and roll appears conservative and that its consumption merely reinforces the capitalist hegemony, there is always a remainder of nonsignifying effects in such calculations. The fact that we think of it as "pleasure" is often used to justify our dismissing it as the sugar coating that makes the ideological pill go down. I will argue that it is much more.[5]

The third feature of the way rock and roll exists within youth cultures is that, oddly enough, the genre cannot be defined solely in musical terms. Different audiences not only define the boundaries of rock and roll differently but are differentially capable of listening to, and finding "pleasure" in, different forms of rock and roll.

---

aware that key theoretical terms, like "pleasure" and "empowerment" remain undefined. I believe this is, albeit unfortunate, unavoidable. Hopefully, they can be understood by the function which they play in the context of my argument.

[5]Throughout the essay, I will use "pleasure" to refer to this broader sense of the asignifying and pleasure (without quotation marks) to refer to the narrower sense of sensuous enjoyment.

These three features suggest that one cannot approach rock and roll by using anyone's experience of it, or even any collective definition of that experience. Yet one cannot deny its popularity, not merely in quantitative and economic terms, but also in terms of its importance in the lives of its fans and its role in the "youth cultures" of the United States. Further, they suggest that one cannot read the political effects of rock and roll off the text (although this does not deny the relevance of the musical/lyrical text). Understanding rock and roll requires asking what it gives its fans, how it empowers them and how they empower it. What possibilities does it enable them to appropriate in their everyday lives? Treating functions/effects in terms of empowerment avoids the textual and social-psychological reductionism of communication theory. It may help to give some rather simple examples of "empowerment": A record is a commodity to be purchased, consumed and disposed of. But within the larger networks I want to investigate, such as accommodation to capitalism may also empower its fans in ways that contradict the consumer economy's attempt to regulate the structures and rhythms of daily life. For the disposability of the commodity also places the record at the disposal of its fans: they can control its uses, use it in new and unintended ways, restructure and recontextualize its messages, etc. Second, a song may, in both its ideological messages and the patterns of its gendered consumption, reproduce the social definitions of sexuality and social roles. And yet, in its restructuring of the body as the site of pleasure, in the ways it makes a space for and inserts the female body and voice into its physical and social environment, it may challenge hegemonic constraints on sexuality, desire and even gender construction. And finally, to combine these two examples, although early rock and roll (especially rockabilly) was marketed as if it were male produced and consumed, women were not only fans of the music, but also sang and even recorded it. The politics of the economic decision not to market such efforts is not the same as the politics of the functioning of the music within the everyday lives of its fans.

Furthermore, looking at the networks of empowerment within which rock and roll functions also points to its potentially oppositional role in American culture. Rock and roll has, repeatedly and continuously, been attacked, banned, ridiculed and relegated to an insignificant cultural status. The fact that so much effort has been brought to bear in the attempt to silence it, makes it reasonable to assume that some struggle is going on, some opposition is being voiced. And despite the changing social sites and discourses of the attack, it is consistently as a way of behaving that rock and roll is seen as dangerous. For example, it is not that the music sounds like black music but that it makes its fans act like "animals" (in the rhetoric of the fifties, blacks). As Duncan (1984, p. 1) says, "My father always blamed it on the rock 'n' roll. The drugs, the sex, the faithless wild boys and girls obeying no authority and bearing no responsibility, playing havoc with America in a mindless quest for the good time they believed was owed them by the world. My father's not stupid." Of course, empowerment may function conservatively as well as oppositionally; this points to a level of empirical analysis beyond the scope of the present essay.

This suggests that we look at the ways of behaving—the practices—that define the rock and roll culture, including the fact that particular texts exist and are popular, which is not the same as being commercially successful. That is, rock and roll is not defined by the *Billboard* charts. Even the briefest study of the rock and roll culture points to the existence of a boundary between popular music and rock and roll, but again, this distinction cannot be made in solely musical terms. Not all popular music is rock and roll, and not all of the fans of popular music are rock and roll fans. Both the music itself (in its self-references, in the fact that performers—from the slick commercialism of Culture Club to the avant-gardism of Fred Frith—struggle to assert that they make "rock and roll"; in the use of cover versions of songs, etc.) and the fans compulsively encapsulate rock and roll. The power of rock and roll depends upon that part of the population which makes a particular investment in it, which empowers it within their lives, which differentiates both the music and themselves. Rock and roll fans (used now in this narrower sense) enact an elitism (an inverse canonization) in their relation to music. Rock and roll does not belong to everyone, and not everything is rock and roll. This is visible in the judgments they make: rock and roll fans distinguish not only between good and bad rock and roll, but also between rock and roll and music which cannot be heard within the genre (they have a variety of names for it: co-opted, sold-out, boring, straight music).[6] While a rock and roll fan may enjoy other forms of popular music, the boundary is always drawn. If there must always be something which is not rock and roll (and which the fan can recognize because he or she knows what is really rock and roll), how does this boundary work?

I will make three general claims about this encapsulation. *First,* it works on the audience as well as the music; it marks them as different without necessarily defining any positive (visible, readable) identity: You are not what you don't listen to, which cannot be simply reduced to you are what you listen to. One cannot predict individual tastes; one can only invoke a "social cartography" of taste (Bourdieu, 1984). Encapsulation creates what I would call "nomination groups" (rather than taste cultures) which function, by naming rock and roll, to create, not subcultures but what are only nominal groups. *Second,* the music always functions in a larger context, a rock and roll apparatus. That is, the way in which particular music is inserted into the everyday lives of its fans depends upon the overdetermined relations between the music and a variety of other social, cultural, economic, sexual, and discursive practices. Rock and roll is always located within a seemingly random collection of events that interpenetrate and even constitute the specific rock and roll culture, including styles of dance, dress and interaction, images of the band and its fans, etc. *Third,* rock and roll's importance in the experience of its fans depends upon its functioning affectively within their everyday lives. A rock and roll apparatus (there are always many competing ones) locates what sorts of "pleasures" or energizing possibilities are available to its fans; it restructures social life by rearranging the sites at which pleasure can be found and energy derived, at which desire and power are invested and operative. For example, the rock and roll culture transforms many of the structures of contemporary boredom (e.g., repetition and noise) into the structures and pleasures of its musical and listening practices. Similarly rock and roll is about transforming the possibilities of an oppressive technological environment and the frustrations of its reproduction of the environment. This is not merely a process of giving them a new meaning; it establishes, for example, a new relation to the material fact of repetition which already colors or inflects any attempt to interpret it. As Chambers (1985) suggests, such groups regularly

---

[6]Much of the following description of "encapsulation" holds true as well for other forms of "popular" culture. See Hall (1981).

transform the modes of subordination (music, fashion, style, consumerism) into their own pertinent realities.[7]

The work of encapsulation might be clarified by comparing it with the common argument that the car has become an extension of the house. Inversely, rock and roll might be seen as an invasion of the house; it creates a kind of "bubble," a mobile environment surrounding its fans, sometimes weak and transparent, sometimes strong and opaque. It thus radically reshapes the real, not merely symbolically, by placing the rock and roll apparatus in a (limited) struggle within and against the structures of everyday life. The functioning of rock and roll within "everyday life" cannot be reduced to or equated with the lived experience of its fans. Experience—the product of struggles among competing and contradictory ideological practices—is only a part of the context in which we live and act in ways over which we have no control and about which we may be unaware (Foucault, 1981). Everyday life, following Baudrillard's (1983, p. 88) notion of the simulacrum, is "not only a game played with signs; [it implies] social rapports and social power." The term is, of course, Lefebvre's. Everyday life (Lefebvre, 1971, p. 14)

> eludes natural, divine and human myths. Could it represent a lower sphere of meaning, a place where creative energy is stored in readiness for new creations? A place that can be reduced neither to philosophical subjective definitions nor to objective representations of classified objects . . . because it is more and other than these? It is not a chasm, a barrier, or a buffer but a field and a halfway house, . . . a moment made of moments (desires, labours, pleasures—products and achievements—passivity and creativity—means and ends—etc.), the dialectical interaction that is the inevitable starting point for the realization of the possible.

Everyday life is the functioning of the social machine as the active context within which experience is itself both determined and determining. Lefebvre proposes a history of everyday life, comparable perhaps to Baudrillard's (1983) "three orders of simulacra." In late capitalism (Lefebvre, 1971, p. 72–73),

> everyday life must shortly become the one perfect system obscured by the other systems that aim at systematizing thought and structuralizing action, and as such it would be the main product of the so-called "organized" society of controlled consumption and of its setting, modernity. If the circuit is not completely closed it is not for want of purpose or strategical intent but only because "something" irreducible intervenes, "something" that is perhaps Desire. . . . The only way to stop the circuit from closing is to conquer the quotidian, attack it and transform it by making use of another form of strategy.

It is precisely as such a strategy, operating within the structure of everyday life that I will shortly introduce as the "postmodern," that rock and roll empowers—not within a dialectic of use and exchange value but rather, between the operation of a historically specific social machine and its ideological mystifications. And it is this strategic space that I am describing as the level of an affective politics.

---

[7]This can be seen embodied in particular songs which take a particularly negative phrase and, through rhythms and repetition, transform it into the site of celebration. For example, Gang of Four's "Anthrax" ("Sometimes I feel like a beetle on its back . . . love will get you like a case of anthrax") or Ack-Ack's "Percentage" ("I'm one of the, one of the, percentage, let's go") or the Talking Head's transfiguration of paranoia into rock and roll.

Thus, I want to locate the effects of rock and roll at the level of an (at least potentially) oppositional politics which produces a rupture between the rock and roll audience (in their everyday lives) and the larger hegemonic context within which it necessarily exists. But how is this politics constructed? There are two analytic moments to this work. The first I have already implicitly described: rock and roll selects and uses pieces of its material environment as the raw material with which to articulate a youth culture or, more accurately, a series of different and allied youth cultures embodied within the various rock and roll apparatuses. In fact, rock and roll at all levels of its existence constantly steals from other sources, creating its own encapsulation by transgressing any sense of boundary and identity. This is the stage of "bricolage." The second moment actively structures this material context into an organization of "pleasure" and power, of the social energy which defines the possibilities for both domination and resistance within everyday life. The rock and roll apparatus is a kind of machine which, like a cookie cutter constantly changing its shape, produces or imprints a structure on the fans' desires and relations by organizing the material pieces of their lives, within the apparatus, along certain axes. The rock and roll apparatus works by inscribing a geography of desire on its youth cultures, on the space within which the audience exists.

I now want to briefly describe the circuits of empowerment within the rock and roll apparatuses, the space into which the musical practices are themselves inserted at particular sites, articulated as having particular meanings and effects. The task is made more difficult by the fact that the position of each axis within the network of social practices—a position which determines its possibilities—is constantly changing because of the continued functioning of the apparatus itself. Nevertheless, the unity and continuity of the rock and roll culture is determined by its construction of a three-dimensional geography.[8] The three dimensions can be described as youth, the body (or pleasure), and "attitude," embodied in a practice of "excorporation."

Most obviously, the energy of the rock and roll apparatus is constructed around the categories of youth and the body. Rock and roll celebrates youth, not merely as a chronological measure but as a difference defined by the rejection of the boredom of the "straight" world. The politics of youth celebrate change, risk and instability; the very structures of boredom become the sites of new forms of empowerment. The powerlessness of youth is rearticulated into an apparatus in which it becomes the site of "pleasure" and power. The "pleasure" of empowerment/empowerment of "pleasure" is, furthermore, articulated around the material pleasures of the body. It is its emphasis on rhythm and dance, and its affirmation of sexual desire which may, occasionally, challenge the dominant gender categories. Rock and roll seeks pleasure in the different ways the body can be inserted into its social environment.

However, it is the third axis of "attitude" that locates the radical specificity of rock and roll as a response to the specific structures of contemporary everyday life—postmodernity. This response is manifested in rock and roll's celebration of surfaces, styles and artifice. For those who have grown up in the United States after the Second World War, existence has qualitatively changed (although one need not assume that this rupture is experienced as such). Obviously, its experience will be determined in part by the ideological struggles within the social

---

[8]For a different and more elaborate discussion of the three axes, see Grossberg (1984c).

machine:[9] the structures of historical consciousness and of meaning, purpose and even order, which have been taken for granted, have apparently collapsed. In Baudrillard's (1983) terms, "reality" has disappeared, leaving only its image; without origins, everything becomes a rerun, another style. Given the rapid rate of continuous change, the increasing knowledge of risk and danger, the sense that the rules for survival no longer guarantee a good life, the commodification of all value, life is increasingly lived in "a controlled panic." If "life is hard and then you die" (as a popular T-shirt says), or "nothing matters and what if it did" (John Cougar), or "if nothing is true, everything is permitted" (Jim Carroll), have become maxims for life, then the insertion of the rock and roll apparatus into the equation becomes a strategy of resistance and more directly, of survival. The rock and roll apparatus not only energizes new possibilities within everyday life, it places that energy at the center of a life without meaning; the postmodern situation. Thus, the program notes for Culture Club's 1984 tour: "It is said that love and hate amount to the same thing. If this is true then feel the energy, if not, any feeling however reactionary is better than none." Moreover, if there is no truth beneath the surface of everyday life which can be identified as the source of meaningfulness and direction, then not only the materiality of "pleasure" but that of style or attitude as well rearticulates the structures of everyday life. Rock and roll rearticulates the powerlessness of confronting the postmodern condition into a celebration of new forms and sites of empowerment.

This postmodern context makes one historical appearance of the generation gap into a permanent difference, and the practice of excorporation defines a response by which the rock and roll apparatus constantly reinscribes a boundary between "us" and "them." It steals and transforms the practices, fragments and signs of other cultures and cultural moments, both those marginalized and repressed by the hegemonic culture and those located in the heart of the hegemony; it relocates them within its own reduction to surfaces—all a matter of attitude (or in its more visible forms, style). It celebrates the very conditions of its oppression in postmodernity by making them into the sites of "pleasure." It takes musical practices and styles from black culture, rural and southern culture, gay culture, working class culture, etc., and relocates them within an apparatus whose differences cannot be defined outside of its "attitude," its practice of excorporation. Thus, rock and roll need not celebrate a liberatory politics of pleasure, nor need it represent the anarchic explosion of possibilities. Rock and roll locates itself in the empowerment, the "pleasure" or energy of transitions.

These three axes circumscribe the boundaries of rock and roll while allowing for the local production of different apparatuses within which both the music and the audiences are defined and empowered. One can describe a rock and roll apparatus in terms of the particular ways it inflects each of the axes, and the ways it uses the pieces of other cultural domains it has excorporated into its own spaces. The particular difference that the apparatus constructs for itself and its fans can be described as an "affective alliance."

I want to use this framework to suggest two of the elements—one specific and one general—which have contributed to the current uncertainty marking the rock and roll culture. The first concerns the appearance and effects of punk rock. Punk was, after all, a watershed of some sort, at least in the sense that every-

---

[9]For a discussion of postmodernism, see Grossberg (1985) and Foster (1983). For a discussion of "attitude," see Unger (1982).

thing that has come after it—and there has been a real explosion of music and styles—must be read as "post-punk." This is not merely another turning of the rather tedious critical circle of authentic and co-opted music. I will argue that the particular structure of the punk apparatus problematized, in certain important ways, our ability to empower rock and roll. Punk made visible a contradiction within the rock and roll apparatus by foregrounding the axis of excorporation. By foregrounding "attitude," it not only problematized the investment in any particular attitude but also, in pleasure as well. It was able to rescue them and thus, to rearticulate the affective power of rock and roll, only by placing the axis of youth at the center of its apparatus, by reinscribing the imperative of generational differences that had marked the historical emergence of rock and roll. It celebrated rock and roll as the music of youth, manic fun and risk even as it implicitly called that attitude into question. Contemporary rock and roll apparatuses have had to confront the contradiction which both animated and perhaps destroyed punk, choosing either to further deconstruct the power of rock and roll by celebrating the very artificiality of any attitude, or to find alternative alliances within which its affective power could be reconstructed. The second element was already operating in the punk apparatus, manifested in its dual existence as both populist (an expression of youth) and avant-garde. It involves the growing historical contradiction within the very axis of youth itself as a social category, making punk's attempt to place it at the center of its apparatus precarious at best. Rock and roll emerged in part as a resistance to the "disciplinization" (Foucault, 1977) of youth in the institutions of the family and schools. In this context, empowerment can be seen as a form of struggle against the hegemonic construction of social categories and identities. Rock and roll found an alternative model in the peer group street cultures of both working class (and immigrant) urban and southern communities. Yet the very resistance which helped construct a youth culture has made rock and roll an agent, in the context of other social changes, in the deconstruction of youth.

Punk: Rock and Roll Against Itself

What is punk? (Listen to the first albums by the Sex Pistols, The Clash, or the Ramones.) The music is loud, fast, simple and abrasive. But punk is what it did and how it worked.[10] First, it challenged the control of the so-called "major" record companies which have, since the sixties, dominated the economics of rock and roll. It was not, however, anticapitalist; for the most part, it substituted small capitalists for big ones and, if Malcolm McLaren (manager of the Sex Pistols) is taken as an example, it used capitalist practices to beat the system (e.g., the Sex Pistols were paid by a number of record companies without ever releasing a record). This is not a criticism: there is nothing wrong with using rock and roll as a form of economic work and mobility. Second, it returned the single to the center of the production of rock and roll, making it easier for new groups to record and release music. Thus it empowered the raw sounds of such records. Third, it rejected the criteria of aesthetic and technological expertise

---

[10]It is important to note that many of the same effects were being produced at the same time by the disco apparatus, arising out of urban black, gay and hispanic subcultures. See Dyer (1979) and Frith (1978).

which had dominated and often defined the musical practice of rock and roll in the seventies. Fourth, it rejected the star system which had become so pervasive and had fractured the relation between musician and fan. And, finally, it consciously sought the minimal musical conditions of rock and roll. To many, it sounds like anarchic noise. Greil Marcus (1980a, p. 452) described it as music stripped down to "the essentials of speed, noise, fury and manic glee."

The significance of punk is commonly located in its supposed working class origins. Punk was "dole queue rock" which translated the unemployment of angry white youths into leisure. There are two problems with this view: first, the impact of punk cannot be explained by its origins, and second, this view of its origins, and second, this view of its origins is factually problematic. It ignores the existence of a punk movement in New York which in fact helped to stimulate the British movement. This American punk (listen to Patti Smith, Television or Talking Heads) was more self-consciously avant-garde, with a more explicit sense of distance, irony, and contradiction than the British music which came to define the movement. Further, even in England, many of those who shaped this apparatus were either art school students or existed on the fringes of debates in politics and the visual arts (e.g., situationism [Frith, 1978, 1980; Frith & Horne, 1983]).

Even the sound of the British punk voice belies its working class origins.[11] The voice (as in Johnny Rotten of the Sex Pistols) appears, at first glance, to be the expression of working class anger and to use working class clichés. But what is heard at one level as class determined is, at another level, a particular sort of consciously chosen inarticulateness—a voice which is anonymous and distant from its own words. The punk singer clearly chose to reject the conventions of both the soul singer and the pop crooner, returning to a particularly "rock and roll" grain of voice. The punk is not the voice of an individual, a class, or a community but rather, the voice of the "crowd," or as I will suggest later, of youth. Its artificiality is comparable to that of the convention of filming documentaries in black and white. The anonymity of the voice is reflected in the chosen anonymity of many of the performers.

This suggests a different reading of punk.[12] Rather than transforming unemployment into leisure, it transformed a history with "no future" (a particular economic appearance of the postmodern condition) into a celebration and empowering of "youth." It triumphed over its visions of a society in decline by embodying them in music and style. It was "music to watch England go down the toilet" (D. Hebdige, personal communication April, 1980). Locating punk in this broader context (which was made to appear to correspond to a particular class formation as much by hegemonic media practices as anything else) makes it a set of strategies for living in the face of the collapse of meaning and increasing paranoia:

> Where there's no future
> How can there be sin
> We're the flowers in your dustbin
> We're the poison in your human machine

[11]The discussion that follows is the product of conversations with Dick Hebdige.
[12]For discussions of punk and its aftermath, see Dancis (1978); Laing (1978, 1985); Hebdige (1979, 1983); Marcus (1980a, 1980b, 1981a, 1981b, 1981c, 1983); Erikson (1980); Frith (1981, 1983); Marchetti (1982); Grossberg (1983–1984); and Savage (1983).

We're the future
Your future. (Coons, 1978, p. 128)

This reading is reinforced by the fact that other, more mainstream rock and roll groups had hits shortly after the punk explosion which, both musically and affectively, confronted the cynicism and postmodernity that punk foregrounded (e.g., Pink Floyd's *The Wall,* J. Geil Band's "Love Stinks").

How then are we to understand punk's effects as a response to postmodernity? We might begin by considering what is, in my opinion, the most emblematic of all punk songs—Sid Vicious (and the Sex Pistols) singing "My Way." The song is composed of two parts: first, a thoroughly awful (wonderful!) and off-key cover of Sinatra's original version which reduces the latter's honesty and sincerity to absurdity and artificiality; second, a thoroughly punk version (fast, noisy, grotesque, etc.) in which the lyrics clearly reflect the violence and horror of "my way" in the contemporary world. The point of the song, its effect, is not to substitute one version for another, or to offer the punk rewrite as the new authentic expression. The obvious parody of the first part renders both Sinatra's absent version and the punk version equally problematic, equally undecidable. The song makes punk into just another style, another musical choice. Someone can now do a cover of Sid Vicious' version as well—an endless chain of signs with no point at which some authentic meaning and sincere expression are given.

Hebdige (1979, 1983) has given a convincing description of punk style as deconstructive. Its fragmented and outrageous style celebrated impotence as a strategy for avoiding surveillance. Punk cut up every style or surface and threw the pieces together. While earlier rock and roll apparatuses had stolen the material of their styles primarily from other marginal cultures, punk stole from its own history (i.e., from other, earlier rock and roll cultures: see the early pictures of the Sex Pistols) and from the heart of the hegemonic culture (e.g., garbage bags, safety pins) and the hegemony's most sacred history (e.g., swastikas). It took these objects, cut them up and threw them back into the face of the nonpunk world (which included old rock and rollers—hippies and heavy metal fans—as well as the straight adult world) as their worst nightmares. In the fifties, kids were prohibited from going out looking like trash. In punk, they went out literally dressed in trash.

Punk foregrounded the axis of attitude, placing its own excorporative practice on its surface. It treated every sign as if there were no meaning behind it; its motto was "Xpose." It demonstrated that anything could be excorporated, treated as a fragment without meaning, history or feeling. Style became, not an identity, but a measure of its effects. Anything could become punk, anything could be used by punk, and so punk was there to be used and used up. Implicit in this practice was the fact that punk style was itself artificial. Yet style was all that punk had; it demonstrated, in its attitude, on its surfaces so to speak, that attitude, style and surface is all that there is.

This particular inflection of the axis of attitude had a significant impact on the way punk articulated the axis of the body and pleasure within its apparatus; in particular, it deconstructed the body as the site of its pleasures. In both its fashions and dance styles, punk cut up and even attacked the body, denying its claims to be privileged. This had a number of intriguingly positive effects: it opened up new possibilities for sexual voices and positions within rock and roll, especially for women,[13] who used punk's techniques to deconstruct and challenge the sexual/gender definitions of both the straight world and the rock and roll culture. It also significantly restructured the possibilities of image and movement. Punk played with the iconography of sex and gender; the body became a fractured surface on which punk could play out its image-games. Such deconstructions of pleasure challenged, not only the ideologies of romance and gender difference (punk was the first rock and roll apparatus that did not rely heavily on songs about romance and love), but the very legitimation of sexual pleasure as well. Pleasure itself had become passe. The crescendo of rock and roll rhythms was replaced by the continuous noise, pulses and droning of punk, suggesting something other than sexual satisfaction. Again, Johnny Rotten summed it up: "What is sex anyway? Just thirty seconds of squelching noise?" And in groups like the Voidoids, Blondie, the Gang of Four, Patti Smith (and later, even more explicitly in Joy Division and Au Pairs), the body appears only to be another artificial site on which style is enacted. Punk questioned the naive celebration of pleasure and its significance as a moment of resistance or transcendence.

A similar result might have been predicted for the axis of youth--that is, youth itself would have been seen as just another pose, in fact, as passe[14] If carried to its "logical" conclusion as a cultural project (and this was perhaps true in the avant-garde articulations of the punk aesthetic), punk made obvious the arbitrariness of any style or attitude, the impossibility of any investment. Bringing glitter rock's (e.g., David Bowie) attempt to display the artificiality of all surfaces to the surface, punk pointed to the construction of an "aesthetics of the fake." As Joe Jackson would later sing, "Look sharp, just keep looking over your shoulder."

Punk's practice recognized, if only implicitly, that all cultural life is constructed. By excorporating even the most innocuous signs, it celebrated the unnatural and denied the very category of the "natural." All it could do was demystify and problematize any construct, any attitude, any style. This would, presumably, have meant rock and roll itself, including punk. When Johnny Rotten said, "All we are trying to do is destroy everything," he presumably meant to include rock and roll's own empowerment. There was, after all, no reason to assume that this self-appointed "Antichrist" would exempt the salvations offered by rock and roll.

In fact, punk did acknowledge rock and roll's status as a commodity and the apparent inevitability of its co-optation. It established a new relation to its own history of rock and roll. As Marcus (1980a) has argued, rock and roll became, not only the first principle of any youth revolt but also that revolt's first target; rock and roll became a weapon against itself. Punk at least opened the possibility of questioning rock and roll's exemption from the oppressively boring world. It placed anyone seeking the affective empowerment of rock and roll in a rather awkward position: one could no longer believe in "the magic that will set you

---

[13]S. Frith (personal communication, September, 1983) has suggested that the differences in the sexual politics of British and American rock and roll may be due, in part, to the fact that women re-entered (and feminist concerns entered) British rock and roll with punk, while in the United States, this had occurred earlier in the decade with the singer-songwriter movement.

[14]"Youth" in rock and roll is always connected to the real frustrations and powerlessness of adolescents, despite attempts to define it in terms of an attitude of "eternal youth." See Christgau (1984).

free.'' This questioning of the power of rock and roll (again, this can be heard in the later, more mainstream recordings of David Bowie, Peter Gabriel, etc.) changed the ways one could listen to rock and roll, not merely by refusing to take rock and roll seriously (rock and roll has always done that) nor even by attacking it directly, but precisely by making rock and roll work against itself. But punk continued to exempt itself by centering its own apparatus upon the privileged axis of youth, the privileged access of youth into its encapsulations. It thus displaced its foregrounded, self-conscious artificiality into a populism of postmodern youth. (The more avant-garde groups that refused this displacement, groups that were already marginalized within the dominant punk apparatus, were able to move more fluidly into the context of post-punk apparatuses.)

Punk emerged at, and responded to, a particular moment in the history of rock and roll. It is, after all, not coincidental that in 1976, the first of the baby boomers were turning thirty. Punk attacked rock and roll for having grown old and fat, for having lost that which puts it in touch with its audience and outside of the hegemonic reality. It attacked rock and roll in the guise of megagroups and arena rock, hippies and baby boomers who had clearly become part of that which was supposed to be outside of rock and roll. If the rock and roll apparatus works when it draws a line between ''them'' and ''us,'' encapsulating its fans in a mobile environment of their own, punk did so more clearly and outrageously than at any point in the seventies, precisely by articulating a particular structure of the apparatus. Even as it deconstructed the naturalistic claims of culture, it reasserted the power of its own expressionism. While it denied that rock and roll represented the emotional life or real social experiences of its fans, it reconnected the music and the fan. When it looked inside itself, it did not find nothing; it found the emptiness of the ''blank generation,'' postmodern youth. Even as it seemed to celebrate anarchy and the pure negativity of its deconstruction (the insanity, dissonance, its threatening difference), even as it projected a potentially expansive pluralism of apparatuses and styles (a pluralism which could arise only after punk celebrated its own death), it re-encapsulated rock and roll within a surprisingly circumscribed range of sounds, styles and attitudes.[15] Deconstruction as attitude was articulated to, and limited by, the axis of youth. Youth remained the site of rock and roll's investment and empowerment, even if it was a youth with neither a past nor a future. By reinvesting the axis of youth at the center of the apparatus and displacing the question of style, punk was able to reaffirm its existence as rock and roll. But this was obviously a strategy/ structure that was condemned to failure. In fact, punk reproduced, almost perfectly, the contradictions—the impossible situation—in which youth and youth culture increasingly found itself.

The Deconstruction of Youth

The place of youth in the rock and roll culture has been unsettled by the conjunction of the history of rock and roll and a series of other social events. In the eighties, the contradictions of ''youth'' are becoming increasingly explicit. We might begin trying to make this visible by returning to the contemporary discus-

---

[15]In my opinion, the best punk and post-punk music foregrounded this contradiction (e.g., the Sex Pistols, the Buzzcocks, the Voidoids).

sions of the death of rock and roll. For the real power of this discourse lies, not in its connection with that part of the audience struggling to rediscover or reinvest its faith in rock and roll but rather, in its pointing to a part of the audience for whom rock and roll is neither possible nor desirable.

The typical description of the crisis of the rock and roll audience goes something like this: There is, apparently, a new generation of youth who have confronted a number of events: (1) Style and culture have been increasingly commodified and incorporated into hegemonic discourses through advertising, fashion and the media. (2) They have been raised under the threat of continuous economic recession. While rock and roll has survived earlier recessions, its fans had previously believed that there was something after the recession and that fun was a sufficient strategy (on the surface) for getting through it. Rock and roll offered an economy of transitions, of magical transformations. (3) Images of youth, which so dominated postwar baby boom America, have been replaced increasingly with images of the baby boomers' attempts to deal with growing old and having responsibility. (4) Rock and roll has become nostalgic. It is not only the music of parents but of advertising as well. How can it possibly mark a difference and constitute some kind of resistance? Its claims to have provided some form of transcendence or revolution have been dissolved in the gray morning of Reagan and yuppies. (This may partly explain why the current explosion of revivals has not often led to a rediscovery of the originals. The originals belong to someone else; they cannot exist as rock and roll anymore.) (5) A new generation of conservative youth has appeared—variously characterized as the "me generation" and the "mean generation"—for whom "Hipness isn't hip anymore" (Truman, 1985, p. 23). (6) New technologies, and in some cases, older cultural forms, have replaced rock and roll as the dominant leisure activities of youth. The result is that, for many young people, rock and roll has become just another moment of hegemonic leisure, background music to which they relate in ways more reminiscent of an earlier generation's relation to Tin-Pan Alley's music.

There is, obviously, a good deal of truth in all of these observations. And young people do seem to have turned to other forms of culture to seek their own strategies of "pleasure" and survival within a context of "controlled panic." This was already visible in the late seventies, in the popularity of absurdist humor. *Saturday Night Live* not only gave youth access to rock and roll but also, to the increasingly adult status of that world. In the popular movies which followed upon that show's success, the painful absurdity of the humor ("It just doesn't matter," as one crucial scene in a Bill Murray film says) became the source of its own pleasure and importance. More recently, the connection between youth and rock and roll is being challenged by the growing investment of youth in the video-computer technology. Video games produce a radical sense of enclosedness. In this, they are like the "walkman" rather than the "ghettoblasters" of the seventies (and later, of breakdancing). But their encapsulation is protective rather than resistant. There are, however, two more significant forms of this new technologically based popular culture. The first is the proliferation of personal computers and the increasing computer sophistication of youth. This not only provides them with a clear-cut space of their own (an apparatus which is defined technologically but which has empowering effects as well), it has become a form of pleasure. Thus, on a recent television show, when a "whiz kid" was asked why he would spend hours programming a computer to do a task that would take a few minutes to work out with a pencil, he responded "Computers are fun, pencils are boring."

Television, too, is being reinserted into this new apparatus. Contrary to common wisdom, the rock and roll generations were not the television generations. Television was new, exciting, but it certainly did not belong to them; they did not control its programming nor did they have a special competence in its unique languages (although they may by now). But that has changed. Television has become so much a part of our taken-for-granted lives that it is now available to the younger generations, to be reappropriated as their own. If youth in the fifties, sixties, and even seventies, would have sacrificed anything rather than give up their music, there is increasing evidence that television plays the same role in the life of younger generations.

Of course, this sliding of the signifier of "youth" from rock and roll to video-computers is made that much easier by the advent of Music Television. MTV has provided what American radio never would—a national network of music. But it has accomplished this only by recontextualizing the music, by demanding that it take on a visual and more particularly, a video, existence. It rearticulates the music into different rhythms and structures. It is interesting to compare MTV with other, earlier attempts to incorporate rock and roll into television (e.g., unlike *American Bandstand,* the video-jockeys of MTV constitute a family without parents). All differences of style—in both the music and audiences—are displaced into the abstract principle of style which can then be actively copied (Goldman, 1984). It is too early to speculate on the effects of this new cultural form. We can note that it is immensely popular among the very young, that the way music works is significantly altered by its (re?) entrance into processes of the visualization of culture, and that it will undoubtedly reshape the listening practices and the investments in the music of these new fans.

I want to suggest—and that is all that I will be able to do here—that there is something else taking place which is radically altering the possibility of rock and roll in a contemporary world. There is a sense in which the category of "youth" as we know it is once again being reshaped. The emergence and shifts of this social category have been the subject of much debate.[16] They are located within a larger network of power that takes the body of the population itself as its object of control, what Foucault (1977, 1978) has described as the various technologies of "disciplinization." Thus, I am neither proclaiming the "end of youth" nor interpreting a mere change in its meaning. I am pointing to its rearticulation, not only as a cultural category, but as a social and material body as well. The very sites and forms of its public existence are being restructured (from marches to malls, from drugs to alcohol, etc.). The issue is not whether the various discourses about youth and childhood are referentially accurate, but that they are themselves part of the context in which youth is organized. The discourses and

---

[16] Two recent arguments for the "disappearance of youth" are Postman (1983) and Meyrowitz (1984). See Rowntree (1968) and Jacques (1973) for class-readings of youth and youth culture. For a good summary of many of the arguments, see Frith (1984). One can find discussions of the crises of the various youth populations (yuppies, baby boomers growing up, and the new youth) in almost every major publication. Particularly useful examples are Wellborn (1981) and Trippett (1981). What I am suggesting is the need for a "genealogy" (Foucault, 1980) of youth. I am grateful to Ellen Wartella and Philip Sellars for their contributions to this discussion.

practices that interpenetrate and surround youth, articulating its very existence—these are what need to be mapped out.

In all the contemporary discussions of youth, we are caught in the uncertainty of generations. Youth today is caught already in the contradiction between those who experience the powerlessness of their age and the generations of the baby boomers who have tried to redefine youth as an attitude. If the former is increasingly uncertain, it is partly because the status of the latter has also become problematic. As more and more people point to the increasingly troubled and adult-like qualities of young people, they are also observing the failure of the baby boomers to accept and arrive at traditional notions of adulthood. But we must not assume that we already understand these relations. If we too quickly reduce the context to simple questions—Is youth disappearing? Are youth and adulthood merging?—we are in danger of ignoring the real struggles and frustrations that still characterize the different groups and their relations to each other and other social groups.

Nevertheless, it is clear that changes are occurring: in the rapidly increasing suicide rate and drug-dependency of youth; in the changing child-rearing contexts and practices; in the increasing willingness to sacrifice educational budgets, to treat juvenile offenders as adult criminals. If contemporary youth has been constructed at the intersection of particular dominant institutions and technologies, its identity depends upon its social location. Following the industrial revolution, the image of childhood as innocence justified children's location within privileged institutions qualified to "protect" and "instruct" them: the school was devoted to the acquisition of the skills of economic and political adulthood; more important was the alliance between schools, medical institutions and the family as the protectors of physical, psychological and moral health (Donzelot, 1979). Such a construction of childhood obviously required an enormous economic investment; society "chose" to keep children out of the labor market and to provide the necessary services.

After the Second World War, with the enormous boom in the number of children, it became even more of an economic priority to keep them out of the labor market and to use this as a way of extending the already expanding service basis of the economy. This large segment of the population was also constructed as consumers. The insularity of childhood was extended to youth (or adolescence) as a unique transitional moment.[17] The transitional status of youth, defined as a time between childhood and adulthood, a time of continued protection, provided the freedom for mobility and for the project of "acquiring" an identity. But just because youth was hegemonically defined with its own specific freedom, it could become something more than transitional. It took on its own privileged identity. This new youth was ambiguously valued (Hebdige, 1983): on the one hand, a time of fun, a time in which one could take risks and, on the other hand, a potential threat, a risk to the hegemonic structures, "delinquency." This specific space of youth, which emerged in the fifties and was intimately connected with the wedding of rock and roll and youth, is being displaced by at least three events: the increasing redistribution of knowledge; changing representations of youth; and the effects of the rock and roll apparatus itself.

[17]It is interesting to note that the other major attempt, albeit failed ones, to construct a youth culture, was in the 1920's, following the First World War. Certainly, the contemporary construction of youth needs to be understood in the context of specific events and developments throughout the twentieth century. See Fass (1977) and Wohl (1979).

To put it quite simply, kids today know too much and they are, at some level, too cynical. There is evidence that, for the first time, new generations of youth do not think that the general context of social life is getting better. Nor do they place particular faith in traditional institutions such as relationships or meaningful and satisfying careers. This is not to deny that they may, individually, seek such impossible pleasures; they simply no longer invest in them in the same ways.[18] Nor do they believe, apparently, in the elusive search for an identity out of freedom; no longer privileging the transitions, they deny the specific identity of youth; they have returned to a conception of youth as training for adulthood with its own leisure activities, its own fun. It is an attitude in which everything is taken both too seriously and, at the same time, as a joke, with a certain irony. Anything can be ridiculed even as one struggles to achieve it. If "ambivalence toward life is their only myth, their only dream, the only context in which they can find comfort" (Moffitt, 1981, p. 6), then "to be modern is to be hard-edged, cooly aggressive; to celebrate the synthetic and the artificial; to reject softness and easy intimacy and fuzzy-headed visions of what life has to offer; to feel the pull of polarization in every fiber. . . . Modern youth is showing America how to tighten its sphincter—and like it" (Rose, 1981, p. 1).

This is of course reinforced by, and reflected in, the incorporation of this new cynicism (notice its similarities to punk's inflection of the affective axis of attitude) into the mainstream of everyday life. Calvin Klein advertises jeans by asking "Is there a real me, or am I just what you see?" Pepsi and others represent relationships through fragmented images of the body. Cartoons reflect the increasing identification of love with domestic violence. In a remake of a Grassroots' hit, the lyrics are changed from "Let others plan their future, I'm busy loving you," to "Let others plan their future, that's one way to get through." Even in media aimed for youth, such statements have become increasingly visible, if not dominant. In the movie of S. E. Hinton's *Rumblefish,* the hero is described by his father: "He can do anything he wants but there's nothing he wants to do." And in a movie popular with kids, *Bless the Beasts and the Children,* at the climactic scene when they finally manage to free the buffalo that are about to be shot, one youth muses about their future in terms of roaming the prairies. Another youth, perhaps 14, responds: "I wish I were young enough to believe that"; and of course, the closing scene shows us that the buffalo are about to be shot anyway. One can see more sophisticated representations of this attitude in the current generation of "new wave" movies (e.g., *Repo Man, Liquid Sky, Buckaroo Bonzai* [Rosenberg, 1984]). One can hear it in Chloe's (the child of the eighties in *The Big Chill*) description of her love affair with a now deceased sixties person: "We got along fine. I had no expectations and he had too many." Or in Oshima's *Cruel Story of Youth:* "We have no dreams so we can't see them destroyed." There is no pathos in Chloe's voice when she asks what it is like to be happy, since she has never known many happy people.

Thus, part of what I am calling the deconstruction of youth has come from the erosion of the boundaries of knowledge in the everyday lives of youth. Knowledge and events have made the cynicism of punk hip, but without the anger and frustration. Youth increasingly begins with the artificiality of all styles, categories and commitments. They are obsessed with the transition into adulthood. Ob-

---

[18]For example, "Young people are now getting married cause they see how their parents followed every desire and got totally disrupted and how the nihilism of 1979 caused nothing but O.D.'s and cancer" (Acker, 1982, p. 78).

viously, the above examples are merely that—examples of a changing system of possible statements. I do not intend to interpret their worldview, merely to point to the fact of their existence and proliferation.

There is also a change in the ways that youth is represented. In the late seventies, movies and television offered few, if any, positive images of, or heroes for, youth. The models which were offered were so simplistic that they could be only taken ironically. Increasingly, youth is often represented only in its absence. This absence may function not only as a real lack, but also by placing youth in a position in which it makes no difference that they are, in fact, young. In a large number of popular horror movies of this period, youth is represented either as pure victim or as pure evil. In fact, it makes no difference that they are young, unless it is as the victims of some unnamed social rage; it only deconstructs the very difference being obliterated. Tom Carson (1984, p. 73) has recently described the new "sour view of children" on prime time television in which either "negative characteristics usually associated with adulthood" are displaced onto children—"children are treated as mercenary and calculating while parents are seen as passive, endearingly hapless"—or they are seen as "alien, inherently Other."

The enormous popularity of Spielberg's films (*Close Encounters, ET, Poltergeist, Gremlins*) is the most recent manifestation of this shifting representational code. These films are all structured around the disappearance of children and their eventual return. The movies offer themselves as a new "fountain of youth"; they project adult fantasies of youth and their surfaces resemble advertising. The category of youth has been appropriated by others who not only define but essentialize it. They speak as if from a position of youth, for youth, but they speak as adults, for adults. Thus it is increasingly common to find the baby boomer heroes and heroines of prime time television confronting their ambiguous relations to both youth and adulthood, appropriating the former category and dissolving it into their reluctance to enter the latter category. Perhaps all this encodes a new resentment of youth by a generation that was never taught to be adults or even to value that identity, and whose identity is still imbricated in their investment in youth. This incorporation of youth into adulthood has taken on a new form in the past few years: the increasing sexualization of youth (and more recently, even childhood, perhaps partly in response to an increasing ambivalence about our willingness to make the necessary personal and economic sacrifices that have constructed the category). This sexualization is also taking place within the rock and roll/youth culture itself. One need only look at the way in which dancers present themselves, not to each other but to the camera, on programs such as *American Bandstand,* to realize that the sexualization of youth has taken on new inflections.

In fact, it was perhaps almost inevitable that rock and roll would define and even more, help bring about its own death, that the rock and roll apparatuses would dismantle their possibility of empowering alliances. Consider where rock and roll constructed its own culture, the physical spaces which it appropriated and created as its own: the street, the jukebox, the party and the "hop/dance." The significance of these spaces is that, to some extent, they all attempt to exist outside of the family and the school. In fact, it is these two institutions which rock and roll has most consistently attacked. Frith and McRobbie (1978–1979) have argued that the antidomesticity of rock and roll is an expression of its basic male orientation and its antifemale ideology. I disagree: the antidomesticity of the rock and roll apparatus is an attack on the place in which its own youth is constructed. It is a resistance to the very disciplinization which is, paradoxically, constitutive of its "youth." Such resistance is a crucial aspect of the rock and roll apparatus. But what if rock and roll begins to succeed in challenging the control of the hegemony over the category of youth? For example, if youth is defined in part by its ambiguous and risky relation to sexual practice (especially intercourse), what happens to it when that relationship is fundamentally changed?

The antidomesticity of rock and roll (as well as its antischool stance) is increasingly supported by other hegemonic discourses and such alliances surely make rock and roll's status problematic. The family as an adequate site for the protection of the child is increasingly under attack. For example, although issues of childbeating and incest have raised by feminists since the nineteenth century, they have never been taken up in widespread public debate until the present moment. And the demand for more flexible social and sexual arrangements similarly challenges the stability and adequacy of the traditional nuclear family. One might add that, similarly, the other institutions which have direct responsibility for the disciplinization, control and construction of youth—schools, medicine, juvenile courts—are coming under broad attack.

Finally, these changes can be related to one other reconstruction of youth and its relationship to the body in the contemporary world. This newly emergent structure makes pleasure something to work for (not merely a political struggle, it is a physical and economic one). Youth is something to be held on to by physical effort. That is, youth has become a state of the body, presumably one which offers its own pleasurable rewards. This emergent cultural formation is most clearly embodied in the current transformation of sports/health into a form of leisure with its own styles, and to the remarkable appearance of the "yuppies" on the public scene. It is interesting to note that this emergent culture not only has grown out of the rock and roll audiences, but often continues to use at least some of the music within its own structures of empowerment (*Flashdance* and Michael Jackson's *Thriller*, two of the most successful albums of 1983, are widely used for various styles of exercise).

The result is that while rock and roll has been crucial in constructing a youth culture, it has also been crucial in eroding the conditions for the particular construction of "youth" upon which it is built, not merely because of its own practices but in conjunction with a whole series of events which have intersected and interacted with it. But if the institutions and disciplines that construct youth are deconstructed, how can rock and roll define itself by its resistance to them? How can the rock and roll apparatus invest itself in an unstable axis of youth? Thus, the relationship between rock and roll and youth has become contradictory: rock and roll exists not within the rise of youth but rather, at the cusp between the rise and the decline of a particular construction of youth, one which so privileges its transitional status as to reify and celebrate transitions. The rock and roll apparatus attacks the very conditions of its existence. The current identification of young people with the video-computer technology does not merely make them different from the straight world, it denies their "youthfulness"; they are better—more adult—than adults. They too are implicated in a complex and contradictory historical process by which the existence of youth is being reshaped and relocated in social, cultural and material space.

Conclusion: Is There Rock after Punk?

We can now return to the task of interpreting the current situation of rock and roll. After punk, the dominant contradiction around which rock and roll was rearticulated was that of "attitude." There were two possible responses. First, the practice of excorporation could be submerged below the surface of the apparatus (a position which characterizes much of the history of rock and roll), allowing the axes of youth and/or the body to dominate its affective empowerment, to define both the center and surface of rock and roll's politics of "pleasure." This helps us explain why heavy metal and new wave[19] defined the split center of a narrower vision of rock and roll in the late seventies. Heavy metal has been and remains a strong affirmation of the difference and pleasures of youth (often ideologically entangled with images of working class culture and fantasy). New wave was largely a synthesis of punk attitudes (and historical roots), pop sensibilities and disco practices. It constructed around itself a number of apparatuses which placed the axis of the body and pleasure at their center. This axis was inflected with different emphases given to dance, fashion, sexuality and romance, as well as to its relation to the axis of youth. A second response to the contradiction of attitude is to continue celebrating, not only foregrounding it but placing it at its center as well; the various practices of "post-punk" (e.g., Joy Division and later Talking Heads) and "new music" (e.g., Laurie Anderson, DNA, Birthday Party) increasingly deconstructed any structure or commitment taken as necessary to rock and roll. Such apparatuses often attempted to restructure notions of the body (i.e., through new structures of sense/noise and rhythms) and youth.[20]

As the deconstruction of youth has become a more effective presence in everyday life, the ability to make such discriminations seems to have disappeared (however oversimplified the categories may already seem). Rock and roll has exploded into an almost maddening proliferation of sounds and styles with no musical center. In fact, it is almost as if rock and roll today were running through, metonymically and synchronically reproducing, rock and roll's entire history. It is also expanding its possibilities, partly by combining and rearranging other styles, partly by "excorporating" a wide range of new musical practices and technologies. And this is true, not only musically but stylistically as well. This can be seen in a new generation of rock and roll movies which move fluidly among, and combine a wide range of rock and roll styles (e.g., *Streets of Fire, Buckaroo Bonzai, Repo Man*). It can also be heard, I believe, in individual records (e.g., Hüsker Dü's *Zen Arcade* contains a history of rock and roll although it is given no coherent shape or order).

However, this description leaves unanswered whether, in this situation, rock and roll is affectively empowered and whether it is or can be oppositional. Recently, I was asked to write an article for an Italian magazine explaining the increasing "conservatism" of U.S.-onian youth, the existence of a generation of rock and roll-ing Reaganites. (Obviously, by contemporary reckoning, this in-

---

[19]"New wave" is a particularly problematic genre term. It is sometimes used as if one can assume that it is the form in which punk and disco were appropriated by commercial interests, thus making it inherently co-opted. Obviously, I refuse such an assumption.

[20]It is important to remember that how a particular musical text is located within apparatuses is not inscribed within the musical practice, and hence, that the same text can function in different, even contradictory apparatuses. Consequently, the lines between these different genres is neither simple nor stable. See Grossberg (1984a).

cludes more than one generation, stretching from the yuppies and baby boomers to the current generation of precollege adolescents.) The question assumes both that they are conservative (in a way that is consistent with our historical understanding of the meanings of the term) and that there is, at least intuitively, a contradiction between youth and rock and roll on the one hand, and conservatism on the other.

I have suggested that one cannot answer this question by separating the music and its audience within the terms of traditional communication models. In such a model, one can assume that the music is determining, that is politics are inscribed within it. One would then argue, for example, that rock and roll has become so much a part of the hegemonic, capitalist system that it has lost any oppositional power. Listening to it contributes to the conservatism of youth, reinforcing the already existing conservatism which enabled them to enjoy the music in the first place. Alternatively, one can assume that the audience (partially determined by its social and historical context) is determining. One then argues that the current generation no longer needs or desires oppositional rock and roll. Both of these views lead to identical political alternatives: one announces the death of rock and roll as an oppositional form; or one awaits and perhaps works for the rebirth of "authentic" rock and roll or an idealistic rock and roll audience. Or finally, one argues for an interaction between music and audiences, leading one to look for and privilege the marginal, the subcultural, that which remains outside the musical and sociological mainstream. Such a view not only takes the latter relationship for granted, it fails to locate it within specific historical contexts (Hall, 1981). Furthermore, by reproducing the unreflective elitism of rock and roll, it recreates all of the problems of elitism within its politics.

I would prefer a politics which attempted to locate the points at which rock and roll continues to struggle. This is, however, a complex matter, for, as I have argued, the energy of that struggle is at the level of an affective resistance to the structures of everyday life. Moreover, even if a particular rock and roll apparatus is effective at this level, there is no guarantee that its resistance will be articulated into an active struggle against hegemonic (ideological, economic and political) structures. These two issues then define the sites at which the battle must be waged for the cultural critic. Is rock and roll working affectively for particular audience fractions and how is it positioned within hegemonic politics? The question must remain open for it is an empirical one. But to say that it is empirical is not to say that it is behavioral, exegetical or phenomenological. How then is it to be answered?

I have attempted to do three things in this article: (1) to lay out a conceptual vocabulary with which we can investigate the politics of rock and roll in more subtle and complex ways, a framework within which rock and roll is a set of strategies for struggle, the nature and effects of which are never predetermined; (2) to argue that at least two significant vectors of change have to be taken into account as we consider the present political position of rock and roll. This is not to deny other vectors of determination, merely to acknowledge that the complex array of changes that have taken place over the last 25 years have changed the relations between rock and roll, youth and society; (3) to suggest a different approach to the empirical question. Let me, in conclusion, make some explicit comments about this last concern.

Admittedly, many of the observations, interpretations and conclusions I have presented are not themselves written on the surface of our social experience. There are many objections that could be raised against my argument. For example, one could disagree with my descriptions of the functioning of rock and roll, or punk. One could reasonably ask if the fact that the punk apparatus had only a marginal presence in the United States, or that it continues to exist, contradicts my reading.[21]

I might respond that all critical arguments are based, in the end, upon relative (and hopefully educated) perspectives and critical dialogue: one offers an interpretation and asks, "this is so, it is not?" However, since I believe that the crucial issues upon which questions of culture turn are political, I would prefer a different model. I have offered a particular reconstruction—at a particular level of abstraction—of a complex and contradictory historical context. The task is comparable to trying to reconstruct a multidimensional jigsaw puzzle without knowing the image represented. Moreover, each level of abstraction has its own appropriate demands for evidence and argument. Alternative constructions are always possible, and the connections between different levels of abstraction (i.e., between what we conveniently label the "theoretical" and the "empirical") must constantly be taken into account. Nevertheless, in the last instance, I would appeal to the political implications of different constructions, to whether they allow us to identify and elaborate sites of resistance and struggle. At this point, the questions of contemporary cultural politics enters a different terrain. "Postmodern theory" (e.g., Baudrillard, 1983; Grossberg, 1984c) argues that contemporary popular media can no longer empower through the production of affective apparatuses and alliances. Rock and roll works, if at all, by inserting fragmented individuals into the contradictions and interstices of the hegemonic structures. Its resistance is hyper-localized. The real "pleasure" of rock and roll in the present situation is precisely that of the dispersion of any stable site or structure of "pleasure" and power. On the other hand, while such forms of struggle may be necessary and even important at the level of everyday life, this should not prevent us from seeing the need, and the possibility, to organize structures and alliances which resist at both the affective and hegemonic levels.

We will not arrive at an adequate practical understanding—"pessimism of the intellect, optimism of the will"—of the current situation in rock and roll by focusing on either the phenomenology of its fans or the message of its texts, even if we locate both within the context of a conservative hegemony. The crucial contradiction, the point at which rock and roll is inserted, is that between everyday life and the ideological struggles of contemporary hegemonic politics. For those ideologies—both of the left and the right—continue to mystify that which rock and roll empowers: the changing structures of our affective existence. However naively optimistic it may seem, I believe that the contemporary rock and roll cultures are "all revved up with no place to go" (Meatloaf).

References

Acker, K. (1982). *Great expectations.* New York: Grove Press.
Baudrillard, J. (1983). *Simulations* (P. Foss, P. Patton, & P. Beitchman, Trans.). New York: Semiotexte.

[21]I would argue that the contemporary punk apparatus, for example, as built around hardcore music, differs significantly from the moment I have described. Further, the question of punk's influence at the affective level cannot be read off of some quantitative measure of its cultural presence.

Bourdieu, P. (1984). *Distinction: A social critique of the judgment of taste* (R. Nice, Trans.). Cambridge, MA: Harvard University Press. (Original work published 1979)

Carson, T. (1984, November 6). Head 'em up, move 'em out. *Village Voice*, p. 73.

Chambers, I. (1981). Pop music: A teaching perspective. *Screen Education, 37*, 35–46.

Chambers, I. (1985). *Urban rhythms: Pop music and pop culture.* New York: St. Martins Press.

Chambers, I. (1988). Contamination, coincidence and collusion: Popular culture, urban culture, and the avant-garde. In C. Nelson & L. Grossberg (Eds.), *Marxism and the interpretation of culture.* Urbana: University of Illinois Press.

Christgau, R. (1984, February 7). Rock 'n' roller coaster: The music biz on a joyride. *Village Voice*, p. 37.

Coons, C. (1978). *1988: The new wave punk rock explosion.* New York: Hawthorn Books.

Dancis, B. (1978). Safety pins and class struggle: Punk rock and the left. *Socialist Review, 39*, 58–83.

Donzelot, J. (1979). *The policing of families* (R. Hurley, Trans.). New York: Pantheon. (Original work published 1977)

Duncan, R. (1984). *The noise: Notes from a rock 'n' roll era.* New York: Ticknor & Fields.

Dyer, R. (1979). In defense of disco. *Gay Left, 8*, 20–23.

Erikson, N. (1980). Popular culture and revolutionary theory: Understanding punk rock. *Theoretical Review, 18*, 13–35.

Fass, P. S. (1977). *The damned and the beautiful: American youth in the 1920's.* New York: Oxford University Press.

Foster, H. (Ed.). (1983). *The anti-aesthetic: Essays on postmodern culture.* Port Townsend, WA: Bay Press.

Foucault, M. (1977). *Discipline and punish: The birth of the prison.* (A. Sheridan, Trans.). New York: Pantheon. (Original work published 1975)

Foucault, M. (1978). *The history of sexuality, Vol. 1: An introduction* (R. Hurley, Trans.). New York: Pantheon. (Original work published 1976)

Foucault, M. (1980). Two lectures. In C. Gordon (Ed.), *Power/Knowledge* (pp. 78–101). New York: Pantheon.

Foucault, M. (1981). Questions of method: An interview. *I & C, 8*, 3–14.

Frith, S. (1978, March 9). The punk bohemians. *New Society*, pp. 535–536.

Frith, S. (1980). Music for pleasure. *Screen Education, 34*, 51–61.

Frith, S. (1981). *Sound effects: Youth, leisure, and the politics of rock 'n' roll.* New York: Pantheon.

Frith, S. (1983). Post punk blues. *Marxism Today, 27*, 18–21.

Frith, S. (1984). *The sociology of youth.* Ormskirk, Lancashire, UK: Causeway Press.

Frith, S. (1978, March). Thesis on disco. *Time Out*, pp. 16–17.

Frith, S., & Horne, H. (1983). Eine kleiner ausflug zu den wahren quellen [Doing the art school bop oder]. *Rock Session, 7*, 279–298.

Frith, S., & McRobbie, A. (1978–1979). Rock and sexuality. *Screen Education, 29*, 3–19.

Goldman, A. (1984, November/December). Analyzing the magic. *People Weekly Extra*, pp. 72–77.

Grossberg, L. (1982). The ideology of communication: Poststructuralism and the limits of communication. *Man and World, 15*, 83–101.

Grossberg, L. (1983–1984). The politics of youth culture: Some observations on rock and roll in American culture. *Social Text, 8*, 104–126.

Grossberg, L. (1984a). Another boring day in paradise: Rock and roll and the empowerment of everyday life. *Popular Music, 4*, 225–228.

Grossberg, L. (1984b). The social meaning of rock and roll. *One Two Three Four, 1*, 13–21.

Grossberg, L. (1984c). I'd rather feel bad than not feel anything at all: Rock and roll, pleasure, and power. *Enclitic, 8*, 94–110.

Grossberg, L. (1985). *Cultural studies, between Marxism and postmodernism: Towards a political theory of media practices.* Unpublished manuscript.

Grossberg, L. (1986a). Teaching and the popular. In C. Nelson (Ed.), *Theory in the classroom.* Urbana: University of Illinois Press.

Grossberg, L. (1986b). If rock and roll communicates then why is it so noisy? *Popular Music Perspectives, 2.*

Hall, S. (1981). Notes on deconstructing 'the popular'. In R. Samuel (Ed.), *People's history and socialist theory* (pp. 227–241). London: Routledge & Kegan Paul.

Hebdige, D. (1979). *Subculture: The meaning of style*. London: Methuen.

Hebdige, D. (1983). Posing . . . threats, striking . . . poses: Youth, surveillance, and display. *Substance, 37–38*, 68–88.

Jacques, M. (1973). Trends in youth culture: Some aspects. *Marxism Today, 17*, 268–280.

Laing, D. (1978). Interpreting punk rock. *Marxism Today, 22*, 123–128.

Laing, D. (1985). *One chord wonders: Power and meaning in punk rock*. Milton Keynes, UK: Open University Press.

Lefebvre, H. (1971). *Everyday life in the modern world* (S. Rabinovitch, Trans.). London: Penguin Press. (Original work published 1968)

Lull, J. (1983, May). *Communication alternatives for the modern youth culture*. Paper presented at a meeting of the International Communication Association, Dallas, TX.

Marchetti, G. (1982). Documenting punk: A subcultural investigation. *Film Reader, 5*, 269–284.

Marcus, G. (1980a). Anarchy in the UK. In J. Miller (Ed.), *The Rolling Stone illustrated history of rock and roll* (2nd ed., pp. 451–463). New York: Random House.

Marcus, G. (1980b, June 24). Wake up. *Rolling Stone*, pp. 40–44.

Marcus, G. (1981a, March). The shock of the old. *New West*, p. 113.

Marcus, G. (1981b, September). Etched in stone. *New West*, p. 124.

Marcus, G. (1981c). Lilliput at the cabaret voltaire. *Triquarterly, 52*, 265–277.

Marcus, G. (1983). The Mekons story. *The Threepenny Review, 14*, 20–21.

Meyrowitz, J. (1984). Television and the obliteration of childhood: The reconstructing of adult/child information systems. *Studies in Communication, 1*, 151–167.

Moffitt, P. (1981, April). R U hip, sixties people? *Esquire*, p. 6.

Postman, N. (1983). *The disappearance of childhood*. New York: Delacorte Press.

Rose, F. (1981, April). Welcome to the modern world. *Esquire*, pp. 29–39.

Rosenberg, S. (1984, July 10). Wheel people. *The Boston Phoenix* (Sec. 3), p. 3.

Rowntree, J., & Rowntree, M. (1968). Youth as a class. *International Socialist Journal, 25*, 25–58.

Savage, J. (1983, February). The punk process. *The Face*, pp. 49–51.

Trippett, F. (1981, April 6). The young: Adult penchants—and problems. *Time*, p. 84.

Truman, J. (1985, January). It's a wonderful life. *The Face*, pp. 20–23.

Unger, C. (1982, July 26). Attitude. *New York Magazine*, p. 24t.

Wellborn, S. N. (1981, December 14). Troubled teenagers. *U.S. News and World Report*, pp. 40–43.

Wohl, R. (1979). *The generation of 1914*, Cambridge, MA: Harvard University Press.

Wicke, P. (1982). Rock music: A musical-aesthetic study. *Popular Music, 2*, 219–243.

Young, C. (1984). Heavy metal: In defense of dirtbags and worthless puds. *Musician, 71*, 40–44.

7

DECISIONS IN
RHETORICAL CRITICISM

Fundamentally, critics must decide what they are trying to do when dealing with material that interests them; in making these decisions they assume a perspective toward their work. The consciousness of a perspective, like the consciousness of anything else, may wax and wane. Since critics work from assumptions that affect the shape of their final materials, they must be aware of their points of view.

This book is based on the contentions that various perspectives can be differentiated from one another and that distinguishing them will aid those interested in criticism to see its potentialities more clearly.

Characteristics of the Perspectives

We would like to review the characteristics of the various perspectives. Table 1 provides a summary of the relationships among these perspectives. We present these characteristics in this form to enable one to compare and contrast them quickly. Furthermore, we hope that presenting them in this form will stress a general truth: that generalizations are possible only at the expense of omitting detail. The characteristics we attribute are abstracted from a large collection of unique writing about rhetoric and rhetorical criticism. Therefore, like any set of labels, ours will have considerable variety, and some theoretical and critical works will be difficult to classify, given our headings.

We have taken the position that rhetorical criticism reflects a perspective. However, at a time when rhetorical criticism is nonparadigmatic and many theories are competing for acceptance, we discover that critics frequently make choices that seem to combine elements of what we have purported to be distinct perspectives. For example, an essay may exhibit a critical orientation that is typical of an experiential perspective, but the vocabulary employed may be neo-Aristotelian, dramatistic, generic, or constructionist. Likewise, it is not difficult to imagine that a critic might use a basically sociolinguistic approach but take a speaker orientation, apparently mixing the methodological features of two different approaches.

We believe that in most cases of mixed forms the assumptions made by the critic will line up substantially with one perspective or another. However, what seems to us to be a hybrid form may prove to be one of a number of instances that demonstrate a fresh perspective. Regardless of the classificatory system, a crossing and overlapping will always reflect a process reality and the arbitrary and ambiguous nature of language.

Basic Choices in Rhetorical Criticism

In the Introduction, we indicated that this is not a handbook on writing rhetorical criticism, but we also indicated that we have included applications of each method because we wanted to maintain a link with the actual writing of

Characteristics of Perspectives

	Traditional	Experiential	Dramaturgical	Sociological	Postmodern
Orientation	speaker	critic	symbolic interactions	institutions norms	contradictions
Assumptions					
Societal change	stable	process	patterned change	involution	paradoxes
Methodology	single and unidirectional causation	open-ended interactions	transactions	organizational control of process	deviations
Reality	direct reflection	socially constructed	symbolically created	societally created	power struggles
Consensus	one theory	atheoretical	structural variations	polytheoretical	antitheoretical

rhetorical criticism. For this reason we would like to discuss some of the basic decisions critics make in executing criticism.

Some writers believe that criticism is an intuitive process for which one has or has not the necessary instinct and experience. Although they recognize that critics implicitly make numerous choices as they engage in the act of criticism, these writers are apt to assert that making these choices explicit tears the process of criticism apart. There is certainly an element of truth to their position; but if we are to think about and teach criticism, we must attempt to delineate at least some of the decisions that rhetorical critics make implicitly or explicitly each time they engage in criticism. We suggest five centers of interest. We do not suggest the order given as an ideal sequence through which the critic should move, nor do we imply that these centers of interest will always be distinct or that they exhaust the possibilities.

1. *Focus.* Critics should find a focus for their work that will unify all the necessary elements of the critical act. Their interest will probably be aroused by some specific public discourse, but they should keep it general for a time, asking, "Just what is it that attracts me? What is it that puzzles me?" Obviously, the *it* is vague. Probably the critic's focal point will gradually take the form of a thesis statement.

Any number of specific concepts could serve as the focus of criticism. Focal points in the traditional perspective tended to be speakers, their ideas and purposes, or their effectiveness in moving audiences. Today critics often give focal attention to larger patterns of discourse, which are seen as arising from a multiplicity of sources, and also to strategies for communicating within on-going, interactive social groups. Actually, any element or relationship involved in the rhetorical act has the potential of serving to focus criticism.

Quite possibly two critics examining the same rhetorical act may select different aspects on which to focus. In analyzing the "confrontation at Columbia University" in the spring of 1968, James R. Andrews focused on the "distinction between persuasion and coercion,"[1] while James F. Klumpp focused on the "interaction of rhetoric and action."[2] Different focal points contributed heavily to quite different conclusions about the events of the student strike and occupation of several university buildings. Andrews strongly argued that the abandoning of persuasion to coercion was not justified, while Klumpp constructed the term *polar-rejective identification* to explain how the Students for a Democratic Society (the SDS) was successful in gaining acceptance without compromise for many of their aims.

In a sense, the critic shapes the event. What we mean by this statement is that our idea of "an event" is always a simplification of a dizzying complex of actions on which we impose boundaries in order to give a sense of singularity: we focus on some aspects and ignore others in perceiving "an event." For example, a presidential campaign is an event so complex it will invite a wide array of foci. Thus, in studying the 1980 presidential campaign, Goodwin F. Berquist and James L. Golden highlighted the role of media specialists' commentaries and criticisms in influencing public perception of the presidential candidates in the

---

[1] James R. Andrews, "Confrontation at Columbia: A Case Study in Coercive Rhetoric," *Quarterly Journal of Speech* 55, 1 (February 1969): 15.

[2] James K. Klumpp, "Challenge of Radical Rhetoric: Radicalization at Columbia," *Western Speech* 37, 3 (Summer 1973): 156.

televised debates,[3] while Martha Stout Kessler emphasized the efforts of surrogate speakers for the presidential candidates.[4]

Critics need to find a focus for their work. When they do they will discover that their decisions have implications for other critical decisions that they need to make.

2. *Vocabulary.* In describing, interpreting, and evaluating discourse, a career, a movement, a dominant strategy, or the like, writers need a critical vocabulary that is instrumental to the sort of interest they are trying to develop. They may look toward established theories for their terms; they may select among them, or they may develop them for their particular tasks. Two important influences on critics' choices of vocabulary will be their past experiences and the necessities imposed by the nature of the materials with which they are dealing. Each of the five perspectives we have discussed provides a broad set of basic choices. Each of the five is associated with more particular approaches or methods that may even *specify* a sequence of terminologies.

3. *Perspective.* Any criticism will automatically have a starting point, even though critics do not consciously make such decisions. However, if these decisions are consciously made (which in some cases will mean that critics seek to uncover their perspectives), they can be more certain that the decisions are consistent with their materials, their purposes, and the sorts of judgments they intend to make. Consciously selecting perspectives from which to approach their work will probably enable critics to make their writing more consistent internally. The importance of the critical perspective is the premise of this book. We encourage study of the characteristics of the perspectives we have outlined and the many examples throughout.

4. *Judgment.* Critics should determine the sorts of judgments they wish to make. We have already indicated that a given criticism may be descriptive, interpretative, or evaluative. Traditional criticism tends to be primarily descriptive, and the criticism typifying the dramaturgical and sociological tends to be primarily interpretative. Experiential and postmodern critics are most likely to accept evaluation as a central responsibility of judgment. Too often, however, we believe that critics have failed to think through the implications of their choices of purpose. Critics must be certain that their purposes are consistent with their theses and the ends they wish to achieve through their work.

5. *End.* Critics must conceive carefully the end they wish to achieve through their work. Do they wish to provide insight into a given body of public discourse? If so, what sort of insight will suffice? Should critics not provide a point of view that most people exposed to the rhetoric would miss? Or are critics primarily interested in building rhetorical theory or influencing society? Although the response to these questions may be "all of the above," probably one will dominate, whether or not the critic is aware of the domination. Our advice is to struggle to become aware.

The underlying motive that influences all decisions of critics is the final result they wish to achieve. If critics are concerned with applying or building theory,

---

[3]Goodwin F. Berquist and James L. Golden, "Media Rhetoric, Criticism, and the Public Perception of the 1980 Presidential Debates," *Quarterly Journal of Speech* 67, 2 (May 1981): 125–37.

[4]Martha Stout Kessler, "The Role of Surrogate Speakers in the 1980 Presidential Campaign," *Quarterly Journal of Speech* 67, 2 (May 1981): 146–56.

their critical vocabulary, and probably their perspective, will have been determined for them. If they are interested in influencing society, they will almost certainly be required to convey an evaluative judgment. On the other hand, so intimately related are these basic choices in writing criticism that selecting a critical vocabulary, perspective, and type of judgment may determine the ultimate end critics can serve.

Whether criticism is an intuitive process or whether choices such as these briefly outlined are made explicitly, they must be made because they are inherent in the critical act. In our opinion, critics will profit in terms of the clarity and insight of their work by striving to become aware of the choices they make and of the implications of these choices.

A fully formed, coherent piece of criticism is an ideal that may always be just beyond the grasp of the critic. But the impulse to criticize is a human one. Developing the capacity to strive carefully and conscientiously toward the ideal is humanizing.

The Future of Rhetorical Criticism

In the first two editions of this book we made statements concerning the future of rhetorical criticism. We present them here unchanged so that readers can view the evolution of our thoughts and because we feel they still have something to say today. To these two statements we are adding yet another predictive postscript.

1971 Statement   The twentieth century has witnessed tremendous scientific advances. These advances have been accompanied by, and perhaps even made possible by, a strong sense of the reality of science and the efficacy of its method. On a strong scientific basis the world, or at least the economically advantaged portion of it, has become increasingly re-formed on a technological basis. So complete have these changes been that some social critics have been referring to the United States, Western Europe, and the Soviet Union as "technocracies."[5]

More recently, however, increasing portions of the citizens of these nations have become convinced that their technical proficiencies have so deeply affected their societies that not only economic means but social existences have been technologized. One concomitant of the technical advances has been a plundering of the natural environment to the degree that life itself is threatened. More and more voices have been raised against the seeming consequences of technical sufficiency and spiritual poverty. Part of the outcry, of course, has arisen because, in spite of the plenty produced by bureaucratized industry, education, and government, economic poverty still exists in pockets in the advanced nations and in large segments of the disadvantaged world. These pockets of poverty are often attributed more to a lack of will than to a lack of ability.

Although it seems foolhardy to us to assert that the blame for these conditions should be laid at the door of science, we are confident that one result has been and will continue to be a resurgence of humanistic scholarship. Humane tradi-

---

[5]For a review of technocratic forces and references to some literature, see Theodore Roszak, *The Making of a Counter Culture: Reflections on the Technocratic Society and Its Youthful Opposition* (Garden City, NY: Anchor Books, 1969), chap. 1.

tions are even making themselves felt in the philosophy of science. Thomas S. Kuhn's work, on which we have depended heavily, placed science in a light much different from that typical earlier in this century and is still the most prevalent viewpoint. Such thinkers as Michael Polanyi and J. Bronowski stress the humane values of science itself.[6]

We believe that there will be an increasing ability in academia and in public interchange to tolerate the pluralistic tendencies that seem endemic in humane studies, and we believe that rhetorical criticism is and will remain consistent with this trend. Within a humane tradition rhetorical criticism will be fundamentally subjective, leaving the field open for numerous approaches.

Increasingly, rhetorical criticism is becoming much broader, as interest and research in communication become more complex. Within the broad scope of that criticism, individual critics are finding, and will need to find, particular focuses if their work is to be productive. Methods will develop from the variety of questions asked and the public communicative processes that are probed.

In his review of the theoretical writing on rhetorical criticism, Barnet Baskerville concluded that "alone among recent writings, Mouat's 'An Approach to Rhetorical Criticism,'[7] rejects pluralism and seeks for a uniform approach."[8] We believe that this criticism is even more valid today than it was in 1967. The forces that brought about the general acceptance of pluralism have, if anything, become stronger since Baskerville surveyed the literature.

We conclude, then, that no paradigm will soon arise to gain the adherence that neo-Aristotelianism had in the 1930s and 1940s. If a pluralistic attitude becomes generally recognized and understood, we should see a lessening of interest in theorizing about criticism and a revitalized concern with criticizing public discourse.

At the very least we should expect a lessening of interest in traditional methods of theorizing. It seems fair to say of academic speech criticism during the first part of the twentieth century that a unified theory was rather well accepted before it was applied to the reality of discourse. The process was deductive. Even when faith in the paradigm began to break down, theorists persisted in the deductive mode. In the future, rhetorical theory will probably be developed more inductively, as abstractions from the study of discourse. In a sense, this development will mean less distinction between theory and criticism.

A productive "closeness" of theory and criticism will result if the abstractions from critical practice take on the character of tentative principles, which are held tentatively, applied, confirmed (to some degree), and modified by further criticism of public discourse. If theory is to be descriptive of the process of public discourse in a rapidly changing society, rhetoric must be a constantly growing and changing body of knowledge.

[6]See Michael Polanyi, *Personal Knowledge: Toward a Post-Critical Philosophy* (New York: Harper Torchbooks, 1964); and J. Bronowski, *The Identity of Man* (Garden City, NY: American Museum Science Books, 1965) and *Science and Human Values* (New York: Harper Torchbooks, 1965); Stephen Toulmin, *Foresight and Understanding* (New York: Harper Torchbooks, 1963) is also relevant, as is, of course, Thomas S. Kuhn, *The Structure of Scientific Revolutions* (Chicago, IL: University of Chicago Press, 1962).

[7]Lawrence H. Mouat, "An Approach to Rhetorical Criticism," in *The Rhetorical Idiom*, ed. Donald C. Bryant (Ithaca, NY: Cornell University Press, 1958), 161–77.

[8]Barnet Baskerville, "Selected Writings on the Criticism of Public Address, Addendum, 1967," in *Essays on Rhetorical Criticism*, ed. Thomas R. Nilsen (New York: Random House, 1968), 189.

Accompanying the pluralism, tentativeness, and change that we predict, we see a shift from the traditional critical interest in speakers (or the sources of discourse) to the interaction that make communication a process. Thus, rhetoric as such will be closer to the center of critical interest. Critics are now assuming that rhetoric is not something added to the deliberation of a set of issues by spokespersons but rather something integrally associated with the reality of whatever those issues are.[9] Although critics will be interested in what speakers, writers, or demonstrators have to say, they will be more concerned with the forces that seem to permeate public discourse, issues, campaigns, or movements.

These generalizations about the future may not be completely accurate, of course, but they are based on what present practice appears to indicate. In concluding, we would like to stress one more potentiality. In the future critics are apt to find themselves dealing rhetorically with rhetorical materials, that is, they are likely to enter the arena of social influence, at least to the extent that the manner in which messages are received and made meaningful will be determined in some part by the general critical sensibilities of audiences. If the critic finds the persuasive implications of his own messages, he should be willing to take responsibility for the evaluations that he will inevitably make.

1980 Postscript   Interests in building rhetorical theory on the one hand and concentrating on concrete events that seem to exhibit specific rhetorical interactions on the other are scarcely mutually exclusive. In fact one can argue that both impulses are interdependent. Nonetheless, there seems to be an ebb and flow between these activities as if between two magnetic poles.

The past decade of work in rhetorical scholarship has been dominated by the former tendency rather than the latter, more by the theoretical than the critical (if one considers the latter as digging into specific events). If we are correct in noting an ebb and flow, we can expect more emphasis on specific critical studies in the next decade.

Another tendency may be even more important. Echoing the ideal we stated as the interdependency of theory and criticism, Caroline D. Hamsher and James W. Chesebro argue that the relationship is so demonstrably close that it constitutes a single distinct field of study.[10] Although we are not as sanguine about the actualizing of the ideal, we believe that the growing trend for writers, when arguing for theoretical constructs, to illustrate them with concrete pieces of criticism is healthy.[11]

---

[9]On this point see Robert L. Scott, "On Viewing Rhetoric as Epistemic," *Central States Speech Journal* 18, 1 (February 1967): 9–17. Excellent examples of well-integrated criticism of the sort we suggest are Edwin Black, "The Second Persona," *Quarterly Journal of Speech* 56, 2 (April 1970): 109–19; and Parke G. Burgess, "The Rhetoric of Moral Conflict: Two Critical Dimensions," *Quarterly Journal of Speech* 56, 2 (April 1970): 120–30.

[10]James W. Chesebro and Caroline D. Hamsher [Caroline Dummond-Ecroyd], "Contemporary Rhetorical Theory and Criticism: Dimensions of the New Rhetoric," *Speech Monographs* 42, 4 (November 1975): 311–34.

[11]Examples of articles introducing a new theory with an application are Thomas S. Frentz and Thomas B. Farrell, "Language-Action: A Paradigm for Communication," *Quarterly Journal of Speech* 62 (December 1976): 333–49; Janice Hocker Rushing and Thomas S. Frentz, "The Rhetoric of 'Rocky': A Social Value Model of Criticism" and "The Rhetoric of 'Rocky': Part Two," *Western Journal of Speech Communication* 42 (Spring 1978): 63–72 and 42 (Fall 1978): 208–21; and Michael C. Leff and G. P. Mohrmann, "Lincoln at Cooper Union: A Rhetorical Analysis of the Text," and "Lincoln at

More and more the perspectives on criticism seem to be taking the shape of tools for interpretation. The implication is that in general the critic's role is best seen as enhancing understanding, recognizing that understanding is a joint product of the environment—including the social and communicative environment—and the actors within that environment. This sort of thrust subordinates both description and evaluation as purposes of criticism. Seeing both rhetorical theory and rhetorical criticism as interpretative may help connect the two more closely and encourage an already active pluralism by shifting concern from what is right or wrong to what is helpful *given a point of view* in understanding events.

When critics do serve the urge to evaluate, an interpretative frame should encourage (1) a declaration of a particular frame within which the evaluation is relevant and (2) a recognition that varied evaluations will inevitably result, given different frames, and even that these often need not be taken as inconsistent with one another.

A spirit of toleration may well relieve rhetorical critics of a feeling that a paradigm in the sense of a single, favored model is not at all necessary for vigorous scholarship that may at once satisfy our need to understand the flow of rhetorical communication formative of society and our need to redefine critical theory. In short, pluralism may be a viable idea for humanistic learning and teaching.

1989 Postscript   The organizing concept of this book has been and remains "perspectives on rhetorical criticism." At its inception the term *perspective* was selected as a contrast to the *paradigm* of traditional rhetorical criticism. We wanted to emphasize the emerging pluralism in critical methods. At the time, we did not realize how prophetic the choice of terms would be because the pluralistic tendencies have not abated—the first edition described three perspectives, the second four, and this one five; and approaches within perspectives have also multiplied.

More particularly, the past two decades of work in rhetorical scholarship constitute an extension of some of the trends we isolated some twenty years go in our 1971 Statement and ten years ago in our 1980 Postscript. At the same time, we detect extensions and elaborations of these trends, new developments, and new prospects that we think are likely dominate rhetorical scholarship in the coming decade and beyond.

Since 1971, technology has exerted an even more significant and ever-increasing role in defining the context in which rhetorical transactions exist. Rhetorical critics have consistently protested the dehumanizing consequences of these technologies. As we did in 1971, we would again call for a humanistic counterstatement to the values that accompany the growing dominance of technology throughout the world.

At the same time, within the last decade, a more passionate restraint has characterized the views of technology held by many rhetorical critics. Technologies have become an enduring if not permanent feature of social reality. Reflecting a more analytical posture, rhetorical critics have systematically examined the emergence of national and transnational technocracies as a context for understanding and assessing rhetoric. Particularly within the past decade, technologies

Cooper Union: A Rationale for Neo-Classical Criticism,'' *Quarterly Journal of Speech* 40 (October 1974): 346–58 and 40 (December 1974): 459–67.

have increasingly been viewed predominantly as communication systems. Certainly, the content of these technologies, particularly televised programs, have received extended attention. Yet for a larger number of rhetorical critics, technologies themselves have increasingly been viewed as message-generating systems. Indeed, a foundation[12] has been provided for suggesting that the formatting or production techniques governing technologies may be influencing message construction and audience apprehension as much as the often-ephemeral content of these systems. This technological emphasis has been reflected in the new journals, such as *Critical Studies in Mass Communication* and *Telematics and Informatics,* created in the 1980s. Few factors in the foreseeable future appear likely to diminish the growing interest by rhetorical critics in technology as a decisive, if not determinant, channel affecting message creation and audience responses to communication.

Of the perspectives and methods used by rhetorical critics to respond to the technological contexts in which human symbol using occurs, we continue to see a shift toward pluralism. Indeed, pluralism has become the dominant characteristic of rhetorical criticism much as the neo-Aristotelian perspective was viewed as the paradigm of the 1930s and 1940s. The increase in the number of perspectives and methods is likely to promote and foster five qualitative changes in rhetorical criticism.

First, while diversity continues, the past decade has witnessed a consolidation and clarification in the perspectives and methods governing rhetorical criticism. Individual critics have been more likely to specify their governing perspective and method overtly in their own criticisms, seeking to specify and clarify the relationship of their works to those of other critics. Particular methods have been more precisely defined and distinguished from other methods, and critics employing these methods have more clearly identified their relationship to the methods established by others.[13] We see little that would alter this trend toward the use of an explicitly stated method in rhetorical criticism within the next decade. Such methodological statements provide a shorthand way of defining the choices of a critic amid the ever-growing volume of rhetorical scholarship while also conveniently specifying the intellectual heritage critical essay seeks to extend.

Second, increasing attention is also likely to be devoted to identifying the substantive relationship between the philosophical foundation of a perspective and the procedures governing a specific method. The nature of the philosophical perspective guiding rhetorical criticism is increasingly receiving the same kind of attention as the particular steps of its method.[14] In this regard, we anticipate that

---

[12]See, for example, Walter J. Ong, *Orality and Literacy: The Technologizing of the Word* (London: Methuen, 1982) and Robert K. Logan, *The Alphabet Effect: The Impact of the Phonetic Alphabet on the Development of Western Civilization* (New York: William Morrow, 1986).

[13]See, e.g., Walter R. Fisher, "Narration as a Human Communication Paradigm: The Case of Public Moral Argument," *Communication Monographs* 51 (March 1984): 1–22.

[14]See, e.g., G. P. Mohrmann, "Fantasy Theme Criticism: A Peroration," *Quarterly Journal of Speech* 68 (August 1982): 306–13 and Ernest G. Bormann, "Fantasy and Rhetorical Vision: Ten Years Later," *Quarterly Journal of Speech* 68 (August 1982): 288–305, although the more explicit attention given to the epistemic functions of rhetoric provides a more universal frame of reference for this observation.

the relationships among philosophy, theory, method, and specific rhetorical interactions will receive more attention within the next decade.

Third, while diversity continues, rhetorical critics are also more likely to become increasingly self-conscious about the judgments guiding their critical evaluations. For some, such as Wander,[15] all rhetorical criticism is inherently ideological. For others, rhetorical criticism has systematically ignored the discourses of women and the unique perspective reflected in these discourses.[16] In all, while the interest in the interpretation process we identified in our 1980 Postscript has continued throughout the 1980s, we have also seen more explicit attention given to the criteria employed during the evaluative process. Thus, in terms of the traditional attention devoted to *description, interpretation,* and *evaluation,* we anticipate that rhetorical critics will increasing view any description as a function of the interpretation scheme and evaluation standards employed by a rhetorical critic. Accordingly, we specifically anticipate that descriptive analyses will diminish as an independent feature of criticism, treated more frequently as a dependent feature of the interpretation and evaluative systems employed by a rhetorical critic.

Fourth, while redefined and employed in rather dramatically different ways, quantitative analyses will no longer appear as clearly outside of the province of rhetorical criticism as they once were. Traditionally, the qualitative analysis has functioned as the dominant metaphor for rhetorical criticism. As we noted when characterizing the first works of rhetorical critics in the 1930s, a literary mode characterized rhetorical criticism. Reflected in both its governing conceptions and style, rhetorical criticism has long been assumed to function within a qualitative mode, analytically and stylistically. Indeed, some have argued that the qualitative concepts and style traditionally associated with rhetorical criticism are antithetical to the use of quantitative data, with rhetorical criticism serving— at best—a "pre-scientific function."[17] While such a generalization may have been true in the 1950s, quantitative data and assessments have increasingly made their way into rhetorical analyses.[18] At the same time, as far as we can determine, the use of quantitative data has not drastically transformed rhetorical criticism, nor has the use of quantitative data created any detectable shift toward a positivistic or behavioral orientation in rhetorical criticism. Rather, the use of quantitative data in rhetorical criticism has initially blurred, and is ultimately redefining, the traditional distinction between the qualitative and quantitative. The redefinition has now reached an explicit level. While recognizing the polit-

[15]Philip Wander, "The Ideological Turn in Modern Criticism," *Central States Speech Journal* 34 (Spring 1983): 1–18. Also see Philip Wander, "The Rhetoric of American Foreign Policy," *Quarterly Journal of Speech* 70 (November 1984): 339–61.

[16]Karlyn Kohrs Campbell, "Style and Content in the Rhetoric of Early Afro-American Feminists," *Quarterly Journal of Speech* 72 (November 1984): 434–45 and Carole Spitzack and Kathryn Carter, "Women in Communication Studies: A Typology for Revision," *Quarterly Journal of Speech* 73 (November 1984): 401–23.

[17]John Waite Bowers, "The Pre-Scientific Function of Rhetorical Criticism," in *Essays on Rhetorical Criticism,* ed. Thomas R. Nilsen, 126–45 (New York: Random House, 1968).

[18]See, for example, James W. Chesebro, "Communication, Values, and Popular Television Series—An Eleven-Year Assessment," in *Inter/Media: Interpersonal Communication in a Media World,* 3d ed., ed. Gary Gumpert and Robert Cathcart, 477–512 (New York: Oxford University Press, 1986).

ical nature of all research analyses, Grossberg has already directly argued for a reconception of "critical theory and the politics of empirical research."[19] As rhetorical criticism evolves in the 1990s and beyond, we fully anticipate that rhetorical critics will increasingly find it useful to identify their philosophical and ideological posture and, within these qualitative contexts, specify the degree to which quantitative claims regarding their position can be provided. This use of quantitative data will be part, we believe, of a larger interest by rhetorical critics in theory and comparative methodology.

Fifth, as perspectives and methods continue to be clarified, we anticipate that attention will ultimately turn to a renewed reconception of the requirements for an adequate rhetorical theory and to the role of comparative methodology in rhetorical criticism. This renewed interest in theory and comparative methodology will not, however, emerge without some rather profound soul searching among rhetorical critics. We specifically anticipate that a part of the tension generating the interest in theory and comparative methodology is likely to stem from a conflict between the stated functions of rhetorical criticism and the emerging nature and definition of rhetorical criticism. As we suggested in the Introduction, rhetorical criticism has traditionally been justified because it serves social ends insofar as it highlights, gives meaning to, and assesses the value of phenomena for others. These uses of rhetorical criticism presume the rhetorical critic is addressing not just the personal concerns of the critic but also the governing self-interests of others. At the same time, rhetorical criticism is increasingly being cast as a private and autobiographical activity, ideological in nature, reflecting the self-interests of the critic. We anticipate that the ideological nature increasingly attributed to rhetorical criticism may be perceived as a denial of the social ends and functions traditionally attributed to rhetorical criticism. We would not be surprised, then, if this tension led to a renewed interest in reconceiving the ends and functions of rhetorical criticism and the nature of theory as universal claims about phenomena and/or in how different methods do and do not achieve the stated ends of rhetorical criticism and satisfy the requirements for an adequate theory, or universal claim, regarding rhetorical interactions. An interest in the relationships among theory, comparative methods, and the functions of rhetorical criticism was expressed by Simons in the late 1970s. He suggested that an adequate theory, or universal claim, about a rhetorical interaction must satisfy specific standards of *logical rigor, predictiveness, provocativeness, manageability,* and *comprehensiveness.*[20]

In all, we anticipate that pluralism will continue to dominate rhetorical scholarship. The shock of the paradigm breakdown in rhetorical criticism in the 1960s has now passed. This is not to say that the pluralistic evolution of rhetorical criticism is at an end. We do not think that it is. The potential perspectives and their related methods that might yet be introduced in rhetorical criticism have yet to be exhausted. While pluralism will continue to be experienced, at the same time, we believe that discussions regarding the nature of rhetorical criticism are

---

[19]Lawrence Grossberg, "Critical Theory and the Politics of Empirical Research," in *Mass Communication Review Yearbook,* vol. 6, ed. Michael Gurevitch and Mark R. Levy, 86–106 (Newbury Park, CA: Sage, 1987).

[20]Herbert W. Simons, " 'Genre-alizing' about Rhetoric: A Scientific Approach," in *Form and Genre: Shaping Rhetorical Action,* ed. Karlyn Kohrs Campbell and Kathleen Hall Jamieson, 33–50 (Falls Church, VA: Speech Communication Association, 1978).

also likely to be influenced by efforts to identify and clarify the differences among the diverse perspectives and methods in rhetorical criticism. We are entering an era in which rhetorical criticism will be more self-conscious in virtually all respects.

In part, the growing dependence on technology in societies will demand such retrospection. Insofar as technologies convey discernible messages to human beings, persuading human beings toward one end rather than others, it remains unclear in what sense a technology can be said to have a self-contained set of motives. In traditional terms, technologies do not contain the kind of built-in motives that govern humanly generated discourse. If a rhetorical critic is to extract a motive within the evolution of technologies, the critic's own imposition of this motive must emerge.

Critical self-consciousness is also likely to be stimulated by a desire to have criticism serve social ends. While admitting an inevitable role in how persuasive phenomena are to be interpreted and evaluated, critics must ultimately link their own personal frame of reference to the self-interests of others. Toward this end, we anticipate that critics will need to clarify their own perspectives, philosophies, and evaluative criteria. In the context of competing perspectives and methods, these clarifications may easily provide a foundation for marshaling quantitative support for their claims in terms of some of the explicit standards governing the formulation of an adequate rhetorical theory.

With time, as these trends begin to interact and function as norms for rhetorical critics, we also think that some common agreements among rhetorical critics of very different persuasions may be in the making. It would be, in our view, extremely inappropriate to anticipate that a new paradigm for rhetorical critics, equal in power to the coherence established by the neo-Aristotelian paradigm of the 1930s and 1940s, is emerging. Indeed, of the several possible scenarios we can cast for the future of rhetorical criticism, none of them includes a return the kind of paradigm which governed rhetorical critics in the 1930s and 1940s. Since the 1960s, rhetorical criticism has been perceived as an arena for conceptual and methodological innovation and creativity. These impulses are not likely to be extinguished for whatever benefits uniformity might bring.

At the same time, the sharp divisions which we have employed to distinguish the traditional, experiential, dramaturgical, sociological, and postmodern perspectives may blur in the decade ahead and beyond. There are ways in which these perspectives can already be conceived, at least theoretically, as complementary. While we have yet to find such an integrating conception in the writings of rhetorical critics, it is conceivable to us that some rhetorical critics could simultaneously maintain the experiential view that society is in a continual state of process, the dramaturgical view that structures must and do regulate societal processes, the sociological view that elements of the societal structure can affect societal structures and determine the direction and rate of societal processes, and the postmodern view that certain symbolic constructions of reality serve human objectives while others do not and should accordingly be revealed as self-destructive human systems.

In our view, efforts towards such transcendence could provide a set of norms which would be acceptable to many rhetorical critics. Whether or not any particular method can consistently and usefully embody all of these principles has yet to be determined. Nonetheless, we fully expect that some rhetorical theorists may slight certain philosophical differences among rhetorical critics typically felt to be at odds with one another in order to identify common links, bridges, or similarities.

The shift towards a transcendent definition of rhetorical criticism is likely to be accompanied and reinforced by a shift towards an interdisciplinary conception of the "rhetorical perspective." Once within the province of sociology, the sociolinguistic approach now clearly possesses a decidedly rhetorical perspective. Likewise, much of the thought and directions proposed by postmodern rhetorical critics has been derived from literary critics most frequently associated with English departments. Literary critics were once defined by their concern for the permanent while rhetorical critics were thought to be concerned with effect.[21] Yet, the distinction between the *permanent* and *effect* is no longer as clear as it might have once been. Endurance is one of several possible effects, and the range of effects can include both the enduring and the ephemeral. Accordingly, for literary critics, the popular culture is now a viable object of study, while few rhetorical critics would hold that a classical literary work cannot legitimately be examined as a persuasive document.

The impact of such interdisciplinary approaches to rhetoric is that the definition of rhetoric itself may once again be expanded. Dramaturgical critics initially shifted the definition of rhetoric from the study of the "available means of persuasion" to its more encompassing focus upon all modes of identification, "showing how a rhetorical motive is often present where it is not usually recognized, or thought to belong."[22] Similarly, as more interdisciplinary links are fashioned, the encompassing concept of *effectiveness* may increasingly function as one of the dominant definitional features employed to characterize the rhetorical perspective.

Thus, while they may not have yet emerged, several principles may take shape deemphasizing the divisiveness that has dominated rhetorical criticism, creating a more integrated center from which diverse modes of rhetorical criticism may be examined. We would continue to hold, as we did in 1980, that "in short, pluralism may be a viable ideal for humanistic learning and teaching." At the same time, concerted humanistic actions may become a required survival strategy in the technologized societies of the 1990s and beyond.

[21]See, e.g., Herbert A. Wichelns, "The Literary Criticism of Oratory," in *The Rhetorical Idiom: Essays in Rhetoric, Oratory, Language, and Drama*, ed. Donald C. Bryant, 5–42 (New York: Russell & Russell, 1966). Wichelns's essay originally appeared in 1925.

[22]Kenneth Burke, *A Grammar of Motives and A Rhetoric of Motives* (Cleveland, OH: Meridian Books/World, 1962), 521.

INDEX

Bernard L. Brock is professor of speech communication at Wayne State University and has taught speech at the University of Minnesota. He received his B.A. from Illinois State University (1954) and his M.A. and Ph.D. from Northwestern University (1961, 1965).

Robert L. Scott is professor of speech communication at the University of Minnesota and has taught speech at the University of Houston. He received his A.B. from the University of Nebraska (1951), and his Ph.D. from the University of Illinois (1955).

James W. Chesebro is professor of communication arts and sciences at Queens College of the City University of New York and Director of Educational Services at the Speech Communication Association in Annandale, Virginia. He has also taught at Temple University, the University of Puerto Rico, and the University of Minnesota. He received his B.A. and Ph.D. from the University of Minnesota and his M.S. from Illinois State University.

The manuscript was prepared for publication by Michael Lane. The book was designed by Mary Primeau. The display type is Avante Garde. The typeface for the text is Times Roman, and the text is printed on 60-lb Finch Opaque.

Manufactured in the United States of America.